Lecture Notes in Computer Science   8852

Commenced Publication in 1973
Founding and Former Series Editors:
Gerhard Goos, Juris Hartmanis, and Jan van Leeuwen

Editorial Board

More information about this series at http://www.springer.com/series/7409

Luca Maria Aiello · Daniel McFarland (Eds.)

Social Informatics

SocInfo 2014 International Workshops
Barcelona, Spain, November 10, 2014
Revised Selected Papers

 Springer

Editors
Luca Maria Aiello
Yahoo Inc.
Barcelona
Spain

Daniel McFarland
Stanford Graduate School of Education
Stanford
California
USA

ISSN 0302-9743
Lecture Notes in Computer Science
ISBN 978-3-319-15167-0
DOI 10.1007/978-3-319-15168-7

ISSN 1611-3349   (electronic)

ISBN 978-3-319-15168-7   (eBook)

Library of Congress Control Number: 2014955457

LNCS Sublibrary: SL3 – Information Systems and Applications, incl. Internet/Web and HCI

Printed on acid-free paper

Springer International Publishing AG Switzerland is part of Springer Science+Business Media
(www.springer.com)

Preface to the SocInfo 2014 Proceedings

This volume contains the papers presented at the satellite workshops at SocInfo 2014, the Sixth International Conference on Social Informatics. Workshops were held on November 10, 2014, in Barcelona, Spain.

SocInfo is an interdisciplinary venue for researchers from Computer Science, Informatics, Social Sciences, and Management Sciences to share ideas and opinions, and present original research work on studying the interplay between socially-centric platforms and social phenomena. The ultimate goal of Social Informatics is to create a better understanding of socially-centric platforms not just as a technology, but also as a set of social phenomena. To that end, we have invited interdisciplinary papers, on applying information technology in the study of social phenomena, on applying social concepts in the design of information systems, on applying methods from the social sciences in the study of social computing and information systems, on applying computational algorithms to facilitate the study of social systems and human social dynamics, and on designing information and communication technologies that consider the social context.

This year SocInfo 2014 included nine satellite workshops: the City Labs Workshop, the Workshop on Criminal Network Analysis and Mining (CRIMENET), the Workshop on Interaction and Exchange in Social Media (DYAD), the Workshop on Exploration of Games and Gamers (EGG), the Workshop on HistoInformatics, the Workshop on Socio-Economic Dynamics, Networks and Agent-based Models (SEDNAM), the Workshop on Social Influence (SI), the Workshop on Social Scientists Working with Start-ups, and the Workshop on Social Media in Crowdsourcing and Human Computation (SoHuman).

First, we would like to thank all the workshop organizers for the amazing work they did in collecting high-quality contributions. We would like to thank the authors of submitted papers as well as the participants for making the workshop day a success. We are extremely grateful to the Program Co-chairs Ingmar Weber, Kristina Lerman, and Fabio Rojas for their support in the workshop day organization. We owe special thanks to Estefania Ricart and Natalia Pou, our Local Co-chairs, who had a vital role in all the stages of the organization. We thank our Publicity Chairs Paolo Boldi, Tsuyoshi Murata, Emilio Ferrara, Barbara Poblete, Symeon Papadopoulos and our Web Chair Michele Trevisiol. Also, last but not least we are grateful to Adam Wierzbicki for his continuous support.

Lastly, this conference would not be possible without the generous help of our sponsors and supporters: Microsoft Research, Facebook, Yahoo, the Stanford Center for Computational Social Science, Barcelona Media, and the FP7 EU project SocialSensor.

December 2014

Luca Maria Aiello
Daniel McFarland

Organization

Organizing Committee

Local Co-chairs

Estefania Ricart   Yahoo Labs, Spain
Natalia Pou   Yahoo Labs, Spain

General Co-chairs

Luca Maria Aiello   Yahoo Labs, Spain
Daniel McFarland   Stanford University, USA

Honrary General Co-chairs

Alejandro Jaimes   Yahoo Labs, USA
Dirk Helbing   ETH Zurich, Switzerland

Program Co-chairs

Ingmar Weber   Qatar Computing Research Institute, Qatar
Kristina Lerman   University of Southern California, USA
Fabio Rojas   Indiana University Bloomington, USA

Publicity Co-chairs

Paolo Boldi   University of Milan, Italy
Tsuyoshi Murata   Tokyo Institute of Technology, Japan
Emilio Ferrara   Indiana University Bloomington, USA
Symeon Papadopoulos   CERTH-ITI, Greece
Barbara Poblete   University of Chile, Chile

Steering Chair

Adam Wierzbicki   Polish-Japanese Institute of Information
Technology, Poland

Web Chairs

Michele Trevisiol   Universitat Pompeu Fabra, Spain

Workshop Organizers

Jeremy Blackburn	Telefonica Research, Spain
Alessandro Bozzon	Delft University of Technology, The Netherlands
Salvatore Catanese	University of Messina, Italy
Otto Chrons	Microtask, Finland
Elizabeth M. Daly	IBM Research, Ireland
Petros Daras	CERTH-ITI, Greece
Gaël Dias	Normandie University, France
Marten Düring	Centre Virtuel de la Connaissance sur l'Europe, Luxembourg
Emilio Ferrara	Indiana University Bloomington, USA
Giacomo Fiumara	University of Messina, Italy
Piero Fraternali	Politecnico di Milano, Italy
Serge Galam	CNRS, France
Alejandro Jaimes	Yahoo Labs, USA
Jaroslaw Jankowski	West Pomeranian University of Technology, Poland
Adam Jatowt	Kyoto University, Japan
Marco Alberto Javarone	University of Sassari, Italy
Huy Kang Kim	Korea University, South Korea
Haewoon Kwak	Qatar Computing Research Institute, Qatar
Yelena Majova	Qatar Computing Research Institute, Qatar
Areti Markopoulou	IAAC/Institute for Advanced Architecture of Catalonia, Spain
Radoslaw Michalski	Wrocław University of Technology, Poland
Bonnie Nardi	UC Irvine, USA
Jasminko Novak	European Institute for Participatory Media, Germany
Daniele Quercia	Yahoo Labs, Spain
Rossano Schifanella	University of Turin, Italy
Ingo Scholtes	ETH Zurich, Switzerland
Paulo Shakarian	Arizona State University, USA
Tiziano Squartini	Sapienza University, Italy
Bogdan State	Facebook, USA
Antal van den Bosch	Radboud University, The Netherlands

Sponsors

Microsoft Research (research.microsoft.com)
Facebook (www.facebook.com)
Yahoo (labs.yahoo.com)
Stanford, Center for Computational Social Science (css-center.stanford.edu)
Barcelona Media (www.barcelonamedia.org)
SocialSensor (www.socialsensor.eu)
IEEE Special Technical Community on Social Networking (stcsn.ieee.net)

Microsoft®
Research

facebook

YAHOO!
LABS

Stanford
Center for Computational Social Science

Barcelona
Media

Φ STC SOCIAL
NETWORKING

Contents

Whats in a Dyad? Interaction and Exchange in Social Media (DYAD)

Exploration on Games and Gamers (EGG)

2nd International Workshop on Computational History (HistoInformatics)

Socio-Economic Dynamics, Networks and Agent-Based Models (SEDNAM)

Workshop on Social Influence (SI)

3rd International Workshop on Social Media in Crowdsourcing and Human Computation (SoHuman)

City Labs

City Labs - Introduction

Elizabeth M. Daly[1], Areti Markopoulou[2], and Daniele Quercia[3]([⊠])

[1] IBM Research, Dublin, Ireland
[2] IAAC/Institute for Advanced Architecture of Catalonia, Barcelona, Spain
[3] Yahoo Labs, Barcelona, Spain
daniele.quercia@gmail.com

Introduction

Social media and digital traces from sensor such as smart cards and mobile phones have played a key role in providing insights into people's activities, opinions and day-to-day lives. These detailed user-generated information streams offer a unique opportunity for cities to understand and engage their citizens. The research domain of smarter cities aims to monitor disruptive events (e.g., emergencies, Olympics), analyze social behaviour, identify citizens' sentiment and understand their interactions with services. On the other side, cities can use their understanding of the citizen to foster stronger relationships with the diverse communities in their constituencies. This understanding could be applied to mobilize people on important issues such as education, health care, political engagement and community awareness. Also, new digital fabrication tools have been recently used to generate adoptable, dynamic and interactive architecture able to evolve together with urban dwellers, and it has been shown that new Internet-of-Things devices could effectively capture physical observations to understand how cities and urban centers work. As a result, cities now provide a living lab where applied research can be carried out to understand citizen and services with a focus on collaborative, user-centred design and co-creation.

This workshop aims to bring together researchers and practitioners to discuss and explore the research challenges and opportunities in applying the pervasive and social computing paradigm to understand cities. We are seeking multidisciplinary contributions that reveal interesting aspects about urban life and exploit the digital traces to create novel citizen-centric applications that benefit not only citizens, but also urban planners and policy makers. The goal is was to attract researchers from communities ranging for computational science, to social science and urban design.

The workshop received 17 submissions and after peer review process we were able to accept 9 papers for presentation. The accepted papers come from a variety of disciplines covering diverse topics: visualizing urban flows, using social media for policy making and historical preservation, privacy management, online campaigning for NGOs, hyperlocal social interactions among apartment residents, failures and risks of smart technologies, crowdsourcing urban design, and the benefits of city labs.

© Springer International Publishing Switzerland 2015
L.M. Aiello and D. McFarland (Eds.): SocInfo 2014 Workshops, LNCS 8852, pp. 3–4, 2015.
DOI: 10.1007/978-3-319-15168-7_1

Program Committee

- Anthony Townsend, New York University
- Charlie Catlett, Argonne National Laboratory
- Colin Ellard, University of Waterloo
- Dani Villatoro, IIIA - CSIC
- Ed Manley, University College London
- Enrique Friasmartinez, Telefonica
- Giovanni Quattrone, University College of London
- Jos Luis De Vicente, CCCB
- Josep Perell, University of Barcelona
- Mar Santamaria, Universitat Politcnica de Catalunya
- Marcus Foth, Queensland University of Technology
- Michael Smyth, Edinburgh Napier University
- Mirco Musolesi, University of Birmingham
- Miriam Roure, MIT
- Neal Lathia, University of Cambridge
- Oleg Pachenkov, European University at St. Petersburg
- Olga Subiros, CCCB
- Prodromos Tsiavos, UCL/GFOSS
- Ramon Riberafumaz, Universitat Oberta de Catalunya
- Raz Schwartz, Cornell Tech NYC
- Rosta Farzan, University of Pittsburgh
- Sarah Gallacher, Intel Collaborative Research Institute
- Sascha Haselmayer, Citymart

Acknowledgments. We thank the conference organizers for allowing us to host the workshop, Tomas Diez for accepting to be our guest speaker, and the program committee members for doing a fantastic job.

FlowSampler: Visual Analysis of Urban Flows in Geolocated Social Media Data

Alvin Chua[1(✉)], Ernesto Marcheggiani[2,3], Loris Servillo[1],
and Andrew Vande Moere[1]

[1] Department of Architecture, KU Leuven,
Kasteelpark Arenberg. 1 – Bus 2431, 3001 Heverlee, Belgium
{alvin.chua,loris.servillo,andrew.vandemoere}@asro.kuleuven.be
[2] Department of Earth and Environmental Sciences, KU Leuven,
Celestijnenlaan 200E – Bus 2411, 3001 Heverlee, Belgium
[3] Department of D3A, University of Marche,
Via Brecce Bianche 10, 60131 Ancona, Italy
ernesto.marcheggiani@ees.kuleuven.be

Abstract. Analysis of flows such as human movement can help spatial planners better understand territorial patterns in urban environments. In this paper, we describe FlowSampler, an interactive visual interface designed for spatial planners to gather, extract and analyse human flows in geolocated social media data. Our system adopts a graph-based approach to infer movement pathways from spatial point type data and expresses the resulting information through multiple linked multiple visualisations to support data exploration. We describe two use cases to demonstrate the functionality of our system and characterise how spatial planners utilise it to address analytical task.

Keywords: Social media analytics · Geovisualisation · Spatio-temporal analysis · Data mining · Flow maps

1   Introduction

Urban (or inter-urban) flow analysis is a particularly important subject in spatial planning that identifies territorial patterns in human movement to inform policymaking. Although many techniques have been devised to carryout such analysis [1-3], the growing volume of geolocated social media data presents spatial planners with new opportunities to formulate evidence based policies that could lead to improvements in the urban environment. A key component in analysing human movement is the notion of trajectory. A trajectory provides information about the position of a person through space and time. By analysing patterns in aggregated trajectories, spatial planners aim to identify pathways where important movement or flows occur. The insights that they gain from analysis are used to conceptualise territorial structures, such as functional urban areas [4], that ultimately determine where and how policies are enacted.

Geolocated social media data is a source of publicly accessible data that contains information, which may be extracted to study urban flows. Since such data typically

© Springer International Publishing Switzerland 2015
L.M. Aiello and D. McFarland (Eds.): SocInfo 2014 Workshops, LNCS 8852, pp. 5–17, 2015.
DOI: 10.1007/978-3-319-15168-7_2

contain a timestamp and can be referenced to specific user identifiers, it is reasonable to construct a social media user's trajectory based on a chronologically ordered set of geolocated data records. While this task may appear to be outwardly trivial, it can be rather challenging for spatial planners to accomplish with generic GIS software, as the data tend to be large and ill structured.

We present FlowSampler, a visual analytics system designed for spatial planners to gather and analyse urban flows in geolocated social media data. This work was motivated by the need for an interactive visual interface that would extract trajectories out of geolocated social media data and summarise them in a flow map [5]. The strength of this system is that it enables spatial planners to formulate and subsequently verify research questions by reconfiguring the interface for analysis at various spatial and temporal granularities. The interactions are carried out through a series of integrated control widgets that allows the spatial planners to directly manipulate the visualisation. We make three contributions in this paper: First, we propose a graph-based approach to construct a flow map from the trajectories extracted from a geolocated social media dataset. Then, we describe a visual analytics procedure to identify pathways with significant movement between sets of locations. Finally, we demonstrate the functionality and scalability of our system with two use cases that characterise the task this system addresses at different spatial and temporal granularities.

2   Data

Recent growth in smart phones usage [6] and emergence of location aware services has enabled large-scale data collection [7] through participatory sensor networks [8]. A key feature that makes such systems particularly relevant for urban informatics [9] is the ubiquity of the sensors, and the existence of infrastructures that enable sensing. Twitter is an example of a participatory sensor network. It is a microblogging service that allows people to share events and news or have conversations in real time [10]. Empirical studies have shown that people generally use Twitter to describe what they are doing or express how they are feeling [11]. Apart from text content, each tweet is accompanied by a range of meta data such as timestamp and geographic location. We refer to geographically referenced tweets as geolocated tweets. Geographic referencing is not exclusive to Twitter but has been a popular concept, implemented in many other social media services. Depending on individual preferences, Twitter users may decide to publically share their activities on other social media. When they do so, the information posted on those services are also publicised on Twitter. Foursquare, an online service for users to share their whereabouts is an example of such a network. Because Twitter offers a relatively simple protocol to access such information, other studies in literature [12, 13] have also collected geolocated data from other social media through Twitter. For these reasons, we developed our system based on geolocated twitter data. Yet, the concepts we describe can be generalizable to a wider class of geolocated social media data with similar characteristics.

Prior to the availability of geolocated social media data, large-scale studies of mobility were mainly based on cellular activity logs [14-17] that track the spatial position of people at different moments in time. To analyse movement in cellular datasets, analyst rely on techniques that partition a given territory into subspaces based on the locations of cellular base stations. The position of a cell phone is then approximated to the location of the base station responsible for routing its signal. An estimated trajectory can then be constructed by chronologically ordering the locations of the base stations that served the cell phone. While this approach has revealed valuable insights about human mobility [14, 15], the spatial resolution in which studies can be conducted depends on the physical geometry of the infrastructure. In comparison to geolocated social media datasets that offer spatial information of up to street level precision, the space partitioning technique implies that studies conducted in territories with sparsely distributed base stations will be limited to relatively low resolution spatial analysis. Moreover, cellular dataset are proprietary in nature. In most cases, obtaining such data tend to require a long time to accomplish due to complicated procedures and long discussions with stakeholders.

3   Related Work

There are many examples that take advantage of the fine spatial granularity offered by geolocated social media data to study cities in greater detail. In popular culture, such datasets have been used to create casual visualisations [18] to engage the lay audience [19]. Several prominent examples include maps that show key paths in transport infrastructure [20], track the use of different languages in cities [21, 22] and reveal the distribution of urban wealth [23]. Previous work in literature have also made use of geolocated datasets for a multitude of purposes such as studying or developing technologies to support land use analysis, crisis management and mobility.

Land Use Analysis. Applications that use geolocated social media data for land use analysis are generally concerned with identifying the type of activities that are most common in specific urban areas. Frias-Martinez *et al* described a straightforward procedure that combines a space partitioning technique with human deduction to identify changes in land use over time [24]. Livehoods, a project by Cranshaw *et al* [12] addresses the same issue but adopts an automatic technique to draw alternative neighbourhood boundaries by clustering nearby locations with similar social activities. Their approach illustrates how the fine spatial resolution offered by geolocated tweets can be used to reveal social-spatial divisions in cities. Kling and Pozdnoukhov [13] developed a more sophisticated system that addresses the same issue. However, their work differs from the former in that they extract a chronologically ordered set of keywords to provide analysts with time stamped contextual information of activity on the ground.

Crisis Management Systems. Apart from land use analysis, geolocated social media data also serve as a source of information in crisis management systems. The task addressed by analyst in this domain involves extracting information to monitor situations and explain how they evolve. Studies such as De Longueville *et al's* analysis of a forest fire near Marseille [25], and Prasetyo *et al's* investigation of how a severe haze affected the residents of Singapore [26], act as some instances to characterise how such data can be used as a quantifiable source of information in times of crisis.

Mobility Analysis. While there exists a diverse range of work that made use of social media data for land use analysis and crisis monitoring, relatively little has been done to tap its potential for understanding human mobility. Traffic and navigation is one application area where such data have been exploited for mobility analysis. Wei *et al* describes an approach for constructing routes that navigate popular landmarks in cities [27]. Likewise, Pan *et al* address the problem of detecting and describing traffic anomalies by monitoring changes in mobility behaviour [28]. Pan's approach however, does not infer routing information from geolocated social media data but analyses it for contextual information that may be useful to describe events occurring on the ground. Character profiling is another application area where geolocated social media data has been applied. Fuchs *et al* presents an analytical approach to extract knowledge about personal behaviour from geolocated social media data by classifying profiles based on movement trajectories [29]. Andrienko *et al* addresses a similar challenge but classifies profiles based on venues instead [30]. A similarity between the existing works that make use of geolocated social media data to derive mobility information is that they focus on very precise patterns. Our work differs from existing applications in that we are more concerned with identifying general flow pathways between locations in a territory rather than the actual transit route or specific points of interest. In this respect, recent work by Gabrielli et al [31] addresses a similar topic as us yet their intent was to identify semantic rather than spatial patterns.

Visual Analytics. There are two broad approaches to conduct data analysis. Automatic algorithms can be used to address well-defined task with a known set of steps [32] while visual analysis is often required to support explorative task that require human deduction and reasoning. Visual analysis is not new to spatial planning as the discipline has a tradition of using maps for thinking and reasoning [33, 34]. There are several visualisation techniques that are relevant for urban flow analysis. Minard's map of Napoleon's Russian campaign [35] is one of the earliest attempts at visualising flows. The map depicts the size of the French army by the width of a band on the map, and depicts the change in its numbers in relation to air temperature throughout the duration of the campaign. Tobler [36] provides some early examples of computer generated flow maps. Flow maps are maps that show the movement of objects from one location to another [37]. The objects that are represented vary by theme. Flow maps rely on a node-link type representation where lines of different widths are used to represent the direction and quantity of objects being moved. An alternative to the node link representation is an origin destination map [38]. Origin destination maps comprises of a set of origin destination matrices arranged in geographic order. The map is interpreted by tracing a point of origin to a corresponding destination in one of the other matrices. While benchmarks [39] have shown that the matrix representation outperforms the node-link representation in task such as search and quantity estimation, node-link representations are reported to be more effective at path finding, an important task in interpreting the direction and sequence of flows.

4 Design

FlowSampler is a visual analytics system that comprises of four visualisations components each highlighting a different attribute in the data. We have chosen a visual analytics approach, as the task we address is exploratory and requires human judgement for pattern analysis and evaluation. By providing a visual interface, spatial planners can establish and fine tune their analytical procedure, identify uncertainty and biases in the data, and communicate their findings in an interactive visual environment. Our system should allow spatial planners to identify significant flow pathways that connect various locations in a given territory. Specifically, we are interested in (1) flow patterns that exhibit characteristics of routine behaviour and (2) sequence of movements that can be used to characterise spontaneous, unexpected, behaviour. Our model considers a flow path to be routine if it contains a large number of trajectories that are made by few people. Conversely, a flow pathway is considered to exhibit spontaneous characteristics when it is infrequently traversed by a large number of people (fig. 1).

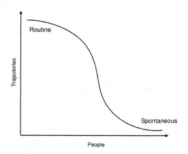

Fig. 1. Model to distinguish between routine and spontaneous characteristics in flow pathways

4.1 Data Transformation

To model urban flows (fig. 1), we propose a data transformation procedure for which we can transform spatial point type data into a graph structure suitable for expressing flow pathways [40]. The procedure consists of two steps. We begin by discretising the territory with an n^2 grid where n^n possible trajectories may occur. Next, we propagate a directed graph $G(V, E)$, where nodes $v_i \in V$ are cells in the grid generated in step 1. A directed edge $E(i, j)$ represents a movement trajectory from node v_i to node v_j if a tweet has been made by a user in cell v_i and cell v_j in chronological order. We adopt two attributes as edge weights: The number of aggregated trajectories $T(i,j)$ and the number of unique people $P(i,j)$ that move between cell v_i and cell v_j. Looping or self directed edges, for instance $E(i, i)$, are also accounted for in the same manner.

4.2   Interface Components

Our interface comprises of four components in a linked, integrated view (fig. 2). It contains a flow map, a time selection widget, a trajectory selection widget and a headcount selection weight. We implemented dynamic zooming in the flow map. Both weight and time selection widgets have dynamic filter ranges for the user to define filter boundaries. Inline with the visual information seeking mantra [41], all filter ranges are set to span the entire distribution while the map is set to the furthest zoom level on initialisation. This provides spatial planners with an overview of the data before further analytical task are carried out. The zoom level of the flow map can be modified with the mouse wheel and the filter range by manipulated by moving the interactive range sliders or selecting individual bars.

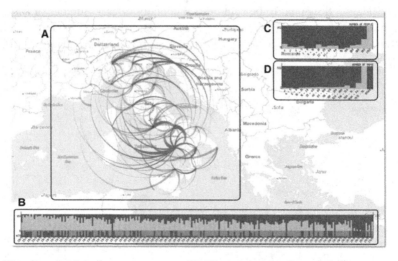

Fig. 2. FlowSampler interface components. (A) Flow map with flow pathways represented as arcs. Red arcs represent incoming flows while blue arcs represent outgoing flows. (B) Time selection widget. (C) Trajectory selection widget (D) Headcount selection widget.

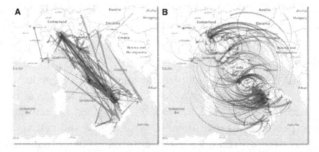

Fig. 3. Comparison between two flow representations. (A) Depending on the physical geometry of the territory and flow patterns in the data, polyline representations may create distracting crossings that are confusing to interpret. (B) Arc representations address this problem by separating the short flow from the long flows.

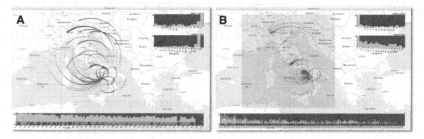

Fig. 4. FlowSampler configured to show flow pathways at two levels of spatial-temporal resolution. (A) Coarse granularity reveals general trends in the data. (B) Fine granularity allows spatial planers to identify outliers and nuances such as movements between locations that only occur at specific hours of the day.

Flow Map. The flow map provides a spatial view of the data. The principle behind flow map is based on a node-link type representation where trajectories are plotted as lines that link origin to destination. While this approach produces maps that are familiar to many people, it does not scale well to large numbers of trajectories. To reduce visual clutter, flow maps merge trajectories that share similar origins and destinations. A line of varying thickness is then use to express the number of trajectories that have been aggregated. Similarly, ellipses of varying diameter are used to represent self-directed flows. We adopt a node-link representation that can be super imposed onto a variety of base maps depending on various planning needs. To reduce ambiguity during interpretation, we represent flows with tapered polylines as recommended in literature [42]. While polylines are effective when flow distances are relatively short, they can become problematic when connections between two distant cells create long diagonal lines that may cause overlap or distracting crossings. To address the problem, we curve the polyline to form an arc. Arcs were chosen for the alternative representation, as they are a computationally cheap solution to avoid distracting crossings by separating the short flows from long flows. A disadvantage of the arc representation however is the added visual complexity it introduces to the display. There are two interactive features that support data exploration. Spatial planners may filter the flow to focus on a specific range of flow pathways in the data or select a cell to highlight the incoming and outgoing flows related to it. We tint selected flows with divergent colours to emphasize directionality.

Time Selection Widget. The time selection widget is an interactive split bar chart where each bar represents a time unit (i.e. week/day/hour) predefined by the spatial planer. Bars are arranged in a chronological order. The height of each bar in the upper half of the bar chart is used to encode the number of trips that occurred during that period while the lower half of the bar chart is used to indicate the total number of flows related to a selected cell. The lower half of the bar chart will be empty if no cells are selected.

Trajectory and Headcount Selection Widget. The trajectory selection widget and the headcount selection widget are histograms that visualise the distribution of the aggregated trajectories and unique people who travelled along a certain flow pathway respectively. The intervals of the histogram are determined by a linear interpolation by default but spatial planners may dynamically switch the display to a logarithmic interpolation in the event of a highly skewed distribution.

5   Use Cases

5.1   Investigating Daily Routine in Trip Making Behaviour

One purpose of FlowSampler is to experiment with alternative approaches to identify the centres of sub regions in territories based on urban flows. The significance of analysing geolocated social media data is that the information extracted may give an alternative image of how functional urban areas are shaped in comparison to existing techniques that mainly analyse home to work commuting information obtained through census data [4].

Using 734,494 geolocated tweets collected from 2,786 twitter users in Belgium over the duration of a year, we generate a flow map consisting of trajectories belonging to 2,194 users. We omit 592 users because of insufficient tweeting activity. Figure 5a. provides a visual summary of the trips that have occurred over the year. From the map, we identify four distinct clusters that reveal a polycentric distribution of movements. To obtain a map that illustrates routine trip making, we remove the flow pathways that exhibit spontaneous characteristics by filtering flows that fall into the lower percentile of the trajectory selection widget and flows that fall into the upper percentile of the headcount selection widget (fig. 5b). The resulting map characterises the routine trip making behaviour of Twitter users in Belgium. To verify the regularity of the remaining flow pathways, we inspect the frequency of these trips with the time selection widget. Through this process, we discovered that majority of the routine movements take place around local communities typically in towns and villages. Yet, we also observe routine intercity travel across contiguous urban areas between three major Belgian cities (fig. 5c).

5.2   Investigating Exceptional Trip Making Behaviour

To demonstrate the scalability of FlowSampler, we describe an orthogonal use case investigating exceptional, short-term transit behaviour that took place over the touristic season in Italy. The dataset we analyse consist of 13,953,814 tweets generated by 344,660 twitter users over a period of three months. For this study, we are specifically interested in identifying movements that converge on, and take place within, Cilento, a national park in southern Italy. From this data, we construct trajectories beloinging to 78,477 twitter users. We omit 266,183 users due to insufficient tweeting activity. The map in figure 6a. illustrates that majority of movement towards Cilento originate from three major Italian cities. We refine the spatial granularity of the map to obtain a more precise boundary over the park and exclude twitter users who were in fact travelling to nearby cities. This reduces the analysis to 1,214 trajectories that transit Cilento. Figure 6b. presents a micro view of the park showing a concentration of twitter users along the coastline. This reveals the extent by which the coastal regions are perceived as privileged destinations in contrast to the inland regions. Visually inspecting the

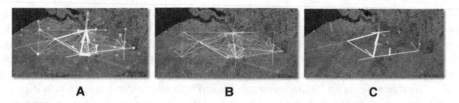

Fig. 5. (A) Flow map aggregated trajectories that have occurred over the course of a year in Belgium. We identify four distinct clusters that show a polycentric distribution of movement. (B) Flow pathways that exhibit spontaneous characteristics are removed from the analysis. (C) Flow pathways that represent the routine trip making behaviour of Twitter users in Belgium. A particularly striking feature in this map is the connection between three major Belgian cities.

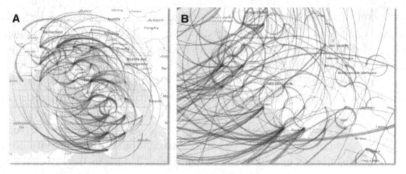

Fig. 6. (A) The arcs highlighted in red indicate that majority of the flow pathways heading towards Cilento Park originate from Milan, Rome and Naples. (B) Micro view of Cilento Park showing a concentration of activity near the coastland.

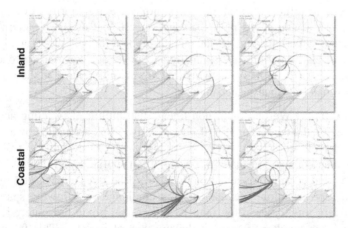

Fig. 7. Comparing the connectivity of coastal regions to inland regions. We observe that flows occurring in the inland regions are limited to adjacent localities while regions along the coastland are better connected. We tint unrelated flow pathways in a lighter shade to improve the legibility of the image.

incoming and outgoing edges of each node reveals an asymmetry in trip making behaviour. Whereas coastal regions appear well connected to other locations, trip making within the inland regions of Cilento tend to be limited to adjacent localities (fig. 7). This finding corresponds to the availability of transport infrastructure as well as to how the coastline is marketed as a key touristic attraction. Filtering the time selection widget further reveals an "inland, coastal, inland" travel pattern between two disjoint inland regions showing that the settlements along the coastline serve as important hubs for transit between locations.

6   Limitations, Uncertainty and Bias

We have described FlowSampler, a visual analytics system that supports the extraction and exploration of urban flows in geolocated social media data. A key advantage of this system is that it enables planners to interactively reconfigure the interface to explore and detect patterns in the data at various spatial and temporal granularities. Furthermore, our system allows spatial planners to include external geographic information in form of base maps to evaluate the significance of patterns that they have identified. To show the functionality and scalability of our system, we presented two use cases that investigate urban flows at different spatial and temporal scales. We identified pathways of routine movement that occur within Flanders, a region in Belgium, over the duration of a year, and traced exceptional transit activity converging on and subsequently occur within Cilento, a national park in Italy over the touristic season spanning three months. While initial deployment of FlowSampler with the spatial planners in our department has resulted in positive feedback, several discussion topics have been raised.

Skewed Demographic. As existing studies indicate that majority of the online social media users are young adults [43], there is concern that the flow patterns we detect only represent a partial slice of the actual population on the ground. While we acknowledge this limitation, we would like to point out that our approach provides equally valuable and alternative insights that are complimentary to the results derived from other urban flow analysis techniques.

Sporadic Activity. We observe a non-linear distribution of tweeting activity in the form of a long tail where a handful of highly active users are trailed by a substantially larger number of people who tweet sporadically. Because highly active users have trajectories that comprise of many more trips than sporadic user, the uneven distribution implies that certain movement pathways will be over emphasized thus skewing the overall representation. We address this challenge by allowing spatial planners to interactively modify the flow map to determine which attribute edge thickness encodes (i.e. the number of trips or the number of people). This facilitates visual comparison between both attributes in order to identify bias in the representation. Another feasible solution is to pre-filter overly active users to remove the bias entirely from the analysis however this narrows the slice of the population being studied.

Privacy. Our system is designed to present information about aggregated movement behavior yet we provide functionalities for the information to be disaggregated. While we acknowledge that it maybe difficult to prevent the recovery of personal information under such circumstances, imposing control measures to displace or distort the data maybe counter productive for the spatial planners.

7   Future Work

There are several avenues for future work. We plan to conduct a comparative study with existing urban flow analysis techniques in order to evaluate and better understand the added value and potential pitfalls that may occur when using geolocated social media data to inform spatial planning. To optimise our system, we will experiment with visualisation techniques such as interactive clustering [44-46] to address challenges with visual clutter. Finally, feedback from spatial planners suggests that contextual data such keywords could be useful for characterising flow patterns. The occurrence of special events such as festivals or strikes can be better understood by combining what people say with what they do.

References

1. Asakura, Y., Hato, E.: Tracking survey for individual travel behaviour using mobile communication instruments. Transportation Research Part C: Emerging Technologies **12**, 273–291 (2004)
2. Witlox, F.: Evaluating the reliability of reported distance data in urban travel behaviour analysis. J. Transp. Geogr. **15**, 172–183 (2007)
3. O'Neill, E., Kostakos, V., Kindberg, T., Schiek, A., Penn, A., Fraser, D.S., Jones, T.: Instrumenting the city: Developing methods for observing and understanding the digital cityscape. In: Dourish, P., Friday, A. (eds.) UbiComp 2006. LNCS, vol. 4206, pp. 315–332. Springer, Heidelberg (2006)
4. Servillo, L., Atkinson, R., Smith, I., Russo, A., Sýkora, L.k., Demazière, C., Hamdouche, A.-I.: TOWN, small and medium sized towns in their functional territorial context, Final Report, Espon (2014)
5. Slocum, T.A.: Flow mapping. In: Thematic cartography and visualization, pp. 360–370. Prentice hall, Upper Saddle River (1999)
6. Demirbas, M., Bayir, M.A., Akcora, C.G., Yilmaz, Y.S., Ferhatosmanoglu, H.: Crowdsourced sensing and collaboration using twitter. In: IEEE International Symposium on a World of Wireless Mobile and Multimedia Networks (WoWMoM) 2010, pp. 1–9. IEEE (2010)
7. Silva, T.H., Vaz de Melo, P.O.S., Almeida, J.M.d., Loureiro, A.A.F.: Uncovering properties in participatory sensor networks. In: Proceedings of the 4th ACM International Workshop on Hot Topics in Planet-Scale Measurement, pp. 33–38. ACM (2012)
8. Burke, J.A., Estrin, D., Hansen, M., Parker, A., Ramanathan, N., Reddy, S., Srivastava, M.B.: Participatory sensing. Center for Embedded Network Sensing (2006)
9. Foth, M., Choi, J.H.-j., Satchell, C.: Urban informatics. In: Proceedings of the ACM 2011 Conference on Computer Supported Cooperative Work, pp. 1–8. ACM (2011)
10. Twitter. https://business.twitter.com/twitter-101

11. Java, A., Song, X., Finin, T., Tseng, B.: Why we twitter: understanding microblogging usage and communities. In: Proceedings of the 9th WebKDD and 1st SNA-KDD 2007 Workshop on Web Mining and Social Network Analysis, pp. 56–65. ACM (2007)
12. Cranshaw, J., Schwartz, R., Hong, J.I., Sadeh, N.M.: The livehoods project: utilizing social media to understand the dynamics of a city. In: ICWSM (2012)
13. Kling, F., Pozdnoukhov, A.: When a city tells a story: urban topic analysis. In: Proceedings of the 20th International Conference on Advances in Geographic Information Systems, pp. 482–485. ACM (2012)
14. Gonzalez, M.C., Hidalgo, C.A., Barabasi, A.-L.: Understanding individual human mobility patterns. Nature **453**, 779–782 (2008)
15. Song, C., Qu, Z., Blumm, N., Barabási, A.-L.: Limits of predictability in human mobility. Science **327**, 1018–1021 (2010)
16. Sevtsuk, A., Ratti, C.: Does urban mobility have a daily routine? Explorations using aggregate mobile network data. In: Proceedings of the 11th International Conference on Computers in Urban Planning and Urban Management (2009)
17. Doyle, J., Hung, P., Farrell, R., McLoone, S.: Population Mobility Dynamics Estimated from Mobile Telephony Data. Journal of Urban Technology **21**, 109–132 (2014)
18. Pousman, Z., Stasko, J.T., Mateas, M.: Casual information visualization: Depictions of data in everyday life. IEEE Trans. Visual Comput. Graphics **13**, 1145–1152 (2007)
19. Grammel, L., Tory, M., Storey, M.: How information visualization novices construct visualizations. IEEE Trans. Visual Comput. Graphics **16**, 943–952 (2010)
20. Citylab.   http://www.citylab.com/commute/2012/02/map-day-how-people-travel-around-city/1131/
21. Twitter Tongues. http://twitter.mappinglondon.co.uk
22. Twitter NYC. http://ny.spatial.ly
23. Business Insider. http://www.businessinsider.com/android-is-for-poor-people-maps-2014-4
24. Frias-Martinez, V., Soto, V., Hohwald, H., Frias-Martinez, E.: Characterizing urban landscapes using geolocated tweets. In: Privacy, Security, Risk and Trust (PASSAT), 2012 International Conference on Social Computing (SocialCom), pp. 239–248. IEEE (2012)
25. De Longueville, B., Smith, R.S., Luraschi, G.: OMG, from here, I can see the flames!: a use case of mining location based social networks to acquire spatio-temporal data on forest fires. In: Proceedings of the 2009 International Workshop on Location Based Social Networks, pp. 73–80. ACM (2009)
26. Prasetyo, P.K., Gao, M., Lim, E.-P., Scollon, C.N.: Social sensing for urban crisis management: The case of singapore haze. In: Jatowt, A., Lim, E.-P., Ding, Y., Miura, A., Tezuka, T., Dias, G., Tanaka, K., Flanagin, A., Dai, B.T. (eds.) SocInfo 2013. LNCS, vol. 8238, pp. 478–491. Springer, Heidelberg (2013)
27. Wei, L.Y., Zheng, Y., Peng, W.C.: Constructing popular routes from uncertain trajectories. In: Proceedings of the 18th ACM SIGKDD International Conference on Knowledge Discovery and Data Mining, pp. 195–203. ACM (2012)
28. Pan, B., Zheng, Y., Wilkie, D., Shahabi, C.: Crowd sensing of traffic anomalies based on human mobility and social media. In: Proceedings of the 21st ACM SIGSPATIAL International Conference on Advances in Geographic Information Systems, pp. 334–343. ACM (2013)
29. Fuchs, G., Andrienko, G., Andrienko, N., Jankowski, P.: Extracting personal behavioral patterns from geo-referenced tweets. AGILE (2013)

30. Andrienko, G., Andrienko, N., Fuchs, G., Raimond, A.-M.O., Symanzik, J., Ziemlicki, C.: Extracting semantics of individual places from movement data by analyzing temporal patterns of visits. In: Proceedings of The First ACM SIGSPATIAL International Workshop on Computational Models of Place (COMP 2013) (2013)

31. Gabrielli, L., Rinzivillo, S., Ronzano, F., Villatoro, D.: From tweets to semantic trajectories: Mining anomalous urban mobility patterns. In: Nin, J., Villatoro, D. (eds.) CitiSens 2013. LNCS, vol. 8313, pp. 25–34. Springer, Heidelberg (2014)

32. Sedlmair, M., Meyer, M., Munzner, T.: Design study methodology: Reflections from the trenches and the stacks. IEEE Trans. Visual Comput. Graphics **18**, 2431–2440 (2012)

33. Thomas, J.J., Cook, K.A.: A visual analytics agenda. IEEE Comput. Graphics Appl. **26**, 10–13 (2006)

34. DiBiase, D.: Visualization in the earth sciences. Earth and Mineral Sciences **59**, 13–18 (1990)

35. Robinson, A.H.: The thematic maps of Charles Joseph Minard* (1967)

36. Tobler, W.R.: Experiments in migration mapping by computer. The American Cartographer **14**, 155–163 (1987)

37. Phan, D., Xiao, L., Yeh, R., Hanrahan, P.: Flow map layout. In: IEEE Symposium on Information Visualization 2005, pp. 219–224. IEEE (2005)

38. Wood, J., Dykes, J., Slingsby, A.: Visualisation of origins, destinations and flows with OD maps. The Cartographic Journal **47**, 117–129 (2010)

39. Ghoniem, M., Fekete, J., Castagliola, P.: A comparison of the readability of graphs using node-link and matrix-based representations. In: IEEE Symposium on Information Visualization, pp. 17–24. IEEE (2004)

40. Guo, D.: Flow mapping and multivariate visualization of large spatial interaction data. IEEE Trans. Visual Comput. Graphics **15**, 1041–1048 (2009)

41. Shneiderman, B.: The eyes have it: A task by data type taxonomy for information visualizations. In: Proceedings: IEEE Symposium on Visual Languages, pp. 336–343. IEEE (1996)

42. Holten, D., van Wijk, J.J.: A user study on visualizing directed edges in graphs. In: Proceedings of the SIGCHI Conference on Human Factors in Computing Systems, pp. 2299–2308. ACM (2009)

43. Duggan, M., Smith, A.: Social media update 2013. Pew Internet and American Life Project (2013)

44. Rinzivillo, S., Pedreschi, D., Nanni, M., Giannotti, F., Andrienko, N., Andrienko, G.: Visually driven analysis of movement data by progressive clustering. Information Visualization **7**, 225–239 (2008)

45. Andrienko, G., Andrienko, N., Rinzivillo, S., Nanni, M., Pedreschi, D., Giannotti, F.: Interactive visual clustering of large collections of trajectories. In: IEEE Symposium on Visual Analytics Science and Technology, pp. 3–10. IEEE (2009)

46. Adrienko, N., Adrienko, G.: Spatial generalization and aggregation of massive movement data. IEEE Trans. Visual Comput. Graphics **17**, 205–219 (2011)

Policing Engagement via Social Media

Miriam Fernandez[✉], A. Elizabeth Cano, and Harith Alani

Knowledge Media Intitute, The Open University,
Walton Hall, Milton Keynes, MK76AA, England
{m.fernandez,amparo.cano,h.alani}@open.ac.uk

Abstract. Social Media is commonly used by policing organisations to spread the word on crime, weather, missing person, etc. In this work we aim to understand what attracts citizens to engage with social media policing content. To study these engagement dynamics we propose a combination of machine learning and semantic analysis techniques. Our initial research, performed over 3,200 posts from @dorsetpolice Twitter account, shows that writing longer posts, with positive sentiment, and sending them out before 4pm, was found to increase the probability of attracting attention. Additionally, posts about weather, roads and infrastructures, mentioning places, are also more likely to attract attention.

Keywords: Social web · Semantic web · Engagement · Police

1 Introduction

Social media is now commonly used to help communicate policing messages to the general public. Many forces have staff dedicated to this purpose and to improve the spreading of key messages to wider social media communities. However, while guidance reports claim that social media can enhance the reputation and accessibility of police staff to their communities [5], research studies have shown that exchanges between the citizens and the police are infrequent. Social media works as an extra channel for delivering messages but not as a mean for enabling a deeper engagement with the public. [2]

Studies targeting citizen engagement towards police forces in social media have been mainly focused on studying the different social media strategies that police forces use to interact with the public [2, 3, 5, 6]. However, it is still unclear which factors drive the attention of citizens towards social media messages coming from police information sources. There are various parameters that can influence engagement on Twitter, such as the characteristics of the content, writing style, time of posting, network position, etc. [1, 8, 9, 10, 11, 12]. Analysing these parameters can help identifying actions and recommendations that could increase public's engagement.

In this paper we present a pilot study developed in collaboration with the Dorset Police, UK. This organisation is moving towards a more engaging style of social media usage and it is interested in scientifically identifying best practices for engaging the public on Twitter. For the purpose of this study we have collected 3,200 posts

© Springer International Publishing Switzerland 2015
L.M. Aiello and D. McFarland (Eds.): SocInfo 2014 Workshops, LNCS 8852, pp. 18–26, 2015.
DOI: 10.1007/978-3-319-15168-7_3

from @*dorsetpolice* Twitter account and we have investigated the key characteristics of those messages attracting the citizen's attention. To investigate engagement towards these messages we propose a combination of Machine Learning (ML) and semantic analysis techniques. Using ML analysis techniques we aim to identify the key language and time features of those messages. In addition, a semantic content analysis is used to investigate the key topics (concepts and entities) associated with engagement.

Our results show that writing longer tweets, with positive sentiment, and sending them out before 4pm, was found to increase the probability of attracting attention. Additionally, citizens are more interested about tweets mentioning places and related with topics such as weather conditions, roads and infrastructures. Note that, this study is not meant to be a representative of all forces, but rather a focused study on @dorsetpolice. Future work will include the analysis of other police forces [4].

The rest of the paper is organised as follows. Section 2 provides an overview of the related work in the area of policing engagement in social media. Section 3 describes the dataset used in this work and the results of the conducted engagement analyses. Conclusions are reported in section 4.

2   Related Work

Previous studies have investigated police adoption in social media by measuring the growth in the number of followers of Twitter police accounts. Crump, J. [2], for example, obtained a positive correlation between the number of followers and the length that an account had been active. This study also investigated the topics of tweets posted by police accounts and extracted four main categories for those topics: patrol (reports from police patrolling), information (police requesting information from the public), partners (messages associated with emergency services or local authorities) and other (messages that did not relate to any of the above categories).

Heverin, H. investigated the use of Twitter by police departments from large U.S. cities (cities with populations greater than 300,000). This study found that the primary use of Twitter by city police departments is informing about crime or incident related information (45.3 % of tweets). Other uses of Twitter included sharing department, event, suspect, prevention, and traffic information. This study highlighted that; overall, city police departments do not use Twitter to converse directly with members of the public.

Other works have analysed policing messages in the context of riots [3] and protests [6]. The work of Denef et al. [3] analyses the Twitter communication by the London Metropolitan Police (MET) and the Greater Manchester Police (GMP) during the London riots in August 2011. The study concluded that, while MET followed an instrumental approach in their communication, in which the police aimed to remain in a controlled position and keep a distance to the general public, GMP developed an expressive approach, in which the police actively decreased the distance to the citizens.

Earl et al. [6] analysed the engagement of citizens (protesters) during the 2009 G20 meetings held in Pittsburgh. This study concluded that, during this event, Twitter was used by the citizens to share information that was formerly monopolized by the police, such as the location of the police or their actions; creating new dynamics in protester and police interactions.

While all these works focus on understanding the different approaches of police communication, and the different topic categories of such communication, none of these works investigate the engagement dynamics of the citizens towards social media policing content. Understanding what are they features of those messages that attract the citizen's attention (How are they written? When are they posted? Which topics they talk about?) may help police forces to enhance the impact that they have on their communities.

3   Engagement Analysis

In this section we present our engagement analysis study. For the purpose of this study we have collected the latest 3,200 posts from the @dorsetpolice Twitter account, published between 2011-12-23 and 2014-06-12. This account has around 14K followers, and over 3.3K tweets in the form of announcements, appeals, crime reports, etc. From the collected 3,200 posts (note that this limit is established by the Twitter API), 733 are not originally written by @dorsetpolice, but are messages retweeted from other sources. Also 74 of the collected posts are not initialisations but replies to other tweets.

To analyse these data we use a two-phase approach. In the first part we apply a machine learning analysis method [1] to identify the key linguistic and time characteristics of those posts attracting attention. In the second part we conduct a semantic analysis to extract the key topics (concepts and entities) of the policing messages. We combine machine learning with semantic technologies to better understand, not only how and when messages should be written to attract attention, but also which topics users are more likely to engage with.

3.1   Expressing Engagement in Twitter

In the Twitter platform, retweeting, favouring and replying are actions that require an explicit interaction from a user towards another one. These actions have been repeatedly considered in the literature of social media as engagement indicators [8, 9, 10, 11, 12]. In total, the posts generated by the @dorsetpolice Twitter account received 30,726 retweets. To provide an overview, the following table shows the top 10 retweeted posts in our collected dataset.

Table 1. Top 10 retweeted posts. Note that mentions and links have been anonymized.

Post	Date	Ret
Regarding tweets to @*user1* - We are aware of the issue and we are actively looking into it.	2012-07-30 22:47:19	6672
Regarding tweets to @*user1* - 17-year-old man arrested this morning at a guest house in the Weymouth area. Enquiries continue.	2012-07-31 07:51:26	5069
RT @*user2*: URGENT ALERT (please RT) Mass ransomware spamming event targeting UK computer users. More... *URL₁*	2013-11-18 09:39:44	1434
RT @*user3*: Today is #WorldMentalHealthDay RT if you agree: We need support and respect. We won't give up. *URL₂*	2013-10-10 09:54:56	853
RT @*user4*: Please RT: Stay away from the shoreline this evening/tomorrow. Coastal paths could be dangerous. Risk of being swept out to ...	2014-01-02 13:48:04	392
RT @*user5*: Have you seen missing person Richard Brockbank from Newbury? *URL₃* @*user6* #findbrocky *URL₄*	2014-05-21 16:46:58	235
RT @*user7*: Severe weather warnings have been issued for the next five days. More info at *URL₆, URL₇*	2014-02-04 16:32:23	217
Wanted Poole man Dean Goodwin has been arrested by armed police in Poole and is in police custody	2012-11-27 18:05:15	177
Someone must recognise suspect from #Bournemouth robbery. Call 101 if you do. Please RT. #CCTV *URL₈*	2014-05-07 22:51:59	159
RT @*missingpeople*: Zara went missing from Wimbourne, Dorset last month. Please #jointhesearch RT and help us find her *URL₉*	2013-06-05 16:21:09	136

As we can see in Table 1, the top two posts talk about the detention of a criminal. The remaining posts focus on a variety of issues, such as sea and weather warnings as well as the tasks of searching for lost people or suspects.

Note that when users retweet they spread the message to their followers (as opposed to favouring or replying) leading to a potential stronger involvement and engagement. In this work we consider retweets as indicator of engagement for the rest of our analysis. Tweets that have been retweeted at least once by the citizens are considered *seed-posts*. Those tweets that have not been retweeted (i.e., have not obtained any direct engagement from the citizens) are considered *non-seed posts*. Table 2 summarises the dataset, and shows the number of seeds vs. non seed posts. As we can see from the table, over the course of nearly 3 years, from 2011-12-23 till 2014-06-12, 86% of the tweets received at least one retweet (*seed posts*).

Table 2. Dataset description (number of seeds vs. non seed posts)

Dataset	Time Spam	Num posts	Seed posts	Non seed posts
Twitter	2011-12-23 2014-06-12	3,200	2,770	430

The next two sections present the analysis of engagement dynamics performed over this dataset. The first part consists on a ML analysis, which aims to detect the linguistic and time patterns of seed vs. non-seed posts. The second part performs a semantic analysis to identify the key topics of seeds vs. non-seed posts.

3.2   Machine Learning Analysis

To identify the key characteristics of those posts generating attention we follow our previous approach [1]. This approach characterises posts by analysing how they are written and when they are published. Our goal is to identify, by using a set of features, the main characteristics of those posts that generate higher levels of engagement. The features considered for this analysis are listed below:

- *Post length*: Number of terms in the post.

- *Complexity*: Cumulative entropy of terms within the posts to gauge the concentration of language and its dispersion across different terms. Let n be the number of unique terms within the post p and fi the frequency of the term t within p. Therefore, complexity is given by:

$$complexity(p) = \frac{1}{n} \sum_{i=1}^{n} f_i (long_n - \log f_i)$$

- *Readability*: This feature gauges how hard the post is to parse by humans. To measure readability we use the Gunning Fox Index[1] using the average sentence length (ASL) and the percentage of complex words (PCW).

$$0.4 * (ASL + PCW)$$

- *Referral Count*: number of hyperlinks (URLS) present in the posts.

- *Informativeness*: The novelty of the post's terms with respect to the other posts. We derive this measure using Term Frequency-Inverse Document Frequency (TF-IDF):

$$\sum_{t \in p} tf_{t,p} \times idf_t$$

- *Polarity*: Average polarity (sentiment) of the post. We are computing sentiment by using SentiStrength,[2] a state of the art method for analysing sentiment in social media data.

- *Mentions*: Number of mentions (references to other users) within the tweets.

- *Time of the day*: Time of the day in which the tweet has been posted.

To extract the key characteristics of those posts generating attention we firstly identify the characteristics of those tweets that are followed by an engagement action (*seed posts*), and we then identify the characteristics of those seed posts that are followed by a high level of engagement (*high number of retweets*).

To perform the first task we train different ML classifiers and select the one that provides a better classification of seed posts, in this case the J48 classifier tree. Once the optimal classifier has been selected, features are removed (one at a time) from the classifier and a drop in performance is measured. Those features that generate a higher performance drop are considered the most discriminative ones, i.e., those ones

---

[1] http://en.wikipedia.org/wiki/Gunning_fog_index
[2] http://sentistrength.wlv.ac.uk/

that better distinguish the seed posts (those generating engagement) vs. the non-seed posts. For more details of the complete analysis process see [1].

Figure 1 shows the result of this analysis. More particularly, the top 4 discriminative features that help distinguishing seed vs. non-seed posts are: post length, complexity, polarity and mentions. Posts that generate some level of engagement are generally longer, present a higher level of complexity (i.e., the post contains many terms which are not repeated often), present slightly more positive than negative sentiment and mention at least one user within the tweet.

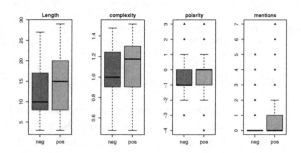

Fig. 1. Features with higher influence on engagement levels

Once we have identified the key characteristics of seed posts, our goal is to determine which are the characteristics of those seed posts that generate higher attention levels. To obtain this information we create a linear regression model where the different features listed above are used to approximate the number of engagement interactions that a tweet is receiving. Significant coefficients (p<0.5) are associated with complexity, mentions and time in the day. More specifically, those tweets generating higher levels of attention contain many terms that are not repeated often, mention several users in the tweet, and are posted between 8:00 a.m and 16:00 p.m. As Dorset Police indicated, for the moment, there are no dedicated resources for actively tweeting, monitoring or responding to comments outside that time range.

3.3   Semantic Analysis

Understanding the content of the posts, and in particular the key topics of interest for the users, is important to understand engagement. For this purpose we have semantically annotated the tweets of our dataset by using TextRazor.[3] This annotator provides us with the entities from all seed and non-seed posts in our dataset, thereby returning a mapping between each post and a list of DBPedia URIs. We can then identify the concepts that are referred to within a post by looking up each entity's rdf:type in the DBPedia ontology and recording these concepts in a list for each post.

---

[3] https://www.textrazor.com/

Table 3. Top entities/concepts for seeds vs. non-seed posts

Top Entity [Types] Seed Posts	Top Entity [Types] NonSeed Posts
Dorset [Place, PopulatedPlace]	Bournemouth [Place, PopulatedPlace]
Bournemouth [Place, PopulatedPlace]	Weymouth,_Dorset [Place, PopulatedPlace]
England [Place, Country, PopulatedPlace]	Dorset [Place, PopulatedPlace]
Flood	Burglary [Crime]
Weather	Dorset_Police [LawEnforcementAgency]
Weymouth,_Dorset [Place, PopulatedPlace]	Closed-circuit_television
Poole [Place, PopulatedPlace]	Poole [Place, PopulatedPlace]
Snow	Twitter [Organisation, Company]
A31_road [Place, Road]	Bridport [Place, PopulatedPlace]
Collision	Driving_under_the_influence
South_West_England [Place, PopulatedPlace]	Assault [Crime]
Dorchester,_Dorset [Place, PopulatedPlace	999_(emergency_telephone_number)
Volvo_XC90 [Automobile]	Traffic
Severe_weather [WeatherHazards, Danger]	Robbery [Crime]
A35_road [Place, Road]	Property_damage [Crime]

Table 3 presents the top entities/concepts for the seed and non-seed posts respectively (top entities are the most frequent ones within our dataset). Note that only the URL label has been selected for better visualisation. However, each of those entity labels corresponds to a specific Wikipedia page, e.g. (http://en.wikipedia.org/wiki/Anti-social_behaviour). Also note that not all the entities identified by TextRazor have associated an rdf:type concept in the DBPedia ontology.

Locations, such as Dorset, Bournemouth, Poole or Weymouth are constant across the two groups of posts. However, seed posts include less focalised locations, such as England and South West England. Additionally, seed posts include entities related with weather (snow, severe weather, flood) as well as road an infrastructures (A31 road, A35 road, etc.). Non seed posts, on the other hand, talk about crimes such as burglary, assault or driving under the influence of alcohol.

As we can see from this first overview, semantic entities help us to understand those topics of interests for the citizens, and to differentiate some of the key themes attracting their attention (e.g., road problems or weather conditions). A further analysis should be performed to investigate deeper which combinations of entities spike higher attention levels, in which context they appear (semantic relations with other tweets), and how they differ from the information explicitly provided by hashtags. These are part of our future line of work.

4   Discussions and Conclusions

This paper presents an analysis of policing engagement via social media. The aim of our work is to understand what are the characteristics of the content posted by police forces that attracts higher attention levels. By understanding these characteristics we could provide guidelines to the police forces of when and how they should write their posts; so that police messages reach to larger audiences and increase engagement within the communities.

To analyse this content we propose an approach that combines ML techniques with semantic technologies. While ML techniques help us to understand the more discriminative language and time features of those posts generating attention, semantic technologies help us to better understand and categorise the topics emerging from the content. Our analyses show that, writing longer tweets, with positive sentiment, and sending them out before 4pm, was found to increase the probability of attracting attention. Additionally, tweets about weather, roads and infrastructures, mentioning locations are also likely to attract attention.

It is important to highlight that this is a preliminary study and therefore have several limitations. First of all, only one social media platform (Twitter) has been considered for this study. Other social media platforms, such as Facebook, or even news media articles, should be taken into account to have a better understanding of the citizens' engagement towards social media policing content. Secondly, only one police Twitter account has been selected for the analysis performed in this work. Engagement dynamics may vary across the accounts of different police institutions [4]. Finally, only retweets have been considered as engagement indicator. Other indicators, in particular replies, should be also considered.

Additionally to expanding the number of platforms, accounts, and engagement indicators, our future work includes a deeper exploration of how semantics can be used to understand policing content. In particular we aim to explore the relations among tweets via the semantic entities and concepts they share. Our final goal is to be able to analyse conceptual evolution of the posts over time periods.

Acknowledgments. Thanks to all @dorsetpolice for their contribution to this work.

References

1. Rowe, M., Angeletou, S., Alani, H.: Anticipating discussion activity on community forums. In: Third IEEE International Conference on Social Computing (SocialCom 2011), Boston, MA, USA, 9–11 October 2011, pp. 315–322 (2011)
2. Crump, J.: What are the police doing on Twitter? Social media, the police and the public. Policy & Internet 3(4), 1–27 (2011)
3. Sebastian, D., Bayerl, P.S., Kaptein, N.A.: Social media and the police: tweeting practices of british police forces during the August 2011 riots. In: Proceedings of the SIGCHI Conference on Human Factors in Computing Systems. ACM (2013)
4. UK Police Twitter Accounts. https://twitter.com/nickkeane/lists/uk-police-force-twitters
5. NPIA: Engage: Digital and Social Media for the Police Service. National Policing Improvement Agency, London (2010)
6. Earl, J., et al.: This protest will be tweeted: Twitter and protest policing during the Pittsburgh G20. Information, Communication & Society 16(4), 459–478 (2013)
7. Bayerk, P.S., et al:. Who wants police in social media. In: Proceedings of the European Conference of Social Media, Brighton, UK (2014)
8. Cha, M., Haddadi, H., Benevenuto, F., Gummadi, K.P.: Measuring user influence in twitter: The million follower fallacy. In: Proc. 4th Int. AAAI Conf. on Weblogs and Social Media (ICWSM), Washington, DC (2010)

9. Gomez, V., Kaltenbrunner, A., López, V.: Statistical analysis of the social network and discussion threads in slashdot. In: WWW 2008: Proceeding of the 17th International Conference on World Wide Web, pp. 645–654. ACM, New York (2008)
10. Naveed, N., Gottron, T., Kunegis, J., Alhadi, A.C.: Bad news travel fast: A content-based analysis of interestingness on twitter. In: Proc. 3rd Int. Conf. on Web Science, 2011, Bon, Germany (2011)
11. Sousa, D., Sarmento, L., Rodrigues, E.M.: Characterization of the twitter @replies network: are user ties social or topical? In: Proceedings of the 2nd International Workshop on Search and Mining User-generated Contents (SMUC), Toronto, Canada (2010)
12. Suh, B., Hong, L., Pirolli, P., Ed Chi, H.: Want to be retweeted? Large scale analytics on factors impacting retweet in Twitter network. In: Proc. IEEE Second Int. Conf. on Social Computing (SocialCom) (2010)

Digital Social Media to Enhance the Public Realm in Historic Cities

Morandi Corinna[1], Palmieri Riccardo[2], and Tomarchio Ludovica[3(✉)]

[1] Dipartimento di Architettura e Studi Urbani-DAStU, Politecnico di Milano,
Via Bonardi 3, 20133 Milano, Italy
corinna.morandi@polimi.it
[2] Hagenauestrasse 13, 104345 Berlin, Germany
riccpalmieri@gmail.com
[3] Politecnico di Milano, Via Ripamonti 9, 20136 Milano, Italy
ludovicatomarchio@gmail.com

Abstract. The research aims at exploring a methodology for the use of *digital social media* (*DSM*) to study and influence people's behaviors within the public realm of an historic city center. Potentialities and limitations, created by the use of digital social media for urban analysis and planning, are spotted regarding the specific conditions of an historic city center with the goal of creating a more livable public realm. The research aims at drafting a general methodology both in data mining both in public places promotion and enhancement, through information and digital connection, referring to the specific case of historic city centers. The research considers the case study of Urbino, in the Marche region (Italy), and carries on different analyses and proposals of intervention based on digital social media.

Keywords: Public realm · Historic cities · Information technologies · Social media · Urban analysis · Information strategy

1   Introduction

The research[1] at issue aimed at defining a methodology to explore the potentialities of digital social media (DSM) to study people's behavior within the public realm of an historic city center and to propose a strategy able to influence it, through information flows and media activities.

The Italian peninsula is constellated by a very conspicuous number of ancient municipalities, where people keep on dwelling, although increasing preservation restrictions. The dichotomy between the spaces of these cities and the expectation of contemporary dwellers is dramatically increasing in time. Particularly, the research fo-

---

[1] The research has been developed within the activities related to a master thesis discussed at *Politecnico of Milan* in April 2013. The thesis *Urbino: can digital technology enhance historic public realm?* was the joint effort of three Politecnico students under the supervision of Prof.ssa Corinna Morandi, Prof. Paolo Ceccarelli and Prof.ssa Agata Spaziante.

© Springer International Publishing Switzerland 2015
L.M. Aiello and D. McFarland (Eds.): SocInfo 2014 Workshops, LNCS 8852, pp. 27–34, 2015.
DOI: 10.1007/978-3-319-15168-7_4

cused on the case of Urbino, a historic city center in Italy, listed as UNESCO heritage and hosting a university pole. The difficulties to intervene with a material transformation of the city could foster the use of digital social media as tools for an intervention that shifts its field of action from the physical dimension to the informational approach. Based on those principles, we tested this praxis on the historic center of Urbino and we present in this paper the adopted methodology and its results.

In the first part of the paper we trace the literature references and define the main features of the case study Urbino.

Then we present the outcome of the analyses obtained by data mining of digital social media. In particular, we focus on how the geographical and social features of Urbino offered unique conditions and we investigate what kind of data are worth to be stored and what analyses are relevant for this specific case.

In the last part we present the strategy to reactivate the public spaces of Urbino based on injecting in the historic fabric new activities connected with the use of digital technology, whose accessibility and interconnection is enhanced by a designed flow of information. This strategy also seeks solidification of the community bonds of Urbino, particularly for students, facilitating a more active citizenship.

2   Relevant Works

Nowadays, information technologies are part of our daily life and are influencing the way we use and experience the space we live. It is important to consider new forms of communication when acting within the city and its spaces, assuming that information may be an ingredient that – as well as uses and physical infrastructures – drives the public realm. According to theoretical framework we referred to, digital technologies are relevant in planning and urban design in different ways:

- In first instance the possibility to consider digital social media data disclosures innovative manners of *analyzing the public realm*. There is a huge amount of invisible data daily produced by citizens: places are embedded with a series of media contents that once revealed might give new insights [2], [8,9], [11], [15,16].
- Secondly a *new approach to design* should be considered: points distant one from the other, working reciprocally once they are digitally connected [1], [4,5], [12]. Referring to *Networked urbanism* means analysing and planning the urban environment with an information based approach, reasoning in terms of *nodes* (points) and *connections* (network); where the nodes are public and semi-public spaces assumed to be the core of not private activities and the *connections*, assuring the exchange among the nodes, are both the physical (roads, streets) and virtual (internet connection, video-streaming, information exchange) tools for communication. In this wider connotation *accessibility* also means "published on the web", while *density* stands for *frequency of intercommunication among different places through virtual information sharing*. Thus, it is possible to create a more liveable system of public spaces considering a series of isolated points that work synergistically as if they were physically co-present and whose activities are "advertised" via media.

- A tool for place making. But communication technologies could also be used in order to drive citizen towards a more active role with the public spaces their cities, to support grass-root common projects and to strengthen the community ties in general terms. DSM are able to create connections among strangers and to provide a platform for a more proactive citizenship [6,7], [14].

3   Urbino: Why It Could Be Assumed as a Case Study

Urbino is a small-sized city located in the "heart" of the Italian peninsula; it is listed under the UNESCO patronage since 1983, thanks to its prominent historic heritage dated back to the Renaissance.

The condition of isolation – both geographical and infrastructural – represented for our research an in-vitro test situation. The number of observable social phenomena is limited and bearable; cases of "contamination" by exogenous factors – meaning social interactions coming from outside the city center – are rare and controllable.

Moreover Urbino hosts a huge university pole, thus students represents a significant slice of the population living within the city center and this conjunction is relevant for two main reasons:

- Digital devices, especially with a socially oriented purpose, are particularly spread among people between 15 and 30 years. Since university students fall entirely in this age-range and since these latter also represent a conspicuous slice of the urban population of Urbino, a preponderant number of users is observable using data coming from digital social interactions;
- Every year, young people arrive in Urbino from all over Italy, in order to attend university, who will leave the city once their education is completed. Students are thus temporary users of Urbino and this condition is cause – and then again effect – of a lack of awareness towards the common value of public spaces. Such indifference is exacerbated due to the failure of these venues in satisfying the needs and demands of the students;

Moreover, the precepts of integral conservation of the architectural and historical heritage, further intensified by the declaration as UNESCO site, made it impossible to offer a tangible answer to the requests of those who live – or should live – in the historic city.

The aim of our research, therefore, was to give indications for a possible strategy of intervention, that could make the public realm of the historic city more suitable to the needs of young people, keeping in mind the neo-born practices influenced by the extensive use of digital social devices.

4   Data Mining Processes to Trace the Public Life of an Italian Historic City Center

The use and spread of digital social devices has produced a vast amount of data that could be collected in real time maps and give new insights to the way people live within the city.

Nowadays a great optimism is perceived towards the possibilities aroused by the collection and the reading of users' generated data, produced by digital social media activities: these types of observations may require a moment of reflection to understand what significant analyses could be drawn out starting from the interpretation of user's generated data; in particular what analyses could be significant in the case of Urbino and more generally for historic cities centers.

As previously introduced, this research finds particularly relevant to consider data from social media in places like Urbino for the following reasons:

- *The observable portion of users is significant to the terms of the research.* In fact, usually, the main users of digital social media are young people under thirty-five years old[2]. Thus, students and young native dwellers are fully covered within this age-range.
- *The results are manageable and thus immediately functional as planning resources.* Urbino is a small town, characterized by a condition of spatial isolation. The data mining from digital social media suits particularly well these conditions: no contaminations with exogenous factors are possible and the number of interactions of the inner members is easily controllable and bearable.[3]

Our main goal was to draw out maps of the social life in public spaces, to incorporate them in a strategy that addresses the whole city center and makes an extensive use of information technologies.

Using data coming from the social network Foursquare we created the Popularity Map and the Attendance Ratio Map, the first registering the most representative places of the city, the latter the type of approach people have towards certain locations (frequently attended venues, occasional venues, special events venues). With the data coming from Flickr, we extracted the Tourist representative poles map, considering what people tend to visit whenever they decide to spend a couple of days in Urbino [11].

Approaching the social network Instagram, the mapping process itself could benefit from the specific physical and social environment of Urbino. In fact Instagram provides several information about the users: apart from the pictures shared – that is a main content itself – it is possible to deduce collateral data concerning the age, gender, profession of the user and where he lives and works.

This enabled us to profile people according to four main categories: the resident, the student – originally not from Urbino, but living and studying in the Marchisan city – the tourist and the commuters – those that even though they are not living inside the historic center of Urbino, reach the city frequently due to working reason or for leisure activities.

The way each Instagram user is assigned to a category follows certain empirical criteria that combine information provided by the users and deducted from the pictures. Applying this methodology of observation to the case of Urbino, by February 2013, it has been possible to identify one hundred sixty Instagram users, which were using the geo-location option in sharing their contents. The profiles have been studied to find out which the most attended places within the historic center were and who the users were. Combining these two inputs we were able to identify which are the most attractive spots of the city for students, tourists, commuters and inhabitants and how their dynamics influence reciprocally.

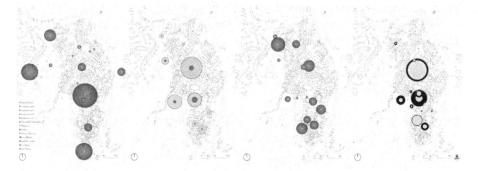

Fig. 1. Maps of Urbino from social networks data mining. From left: *Tourist representative poles* Map, *Popularity* Map, *Attendance Ratio* Map, *Instagram* Map (Source: Palmieri, Stojanovic, Tomarchio, Urbino: can digital technology enhance historic public realm?, 2013)

As a result of this assumption, we discovered how certain areas packed with touristic attractions where instead not popular at all among tourists. The other way round, it was possible to map selected places well known among the students, but absolutely not perceived through the sieve of the traditional analysis.

In order to draw these conclusions we crossed data coming from social networks with those that are normally observed in the city with a traditional analysis (eg. mapping building uses, analyzing flows of people and mental maps). Trying to abstract and synthesize the enormous number of potential outcomes of these collected data overlapping, it could be possible to identify three main categories:

- *Discovery*. The digital analysis reveals the existence of certain urban spots that are not detectable by means of traditional analysis.
- *Matching*. The digital analysis spots a series of evidences actually corresponding to those individuated through the use of the traditional one.
- *Denial*. The digital analysis reports no or little evidences referred to a point that at a classical observation seems to be a major one.

Discovery and Denial areas where those on which the next part of our research focused, exploring what kind of information strategy could be used in a historic city center to enhance its liveability.

5   A Strategy to Enhance the Public Life of Historic City Centers

The purpose is to define a strategy that uses digital technologies to address the public spaces in a historic city.

The strategy aims at:

- Strengthening the community ties creating tools to reinforce the common attachment and interest toward venues [6,7] [14];
- Extending the public uses of places, including activities that are at least partly performed using new tools and media;
- Creating a holistic system among the public spaces of the historic center, so that what happens in one place is immediately shared with the others, using real time communication as a way to create contamination of uses and generate unexpected activities.
- Inform people about the existence of certain public spaces and opportunities and thus influence the way they use the venues.

From the previous analyses we selected two types of spaces, object of our intervention: the anchor points – venues turning out to be the most popular and attended by the city dwellers – and action points – beautiful open spaces, practically unknown and not used by the citizens, where it would be possible to established new activities to revitalize the area.

We decided to introduce in the action points new programs, partially performed by new media technologies: common screens for media streaming, working area with Wi-fi connection and sockets, but also spots to access common media contents showing past events in that venue. The public life in both these points, action and anchor, will work within a holistic system created by an information infrastructure, through which users could talk, describe, get to know about the venues and activities.

The design of the infrastructure requires both the design of an application that stores user-generated information and the strategic planning of places and devices through which people could access this information. These two points will be crucial in deeply influencing the target of user that will be exposed to the data. In fact, if the distribution was limited to smart phone owners only, a large piece of population will be cut out. Moreover the way we access spatial information determine also the way we navigate the space. The common way to experience the city used to be stumbling upon activities, with the result that close events could influence and contaminate each other. But nowadays, the discovery of space is at least partly up to the use of social media: people tend to look at their network database to decide where to go, moving from one point to the other, following the Google Maps pin, with an indifferent attitude toward the physical reality around them. Our proposal is then to combine those two ways of experiencing the space. Create a user-generated database of events and interactions that is shared not only in social networks, but also in physical places. In fact in each of the anchor point, a screen may visualize events and information about other venues in the city. Moreover, anchor points and action points could be directly linked each other with a video streaming connection, thus contaminating the respective uses.

The data base of information shared in the screens is generated by an application, called OpenUrbino: this social communication software is designed in order to create an online database of information – that could be redistributed upon the territory in specific spots, as previously described – but also in order to "enhance" local communities. Communication technologies have proved they could help processes where citizens are engaged as co-makers and co-creators of the public domain.

The application OpenUrbino specifically designed for the historic center of Urbino aims at achieving those goals. The design of the application, still a beta version for exclusive use within the research, is already partly coded and will be soon released.

In order to help in creating the local community ties, OpenUrbino lets people share localized media contents they have been producing on popular social networks (Instagram, Foursquare, Facebook, to mention but a few), not only with friends but also with strangers who are - or will be - in the same location. The application doesn't work as a competitor of other social networks, but rather like a digital social traces search engine. The proposed goal is to share activities and memories with strangers who are actually neighbors, tourists, thus reinforcing the sense of community. The application is designed in order to share social media contents about places, to browse the venues where there is a major number of contributions (for instance in the previously discussed Popularity map); but also to start and foster projects of common interest, to share public events and then to look at what is happening in real time in the area. Open-Urbino creates a huge database: for each venue there are several media experiences recorded, showcasing activities and uses, lists of events, lists of participants, all updated in real time.

6   Conclusion

The research aimed at drawing a methodology on how to use the resources offered by digital social media in analyzing the use of public spaces and in promoting activities to enhance their attractiveness and liveability for an historic Italian city center. The historic dimension was pretty significant in term of the research because it offered a network of public venues with high quality spaces, easily accessible by pedestrians and public transportations. Since the physical components that affect the public realm are considered as quite untouchable resources, different actions were required.

The research demonstrated to have a clear principle of reproducibility, offering the chance to elaborate a methodology of intervention that operates on the public realm in a non-invasive and basically low cost way. Thus, this methodology explored for this case study could be extended, being pertinent and applicable to a conspicuous number of Italian municipalities, similar to Urbino under many aspects.

References

1. Choi, J.H.-J., Seeburger, J.: Sapporo world window: urban interaction through public and private screens. In: IEEE Pervasive Computing and Communications Workshops (PERCOM Workshops) (2011)
2. Ciuccarelli, P., Lupi, G., Simeone, L.: Visualizing the Data City: Social Media as a Source of Knowledge for Urban Planning and Management. Springer (2014)
3. De Waal, M., De Lange, M.: What is ownership and why does it matter? vol. 30, p. 40. Stichting Archis, February 2012
4. Dupuy, G.: Urban networks – network urbanism, pp. 121–137. Techne Press, Amsterdam (2008)
5. Firminio, J.R., Graham, S.: Typology for virtual cities: the interplay between physical and virtual urban spaces. In: EDA 2001 – European Digital Architect, Prague (2001)
6. Paay, J., Kjeldskov Foth, J.: Bjørnetjeneste: Using the city as a backdrop for location-based interactive narratives. In: Foth, M., Forlano, L., Satchell, C., Gibbs, M., Donath, J. (eds.) From Social Butterfly to Engaged Citizen: Urban Informatics, Social Media, Ubiquitous Computing, and Mobile Technology to Support Citizen Engagement. The MIT Press, London (2011)
7. Klaebe, H.G., Foth, M., Burgess, J.E., Bilandzic, M.: Digital storytelling and history lines: community engagement in a master-planned development. In: Proceedings of the 13th International Conference on Virtual Systems and Multimedia: Exchange and Experience in Space and Place. Australasian Cooperative Research Centre for Interaction Design Pty, Limited, Brisbane (2007)
8. Kleinberg, J.M.: Challenges in mining social network data: processes, privacy, and paradoxes. In: Proceedings of the 13th ACM SIGKDD International Conference on Knowledge Discovery and Data Mining. ACM, New York (2007)
9. Manovich, L.: Trending: The Promises and the Challenges of Big Social Data. Debates in the Digital Humanities (2011)
10. Morandi, C., Rolando, A., Di Vita, S.: ICT: interfacce tra persone e luoghi. TEMA 6 (2013)
11. Morandi, C., Palmieri, R., Stjanovic, B., Tomarchio, L.: Digital mapping: the analysis of the social realm of Urbino. NUL-New Urban Languages. Planum 2(27) (2013)
12. Salingeros, N.: Theory of the Urban Web in Principles of Urban structure. Techne, Delft (2005); Salingeros, N.: The information Architecture of Cities in Principles of Urban structure. Techne, Delft (2005)
13. Salingaros, N.: P2P Urbanism, p. 14. Umbau-Verlag, Solingen (2011)
14. Shirvanee, L.: Locative Viscosity: Traces of Social History in Public Spaces. Leonardo Eletronic Almanac 14(3) (2006)
15. Ratti, C., Williams, S., Frenchman, D., Pulselli, R.: Mobile Landscapes: Using Location Bata from Cell Phones for Urban Analysis. Environment and Planning B: Planning and Design (2006)
16. Townsend, A.: Augmenting Public Space and Authoring Public Art: The Role of Locative Media. ArtNodes E-Journal (2008)

Privacy Preserving Energy Management

Holger Kinkelin[1]([⊠]), Marcel von Maltitz[1]([⊠]), Benedikt Peter[1],
Cornelia Kappler[2], Heiko Niedermayer[1], and Georg Carle[1]

[1] Technische Universität München, Boltzmannstr. 3, 85748 Garching, Germany
{kinkelin,vonmaltitz,peter,niedermayer,carle}@net.in.tum.de
[2] deZem GmbH, Sybelstr. 63, 10629 Berlin, Germany
cornelia.kappler@dezem.de

Abstract. The improvement of energy efficiency is an important target
on all levels of society. It is best achieved on the basis of locally and temporally fine-grained measurement data for identifying unnecessary use of
energy. However, at the same time such fine-grained measurements allow
deriving information about the persons using the energy. In this paper we
describe our work towards a privacy preserving system for energy management. Our solution follows the privacy by design paradigm and uses
attribute-based cryptography and virtualization to increase security.

1 Introduction

The increase of energy efficiency is an important target on all levels of society.
According to studies [SZ11] [V. 09], it is best achieved when users receive information about their energy consumption such as how much is consumed, when,
by which device, in what form. Furthermore, the effectiveness of this measure is
best, when information is given close to the point in time energy is consumed
[Fis07]. The smart meters increasingly installed in European homes, reporting
consumption with a resolution of 15 minutes, are a first step in this direction.

What is true of the individual energy user is also true for *energy managers*,
responsible for decreasing the energy consumption of their organisation, e.g. a company, an office building or a factory: In this context, the collection of energy consumption measurements is usually embedded in an *energy management system*
(EMS) such as ISO 50001 [fSI11], which provides a continuous improvement
process supporting the discovery and realization of energy saving potentials. Consumption measurements are compiled using a wide variety of methods, ranging
from manual reading of meters to data loggers automatically providing measurement data collected from buildings equipped with thousands of sensors.

A central parameters in the design of an EMS is the resolution of the measurements, both in space and in time. The low end of the spectrum is the single
aggregated consumption number manually collected once per year. The advanced
end of the spectrum provides real-time measurement data with a temporal resolution of seconds and spacial resolution down to the individual device, plus
additional information e.g. on weather or building and device status. The better
the resolution, the more targeted and efficient the energy saving measures. For

© Springer International Publishing Switzerland 2015
L.M. Aiello and D. McFarland (Eds.): SocInfo 2014 Workshops, LNCS 8852, pp. 35–42, 2015.
DOI: 10.1007/978-3-319-15168-7_5

example, a heating system which is not configured properly and thus working at inappropriate hours can be discovered quickly, just as open fridge doors or lights left on.

The problem addressed in this paper is that an EMS can be abused and turned it into a system that monitors e.g. employees via their energy consumption. In Fig. 1 we depict the power consumption of a computer workplace, which shows that it is easy to derive information about the user's workday.

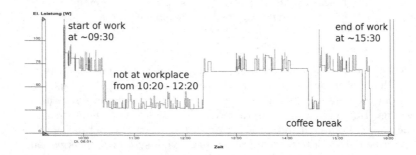

Fig. 1. Detailed energy monitoring tells much about a user's behavior

Correlating energy logs with other information sources, e.g., the system keeping track of working times of employees, is just a further step. It is problematic that the time an employee spends working at her computer can thus be compared to her "claimed" working time.

We conclude that the high resolution measurements (desirable and necessary for improving energy efficiency) and personal privacy appear to be contradicting requirements. When an EMS based on high-resolution measurements is established in an organization, usually the work council is involved and any objections are addressed. This makes the introduction of the EMS more complicated and eventually may endanger its successful operation.

In this paper we present our work towards an EMS that tries to resolve this apparent contradiction. The solution can be applied to similar use-cases where access rights to privacy-sensitive data streams have to be enforced. We first detail the problem in Chapter 2 and outline background information in Chapter 3. Our approach is discussed in chapters 4 and 5.

2   Analysis

2.1   Are Energy Logs Personal Data?

According to the European Data Protection Directive, *personal data* is defined as "any information relating to an identified or identifiable natural person" [Par95]. Especially when office rooms are used by only one person it is straight forward to relate energy logs of this room to this person. Hence, energy logs need to be considered as personal data and data protection laws have to be applied.

2.2   EMS User Groups and Their Access Rights

Before introducing different roles in the EMS, we must introduce several assumptions about a building. A building is provided and managed by an authority we call *Building Supplier* (BS). Different *spaces* of the building (multiple floors, rooms, etc.) can be rented by *Building Customers* (BC), for instance, companies. BCs pay money to the BS for rented space and consumed energy (electrical power, heating, etc.).

Based on above assumptions, we introduce user groups in the EMS. Each user is represented in the EMS by processes that automatically analyze data accessible for this user.

Building User (BU): a person working in the building. By default she is allowed to retrieve energy measurement data in full granularity concerning herself. A BU belongs to a BC. *Energy Manager* (EM): belongs to a BC. Her duty is finding unnecessary energy consumption in the company and optimizing the situation. Hence she needs to access detailed energy logs of the entire space rented by the BC. This data set comprises personal data of several BUs. *Energy Accountant* (EA): belongs to the BS. Her tasks include billing of energy by BCs. For the EA a spatially and temporally aggregated view on energy logs, i.e., the sum of energy spent within the space of an BC, is sufficient.

2.3   Design Strategies for Privacy by Design vs. Energy Control

Hoepman defined in [Hoe12] eight design strategies for privacy by design systems. These strategies are derived from data protection laws, such as [Par95]. In the following we introduce the most relevant strategies and assess their applicability.

Strategy #1 - Minimize: "The amount of personal data that is processed should be restricted to the minimal amount possible." [Hoe12] As already described, collecting data with high resolution is essential for an EMS. Otherwise, the successful operation of the EMS is compromised. Hence, this strategy can not be applied.

Strategy #2 - Hide: "Any personal data, and their interrelationships, should be hidden from plain view." [Hoe12] This design strategy does not conflict with an EMS and can be implemented by access control mechanisms.

Strategy #3 - Separate: "Personal data should be processed in a distributed fashion, in separate compartments whenever possible." [Hoe12] This strategy does not conflict with an EMS. However, distributed processing and storage has a bigger overhead in administration than a centralized system.

Strategy #4 - Aggregate: "Personal data should be processed at the highest level of aggregation and with the least possible detail in which it is (still) useful." [Hoe12] Aggregation will reduce resolution. Hence, this strategy is basically equal to strategy #1 and can only be applied in selected cases, e.g. for the EA.

Furthermore a system following privacy by design should also obey the following remaining principles. It should **inform** (#5) a user when her personal data is processed as well as preferably putting her in **control** (#6) of her data and its distribution. Furthermore, the system's compliance to legal requirements must be **enforced** (#7) while being able to **demonstrate** (#8) this property.

3   Background

3.1   (Hardware) Virtualization

Hardware virtualization is a technology able to execute several *virtual machines* (VMs) on the same physical hardware, e.g., a server. An individual operating system and any desired set of applications can be installed in a VM. As a result, virtualization is a quite popular technology today and used to cut down hardware costs in companies, or as basis for Cloud computing. [Cit12]

Besides the direct benefits of virtualization, it is often used as a security mechanism when several critical processes on the same machine need to be isolated. Instead of only relying on the operating system's ability of processes isolation, the virtualization system adds another isolation layer. This layer makes it more difficult to take control over one process after compromising the other. However, isolation by virtualization is not impeccable. [RW10]

3.2   Attribute Based Encryption

Attribute based encryption (ABE) is a crypto system initially proposed by Sahai and Waters [SW04]. It consists of a trusted Key Generator (KG), which initially creates and owns a master key and a public key. The KG's purpose is to create private keys for other users using its master key. These private keys will include attributes of its owner, e.g., her identity, her security clearance, etc.

Besides their private key, users of an ABE crypto system possess the global public key, which allows them to encrypt data. A unique property of a specific ABE type, called *cipher text policy ABE* (CP-ABE) [BSW07], is that a policy is integrated into the cipher text that expresses who is able to decrypt it. Policies can include required attributes (attribute `admin` is set), inequalities (`clearance > 3`), and even complex boolean expressions. An entity that tries to decrypt data will only succeed if the attributes of her private key conform to the specified policy. Hence, CP-ABE offers powerful, cryptography-based access control to data.

4   Approach

4.1   Abstract EMS Architecture

A high-level architecture showing the most important components of an EMS is depicted in Fig. 2. A *data logger* equipped with *sensors* measures electrical consumption. It outputs a stream of data elements, each consisting of the logger's identity, the identity of the sensor, the measurement value and a time stamp.

Next, the data stream is pre-processed and stored. The *combiner* enriches the data stream with additional *knowledge* about the monitored system. For instance, the combiner knows that sensor "a" attached to data logger "x" measures the electrical consumption in BU Dave's office. Hence, the combiner assigns the measurement value to Dave. The enriched data stream is finally stored within a data sink from where it can be accessed after authorization by the different user groups defined before.

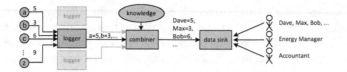

Fig. 2. Abstract EMS Architecture

4.2 Limitations of Privacy Enhancing Services

Typically, privacy protection would be added by a separate layer or module implementing e.g. access control mechanisms. This approach has benefits when existing systems need to be extended with privacy preserving features. The downside is, that circumvention of the mentioned module allows raw access to the unprotected data (e.g. the database files on the server). In consequence the effectiveness of privacy preservation does not only depend on the given mechanism but also on the security of the overall server infrastructure.

4.3 Logically Distributed EMS Based on CP-ABE and Virtualization

Our approach to create an EMS architecture with privacy by design is based on the idea to combine CP-ABE with isolation offered by hardware virtualization. Above architecture can simply be extended after the combiner, see Fig. 3.

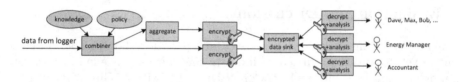

Fig. 3. Privacy by Design EMS Architecture

In order to allow processes acting for a specific user to find accessible data elements, CP-ABE encrypted index structures are created for every user. A pointer as well as a random AES key are created and appended to this index document. In the cipher text, a policy is embedded which makes sure that only a specific BU, e.g., Dave, and (EM Dave), the EM of the company Dave belongs to will be able to decrypt the data element. In the example Dave and (EM Dave) would both get their own index document containing the same key and a pointer.

After the combiner assigned a data element to a BU, the *encrypter* component encrypts the data using AES and the AES key. The encrypted data element is then stored within a database using the pointers as (unencrypted) index fields. By sharing the AES key, each data point has only to be stored once, even if multiple users are allowed to retrieve it. Other incoming data elements are processed analogously.

While a process with a valid private key is able to find encrypted data blocks, it is not possible to do reverse queries. Therefore, one cannot gain information on who may decrypt a specific data block. This is an important feature, because otherwise it would be possible to link appearance of persons to specific points in time (e.g. Dave and Bob were present in the same room).

Here the strategy of data *hiding* is applied: The energy data itself is protected from unauthorized access as well as the access policy.

Hardware virtualization is used to isolate processes concerned with above processing of incoming data from processes that analyze data. For every user of this system an individual VM is provided. Within a VM, the private CP-ABE key of the user resides, which allows the analysis processes to decrypt data elements accessible by this user. Please note, data analysis might also be performed on a different physical machine. This allows the desired *separation* of critical data.

Aggregation of data elements, e.g., to provide data needed by the EA, is also performed within a separate VM. After assigning an incoming data element to a BU, the combiner sends the unencrypted data element to the responsible aggregation process. This process understands that the element belongs to a BC it is responsible for and adds the new value to the sum of energy spent by all BUs that belong to the BC. The element itself is then discarded. After the applicable aggregation period is over, the aggregation process encrypts the aggregated value for the EA and stores the result in the database. This part realizes the *aggregation* of data to remove undesired fine-granularity of information. This approach also supports, to a small degree, the *minimization* of the amount of persisted data.

5   Evaluation and Discussion

As we are describing work in progress we cannot provide a thorough performance analysis yet. However, our first tests indicate that our reference implementation running on a machine with an Intel Core 2 Duo CPU with 2.5Ghz, 8GB of RAM and a conventional hard drive easily copes with the data stream produced by the energy logger deployed at our group. Additional tests showed that we are able to scale it up to 2 Million data elements per hour without performance issues.

The increased complexity of our EMS (privacy by design, CP-ABE-based access control; logically distributed) compared to a simple EMS (privacy functions, access control by authentication and authorization; centralized) is worth the effort when we compare security features of both systems. In case an attacker gains access to the simple EMS, she would be able to access the database containing energy logs of the entire building and could eavesdrop on incoming data elements. In our EMS we need to differentiate. In case the attacker gains access to the VM of a BU, only this BU's data elements are accessible. In case the attacker gained access to an EM's VM, all data elements accessible by this EM can be accessed. The logger's data stream is not affected in both cases. In case a VM with an aggregation process is compromised, the attacker will be able to eavesdrop all data elements sent to the aggregation process. At the worst, this would be the energy consumption of the entire building. However, the attacker is unable to access detailed energy logs of the past. Compromising the VM running the combiner and encryptor would have a similar effect on incoming data elements. However, the attacker has no access to past energy logs.

Our system is protecting measurement data and not meta data of requests. An observer logging user requests will not see the data, yet she can observe if a user (in the sense of IP address) is requesting data for a given time interval.

As explained, our EMS is able to effectively limit the effects of attacks and increase the effort an attacker must spend to gain access on all data. For increased security, VMs can be monitored by Host Intrusion Detection Systems (HIDS). When the HIDS detects that a VM is compromized, the VM can be shut down in order to prevent all unencrypted information from being compromised. An identical VM can then be restarted from an integrity protected VM image.

6 Related Work

Smart meters report the power consumption of a building e.g. every 15 minutes to the energy provider. However, even this information is sufficient to allow the energy provider an overall footprinting of the household. To circumvent this problem, technologies such as homomorphic encryption are used. The basic idea of such systems is that multiple parties, e.g., the smart meters located in one street, cooperate in order to calculate the sum of consumed power within this street. For the energy provider this information is still sufficient in order to control energy production. Secure multiparty computation using homomorphic encryption [GJ11] now guarantees that neither the individual smart meters nor the energy provider learn about the energy consumption of single households, as all computations are performed on encrypted values. This type of work is an example where privacy can be increased by aggregation.

7 Conclusion and Future Work

Energy management systems (EMS) are needed in smart buildings to decrease energy consumption. However, there is a conflict between the need for fine-grained energy measurements and the right on personal privacy of affected persons. We analyzed strategies for designing privacy preservation in systems processing personal data and assessed their applicability on EMS. We then outlined our approach which combines the features of attribute-based encryption to enforce strong access control and of virtualization to gain isolation of processes handling personal data. A first evaluation of our prototype's performance showed that it is easily capable to handle the energy measurements of the installation in our building. Furthermore, a discussion of security features showed the clear advantages of our system compared to a centralized system.

Up to now we addressed mechanisms that increase privacy properties of an EMS. However, to achieve compliance to privacy regulations further properties, such as informing a user and demonstrating the system's abidance to legal requirements need to be addressed, i.e. to have no secret surveillance functions.

We plan to address this issue based on our preliminary work on Trusted Computing and attestation technologies [KDC14].

Acknowledgments. This work has been supported by the German Federal Ministry of Education and Research, projects IDEM (grant 01LY1217C) and BaaS (grant 01IS13019G) as well as by the European Commission, FP7 project EINS (grant 288021).

References

[BSW07] Bethencourt, J., Sahai, A., Waters, B.: Ciphertext-policy attribute-based encryption. In: Proc. of the 2007 IEEE Symposium on Security and Privacy (2007)

[Cit12] Citrix Systems Inc., The Xen Project. Website (2012). http://www.xen.org/ (last accessed on July 09, 2013)

[Fis07] Fischer, C.: Influencing electricity consumption via consumer feedback. In: Proc. of the ECEEE 2007 Summer Study, June 2007. http://www.tips-project.org/download/TIPS_DP8_Fischer.pdf (last accessed on July 08, 2014)

[fSI11] International Organization for Standardization (ISO). Energy management systems requirements with guidance for use (iso 50001:2011), June 2011. http://www.iso.org/iso/home/standards/management-standards/iso50001.htm (last accessed on September 16, 2014)

[GJ11] Garcia, F.D., Jacobs, B.: Privacy-friendly energy-metering via homomorphic encryption. In: Cuellar, J., Lopez, J., Barthe, G., Pretschner, A. (eds.) STM 2010. LNCS, vol. 6710, pp. 226–238. Springer, Heidelberg (2011)

[Hoe12] Hoepman, J.-H.: Privacy design strategies (2012). http://arxiv.org/abs/1210.6621 (last accessed on July 08, 2014)

[KDC14] Kinkelin, H., Dorner, M., Carle, G.: Lokale Integritätsverifikation von Systemen durch Java Smart Cards. Tagungsband des 24. SmartCard Workshop, February 2014

[Par95] The European Parliament. Directive 95/46/EC. Website, November 1995. http://eur-lex.europa.eu/LexUriServ/LexUriServ.do?uri=CELEX:31995L0046:en:HTML (last accessed on July 08, 2014)

[RW10] Rutkowska, J., Wojtczuk, R.: Qubes OS Architecture Version 0.3. White paper, Invisible Things Lab, January 2010

[SW04] Sahai, A., Waters, B.: Fuzzy identity based encryption. Cryptology ePrint Archive, Report 2004/086 (2004). http://eprint.iacr.org/2004/086 (last accessed on July 08, 2014)

[SZ11] Amt für Hochbauten Stadt Zürich: Schlussbericht Nutzerverhalten beim Wohnen. Website (2011). http://www.mehralswohnen.ch/fileadmin/download/1107_Bericht_Nutzerverhalten.pdf (last accessed on September 18, 2014)

[V. 09] Bürger, V.: Öko-Institut. Identifikation, Quantifizierung und Systematisierung technischer und verhaltensbedingter Stromeinsparpotenziale privater Haushalte. Study (2009)

DaTactic, Data with Tactics: Description and Evaluation of a New Format of Online Campaigning for NGOs

Pablo Aragón[1]([✉]), Saya Sauliere[2],
Rebeca Díez Escudero[2], and Alberto Abellán[2]

[1] Barcelona Media, Barcelona, Spain
pablo.aragon@barcelonamedia.org
[2] Oxfam Intermón, Barcelona, Spain

Abstract. Social media has emerged as a powerful communication channel to promote actions and raise social awareness. Initiatives through social media are being driven by NGOs to increase the scope and effectiveness of their campaigns. In this paper, we describe the *#DaTactic2* campaign, which is both an offline and online initiative supported by Oxfam Intermón devised to gather activists and NGOs practitioners and create awareness on the importance of the 2014 European Parliament election. We provide details regarding the background of the campaign, as well as the objectives, the strategies that have been implemented and an empirical evaluation of its performance through an analysis of the impact on Twitter. Our findings show the effectiveness of bringing together relevant actors in an offline event and the high value of creating multimedia content in order to increase the scope and virality of the campaign.

1 Introduction

Social media have become a central tool to increase awareness of social issues and political change. Online social networks have emerged as a channel through which discussion is promoted, supporters and activists are organized and tactics during urban demonstrations and protests are defined. Social media have also become a new paradigm for the creation of collective identities and for sharing alternative storytelling outside traditional offline media through the logic of connective action[2].

This emerging form of activism can overcome academics and users´ disappointment with regard to slacktivism - the perception that these tools and their use are too superfluous, superficial or ephemeral[11]. However, the catalytic role of social media in the recent new social movements (e.g. the Arab Spring, the Spanish 15M movement or the Occupy Wall Street movement) is currently being confirmed from a sociological and political point of view[5,13]. Research carried out from a Social Network Analysis (SNA) perspective on recent mobilizations has allowed to create key concepts and identify clear evidence on networks and

© Springer International Publishing Switzerland 2015
L.M. Aiello and D. McFarland (Eds.): SocInfo 2014 Workshops, LNCS 8852, pp. 43–51, 2015.
DOI: 10.1007/978-3-319-15168-7_6

communication [6–9]. This knowledge is currently presented under a very technical and academic format, thus restricting activists and social practitioners´ access to this useful know-how for their future advocacy work. Among other objectives, the *#DaTactic* initiative intends to fill this knowledge gap. Our proposal is that the new format of *#DaTactic* is opening a door to social media´s potential for the achievement of social good through collective strategy, in order words, *data science for social good*.

As of October 2014, two editions of *#DaTactic* events have taken place. Organized as "training-action" events, each edition had that double objective. With regard to *training*, the aim is to easily share knowledge about SNA for social action. As for *action*, the objective is to carry out collectively a specific social media process using digital tactics based on the insights regarding digital methods[12]. In that sense, *#DaTactic* aims to offer an entirely new offline/online format for NGOs and activists by using SNA techniques prospectively, informing about digital tactics and reaching out to a broad range of communities in order to obtain a broader scope.

This article will first introduce the origin of the *#DaTactic* initiative. After a brief description of the first edition, this article will focus on *#DaTactic2*, which took place simultaneously in Barcelona and Madrid on May 22, 2014. The action *#OccupyEP2014* intended to show the importance of the European Elections and encourage Spanish citizens to vote by implementing a collective social media strategy. Then, we evaluate if the digital tactics were successful and whether the hypotheses of creating multimedia content and gathering offline profiles to increase online impacts are valid. Finally, we conclude with a discussion about the results obtained from the analysis of *#DaTactic2*.

2   DaTactic: Data with Tactics

2.1   Context and Origin: *#DaTactic1* / *#LaAyudaImporta*

In November 2013, Oxfam Intermón[1], in collaboration with the Outliers collective[2], began to explore the digital sphere concerning Cooperation and International Development in Spain. Inspired by Internet research methodologies designed by the Digital Methods Initiative[3] of the University of Amsterdam, the research consisted in identifying social network structures and dynamics, as well as subjects of debate in different social media channels related to the issue. Some of the findings of digital research were significant and the *#DaTactic* team determined that they could shape a more strategic and tailor-made social network.

The idea to organize a *#DaTactic* emerged from that scenario, based on the team´s willingness to give back to these communities the processed data and share knowledge on best practices in social media (in the context of "open"

---

[1] http://www.oxfamintermon.org/
[2] http://outliers.es/en
[3] https://www.digitalmethods.net/Dmi/DmiAbout

philosophy). On April 8, 80 persons coming from different cities joined in Madrid for a face-to-face encounter. The first event was totally experimental but the action *#LaAyudaImporta* was successful in reaching new audiences, becoming a trending topic in Madrid and Spain[4] and catching the attention of some major politicians. Then, the audience showed interest in participating in a new edition of *#DaTactic* and the 2014 European Parliament election was targeted as the next scenario.

2.2   Strategy and Tactics: *#DaTactic2 / #OccupyEP2014*

On May 22 - three days before the European Election Day in Spain - the second edition of *#DaTactic (#DaTactic2)* took place simultaneously in Madrid and Barcelona. With over 100 offline participants in the two cities, the overall objective was to increase Spanish citizens´ votes for the European Elections. At that time, the elections surveys indicated a rate of abstention around the 70%. Prior to the event, participants were invited to collaborate in the elaboration of a clear narrative to reach this objective. Two main lines were identified to effectively communicate and convince Spanish citizens about the importance of the election.

First, the team sought to provide information about the importance of the European Parliament (after the Lisbon Treaty) and the impact of European Union decisions in daily life. Many significant decisions (e.g. Transatlantic Trade and Investment Partnership) are made at a European level that is distant from citizen control and awareness.

Second, at a more domestic level, the team sought to inform that voting in the European election could change the current - and highly criticized - two-party Spanish political rotation. European election formula would reflect political diversity more faithfully than the system established for Spanish general election. In order to achieve this goal, the participants carried out political analyses of the lists of candidates and their political proposals to provide citizens materials and information to help them in their vote decision. The participants also included images and data visualizations along with this information in order to communicate the potential impact of voting more effectively [5].

Finally, to foresee the network behaviour and define tailor-made digital tactics, the team carried out a series of analysis on Twitter data. Conversations concerning the European Elections were mapped through hashtags such as *#EP2014* and some critical ones[6].

#DaTactic2 followed the double objective mentioned above: *training* and *action.* On the one hand, the *training* approach consisted in two sessions focused on management of social media communities, how to carry out real-time monitoring of an online campaign with tools like NetVizz[3] and Gephi[1], and how

---

[4] http://www.trendinalia.com/twitter-trending-topics/spain/spain-140408.html
[5] Infographic example: http://pbs.twimg.com/media/Bn8n1B4CAAEMupH.jpg
[6] #SalDelBipartidismo,   #sinovotasellosserien,   #AsaltoUE,   #NoVotisInjusticia, #TTIPNoGracias, #StoppTTIP.

to evaluate Twitter actions in a strategic way. On the other hand, the *action* approach was designed to raise awareness on the importance of the European election. Different groups were organized in Barcelona and Madrid with a specific focus on:

1. Disseminating major European issues
2. Bringing European politics closer to Spanish citizens

The digital tactics set forth in this edition were:

1. Inviting journalists, media and NGOs to the offline event to generate a cohesive community responsible of diffusing the online campaign.
2. Creating multimedia content (mostly images) as part of a viral strategy in order to reach different audiences and counteract to more technical message.
3. Mentioning and questioning politicians to ask their opinion on key European issues or on their political programs.

3   Evaluation

The evaluation of the strategies described above relies on a dataset that consists of 10,424 tweets and retweets. The messages were extracted through the Twitter Streaming API that returned the public messages during 22-30 May 2014 which match the term OccupyEP2014, selected as the official hashtag of the campaign. The dataset is composed of 2,945 original tweets (28%) and 7,479 retweets (72%) to the original tweets. 4,044 users were involved in the campaign tweeting or retweeting at least one message. Table 1 shows the number of messages per day revealing that most of them (84%) were produced the launch day.

Table 1. Number of messages per day

Date (May 2014)	22	23	24	25	26	27	28	29	30
#Messages	8 749	826	334	302	110	27	29	34	13

We analyze the scope of the campaign according to the visibility of the hashtag as trending topic (TT) on Twitter during the launch day. Table 2 shows the length and position of *#OccupyEP2014* in the general/politics rankings of longest TTs for different locations. Data regarding TTs have been extracted from the online website Trendinalia[7]. We only focus on Spanish locations because the hashtag did not become TT in any region out of Spain. The hashtag was visible as a TT in Spain for more than 5 hours and was also TT in most of Spanish locations except for Valencia and Bilbao. In Table 2, we differentiate two rankings (general/politics): the first one is the original ranking from Trendinalia (TTs are sorted by length) and the second one is a subset focused just on political topics.

---

[7] http://www.trendinalia.com/twitter-trending-topics/spain/spain-140522.html

For most locations, #OccupyEP2014 was the second longest TT related to politics after #VotandoPodemos, campaign hashtag of the emerging political party PODEMOS. We also note that the highest length of #OccupyEP2014 occurred in the local regions of Madrid and Barcelona. Although these two regions are the largest Spanish cities and presumably the locations with the greatest number of users on Twitter, #OccupyEP2014 had the greatest scope in the cities which held the two offline #DaTactic2 events.

Table 2. Length and position of the hashtag #OccupyEP2014 in the general/politics rankings of the Spanish locations available on Twitter. Data from the cities which hosted #DaTactic2 offline events are bolded. Source: trendinalia.es

Location	Population	General position	Politics position	Length
Spain	46 525 002	13	2	05:25
Madrid	**3 255 944**	**12**	**2**	**08:20**
Barcelona	**1 621 537**	**16**	**1**	**06:05**
Valencia	852 208	-	-	-
Seville	703 206	13	2	05:25
Zaragoza	674 317	79	10	00:10
Malaga	568 305	13	2	05:10
Murcia	436 870	26	2	02:20
Palma	401 270	15	2	04:35
Las Palmas	381 847	36	7	01:30
Bilbao	354 860	-	-	-

3.1   Diffusion Network Structure

To understand the diffusion dynamics of the campaign on Twitter we analyze the retweet-network of the tweets from the dataset. We build a directed graph whose nodes are users and the edges represent users who retweeted tweets from other users (see Figure 1). The weight of each edge indicates the number of retweets between the corresponding adjacent nodes. The resulting graph consists of 3,929 nodes and 6,459 edges. The clustering coefficient of the graph is 0,029.

Then, we apply the Louvain Method[4], a community detection algorithm based on the modularity of the graph, and we identify 61 communities. For each community, we build a sub-graph with the corresponding nodes and the inter-community edges. We calculate the clustering coefficient of each sub-graph and we identify (1) the node with the highest in-degree (HI), (2) if HI participated in the offline #DaTactic2 event (Madrid or Barcelona) and (3) the type of user HI is (citizen platform, personal account, journalist, politician, ngo, religious platform). The results of the communities formed by more than 10 nodes are presented in Table 3. We observe that, in general, communities whose HI participated in the offline event acquire higher levels of clustering. In fact, the average clustering coefficient of those communities is 0.036 (SD=0.023) while the communities whose HI did not participate in the offline event is 0.009 (SD=0.001).

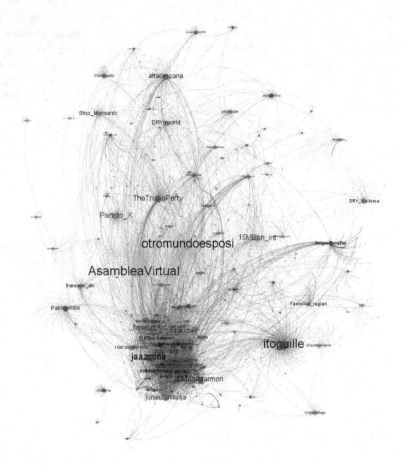

Fig. 1. Retweet graph of *#OccupyEP2014*. Nodes are sized by in-degree and colored by the clustering algorithm. The graph is drawn using the OpenOrd layout algorithm[10].

Among these last communities, the only ones with comparable levels of clustering are the ones whose HI is related to the Spanish 15M networked social movement (*@DRYmadrid* and *@Partido_X*) or NGOs (*@attacespana* and *@AmigosTier-raEsp*).

3.2   Impact of Images

To assess the value of images on tweets, out of the 2,945 original tweets, we make a distinction between the tweets that contained an image and the ones that did not. Afterwards, for each tweet, we calculate the number of received tweets and we present in Figure 2 the distribution of tweets over the number of retweets they received. We only consider tweets from 0 to 15 received retweets (>92%) to exclude outliers in the visualization. The results prove the expected

Table 3. Communities, with more than 10 nodes, detected through the Louvain method (N=number of nodes; E=number of edges; HI: node with the highest in-degree in the community subgraph; HI_P: if HI participated in the offline event; HI_category: category assigned to HI; C_c: clustering coefficient of the community subgraph). The communities whose HI participated in the offline event are bolded.

Id	N	E	HI	HI_P	HI_category	C_c
1	387	386	@AsambleaVirtual	no	citizen platform	0
2	**345**	**537**	**@jaazcona**	**yes**	**personal**	**0.057**
3	**334**	**410**	**@lidiaucher**	**yes**	**personal**	**0.035**
4	**294**	**294**	**@otromundoesposi**	**yes**	**personal**	**0.029**
5	263	267	@itoguille	no	personal	0.007
6	**260**	**381**	**@fanetin**	**yes**	**journalist**	**0.05**
7	211	232	@DRYmadrid	no	citizen platform	0.025
8	188	221	@Partido_X	no	politician	0.031
9	**180**	**199**	**@AlberAG**	**yes**	**personal**	**0.038**
10	156	175	@attacespana	no	ngo	0.04
11	**137**	**201**	**@frmat**	**yes**	**personal**	**0.089**
12	**117**	**118**	**@15MBcn_int**	**yes**	**citizen platform**	**0.004**
13	**117**	**121**	**@TheTroikaParty**	**yes**	**citizen platform**	**0.016**
14	106	117	@AmigosTierraEsp	no	ngo	0.029
15	92	92	@Lineasdefuga	no	personal	0
16	88	88	@Famelica_legion	no	citizen platform	0
17	79	79	@Stop_Monsanto	no	citizen platform	0
18	71	72	@elpidiojsilva	no	politician	0
19	**65**	**69**	**@serg_manero**	**yes**	**journalist**	**0.013**
20	64	66	@PatriHorrillo	no	journalist	0.025
21	53	52	@JovenesIUCM	no	politician	0
22	49	48	@arqueoleg	no	personal	0
23	44	44	@RazonFe	no	religious platform	0
24	**38**	**40**	**@CeliaZafra**	**yes**	**personal**	**0.03**
25	35	34	@elNota_Lebowski	no	personal	0
26	30	29	@Resetgr	no	personal	0
27	12	11	@3Blackhawk	no	personal	0

hypothesis: the tweets with images were more likely to be re-diffused and get viral. In particular, almost half of tweets without images were not retweeted, whereas only 30% of tweets with images received no retweets.

3.3   Mentions to Political Candidates and Potential Allies

#DaTactic2 participants mentioned 27 political candidates on Twitter. 8 of them interacted and replied to the questions and 8 non-mentioned politicians used the hashtag to spread their ideas about the European election. In addition, the participants mentioned potential allies to spread the actions.

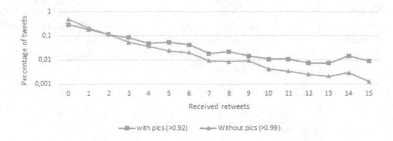

Fig. 2. Distribution of tweets by the number of received retweets

The allies were organized in three categories:

- 60 profiles related to NGOs (institutional profiles),
- 35 profiles related to media (digital newspapers and blogs)
- 60 profiles related to journalists

The analysis of the dataset reveals that the mentioned profiles on Twitter had a notable rate of collaboration:

- NGOs: 32 profiles were engaged (53%)
- Media: 11 profiles were engaged (31%)
- Journalist: 15 profiles were engaged (25%)

4   Discussion

In this paper we have offered an overview of *#DaTactic*, a new methodology for enabling citizen and NGO initiatives through social media. The results of the evaluation of its second edition have provided valuable insights about the usefulness of the proposed strategies. First, we have confirmed that the communities of users who participated in the offline event exhibited a more cohesive structure. We also note that NGOs communities and networked social movements (e.g. 15M movement) should be taken into account when oline campaings are launched. The event included training sessions as well as specific sessions to prepare contents to be diffused, which were mostly images. The distribution of tweets over the number of received tweets shows that the tweets that contained images were more likely to be retweeted. Consequently, we confirm our hypotheses of creating multimedia content and gathering offline profiles to increase online impacts. Finally, although most politicians ignored the mentions on Twitter related to *#OccupyEP2014*; we report that NGOs, media and journalists are valuable actors to increase the visibility of online campaigns.

Acknowledgements. We would like to thank Tamara Izko for her valuable suggestions that helped to improve the manuscript.

References

1. Bastian, M., Heymann, S., Jacomy, M., et al.: Gephi: an open source software for exploring and manipulating networks. ICWSM **8**, 361–362 (2009)
2. Bennett, W.L., Segerberg, A.: The logic of connective action: Digital media and the personalization of contentious politics. Information, Communication & Society **15**(5), 739–768 (2012)
3. Rieder, B.: Studying facebook via data extraction: the Netvizz application. In: Proceedings of the 5th Annual ACM Web Science Conference, pp. 346–355. ACM (May 2013)
4. Blondel, V.D., Guillaume, J.-L., Lambiotte, R., Lefebvre, E.: Fast unfolding of communities in large networks. Journal of Statistical Mechanics: Theory and Experiment **2008**(10), P10008 (2008)
5. Castells, M.: Networks of outrage and hope: Social movements in the internet age. John Wiley & Sons (2013)
6. González-Bailón, S., Borge-Holthoefer, J., Rivero, A., Moreno, Y.: The dynamics of protest recruitment through an online network. Scientific reports, 1 (2011)
7. Howard, P.N., Duffy, A., Freelon, D., Hussain, M., Mari, W., Mazaid, M.: Opening closed regimes: what was the role of social media during the arab spring? (2011)
8. Khondker, H.H.: Role of the new media in the arab spring. Globalizations **8**(5), 675–679 (2011)
9. Lotan, G., Graeff, E., Ananny, M., Gaffney, D., Pearce, I., et al.: The arab spring—the revolutions were tweeted: Information flows during the 2011 tunisian and egyptian revolutions. International Journal of Communication **5**, 31 (2011)
10. Martin, S., Brown, W.M., Klavans, R., Boyack, K.W.: Openord: An open-source toolbox for large graph layout. In: IS&T/SPIE Electronic Imaging, pp. 786806–786806. International Society for Optics and Photonics (2011)
11. Morozov, E.: The net delusion: The dark side of Internet freedom. PublicAffairs (2012)
12. Rogers, R.: Digital methods. MIT Press (2013)
13. Toret, J., Calleja, A., Marín, Ó., Aragón, P., Aguilera, M., Lumbreras, A.: Tecnopolítica: la potencia de las multitudes conectadas. el sistema red 15m, un nuevo paradigma de la política distribuida. IN3 Working Paper Series (2013)

Online Communication in Apartment Buildings

Vadim Voskresenskiy[1]([✉]), Kirill Sukharev[1],
Ilya Musabirov[1,2], and Daniel Alexandrov[1]

[1] National Research University Higher School of Economics,
16 Ulitsa Soyuza Pechatnikov, St. Petersburg 190121, Russia
{vadimvoskresenskiy,ksuharev}@gmail.com,
{imusabirov,dalexandrov}@hse.ru
[2] Uppsala University, Uppsala, Sweden

Abstract. In this paper we explore main patterns of communication
and cooperation in online groups created by residents of apartment buildings in St.Petersburg on the *VK* social networking site (SNS). Using
word-frequency analysis and Latent Dirichlet Allocation (LDA), we discovered main discussion topics in online groups. We have also found that
communication between neighbors in these groups is predominantly connected with material needs and directed at solving common problems,
e.g. related to building improvement, houseowner associations (HOA)
and in-fill constructions near their house. Based on online observations
of city activists, we suggest that dynamic nature of SNS creates online
communities that initially are dedicated to resolving particular problems,
however the connections that get established between users during this
process prevent such groups from falling apart even after the resolution
of the original issues.

Keywords: Online communities · Homeowners · Neighbors cooperation

1 Introduction and Related Work

The Internet has become an ubiquitous part of our life. That gives people a
chance to cooperate and discuss online a range of social problems including
urban environment. There are great many message boards for neighborhoods
where people can discuss various problems or coordinate actions together. However users have to register their own account before communicating with other
participants of such message boards. Recently, due to rising popularity of social
networks (e.g. *VK* in Russia, Facebook, etc.), new social neighborhood networking groups have been brought up into existence. Entry barriers to these groups
were low, which made communication easier for people who wanted to solve
problems connected with their apartment house. Our paper is concerned with
study of cooperation between residents of apartment buildings in networking
groups created on VK, the largest Russian social networking site.

Daly, Dahlem and Quercia[2] studied communication between residents on
the most popular neighborhood online forum in Dublin. Researchers found that,

© Springer International Publishing Switzerland 2015
L.M. Aiello and D. McFarland (Eds.): SocInfo 2014 Workshops, LNCS 8852, pp. 52–55, 2015.
DOI: 10.1007/978-3-319-15168-7_7

compared to mature neighborhoods, new networking neighborhood groups had higher online social activity, which is often aimed at mutual help in improving living conditions. Authors suggested that higher online social activity in new neighborhoods could be explained by absence of pre-existing physical community. Limei Li[3] argued that communication on online forums between homeowners has instrumental function in organizing collective action and building neighborhood community.

The aim of this paper is to discover patterns of cooperation for solving housing problems in the *VK* social network. For this purpose, we analyzed topics of discussions in groups created by residents of apartment building. This research focuses on online groups related to one house, residents of which apparently share a range of problems.

2   Methodology

(*Vkontakte(VK)*) is a social networking site (SNS) with over 200 million accounts. It offers a platform for communities where users can discuss topics of their interests. Users can communicate either in a continuous message flow on the group 'wall', or in discussions sections that have their own specific subtopics.

We collected text data of apartment buildings networking groups by using VK Application Programming Interface (API). We looked for groups related to neighborhood communities in apartment buildings for all streets of Saint-Petersburg. Out of total 2232 groups, we have filtered out spam and irrelevant search results, which left us with 420 groups for further analysis, 199 of which were open for data collecting. Groups were distributed evenly and covered all districts of the city, apart of industrial areas.

For exploratory analysis of the content of group discussions, we treated messages from each group as a single document and used Principal Component Analysis on a term-document matrix.

For more detailed analysis of topics in the VK groups, we used Latent Dirichlet Allocation (LDA)[1]. We aggregated all posts and comments for each group into a single document. After that, we applied lemmatization algorithm[4] and used resulting text to generate topic models. Topic models had to identify 100 topics, which contained significantly interconnected words in text documents.

After that, we clusterized the document-topic matrix to find groups with a similar topical structure and performed further analysis of each cluster.

3   Results

Daly, Dahlem and Quercia[2] found that activity of users in city forums and topic structure differ between apartment buildings, street and area groups. In our research we found that on a street or district level there were very few groups dedicated to urban topics.

Our three-factor PCA model has shown that discussions of car parking and administrative topics were two major factors responsible for the best part of diversity in group discussions. On the other hand, casual communication based on socialization between residents was not playing any visible role in the group interactions.

Further exploration of group clusters based on similarity of LDA generated topics (Table 1) has allowed us to discover some patterns of cooperation.

Table 1. Group clusters and topics

Group Cluster	Topic Label	Key Words
HOA	Services	service company maintenance organization HOA expert technical
	Advertisement	installation system equipment surveillance solution account access control complexity
Administrative topics	internal improvement	water hot pipe staircase job cold district problem replacement quality
	collective action	information document problem solve case decide(v.) start(v.) respect(v.)
Protests against in-fill constructions	infill constr. 1	playground science builder building child st.petersburg governor avenue building
	infill constr. 2	house construction land(adj.) kids district land(noun) hearing courtyard garden

The administrative cluster includes groups where residents discuss work of HOA or management companies, state of their buildings and their surrounding areas. We have identified two types of such groups: created by residents and created by board of HOA. Communities hosted by the board of HOA are filled with spam messages and have low social activity. In contrast, groups created by residents show significantly higher social activity. In these groups, people look for ways to resolve their problems with improvement of living conditions and to organize collective actions for this purpose. They share photos of leaking ceilings, dirty staircases, broken windows etc., criticize management companies or HOA, and discuss ways of resolving their problems.

We also found a set of seven groups dedicated to protection of public locations (squares and yards). Five of these groups are located in one district of St.Petersburg. Members of these groups try to prevent in-fill constructions in the surrounding area. It should be noted that a number of people belong to several groups at once (30 individuals out of 570). We suggest that these people represent a group of local activists whose relationships are built on mutual help and support.

In these groups, activists post information about meetings with local authorities and organize or plan rallies against actions of building developers. Discussions are usually moderated by administrators who are also the most active posters. A large number of reposts from walls of other protests groups and absence of spam messages (which are deleted by administrators) are two main features of these groups. Communication between group members is often supported by snapshots made during rallies or legal acts pointing at illegal sealing constructions. The life cycle of these groups depends on the offline situation in general; we suggest that death of communication in virtual group is triggered by the end of fighting.

4   Discussion

As well as [2], we find that online communication between residents of apartment buildings is based on their material needs and aimed at solving their common problems. By using social networking, neighbors can coordinate collective actions targeted at improvement of their living conditions and communal property. This type of activity can be found in communities created by residents, but not in those created by management companies.

People also try to create independent rules and informal sanctions for those residents who don't comply with established norms. One of such topical issues is parking on apartment building area, which is neither strictly regulated nor enforced in Russia. Our hypothesis is that discussion of parking lots is more intensive in groups of large housing complexes with enclosed areas.

We suggest that, due to the dynamic nature of SNS, the resolution of an issue and the resulting communication decay in a group (which is common for group clusters targeted against in-fill construction) does not necessary mean community breakdown. We assume that there is a community of urban activists who are highly concerned not only with local home improvement, but also with citywide urban environment problems. As they organize collective actions and strive to resolve relevant issues, they move from one group to another.

In our future research, we will try to explore lifecycle patterns and interconnections in different types of communities.

Acknowledgements. We are grateful to Paul Okopny, Ekaterina Mekhnetsova, and Viktor Karepin for their ideas and help with this research. Ilya Musabirov's contribution was produced during his Swedish Institute scholarship period at Uppsala University.

References

1. Blei, D.M., Ng, A.Y., Jordan, M.I.: Latent Dirichlet Allocation. J. Mach. Learn. Res. **3**, 993–1022 (2003)
2. Daly, E.M., Dahlem, D., Quercia, D.: The new blocs on the block: Using community forums to foster new neighbourhoods. In: Proceedings of the 2014 ACM Conference on Web Science, pp. 52–61. ACM, New York (2014)
3. Li, L., Li, S.: Becoming homeowners: The emergence and use of online neighborhood forums in transitional urban China. Habitat International **38**, 232–239 (2013)
4. Segalovich, I.: A fast morphological algorithm with unknown word guessing induced by a dictionary for a web search engine. In: MLMTA, pp. 273–280. Citeseer (2003)

Experiments for a Real Time Crowdsourced Urban Design

Gonzalo Reyero Aldama[1(⊠)] and Federico Cabitza[2]

[1] Nebrija Universidad, Calle Pirineos 55, 28029 Madrid, Spain
greyero@nebrija.es
[2] Università degli Studi di Milano-Bicocca, Viale Sarca 336, 20126 Milan, Italy
cabitza@disco.unimib.it

Abstract. We present a case study that encompassed an interactive urban design workshop held in Nebrija Architecture University in Madrid, Spain, in March 2013. In this workshop, an urban survey was held and an urban intervention proposal was participatorily developed for an empty plot in a nearby neighborhood. Different online collaborative design tools and data mining were used and monitored over the span of a year, and results were analyzed last March 2014. The findings show that collaborative tools help distribute work and gather knowledge from different sources, but seldom are the span and intensity of these work stages taken into consideration. The timeline and completion of the agenda was a key element during the workshop, determining the success or failure of many of the tools used depending on the time dimension. This temporal dimension still retro-feeds the work process, as some of those tools have become obsolete or redundant in a matter of few months. The lessons learned will lead to future studies on this subject.

Keywords: Collaborative design · Crowd sourcing · Time-sourcing · Time-sensitive design · 4D design

1   Introduction

In March 2014 we organized a workshop that was originally aimed at developing an existing small scale urban intervention in Tetuan, a 150,000 inhabitants neighborhood close to the faculty building in Madrid (Spain), by collecting all relevant data, from project inception to its final completion. In this paper we report how the target area was identified, how stakeholders were defined, how the design process evolved and how human and material resources were mobilized until the project completion. Moreover, the follow up and the real use of the project's installation was monitored over the span of a year.

The aim of the workshop was to study all stages of a real previous intervention, analyze the whole process, and propose an alternative way to carry it on, in order to optimize each design stage by reengineering the whole process adopting open source software that was available to anyone outside the design community. In so doing, we aimed to define a method to replicate similar processes in the neighborhood [1].

© Springer International Publishing Switzerland 2015
L.M. Aiello and D. McFarland (Eds.): SocInfo 2014 Workshops, LNCS 8852, pp. 56–63, 2015.
DOI: 10.1007/978-3-319-15168-7_8

As several options adopted during the process actually failed we want to focus here on the lessons learned and define a set of convenient and efficient tools to crowdsource user opinions about any related issue and collaboratively design a urban solution.

The target of our analysis was an existing small scale urban intervention that created an "urban oasis" with multiple possible uses on an empty plot with no planned use (see Figure 1). This was an intervention designed by a local architecture studio for the area. The designers involved got to know the plot by taking some walks in the area surroundings. More than 500 empty plots like these exist in Tetuan neighborhood, where "a-legal" (but not necessarily illegal) uses like temporary urban gardens, bike parks or just meeting places are installed, and coexist with daily activities. An actual map of the interventions is currently up to date on the openstreetmap platform, and a network of uses is being built.

Fig. 1. Time-lapse from initial state to project completion

In our study we focused on the traditional project process itself, irrespective of the intended use of the installation. This process was articulated in four stages, namely:

1. Urban study walks.
2. Plot allocation.
3. Design.
4. Result publishing: call for users.

A first identified concern regarded the lack of "visibility" of the whole process, which generally is opaque to the intended end-users of the final installation. Once completed, the intervention needed to be "published" and shared with the neighborhood inhabitants to find a use with their collaboration.

The workshop proposed to reverse the traditional process and find a way to crowdproduce the project in a bottom-u manner. To this aim, the field study included a urban survey that involved both university students and the neighborhood inhabitants, in order to collect their impressions and thoughts on a number of issues related to the intervention, like the detection of the most suitable areas for its deployment and of the needs for specific uses. This poses an interesting analogy between this activity and the task of requirement elicitation in software engineering.

All the software applications used was open source to evaluate their applicability to this kind of projects. The alternative process was conceived to be almost a reverse sequence of the traditional one, where to discuss a previous agenda and give it a strong initial visibility were considered as important as the development of the process itself.

2   An Alternative Process

Accordingly, publishing the problem at hand was made first, and framed as part of a bigger scale strategy aimed at the whole Tetuan district to regenerate the most deteriorated areas of that large city area. The idea behind this was that developing awareness of the problem was key to create a collective sense of appropriation of the solutions achieved [1]. The new process was then articulated in the following steps:

5. Calling for contributions.
6. Problem mapping.
7. Survey-based collection of problems, needs and desired uses.
8. Urban-to-detail scale Modeling.
9. First Collective Publishing.
10. External feedback provision.
11. Mapping material resources (donations, work contributions, etc.)
12. Execution.
13. Final Publishing and dissemination of results.

As said , even more than the design process, the focus was to design a sustainable and effective process, and engage stakeholders along its enaction and unfolding to improve knowledge and appropriation. In what follows we will describe each step in some detail.

2.1   Calling for Contributions

In this firs step, we aimed to call for crowdsourced contribution through traditional social networks and put the problem on the table, so to say. To this aim, we composed a Web page and shared it through a public folder on the Dropbox platform[1]. This was meant to allow all participants to edit the page content without any particular installation or knowledge of file transfer protocols like FTP or the like. Moreover, we created a Facebook page with a wall to post comments, a Twitter hashtag, and a WhatsApp chat group. These efforts notwithstanding at the beginning user engagement was low. To increase it, we invested more efforts in proposing the use of some more interactive tools, like the online survey already mentioned and state-of-the-art 3D online modeling tools, whose online resources were linked in the Web resources mentioned above. We noticed a positive impact in the collaborative discussion and traced back this phenomenon to a stronger feeling of the users involved to be contributing with "real inputs" to the project, and not just with "messages in a bottle". This could be also related to a climb in the participation ladder[2] from the consultation level, i.e., a kind of tokenism, to a preliminary form of partnership, which is associated with a higher empowerment of the citizens involved.

---

[1] The page is still accessible at th following URL:
https://dl.dropboxusercontent.com/u/5322317/Tetuan/web/index.html.

2.2   Problem Mapping

In this step we literally wanted to "map" potentially problematic areas in the neighborhood, and to this am we employed a collaborative online map editor. In this tool, overlaps and location pictures indicated the most degraded areas (see Figure 2). Spots indicated human and material resources and the indicative timeline of the intervention.

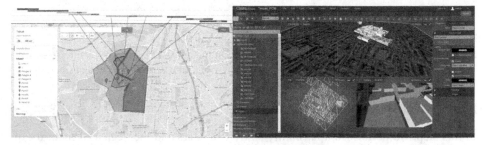

Fig. 2. Google maps engine collaborative work time sensitive map, Google timeline map diagram of future interventions and clara.io 3d open editor

To this regard, our next research will be aimed at employing 4D models, that is, visual representations of the evolution of the 3D model over time from inception to its completion. The potential of 4D modeling is still untapped, especially for its capability to link designs and maps with time- or schedule-related information. To this aim, we will implement a mashup of different open-source tools, like Google Map timeline, and the data sets collected in this user study.

2.3   Online Survey

In this step we designed, tested and deployed an online questionnaire to probe prospective users about potential uses, perceived lack of services, and other usually hard to pinpoint factors such as familiarity with new technologies, sense of neighborhood belonging and conviviality. To this aim the Limesurvey platform was used for its flexibility and power, as we needed to integrate in some of the questionnaire pages interactive maps. These latter interactive maps were used: to ask the survey respondents to insert points of interest in terms of "flags", to indicate potential areas of interventions or lack of services (to be chosen in a predefined list of essential city services); draw polygonal maps, both to circumscribe vaster areas of interventions and to probe the respondents' knowledge of the neighborhood borders; and choose between alternative solutions and pictures of the city surroundings, to understand which places were considered more enjoyable and which more deteriorated, like in the Urbanopticon project [3]. As the survey is still open, we are collecting new responses on a daily basis. So far, we have collected 56 complete questionnaires, while other tens of unfinished questionnaires (i.e., filled in only partially) were used to extract some useful indication nevertheless.

Fig. 3. Screenshots from the online questionnaire. On the left, an example of picture selection; in the middle an example of area drawing, and on the right, of insertion of points of interest.

2.4   Urban to Detail Scale Modeling

In this step, we performed a feasibility study to understand the degree of maturity of state-of-the-art tools that could be adopted in order to enable and support massive online 3D design, like Sketchup and Clara.io online open editor [4]. In this process, we favored either open-source or freeware solutions and considered online accessibility a top priority requirement. User-friendliness and the availability of multiple format for exporting the design models were also considered. We discarded a number of tools, mainly for their "closed" nature, also from the point of view of simple configuration and tailorization, for interoperability problems and lack of support of collaborative processes (e.g., data sharing and messaging). As a general finding, real-time response and feedback of the editing environment was considered critical to keep engagement sufficient to gather useful contributions from the "crowd". In figure 4 the detail scale is shown.

2.5   Collective Publishing

In this phase we wanted to share all the prospective models participatorily built to the public, so that the best option could be detected on the basis of the votes collected for each alternative solution. To this aim we exported the models in obj format on a Web GL 3D engine, which is a format that most desktop computers and even mobile devices can handle and manipulate natively. Figure 4 depicted the best solutions identified in this phase.

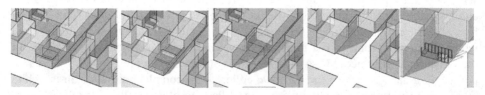

Fig. 4. Main design options chosen among 16 other

To this respect a number of open format were actually available (like kml, dxf, obj, csv, xml) to convert user ratings into graphics attached to geographical data or 3D models. In order to shorten the digital divide a mostly visual language was considered the best solution to adopt to get the opinion also of people not familiar with all these formats. As said above, the focus of the project was not on the technological side, but aimed at understanding what specific combination of tools could engage users more effectively and to what extent this toolset could be adapted to different, but yet strongly related, concerns and goals.

2.6   Feedback Provision

Results were published in real time in public Dropbox repositories and standard Web resources, for over 6 months, gathering feedback through different communication channels that encompassed stakeholder meetings, emailing, phone calls, and Web forms. In particular, feedback was collected through emails, model sharing and open-ended interviews. At a preliminary analysis, no particular difference in engagement was detected between different age or gender groups.

2.7   Completion

In this step we proposed an idea for a crowdsourced call for 3D printed parts of a larger model, without further details. To this respect, market is almost frantic in proposing more powerful and stable solutions: during the study at hand new powerful and easier 3D print tools have been released (e.g., reprap, tinkercad, autodesk 123d). The future work will leverage the contributions of the building and construction de partment of the university to develop a mock-up of the proposal in the next workshop.

2.8   Final Publish and Maintenance of a Web Site

A follow-up site was published and it is still accessible, where contents are updated and planned events advertised periodically. Something important that deserves a comment is that online social networks didn't really help as process starters or working platforms, but rather as follow up sites. The whole experiment served as a touchstone for the developing of new communication interfaces between designers and citizens.

3   Final Remarks

This preliminary user study has provided indications in the intersection of several fields like urban planning, community informatics and 3D modeling, and addressed related ambits of research like: how to collect knowledge from large communities of citizens [5], real time testing of ideas, citizen agency in the design process. As it is clear from the concise outline of the project reported above, further work and new field studies and workshops are needed before definitive finding can be proposed to the research community. That notwithstanding, some ideas can be extracted from the experience and shared in the following points:

- The scope of the project was not to evaluate classic parameters of urban design and planning such as cost or quality of execution, but rather aspects subject to temporality like the interest and degree of appropriation that this project could raise among the neighborhood inhabitants. To this aim, the designers created the collaborative platform, by simply integrating off-the-shelf, but yet state-of-the-art, Web-based technologies, and called for ideas and contributions. Notably, online social networking sites like Facebook and Twitter did not really help as process triggers or working platforms, but rather as scaffolding resources and follow-up resources of dissemination. To this respect, the user study reported here provides motivations for the development of better interfaces that could improve communication and knowledge sharing between designers and citizens [6].
- All stakeholders tended to engage for a longer time when they felt to be part of the process and could appropriate it [7].
- Content, in the sense of use program, must be planned in advance, allowing some "slack room" for spontaneous or unexpected evolution [8].
- A determined life cycle or intervention agenda and its evolution must be thought ahead of the beginning of the process. There is a new temporal dimension to urban design [9].
- Design on itself is just a stage among many others in the overall process of shaping a final installation in city areas. Cost control, planning, scope and the final closing of the project are other key steps to the final success [10]
- Arnstein described citizen participation adopting the metaphor of the ladder [2], where the two first critical steps were to "educate" opinions into people and get them back from the crowd as a substitute for genuine participation.
- Open access software tools are increasingly appearing and blurring the limits between designer and the end user [11]. The client, as in other fields, is becoming a responsible and empowered end user.

These and other lessons learned from this year long experience were gathered and an agenda has been established for the next months. We realized that the design and execution stages worked reasonably well but the quality and timing of the input proved to b critical and therefore must be improved. Citizens must be persuaded that surveys of urban design are truly aimed at gathering their opinions, as a preliminary but necessary means so that the design community can take their ideas seriously. Even more than this, new Web 2.0 tools and visual 3D modeling suites can be integrated as effective tools to have designers and citizens communicate, collaborate and put collective ideas into action.

How these tools and procedures should be adapted so to become suitable for other collaborative initiatives of social, cultural or sustainable nature is still an open problem that deserves more studies, where the main challenges lie in the heterogeneity of the stakeholders involved and hence of the requirements to satisfy.

In particular, we will aim our next research efforts in considering the temporal dimension along which this kind of projects unfold, and also the visibility dimension of such a project trajectory, all together with its partial and final outputs. In this latter case, effective indicators of citizen awareness, engagement, adoption and appropriation of the final installation should be investigated and tested in the field, by combining quantitative and qualitative techniques.

References

1. Brabham, D.C., Sanchez, T.W., Bartholomew, K.: Crowdsourcing public participation in transit planning: preliminary results from the next stop design case. In: TRB 89th Annual Meeting Compendium (2010)
2. Arnstein, S.R.: A ladder of citizen participation. Journal of the American Institute of Planners **35**, 216–224 (1969)
3. Quercia, D.: Urban: crowdsourcing for the good of London. In: Proceedings of the 22nd International Conference on World Wide Web Companion, pp. 591–592. International World Wide Web Conferences Steering Committee (2013)
4. Rosenman, M.A., Gero, J.S.: Modelling multiple views of design objects in a collaborative cad environment. Computer-Aided Design. **28**, 193–205 (1996)
5. Cabitza, F., Simone, C.: Investigating the role of a web-based tool to promote collective knowledge in medical communities. Knowledge Management Research & Practice **1**, 392–404 (2012)
6. Orlikowski, W.J.: Material Knowing: The Scaffolding of Human Knowledgeability. European Journal of Information Systems **15**, 460–466 (2006)
7. Seltzer, E., Mahmoudi, D.: Citizen Participation, Open Innovation, and Crowdsourcing: Challenges and Opportunities for Planning. Journal of Planning Literature **28**, 3–18 (2013)
8. Robinson, M.: Design for unanticipated use. In: Third European Conference on Computer-Supported Cooperative Work, pp. 187–202. Kluwer Academic Publishers, Milano (1993)
9. Carmona, M.: Design coding: mediating the tyrannies of practice. In: Urban Design in the Real Estate Development Process, pp. 288–303 (2011)
10. Sanders, E.B.-N.: Generative tools for co-designing. In: Scrivener, S.A.R., Ball, L.J., Woodcock, A. (eds.) Collaborative Design, pp. 3–12. Springer, London, London (2000)
11. Van Abel, B., Evers, L., Troxler, P., Klaassen, R.: Open design now: why design cannot remain exclusive. BIS Publishers (2014)

How Can City Labs Enhance the Citizens' Motivation in Different Types of Innovation Activities?

Ignasi Capdevila(✉)

newPIC / ESG Management School, Paris, France
icapdevi@esgms.fr

Abstract. There is a wide diversity of city labs for collaborative innovation. However, in all cases their success depends on motivating citizens to participate in their activities. This article builds on the literature on innovation dynamics in Living Labs to link them with other kinds of City Labs. The contribution of this article consists on building on the types of innovation mechanisms in Living Lab networks (Leminen, Westerlund, & Nyström, 2012; Leminen, 2013) by relating each type to a different theoretical innovation logic (methods for creativity; social innovation; open innovation; user innovation). Each logic is related to a different type of localized space of collective innovation (Fab Labs, co-creation spaces, Living Labs, coworking spaces and hackerspaces) and participants' motivation to collaborate. The literature review on the main characteristics of each logic provide some guidelines for City Labs practitioners about how to motivate citizens.

Keywords: Motivation to collaborate · Hackerspaces · Coworking spaces · Fab Labs · Open innovation · Social innovation · User innovation · Living Labs · City labs

1   Introduction

There is still a lack of common understanding about how to increase the citizens' involvement, in part due to the heterogeneity of practices and concepts behind City Labs.

The term City Lab can be used as an umbrella term under which a large diversity of projects and activities can be included. Often, definitions of the concept are close to the ones of other kinds of localized spaces of collective innovation (LSCI) like makerspaces, hackerspaces, Living Labs, Fab Labs, co-creation spaces or coworking spaces. Different denominations are related to different types of innovation logics and to different participants' motivations dynamics. Thus, the study of the innovation dynamics of other types of LSCI will contribute to understand the diversity of practices within Living Labs and the most efficient ways to motivate and engage participants. By analyzing the motivation of participants in the innovation dynamics of different LSCI, the article aims to provide some guides to city labs practitioners to increase the engagement of citizens.

© Springer International Publishing Switzerland 2015
L.M. Aiello and D. McFarland (Eds.): SocInfo 2014 Workshops, LNCS 8852, pp. 64–71, 2015.
DOI: 10.1007/978-3-319-15168-7_9

2   Different Approaches to City Labs

The typology based on the coordination and participation approaches in Living Lab networks (Leminen et al., 2012; Leminen, 2013) is especially convenient for disentangling the different citizens' motivations in City Labs as it focuses on the stakeholders' role in the innovation processes rather than on the processes, methodologies or systems.

According to this view, four approaches are identified, based on the different roles of Living Labs as providers, users, utilizers, and enablers (Westerlund & Leminen, 2011):

1. Provider-driven mechanism: The innovation activities of the Living lab aim to develop a solution for participants or other stakeholders, or have an educational purpose.
2. Enabler-driven mechanism: Taking a bottom-up approach, the activities focus on fulfilling the needs of a local community or association like improving the local social development where the Living Lab is located.
3. Utilizer-driven mechanism: The participants' activities are designed to develop or improve the product or service of a third-party (the utilizer).
4. User-driven mechanism: The participants collaborate to develop their own personal ideas or projects. Living labs activities focus on fulfilling the needs of individual users or user communities.

3   Enhancing Motivation in Different Localized Spaces of Collective Innovation

3.1   Methods and Techniques to Channel Collective Creativity (Provider-Driven Activities)

Innovation through collective participation is facilitated by the use of methodologies that guide participants' creativity to reach innovative solutions to current problems. There are a multiple methods, techniques and approaches that have been developed by academics and practitioners to ignite and channel the participants' creativity and imagination like TRIZ, C-K, Creative problem solving (CPS) or design thinking.

Co-creation activities following a given method can take place in virtual or localized environments. Localized spaces offer the advantage of facilitating the sharing of tacit knowledge and face-to-face interaction. They also allow the use of physical objects and the construction of prototypes that support the creation process (T. Brown, 2008). Consequently, Design Thinking and other similar innovation methodologies will benefit from taking place in spaces optimized for the construction of prototypes and models (Kelley, 2001), like Fab Labs.

The Fab Lab concept originated in MIT's interdisciplinary Center for Bits and Atoms where a first lab was put in place empowering students to make (almost) anything (Gershenfeld, 2005) by the use of new technological tools for rapid prototyping like 3D printers, laser cutters, and programmable sewing machines that allow small-scale production. They serve a wide spectrum of users, from youth, inventors as well as companies and students. They also serve multiple uses like teaching, professional development, applied research and research services.

3.2   Social Innovation Focus (Enabler-Driven Activities)

Social innovation can be defined as "innovative activities and services that are motivated by the goal of meeting a social need and that are predominantly developed and diffused through organizations whose primary purposes are social." (Mulgan, Tucker, Ali, & Sanders, 2007). Thus social innovation is differentiated from traditional business innovation as the latter is characterized by the profit maximization and the commercial exploitation of innovative endeavors. Between these two extremes, there is a large gray zone that includes other types of innovation that have both an economic and social goal, for instance, like innovation in social entrepreneurship.

The mere social collective benefit of the resulting social innovation is not sufficient to engage participation. The successful evolution of a social innovation, as in the case of any type of innovation, requires convincing new followers to adopt it. In the case of social innovation, the main types of resistance to people's participation are related to the short/term efficiency loss, the fear of risks and the loss of the current status quo, the resistance to change and the strong social ties (Mulgan et al., 2007). Consequently, to motivate participation, the promoter has to convince of the long-term benefits of participation, compared to a potential efficiency decrease and resistance to change in the short-term.

Changing mentalities, routines and practices is one of the biggest challenges of social innovators. Thus, participants in social innovation activities will be more inclined to contribute if they are already sensitive to social issues and share the values of social innovation. Local impact might also facilitate the participation of citizens. Short-term positive results can motivate and engage a larger local community, however, the lack of visible results or not implementing the results of the collaborative efforts might result in participants' deception and demotivation.

Grassroots emerging spaces, like coworking spaces focused on social innovation are deeply embedded in the local social environment and represent platforms for participation in social innovation for the local community.

Coworking spaces with a social innovation focus are not only platforms of interaction and collaboration among social innovators and entrepreneurs but also attract individuals interested in collaborating in social innovation initiatives.

The social entrepreneurs and innovators in coworking spaces tend to dedicate their efforts in the benefit of the local community. Communities that emerge in such spaces are in general self-managed, autonomous, and do not depend on public funds. This aspect allows the community to be deeply embedded in the local community and attract the participation of neighbors. However, despite the social goal of social entrepreneurs, their for-profit focus can refrain them from getting involved in pure social innovation.

3.3 Open Innovation Focus (Utilizer-Driven Activities)

The term open innovation has been used to refer to a system where innovation is not developed exclusively internally within a firm, but using external sources (Chesbrough, 2003; Laursen & Salter, 2006).

To link the firms internal innovation process and the external sources of knowledge and expertise, open innovation often requires the intervention of intermediaries (Chesbrough, 2006). Such innovation intermediaries might be virtual online platforms (like Innocentive or Nine Sigma) than allow the interaction of external participants to respond to the firms' needs and proposed challenges. Additionally, localized spaces of collective innovation like Living Labs can also fulfill this role of intermediary, facilitating the users' participation and coordinating innovation processes (Almirall & Wareham, 2010).

Participants in open innovation activities accept to contribute to an innovation process in order to develop a new product or service for an organization that will commercialize the innovative endeavor in the market.

Open innovation participation often uses virtual online platforms as intermediaries. Virtual open innovation processes are however not out of this world as "innovation processes [...] do not happen in a void but are carried out somewhere – they literally take place" (Haner & Bakke, 2004, p. 5).

Face-to-face interaction offers though advantages for collaborative innovation. Even in the case of virtual teams, the periodic co/location of the members facilitates the success of the innovation project (Gassmann & von Zedtwitz, 2003; Leonard & Swap, 1999).

Localized activities of open innovation can take place in different spaces. Experiences of organizing open innovation workshops in Living Labs have encounters difficulties of both attracting participants and firms.

3.4 User Innovation Focus (User-Driven Activities)

An important differentiation has to be made between the role of users in open innovation and in user innovation. While in the open innovation model, users participate in the innovation process responding to the challenges proposed by a firm, in the user innovation concept, users innovate in a self-motivated and autonomous way (von Hippel, 1994, 2005, 2007).

Users often innovate in user communities, critical in the processes of prototyping, developing and diffusing solutions to their needs. Collaboration within communities accelerates the development and simultaneous experimentation of novelties (Shah, 2005). These communities are characterized by being emergent, autonomous and by sharing knowledge openly. These communities contrast with the dynamics in traditional corporate R&D departments where new knowledge and innovations are internally kept.

These communities are characterized by the voluntary participation of loosely-affiliated users with common interests. Communities members engage in the development and testing on innovations through an iterative process of trial and error where members give feedback to one another to advance in the development and improvement of products. These communities are intimately related to practice, and can be assimilated to the communities of practices (J. Brown & Duguid, 2000; Wenger, 1998a). Even if community members might interact through virtual communication, temporary co-location allow the common practice of the hobby (i.e. in the case of sports) or the sharing of tools and machines needed for prototyping. Face-to-face interaction also reinforces the community identity and facilitates the transfer of tacit knowledge (Lave & Wenger, 1991; Wenger, 1998b).

The open sharing of knowledge, information and innovations are crucial in the collaborative work if innovation communities. Users are motivated to share their innovative work and engage in collaboration, however, user-innovators might also be motivated to not diffuse their work to third-parties. The appropriation of the innovation by a third party could impede a further development by users. Innovation communities might put in place several mechanisms to forbid external actors to take advantage of their innovations. For instance, the public exhibition or documentation of innovation, or registering innovations with open licenses that avoid the commercialization or appropriation of the innovations.

Beyond the intrinsic motivation, innovation communities and users might also engage in entrepreneurship practices and commercialize their own innovations, mainly in the cases of wide adoption of the innovation with the consequent appearance of potential buyers (Shah, 2005).

Even though hacker spaces or other similar terms like hacklabs (Maxigas, 2012) do not respond to a clear definition, they could be straightforwardly defined as being communities' workspaces which operate on the principles of hacker ethics (Farr, 2009; Himanen, 2009; Levy, 2001). They are driven by an open culture that, through a sharing attitude and a peer-to-peer approach, can enhance the development of distributed networks and social bonds (Bauwens, 2005). Emerging from the counter culture (Grenzfurthner & Schneider, 2009), hackerspaces are a large set of differing places, with one ubiquitous feature: a community of enthusiasts sharing a common motivation (Schlesinger, Islam, & MacNeill, 2010). Altruism, community commitment, meeting other hackers in the real world and having fun seem to be the most important factors of motivation (Moilanen, 2012).

4   Managerial Implications

One of the biggest challenges that City Labs' managers encounter is to engage citizens in their innovation activities. Research on motivation in creativity and innovation has underlined the crucial role that intrinsic motivations plays in engaging participation (Amabile, 1996). In the cases of a bottom-up innovation modes, participants co-develop innovation projects for their own benefit. In the case of enabler-driven activities, the innovation project would impact the social local environment of participants. In this case, the rationale that could motivate participants would be "I am here to contribute to a project for my society". In user-driven activities, participants are empowered to develop their own innovative projects for their own private benefit.

In bottom-up innovation modes, managers should focus on providing the required tools and needed resources for reaching successfully the emerging project goal. However too much intervention or over-management could be counterproductive. In enabler-driven activities, participants should manage their own-created expectations with the available resources. Otherwise, they could feel demotivated if finally the forecasted results are not fulfilled. In the case of user-driven activities, emergent user communities might be reluctant to management control, as has been referred in the literature on communities of practice (Wenger, 1998b).

In provider- and utilizer-driven activities, participants might be more motivated by participating in the innovation process rather than by benefiting of the final product resulting from the collaboration. In these cases, managers could increase the participants engagement by focusing on designing an attractive and enriching ideation process. Provider-driven activities allow the participation of a wide spectrum of participants that encourages the combination of different knowledge bases. Methodologies, tools and techniques facilitate the guidance and coaching all along the process, ensuring its consistency, replicability and control. However, following a too strict process protocol risks to reduce opportunities for unexpectedness and improvisation that could benefit creativity and imagination. In the case of utilizer-driven activities, the commercial exploitation of the collaborative innovation by a firm could refrain participation unless if participation is incentivized by monetary rewards. However, managers should not only focus on extrinsic motivation of participants, and also focus on nurturing a creative and enjoyable environment to attract engagement more based on intrinsic factors of motivation.

5   Conclusion

The article underlines the uniqueness of City Labs as they represent spaces where different types of innovators can interact and thus benefit from synergies, diversity and cross-pollination of ideas. The different approaches are however not mutually incompatible, and might be implemented simultaneously in different collaborative projects in a same City Lab. Nevertheless, in some cases, a conflict between logics might create a cognitive dissonance in the participants and thus inhibit participation. By clarifying the different logics and individuals motivations, the article aims to provide guidelines to City Lab managers and practitioners to maximize the participation and therefore ensure the sustainability of the City Lab activities.

The comparison of types of activities in City Labs, theoretical innovation approaches, and types of LSCI that has been developed in this article presents some limitations. First, in an effort of simplification, LSCI have been only related to one type of innovation. However, reality is more complex and each kind of space might present several types of innovation activities. Second, there is also a great diversity of practices among spaces of a same LSCI type. For instance, some Fab Labs do similar activities as hacker- or makerspaces. The differences identified in the analysis have underlined the context of innovation rather than the specific practices. For instance, even if practices between Fab Labs and hackerspaces are comparable, the approach is different: hackers are firstly driven by their hacker ethic, while Fab Labs are ruled by their common charter.

The contribution of this paper is threefold: managerial, conceptual, and theoretical. First, through a literature review on innovation modes and their motivation logic, the article provides some useful perspectives for City Labs managers on how to engage participants. Second, conceptually, the comparison of different LSCI has contributed to understand new phenomena of localized collaboration and innovation, as well as their differences and similarities. Third, the article contributes to the theorization of City Labs by using different innovation theories.

References

1. Almirall, E., Wareham, J.: Living labs: arbiters of mid- and ground-level innovation. In: Oshri, I., Kotlarsky, J. (eds.) Global Sourcing of Information Technology and Business Processes. LNBIP, vol. 55, pp. 233–249. Springer, Heidelberg (2010)
2. Amabile, T.M.: Creativity in Context. Westview Press, Boulder (1996)
3. Bauwens, M.: P2P and Human Evolution: Peer to peer as the premise of a new mode of civilization. Ensaio, Rascunho, 1–73 (2005)
4. Brown, J., Duguid, P.: The social life of information. Harvard Business Press (2000)
5. Brown, T.: Design Thinking. Harvard Business Review **86**(6), 84–92 (2008)
6. Chesbrough, H.W.: Open innovation: The new imperative for creating and profiting from technology (2003)
7. Chesbrough, H.W.: Open business models: How to thrive in the new innovation landscape (2006)
8. Farr, N.: hackerspaces | flux | Respect the Past, Examine the Present, Build the Future (2009).   http://blog.hackerspaces.org/2009/08/25/respect-the-past-examine-the-present-build-the-future/. (Retrieved March 22, 2013)
9. Gassmann, O., von Zedtwitz, M.: Trends and determinants of managing virtual R&D teams. R&D Management **33**(3), 243–262 (2003)
10. Gershenfeld, N.: Fab: The coming revolution on your desktop–from personal computers to personal fabrication. Basic Books (2005)
11. Grenzfurthner, J., Schneider, F.: Hacking the Spaces (2009). http://www.monochrom.at/hacking-the-spaces/. (Retrieved March 08, 2013)
12. Haner, U.-E., Bakke, J.W.: On how work environments influence innovation – a case study from a large ICT company. In: Proceedings of the XV Annual Conference of the International Society for Professional Innovation Management (ISPIM), Oslo 20–24 June 2004
13. Himanen, P.: The hacker ethic. Random House Publishing Group (2009)
14. Kelley, T.: Prototyping is the shorthand of innovation. Design Management Journal (Former Series) **12**(3), 35–42 (2001)
15. Laursen, K., Salter, A.: Open for innovation: the role of openness in explaining innovation performance among UK manufacturing firms. Strategic Management Journal **27**, 131–150 (2006). doi:10.1002/smj.507
16. Lave, J., Wenger, E.: Situated learning: Legitimate peripheral participation. Cambridge University Press (1991)
17. Leminen, S.: Coordination and Participation in Living Lab Networks. Technology Innovation Management Review, pp. 5–14, November 2013
18. Leminen, S., Westerlund, M., Nyström, A.: Living Labs as Open-Innovation Networks. Technology Innovation Management Review, pp. 6–11, September 2012

19. Leonard, D., Swap, W.: When Sparks Fly: Igniting Creativity in Groups. Harvard Business School Press, Boston (1999)
20. Levy, S.: Hackers: Heroes of the computer revolution. Penguin Books, New York (2001)
21. Maxigas: Hacklabs and hackerspaces – tracing two genealogies. Journal of Peer Production **2**, 1–10 (2012)
22. Moilanen, J.: Emerging hackerspaces – peer-production generation. In: Hammouda, I., Lundell, B., Mikkonen, T., Scacchi, W. (eds.) Open Source Systems: Long-Term Sustainability. IFIP AICT, vol. 378, pp. 94–111. Springer, Heidelberg (2012)
23. Mulgan, G., Tucker, S., Ali, R., Sanders, B.: Social innovation: what it is, why it matters and how it can be accelerated. Skoll Centre for Social Entrepreneurship, Ox (2007)
24. Schlesinger, J., Islam, M.M., MacNeill, K.: Founding a Hackerspace. wpi.edu (p. 69). Worcester (2010)
25. Shah, S.: Open beyond software. *SSRN 789805* (2005)
26. Von Hippel, E.: "Sticky information" and the locus of problem solving: implications for innovation. Management Science **40**(4), 429–439 (1994)
27. Von Hippel, E.: Democratizing innovation. MIT press, Cambridge (2005)
28. Von Hippel, E.: The sources of innovation (2007)
29. Wenger, E.: Communities of Practice: Learning as a Social System, pp. 1–10, June 1998
30. Wenger, E.: Communities of Practice: Learning, Meaning, and Identity. Cambridge University Press, Cambridge (1998)
31. Westerlund, M., Leminen, S.: Managing the challenges of becoming an open innovation company: experiences from Living Labs. Technology Innovation Management Review, pp. 19–25, October (2011)

Criminal Network Analysis and Mining (CRIMENET)

Criminal Network Analysis and Mining (CRIMENET 2014) - Introduction

Emilio Ferrara[1]([✉]), Salvatore Catanese[1], and Giacomo Fiumara[2]

[1] School of Informatics and Computing Bloomington,
Indiana University Bloomington, Bloomington, IN 47408, USA
`ferrarae@indiana.edu`
[2] Dipartimento di Matematica e Informatica, Universitàdegli Studi di Messina,
Messina 98100, Italy

Mobile phone networks, social network platforms, social media and over-IP messaging systems represent typical examples of the multitude of communication media broadly adopted in nowadays society. One aspect that has vast societal impact is the abuse of such platforms: the possibility that criminals can exploit these communication channels to organize and coordinate their illicit activities has been proved real. Criminal Networks (CNs) differ from well-studied Social Networks in a number of ways, including their size (usually the number of members is low), the lack of knowledge of their structure and organization (information about members and their relations is incomplete) and the different types of dynamics of interactions (digital communications, economic transactions, face-to-face interactions, etc.). Therefore, in recent years (say, after 9-11-2001) Criminal Network Analysis has grown as an outstanding, almost independent research area. The ability to detect criminal behavior across different interaction media is of paramount importance to avoid abuse and fight crime. For this reason, computational tools and models have been recently proposed to study criminal behavior in online platforms and mobile phone networks.

Scope

An objective of the event is to create a fully interdisciplinary venue, bringing together scientists from disciplines including, among others, physics, sociology, mathematics, computer science, information technologies, policy and law enforcement agencies.

This event is intended to be of particular relevance for some of the conference research topics, namely Social network analysis and mining, Mining social big data, Web mining and its social interpretations, Security, privacy, trust, reputation and incentive issues, Real-time analysis or visualization of social phenomena and social graphs.

Particular attention will be devoted to the following topics:

- CN analysis techniques;
- Community detection in CNs;

© Springer International Publishing Switzerland 2015
L.M. Aiello and D. McFarland (Eds.): SocInfo 2014 Workshops, LNCS 8852, pp. 75–77, 2015.
DOI: 10.1007/978-3-319-15168-7_10

- Flow of information in CNs;
- Visualization techniques in CNs;
- Spatio-temporal analysis in CNs;
- Simulations and real-case studies of attacks to CNs;
- Crime on the Web and crimes using the Web.

This is the first edition of the workshop. Our aim is to attract researchers and practitioners, from academia (e.g. computer science, mathematics, sociology) and law enforcement agencies.

Keynote Speaker

Serge Galam   CEVIPOF - Centre for Political Research, Paris

Program Commitee

Jisun An	Qatar Computing Institute
Andrea Apolloni	London School of Hygiene and Tropical Medicine
Giovanni L. Ciampaglia	Indiana University
Michele Coscia	Harvard University
Martina Deplano	University of Turin
Pasquale De Meo	University of Messina
Bruno Goncalves	Aix-Marseille Universitè
Przemyslaw Grabowicz	Max Planck Institute for Software Systems
Marco Alberto Javarone	University of Cagliari
Mariantonietta La Polla	CNR Pisa - IIT
SangHoon Lee	University of Oxford - Internet Institute
Jared Lorince	Indiana University
Emanuele Massaro	Carnagie Mellon University
Luca Pappalardo	CNR Pisa - KDD Lab
Nicola Perra	Northeastern University
Giovanni Petri	ISI Turin
Giancarlo Ruffo	University of Turin
Yana Volkovic	Barcelona Media Foundation
Claudia Wagner	GESIS - University of Koblentz
Tim Weninger	Notre Dame University

Statistics on Accepted Papers

Submitted: 7
Accepted: 6

Accepted Papers

Fatih Özgül and Zeki Erdem
Understanding Crime Networks: Actors and Links

Donatella Firmani, Giuseppe F. Italiano and Luigi Laura
The (not so) Critical Nodes of Criminal Networks

Jess Espinal-Enrquez, Jesus Mario Siqueiros-Garca, Rodirgo Garca-Herrera and Sergio A Alcal
A Literature-Based Approach to a Narco-Network

Sarah White, Tobin Yehle, Hugo Serrano, Marcos Oliveira and Ronaldo Menezes
The Spatial Structure of Crime in Urban Environments

Marco Alberto Javarone and Serge Galam
Emergence of Extreme Opinions in Social Networks

Gemma Galdon Clavell and Philippe M. Frowd
Using societal impact assessment (SIA) to improve technological development in the field of crime prevention

Understanding Crime Networks: Actors and Links

Fatih Ozgul[1][(✉)] and Zeki Erdem[2]

[1] Faculty of Security Sciences, National Police Academy, Golbasi, Turkey
fatih.ozgul@istanbul.com
[2] TUBITAK BILGEM, Gebze, Kocaeli, Turkey
zeki.erdem@tubitak.gov.tr

Abstract. In order to understand crime networks, criminological and practical knowledge should be merged. Criminals are similar, criminals are different. Crime networks can be categorized but still the links, actors, and characteristics are different. This paper gives a literature review of crime networks from criminological as well as network analysis views.

Keywords: Crime networks · Analysis of crime networks

1 Crime Networks

Crime networks are social groups whose members gather to obtain a political or financial gain, by breaching law of a particular country and this action is accepted as "crime" in this country's criminal justice system, where they have an organization to serve their purpose, and they are reluctant to use means of violence and weapons to this end. In recent years, there have been more and more studies into criminal activities that require a certain form of collaboration and organization. Terms like group crime, gangs, corporate crime, organized crime, and terrorist networks are used to define various types of crime networks. Throughout the decades criminologist tried to explain crime networks form different perspectives. Crime networks are made up with people and connections between them, so they are expected to be diverse in nature. It is difficult to come up with a comprehensive theory in order to explain the criminal networks as a social construct [1]. Shaw and McKay [2] explain that lower socioeconomic class slum areas of major cities is the source of unique and independent value system which causes offenders break the law because of their adherence to the value system [3]. Further studies contended that the crime is not restricted to slums and lower level class it is more related to learning through cultural transmission. If a person grow up in a place where there are successful criminal role models running activities such as prostitution, drug trafficking, gambling and so on, he could be a member of a street gang than recruited by an organized crime network since high probability of being able to have close contact with criminal role models, learn from them and imitate them [4] [5]. Sellin also extend another explanation from the cultural conflict perspective. He argues that when different cultures get in touch with each other there could be conflict with values, traditions etc. This could create problems to achieve equal opportunities therefore neighborhood may become a ground for organized crime and street gangs [6]. For example, Irish, Jews, Italians, African

© Springer International Publishing Switzerland 2015
L.M. Aiello and D. McFarland (Eds.): SocInfo 2014 Workshops, LNCS 8852, pp. 78–86, 2015.
DOI: 10.1007/978-3-319-15168-7_11

Americans, Russians, and Asians are prominent crime networks in the US. Another explanation is come from theory of strain. It basically stress that strain between means end ends may result frustration afterwards joining a crime network. Lack of legitimate avenues to achieve goals is either closed or very limited to different segment of the society therefore criminal solution and joining crime networks could be considered as the best response for some people [7]. Cloward and Ohlin [6] take this approach one step ahead and argued that availability and stability of illegal business varies depends on the quality of relationship between underground and legal world. If a crime network knows how to deal with legal structure through corruption of politician and judicial system it become shining star in the society attract people join this network [8]. From all explanation above it could be excerpt that poor urban neighborhoods provide nice opportunities for crime networks. Being part of this crime network could be a forced choice rather a volunteer one because lack of availability of legitimate avenues.

Crime networks are not simply social networks operating in criminal context. The covert settings that surround them call for specific interactions and relational features within and beyond network. When secrecy is a "necessary condition" and risk is a fundamental factor, trust, personal vouching, and social tie strength all increase in importance. Risk and concealment are the most important features in crime networks [9]. All social networks face some level of control, but a crime network faces more intensive and systematic control from external and internal forces. For instance, crime networks generally hide their members and conceal their activities. Crime network structure often protects some participants when their illegal activities are no longer secret and participants become the target of investigation by external forces. Increasing protection after detection can take a variety of forms such as limited physical interaction between network participants, the minimization of communication channels, the creation of internal organizational buffers to detach participants from another, and decentralization of management to shelter leaders [9]. Some previous research has shown that most crime networks are not dominated by centrally controlled organizations with a clear hierarchy and strict division of tasks. Rather, they operate in an informal and flexible way. For instance, organized crime is a collection of criminals and criminal groups that enter into collaboration with each other in varying combinations and in order for crime networks to function within a geographical distance and in a time period to match supply and demand [10, 11, 12, 13] Crime networks also presence to tightly knit, hierarchical, monolithic, and intensely regulated, while other type of crime networks are confronted this position by emphasizing the difficulties for criminal collectives to organize in such overly regulated forms and they insist on loose and decentralized nature of most criminal groups. These researchers also emphasize that offenders are not simply abiders of rules and they consequently organize themselves in ways that are the least possibly regulated. Another claim about crime networks is they merge hierarchy and decentralization by creating criminal settings which are traditionally hierarchical become more decentralized once loyalty and formal order were displaced by individual expertise and an entrepreneurial spirit [9].

Canter [14] suggests that two dominant trends are identified for crime networks; first the size of the network, second the product of the centrality of leadership. Using these criteria, three types of criminal organization are specified. They are ad-hoc groups, oligarchies, and organized criminals. Ad-hoc groups are with relatively little structure, sometimes with just the presence of key central figures. Oligarchies are the kind of networks where their communications appear to be controlled by a small group of people. Organized criminals are the closest to being an illegal organization with most of differentiation, indicating a management hierarchy. Ad-hoc groups are the smallest sized groups whereas organized criminals are the largest sized ones. For instance, he suggests that hooligan groups are less structured whereas drug dealing networks are the most structured were found for all types of criminal activity.

Crime networks may be clandestine but other than their management principles are quite common to any other goal-oriented network: it's all about integrating people, information and technology. If I consider organized crime for example, as a complex and dynamic set of goal-oriented processes, crime networks are designed to optimize their efficiency and effectiveness. One of the main problems in human resource management is to fit right people with necessary competencies, skills, and expertise into right jobs in order to optimize overall performance. Another cornerstone for organizational success is to create competitive advantages through social connections that facilitate the achievements. Crime networks are largely depending on their human capital, contacts and ties. People and organizations that have better access to valuable social resources are more successful in their performances [15].

2   Importance of Actors and Links

Just like ordinary social networks, crime networks consist of two sorts of elements: actors and links between actors. In most studies of social networks, the actors are persons with characteristics and features such as age, sex, education, criminal record, physical strength, or temperament. A relationship may or may not exist between two actors. The existence of a relationship indicates that both actors are linked to each other via a link. Just like people, these relationships between actors also have characteristics. Some characteristics of social links and relationships are distinguished. Examples of these are the frequency of contacts, age, duration of the relationship, the degree to which the relationship is affective or instrumental, whether the relationship is hierarchical, and the degree to which the relationship is homogenous (e.g., between people with similar personal or background characteristics). There are examples of classifications of links between criminals. For example, much of the Canadian police uses the Long Matrix on organized crime, or Sleipnir Scale [16] to measure the relative strength, or threat, of criminal organizations. Sleipnir scale attaches a numeric value to the threat posed by crime networks. In the Sleipner system, criminal organizations are graded according to nineteen different attributes such as ability to corrupt public officials, propensity to use violence capacity to discipline its membership. At the end of this grading process, a criminal organization receives a score between 0 and 760 [17].

Social relationships show multiple directions and characteristics simultaneously. From this great variety of social relationships, it can be assumed that the social world of criminals is vibrant. If criminals and their mutual collaborative relationships with others are filtered, then someone can easily find out that relationships between criminals are just the top of iceberg as compared to criminals' relationship to rest of people. Social links are connections between actors that indicate some form of activity or bonding between actors. Strong links are close solid and trusted relationships such as family and friends. Weak links include less intimacy such as co-worker. Both strong and weak links bring their own benefits and disadvantages. The major benefit of strong links is that people are more willing to help and share the same norms and values which increase the ability to access instrumental resources. On the other hand, similar people tend to have identical qualities and circulate in the same social circles which mean they share identical resources as well. But for weak links, things are different. The available pool of resources may be more limited because of the limited willingness of other people to help, but weak links are more likely to connect people from different social circles. This is known as the strength of weak links [18]. The fundamental dilemma for criminals to balance their need for strategic initiatives based on a broad access to instrumental resources via weak links and their need for trusted and solid collaborations that facilitate secrecy, protection and the enforcement of norms and sanctions [19, 20, 15].

3   Analysis of Crime Networks

Analysis of crime networks mostly refers to the discovery of members of within a crime network, finding out their relationships with each other, and underlying organizational structure of its network. It involves identifying the world of intended crime networks, their interaction, interactions of subgroups and cliques within these networks. Each crime network has also special characteristics; so each network bear specific behavioral heuristics, crime committing habits, associations with other criminals in order to provide transfer specific tools and capabilities. Significant behavioral characteristics of criminals reflect the characteristics of relationships in crime networks. Some of those features are: Offender demographics information such as surname, country of origin, hometown, choice of locations for committed crimes which represents the natural habitat of criminals to operate, modus operandi information which shows the skills of criminals, features of crimes (e.g. crime date, location) committed which describes the acts of a crime network, co-offending information which shows previous associations and collaborations between criminals. There are three analysis methods that are important when analyzing criminal networks:

• Structural analysis investigates the characteristics of the network structure as a whole. For instance, what kind of crime network is this? Are they structured hierarchically or more informal? How serious is the emerging network? So, structural analysis of criminal networks gives a general about the type of network [21].

• Positional analysis investigates the characteristics of the position that a criminal occupies in network structure. For instance, the key players in the network must be kept in physical surveillance, their communications must be eavesdropped and their all correspondence must be found out. Positional analysis of crime networks gives an idea about particular persons in the network must be focused.

• Relationship analysis investigates the characteristics of relationships between network and people. For instance in many countries, whistle blowers within the crime networks can be excluded from prosecution if they give satisfying amount of information to the police. Relationship analysis of crime network gives an idea about relationships within crime networks and their members.

Based on the existing crime networks most famous types of crime networks are as follows:

3.1 Organized Crime and Drug Dealing Networks

Criminal groups that are engaged in drug smuggling and mafia are usually based on collaborations between members of cohesive and often ethnically homogenous social networks. This seems to be much less the case in human trafficking and the trade of stolen goods [22]. Trust is principally important in activities that are linked to major criminal and financial risks. Small world networks, which are characterized by high density and a large proportion of affective relationships, are pre-eminently suited to criminal collaborations where a great deal of mutual trust is needed [27]. Small world networks would seem to be supported by the finding that collaboration in the smuggling and wholesaling of heroine takes place primarily by criminals who are mutually embedded in cohesive networks. Drug distribution networks, which exist both in wholesale markets and in the less risky street trade, are less cohesive than smuggling networks. One hypothesis is that collaborative relationships between people who jointly participate in cohesive networks are more durable and stable than collaborative relationships between people who participate in less cohesive networks [22]. This hypothesis is based on the contents of police files of criminal investigations, in which more long-term collaborative relationships are recorded. It is expected, therefore, that the collaboration between criminals in cohesive networks will be of a longer duration, because their mutual relationships are not merely instrumental, while people who participate in looser networks often restrict their collaboration to just one or a few criminal projects. Mafia-type organized crime and drug dealing networks are of various sizes. There are many ethnical originated criminal networks all over the world. Members of clans in Diaspora or in ethnic/religious minority community develop strong ties with family members and relatives. When they grow up, they find themselves in a strongly structured extended family ties. Within these strong ties, they find relatives and friends identical to them; they therefore operate in homogenous networks, able to reach some abundant and redundant resources of knowledge, materials, and people. When they grow up, they develop weak ties with other community members or strangers where they bridge different social circles and diverse networks. Having bridge position bring some opportunities to access limited resources. Many mafia-type organized crime and drug dealing networks within this manner. First they realize the demand for illegal goods and services in countries/cities they migrated to. They also know where they can find them, use human labor to bring them over to the customers they demand for. Members of clans and extended families are generous enough to provide human labor, trust, and secrecy which they desperately need for doing such business. The strategic benefit for having both strong and weak ties for illegal activities is defined as being criminal brokers. The strategic benefits associated with being in a unique bridging position between other actors are the basis for Structural Holes Theory [19]. If two non-redundant groups of actors are focused on their own in-group activities without paying too much attention to activities of the other, there is a hole in the social structure [15]. Actors who span structural holes or social gaps and who position themselves in between the groups create competitive benefits. Criminal brokers are able to find rewarding opportunities and power via information benefits and controlling benefits between parties. As a result, between central actors are more creative, identify opportunities fast, know exactly where to find right people and create higher returns on investment. Research indicated that brokers in transnational crime who bridge the connections between sources, transit and destination countries are often ethnically homogenous to the counterparts they work with. Their relations are mostly based on trusted friendship or family ties [22, 12]. As a result, organized crime and drug network characteristics are mostly non-hierarchical, and cell-based, members of the networks have strong trust in each other and they prefer to operate in secrecy.

3.2   Terrorist Networks

Terrorist organizations often operate in a network in which individual terrorists cooperate and collaborate with each other to carry out attacks. Despite the motivational and group dynamics differences between organized crime and terrorist groups, they share the same loosely connected and fluid as hoc organizational principles [15]. The same topology of cellular structures applies to "home-grown" terrorist networks [20]. Terrorist organizations often operate in a network in which individual terrorists cooperate and collaborate with each other to carry out attacks. According to Sageman [20], home-grown terrorists are citizens of the western countries, they were born in western countries, educated there and they are non-immigrant. The other type of terrorists are the ones where they are born in their originated country, but migrated to western countries after they are grown-up, and they conceal their ideology while living in. Most members of those terrorist networks are not aware of other cells which are geographically very close to them. They share the same ideology, meet each other on internet, but they only know each other with nicknames. That is why they are more difficult to follow, more complex, and unpredictable. Since September 11, 2001, (e.g. 9-11), there has been a considerable increase in interest from the police and intelligence agencies to use social network analysis as a research tool [9]. But studies of terrorist network structure have generated little actionable results. This is due to the difficulty in collecting and accessing reliable data and the lack of advanced network analysis methodologies in this field. When analyzing terrorist networks, analysts often focus on characteristics of the network structure in order to gain insight into the following questions [23].

- •Which terrorist is highly/less connected?
- •Which terrorists are connected to highly connected terrorists?
- •Who is depending on whom?
- •On whom do many terrorists depend?
- •What is the efficiency of the network?
- •Who is the most important person in the network?
- •What are the various roles of terrorist in the network?
- •Which terrorists are key players?
- •How can police use (often incomplete and faulty) network data to disrupt and destabilize terrorist networks?

Knowledge of these structural characteristics helps in revealing vulnerabilities of terrorist networks and may have important implications for investigations. Analysts of terrorist networks face the difficulty of building an accurate map of these groups.

Valdis Krebs [24], who has used network analysis to provide an extensive analysis of the 9-11 hijackers' network, explains three problems he encountered very early on. Relying on the work of Sparrow [25], he states that three problems are likely to plague the social network analyst, regardless of context. These are:

•Incompleteness - the inevitability of missing nodes and links that the investigators will not uncover.
•Fuzzy boundaries - the difficulty in deciding who to include and who to exclude.
•Dynamic - these networks are not static, they are always changing.

Usually, terrorist network members who occupy central positions should be targeted for removal or surveillance. A central member may play a key role in a network by acting as leader who issues commands and provides steering mechanisms, or by serving as gatekeeper that ensures information or goods flows effectively among different components of the networks [23]. Counter-terrorist forces usually use assassination to disrupt terrorist networks. But sometimes "taking out" the leadership doesn't stop terrorism by itself. Carley and Dombrowski [26] proposed a well-constructed set of criteria for requirement of "taking out the key players" operation, if not;

•The rate of information flow through the network has been reduced (perhaps to zero).
•The network, as a decision making body, cannot reach a consensus.
•The ability of the network to accomplish tasks is impaired.

Evidence indicates that terrorist networks are not susceptible to these measures of disruption due to leadership removal. The reason is that in a distributed terrorist network, intra-networking between emergent leaders radically reduces the impact of leadership removal. The removal of leadership from a distributed network is rapidly repaired. The analysis indicates that assassination is not effective in disrupting terrorist networks. In fact, leadership removal may make the network denser to future analysis given the emergence of new leadership that may not be known and new future leadership may be technologically sound.

3.3   Theft and Violence Networks

Theft networks and violence networks are different from organized crime and terrorist networks. Violent crimes are committed more frequently than organized crimes. Theft networks are also very common. When the ages of members are considered, it is a well-known fact that theft and violence networks are dominated by youngsters and members of these networks are belongs to peer-groups [27, 28, 29]. In theft and violence networks co-offending is important feature to link criminals [30, 31]. But not all theft and violence networks are operated by peer-groups. The expertise of knowledge is required to operate for their team building function. According to some domain experts, in theft network, in general, four types of roles are sought for. Those are masters, who are needed for leadership and exchange of goods, laborers who are needed for labor intensive jobs, craftsmen who are needed for required specific knowledge and modus operandi skills, and locators who know a geographical location very well.

In terms of stability [28] in crime networks, there are two types of actors (e.g. criminals); life course persistent criminals begin offending in early ages, engage in an array of offences and persist over the life course. On the other hand adolescent limited criminals begin offending later, engage in group based delinquent acts that are indicative of teenage rebellion, but then adolescent limited criminals tend to be in general decline of criminality.

4   Conclusion

We investigated the key literature to understand crime networks and main characteristics of them. Due to fuzziness [24, 25, 32] of links, relationships and actors, it is always difficult to find out the real world of criminals. Criminological findings and social network analysis practice hand in hand may produce better understanding and analysis of crime networks.

References

1. Shaw, C.R., McKay, H.D.: Juvenile Delinquency and Urban Areas. University of Chicago Press, Chicago (1942)
2. Burgess, R., Akers, R.L.: A Differential Association-Reinforcement Theory of Criminal Behavior. Social Problems **14**, 363–383 (1966)
3. Bandura, A.: Social Learning Theory. General Learning Press (1971)
4. Sellin, T.: Culture Conflict and Crime. Social Science Research Counsel, New York (1938)
5. Merton, R.: Social Theory and Social Structure. The Free Press, Glencoe (1957)
6. Cloward, R.A., Ohlin, L.E.: Delinquency and Opportunity: A Theory of Delinquent Gangs. Free Press, New York (1960)
7. Scott, J.: Social Network Analysis: A Handbook. SAGE Publications, London (2005)
8. Wasserman, S., Faust, K.: Social Network Analysis Methods and Applications. Cambridge University Press, Cambridge (1994)
9. Morselli, C.: Inside Criminal Networks. Springer Science+Business Media LLC, New York (2009)
10. Reuter, P.: Disorganised Crime, illegal markets and the Mafia. MIT Press, Cambridge (1986)
11. Fijnaut, C., Bovenkerk, F.: Organised Crime in Netherlands. Kluiwer Law International, Hague (1998)
12. Kleemans, E.R., van den Berg, E.A.I.M.: Organised crime in Netherlands - Georganiseerde Criminaliteit in Nederland. WODC, Hague (1998)
13. Klerks, E.R.: Big in Hash: Theory and Practice of Organised Criminality - Groot in de Hash: Theorie en Praktijk van de Georganiseerde Criminaliteit. Erasmus University, Rotterdam (2000)
14. Canter, D.: A partial order scalogram analysis of criminal network structures. Behaviormetrika **31**(2), 131–152 (2004)
15. van der Hulst, R.C.: Introduction to Social Network Analysis as an investigative tool. Trends in Organised Crime **12**, 101–121 (2009)

16. Strang, S.: Project SLEIPNIR: an analytical technique for operational priority setting. In: International Conference on Intelligence Analysis, Ottawa, Canada, Central Intelligence Agency (2005)
17. Schwarts, D.M., Rouselle, T.D.A.: Using social network analysis to target criminal networks. Trends in Organised Crime 12, 188–207 (2009)
18. Granovetter, M.: The strength of weak ties. American Journal of Sociology 78, 1360–1380 (1973)
19. Burt, R.S.: The network structure of social capital. JAI Press, Greenwich (2000)
20. Sageman, M.: Understanding Terror Networks. University of Pennsylvania Press, Philadelphia (2004)
21. Wasserman, S., Faust, K.:Social Network Analysis Methods and Applications. Cambridge University Press (1994)
22. Bruinsma, G., Bernasco, W.: Criminal Groups and transnational illegal markets. Crime, Law & Social Change 41, 79–94 (2004)
23. Memon, N., Larsen, H.L.: Practical approaches for analysis, visualization and destabilizing terrorist networks. In: Proceedings of the First International Conference on Availability, Reliability and Security, pp. 906–913. IEEE Computer Society (2006)
24. Krebs, V.: Mapping networks of terrorist cells. Connections 24(3), 43–52 (2002)
25. Sparrow, M.K.: Network vulnerabilities and strategic intelligence in law enforcement. Journal of Intelligence and counterintelligence 5(3), 255–274 (1991)
26. Carley, K., Dombrowski, M.: Destabilizing Dynamic Covert Networks, 8th International Command and Control Research and Technology. National Defence War College, Washington DC (2003)
27. Finckenauer, J.O.: Mafia and Organized Crime A Beginner's Guide, p. 11. Oneworld Publication, Oxford (2007)
28. Moody, J.: Peer influence groups: identifying dense clusters in large networks. Social Networks 23, 261–283 (2001)
29. McGlorin, J.M., Sullivan, C.J.: Investigating the stability of co-offenders among a sample of youthful offenders. Criminology 46(1), 155–187 (2008)
30. McCord, J.: Co-offending and Patterns of Juvenile Crime. National Institute of Justice, Washington DC (2005)
31. Felson, M.: The natural history of co-offending. Trends in Organised Crime 12, 159–165 (2009)
32. Klerks, P.: The Network Paradigm Applied to Criminal Organisations: Theoretical nitpicking or a relevant doctrine for investigators? Recent developments in the Netherlands. Connections 24(3), 53–65 (2001)

The (not so) Critical Nodes of Criminal Networks

Donatella Firmani[1]([✉]), Giuseppe F. Italiano[1], and Luigi Laura[2]

[1] University of Rome "Tor Vergata", Via del Politecnico 1, 00133 Rome, Italy
firmani@ing.uniroma2.it, giuseppe.italiano@uniroma2.it
[2] University of Rome "Sapienza", Via Ariosto 25, 00185 Rome, Italy
laura@dis.uniroma1.it

Abstract. One of the most basic question in the analysis of social networks is to find nodes that are of particular relevance in the network. The answer that emerged in the recent literature is that the *importance*, or *centrality*, of a node x is proportional to the number of nodes that get disconnected from the network when node x is removed. We show that while in social networks such important nodes lie in their *cores* (i.e., maximal subgraphs in which all nodes have degree higher than a certain value), this is not necessarily the case in criminal networks. This shows that nodes whose removal affects large portions of the criminal network prefer to operate from network peripheries, thus confirming the intuition of Baker and Faulkner [4]. Our results also highlight structural differences between criminal networks and other social networks, suggesting that classical definitions of importance (or centrality) in a network fail to capture the concept of key players in criminal networks.

Keywords: Articulation points · Social networks · Criminal networks

1 Introduction

In recent years several tools from Social Network Analysis (SNA) have been applied to the study of criminal networks; however, citing the words of Morselli [18]: *"Criminal networks are not simply social networks operating in criminal contexts. The covert settings that surround them call for specific interactions and relational features within and beyond the network"*. Indeed, it is known that criminal networks differ substantially from social networks (in short, SNs); this is mainly due to the trade-off between security and efficiency which directly affects their underlying network structure [10]. Sparrow, in a seminal paper [23], listed four peculiar features of criminal networks: i) limited size, ii) information incompleteness (i.e., criminal network data is inevitably incomplete) iii) undefined borders, i.e. it is not easy to discover all the connections of a node;

This paper has been partially supported by MIUR, the Italian Ministry of Education, University and Research, under Project AMANDA (Algorithmics for MAssive and Networked DAta).

© Springer International Publishing Switzerland 2015
L.M. Aiello and D. McFarland (Eds.): SocInfo 2014 Workshops, LNCS 8852, pp. 87–96, 2015.
DOI: 10.1007/978-3-319-15168-7_12

and, iv) dynamics, that is, many of the useful networks questions depends heavily on the temporal dimension. In this scenario, SNA tools are limited, due to these intrinsic differences.

One of the most basic questions associated to the analysis of a network is *who are the key players*, or *who are the central nodes in the network*? Node-centrality measures introduced in the recent literature, such as degree, betweenness and closeness centrality, just to name a few (see [8] for a good survey) can successfully identify most key players in social networks. Quite on the contrary, in criminal networks, the most important actors do not necessarily display high centrality scores [4]. More recently, node-centrality measures that look at how some graph invariant changes when some nodes or edges are deleted have been studied for example in [9], but no results are known for criminal networks.

In this paper we show that criminal networks can suffer high disconnection when few nodes are deleted. However, while in social networks nodes whose removal disconnects most nodes from the network belong to their cores, in criminal networks this is not the case. This suggests that, on the one hand, and differently from most social networks, nodes that pulls together the network deliberately operate from network peripheries, thus being protected from detection; on the other hand, the key players in the network may not be the ones whose removal affects large portions of the network.

Related Work. The seminal work of Sparrow [23] is considered as the starting point of the academic research on the use of SNA tools to the study of criminal networks. The interested reader is referred to the books of Morselli [18] and to the very recent one of Masys [16] for a broad coverage of research on criminal networks. There are nowadays several tools devoted to the analysis of criminal networks using tools from SNA; we refer the interested reader to the survey of Xu and Chen [25] and we also cite the recent *LogAnalysis* of Ferrara et al. [11,12].

Schwartz and Rouselle [20] addressed the problem of identifying central actors in the network, building on the previous work of Borgatti [7,9] for the *key players* problem. Duijn et al. [10] focused on the dynamics of the interaction between disruption and resilience within criminal networks, concluding that the disruption of the criminal cannabis network they studied is relatively ineffective. Mainas [15] presented an exhaustive analysis of two criminal networks, a drug-trafficking and a terrorists group, which are the ones studied in this paper.

The concept of *critical nodes* has been introduced in [2], building upon the concepts of *articulation points* and *core* of a connected network, that are respectively the nodes whose removal disconnects the network, and the subset of the nodes obtained by repeatedly pruning the nodes of low (fixed) degree. Precisely, the critical nodes are defined as the articulation points belonging to the network core. Using different samples of the Autonomous Systems network[1], Ausiello

---

[1] The network of routers comprising the Internet can be organized into sub-graphs called Autonomous Systems (AS) and we can construct the ASes communication network from the BGP (Border Gateway Protocol) logs. More information about this dataset can be found at http://snap.stanford.edu/data/as.html.

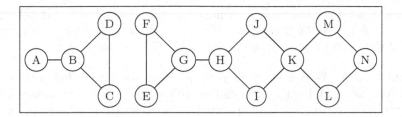

Fig. 1. An example graph with two connected components (nodes A, B, C, D and E, F, G, H, I, L, M, N) and four articulation points (B, G, H, K)

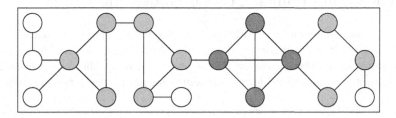

Fig. 2. An example graph, its 2-core (light and dark grey nodes), and its 3-core (dark grey nodes). Nodes in the 3-core are a subset of the nodes in the 2-core of the graph.

et al. show that: (1) the removal of few critical nodes can affect large portions of the network, thus they are central in a very strong sense [2], and (2) the critical nodes have orders of magnitude higher centrality scores than other nodes [3].

Structure of the Paper. In the next section we recall few preliminary notions. In Section 3 we discuss some properties of the main notions used in this papers: articulation points, critical nodes and network cores. Our experimental results are discussed in Section 4, whilst Section 5 addresses concluding remarks.

2   Preliminaries

Given an unirected graph $G = (V, E)$, a **connected component** is defined as a maximal set of nodes $V' \subseteq V$ such that, given $u, v \in V'$, there is at least one path between u and v in G. Furthermore an **articulation point** is defined as a node $v \in V$ such that its removal from the graph G increases the number of connected components in G (see Figure 1). A connected graph G is *biconnected* if the removal of any of its nodes leaves the graph connected. Therefore, a biconnected graph contains no articulation point.

Coreness. The concept of coreness was introduced in [21] and [6]. The *k-core* of a graph is defined as the unique subgraph obtained by recursively removing all nodes of a degree less than k. A node has coreness value l, if it belongs to the l-core but not to the $(l+1)$-core. We denote with G^k the k-core of graph G. Figure 2 shows an example graph G, its 2-core G^2, and its 3-core G^3.

Critical Nodes. As we mentioned in the previous section, we follow the definition of Ausiello et al. [2], that defines the critical nodes as articulation points of the network cores. In the following sections, unless specified otherwise, we refer as "critical nodes" to the articulation points of the 2-core.

3   Articulation Points, Critical Nodes and Cores

Before discussing the experimental results in the next section, we discuss briefly few properties of the main concepts used in of our analysis: articulation points, critical nodes and network cores. We begin by proving the following lemma, which shows the connection between articulation points and critical nodes.

Lemma 1. *Let G be an undirected connected graph. The critical nodes of G (i.e. the articulation points of G^2) are articulation points of G.*

Proof. Assume by contradiction that node x is a critical node of G, but not an articulation point of G. If x is a critical node of G this means, by definition, that the removal of x from G^2 disconnects at least one node from G^2. Consider a generic node y that gets disconnected from G^2 when node x is removed. Since the removal of x disconnects y in G^2, this means that all the paths from y to nodes in G^2/x pass through node x. Let w be a generic node in G^2/x. By hypothesis, y does not get disconnected from G if we remove x, since x is a critical node but not an articulation point; this means that y in G is connected to one or more nodes that get pruned in G^2. Let z be one of these nodes. Since x and y are connected in G^2, and G is connected, we can consider the following four paths: 1) the path from x to y in G^2, which does not use z, 2) the path from y to z in G, which does not include x, 3) the path from x to w in G^2, which does not use y nor z, 4) the path from z to w in x. If we consider these paths together, it is easy to see that we obtain a graph that includes a cycle, in which one of the following holds: either z belongs to the cycle, or another node $z' \notin G^2$, connected to z through a simple path, belongs to the cycle. In both cases, we have a node of degree two (since it belongs to a cycle), either z or z', that does not belong to G^2. This is a contradiction, since all the nodes in the cycle should belong to G^2.   □

It is easy to see that the converse of Lemma 1 does not hold. Furthermore, this relation does not hold for higher level cores, that is, an articulation point of the 3-core is not necessarily an articulation point of the 2-core of the graph.

Let us define the *impact* of a node v as the number of nodes that get disconnected from the largest connected component when v is removed. Lemma 1 provides support to the intuitive fact that the critical nodes have a bigger impact than the generic articulation points: indeed, if an articulation point x gets pruned in the computation of the 2-core, this means that it is connected to other nodes that get pruned and to exactly one node of G^2. Thus, this node of G^2 is, by definition, an articulation point, since its removal disconnects x and all the nodes connected to it, and its impact is at least equal to the impact of x plus one[2]. In particular, for each articulation point not in G^2 there should be a critical node in G^2 with higher impact. In the next section we will see that, whilst all the considered real social networks confirm this intuition, criminal networks exhibit consistently a different behavior.

4   Experimental Results

In this section we describe our experimental results. In particular, before detailing our findings, we describe the datasets and the metrics we considered.

4.1   Datasets

In Table 1 we show the type, the number of nodes (n), the number of edges (m) and the repository of the networks in our dataset. Our criminal networks include Drug-Traffic, a network collected in November 2007 during a police investigation against a drug-trafficking group, and Terrorists, collected over a period of several years of an ongoing intelligence operation against terrorism. The social networks we considered include Karate, which is amongst the most studied in SNA after its first appearance in the work of Zachary [26], and describe the friendship relations in a karate club in a US university in the 1970s. Science is a co-authorship network of scientists compiled by Newman [19], whilst Facebook collects friends' lists of survey participants; it has been collected by McAuley and Leskovec [17]. Among social networks, we also consider two *fictitious* social networks; the first one, Lindenstrasse, has been used in the Graph Drawing Conference contest in '99 [14] and describes the relationships between the characters of the german soap opera Lindenstrasse. The other dataset, Marvel, describes the relationships in the Marvel Comics Universe (thus including, amongst many many others, superheroes like Spiderman, Capitan America, and Iron Man); it has been collected by Alberich et al. [1]. For the sake of comparison, we also consider three networks from different domain application areas: Airlines, that describes airlines connections in US cities, PowerGrid, collected by Watts and Strogatz [24], which represents the topology of the Western States Power Grid of the United States, and ASes, which is snapshot of the structure of the Internet at the level of autonomous systems, collected by Newman from 2006 data. We refer the interested reader to the cited repositories and references for more details about each dataset and their format.

---

[2] Note that, since the impact is defined as the number of nodes that gets disconnected by the main connected component, it might be the case that the pruned nodes are more than the ones in G^2, thus the impact of an articulation point might be bigger than the one of the node that connects it to G^2.

Table 1. The network datasets analyzed in this paper

Name	Type	Nodes (n)	Edges (m)	Source
Drug-Traffic	Criminal Network	2749	13578	Mainas [15]
Terrorists	Criminal Network	4275	7874	Mainas [15]
Karate	Social Network	34	78	GEPHI [13]
Science	Social Network	1589	2742	Pajek [5]
Facebook	Social Network	4039	88234	SNAP [22]
Lindenstrasse	Fictitious SN	233	325	Pajek [5]
Marvel	Fictitious SN	10822	314054	GEPHI [13]
Airlines	Other	235	1297	GEPHI [13]
PowerGrid	Other	4941	6594	GEPHI [13]
ASes	Other	22963	48436	GEPHI [13]

4.2 Metrics

We recall that the *impact* of a node v is given by the number of nodes that get disconnected from the largest connected component when v is removed. In our analysis, we compute for each network in our dataset the following information:

1. the number of articulation points, in short APs;
2. the number of critical nodes, in short CNs;
3. the number of critical nodes in the 3-core, in short CN^3s;
4. the number of CNs and CN^3s that belong to the top K articulation points, sorted by the impact, where K is respectively the number of CNs or CN^3s.

Let us clarify (4) with an example: the Marvel network has 107 APs, 3 CN, and 2 CN^3s. The top five APs have impact values equals to $\{39, 27, 15, 13, 12\}$. The three CNs have impact values equals to $\{39, 4, 3\}$, whilst the two CN^3 have both impact equals to 1. Of the three CNs only the first one belongs to the top three APs. Of the two CN^3, none belongs to the top two APs. We call this ratio the "membership ratio", as detailed in the followng.

Membership and Weighted Impact Ratio. We formally define the *membership ratio* as $\frac{|CNs \cap (Top\ APs)|}{|CNs|}$. For example, this ratio equals $\frac{1}{3}$ in the case of the CNs of the Marvel network. We can consider this ratio as a measure of the relative importance of the CNs (and CN^3) when compared to the superset of the APs. Another measure of the relative importance of CNs (and CN^3) that we will use in the next section is the *weighted impact ratio*: the sum of the impacts of the CNs (or of the CN^3) divided by the sum of the top K APs. It is easy to verify that this value ranges from 0 to 1. For example, in the case of the Marvel network, the weighted impact ratio is equal to $\frac{39+4+3}{39+27+15} = \frac{46}{81} \approx 0.56$ for the CNs. In Figures 3 (CNs) and 4 (CN^3s) we report, for each network, the membership ratio and the weighted impact ratio as percentage values.

4.3 Experimental Findings

In Table 2 we show, for each considered network, the size and the number of articulation points of the largest connected components and of G^2 and G^3.

Table 2. In this table we report, for each network, the size of its largest connected components and its 2-core and 3-core, together with the number of articulation points in each of these components

	G		largest CC			G^2			G^3		
	n	m	n	m	APs	n	m	APs	n	m	APs
Drug-Traffic	2749	13578	1554	2216	280	454	1116	15	163	588	0
Terrorists	4275	7874	4085	6358	521	1303	3576	77	681	2440	7
Karate	34	78	34	78	1	33	78	1	22	55	1
Science	1589	2742	379	914	57	352	887	44	265	736	1
Facebook	4039	88234	4039	88234	11	3964	88159	7	3856	87952	1
Lindenstrasse	233	325	233	325	74	123	215	1	12	19	0
Marvel	10822	314054	10822	314054	107	10543	313775	3	9935	312565	2
Airlines	235	1297	235	1297	9	201	1263	2	162	1190	1
PowerGrid	4941	6594	4941	6594	1229	3353	5006	94	231	479	1
ASes	22963	48436	22963	48436	1870	14966	40439	10	4383	19678	1

We note that, in almost all the considered networks, the number of critical points is much smaller than the number of articulation points. The most notable exception is Karate, which has only one articulation point that is also a critical node.

In Table 3 we show the impact of nodes removal: we report for each network, the maximum impact of an articulation point (AP), of a critical node (CN), and of a critical node of the 3-core (CN^3). We also report the number of CNs and CN^3s that are in the top K articulation points, as in Section 4.2. It is impressive to see that in all the considered social networks the top APs are exactly the CNs, whilst this does not happen in the criminal networks. In the case of fictitious SNs, in Lindenstrasse there is only one critical node that is the one with maximum impact. The same does not hold in the Marvel network, where there are few APs and CNs, if compared to the size of the whole network. For the other network types, exactly half of the CNs belong to the top APs in both Airlines and PowerGrid; it is interesting to notice that in the Autonomous System network dataset, we have only 3 CNs in the top APs, but this three are the first, the second and the fourth, thus confirming the findings of Ausiello et al. [2].

Our findings can be summarized by the plots in Figure 3 and 4. In Figure 3 we show, for each network, the membership ratio and the weighted impact of the critical nodes ratio as percentage values. Here it is possible to distinguish, at a glance, criminal networks from social networks: all the considered social networks have the maximum values in these ratios. The same happens also for the fictitious Linderstrasse; in the ASes networks, with only three CNs in the top ten APs, the total weighted impact ratio is slightly more than 50%. Finally, in Figure 4 we consider the CN^3s for all the networks except Drug-Traffic and Lindenstrasse, that have no CN^3s, i.e. their 3-core G^3 is biconnected. We see a clear difference between the real (not fictitious) social networks and Terrorist.

From the results shown it seems that there is a strong difference between criminal networks and real social networks, if we focus on the relative importance of CNs and APs. The fictitious networks considered have two different behaviors:

Table 3. In this table we report, for each network, the number of APs, of CNs and CN^3 and their maximum impact. We also report, for CNs and CN^3, the number of them included in the top APs, sorted by their impact.

	1CC	G^2		G^3		Max Impact
	APs	CNs	CNs in TOP APs	CN^3s	CN^3s in TOP APs	AP CN CN^3
Drug-Traffic	280	15	8	0	–	172 57 –
Terrorists	521	77	40	7	2	83 83 83
Karate	1	1	1	1	1	7 7 7
Science	57	44	44	1	1	60 60 60
Facebook	11	7	7	1	1	197 197 197
Lindenstrasse	74	1	1	0	–	13 13 –
Marvel	107	3	1	2	0	39 39 1
Airlines	9	2	1	1	1	11 11 11
PowerGrid	1229	94	47	1	0	106 106 8
ASes	1870	10	10	1	1	333 333 333

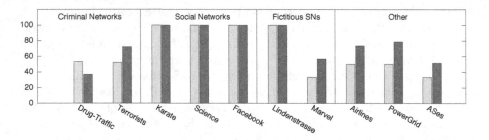

Fig. 3. Overall impact of Critical Nodes: the *membership ratio* (yellow) and the *weighted impact ratio* (red) as percentage values ranging from 0 to 100%. (Best viewed in colors).

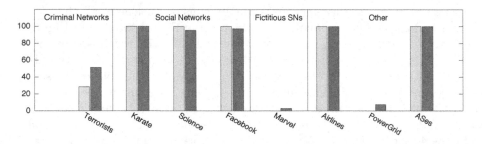

Fig. 4. Overall impact of CN^3, the Critical Nodes of the 3-core:the *membership ratio* (yellow) and the *weighted impact ratio* (red) as percentage values ranging from 0 to 100%. (Best viewed in colors).

Linderstrasse seems a real social network, whilst Marvel does not, and this appears to be consistent with the findings of Alberich et al. [1]. The networks classified as "other" exhibit a different behavior, but this seems due to their physical nature: all of them are, in some sense, infrastructure networks, and thus we do not expect them to behave like social networks for centrality aspects.

5   Conclusions

In this paper we showed that, if we focus on critical nodes, criminal networks and social networks exhibit a consistently different behavior, and critical nodes "deserve their name" only in the case of social networks. We analyzed two criminal networks, from [15], and compared them with real and fictitious social networks, and also networks from different application domains. Our findings confirm, from a different perspective, what observed by Baker and Faulkner [4]: in criminal networks important actors are not the ones whose removal affects a large portion of the network.

Acknowledgements. We are indebted to Efstathios D. Mainas for making their criminal network datasets in [15] available to us.

References

1. Alberich, R., Miro-Julia, J., Rossello, F.: Marvel Universe looks almost like a real social network. eprint arXiv:cond-mat/0202174, February 2002
2. Ausiello, G., Firmani, D., Laura, L.: Real-time analysis of critical nodes in network cores. In: IWCMC, pp. 42–46. IEEE (2012)
3. Ausiello, G., Firmani, D., Laura, L.: The (betweenness) centrality of critical nodes and network cores. In: Saracco, R., Ben Letaief, K., Gerla, M., Palazzo, S., Atzori, L. (eds.) 2013 9th International Wireless Communications and Mobile Computing Conference, IWCMC 2013, Sardinia, Italy, July 1–5, 2013, pp. 90–95. IEEE (2013)
4. Baker, W.E., Faulkner, R.R.: The social organization of conspiracy: Illegal networks in the heavy electrical equipment industry. American Sociological Review, 837–860 (1993)
5. Batagelj, V., Mrvar, A.: Pajek datasets (2006)
6. Batagelj , V., Zaveršnik, M.: Generalized cores. Preprint 799, University of Ljibljana (2002)
7. Borgatti, S.P.: The key player problem. In: Dynamic Social Network Modeling and Analysis: Workshop Summary and Papers, p. 241. National Academies Press (2003)
8. Borgatti, S.P.: Centrality and network flow. Social Networks **27**(1), 55–71 (2005)
9. Borgatti, S.P.: Identifying sets of key players in a social network. Computational & Mathematical Organization Theory **12**(1), 21–34 (2006)
10. Duijn, P.A.C., Kashirin, V., Sloot, P.M.A.: The relative ineffectiveness of criminal network disruption. Scientific Reports **4** (2014)
11. Ferrara, E., De Meo, P., Catanese, S., Fiumara, G.: Detecting criminal organizations in mobile phone networks. Expert Systems with Applications **41**(13), 5733–5750 (2014)

12. Ferrara, E., De Meo, P., Catanese, S., Fiumara, G.: Visualizing criminal networks reconstructed from mobile phone records. In: Hypertext 2014 Extended Proceedings: Late-breaking Results, Doctoral Consortium and Workshop Proceedings of the 25th ACM Hypertext and Social Media Conference (Hypertext 2014), Santiago, Chile, September 1–4, 2014 (2014)
13. GEPHI sample datasets. https://wiki.gephi.org/index.php/Datasets
14. GD99 Graph Drawing Conference Contest. http://kam.mff.cuni.cz/conferences/GD99/contest/rules.html
15. Mainas, E.D.: The analysis of criminal and terrorist organisations as social network structures: a quasi-experimental study. International Journal of Police Science & Management 14(3), 264–282 (2012)
16. Masys, A.: Networks and network analysis for defence and security. In: Proceedings of the 2013 IEEE/ACM International Conference on Advances in Social Networks Analysis and Mining, pp. 1479–1480. ACM (2013)
17. Mcauley, J., Leskovec, J.: Discovering social circles in ego networks. ACM Trans. Knowl. Discov. Data 8(1), 4:1–4:28 (2014)
18. Morselli, C.: Inside criminal networks. Springer (2009)
19. Newman, M.E.J.: Finding community structure in networks using the eigenvectors of matrices. Phys. Rev. E 74, 036104 (2006)
20. Schwartz, D.M., Rouselle, T.D.A.: Using social network analysis to target criminal networks. Trends in Organized Crime 12(2), 188–207 (2009)
21. Seidman, S.B.: Network structure and minimum degree. Social Networks 5(5), 269–287 (1983)
22. SNAP: Stanford Network Analysis Project. http://snap.stanford.edu/
23. Sparrow, M.K.: The application of network analysis to criminal intelligence: An assessment of the prospects. Social Networks 13(3), 251–274 (1991)
24. Watts, D.J., Strogatz, S.H.: Collective dynamics of 'small-world' networks. Nature 393, 440–442 (1998)
25. Xu, J., Chen, H.: Criminal network analysis and visualization. Commun. ACM 48(6), 100–107 (2005)
26. Zachary, W.W.: An information flow model for conflict and fission in small groups. Journal of Anthropological Research 33, 452–473 (1977)

A Literature-Based Approach
to a Narco-Network

Jesús Espinal-Enríquez[1,3](✉), J. Mario Siqueiros-García[2],
Rodrigo García-Herrera[1], and Sergio Antonio Alcalá-Corona[1]

[1] Department of Computational Genomics, National Institute of Genomic Medicine,
Periférico Sur 4809, Arenal Tepepan, Tlalpan, México
jespinal@inmegen.gob.mx
[2] Institute for Research Applied Mathematics and Systems,
National University of México, Ciudad Universitaria, México, Mexico
[3] Center of Sciences of Complexity, National University of México,
Ciudad Universitaria, México, Mexico

Abstract. In this work we used a combined text-mining/manual-curing
approach in order to mine the Spanish-written book "Los Señores del
Narco" and identify the narco social network. In our method, nodes
are book characters and links are created when the closeness between
those characters is under a certain threshold value along the text. Results
show the network of the principal drug-dealers of México as well as some
politicians or members of the national police department. A community
analysis shows some separated groups corresponding to well-known drug
cartels. The analysis presented here remarks the importance of the text
mining tools to understand relationships among individuals –specially
the qualitative character of the interactions– which could be difficult by
using other approaches.

Keywords: Narcotraffic · Narco-network · Text-mining · Manual
curing · Communities · Drug cartels · Los Señores del Narco

Introduction

México has placed itself as an strategic spot for connecting cocaine producers
from Colombia, Bolivia and Peru and the biggest consumer market in the world.
It also has become an important producer and exporter of natural and synthetic
drugs. Since the 1990's, drug-related violence in México has increased significantly due to the pressing demand from the American government for the Mexican authorities to fight drug-dealers. In January of 2007, the former mexican
president, Felipe Calderón, started an official "battle against narco", resulting
in dozens of thousands of casualties among security forces, drug-dealers and
civilians[1].

Prominent characters of this convoluting scenario are the kingpins of each
narcotraffic group, like Joaquín Guzmán, a.k.a. "El Chapo Guzmán", who leads
the Sinaloa Cartel (cartel is the term used to refer an organized drug group);

L.M. Aiello and D. McFarland (Eds.): SocInfo 2014 Workshops, LNCS 8852, pp. 97–101, 2015.
DOI: 10.1007/978-3-319-15168-7_13

Heriberto Lazcano, a.k.a. "El Lazca" or "Z3", leader of the "Los Zetas" group; as well as politicians and police officers of practically any rank [1–4].

The problem of narcotraffic has been documented along these years. Nevertheless, the most comprehensive book on the topic is the one written by the journalist Anabel Hernández, "Los señores del Narco" (*The Lords of Narco*) [3]. Anabel Hernández's book is a chronological narration of the existing relationships between the principal drug cartels in México, the political class and police agents. Our work is based on the aforementioned book. Using text-mining tools, combined with manual curing, we built a network of all characters appearing in the book.

Methodology

To construct the narco-network we read several books about narcotraffic in México. We looked for the most comprehensive one in terms of the information given about the characters. We chose the book "Los Señores del Narco". We converted the PDF file into a plain text version, by using the "pdf2txt" command from the GNU/linux command line. We used Python's 3.0 version of the Natural Language Toolkit (NLTK) library to identify names, surnames and aliases of each character. NLTK's most complete corpus is for English language. Since the book we mined is written in Spanish, it was necessary to develop a manual curing of the names list appearing in the text. We extracted a vector of names, surnames and aliases of the entire book. In order to obtain the full list of characters, we constructed a set of triplets of the names because in Latin America people often use one name and two surnames; however, several of the characters have two or more names and two or three aliases as is customary in drug-dealer groups. To correct this, we manually cured the triplets list. Another problem in the process of text mining was that most characters are mentioned in more than one form. For example, the author refers to "El Chapo Guzmán" in seven different ways. In order to tackle this problem, we developed a Perl's style dictionary data structure to relate every alias to a unique identifier for each character. This part was also manually cured. Once we had our list of names ready, we wrote a script to identify the position of each character in the text, in order to have a measure of closeness between them. We set 200 bytes as a maximum distance among two characters, because 200 is an average size of a paragraph in the book. Characters are connected if they appear at distances shorter than 200 bytes. We established the weight of the links by counting the number of repeats of each co-ocurrence. We generated a connectivity matrix, we plotted it using Cytoscape v.3.1.1 [5] and found its communities by using the *GNU General Public License* implementations [6][7] of two random-walks based algorithms, the Rosvall and Bergstorm's Infomap algorithm [8] and van Dongen's MCL algorithm [9]. We compared those results and analyzed them.

Results

Network Analysis

The network has 1037 characters and 6405 links. In Figure 1, we depict only the main component (981 nodes and 6342 links).

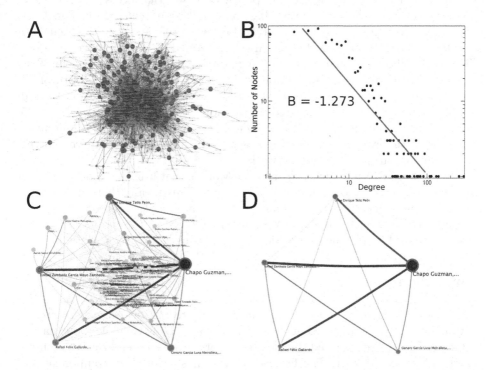

Fig. 1. Mexican narco-network constructed from the book "Los Señores del Narco", from Anabel Hernández. A) The Figure shows only the giant component, however, the network presents 30 connected components. The size of the nodes represents the node degree and the edge width is related to the number of repeats of each pair of nodes along the whole book. B) Node degree distribution of the whole narco-network. A fitted power law is also depicted. This power law has an exponent $b = -1.273$. C) *Infomap*-based communities of the narco-network. The size and color of the circles are proportional to the number of elements in the community. The color and width of the blue links reflect the flow of information among the communities. The biggest node corresponds to the "Chapo Guzmán" community. In D) we depict the top five communities, to emphasize the flow of information among them.

A remarkable point is that the average clustering coefficient is relatively high $\langle C \rangle \approx 0.623$. The average shortest path length is $\langle l \rangle \approx 3.25$. Such values may suggest a *small world* network with an associated community structure [10].

The degree distribution follows a power law with an exponent close to -1.273 (Figure 1B) [11–14].

Infomap algorithm identified 87 different communities (Figure 1C). The MCL algorithm showed 60 communities. In the infomap community structure, the groups vary in the number of elements from 2 to 585 nodes for each group. The biggest community includes the main characters of narcotraffic in México as well as some important members of politics and security forces, most of them linked to the "Sinaloa Cartel". Other big communities present drug-dealers from other well-known groups like the "Beltrán-Leyva Cartel" and the "Los Acuario" kidnapping band, an organized criminal group formed by some important police officers [15]. Those communities are also strongly connected among them. This is observed in Figure 1C. Using Infomap we could generate the network of all communities. From such graph we extracted and studied the subgraph formed by those communities that included 47 or more members (Figure 1D). The 5 communities that form the subgraph, include the most populated communities and some of the strongest interactions between communities compared to the rest of interactions in the whole network.

One of the most salient feature of our network is that it is an almost complete subgraph of 5 nodes (communities) and 9 links. This means that three of the five communities have a degree of four and the remaining two communities have a degree of three. Such topology is consistent regardless the number of nodes added to the subgraph, the "semi-clique" remains as can be seen in Figure 1D.

Conclusions

Using text mining tools as well as manual curing techniques we constructed a network of the characters present in the most comprehensive book about narcotraffic in México. We analyzed the global network properties and the community structure associated to it. The features of the most connected component are consistent with what is generally known about the organized-crime community. The small-world structure of this network suggests that the relationships among politicians, security forces and criminal groups are very close and functional. We think is worth noticing the presence of a subgraph formed by the most populated communities with the strongest connections. We might suggest that such subgraph stands as a topological backbone that organizes the rest of the network and also, as the basic structure responsible for the patterns of information flux among all nodes in the whole communities network. The absence of an edge connecting two of the five communities in the subgraph is quite remarkable and it demands further work, from the perspective of complex networks and from a historiographic approach as well.

By addressing criminal organization properties from a literature-based perspective, we have traversed several difficulties regarding the non-automated methodology to construct the network. To find the names in Spanish language with NLTK library was complicated. A more automated strategy would allow us to mine more books and in this way to present a more robust network. Another issue to consider is that this book is a deep journalistic research but it reflects the opinion of the author. Further steps towards a better methodology must include more authors, compare them and preserve the emergent similarities. To fit the distance among characters to establish a link could be tuned by averaging the distance among characters or just by separating paragraphs, since an idea presented in a paragraph is often independent of the ideas presented in the following ones. The main message that we want to stress is that a literature-based approach could serve to analyze criminal network properties with some accuracy and give us information not easily discernible by only reading the texts. The road to have a tool that could mine any text is a long one. However, we believe that it could be a valuable effort.

Acknowledgements. Authors acknowledge to their institutions for the partial support to the development of this work.

References

1. Guerrero-Gutierrez, E.: Drugs and violence: México's addiction (2010). http://www.bbc.com/news/world-latin-america-11174174
2. Reveles, J.: El Cártel Incómodo. Grijalbo (2011)
3. Hernández, A.: Los Señores del Narco. Grijalbo (2010)
4. Osorno, D.E.: El Cártel de Sinaloa. Grijalbo (2011)
5. Shannon, P., et al.: Cytoscape: a software environment for integrated models of biomolecular interaction networks. Genome Res. **13**, 2498–2504 (2003)
6. Edler, D., Rosvall, M.: The MapEquation software package (2013). http://www.mapequation.org
7. van Baal, J., Benner, P.: Debian mcl package. http://micans.org/mcl
8. Rosvall, M., Bergstrom, C.T.: Maps of random walks on complex networks reveal community structure. Proceedings of the National Academy of Sciences **105**(4), 1118–1123 (2008)
9. Van Dongen, S.M.: Graph clustering by flow simulation. PhD thesis, University of Utrecht (2000)
10. Watts, D.J., Strogatz, S.H.: Collective dynamics of 'small-world' networks. Nature 393, 440–442
11. Zipf, G.K.: Human behavior and the principle of least effort, p. 573. Addison-Wesley Press, Oxford (1949)
12. Barabasi, A.L., Albert, R.: Statistical mechanics of complex networks. Rev. Mod. Phys. **74**, 47 (2002)
13. Newman, M.E.J.: The structure and function of complex networks. SIAM Rev. **45**(167), 256 (2003)
14. Newman, M.E.J.: Networks: An Introduction. Oxford University Press, New York (2010)
15. Hernandez, A., Saviano, R.: Narcoland: The Mexican Drug Lords and Their Godfathers Verso Books (2013)

The Spatial Structure of Crime
in Urban Environments

Sarah White[1], Tobin Yehle[2], Hugo Serrano[3], Marcos Oliveira[3],
and Ronaldo Menezes[3(✉)]

[1] College of Arts and Sciences,
University of North Carolina at Chapel Hill, Chapel Hill, USA
sarahw14@live.unc.edu
[2] School of Computing, University of Utah, Salt Lake City, USA
tobin.yehle@utah.edu
[3] BioComplex Laboratory, Florida Institute of Technology, Melbourne, USA
{hbarbosafilh2011,moliveirajun2013}@my.fit.edu, rmenezes@cs.fit.edu

Abstract. It is undoubtedly *cliché* to say that we are in the Age of Big
Data Analytics or Data Science; every computing and IT publication
you find talks about Big Data and companies no longer are interested
in software engineers and analysts but instead they are looking for Data
Scientists! In spite of the excessive use of the term, the truth of the matter is that data has never been more available and the increase in computation power allows for more sophisticated tools to identify patterns
in the data and on the networks that governs these systems (complex
networks). Crime is not different, the open data phenomena has spread
to thousand of cities in the world, which are making data about crime
activity available for any citizen to look at. Furthermore, new criminology studies argue that criminals typically commit crimes in areas in
which they are familiar, usually close to home. Using this information we
propose a new model based on networks to build links between crimes
in close physical proximity. We show that the structure of the criminal
activity can be partially represented by this spatial network of sites. In
this paper we describe this process and the analysis of the networks we
have constructed to find patterns in the underlying structure of criminal
activity.

Keywords: Network science · Crime mapping · Social disorganization ·
Routine activity

1 Introduction

The understanding of crimes, the organizational process in criminal activities,
and the emergence of crime spots in certain regions of a city can lead to the
creation of better tools to enable more effective law enforcement, culminating
in safe cities. The increasing amount of criminal data available nowadays may
be used to guide this understanding of crime. For instance, information about

© Springer International Publishing Switzerland 2015
L.M. Aiello and D. McFarland (Eds.): SocInfo 2014 Workshops, LNCS 8852, pp. 102–111, 2015.
DOI: 10.1007/978-3-319-15168-7_14

crime is usually accompanied by location metadata indicating where the criminal activity occurred. This type of spatial data has been used to understand delinquent behavior back in the 1920s [1, 2], and many theories have been proposed to explain the existence of areas of concentrated crime, referred as hotspots [3–7].

These hotspots are related to the fact that criminal activities do not occur uniformly across a region [8, 9]. The theories of social disorganization, social control and collective efficacy explain this phenomenon by means of the residents of the area considered [6, 7]. These studies recognize the active role of the environment on the criminal activities. For example, many aspects of the community lead to the inability of the neighborhood to publicly control the behavior of people, and thus to the increase of the likelihood of crime [10]. Moreover, prior work shows that crimes happen close to each other are carried out by people with familiar with similar geographical areas [11].

The hotspot analysis is an approach used to find regions with these aforementioned issues [8] and has been one of the main artifacts in the analyses of crime incidence [12]. In some sense, hotspot analysis is similar to a histogram because it allows to depict the crime frequency (or similar measure) in sub-regions of a certain region. Thus, any information about the relation between crimes is not present in this analysis—any criminal structure that could be underlying the criminal activity is not included.

In order to capture this structure, we propose to analyze crime activity using a network framework. The rationale here is that criminal activities rely heavily on different types of networks, such as a social network within gangs and the word-of-mouth flow of information regarding illegal market [13–15]. The presence of these relations suggests that network science can be a powerful tool for analyzing criminal activity.

In this paper, we define a crime network in which crimes are connected if they occur nearby. We used data of crime incidents from US police department records to generate complex networks of criminal activity in Los Angeles, CA, and Miami, FL and we found borders between communities in these structures using an approach adapted from Thiemann et al. [16]. Finally, in order to show that these networks capture real-world phenomena, we compared these borders to similar boundaries in demographic data. We found statistically significant variations that indicates the structure of the crime networks reflects real-world phenomena that cannot be accounted for by demographic differences.

2 Background

2.1 Criminology

There exist two theories in criminology that are of interest to us: the *routine activity* and *social disorganization* theories. The former argues that criminal activity occurs at the convergence of three things: a potential offender, a lack of guardianship or supervision, and a target [17]. The latter contends that criminal activity is the result of the social and physical environments of the neighborhood at hand [18]. Both theories seek to model crime phenomena using spatial and geographical context. For example, elevated crime rates are expected in a neighborhood that lacks a strong social community and access to resources.

The routine activity theory asserts that crime is a convergence between criminal opportunity and a potential offender, where this convergence serves as a point in time and space. The opportunistic nature of this theory means that criminal activity typically occurs in the sphere of familiarity of the criminal. Despite this sphere of familiarity being peculiar to the individual, areas of high traffic, such as downtown areas, lie within the sphere of familiarity of many individuals. This aspect is also related to the fact that criminals typically commit crimes within a short distance from their home [11].

Metropolitan areas are typically organized by regions of different land use through the natural development of urban centers and unnaturally through zoning laws. These different land uses include: residential use, commercial use, and industrial use. The presence of types of crimes differs between these land uses; neighborhoods with residential housing and no commercial businesses are perceived as *safe* and non-residential land uses are correlated with an increase in criminal activity [19]. Non-residential areas is typically found to have higher traffic in comparison to residential areas, consequently they witness to more crime. Also, the places within these areas, such as shopping centers or public parks, coincide with an increase in *foreign* or non-residential presence. The presence of such *strangers* negatively impacts a neighborhood's social structure.

Street networks influence human mobility and thus the potential offenders mobility. In fact, the convergence of a potential offender with a criminal opportunity is much more likely to occur and be exploited on a street that is relatively accessible and frequently traveled [17]. Street networks are not only correlated with an increase in crime incidence but additionally have a relationship with the typical *journey-to-crime* length of an offender [11]. Roadways and public transportation link together different areas of a criminal's sphere of familiarity and facilitate travel outside of a criminal's immediate neighborhood. The type of crime can affect the *journey-to-crime* length. For example, violent crime trips are shorter in length than property crime trips [11].

Both of aforementioned theories serve to explain crimes in terms of the spatial context of the neighborhood. By the social disorganization theory, a break down in the social structure of a neighborhood causes the elevated crimes rates. On the other hand, the routine activity theory implies that the higher traffic associated with non-residential land use is the cause of such crime rates.

2.2 Network Science

In order to find the areas of crimes, we used the algorithm *label propagation* for community detection applied to the network of crimes we created [20]. The stochastic output of the method is essential to our analysis of crime borders, because the borders have strength based on the frequency of the community pertinence [16]. Label propagation finds communities by assigning community labels to vertices matching the most common label of their neighbors. The procedure starts by assigning an unique label to each vertex. In each iteration the label of each vertex is assigned to be the most common label of its neighbors in the previous iteration, breaking ties randomly. If the edges have weights it assigns the label connected by the highest weight. The label propagation algorithm has complexity of $O(m)$, where m is the number of edges in the graph [20]. Therefore, this algorithm is both fast and stochastic which makes it a perfect choice for our chosen method of producing borders between communities.

3   Identifying Borders of Crime

3.1   The Dataset

In order to create the networks and their borders, a collection of police department records in the USA that spans the time frame 2007 through 2010 was gathered from *SpotCrime*[1]. Each crime event in the dataset is characterized by description, address, geotag, type, date, and time. The types of crimes are arrest, assault, vandalism, burglary, theft, robbery, shooting, and other. Using the geotag of each crime we derived the ZCTA (ZIP Code Tabulation Area) it belonged to. We used the data from Los Angeles, CA, and Miami, FL to construct our model because they are large metropolises, geographically different, culturally diverse, and have different demographics.

To compare the crime borders against socio-economic and demographic borders inherent to the metropolises considered, we clustered ZCTA of the respective areas based on features extracted from US Census data of the American Community Survey for 2007-2011 (the time period most similar to the time span of the crime records). Then, these clusters are compared with the crime borders. The features used to cluster were: percent of population with a high school degree, joblessness, poverty rate, median income, percent of population receiving public assistance, percent of households that have moved in the past year, percent of properties that are vacant, percent of renter-occupied households, and percent of female-headed households. These variables are based on the work of Willits et al., which shows that they accounted for over 70% of the variance between neighborhoods at the block level [18]. Finally, these clusters are reduced to borders in order to compare with the crime borders. Thus, a border of this kind exists between two ZCTA if they are geographically adjacent and are not in the same cluster.

3.2   Building Networks and the Borders

The networks analyzed in this paper have each vertex representing locations and these vertices are connected if the crimes associated with the vertices occurred within a certain distance. This method of linking crimes is based on previous findings that criminals generally act in a small area, and the crimes occurring near to other crimes are committed by the same, or similar people [11].

---

[1] http://www.spotcrime.com

The choice of the location information that each vertex represents also defines the resolution of the network. For example, if the vertices represent the ZCTA of the location, the structure within this place is lost. However, this approach leads to reduction of computational cost of analysis, as well as to simplification of the results. In order to create this structure, a network where each vertex represents a single crime is built, then the crimes and their edges are collapsed into a network with fewer connections. Thus, the edges between crimes in different regions are represented by a single edge with weight equal to the number of original edges. On the other hand, the edges between crimes in a single region are treated as self edges and are removed.

The borders between vertices in the networks are analyzed by assigning to each vertex an associated map area. The vertices in the ZCTA-level networks contain all crimes in a single ZCTA, thus the shape of the ZCTA that each vertex represents is the physical region for the vertex. For the crime-level networks we used Voronoi maps. The region associated with each crime is the Voronoi cell surrounding that crime. Once the vertices in a network have an associated physical area, any communities in the network are a union of the areas of each node belonging to the community. Since each node belongs to a single community, the areas of all the communities completely cover the area of the network.

The analysis of the borders are not only concerned with their location, but the borders' strength is also a subject of study. The use of a stochastic community detection algorithm allows us to measure the probability of a border occurring as well as its physical position. The borders for many runs of a community detection algorithm are overlaid, and overlapping borders are combined. The weight w_{ij} of the border between two adjacent regions i and j is defined as:

$$w_{ij} := \frac{1}{R} \sum_{r=1}^{R} \delta(c_i^r, c_j^r) \tag{1}$$

where R is the number of runs of the community detection algorithm, c_i^r is the community of region i in the rth run of community detection, and $\delta(a, b)$ is 1 if a and b are different community labels, and 0 otherwise. This results in the weight of each border being the number of times the regions it divides appear in different communities normalized to a maximum value of 1.

3.3   Comparing Borders

The comparison between different sets of borders for the same region is made with the *absolute cross correlation* of a network representation of the borders [16]. A set of borders can be embedded in a network by representing the physical regions as vertices, and the borders between them as edges connecting adjacent regions. These edges have weights representing the strength of the borders between the regions. The absolute cross correlation is the normalized scalar product of the weights of edges in two networks. For two border networks b and b', the cross correlation is defined as:

$$c(b, b') := \frac{\sum_{e \in E} b(e)b'(e)}{\sqrt{\sum_{e \in E} b(e)^2}\sqrt{\sum_{e \in E} b'(e)^2}} \tag{2}$$

where $b(e)$ is the weight of edge e in b, and E is the set of edges in the two border networks. Equation 2 leads to high values when borders overlaps and borders not overlapping produce low values. However, different weight distributions of networks produce vastly different cross correlations, thus this evaluation by itself does not give meaningful results [16]. To compare the cross correlation between network, the comparison is made with a random null model in such way that a z-score is used to compare the cross correlations of different sets of networks.

However, the border network represents associations between adjacent regions, thus adding or removing edges from the graph in order to randomize it is not possible. Furthermore, cross correlation requires two networks with the same set of edges. For this reason, the weights of the borders are redistributed to find a random network using the iterative border redrawing method used by [16]. This method is a random process which iteratively redraws borders until a sufficiently random set of borders is achieved.

4   Results

The spatial distribution of different types of crimes is strongly influenced by factors such as education, income levels, family structure and organization of public spaces [18]. In this section we investigate whether the network structures that support the criminal activities also influence the spatial distribution of crimes and how criminals move in space. In other words, we compare the structure of the borders generated from crime networks with borders of areas clustered by their socio-demographic characteristics. The intuitive notion here is that the more influential networks used by criminals from different areas (e.g. transportation and social networks) the stronger the relationship between these areas will be in the crime network that we generate. Conversely, the smaller the influence of these networks, the weaker the connection between the network crime areas in and hence the stronger the borders between these areas.

This intuition is a plausible assumption once the distribution of distances traveled by offender from their places of residence to crime locations is characterized by the predominance of short trips with sporadic long trips. This distances vary with many factors such as the type of crime, gender and age of the offender, but the average trip length is approximately 1.6 miles with 84% of trips being shorter than 3.1 miles and only 7 % of the trips were longer than five miles [11].

In order to test whether the borders of crimes were capturing some underlying network structure we compared them against borders generated by demographic data. To ensure the comparison reflects the location, not the number of borders, we needed the demographic data and the crime data to have a similar number of communities. To get borders in the demographic data of roughly the same resolution as the borders in the crime networks we cut the dendrogram of demographic clusters at four heights resulting in a similar number of communities in both data sets. The three methods of hierarchical clustering and the four levels we cut each dendrogram at left us with 12 sets of demographic borders to compare each network to. The clusters for single linkage tended to be much more sparse than the other two methods of clustering so we dropped all but the most fine resolution of borders for single linkage. This left us with nine sets of borders for each metropolitan area we analyzed. Figure 1 shows the spatial representation of the borders structures compared to the socio-demographic characteristics

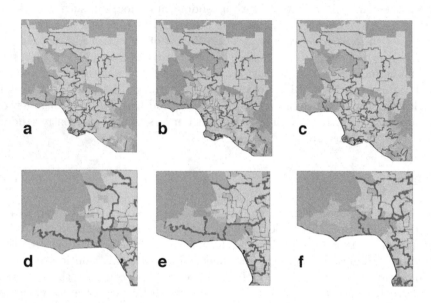

Fig. 1. Los Angeles Metropolitan Area – the structure of the borders (blue curves) for different crime types overlaying the ZCTAs clustered by their socio-demographic characteristics. (**a**) When we compare the borders of thefts with borders of socio-demographic clusters we can observe that in most cases the two sets do not coincide, suggesting that thefts tend to occur close to the socio-demographic borders. In fact, the theft borders partially correlate with the administrative limits of Los Angeles County regions such as Central L.A., Harbor, South L.A., Westside and San Gabriel Valley. (**b**) Similarly, burglary borders show a strong correlation with the county regions. Also, both theft and burglary borders set show a strong correlation. (**c**) The assault borders on the other hand seems to follow a different regime when compared to property crimes such as theft and burglary once their positions do not coincide. It is possible to see that assault borders tend to create subregions within socio-demographic clusters, particularly in dense areas such as Central L.A. Even though the borders of property crimes coincide in many areas of L.A., it is possible to observe some interesting dissimilarities such as a strong theft border across the center of the San Francisco Valley (**d**) that is nos present on the burglary borders set (**e**). Also, the strong borders of theft and burglary networks between Malibu and the Santa Monica Mountains show that the mountains represent a real topological barrier between Malibu and Calabasas and Agoura Hills. (**f**) Such borders, on the other hand, does not exist on the assault networks.

for the Los Angeles Metropolitan Area. Figures 1(a), 1(b) and 1(c) depict respectively the borders for theft, burglary and assault, and a zoom in Santa Monica area is shown in figures 1(d), 1(e) and 1(f).

A lack of correspondence between the socio-demographic characteristics and the borders of crimes networks suggests that such structures are not just a proxy for the characteristics of the an area. But before we assume that the borders structures are representing some underlying network phenomena, we need to validate it against a null model. In order to carry this analysis out, we chose to generate random borders based on the demographic borders and reuse these for the comparison to each set of crime borders. For each of the 9 sets of demographic borders there were networks for each of four years (2007-2010), five distance parameters (0.1, 0.8, 1.6, 2.4, and 3.2 miles), and four types of crimes (all types, assault, burglary, and theft), for a total of 80 networks. This left us with 720 z-scores over a range of parameters for each city we were interested in.

Figure 2 highlights some of the different correlations between crime types, cities, and distance between crimes. For both of Miami and Los Angeles we saw more than a single standard deviation between other crime types for at least one of the five distances we analyzed. The fact that different crime types have statistically significant differences in correlation with the socio-economic boundaries in a city shows the structure of the crime networks are driven by

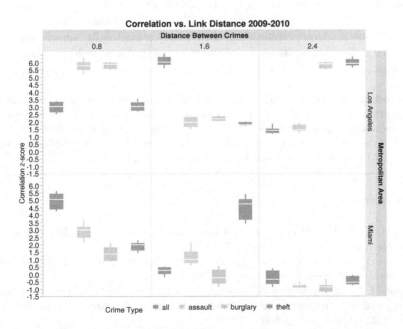

Fig. 2. As the distance between associated crimes changes the correlation with the demographic borders also changes. The varying patterns of this change for different crime types shows the crime networks have different structure for different types of crime.

different underlying phenomena. From this we concluded the structure of the crime networks could be used to find interesting patterns in the structure of criminal activity in a metropolitan area.

5   Conclusions and Future Works

The reliance of criminal activities on different types of networks makes network science an obvious choice for analyzing criminal activity. Using assumptions about the spatial distribution of crimes, we proposed a new model in which networks are built with links between crimes in close physical proximity. We showed that there exists an underlying structure of criminal activity that can be represented by the spatial distribution of the crimes. The model we propose allows the construction of criminal networks without the need for gathering extra data about individual criminals or patterns of crimes. No additional work is required to gain insights available from this new model because the data we used to construct the networks is already a part of law enforcement bookkeeping. The growth of computational resources available to law enforcement agencies allows for more complex analysis than the heatmaps that have been useful in the past.

For Los Angeles, CA and Miami, FL, we generated networks for multiple spatial distances, ranging from 0.1 miles to 3.2 miles, and various crime types. We showed that these networks capture real-world phenomena, by comparing borders between communities of crimes. We compared these borders to similar boundaries in demographic data and found statistically significant variations, which indicates the structure of the crime networks is reflecting real-world phenomena.

Acknowledgments. The authors acknowledge support from NSF grant No. 1263011 and NSF grant No. 1152306. Any opinions, findings, and conclusions or recommendations expressed in this material are those of the authors and do not necessarily reflect the views of the NSF. Marcos Oliveira would like to thank the Science Without Borders program (CAPES, Brazil) for financial support under grant 1032/13-5.

References

1. Shaw, C.R., McKay, H.D.: Juvenile delinquency and urban areas (Revision of 1942 ed.). University of Chicago Press (1969)
2. Shaw, C.R., Zorbaugh, F.M., McKay, H.D., Cottrell, L.S.: Delinquency areas. University of Chicago Press (1929)
3. Taylor, R.B., Gottfredson, S.D., Brower, S.: Block crime and fear: Defensible space, local social ties, and territorial functioning. Journal of Research in crime and delinquency **21**(4), 303–331 (1984)
4. Sampson, R.J., Raudenbush, S.W., Earls, F.: Neighborhoods and violent crime: A multilevel study of collective efficacy. Science **277**(5328), 918–924 (1997)
5. Bursik Jr., R.J., Grasmick, H.G., et al.: Neighborhoods & Crime. Lexington Books (1999)

6. Morenoff, J.D., Sampson, R.J., Raudenbush, S.W.: Neighborhood inequality, collective efficacy, and the spatial dynamics of urban violence*. Criminology **39**(3), 517–558 (2001)
7. Jobes, P.C., Barclay, E., Weinand, H., Donnermeyer, J.F.: A structural analysis of social disorganisation and crime in rural communities in australia. Australian & New Zealand Journal of Criminology **37**(1), 114–140 (2004)
8. Eck, J.E., Chainey, S., Cameron, J.G., Leitner, M., Wilson, R.E.: Mapping Crime: Understanding Hot Spots. National Institute of Justice (2005)
9. Furtado, V., Melo, A., Coelho, A.L.V., Menezes, R.: Simulating crime against properties using swarm intelligence and social networks. In: Artificial Crime Analysis Systems: Using Computer Simulations and Geographic Information Systems, pp. 300–318 (2008)
10. Kubrin, C.E., Weitzer, R.: New directions in social disorganization theory. Journal of Research in Crime and Delinquency **40**(4), 374–402 (2003)
11. Levine, N., Lee, P.: Journey-to-crime by gender and age group in manchester, england. In: Crime modeling and mapping using geospatial technologies, pp. 145–178. Springer (2013)
12. Jefferis, E.: A multi-method exploration of crime hot spots: a summary of findings. US Department of Justice, National Institute of Justice, Crime Mapping Research Center, Washington, DC (1999)
13. Sparrow, M.K.: The application of network analysis to criminal intelligence: An assessment of the prospects. Social networks **13**(3), 251–274 (1991)
14. McIllwain, J.S.: Organized crime: A social network approach. Crime, Law and Social Change **32**(4), 301–323 (1999)
15. Klerks, P.: The network paradigm applied to criminal organisations. Transnational organised crime: perspectives on global security, p. 97 (2003)
16. Thiemann, C., Theis, F., Grady, D., Brune, R., Brockmann, D.: The structure of borders in a small world, November 2010
17. Beavon, D.J.K., Brantingham, P.L., Brantingham, P.J.: The Influence of Street Networks on the Patterning of Property Offenses, Crime prevention studies (1994)
18. Willits, D., Broidy, L., Gonzales, A., Denman, K.: Place and Neighborhood Crime: Examining the Relationship between Schools, Churches, and Alcohol Related Establishments and Crime. Institute for Social Research, March 2011
19. Foster, S., Wood, L., Christian, H., Knuiman, M., Giles-Corti, B.: Planning safer suburbs: Do changes in the built environment influence residents' perceptions of crime risk? Social Science & Medicine **97**, 87–94 (2013)
20. Raghavan, U.N., Albert, R., Kumara, S.: Near linear time algorithm to detect community structures in large-scale networks. Phys. Rev. E **76**, 036106 (2007)

Emergence of Extreme Opinions
in Social Networks

Marco Alberto Javarone[1] (✉) and Serge Galam[2]

[1] Dept. of Mathematics and Computer Science, University of Cagliari, Cagliari, Italy
marcojavarone@gmail.com
[2] CEVIPOF Centre for Political Research, CNRS and Sciences Po, Paris, France
serge.galam@sciencespo.fr

Abstract. The emergence and spreading of "extreme opinions" are studied in networks with agents sharing mild opinions. The turning extreme shift is driven by social group meetings. The extremization process is apprehended according to the social psychology phenomenon of group polarization and illustrated in the case of terrorism. In particular the focus is on the dynamics of emergence of "passive supporters" from which terrorists can then be recruited. Becoming a passive supporter being considered as taking an extreme opinion, group polarization is shown to play an important role for increasing the transition probabilities from mild opinion (e.g., anti-western feeling) to its extreme form (e.g., passive supporter or terrorist). Accordingly a simple agent-based model is defined to implement interactions among agents on networks. Three opinions are considered, pro-western opinion, anti-western opinion and extreme anti-western opinion. The latter may lead people to become passive supporters and, potentially, terrorists. Results of simulations show that a substantial fraction of anti-western agents adopt the extreme opinion exhibiting an emergent phenomenon which may shed some new light on real social phenomena of political violence.

Keywords: Emergent phenomena · Group polarization · Opinion dynamics · Sociophysics

1 Introduction

Social dynamics [1,2] and, in particular the subfield of opinion dynamics [1–3], deal with the emergence and the spreading of information and opinion in groups of individuals. Several authors investigated these issues by defining models, as the voter model [4], able to represent simplified scenarios of opinion spreading. Usually, models are devised to analyze systems with only two opinions, simplified dynamics as directed spreading of opinions from an agent to one of its neighbors, and opinion spreading by a majority voting rule [5]. In order to model social phenomena, as opinion dynamics, agent-based models constitute a powerful framework —see [6][7], that can be combined with the modern network theory [8]. In this work, we focus on the emergence of extreme opinions in groups

© Springer International Publishing Switzerland 2015
L.M. Aiello and D. McFarland (Eds.): SocInfo 2014 Workshops, LNCS 8852, pp. 112–117, 2015.
DOI: 10.1007/978-3-319-15168-7_15

of people. In particular, we consider the theory of group polarization studied in social psychology [9]. Group polarization is a collective phenomenon that can take place when groups of people are taking a decision, i.e., when they are taking an opinion or forming a new one. In particular, this social phenomenon leads a group of people to form an extreme opinion. In this context, the attribute "extreme" is used in comparison to the opinion that each person, belonging to the group, had individually [9]. We propose an agent-based model considering a system with three opinions, i.e., two opposite opinions and one representing the extreme form of one of them. First two opinions are related to pro-western and anti-western feelings. Instead, the third opinion is "terrorist". In this context, the word "terrorist" is used with a more general meaning, as it is referred also to the behavior of "passive supporters" [10], that in real scenarios cannot be properly defined as terrorists. Results show that a great amount of anti-western agents becomes terrorists as result of interactions among agents, having the same conflicting opinion (i.e., anti-western feeling), in an adaptive network [11]. The remainder of the paper is organized as follows: Section 2 introduces the model for studying the emergence of extreme opinions in an agent population. Section 3 shows results of numerical simulations. Eventually, Section 4 ends the paper.

2   The Model

We consider a system with N interacting agents provided with an individual opinion, i.e., pro-western (hereinafter pw) and anti-western (hereinafter aw) feeling. Then, these opinions are mapped to states $s = \pm 1$. Agents are arranged on a small-world network, hence they can interact with their neighbors; although we impose that they cannot change opinion (or state) from $+1$ (i.e., pw) to -1 (i.e., aw), and vice versa, over time. Now, we suppose that one agent of the network is a terrorist leader (hereinafter TL), with an opinion $s = -2$ representing an extreme form of the anti-western feeling (i.e., $s = -1$). At each time step, TL tries to recruit other agents, among those with the aw feeling, in order to organize secret meetings. Each aw agent (i.e., having $s = -1$) will accept the invitation, to attend secret meetings, with probability $p^r \in [0,1]$ (equal for all aw agents). As aw agents accept to attend secret meetings, they generate new connections among them. Hence, we are dealing with an adaptive network [11], whose main result is represented by the emergence of a sub-community of aw agents. Since participants of secret meetings tend to generate connections with the other participants, the sub-community tends to approach a fully-connected structure over time. According to social psychology theory of "group polarization", a small set of people with the same idea can be lead to take the idea to the extreme level, when they interact among themselves. Therefore, in the proposed model, a small set of aw agents can become terrorists due to interactions with other aw agents. In particular, we map the phenomenon of group polarization to the parameter p^t. The latter represents the transition probability from aw agent to a terrorist one and, moreover, p^t is computed by the density of aw agents and of terrorists present in the social circle of each participant of secret meetings. The recruiting of aw agents, in these secret meetings, is the underlying mechanism responsible for the variation of the social network over time. The proposed model considers also that some participants quit to attend secret meetings after a while. Hence, this last circumstance is represented by the probability p^{out} which depends on the density of pw agents in the social circle of participants. Considering the ith recruited agent (i.e., one of the meetings' participants), its p^t and p^{out} are computed as follows

$$\begin{cases} p_i^t = f(\sigma_i^-, \sigma_i^{--}) \\ p_i^{out} = \sigma_i^+ \end{cases} \tag{1}$$

with σ_i^- and σ_i^{--} densities of aw and terrorist agents in the social circle of the ith agent, respectively; and σ_i^+ density of pw agents in the social circle of the ith agent. The function $f(\sigma_i^-, \sigma_i^{--})$ has been devised in order to consider the presence of both aw and terrorist agents among neighbors of the ith agent. In particular, it has been defined as follow:

$$f(\sigma_i^-, \sigma_i^{--}) = \frac{S_j^- + S_j^{--}}{N_i} \tag{2}$$

with N_i number of neighbors of the ith agent (i.e., cardinality of its social circle), and S_j^- and S_j^{--} total number of its neighbors in the state -1 and -2, respectively. In a similar way, we compute $\sigma_i^+ = S_j^+/N_i$, with S_j^+ number of neighbors, of the jth agent, in the state $+1$. Therefore, the underlying mechanics to modify the state of aw agents (from -1 to -2), or to let them quitting secret meetings, is based (stochastically) on the majority voting rule. Eventually, recall that probabilities p^t and p^{out} are computed only for recruited agents and, moreover, as a recruited agent quits secret meetings, it will be also removed from the sub-community of aw agents generated among all participants. Agents who quit meetings cannot be contacted again by TL. It is worth to note that by this mechanism (i.e., the probability that agents quit meetings), a pure fully-connected structure cannot be reached by the sub-community of participants, although the density of internal edges still remains high.

3   Simulations

We performed many numerical simulations of the proposed model in order to analyze its outcomes in a small population of $N = 900$ agents. At the beginning, the two opinions, pw and aw, are equally spread in the population, therefore connections between pw and aw agents avoid aw agents become terrorist ones. On the other hand, as aw agents begin to attend secret meetings, the transition from the state aw to terrorist is more likely due to the increasing number of connections among aw agents in the sub-community of participants. The algorithm to implement the proposed model is composed by the following steps:

1. Define a network with N agents provided with a state $s = \pm 1$, equally distributed

2. Select one random agent and change its status s to -2, then it plays the role of TL
3. At each time step:
   - TL contacts one aw agent —say the jth agent, randomly chosen, for inviting it to attend secret meetings; then, the jth agent accepts with probability p^r. In the event the jth agent accepts, it is added to the sub-community of "potential terrorist" (i.e., it is added to the list of participants of secret meetings);
   - each participant agent computes its probability to become a terrorist p^t and, in the event of a negative result (i.e., it does not become terrorist), it computes the probability to quit secret meetings (i.e., p^{out}). Now, if the result is positive (i.e., it quits meetings), the agent will not be contacted again by TL, then its status will never change.
4. Repeat from (3), until the terrorist opinion emerges in the population, or a maximum number of time steps is elapsed.

It is worth to recall that, as an aw accepts invitation, at each time step it generates a new connection with a random agents belonging to the sub-community. Eventually, the emergence of the terrorist opinion (i.e., $s = -2$) does not consider the presence of the TL agent, as it has already a state $s_{TL} = -2$. Notably, it is possible to analyze the proposed model in order to study the increasing of terrorist agents over time. Figure 1 shows results of numerical simulations.

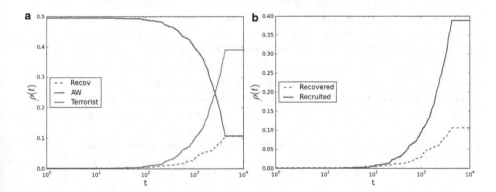

Fig. 1. a Density of agents having the opinions aw and Terrorist, over time. The density of aw agents decreases until it reaches the density of recovered ones (i.e., those who quit secret meetings). **b** Comparison between the amount of recovered agents vs that of recruited agents, over time. Results are averaged over 10 different simulation runs.

4 Discussion and Conclusions

In this work, we analyze a social phenomenon called group polarization, deemed relevant in social psychology. In particular, we are interested in modeling this phenomenon, under a sociophysical perspective, due to its relations with the terrorism dynamics. Group polarization is a collective phenomenon emerging from people's interactions; hence agent-based approaches, combined with the framework of modern network theory, allow to devise suitable models for studying these dynamics. In the proposed model, we consider a system with three opinions: two opinions are initially spread in the agent population, whereas a third opinion (representing the extreme form of one of the initial opinions) emerges as results of agents' interactions. Moreover, we impose that agents can change opinion only to become extremists (i.e., terrorists or passive supporters). As said before, at the beginning only two opinions exist in the system, with the exception of one agent, randomly chosen, that plays the role of the terrorist leader (i.e., TL). Hence, TL is provided immediately with the extremist opinion (i.e., $s_{TL} = -2$). The role of the terrorist leader is to group agents having the opinion which allow the transitions from -1 to -2. Grouping agents is represented by the task of recruiting them to organize secret meetings. Agents that accept the invitation take part to the sub-community of potential terrorists (or passive supporters). As agents attend meeting, they generate new connections over time, increasing the risk of group polarization. On the other hand, if they do not change opinion, at each step there is a probability they quit meetings. In this last case, they are removed from the sub-community and all edges with the other attendees are deleted. Therefore, the dynamics of the proposed model entail the structure of the network, where agents are arranged, varies over time. Simulations show that a great fraction of agents which take part to secret meetings undergoes the phenomenon of group polarization, changing its status from $s = -1$ to $s = -2$. Therefore, considering a real scenarios the proposed model is more suitable to describe the emergence of passive supporters [10] than that of terrorists. In particular, considering the biography of famous anti-occidental terrorists [12], a neat terrorist opinion can be viewed as an extreme form of the passive supporter state. As for future work, we will consider network strategies [13] to reduce the probability anti-western agents will become terrorists.

Acknowledgments. This work was supported in part from a convention DGA-2012 60 0013 00470 75 01.

References

1. Galam, S.: Sociophysics: a review of Galam models. International Journal of Modern Physics C **19–3**, 409–440 (2008)
2. Castellano, C., Fortunato, S., Loreto, V.: Statistical physics of social dynamics. Rev. Mod. Phys. **81–2**, 591–646 (2009)
3. Sznajd-Weron, K., Sznajd, J.: Opinion Evolution in Closed Community. International Journal of Modern Physics C **11–6**, 1157 (2000)
4. Sood, V., Redner, S.: Voter Model on Heterogeneous Graphs. Phys. Rev. Lett. **94–17**, 178701 (2005)
5. Galam, S.: Social paradoxes of majority rule voting and renormalization group. Journal of Statistical Physics 61 (1990)

6. San Miguel, M., Eguiluz, V.M., Toral, R. Binary and Multivariate Stochastic Models of Consensus Formation. Computing in Science and Engineering **7–6**, 67–73 (2005)
7. Castello, X.. Eguiluz, V.M., San Miguel, M.: Ordering dynamics with two non-excluding options: bilingualism in language competition. New Journal of Physics 8 (2006)
8. Albert, R., Barabasi, A.L.: Emergence of Scaling in Random Networks. Science **286**(5439), 509–512 (1999)
9. Aronson, E., Wilson, T.D., Akert, R.M.: Social Psychology. Pearson Ed., (2006)
10. Galam, S., Mauger, A.: On reducing terrorism power: a hint from physics. Physica A: Statistical Mechanics and its Applications **323**, 695–704 (2003)
11. Gross, T., Hiroki, S.: Adaptive Networks: Theory. Models and Applications. Springer, Heidelberg (2009)
12. Islamic Terrorism. http://en.wikipedia.org/wiki/Islamic_terrorism
13. Javarone, M.A.: Networks strategies in election campaigns. Journal of Statistical Mechanics: Theory and Experiments P08013 (2014)

Using Societal Impact Assessment (SIA) to Improve Technological Development in the Field of Crime Prevention

Gemma Galdon Clavell[1,2(✉)] and Philippe M. Frowd[1]

[1] Eticas Research and Consulting, Barcelona, Spain
{gemma,philippe}@eticasconsulting.com
[2] Universitat de Barcelona, Barcelona, Spain
gemma.galdon@ub.edu

Abstract. Geographical information systems (GIS), intelligence-led policing, and automation of border controls are approaches to crime prevention heavily reliant on technology as a fix for faster data gathering and processing. This paper proposes a four-part societal impact assessment (SIA) methodology as a means of accounting for the impacts of crime prevention technologies from the standpoints of desirability, acceptability, ethics, and data management. The paper provides empirical material in two short cases on crime-mapping and automated border control.

Keywords: Societal impact · Border control · Data protection · Crime mapping · Security technologies · Technological development · Privacy

1 Introduction

A number of technologies have emerged to better allow law enforcement agencies to thwart criminal networks but also to attenuate urban insecurity. These have included geographical information systems (GIS), intelligence-based policing, monitoring of social media, the use of unmanned aerial vehicles (UAVs) and automation of immigration controls. In each of these cases, technology operates as a fix to improve data gathering, facilitate decision-making, or speed up security procedures. However, the adoption of new technologies, in order to guarantee their efficacy and to minimize their negative externalities, should be subject to a clear and comprehensive set of assessment guidelines. All too often, such technologies have led to unwanted effects: disproportionate targeting of identifiable groups, excessive costs, and more. In light of this, this paper argues for a greater attention to societal impacts in the development of crime-fighting technologies, doing do by drawing on existing practices in urban crime management through GIS as well as on the ongoing automation of border controls in Europe. The paper begins by providing a working definition of societal impact assessment (SIA) as a means of developing a four-part framework for the assessment of security technologies and projects. The primary takeaway point from this paper is that developers and operators of digital crime-fighting technologies, in order to maximize *both* effectiveness and social responsibility, should endeavour to include a holistic

© Springer International Publishing Switzerland 2015
L.M. Aiello and D. McFarland (Eds.): SocInfo 2014 Workshops, LNCS 8852, pp. 118–124, 2015.
DOI: 10.1007/978-3-319-15168-7_16

social impact awareness into their products and procedures. In this way, the paper provides both theoretical development as well as operational examples showcasing the potentials of a societal impact lens.

2   Societal Impact Assessment (SIA)

Societal impact assessment focuses on the potential consequences of policies, programs, projects and technologies. It is the evaluation of the risks, externalities and consequences of technologies, policies, programs, and systems. Societal impact includes the intended and unintended consequences of development, and these consequences can be changes in people's way of life; their culture; a community's cohesion and trust, stability, character, services and facilities; political systems; environment; health and wellbeing; personal and property rights and/or fears and aspirations concerning safety and future.[1]

According to the ASSERT project,

> SIA is the process of understanding, managing and responding to the societal impacts that arise from security research and the application of innovative security measures. The use of the term societal (rather than social) connotes the inclusion of anything affecting human, natural or artefactual systems, rather than just those effects that impact upon humans and their interactions. It also allows us to distinguish the process from social impact assessment [...][2]

SIA's origins are multiple, and it comes from a long line of methods of assessing impacts of technologies as well as impacts on the environment. SIA can trace its proverbial 'roots' to impact assessment methods such as constructive technology assessment (CTA) as well as environmental impact assessment (EIA) and privacy impact assessment (PIA). Each of these strives to provide some form of holistic view of what a particular project, technology or program's effects (both negative and positive) might be.

The value-addition of societal impact is that it takes into account technology and design as much as social/human impacts, which allows considerations relating not only to rights and ethics questions but also to elements such as design, cost-benefit analysis and project management. SIA is therefore not only a critical tool from the sociological standpoint, but a useful approach for designers, engineers and end users to better design and implement crime-fighting technologies.

---

[1] Vanclay F.: Social Impact Assessment: International Principles. International Association for Impact Assessment, Special Publication Series no.2, 8 (2003).

[2] Barnard-Wills, D., Wadhwa, K., Wright, D.: ASSERT Project Deliverable 3.1: Societal Assessment Manual and Toolkit, 9 (2014).

So what might a framework attuned to societal impact look like? This paper proposes a four-pronged approach centred on *desirability*, *acceptability*, *ethics*, and *data management*.

2.1   Desirability

The desirability of a program refers to the very need for a solution. To think about desirability is to define the **problem** to be resolved and ensure that the design of the solution is collaborative, accounts for societal impact, and is well governed. Assessing the desirability of a project is helpful for designers as it may help to determine whether a particular **solution** is needed at all, or whether it is best to have a 'do-minimum' or 'do-nothing' solution. This can be achieved through **cost-benefit analysis** which takes into account key factors such as utility, impact and costs in an economic but also societal sense. The desirability of a security technology should also be guided by the organizational needs of the implementer, such as **staffing** which includes training and resource allocation. Personnel may need training in societal impact as well as on use of the technology chosen, and scarce resources (especially in the public sector) may be diverted for little gain. Desirability of a technology may be affected by how well it is **governed**. Assessment should include an attentiveness to accountability procedures, enforcement mechanisms, and how well best practices are formulated and applied.

2.2   Acceptability

The acceptability of a security technology builds on desirability to include public debate and consent. Acceptability is fundamentally more public-facing, and includes an emphasis on **choice**, **consent** and **control**. Technologies or programs require accountability on the part of an informed user base and broader public, and as such designers should provide adequate **information** to the public, and frequently gather the informed and voluntary **consent** of the public or intended users of a technology. Consent is an essential part of how well a technology is accepted precisely because it allows users control over their data as well as over the outcome of the technological deployment, which in its turn can impact **trust**. Acceptability of a technology or policy is also shaped by an understanding of the societal **context**, which includes overarching societal values and to what extent they might limit what users are willing to accept. Finally, **proportionality** is a key test of whether a particular technology is acceptable or not, ensuring that the effects of a solution are kept in relation to the problem it is trying to solve: for example, collection of personal data for crime mapping may be disproportionate once it begins to impact on the presumption of innocence.

2.3   Ethics

Ethics refers to the values and moral standards that guide a particular innovation or technology. Ethics are reflected in some formal documents such as those laying out **fundamental rights**, but are also composed of more intangible **values**. These are continually in flux but in democratic societies tend to include freedom of movement, freedom of assembly, the right to free speech, freedom from discrimination, equality guarantees, and so on. Taking ethics into account necessarily means guaranteeing **inclusivity**. Inclusivity recognizes differences in accessibility, such as disability, but also imbalances in social power and access to social capital. It therefore accounts for the fact that some groups may be more affected than others and that access to services may not be equal. An ethical approach should also take into account the **precautionary principle** by which the onus is on designers, rather than the public or end users, to justify the deployment and potential risks associated with a security technology. With this onus on designers and developers comes an additional responsibility to clearly lay out the vision of **security** that is part of the technology being designed, and justify exactly what threats and being secured against, and who is being secured.

2.4   Data Management

Privacy and personal data protection is a legal and societal question. Taking into account data management compels engineers and other data managers to **follow existing law** but encompasses principles such as **minimization** and **anonymization** of data collected, as well as design techniques such as **privacy by design** (which advocates building privacy into technologies) and tools such as **privacy-enhancing technologies** (user tools for anonymity and data protection). An attentiveness to data management questions urges a careful consideration of what data is collected, from whom, for what purpose, and what rights the user has to deletion and **redress**.

3   Assessment of Existing Crime-Fighting Technologies

3.1   Crime Mapping by GIS

Police forces have increasingly sought to technologize policing tools, and GIS mapping has become an important tool for policing through a better grasp of the different layers of the very urban space of law enforcement. GIS is a compounded system made up of hardware, software and informational processes. It is designed for the gathering, management, analysis, modelling, and display of geographical data. It is primarily used for the purpose of establishing patterns, correlations to visualize often undetectable or previously unseen data.[3] For example, GIS systems can plot as well as overlay different sets of overlapping data such as urban grids, topographical maps, land use patterns and satellite imagery.

Technologies for GIS mapping of crime have been developed in order to make policing more *efficient*. Some of the earliest GIS systems were deployed before the digital age by police departments in the United States, with the St. Louis police using this technology to improve the efficiency of its patrol routes based on the SYMAP punch card system developed at Harvard University. In the 1990s, the New York Police Department began to explicitly deploy systems to make policing a strategic and intelligence-led operation based on crime statistics, beginning with COMPSTAT

---

[3] Galdon Clavell, G., Pybus Oliveras, M.: Crisis Economics y Gestion de la Inseguridad Ciudadana: Los Mapas de Delincuencia. Revista Catalana de Seguretat Publica 24, 79-105 (2011).

(Computer Statistics). With the development of complex ICTs, a range of GIS tools now includes CrimeStat, CrimeWiew, Spatian Analyst, HotSpot Detective Vertical Mapper, SpaceSat, and many more. The ClearMap system deployed by the Chicago Police not only relies on statistics but also on geolocation of crime through GPS coordinates and is integrated with databases of sex offenders. The development of GIS-based crime mapping is inseparable from a faith whereby investments in technology, irrespective of budgetary situation, are considered good investments. In the case of crime mapping, the technological possibilities of mapping technology have actively shaped policing tactics. What could a lens attuned to societal impact add to the study of police mapping practices? What kinds of new questions could be raised in terms of desirability, acceptability, ethics, and data management? These are reflected in some of the sample assessment questions provided in Table 1, below.

Table 1. Potential questions to be asked of GIS-based crime mapping

Desirability	**Acceptability**
• Has there been any cost-benefit analysis carried out in relation to the purchase of GIS equipment? • What alternative options exist to better combat crime by geographic area, and how are they to be weighted? • Has implementation been accounted for, including staffing and training?	• To what extent are the public aware of, and specifically consenting to, the use of GIS mapping? • How have the public been informed of the use of GIS information for policing? • At the institutional level, have personnel been consulted about their perspectives on GIS mapping techniques?
Ethics	**Data management**
• How does the use of crime mapping potentially exclude identifiable or vulnerable groups? • What measures are in place to ensure that the use of GIS mapping remains limited to its original mandate? • Have key values such as freedom of movement been assessed in light of the use of GPS systems? • Could crime mapping lead to hot-spot policing and a disproportionate police presence in vulnerable areas?	• Are those who have police contact (e.g. arrest) aware of the collection of their data? • How is data kept secure, and who has access to the databases the system connects to? Are searches of the database logged? • Have privacy by design principles been considered in the design of the GIS system itself?

Table 2. Potential assessment questions for automated border control

Desirability	Acceptability
• Do ABC gates provide any cost savings for their operators, or time savings for their users, and in what relation do these benefits sit in relation to the economic cost of these systems? • What have countries outside the EU tended to adopt for automation of border control, and how can this experience shape the EU's own deployment? • How can gate designers and engineers be trained on societal impact in a way that is meaningful and can be translated into their professional routines?	• How do ABC systems conform to existing law (such as the Schengen Borders Code), particularly in relation to their automation of border procedures? • What is the public perception of ABC gates, and how has this been measured? • What measures are in place to inform travellers of the presence of ABC gates and ensure that they use them with freely given consent? • What data is published about the efficacy of ABC gates and is it publicly available?
Ethics	**Data management**
• Is the use of biometrics for border control potentially encouraging the broader use of biometrics throughout society? • What provisions have been made in the physical and human interface design of the gates to ensure that they are accessible to persons with disabilities? • What ideal of security is put forth by these gates, and do they contribute to an ideal of borders as primarily security-related spaces? • Is the autonomy of travellers protected by the ability to opt-out or use fallback measures of equal quality? • To what degree does automation potentially remove agency from the traveller or lead to inequality?	• What transfers of biometric information are put in place? • What are the rates of false rejection in the biometric matching? • Is biometric data stored locally, or on an off-site database, and is it deleted immediately after each traveller passes? • What steps have been taken to avoid unnecessary polling of databases?

3.2   Automation of Border Control

Several European states have, over the last decade, attempted to automate elements of their border management processes. This has included but not been limited to passport/ID control, with visa issuance and entry/exit tracking increasingly automated and interlinked. Sweden has automated elements of its visa issuance and verification system and interlinked it with its diplomatic missions abroad, while states such as France and Germany provide automated border control (ABC) for biometric passport holders at some main airports. A majority of states in Europe now have some form of automation of border procedures. Automation of border control is partly an issue of convenience, as it theoretically speeds up border crossing. However, ABC also serves to prevent identity fraud and to stifle criminal networks proliferation of forged documents. The adoption of biometric travel documents, called for by international norms (like the International Civil Aviation Organization's Doc 9303) and by EU directives (such as Council Regulation EC 2252/2004) specifically aims to combat this threat and these documents are the backbone of border control automation.

In the pursuit of a more harmonized and societally-conscious solution, at least for states participating in all aspects of the Schengen Agreement, the EU has funded a number of studies, including two large projects–FASTPASS and ABC4EU–under its Seventh Framework Programme (FP7) research funding. These projects are oriented towards assessment of the legal possibilities of automation of border control and, due to their public-private nature, are building and deploying prototype units to test elements of border control automation, from document verification to biometric matching to user interface. In each project, but particularly in ABC4EU, there has been an opportunity to introduce an awareness of societal impact from the beginning of the development process, to ensure that the designers of the gates are trained on societal impact and that the final product is reflective of the broad societal consensus. Some of the questions asked of ABC gates are included in Table 2, below.

4   Conclusion

This paper has explained some of the essentials of SIA and set out a four-pronged framework for assessment of security technologies. It has then used two examples of current crime-fighting tools to suggest some beneficial applications of such an approach. Going forward, SIA can prove itself to be a fruitful lens not only for critics of similar security technologies, but also for their designers. The SIA approach ensures that fundamental rights are respected, that societal impacts (and project impacts) are considered, and that technologies are able to carry out their security functions without compromising the type of society in which we wish to live.

References

1. Barnard-Wills, D., Wadhwa, K., Wright, D.: ASSERT Project Deliverable 3.1: Societal Assessment Manual and Toolkit, 9 (2014)
2. Clavell, G.G., Oliveras, P.M.: Crisis Economics y Gestion de la Inseguridad Ciudadana: Los Mapas de Delincuencia. Revista Catalana de Seguretat Publica **24**, 79–105 (2011)
3. Vanclay, F.: Social Impact Assessment: International Principles. International Association for Impact Assessment, Special Publication Series no. 2, 8 (2003)

Whats in a Dyad? Interaction and Exchange in Social Media (DYAD)

What's in a Dyad? Interaction and Exchange in Social Media - Introduction

Rossano Schifanella[1]([⊠]), Bogdan State[2], and Yelena Mejova[3]

[1] Computer Science Department, University of Turin, Turin, Italy
schifane@di.unito.it
[2] Facebook Inc. and Stanford University, Stanford, USA
[3] Qatar Computing Research Institute, Doha, Qatar

Abstract. Scientists are now on the cusp of gaining a computational understanding of social interaction by means of online conversational data in the form of blog posts, emails exchange, comments threads, or interest-based discussions. Online interactions can be conceptualized as a social exchange, and also as a process from which meaning emerges through dialogue between the two partners. This workshop creates an interdisciplinary venue for plentiful dialogue and exchange that aims to shed light at the understanding of social structure through a computational focus on the mechanics of the dyad.

Description

A great deal of work has used computational methods to investigate the intensity, structure, topic and sentiment of social interactions. Researchers have developed a variety of tools to mine the syntactic and semantic aspects of textual messages recorded through computer-mediated interactions. At the same time, the structure of online social networks has intrigued computational researchers.

The workshop objective stems from the observation that neither information alone nor structure in isolation can be considered fully responsible for the complexity of social life, whether on- or offline. It wants to explore the connections between the textual and structural approaches to computational social science and show how online interactions can be conceptualized as a social exchange, the richness and complexity of which demands more elaborate modeling than most research into large social networks has achieved so far. An interactional view of social ties will enable researchers to gain a computational understanding of the social construction of meaning, ultimately leading to a deeper interpretation of social structure both at the dyadic and group levels.

The first edition of the DYAD workshop was held in Barcelona, Spain in conjunction with the 6th International Conference on Social Informatics (SocInfo 2014) on November 10th 2014, and it allowed for a greater role for exchange and interaction as concepts routinely used in the research of online platforms.

Though the study of dyadic interaction is based on a well-established theoretical scholarship with a long tradition, an increased focus on dyadic interaction

© Springer International Publishing Switzerland 2015
L.M. Aiello and D. McFarland (Eds.): SocInfo 2014 Workshops, LNCS 8852, pp. 127–129, 2015.
DOI: 10.1007/978-3-319-15168-7_17

in the computational realm would undoubtedly also benefit the further development of social theory. The computational turn helped bring massive online scale to many problems which could previously only be studied in the laboratory. We expect this transposition therefore to elicit the need for the development of new concepts as well as the deeper understanding of old ones, a goal to which we hope the DYAD workshop contributed through the exploration of a number of rich perspectives.

Accepted Papers

We included in the program of the first edition of the workshop the following 4 out of 7 papers that represent a sample of the rich topical variety that is intrinsic in online dyadic communication:

- *"Triad-based Role Discovery for Large Social Systems"* where Derek Doran proposes a methodology to identify user roles using triad consensuses of ego-networks.
- *"A Tool-based Methodology to Analyze Social Network Interactions in Cultural Fields: the Use Case MuseumWeek"* by Antoine Courtin, Brigitte Juanals, Jean-Luc Minel, and Mathide de Saint Léger. The paper analyzes institutional communication in a cultural mediation scenario that includes Twitter campaigns of several European museums.
- *"Detecting Presence of Personal Events in Twitter Streams"* in which Smitashree Choudhury and Harith Alani detect personal events, including marriage, job change, and the death of relatives, in the user's Twitter stream.
- *"Digital Addiction Ontology for Social Networking Systems"* where Amen Alrobai and Huseyin Dogan propose an ontology for the analysis of digital addiction.

Program Committee

Saiph Savage	UC Santa Barbara
Nicholas Diakopoulos	Columbia University
Emre Kiciman	Microsoft
Haewoon Kwak	Qatar Computing Research Institute
Michael Mäs	ETH Zürich
Salvatore Scellato	University of Cambridge
Mirco Musolesi	University of Birmingham
Giovanni Luca Ciampaglia	Indiana University
Emilio Ferrara	Indiana University
Emma Spiro	University of Washington
Vincent Buskens	Utrecht University
Brandy Aven	Carnegie Mellon
Damon Centola	University of Pennsylvania

Giancarlo Ruffo	University of Torino
Farshad Kooti	University of Southern California
Eytan Adar	University of Michigan
Frank Schweitzer	ETH Zürich
Brian Keegan	Northeastern University
Aek Palakorn Achananuparp	Singapore Management University (LARC)
Fabio Celli	University of Trento
Chenhao Tan	Cornell University
Airi Lampinen	Helsinki Institute for Information Technology
Emilio Zagheni	Queens College
Ka-Yuet Liu	UCLA
Andrea Tagarelli	University of Calabria

Sponsors

We acknowledge the generous contribution of Facebook Inc., the official sponsor of the program.

Triad-Based Role Discovery
for Large Social Systems

Derek Doran[✉]

Department of Computer Science and Engineering, Kno.e.sis Research Center,
Wright State University, Dayton, OH, USA
derek.doran@wright.edu

Abstract. The *social role* of a participant in a social system conceptu-
alizes the circumstances under which she chooses to interact with others,
making their discovery and analysis important for theoretical and practical purposes. In this paper, we propose a methodology to detect such
roles by utilizing the conditional triad censuses of ego-networks. These
censuses are a promising tool for social role extraction because they capture the degree to which basic social forces push upon a user to interact
with others in a system. Clusters of triad censuses, inferred from network
samples that preserve local structural properties, define the social roles.
The approach is demonstrated on two large online interaction networks.

1 Introduction and Motivation

Why do users choose to participate and interact with others in a social system?
This fundamental question lies at the heart of many sociological studies that
examine the way people interact within a community. A *social role* is a powerful
conceptualization for reasoning about the nature of these interactions and can
be used to infer why users choose to participate. It is defined as a descriptive
label that expresses the circumstances and reasons under which a user interacts
with others in a community [1]. Social roles determine the set of interaction
partners of an ego, and have a direct affect on choose they interact with. The
concept is theoretically based on a notion of the user's *position* in a network
of interactions; how one decides to embed themselves among others, based on
who they choose to forge relationships with, can explain how they are perceived
and their ability to spread information or influence [2]. Such perceptions and
abilities factor into why and how a user interacts with others [3]. Practically, the
delineation of users by their social role facilitates the analysis and interpretation
of complex social networks by simplifying them from interactions among users to
interactions among roles [4]. It also lets researchers perform comparative studies
of different communities by comparing the structure of interactions among roles
common to many contexts. Role analysis can also help us identify the kinds of
roles (and hence users) that may become influential [5], and reveal latent social
structures within social systems [6]. Furthermore, meta-analysis of the kinds of
roles and the interactions among them can help designers create effective physical
and digital spaces for communities and organizations to grow within [7].

© Springer International Publishing Switzerland 2015
L.M. Aiello and D. McFarland (Eds.): SocInfo 2014 Workshops, LNCS 8852, pp. 130–143, 2015.
DOI: 10.1007/978-3-319-15168-7_18

Two users exhibit the same social role if they are in "regularly equivalent" positions [8]. Finding such positions, however, is analogous to searching for a k-coloring of a network with k unknown a priori (an NP-hard problem [9]). The vast scale of many online social systems thus make it infeasible to precisely identify the social roles within them. Researchers have instead turned to approximation methods that define roles based on the *structural similarity* of users' ego-networks [7,10,11]. Such methods capture the notion that users exhibiting *similar patterns of interactions with others* contribute towards and utilizes a social system in comparable ways, and thus, take on similar social roles. However, present approaches find similarities among structural ego-network features that reflect their overall shape, instead of micro-level features that better reflect a users' embedding within their peers. The resulting groups of social roles may thus consist of discordant ego-networks with few common interaction patterns and motifs. Some methods even need to apply further, potentially distorting post-processing steps [10,11] to the roles that are mined.

This paper introduces a new approach to detect the social roles users exhibit in large social systems. It evaluates the similarity of ego-networks according to their *conditional triad census*, which is a vector capturing the different types of three way relationships it is composed of. This representation holds more promise for discovering roles becacuse triad types are indicative of specific sociological forces that drive interactions at a basic level, and hence, speak closely to the social role concept. Users are ground into roles by clustering the conditional triad censuses of their ego-networks. Two large social systems are used to test our approach: an online social network and collaborative editing platform.

This paper is organized as follows: Section 2 gives an overview and assessment of the related work. Section 3 introduces the concept of a conditional triad census. Section 4 presents a method to detect roles based on conditional triad censuses. Section 5 analyzes the structure of the social roles mined from large social systems. Conclusions and directions for future work are offered in Section 6.

2   Related Research

Broadly, previous work for studying social roles in large or online social systems may be divided into two types: (i) implied role analysis; and (ii) automatic social role extraction. Implied role analysis predefines the set of social roles users in a social system are expected to exhibit based on an analyst's understanding of how interactions within it occur. For example, Nolker *et al.* predefine members of a Usenet group into the roles *leader, motivator*, and *chatter* [12] based on their own hypothesis about the nature of Usenet interactions. Golder *et al.* also studied Usenet groups but proposed a different taxonomy of roles that include *celebrity, ranter, lurker* and *troll* [13]. Gliwa *et al.* examined collections of online bloggers and defined roles such as *selfish influential user, social influential blogger*, and *standard commentator* [5]. Welser *et al.* defined the roles *substantive experts, technical editors, counter vandalism*, and *social networkers* for Wikipedia users [14]. These implied role analyses are based off of social roles that are presumed to exist without evaluating any interactions in the network first. Thus, studies may define different sets of implied roles over the same kind of online social system, inducing conflict or confusion. For example, it is unclear if the Usenet roles *leader, motivator,* and *chatter* [12] compatible with the alternative set *celebrities, ranters, lurkers, trolls,* and *newbie* [13], when one set is more suitable than the other, and if the cross-product of the two sets (e.g. *leader-celeberty; chatter-lurker,* etc.) is a valid collection of roles. Furthermore, implied role analyses search for evidence of the roles they assert to exist prior to analysis. However, one can find statistically significant evidence for almost any model when data sets are very large [15].

Instead, automatic role extraction methods lets a social system 'speak for itself' by defining roles purely based on observed data. Hautz *et al.* categorized users in an online community of jewelry designers by mapping out- and in-degree distributions and frequency of interactions to "low" and "high" levels [7]. Zhu *et al.* identify social roles across phone call networks based on ego-network clustering coefficients and mean geodesic distances between users [10]. Chan *et al.* discover roles using over fifty behavioral and structural features of users across the post/reply network of online forums [11]. However, such role extraction methods commonly use quantitative structural and behavioral features that may not speak to the nature of a user's role. For example, clustering coefficients and degree distributions quantify the totality of an ego-network's structure, even though it is the specific kinds of interaction patterns within them that reflect one's social role [3]. To overcome this limitation, we next introduce a role extraction method that represents of ego-networks by their conditional triad census.

3   Conditional Triad Census

In social network analysis, a *triad* is defined as a group of three individuals and the pairwise interactions among them [16,17]. They are the smallest sociological unit from which the dynamics of a multi-person relationship can be observed [18]. For example, third actors may act as a moderating force that modifies the relationship among two others [19]. Figure 1 captures the 36 different *conditional triads*, or ways an individual can be oriented towards two alters within a triad [20]. We define the *conditional triad census* of an ego-network is defined by a 36-element vector whose i^{th} component corresponds to the proportion of triads in the ego-network that are of type i.

Observational data has been used to develop theories that associate the configuration of a triad to underlying effects that promote specific kinds of social interactions [21,22]. For example, triad 5 has an ego that receives interactions from two alters but chooses not to reciprocate. Ego-networks largely composed of this triad suggest that the ego receives many interactions but, for possibly selfish reasons, seldom chooses to reciprocate. By summarizing how frequently each kind of triad appears, a conditional triad census can thus model the strength of the different social forces that explain the nature of an ego's interactions.

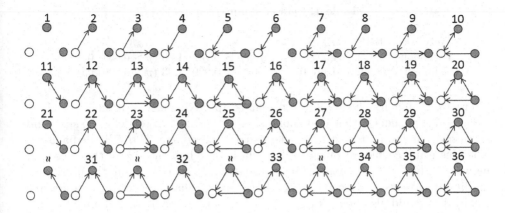

Fig. 1. Types of conditional triads

These forces, taken together, represent the circumstances and reasons why an ego participates in a social system, and thus, can explain her social role. Thus, we argue that searching for ego-networks whose conditional triad censuses are similar will lead to a meaningful grouping of users into social roles.

4   Extracting Social Roles

This section explains the process for extracting social roles based on conditional triad censuses. It first requires a careful sampling of the networks to make the computation of censuses scalable to the size of large social systems. k-means clustering is subsequently used to separate users by the social roles they exhibit.

We first introduce data from two popular online social systems, namely Facebook and Wikipedia, to demonstrate our methodology. These systems were chosen because users participate within them for different purposes, because of the distinct way interactions in the networks are defined, and because the interactions captured in our data represent strong associations. Facebook is used as a platform to informally share personal information, photos, and events with friends and family. We built its interaction network by placing a directed edge from user a to b if a posts at least one message on the wall (a collection of public messages) of b. Wikipedia is an online encyclopedia with articles that are written and edited by an open community of users. Interactions on Wikipedia are defined by the modification of content contributed by another user; we add a directed edge from a to b if a edited the text, reverted a change, or voted on approving an action to an article made by b. We built interaction networks for Facebook and Wikipedia using publicly available datasets [23,24].

Table 1 presents summary statistics for these interaction networks, illustrating how they vary in size, shape, and user behaviors. The Facebook network has the smallest number of users (46,952). The Wikipedia network is almost three times the size of Facebook, with 138,592 users and 740,397 distinct pairwise

Table 1. Dataset summary statistics

Network	$|V|$	$|E|$	$\bar{d}$	α_{in}	α_{out}	$\bar{C}$
Facebook	46,952	264,004	37.36	1.61 $(p > 0.732)$	1.68 $(p > 0.964)$	0.085
Wikipedia	138,592	740,397	10.68	1.54 $(p > 0.999)$	1.83 $(p > 0.999)$	0.038

interactions, but its clustering coefficient is approximately 55% smaller. These measurements suggest that Facebook users have a greater tendency to surround themselves in within more connected ego-networks compared to Wikipedia users. The clustering coefficient of the Wikipedia is over half the size of the Facebook network. This could be explained by users who generally limit themselves to modifying articles written by a specific group (perhaps representing a specific topic), but could also be making minor edits (e.g., spelling or grammar) across the entire site. Users may thus have a tendency to organize into clusters based on their expertise, but because they also interact with all types of other groups by making simple technical edits, the clustering coefficient of the network is suppressed.

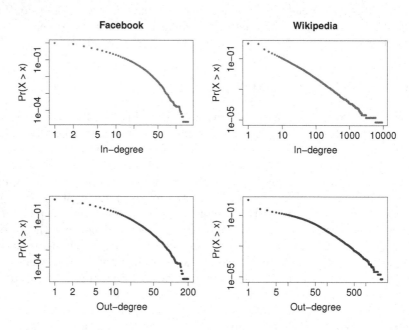

Fig. 2. Facebook (left) and Wikipedia (right) degree distributions on log-log scale

We also examine the in- and out-degree distributions of each network, presented in Figure 2, and note that they all exhibit a power-tailed shape. We test for power-law behavior using a maximum likelihood estimate approach [25] and list the resulting power-law exponent $\alpha_{in,out}$ in Table 1. We find the estimates of the power-law exponent to be very reliable $(p > 0.95)$ except for the in-degree distribution of Facebook, which may be because its range only covers two orders of magnitude. All of the distributions exhibit a similar exponent $(1.54 < \alpha < 1.83)$. A larger power-law exponent indicates that the distribution drops to zero faster in its right-tail [26], hence we are it is less likely to find a user who interacts with (receives interactions from) an unexpectedly high number of others on Wikipedia (Facebook) compared to Facebook (Wikipedia).

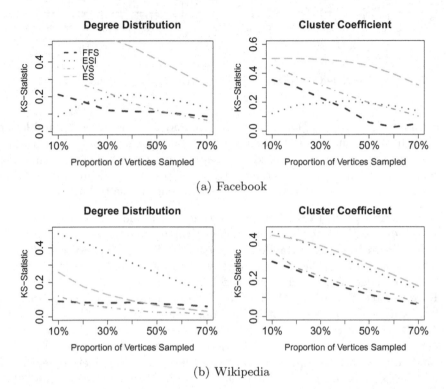

(a) Facebook

(b) Wikipedia

Fig. 3. Comparison of graph sampling methods

Network Sampling. Computing the conditional triad census of every ego-network requires us to examine the configuration of $O(\binom{|V|}{3})$ triples in the network. Given the large size of these online social systems, even advanced algorithms that compute censuses in $O(|V|^2)$ [27] or $O(|E|)$ [28] time may be impracticably slow. However, since the components of a conditional triad census is the *proportion* of a triad type in an ego-network, the census of a smaller but similarly structured ego-network would yield a similar census. We therefore explore ways to approximate conditional triad censuses in the full network from a carefully selected network sample. A sample of a network G is a new network $G_s = (V_s, E_s)$ where $V_s \subset V$, $E_s \subset E$, and $|V_s| = \phi|V|$ with $0 < \phi < 1$. The configuration of triads within an ego-network critically rely on two local structural properties, namely, its degree distribution and the users' clustering coefficient. For example, ego-networks with high degree will naturally tend to have triads with relations

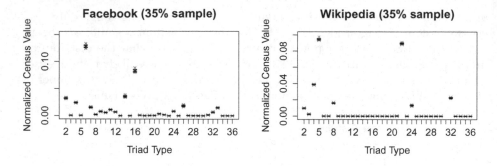

Fig. 4. Triad Role Census Sample Values with 95% Confidence Intervals

among multiple alters (e.g. triads in rows 3, 5, and 7-10 in Figure 1), and lower (higher) cluster coefficients indicate a greater proportion of open (closed) triads.

We consider four commonly used [29] graph sampling techniques for choosing V_s and E_s, and compare how well they are able to preserve the degree distribution of a users' ego-network and her clustering coefficient. These techniques are:

1. **Vertex Sampling (VS):** Let V_s be a random sample of $\phi|V|$ vertices from V and define E_s to be the set of all edges among the vertices in V_s from G.
2. **Edge Sampling (ES):** Randomly choose an edge $e = (v_1, v_2)$ from E, add it to E_s, and add v_1 and v_2 to V_s if they have not yet been added. Continue to choose edges from E until $|V_s| = \phi|V|$.
3. **Forest Fire Sampling (FFS)** [30]: Choose a random vertex v from V, randomly select $p/(1-p)$ of its outgoing edges, and add theses edges to E_s. Place every vertex incident to those added to E_s into a 'burned' set V_* and update V_s by $V_s = V_s \cup V_*$. Randomly choose a burned vertex from V_*, randomly select $p/(1-p)$ of its outgoing edges, and recursively repeat until $|V_s| = \phi|V|$. We use $p = 0.7$ based on the method author's suggestion [30].
4. **ES-i (ESI)** [29]: Randomly choose an edge $e = (v_1, v_2)$ from E and add v_1 and v_2 to V_s if they have not yet been added (note that e is not added to E_s). Continue sampling until $|V_s| = \phi|V|$. Finally, define E_s to be the set of all edges among the vertices in V_s from G.

We used the Kolmogorov-Smirnov distance metric $D = \sup_x |F_s(x) - F(x)|$ to compare how closely the degree and clustering coefficient distributions F_s of a sample taken with each method follow the distribution in the original network F. Figure 3 compares the average D of 100 samples taken at different levels of ϕ. We find that FFS does the best job at preserving both degree and clustering coefficient distributions for $\phi \geq 0.33$ on Facebook. It also best preserves the cluster coefficient distribution on Wikipedia, and performs similarly to VS in maintaining the degree distribution at $\phi \leq 0.35$. We further plot the average value of all conditional triad census components from $n = 20$ independently generated FFS samples of each network for $\phi = 0.35$ (we exclude triad 1 due to disproportionately high frequency) and their 95% confidence intervals in Figure 4. We find the sampling distribution of census proportions using FFS to have very small confidence intervals, indicating that the conditional triad censuses from any $\phi = 0.35$ sample is stable and may reasonably approximate the true censuses of the full network. We thus consider an FFS sample at $\phi = 0.35$ for the clustering analysis.

Census Clustering We use k-means clustering, a common and flexible algorithm for discovering latent groups in data [31,32], to separate users into roles. We use the ℓ^2-norm of the difference of two censuses from the FFS sampled network to measure their similarity. Since Figure 4 shows how many components are close or equal to 0, and hence are not useful dimensions to differentiate censuses, we reduce the dimensionality of our data using PCA [33]. As the scree plots in Figure 5 (a) and (b) show, we can reduce the complexity of the data from 36 to 6 and 3 dimensions for Facebook and Wikipedia, respectively, while preserving over 85% of the variation in the original data.

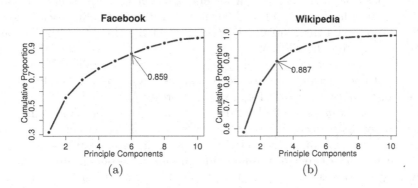

Fig. 5. Principle Component Analysis Scree Plots

k-means clustering requires us to choose the number of clusters k to divide the data into beforehand. We use the silhouette coefficient metric [34] $SC_{\hat{C}^k}$ to evaluate differences in quality between divisions of censuses into k clusters. Larger values of $SC_{\hat{C}^k}$ correspond to a superior partitioning where the distance between clusters is large and the distance between vectors within cluster is small. For a given value of k, we ran 50 k-means clusterings over the PCA-reduced data using different random initializations of the centroid positions. Figures 6 (a) and (b) plots the average $SC_{\hat{C}^k}$ of these 50 trials for $2 \leq k \leq 9$. They reveal peaks at $k = 3$ and $k = 2$ clusters of the Facebook and Wikipedia censuses, respectively.

5   Role Analysis

To study the kinds of social roles that emerge from our clustering analysis, we identified the centroid positions C_i^* of each cluster C_i and searched for the user u_i^* whose conditional triad census is located closest to C_i^*. We define u_i^* as

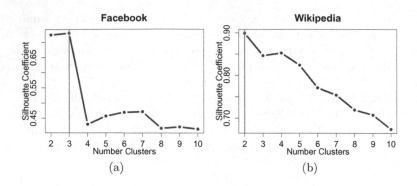

Fig. 6. k-means Clustering Silhouette Coefficients (bottom)

the "central user" of role i whose ego-network is the role's "central structure". Due to its position in the cluster, this "central structure" represents the way a prototypical user having this role embeds herself within the online social system.

Figure 7 presents the central role structures of the three social roles found on Facebook within the FFS $\phi = 0.35$ network sample. We label these roles and list the proportion of users falling under each role in Table 2. In these figures, the red node corresponds to the central user and the blue nodes are the members of their ego-network. Figure 7(a) represents a social role the majority of all Facebook users (56.6%) fall into with a central user who is embedded between many disconnected groups of others. They lie in an entrenched position critical for maintaining connectivity between the groups, and hence, act as a gatekeeper who can control the flow information from one group to another. However, given the fact that Facebook is used as a platform for social sharing, users may be embedded in such positions simply because it allows them to manage interactions within distinct groups of friends and contacts. For example, one can envision the user in Figure 7(a) to be sitting between groups that may correspond with colleagues at work, relatives, personal friends, and acquaintances. This structure may thus represent users that use the network to manage and facilitate communication with many non-overlapping social circles. By contrast, the 28.4% of users falling into the role represented by the central structure of Figure 7(b) find themselves surrounded by a web of interactions that occur between their first-degree connections. This minority of users cooperate with a variety of other interlinked colleagues participating in a free exchanged of information compared to the siloed, disconnected communities seen in Figure 7(a). participate in a single, tight-knit community of others, and thus correspond to users who use Facebook only to interact within a small group rather than as a tool for managing disconnected social circles.

Figure 7(c) corresponds to the 15% of users who are not embedded within a cohesive community or are entrenched between groups of others, but are positioned at the periphery of an active alter's neighborhood. These users thus exhibit little activity on the site, and are connected to one who prolifically shares information. This central structure thus suggests that these users are in a role

Table 2. Mined social roles

Facebook	Role label	Structure	Proportion of users
	Entrenched Member	Figure 7(a)	56.6%
	Cooperative Colleague	Figure 7(b)	28.4%
	Casual Participant	Figure 7(c)	15.0%
Wikipedia	Role label	Structure	Proportion of users
	Specialist Attractor	Figure 7(d)	89.7%
	Generalist Attractor	Figure 7(e)	10.3%

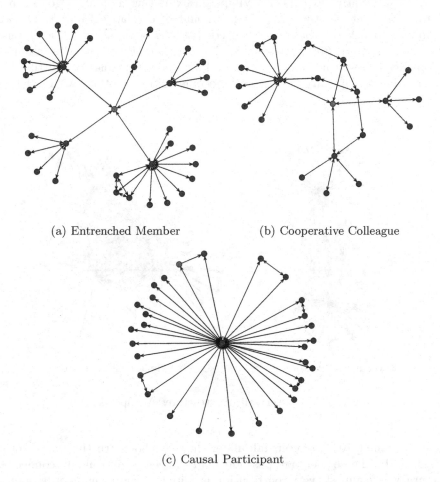

(a) Entrenched Member   (b) Cooperative Colleague

(c) Causal Participant

Fig. 7. Mined central role structures: Facebook

that is not productive to the growth or dissemination of information; they are on Facebook only to consume information from a single popular other, and hence simply participate in the network casually.

The density of the central structures of the two Wikipedia social roles shown in the bottom of Figure 8 is a result of the many different ways interactions are defined, as explained in Section 4. The social role taken on by the majority of users (89.7%) are represented by the structure in Figure 8(a). Here, we find the central user to be serving as a bridge between two sets of very active others (the two hubs) that are not strongly connected. It is interesting that these two others frequently edit articles written by many others, yet they seldom edit content added by the same individual. Such behaviors may emerge when two domain-specific specialists are only editing articles that only fall under their purview. This hypothesis is substantiated by previous research that found users labeled as substantive experts on Wikipedia exhibiting a similar ego-network structure [14]. Yet we still see a small amount of overlap between these two contributors, which may be done when editing Wikipedia articles that discuss many different topics. Since most Wikipedia articles do cover topics from multiple domains [35], we conclude that users falling under this role are contributors who write interdisciplinary articles that become edited by others with different expertise.

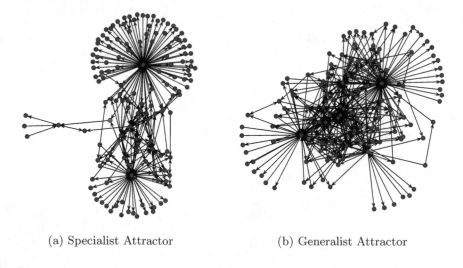

(a) Specialist Attractor   (b) Generalist Attractor

Fig. 8. Mined central role structures: Wikipedia

The remaining 10.3% of users fall under the role whose structure represented in Figure 8(b). These users are positioned in the center of a highly connected structure, where almost every contribution is edited by a large number of others. We still observe users in hub positions that make edits to the work of separate collections of others, but unlike Figure 8(a), the hubs are strongly connected to each other. A plausible explanation for such structures are generalist editors who perform basic tasks such as spelling, grammar, and hyperlink corrections to contributed content that may have also been reviewed by specialists. Such technical editors may even be edited by other technical editors, as the language and wording of an article becomes more defined, adding to the density of this structure This explanation is also compatible with past observations of Wikipedia editors [14].

6   Conclusions and Future Work

This paper presented a novel methodology to detect social roles through the use of conditional triad censuses. This data-drive detection approach was applied to two different online social systems and extracted central structures that reflect intuitive reasons why users participate on Facebook and Wikipedia. This analysis made no assumptions about the roles users exhibit in the network prior to analysis. Future work will compare roles extracted by conditional triads over the same networks but under alternative definitions of network interactions. It will also analyze the differences between cluster-based role detection and using quantitative approximations of regular equivalence [36]. The feasibility of multiple role assignments with fuzzy clustering techniques will also be explored.

References

1. Lorrain, F., White, H.C.: Structural equivalence of individuals in social networks. The Journal of Mathematical Sociology 1, 49–80 (1971)
2. Zaheer, A., Bell, G.G.: Benefiting from network position: firm capabilities, structural holes, and performance. Strategic Management Journal 26, 809–825 (2005)
3. Scott, J., Carrington, P.J.: The SAGE handbook of social network analysis. SAGE publications (2011)
4. White, H.C., Boorman, S.A., Breiger, R.L.: Social structure from multiple networks. i. blockmodels of roles and positions. American Journal of Sociology, 730–780 (1976)
5. Gliwa, B., Zygmunt, A., Koźlak, J.: Analysis of roles and groups in blogosphere. In: Proc. of the 8th Intl. Conference on Computer Recognition Systems, pp. 299–308 (2013)
6. Laniado, D., Tasso, R., Volkovich, Y., Kaltenbrunner, A.: When the wikipedians talk: network and tree structure of wikipedia discussion pages. In: Intl. Conference on Weblogs and Social Media (2011)
7. Hautz, J., Hutter, K., Fuller, J., Matzler, K., Rieger, M.: How to establish an online innovation community? the role of users and their innovative content. In: Hawaii Intl. Conference on System Sciences, pp. 1–11 (2010)
8. Luczkovich, J.J., Borgatti, S.P., Johnson, J.C., Everett, M.G.: Defining and measuring trophic role similarity in food webs using regular equivalence. Journal of Theoretical Biology 220, 303–321 (2003)
9. Khot, S.: Improved inapproximability results for maxclique, chromatic number and approximate graph coloring. In: Proc. of IEEE Syomposium on Foundations of Computer Science, pp. 600–609 (2001)
10. Zhu, T., Wang, B., Wu, B., Zhu, C.: Role defining using behavior-based clustering in telecommunication network. Expert Systems with Applications 38, 3902–3908 (2011)
11. Chan, J., Hayes, C., Daly, E.M.: Decomposing discussion forums and boards using user roles. In: Intl. Conference on Weblogs and Social Media, vol. 10, pp. 215–218 (2010)

12. Nolker, R.D., Zhou, L.: Social computing and weighting to identify member roles in online communities. In: The 2005 IEEE/WIC/ACM International Conference on Proceedings of the Web Intelligence, 2005, pp. 87–93 (2005)
13. Golder, S.A., Donath, J.: Social roles in electronic communities. Internet Research **5**, 19–22 (2004)
14. Welser, H.T., Cosley, D., Kossinets, G., Lin, A., Dokshin, F., Gay, G., Smith, M.: Finding social roles in wikipedia. In: Proc. of ACM iConference, pp. 122–129 (2011)
15. Fayyad, U.M., Piatetsky-Shapiro, G., Smyth, P., et al.: Knowledge discovery and data mining: Towards a unifying framework. In: Proc. of ACM Conference on Knowledge Discovery and DAta Mining, vol. 96, pp. 82–88 (1996)
16. Simmel, G., Wolff, K.H.: The Sociology of Georg Simmel. Macmillan Publishing Co. (1950)
17. Faust, K.: Very local structure in social networks. Sociological Methodology **37**, 209–256 (2007)
18. Davis, J.: Sociometric Triads as Multivariate Systems. Journal of Mathematical Sociology **5**, 41–59 (1977)
19. Baum, A., Shapiro, A., Murray, D., Wideman, M.V.: Interpersonal Mediation of Perceived Crowding and Control in Residential Dyads and Triads. Journal of Applied Social Psychology **9**, 491–504 (1979)
20. Burt, R.S.: Detecting role equivalence. Social Networks **12**, 83–97 (1990)
21. Holland, P., Leinhardt, S.: An Omnibus Test for Social Structure Using Triads. Sociological Methods and Research **7**, 227–256 (1978)
22. Doran, D., Alhazmi, H., Gokhale, S.: Triads, transitivity, and social effects in user interactions on facebook. In: Proc. of IEEE Intl. Conference on Computational Aspects of Social Networks, pp. 68–73 (2013)
23. Viswanath, B., Mislove, A., Cha, M., Gummadi, K.: On the evolution of user interaction in facebook. In: Proc. of 2nd ACM Workshop on Online Social Networks (2009)
24. Maniu, S., Abdessalem, T., Cautis, B.: Casting a web of trust over wikipedia: an interaction-based approach. In: Proceedings of the 20th International Conference Companion on World Wide Web, ACM, pp. 87–88 (2011)
25. Clauset, A., Shalizi, C.R., Newman, M.: Power-Law Distributions in Empirical Data. Technical report. arXiv:0706.1062v2 [physics.data-an] (2009)
26. Lipsky, L.: Queueing Theory: A Linear Algebraic Approach, 2nd edn. Springer-Verlag (2009)
27. Moody, J.: Matrix methods for calculating the triad census. Social Networks, 291–299 (1998)
28. Batagelj, V., Mrvar, A.: A subquadratic triad census algorithm for large sparse networks with maximum degree. Social Networks **23**, 237–243 (2001)
29. Ahmed, N.K., Neville, J., Kompella, R.: Network sampling: from static to streaming graphs. arXiv preprint. arXiv:1211.3412 (2012)
30. Leskovec, J., Faloutsos, C.: Sampling from large graphs. In: Proc. of ACM Conference on Knowledge Discovery and Data Mining (2006)
31. He, X., Zha, H., Ding, C.H., Simon, H.D.: Web document clustering using hyperlink structures. Computational Statistics & Data Analysis **41**, 19–45 (2002)
32. Gasch, A.P., Eisen, M.B.: Exploring the conditional coregulation of yeast gene expression through fuzzy k-means clustering. Genome Biol **3** (2002)

33. Jackson, J.E.: A User's Guide to Principal Components. John Wiley & Sons (2004)
34. Tan, P.N., Steinbach, M., Kumar, V.: Introduction to Data Mining. Addison-Wesley (2006)
35. Medelyan, O., Witten, I.H., Milne, D.: Topic indexing with wikipedia. In: Proceedings of the AAAI WikiAI Workshop, pp. 19–24 (2008)
36. Newman, M.: Networks: an introduction. Oxford University Press (2010)

A Tool-Based Methodology to Analyze Social Network Interactions in Cultural Fields: The Use Case "MuseumWeek"

Antoine Courtin[1]([⊠]), Brigitte Juanals[2], Jean-Luc Minel[2],
and Mathide de Saint Léger[2]

[1] Labex Les Passés dans le présent, Nanterre, France
antoine.courtin@mac.com
[2] MoDyCo, Université Paris Ouest Nanterre La Défense, Nanterre, France

Abstract. The goal of this paper is to present a tool-based methodology which has been developed to analyze messages sent on the Twitter social network. This methodology implements quantitative and qualitative analyses, which were benchmarked with the "MuseumWeek" event.

Keywords: Cultural mediation · Twitter · Machine learning categorization

1 Introduction

Since the nineties, in the cultural field of museums, continuous developments in information and communication technologies have affected not only modes of disseminating and displaying cultural and scientific knowledge, but also modes of communication involving audiences[10,26,27]. In this sector which is undergoing in-depth transformation, our research aims to investigate the relationship between the cultural sector and communication industries in order to reveal their operative logics. Special emphasis is placed on cultural dissemination processes and the hybridization between museum institutions and communication companies which recently entered this field.

Among large-scale socio-technical changes, one of our research field deals with the uses of digital social networks, which play an increasing role in access to information, culture and education[17]. In this context, the overall goal of this paper is to present a tool-based methodology which has been developed to analyze messages sent on the Twitter social network. To design, implement and test this methodology, we selected the European communication event MuseumWeek, which was launched in March 2014 by the American company Twitter in the European museum field. We will focus on the French coverage of this event. A comparison between French and United Kingdom user's behavior is currently underway[7]. The outline of the paper is the following. First in Section 2, we describe the entanglement between communication industries and museums. We will point out the cultural and marketing aspects which are at stake. In Section 3, we present the MuseumWeek event directives. In section 4, results from quantitative and qualitative analyses are discussed. Finally, we conclude in Section 5.

© Springer International Publishing Switzerland 2015
L.M. Aiello and D. McFarland (Eds.): SocInfo 2014 Workshops, LNCS 8852, pp. 144–156, 2015.
DOI: 10.1007/978-3-319-15168-7_19

2   The Circulation of Cultural Content on Social Networks: An Industrial and Cultural Issue for Museums

The theoretical basis of our research is situated in the sociology of culture, the sociology focused on the study on audiences, as well as in the cultural-industry sector and in the communication industries. By changing the conditions of access to cultural contents, digital technologies have destabilized the socio-economic equilibrium of museums and the way they manage the publication of information and knowledge. Stakeholders in communication industries and internet now play an increasing role within cultural industries[6]. In this respect, this operation can be considered emblematic of development strategies of Internet companies in the cultural field[2,3,13,24]. In order to apprehend the entanglement between communication industries and museums on social networks, we set up a two-year interdisciplinary study[12] which combines fieldwork and interviews of community managers in charge of communication in several French social network museums. The corpora harvested in these fields were analyzed with textual and statistical analysis tools. In the international context of multimedia convergence, stakeholders coming from the Internet market, computing and communications industry have penetrated the cultural sector of museums, relying on their platforms of goods and services. This new configuration gives rise to the renegotiation of the control of information dissemination channels between the two categories of stakeholders, namely cultural organizations and industrial companies [13]. In this respect, museums are in the same position as cultural industries [5]. An increasing number of museums have generalized the use of social networks, among other digital media and electronic artefacts [11]. Two American companies, Facebook and Twitter, have captured the lion's share of this competitive international market. Their business model is based on the attendance and the participation of audiences and organizations.

Social networks[8] have now become editorial spaces for cultural organizations but they are difficult to comprehend because they are both places to attract audiences and places to produce and share cultural content [13]. We have designed a tool-based methodology to deal with this problem. First of all, we identify and describe different categories of stakeholders (primarily community managers, who are professionals, and audiences) who interact on social networks. Second, we analyze actions and modes of interaction, such as sending tweets or retweets. Finally, we partially describe the tweet contents exchanged. In this paper, we focus on a specific use case, the MuseumWeek event.

Analysis of tweets has led to a great deal of research [29], on topics such as election forecasts [25], the stock market [4], dramatic events [15,21], and especially sentiment analysis [18,23,28], but we are not aware of research in the cultural field combining analyses of messages from professionals such as community managers and the general public.

3   The Case of the MuseumWeek Communication Event

During 2013, several museums supported by the French Ministry of Culture engaged in dialogue with Twitter in order obtain a certified account[1] or the creation of a new category to improve their visibility on this media. In February 2014, Twitter invited a group of twelve French museums (hereinafter referred to as GM 12) to a meeting in Paris to propose the framework of the MuseumWeek communication event. Twitter UK likewise organized a meeting with seventy museums in the United Kingdom for the same purpose. At the end of February, a European event, called MuseumWeek (with the generic hashtag #MuseumWeek) was designed and planned to take place during one week (from the 24th to 30th March 2014). The organizational principle of this event was simple: each day was dedicated to a theme, with a specific hashtag. All users were encouraged to use the hashtag of the day as well as the generic one in their tweets. Despite the fact that this instruction was disadvantageous to communicate within the format of 140 characters per message, 69% of users kept to this obligation. Table 1 shows day-themes and their associated French hashtags. 31 592 French tweets were automatically harvested by using the API provided by Twitter (twitter.com/search-advanced). A query searching for tweets containing the hashtag #Museumweek and sent during the week of the event was carried out. Each record harvested contains the identification of the sender, the text of the tweet and the day-of-issue. We completed these data by analyzing the profile of the tweet accounts. This enabled us to categorize all the accounts; 103 institutional accounts (CI) were manually identified based on our knowledge of the cultural field and 7 746 accounts (OA) were automatically categorized (table 2) using Natural Language Processing techniques such as regular expressions and Python scripts to analyze the profile written by the account owner. It must be pointed out that we predefined these categories and that each account is assigned to only one category. Two kinds of analysis were conducted on this corpus: the first one focused on attendance, and the second on the content of tweets.

Table 1. Themes and hashtags of the MuseumWeek event

Day	Theme	Hashtag
Monday	Discovering behind the scenes	#CoulissesMW
Tuesday	Checking our knowledge	#QuizzMW
Wednesday	Sharing our coup de coeur	#LoveMW
Thursday	Free imagination	#ImagineMW
Friday	Taking time to share	#QuestionMW
Saturday	Appreciating museum architecture building	#ArchiMW
Sunday	You are the Artist	#CreaMW

---

[1] For more on certified accounts on Twitter : https://support.twitter.com/articles/269158-faq-sur-les-comptes-certifies.

4   Analysis of Interactions

Table 2. Sub-categories of senders of other accounts (OA)

Generic categories	Specific categories	Comments
Other accounts (OA) 7746 accounts	Professionals of cultural organizations (PIC)	Museum workers (community managers, curators)
	Museogeeks (Msk)	Neologism to describe digital enthusiasts in museums
	Private individuals (Cdp)	
	Legal persons (PM)	Newspapers, Non profit-making associations
	Non registered cultural heritage organizations (NRIG)	

4.1   Quantitative Analysis on Attendance

Global Analysis

Quantitative analysis attendance provides several important results. First, the attendance curve (figure 1) declines regularly (36%) from the beginning, with two rebounds, one on the theme Sharing our coup de coeur, which is also the peak of attendance, and the other on the architecture of museum buildings. It should be noted that these themes are those which concern the individual accounts most. This fact is confirmed by the categorized curve (figure 1) which shows a flat curve for the CI and PM accounts and a two-peak curve for PIC and CdP accounts.

The second result concerns the distribution of the number of tweets sent by users. Figures 2,3 and 4, where tweets sents are grouped by 20 from 1 to 320, shows a marked difference in the practices of CI and OA accounts. CI accounts (103) sent 6188 tweets and OA (7746) sent 25404 tweets. Most importantly, the kind of tweets are very different (cf. figure 2). CI accounts are what we call authors, that is to say they wrote their tweets, while OA accounts are what we call relay runners, which means that they retweeted an original tweet. It must be pointed out that Re-tweet is a functionality of the Twitter interface software.

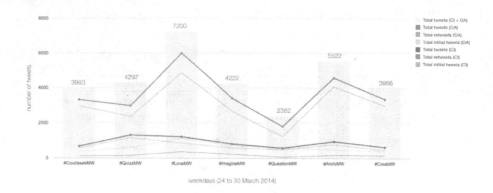

Fig. 1. Attendance and categorized curves

The third finding concerns the number of tweets sent by account. 64 % of OA accounts sent one tweet, while the same proportion of CI accounts sent 55 tweets.

In order to assess the participants level of commitment in the writing of contents, we analysed more thoroughly the behaviour of each account. To achieve this, we computed three indicators as follows (where NOTW is the number of original tweets sent by a user; NRETW is the number of retweets sent by a user; NTWINIT is the total number of original tweets; NTRETW is the total number of original retweets).

IPG   = (NOTW+NRETW) / (NTWINIT+NRETW) : computes the score of global participation of an account;

IPL   = NOTW / NTWINIT : computes the score of an account as author;

IPR   = NRETW / NTRETW : computes the score of an account as relay runner.

The ranking of all the accounts for the IPG indicator shows that the first three are OA accounts, followed by almost all the CI accounts. The first ten IPL are CI accounts, and among the first ten IPR, seven are OA and three are PM. In a nutshell, while the participation of individual users in the event was high, their commitment was relatively weak. As table 2 shows, the OA population is complex but specific categories help to identify trends. Hence, figure 5 shows two major categories: loyalty towards the event (those who tweeted with whole hashtags) but also the twenty most active senders. Although often decried [9], one can note the presence of two robots (1590 tweets, 100% of retweets, 1617 followers) which played an intermediary role between the various countries involved in the event.

Specific Analysis of Museums' Participation

Among the 103 institutional accounts, twelve museums, called GM12 here (see section 3), were the co-founding members of the MuseumWeek event. Consequently, we decided to study their communicational practices during this event

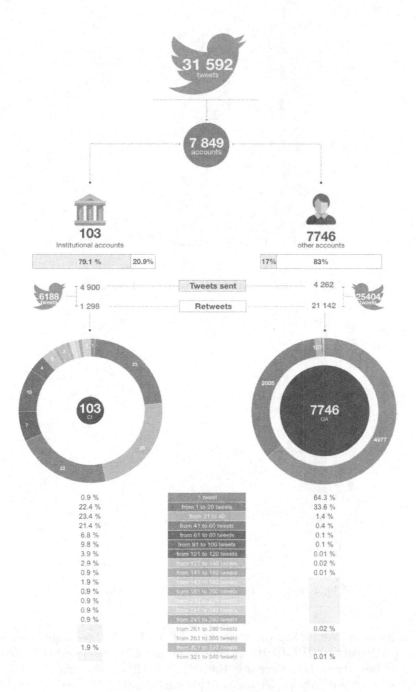

Fig. 2. Distribution of number of tweets sent

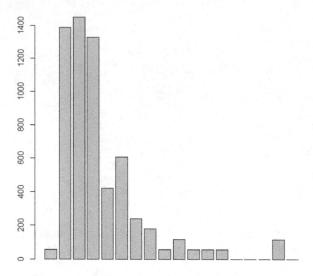

Fig. 3. Barplot of all tweets sent by CI accounts

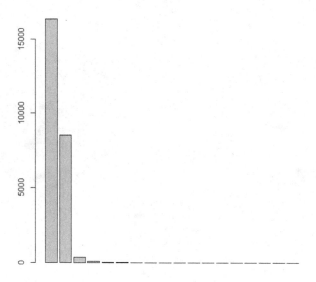

Fig. 4. Barplot of all tweets sent by OA accounts

more thoroughly. We ranked the members of GM12 with three indicators, IPG (global participation), IPL (participating as author of tweets) and IPR (participating as relay runner). As regards the IPG and IPL indicators, the study of ranking of twelve museums (let us call this ranking RIPG) shows three partitions: a top partition composed of 8 members of the GM12 characterized by strong participation; a small partition of two members located at the end of the

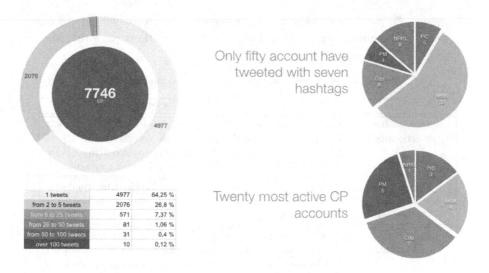

Fig. 5. Zoom on characteristics of OA accounts

first quartile; and a third partition, also composed of two members, located at the bottom of the ranking. As it was difficult to explain this result by intrinsic characteristics of the museums themselves (historical, fine arts, modern art, etc.), we hypothesized that the profile of the community manager (CM) could be an explanation, and the interviews with CMs confirmed this hypothesis. As regards the IPR indicator, the study of ranking of twelve museums (let us call this ranking RIPR) shows no real pattern and no correlation with the previous ranking. Four members of GM12 are at the top of the ranking, but the Centre Pompidou which is a leader in RIPG is no longer present. The Grand Palais museum which is at the bottom of the RIPG ranking is in the first third of the RIPR ranking. The analysis of museums participation allows us to highlight their publishing policies. In this field, two conceptions of the publishing policies conducted by museums emerge. This division reflects different conceptions of authorship concerning the publication of contents.

On the one hand, a selective policy of control of the contents of the tweets sent by the museum, which is reluctant to relay content of which it is not the author. And, on the other hand, a policy of display or more exactly of presence, whatever the kind of messages sent.

4.2   Content Analysis of Tweets

The goal of this analysis is to go beyond the quantification of the stream of tweets (see section 4.1) and to analyze their contents. As the size of the dataset precluded human analysis, a machine learning approach was chosen. Many studies using this kind of approach have been published [1,14,19,20,23], but the majority of them focus on the polarity of messages whereas we needed to categorize the content of a message more precisely. A linguistic analysis [22] carried out on 800 tweets of the initial corpus provided a set of annotations (cf. table 3).

Table 3. Set of annotations for automatic classification

Class	Comment	Example of tweets
Interaction between accounts	A user sends a tweet to one or several specific recipients	@jeanfidu94 Oui, vous pouvez les retrouver sur http://t.co/WcoRmjabFd #CreaMW #MuseumWeek
Encouraging contributions to contents	tweet calling for a reac-tion, asks a question	#LoveMW Et vous, quel est votre meilleur souvenir d'exposition au @MuseeOrsay ?
Promoting a museum	tweet promoting a muse-um, giving information about a feature of the museum, announcing an exhibition	#QuizzMW Connaissez-vous les Ateliers du 12 ? Le nouvel espace pdago-gique de la #MEP : http://t.co/eF3Ny5aL6j #MuseumWeek
Expressing an experience	Tweet telling a story, giving an opinion, sharing feelings	J'ai aussi un coup de coeur pour @Le_Museum et sa grande galerie ! #LoveMW http://t.co/tkNgkx0PBL

Then three researchers, one linguist, one sociologist and one specialized in cultural mediation manually annotated 553 original tweets, that is to say without any retweets, to build the training set for the classifier. They also defined features used by the classifier by studying 173 tweets and by identifying the most frequent tokens. Finally, the 30 features used for classification are linguistic (mainly lexis), semiotic (smileys), positional and tweet-specific (interaction between accounts). For example, clitic pronouns (vous, nous, je, moi, etc.) are used to identify "expressing an experience", as well as lexical markers such as (aimer, beau, plaisir, trsor, amour, etc). Some specific data were also used: first, metadata about accounts such as CI or OA; second, specific marks [13] such as URL links, the modified tweet (MT) mark and the number of hashtags in the tweet. Note however that the annotation assigned to the tweet by the classifier is the result of a probability calculation.

The classifier [22] combines Naive Bayes and Vector Support Machine algorithms and performs a multi-label classification [16]. This kind of classification was necessary because the linguistic analysis showed that a tweet could belong to two classes. For example a tweet such as "@ioster #QuestionMW On va tudier la question ! En attendant n'hsitez pas profiter des magnifiques collections: @PBALille @MHNLille..." could be classified as both "Interaction between accounts" and "Promoting a museum". These two algorithms, Naive Bayes and Vector Support Machine, were applied on the corpus and their results were then compared. If the same class was assigned by both, it was kept, otherwise none of the classes were assigned.

Several bench-marks showed that this method gives the best F0.5 measure, which puts more emphasis on precision than recall [16].

Our classifier gave an F0.5 measure which varied between 0.67 and 0.53, depending on the partition of the corpus being analyzed. These scores are slightly lower than those of the state of the art (approximately 0.70) but it should be pointed out that our set of classes is larger. The Kappa indicator, with three jurors, was between 0.76 and 0.41, depending on the classes compared, which can be considered rather good. Note that several classes can be assigned to the same tweet (they are not mutually exclusive), but rarely more than two, which explains why the sum of percentages may be greater than 100%. Table 4 shows the results obtained on the corpus without retweets (9 511 tweets). The largest class (41%) is Interaction between accounts. This result shows that the social network Twitter was largely used by the users as a way to interact with professionals and with each other, which was one of the goals of the founders of the MuseumWeek event.The score of the second class Promoting a museum (39%), very close to the first one, confirms the marketing trend evolution of some museums. By contrast, the cultural mediation objective, which is partially measured by the class Encouraging contributions to contents (17%) was poorly represented.

Table 4. Percentage of classes in several corpora

	Interaction between accounts	Promoting a museum	Expressing an experience	Encouraging contributions to content	Not classified
Corpus of initial tweets (9511)	41%	39%	33%	17%	2.3%
Muse du Quai Branly (234)	23%	0%	64%	12%	0%
Centre Pompidou (291)	28%	0%	59%	10%	6%
Cit des Sciences (208)	32%	0%	62%	20%	12%

In order to analyze the communication practices of the community managers, the classifier was applied on three specific partitions of the corpus (Table 4): one composed of tweets sent by the Muse du Quai Branly, the second by the Centre Pompidou and the third by the Cit des Sciences. These three museums were chosen because they are the top three leaders (see section 4.1) of the event. The contrast with the global corpus is striking.

First of all, none of three community managers of these museums sent a tweet to promote his/her museum. Second, a mean of 62% (from 59% to 64%) of their tweets aimed at Expressing an experience. Third, there was a slight difference (from 23% to 32%) in communication practices between them concerning the Interaction between accounts, but far behind the score for the whole corpus (41%). Finally, three community managers sent few tweets, in line with all users, for Encouraging contributions to contents, which showed that they privileged exchanges and community animation rather than cultural mediation.

5   Conclusion

This paper has presented a framework for the analysis of a social network event in the cultural heritage field illustrated with an experiment on the MuseumWeek event co-organized by Twitter and a group of museums supported by the French Ministry of Culture.

First, we would like to summarize our tool-based methodology to analyze social network interaction. In the first step, based on a Tuser taxonomy built by experts in the studied field, all the tweet accounts are categorized. As the size of the dataset precluded human analysis, we propose to used NLP tools (regular expressions and more sophisticated scripts if necessary) to automatically categorize accounts. In the second step, a quantitative analysis of the attendance stream is carried out in order to compute temporal trends and user practices. We propose to focus on two specific Twitter practices, which we will call author and relay-runner. Thanks to the Tuser taxonomy, it is possible to study specific segments of users. In the third step, we propose to categorize the content of tweets. First of all, it is necessary to build another taxonomy Tcontent, based on linguistic analysis and on lexicometric tools (lexical frequency or tf*idf score). Here again, as the size of the dataset precluded human analysis, we propose to use machine learning tools, especially multi-label classification. The last step is the classical step of interpreting findings given the assumptions and theoretical framework of the study.

Within this methodology, this paper focuses on completing steps 2 and 3. A multi-label classifier was built in order to partially analyze the content of a large corpus of tweets.

It is interesting to compare our results with different opinions expressed during a debriefing meeting organized by the French Ministry of Culture and Twitter in May 2014 which was attended by around 60 community managers who participated in the MuseumWeek event. Both representatives from the French Ministry and Twitter expressed their satisfaction with the successful performance and announced a second edition for 2015 with some adjustments, whereas community managers were more cautious.

References

1. Agarwal, A., Xie, B., Vovsha, I., Rambow, O., Passonneau, R.: Sentiment analysis of twitter data. In: ACL, Workshop on Language in Social Media, pp. 30–38 (2011)
2. Ballé, C.: Mussées, changement et organisation. Culture et Musées **2**, 17–33 (2003)
3. Benhamou, F.: L'economie de la culture. La Découverte, Paris (2000)
4. Bollen, J., Mao, H., Zeng, X.: Election Forecasts with Twitter: How 140 Characters Reflect the Political Landscape. Journal of Computational Science **2–1**, 1–8 (2011)
5. Bouquillion, P., Miège, B., Moeglin, P.: L'industrialisation des biens symboliques. Les industries créatives en regard des industries culturelles. PUG, Grenoble (2013)
6. Bouquillion, P.: Concentration, financiarisation et relations entre les industries de la culture et industries de la communication. Revue française des SIC (2012)
7. Courtin, A.: Information visualization and data collection: a challenge to analyze the actions of cultural institution professionals on social networks. In: Museums and the Web 2015 (submitted 2015)
8. Ellison, N., Boyd, D.: The Oxford Handbook of Internet Studies. Oxford University Press (2007)
9. Ferrara, E., Varol, O., Davis, C., Menczer, F., Flammini, A.: The Rise of social Bots. Tech. Rep. 1407.5225, arXiv (2014)
10. Grinter, R.E., Aoki, P.M., Hurst, A.S.M.H., Thornton, J.D., Woodruff, A.: Revisiting the visit: Understanding how technology can shape the museum visit. In: Association for Computing Machinery Conference on Computer Supported Cooperative Work, pp. 146–155. ACM press, New Orleans, LA (2002)
11. Johnson, L., al.: The NMC Horizon Report: 2012, 2013, Museum Edition. The New Media Consortium, Austin, Texas (2012)
12. Juanals, B.: Médiation culturelle et circulation des connaissances à l'ère numérique: information institutionnelle, pratiques éditoriales, pratiques informationnelles et dispositifs socio-techniques. Tech. rep., University Paris Ouest Nanterre La Défense, Labex "Les passés dans le présent (2013)
13. Juanals, B.: Museums as Reterritorialization Spaces in the Digital Age: between Knowledge Publishing and Institutional Communication. Journal of Inclusive Museum p. 8 (Accepted 2014)
14. Kouloumpis, E., Wilson, T., Moore, J.: Twitter sentiment analysis: The good the bad and the OMG! In: fifth international conference on weblogs and social media (2011)
15. Lin, Y., Keegan, B., Margolin, D., Lazer, D.: Rising tides or rising stars?: Dynamics of shared attention on Twitter during media events. CoRR abs/1307.2785(5), 127–165 (2013)
16. Makhoul, J., Scwartz, R., Weischdel, R.: Performance Measures for Information Extraction. In: DARPA Broadcast News Workshop, pp. 249–252 (1999)
17. Millerand, F., Proulx, S., Rueff, J.: Web social. Mutation de la communication. Presses de l'université du québec edn (2010)
18. O'Connory, B., Balasubramanyan, R., Routledge, B., Smithy, A.: From Tweets to Polls : Linking Text Sentiment to Puvlic Opinion Time Series. In: 48th International AAI Conference on Weblogs and Social Media (2010)
19. Pak, A., Paroubek, P.: Twitter as a corpus for sentiment analysis and opinion mining. In: LREC 2010, pp. 1320–1326 (2010)
20. Pang, B., Lee, L.S.V.: Thumbs up? Sentiment Classification Using machine Learning Techniques. In: ACL-02 Conference on Empirical Methods in Natural language Processing, pp. 79–86 (2002)

21. Sakaki, T., Okazaki, M., Matsuo, Y.: Earthquake Shakes Twitter Users : Real-time Event Detection by Social Sensors. In: 19th International Conference on World Wide Web, pp. 851–860 (2010)
22. Seminck, O.: Prototype d'un Classifieur de Tweets à Buts Communicatifs. Tech. rep., University Paris Ouest Nanterre La Défense (2014)
23. Thelwall, M., Buckley, K., Paltoglou, C.D., Kappas, A.: Sentiment Strength Detection for the Social Web. Journal of the American Society for Information Science and Technology **63**(1), 163–176 (2010)
24. Tobelem, J.M.: De l'approche marketing dans les musées. Culture et Musées **2**, 49–70 (1992)
25. Tumasjan, A., Sprenger, O., Sandne, R.P., Welpe, M.: Election Forecasts with Twitter: How 140 Characters Reflect the Political Landscape. Social Science Computer Review **29–4**, 402–418 (2011)
26. Watkins, J., Russo, A.: New media design for cultural institutions. In: Proceedings of the 2005 conference on Designing for User eXperience. AIGA: American Institute of Graphic Arts (2005)
27. Weilenmann, A., Hillman, T., Jungselius, B.: Instagram at the museum: Communicating the museum experience through social photo sharing. In: Proceedings of the SIGCHI Conference on Human Factors in Computing Systems, CHI 2013, pp. 1843–1852. ACM, New York, NY, USA (2013). http://doi.acm.org/10.1145/2470654.2466243
28. Welfare, T., Lampos, V., Cristiani, N.: Effects of the Recession on Public Mood in the UK. In: 21st International Conference Companion on World Wide Web, pp. 1221–1226 (2012)
29. Zimmer, M., Proferes, J.: A topology of Twitter research: disciplines, methods, and ethics. Journal of the American Society for Information Science and Technology **66–3**, 250–261 (2014)

Detecting Presence of Personal Events in Twitter Streams

Smitashree Choudhury[(✉)] and Harith Alani

Knowledge Media Institute, The Open University, Milton Keynes, UK
smitashree.choudhury@open.ac.uk

Abstract. Social media has become a prime place where many users announce their personal events, such as getting married, graduating, or having a baby, to name a few. It is common for users to post about such events and receive attention from their friends. Such events are often sought after by social platforms to enrich users timelines, to create life-log videos, to personalize ads, etc. One important step towards accurately identifying an event is learning the signals that indicate the presence of such events. In this paper we generate an event/non-event classification model using a mixture of content and interaction features. We experiment with two categories of interaction features; activity, and attention, and reached a Precision of 56 % and 83 % respectively, demonstrating the higher importance of attention features in personal event detection.

Keywords: Life event detection · User attention · Social web

1 Introduction

Surveys show that currently 74% of adult users of the Web use social networking sites[1]. Such social platforms are quickly becoming digital archives of personal lives, where users often store, share, and access personal content[2]. Attention has been on the rise by industries and researchers towards using such life-logs for other services, such as generating life videos, scrapbooks [4], or personalized advertising [1]

One core aspect for such applications is the identification of events from the personal social life stream of users. Some of the challenges in identifying such events include finding out when the event took place, whether the event is a personal one or not, the type of the event, how memorable or interesting it is to the user, etc. Identifying such events from social media content is non-trivial mainly because of its informal linguistic style. For example, the post *"3 more days for my wedding"* gives a clear indication of a personal event that is taking place in 3 days. However, identifying events from posts such as *"Three more days for the big day ? or Congratulations!"* is more challenging, and needs additional information on context, time, target, etc.

---

[1] http://www.pewinternet.org/fact-sheets/social-networking-fact-sheet/

© Springer International Publishing Switzerland 2015
L.M. Aiello and D. McFarland (Eds.): SocInfo 2014 Workshops, LNCS 8852, pp. 157–166, 2015.
DOI: 10.1007/978-3-319-15168-7_20

Many existing studies on event detection from text streams are focused on detecting general public events, such as sports, social and political protests, natural disasters , etc. Such approaches rely on the fact that the same event is reported by a large number of users, and within a rather narrow time frame. In this paper, we are concerned with the identification of the occurrence of personal events, from the posts stream of an individual user. To this end, we investigate using localised interaction features to generate a model for detecting salient life events from a user's timeline.

We attempt this by identifying various user centric attributes reflecting their activity patterns, as well as the attention they receive from their immediate social network (friends and followers). Events discovery normally follow two stages; (1) identifying the moments (time periods when an event is detected), and (2) identifying the type of the event (e.g. birthday, marriage). In this paper we are mainly concerned with step 1. Step 2, which we tackled in [5] is out of the scope of this paper. To show the feasibility of our approach, we apply our method to all the tweets of 250 users. Contributions of this paper are:

– Propose an approach for detecting the presence of personal events from the Twitter streams of individual users
– Investigate the use of non-textual features in personal event detection.
– Compare the value of activity and attention features in identifying personal events.

The rest of this paper is organised as follows. Section 2 describes related work, followed by Section 3 that describes our dataset and features. Section 4 details the experiment on event detection followed by discussion in section 5. Finally we conclude with a brief summary in section 6.

2   Related Work

To the best of our knowledge, very little work has been done on personal life event detection from social media content. Previously we experimented with using supervised model to detect five types of common personal events from a collection of tweets from random users[5]. One similar study was done by Eugenio and colleagues [6], where they used supervised models to detect employment and marriage events, using unigrams, retweet history, and semantic role labels. They found unigrams to be the most effective for detecting these two event types. This paper aims to detect events of both categories (known and unknown) using simple interaction features only. Authors from [14] worked on similar study like [5]. to detect life events such as marriage, vacation, child birth so for personalised service offerings depending on customers situational context.

There is much research on detecting various kinds of public events from social media, such as earthquakes [7], elections [9], news events [8], and generic social events[10]. Authors in [7] were able to calculate the epicentre of an earthquake by analysing Tweets and their time delays. Benson and colleagues [3] used a graphical model to join multiple Tweets to detect concert events using a city calendar as a guide. Another study by Agarwal and colleagues [15] detected local events such as a factory fire and a labour strike from Twitter streams using a combination of location dictionaries and event correlations across multiple tweets.

Event detection from social media was not limited to text. For example, Chen and Roy [11] discovered social events from Flickr photos by using user tags, time, and geographical coordinates. Firan et al. [12] explored tags, title and description to classify pictures into event categories. Some of the popular approaches used for event detection are spatio-temporal segmentation [16], burst analysis in word signals[13], clustering as well as topic detection techniques. Our work differ from the above in that we focus on detecting the presence of personal events from the Twitter stream of individual users rather than from a time period with multiple users (i.e, aggregation of tweets from many users) as in most public event detection tasks.

Prior works [5][6][14] on personal life event detection mainly focused on lexical features to detect and classify list of pre-determined events. We differ from them as our target is to detect both common and not so known life events, for e.g. a highly controversial publication from a writer or journalist may not be considered as one of the important life event for normal people. Hence our objective is to utilise features uniform to all users but differs in degree.

3   Experimental Design

3.1   What Is a Personal Event?

We are mainly concerned with those events affecting individuals life. Examples of such events include common events such as birthday, marriage, new job or death of family members or infrequent events such as professional achievement. For example, an award ceremony can be treated as public event but at the same time, it can be regarded as personal event for the award winner. A list of personal life events are listed in [17].

3.2   Dataset

Our dataset consists of more than 500000 tweets from 250 users over 4 years starting from 2010. Metadata of each tweet was collected, including its date, time, hashtag, mention, number of favourites, number of re-tweets, and a status code to indicate if a tweet is original or a re-tweet. In this preliminary work, we started with a small dataset and selected these 250 users as they are included in one of the author'sTwitter timeline.

In addition to collecting the tweets created by the users themselves, we also collected tweets where the user is mentioned, replied to, or re-tweeted by other users. We use such information to reflect the amount of interaction and attention a user receives on Twitter at any given time. Out of the 250 users, we filtered out those who have less than 30 tweets or less than 10 days of activity, resulting in 220 users and their English tweets. user demographic is mixed (male- 56% and female=44%) age range spans from early 20s to 60+. User set included journalists, academics, scientists,politician, activists, students. In his work, we have not explored any user specific content reporting style e.g. wether different users report different type of content on Twitter, which can be an interesting aspect to explore in our future work.

3.3   Ground Truth Annotation

To the best of our knowledge, there are no external gold standards available for personal events from social media streams. To this end, we manually annotated the twitter streams of 100 randomly selected users with personal events, if they exist. The annotation was done by the lead author, and verified by an external annotator (female, 31 years old) who is working in IT sector and well versed with social media use . The basic guideline for annotation is to read a day's content for each user and decide any significant event occurred during the day. The annotation process produced 43 events from 39 users. These events were of a variety of types, such as marriage (3), job promotions (6), new job (5), physical attack (1), passing an exam (6), health test (2), resignation (3), award nominations (7), book release(3), death of near relatives (2) and Miscellaneous (5). The days of these events were labeled as of class Event. We also randomly selected "non-event" days from the dataset. Annotated data ratio between event and non-event records is 1:3 (43 event days to 150 non-event days). The annotation setting did not allow for the calculation of inter annotator agreement. However, in future work we plan to use crowdsourcing to enhance and expand our annotation task.

3.4   Classification of Personal Events

Given a user's timeline, segmented into N time intervals, our objective is to classify each interval as eventful or not, i.e., if the day contains any significant personal event related to the concerned user or not. Accordingly, we extracted the following features:

Feature Engineering. Tweets were tokenized to extract meta features such as hashtags, tokens, and links. We extracted multiple features concerning the activity and attention of a user. We also computed the sentiment score for each tweet. Activity Features measure users activity in a single day:

- Number of tweets per day: Total number of tweets created by the user in a day.
- Number of retweets per day: Total numbers of re-tweets made by the user.
- Number of replies per day: Total number of replies made by the user to other users.
- Number of mentions per day: Total number of mentions.

Attention features (attention is defined as "Notice taken of someone or something" in terms of reply and retweets) reflect how many times the user is addressed/talked about by other users on a given day:

- Retweeted: Number of retweets received by the user is computed by adding the retweets counts of all the tweets created by the user on the same day.
- Replied: Number of replies received by the user from other users per day.
- Mentioned: Number of mentions made for the user within a day (excluding RTs and replies).

After computing the features, we created time series for each user based on individual features. The aim is to enable the classification of events from tweets during specified time intervals. The assumption is that important personal events are more likely to be reported over multiple tweets (including tweets, replies, retweets). The dataset is then divided into user specific buckets, where each bucket is a collection of a 1 day interval. Accordingly, each user is represented by 7 time series data (4 activity features, 3 attention features) corresponding to their timeline period. Assuming T_c as the current time, time series of feature f is written as a sequence:

$$S_f = [s_f(1), s_f(2), ..s_f(t)] \tag{1}$$

$s_f(t)$ at each sample point t is given by the relative frequency of the feature which is computed by :

$$s_f(t) = \frac{\text{frequency of feature (e.g. tweets) for the day (t)}}{\text{Total feature score(e.g. tweets)}} \tag{2}$$

Feature Statistics. Tweet volume per user follows a familiar skewed distribution (fig.1), while most users tweeted 1-3 tweets per day (Mean=3.26 and SD=4.36) few users were very active (more than 25 tweets per day). On the other hand, attention is limited compared to activity. The average number of days of attention is significantly lower than the number of activity days of a user (mean=58.62/135.53). This highlights that not all users activities on Twitter were generating attention.

4   Experiment and Evaluation

In this section we compare the performance of the proposed approach in classifying daily sets of tweets into those about a personal-event from those that are not, then analyse the relevance of individual features. As described in the feature engineering section, we consider that the tweets, re-tweets, and replies posted by the user to reflect her activity levels, whereas the replies, re-tweets, and mentions she receives from others are reflections of attention. We used our ground truth annotations to evaluate the classifier, with 5-fold cross-validation. That is, the annotated instances are randomly split into 5 subsets: 4 subsets were used to

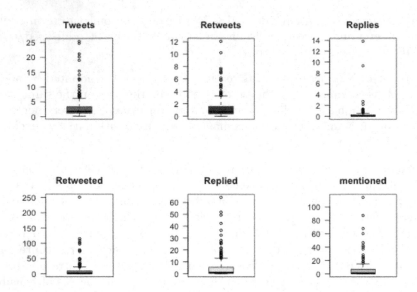

Fig. 1. Distribution of activity and attention features in the dataset

train a classifier and the remaining subset used as test data. The final result is averaged over 5 iterations so that each subset can be used as a test case once. We built three classifiers, Activity-model (AM), Attention model (ATM) and a Hybrid model (HM) which combines both activity and attention into a single model. AM, ATM, and HM take activity, attention, all features respectively, of users on any single day and classify it as event or non-event. We use AUC (i.e. Area under the ROC curve), Precision, Recall and overall Accuracy scores for evaluating the models.

AM gave 54.28% (AUC=53% and Precision=66%) classification accuracy by the best performing classification algorithm (NB) while most of the other learning techniques scored either close to the baseline (53.12% ZeroR where the no-event majority class is selected) or even lower than the baseline method. The average accuracy score over four different classifiers is (46.2%) (table 1). This leads to the conclusion that users activity alone is not a good indicator of personal life events.

Table 1. Classification scores for Activity Model (AM)

Classification	Precision	Recall	AUC	Accuracy
ZeroR	42%	52%	43%	42.85%
NB	66%	23%	41%	54.28%
LR	25%	11%	27%	40%
J48 / RF	39%	42%	42%	42.85%
SVM	40%	11%	47%	48.57%

The second model, ATM, performed better with a score of 83.87% classification accuracy (table 2) We computed with multiple classification algorithms with
different parameters. Each classifier classified the data 3 times and averaged the
results. Two best performing techniques are logistic regression and Nave Bayes
(NB), closely followed by SVM. The AUC under the best performing classification is 81% for ATM. It gave us on average 20 false negatives (FN) and 5 false
positive (FP) and the error rate for the five-fold cross validation is 22%. Moreover, the classifier is linear and uses only three interactive attributes to classify
the day as event or non-event.

Table 2. Comparisons of various classification techniques for ATM model

Classification	Precision	Recall	AUC	Accuracy
ZeroR	39%	55%	47%	55.55%
NB	88%	61%	81%	81.64%
LR	90%	69%	76%	83.87%
J48 / RF	75%	61%	65%	70.96%
SVM	88%	61%	74%	80.64%

NB, SVM and LR come with high precision (88% to 90%) compared to the
tree based algorithms such as J48 and Random Forest (P=75%). One measure of
the quality of a binary classifier is Mathews correlation coefficient (MCC) which
is computed using the results of the confusion matrix:

$$\frac{((P.N) - (p.n))}{\sqrt{(P+p)(P+n)(N+p)(N+n)}} \tag{3}$$

Where, P is true positives and N is true negatives, p is false positives and n
is for false negatives and the range is between [-1,1], a value of 1 reflects a perfect classification (e.g. p+n=0) and a negative correlation value of -1 (P+N=0)
reflects a completely useless model. The MCC in our case is 0.71 indicating a
reasonably good classification quality.

The final model is the Hybrid Model (HM), which takes into account both
the activity and attention features and presents a day d_i as a vector of seven
features for classification. As with previous two cases, we trained and tested
the model using various learning algorithms and the top four results are shown
in table 3. Results show that the HM model performed less than ATM, with
the highest classification accuracy reaching just over 77% from simple logistic
regression. The error rate from the five-fold cross validation is higher than the
attention model (25% compared to 22% of ATM).

The recall-precision curve in figure 2, shows that when recall is about 60%,
precision peaks (close to 90%) and gradually declines to 45% towards a total
recall score.

4.1 Feature Regression Analysis

In this section we analyze and compare the effectiveness of our features individually on event presence classification. To save space, in table 4, we only show

Table 3. Shows the scores from multiple classifiers for the hybrid feature based model
HM

Classification	Precision	Recall	AUC	Accuracy
ZeroR	54%	51%	43%	51.42%
NB	83%	66%	75%	76.66%
LR	81%	72%	74%	77.14%
J48 / RF	81%	60%	69%	73.33%
SVM	92%	33%	66%	66.66%

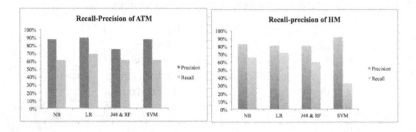

Fig. 2. Recall and Precision score for ATM and HM models

the results for the HM model, which uses all our features. Here we incremen-
tally remove one feature from the learning model and re-classify the data and
recorded the difference in performance at each step.

Table 4. Losses and gains in performance due to the absence of specific features in the
model (first column indicates removal of that feature from the model) and compared
against the best classifier (Logistic regression)

Features	Accuracy	Recall	Precision	AUC
HM with all features	77.14%	72%	81%	74%
-Mentioned (attn.)	-14.29	-.18	-.15	-.06
-Replied (attn.)	0	0	0	-.03
-Retweeted (attn.)	+2.86	+.05	+.01	+.05
-Mention (act.)	+0.14	-.06	-.01	-.03
-Replies (act.)	+0.14	-.06	-.01	+.02
-Retweets (act.)	-8.57	-.18	-.05	-.05
-Tweets (act.)	0	0	0	0

Results suggest that for the HM model, the removal of mentioned feature
results in a loss of more than 14 points in accuracy (18.5%), while the absence
of Retweeted results in a positive gain in accuracy (+4%), and around +0.7%
for Recall and AUC. It is interesting to see that the number of Tweets does not

seem to have any impact on classification, which once again shows that tweeting activity is not an indication of the presence of personal events.

5   Discussion and Future Work

This work was mainly concerned with learning the value of attention and activity features in classifying event and non-event tweet sets. The type of events considered in this work is personal events. Next we plan to run the same analysis to classify public or general events, to see if the models and features perform any differently, which would emphasise the need for personal-event-specific models. Our results showed that attention features are more likely to predict an event (i.e., a day when a personal event was tweeted out) than the activity based model. Feature regression analysis indicates that the performance of the attention-based model could be improved further, by dropping less influencing features. There is a clear need for a larger and better gold standard. We plan to extend this using multiple annotators, additional datasets, and a well-defined list of types of personal events to guide the annotators. This will also enable us to calculate inter-annotator agreement to filter out disagreed event annotations.

We observed that for most users their event window shows a very similar curve of a rapid peak and drop around the event day. However, this momentum seems to continue across multiple days for users with larger social networks. This indicates the need to study the impact of the network size of our event classification models. We also plan to compare against additional baseline approaches, such as word burstiness and topic models. Nevertheless, such models are less likely to fit our use case, which is focused on the twitter streams of individual users, and on their personal events, which might not generate high enough signals for such models.

We would also like to investigate the impact of our approach across different platforms. Hence we will reapply the models on data from Facebook and perhaps other platforms.

6   Summary

This paper investigated a number of user activity and attention features to detect the personal life events in tweets. Focus was on identifying whether the day-load of tweets from users contained the reporting of any personal events. When comparing against our ground truth from 220 users, the classification build that was based on attention features performed best, followed by the hybrid model, then the activity based model. With the attention based model, we achieved 90% Precision, 69% Recall, and 84% Accuracy.

Acknowledgments. This work was supported by EPSRC project ReelLives (EP/ L004062/1).

References

1. Good, K.D.: From scrapbook to Facebook: A history of personal media assemblage and archives. New Media and Society, 557–573 (2013)
2. Rawassizadeh, R.: Towards Sharing Life-log Information with Society Behav. Inf. Technol. **31**, 1057–1067 (2012)
3. Benson, E., Haghighi, A., Barzilay, R.: Event discovery in social media feeds. In: Artificial Intelligence, pp. 389–398. ACM (2011)
4. Tjondronegoro, D., Chua, T.: Transforming mobile personal life log into autobiographical multimedia eChronicles. In: Proceedings of the 10th International Conference on Advances in Mobile Computing & #38; Multimedia, pp. 57–63. ACM, New York (2012)
5. Choudhury, S., Alani, H.: Personal Life event detection from social media. In: Proceedings of the 1st International Workshop on Social Personalisation, Santiago (2014)
6. Eugenio, B.D., Green, N., Subba, R.: Detecting life events in feeds from twitter. In: Proceedings of the IEEE Seventh International Conference on Semantic Computing, pp. 274–277 (2014)
7. Sakaki, T.: Earthquake shakes twitter users: real-time event detection by social sensors. In: Proceedings of the 3rd ACM SIGSPATIAL International Workshop on Location-Based Social Networks (2009)
8. Jackoway, A., Samet, H., Sankaranarayanan, J.: Identification of live news events using twitter. In: Proceedings of the 19th International Conference on World Wide Web, Chicago, pp. 25–32 (2011)
9. Soler, J.M., Cuartero, F., Roblizo, M.: Twitter as a tool for predicting elections results. In: Proceedings of the International Conference on Advances in Social Networks Analysis and Mining, Istanbul, Turkey, pp. 1194–1200 (2012)
10. Ilina, E., Hauff, C., Celik, I., Abel, F., Houben, G.-J.: Social event detection on twitter. In: Brambilla, M., Tokuda, T., Tolksdorf, R. (eds.) ICWE 2012. LNCS, vol. 7387, pp. 169–176. Springer, Heidelberg (2012)
11. Chen, L., Roy, A.: Event detection from flickr data through wavelet-based spatial analysis. In: Proceedings of the 18th ACM Conference on Information and Knowledge Management, Hong Kong, pp. 523–532 (2009)
12. Firan, C.S., Georgescu, M., Nejdl, W., Paiu, R.: Bringing order to your photos: event-driven classification of flickr images based on social knowledge. In: Proceedings of the 19th ACM International Conference on Information and Knowledge Management, Toronto, pp. 189–198 (2010)
13. Weng, J., Yao, Y., Leonardi, E., Lee, F., Lee, B.S.: Event detection in twitter. In: Proceedings of the Fifth International AAAI Conference on Weblogs and Social Media, Berlin, pp. 401–408 (2011)
14. Cavalin, P., Maira, G., Pinhanez. C.: Towards personalized offer by means of life event detection on social media and entity matching. In: Proceedings of the 1st International Workshop on Social Personalisation, Santiago, Berlin, pp. 401–408 (2014)
15. Agarwal, P., Vaithiyanathan, R., Sharma, S., Shroff, G.: Catching the long-tail: extracting local news events from twitter. In: ICWSM (2012)
16. Papadopoulos, S., Zigkolis, C., Yiannis, C., Vakali, A.: Cluster-Based Landmark and Event Detection for Tagged Photo Collections. IEEE MultiMedia, 52–63 (2011)
17. Judith, G., Bluck, S.: Looking back across the life span: A life story account of the reminiscence bump. Memory & Cognition **35**(8), 1928–1939 (2007)

Digital Addiction Ontology for Social Networking Systems

Amen Alrobai[✉] and Huseyin Dogan

Bournemouth University, Poole, UK
{aalrobai,hdogan}@bournemouth.ac.uk

Abstract. Digital Addiction (hereafter referred to as DA) is an emerging, perhaps controversial, issue that is expected to profoundly impact modern societies. Different types of addiction, such as drugs, gambling and alcohol, have clear standards, regulations and policies on how to manufacture, market and sell them. In great contrast, DA has received little recognition or guidance in Human-Computer Interaction (HCI) and social media research communities. These communities are required to support software industry to provide ways to develop products that are more aware of DA. This research focuses on conceptualising DA to advance the understanding of how the design of social networking systems might influence human behaviour in a way that facilitates addiction. This paper presents an initial ontology and logical models for DA, and discusses potential HCI related implications.

Keywords: Digital Addiction · Social Networking · Human Computer Interaction · Software engineering · Ontology

1   Introduction

Digital Addiction (DA), also known as Internet Addiction Disorder, is a high degree of uncontrollable engagement in certain interactions facilitated by some software products. They can provide pleasure and compensate lack of some social skills, but in a way that might harm a person socially and psychologically [1]. The introduction of social software systems and the increasingly notable cases in which people feel addicted to their use, have led to increasing interest to explore this phenomenon. While models [2] have been proposed for a better understanding of DA, these efforts are still without clear reference to the software design.

Some studies (e.g. [2,3]) suggest investigating the "object of addiction" rather than treating the Internet as a one entity, which leads to ignoring the peculiarity of the applications within this medium. In conclusion, the author [2] argues that:

> "Some applications might serve as triggers for the reinforcement of continuous use. This means that patients should stop navigating particular web sites or even certain applications".

This quote raises several important questions. What are the triggers built into these applications? Are there any software-based solutions to support positive behavioural

© Springer International Publishing Switzerland 2015
L.M. Aiello and D. McFarland (Eds.): SocInfo 2014 Workshops, LNCS 8852, pp. 167–175, 2015.
DOI: 10.1007/978-3-319-15168-7_21

change, rather than imposing access restriction policies? This paper presents an approach to address the first question. The findings will be used to derive an initial ontology for digital addiction.

2   Digital Addiction as an HCI Issue

Despite the impact of DA, it is still outside the boundary of the HCI community. DA is still seen as a problem on the users' side more than a responsibility of the software and the design of user interactions. Only a limited number of studies have addressed the role of software design and hence social networking system design in DA [4,3]. These studies mainly focus on the attractive features of the Internet itself as a medium. Consequently, software features and how their interactions might influence human behaviour are ignored. Current treatments are limited to educational programmes including rehabilitation programmes, Internet access restriction, and some cognitive behavioural therapy (CBT) techniques [2].

A way of investigating DA is the collection of data on user interaction with social networking sites, i.e. behavioural observations and user comments, i.e. attitudinal responses. For example, several studies [5,6] have shown that user satisfaction is not severely affected, even when social software sites have poor compliance to usability principles. The question here is why users are still satisfied. It is necessary to incorporate a broader scope of user experience (UX) and include a mixture of data capture methods to address this question. Video gaming which can be classified under Specific Pathological Internet Use [3] (i.e. content-driven) is outside the scope of this research. However, the literature on both video gaming with its related special attributes, e.g. presentation, flow experience, competition and storyline [7,8] and gambling [9] can still provide insights into the correlations between HCI, Social Networking and DA.

3   Methodology

A qualitative study taking grounded theory approach is conducted to understand: (1) DA with respect to social software design; (2) addictive attributes influencing user interaction; and (3) the role of context and triggering cues. The current research models DA from a conceptual perspective by using the techniques described below.

3.1   Logical Models

The literature lacks a standardised definition of DA. Consequently, an approach called "logical modelling" [10] is used to analyse different definitions in order to extract the concepts and relationships between them. A definition of DA was derived as a result of the logical model analysis. The relationship between the concepts defined as concept multiplicity [11] has helped to identify the key and common correlations between the definitions analysed. The existing definitions of DA do not emphasise the role of HCI, so we have created our own definition in a way that it is still recognised in other communities.

3.2   Content Analysis

Content analysis is a method for producing new knowledge through a systematic analysis process of textual and multimedia information coming from different sources, e.g. interviews, printed publications, broadcast programmes and websites [12]. The current research involved selection and analysis of publications written by professionals with an expertise in addiction-related domains from academia and industry. Posts on DA related web discussion forums were also analysed. A directed and conventional content analyses was applied as a qualitative technique to draw some inferences [13]. The former started with relevant theories, e.g. disinhibition effect [14], to guide the coding process, while the latter is used to derive further coding categories directly from the text.

3.3   Ontology Development

Ontology is defined as "an explicit specification of a conceptualization" [15]. In software engineering, ontology is seen as a promising approach to higher-level issues such as modularisation, distribution and reusability [16]. Given the inherent diversity of users and software features and the multidisciplinary nature of DA, we have selected the ontological approach to facilitate subject-matter discussions and knowledge sharing, and to act as a knowledge repository. The outputs of content analysis are used to conceptualise DA components in the form of an ontology to facilitate knowledge sharing, communication and collaboration.

4   Preliminary Results

4.1   Digital Addiction Logical Models

Four definitions were identified: Problematic Internet Use [17]; Generalized Pathological Internet Use [18]; Internet Addiction [1] and (4) Technological Addiction [19]. In these definitions, different terms are used to describe the object of addiction e.g. Internet-, Technological-addiction and Online-addiction. In addition, different terms are used to describe behaviour, e.g. Addiction, Generalized Pathological, Problematic and Compulsive. They are used either interchangeably or based on the focus and emphasis of the publications. These definitions have been analysed to derive the logical models. The steps for using the logical model representational notations are described [10] and implemented in similar cases [20]. Below are two examples of logical models.

(1) Definition: **Problematic Internet Use** *is a multidimensional syndrome that consists of cognitive, emotional, and behavioural symptoms that result in difficulties with managing one's offline life.*

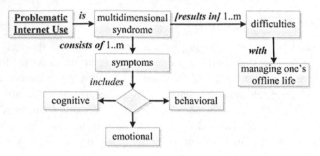

Fig. 1. Logical model of the Problematic Internet Use definition by [17]

(2) Definition: **Generalised Pathological Internet Use** *is conceptualized as a multidimensional overuse of the Internet itself that results in negative personal and professional consequences.*

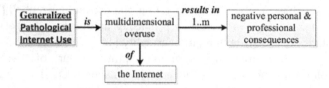

Fig. 2. Logical model of the Generalised Pathological Internet Use definition by [18]

Logical models have also been developed for two further definitions. Relationships between concepts, principles and terminology were created. These four models were then reduced and summarised in a concluding logical model, as shown in Figure 4, which forms the basis of our new definition.

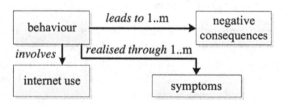

Fig. 3. Summary of the four logical models

Our proposed definition emphasises the role of software as an object of addiction as well as HCI as a responsible community. The following changes were applied.

- Replacing *Internet* Addiction with the term <u>Digital</u> Addiction as the main concept. This is due to the role of digital devices such as smart phones which help to accelerate addiction [2].
- Replacing the term *behaviour* with the agreed disorder, i.e. *compulsive-impulsive use* based on the standard classification on mental disorders [21].
- Discarding the term *consequences*, as the term *compulsive/impulsive use* would implicitly convey the negative impact.

- Using the term *to reach certain requirements* to denote interaction requirements.
- Replacing the term *Internet* with *software-mediated operations* to emphasise the diverse impact of different software products.

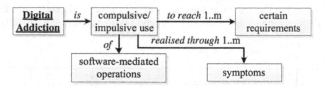

Fig. 4. The logical model of the HCI definition of DA

The authors proposed their own working definition based on the analysis of logical models of definitions: Digital Addiction is the compulsive and/or impulsive use of software-mediated operations to reach certain requirements and it is realised through multiple symptoms. The message to be communicated via this definition is that Internet should not be treated as an object of addiction, rather enabled through certain software-mediated operations and user requirements should be considered in searching for less addictive alternatives [22].

4.2   Initial Ontology of Digital Addiction

This systematic approach for extracting the concepts of DA has helped us to derive the first version of the ontology. The initial ontology, as shown in Figure 5, is derived from reviewing the literature and conducting content analysis. Table 1 shows some statistical data related to the ontology development process. There are 83 concepts extracted and organised in three main categories/dimensions (users, software and culture) and other 17 sub-categories. These concepts, which are revolving around addiction factors, are extracted from 30 different sources, ranging from peer-reviewed articles and books to formal speeches and online articles written by experts in the DA domain. These sources cover wide range of disciplines such as Neuroscience, Management, HCI, Cyber Psychology, Sociology, Marketing, Human Factors and Requirements Engineering. Table 2 illustrates how concepts are extracted from the text.

Table 1. Statistical information about the ontology development activity

	Quantity
Concepts	83
Main Categories	3
Sub-categories	17
Domains	17
Sources	30

Table 2. An example of an ontological term extracted from [23]

TERM EXTRACTION:	
"...developed an incentive-rewarding mechanism specific to SNSs in which users receive incentive rewards in proportion to their number of page views (how many times their page is browsed by others) but alters the reward amount for public and private content to compensate for the different perceived risks experienced. We expect our mechanism to motivate users..."	
Individuals	Privacy
Properties	affects_
Classes	Rewarding
Properties	N/A
Classes	N/A

This approach to information extraction can help to make the concepts, terms and relationships more traceable as well as providing contextual information. Each attribute in the ontology can be studied further to assess its impact on user behaviour.

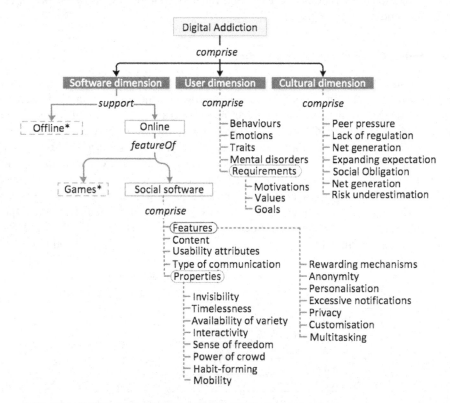

* Games and offline applications are out of the scope of our research

Fig. 5. The initial ontology for DA

Analysing online interaction data can help to reveal how rewarding mechanisms in social software are linked to user requirements (i.e. motivations, values and goals). This cannot be taken into account with the isolation of other factors (e.g. personal traits). For example, what are the online interactions that can trigger addictive behaviors for users looking forward more social recognition? What are the software features/interactions that are used more for this type of users? How would the social structure and given roles in a particular social software influence the addiction behaviours? Therefore, studying the interaction between individuals and the software without analysing the human behavioural elements and social structure might provide misleading answers. Therefore, while ontology was first created to add meaning to the concept of DA, it can be exploited through developing less addictive social software systems by filtering certain elements. We will elaborate on that more in the next section.

5   Discussion

User requirements, perceptions and expectations are little known in most DA cases. This research attempts to address such issues. This paper reported ongoing research activates with some initial results. These results including the preliminary ontology still needs to undergo further iterations and evolve as a result of analysing further literature and running validation exercises.

This research has identified the following key challenges relating to DA:

- The diversity of software features and user traits, requirements and even patterns of use will increase the complexity of understanding DA.
- The level of acceptance of software that might provide a less attractive user experience.
- DA relates heavily to user perceptions, expectations and personal requirements, which are not easy to express in words for most users, i.e. tacit [24], fuzzy in nature, private and sometimes very sensitive.
- How can we develop DA factors and measures to detect addictive behaviours? What can we detect?
- How, or even whether, users would like to be aware of DA when they have it? What decisions should the software designers take when developing such systems? What decisions should the users take when interacting with the social software?
- There is a well-known debate on the causes of DA [25] in that some would argue that Internet/social software is just a medium and irresponsible for the problematic use. However, we argue that while social software is not the "main" cause in all DA cases, some addiction themes can be mitigated through the software itself, as such addressing DA through different stages of SDLC can play a vital role here.

In our research we will focus on some aspects of the ontology. For example, the correlation between addicts motivations and social software features and functionalities. The analysis of online interactions should reveal some of the appealing features that can be mapped to addicts' motivations, e.g. exhibitionism. This idea might be very interesting to different communities. For example, self-adaptive systems can derive better adaptation decisions driven by users requirements. It would partially answer what to observe and what are the features that can be adapted. Future studies will address different parts of the ontology to answer when, how and, probably, where they can be adapted. What we mean by adaptation is some filtering options, such as persona-based filtering options, attribute-based filtering options and extra filtering performed based on extracts of the DA modelling.

One way of exploiting the research findings is to investigate how to design a Rehab and/or Regulation Software for users who are addicted. This can be used in psychotherapeutic treatment. This output can also be a third party application that can still access social networking websites and apply such techniques to regulate addiction based on the finalised DA ontology. This research will also review rehabilitation programs for Game Addiction to discover whether a Rehab Software is required for DA.

6   Conclusions and Future Work

This paper attempts to make the DA more widely recognised in the HCI and Social Networking communities. It is anticipated that this paper leads to a more holistic view of the reasons and potential treatments for DA as a result of the analysis of working definition of DA as presented in this paper. An initial DA ontology was developed by utilising a content analysis approach. This is still to be validated through subject matter experts to finalise the conceptualisation of DA. Further empirical investigations planned include expert interviews, user exploratory surveys, diary studies and controlled usability studies.

Exploratory surveys will target end-users to examine social software applications in more depth, focusing on their features and functionalities. The survey will comprise of two parts; (1) user profiling according to their addiction level; (2) classifying the features, functionalities and interactions of social networking sites according to their addictive level. The survey will guide us in seeking to identify the software's problematic aspects, i.e. those that are likely to accelerate addiction. The targeted population will include adults, adolescents, addicts and non-addicts.

Diary studies will assist capturing users' interaction with minimal interference. The planned diary study approach developed [26] will be used to identify both problematic attributes and their triggers. Participants will set up a plan for their tasks and planned interactions with social software for the next day. Then, they will record their actual use. This will enable a cross comparison of planned and performed activities. The main risk with this method is the user's commitment when recording the required information.

Acknowledgements. The research is supported by the Graduate School in Bournemouth University.

References

1. Ha, J.H., et al.: Psychiatric comorbidity assessed in Korean children and adolescents who screen positive for Internet addiction. Journal of Clinical Psychiatry (2006)
2. Young, K.S., de Abreu, C.N.: Internet addiction: A handbook and guide to evaluation and treatment (2011)

3. Griffiths, M.: Does Internet and computer addiction exist? Some case study evidence. CyberPsychology and Behavior **3**, 211–218 (2000)
4. Hammersley, R.: Personal e-mail communication to ADDICT-L discussion group (1995)
5. Hart, J., et al.: Exploring the facebook experience: a new approach to usability, pp. 471–474 (2008)
6. Thompson, A.-J., Kemp, E.A.: Web 2.0: extending the framework for heuristic evaluation, pp. 29–36 (2009)
7. King, D., Delfabbro, P., Griffiths, M.: Video Game Structural Characteristics: A New Psychological Taxonomy **8**, 90–106 (2010)
8. Goh, D.H., Ang, R.P., Tan, H.C.: Strategies for designing effective psychotherapeutic gaming interventions for children and adolescents. Comput. Hum. Behav. **24**, 2217–2235 (2008)
9. Schüll, N.D.: Addiction by Design. Princeton University Press (2012)
10. Dickerson, C.E.: Towards a logical and scientific foundation for system concepts, principles, and terminology. IEEE (2008)
11. Dogan, H., Barot, V., Henshaw, M., Siemieniuch, C.: Formalisation and mapping of terminologies for Systems of Systems Engineering thesaurus. Presented at the 2013 8th International Conference on System of Systems Engineering (SoSE) (2013)
12. Lazar, J., Feng, J.H., Hochheiser, H.: Research methods in human-computer interaction (2010)
13. Hsieh, H.F.: Three Approaches to Qualitative Content Analysis. Qual. Health Res. **15**, 1277–1288 (2005)
14. Suler, J.: The online disinhibition effect. CyberPsychology and Behavior **7**, 321–326 (2004)
15. Gruber, T.R.: A translation approach to portable ontology specifications. Knowledge Acquisition **5**, 199–220 (1993)
16. Hesse, W.: Ontologies in the Software Engineering Process (2005)
17. Caplan, S.E.: A social skill account of problematic Internet use. Journal of Communication **55**, 721–736 (2005)
18. Davis, R.A.: A cognitive-behavioral model of pathological Internet use. Comput. Hum. Behav. **17**, 187–195 (2001)
19. Griffiths, M.: Gambling on the internet: A brief note. J. Gambling Stud. **12**, 471–473 (1996)
20. Dogan, H., de C. Henshaw, M.J., Ragsdell, G.: The Risk of Information Management Without Knowledge Management: A Case Study. J. Info. Know. Mgmt. **10**, 393–408 (2011)
21. Block, J.: Issues for DSM-V: Internet Addiction. Am. J. Psychiatry **165**, 306–307 (2008)
22. Alrobai, A., Phalp, K., Ali, R.: Digital addiction: a requirements engineering perspective. In: Salinesi, C., van de Weerd, I. (eds.) REFSQ 2014. LNCS, vol. 8396, pp. 112–118. Springer, Heidelberg (2014)
23. Yogo, K., et al.: Incentive-rewarding mechanism to stimulate activities in social networking services. International Journal of Network Management **22**, 1–11 (2012)
24. Gacitua, R., et al.: Making Tacit Requirements Explicit. Presented at the 2009 Second International Workshop on Managing Requirements Knowledge (MARK) (2009)
25. Widyanto, L., Griffiths, M.: internet addiction: a critical review. International Journal of Mental Health and Addiction **4**(1), 31–51 (2006)
26. Newman, W.M.: Busy days: exposing temporal metrics, problems and elasticities through diary studies. In: CHI 2004 Workshop on Temporal Issues in Work (2004)

Exploration on Games and Gamers (EGG)

EGG 2014: Exploration on Games and Gamers - Introduction

Haewoon Kwak[1]([✉]), Jeremy Blackburn[2], and Huy Kang Kim[3]

[1] Qatar Computing Research Institute, Doha, Qatar
hkwak@qf.org.qa
[2] Telefonica Research, Barcelona, Spain
jeremyb@tid.es
[3] Korea University, Seoul, South Korea
cenda@korea.ac.kr

Keywords: Online games · Game design · Gamer behavior · Social dynamics · Virtual space

1 Introduction

With the remarkable advances from isolated console games to massively multiplayer online role-playing games, the online gaming world has become invaluable assets for the research of social dynamics [7]. Online game players interact with each other in various ways, as they do in the real world. More importantly, interactions could be easily quantified and logged in detail. The huge volume of behavioral data collected from online games helps researchers study human nature in an unprecedented scale. For instance, Szell et al. observe six different types of in-game interaction (e.g., friendship, communication, trade, enmity, aggression, and punishment) and analyze the inter-dependence of social networks based on each type [12]. Their rich modeling of human society demonstrates competitive advantage of user behavior data collected in online games.

Considering the time and financial investment people put into games, the research community has shown increasing interest in studying games from a variety of perspectives. Studying video games as a scientific endeavor can have huge impact for the industry. Quantification and empirical evidence can inform game developers on design decisions, aid in the advancement of gaming technology, and provide new insight into the minds of gamers.

There are also important social problems facing gaming. Consider unethical actions such as toxic behavior and cheating. Due to the reliance of social interactions in multiplayer games, both of these issues threaten the community of gamers [1,2,4,11]. As expected from controlled laboratory experiments and intuition, cheating has been shown to display contagious properties, where the behavior will spread from friend to friend. Toxic behavior, which is violations of social norms to cause harm to individuals and the larger community, has only recently begun to be understood. A deeper understanding of bad behavior in online games could lead to detection and mitigation strategies, and can have

L.M. Aiello and D. McFarland (Eds.): SocInfo 2014 Workshops, LNCS 8852, pp. 179–182, 2015.
DOI: 10.1007/978-3-319-15168-7_22

impact on the understanding of other forms of bad behavior, such as contraband networks [5] or even cyberbullying.

2   Scope of Workshop

At the Exploration on Game and Gamers workshop, we welcome interdisciplinary research related to a deeper understanding of games and gamers. We desire both quantitative and qualitative work on social interactions in online games. For example, analysis on and systems support for social interactions and how they influence, and are influenced by, gameplay. We are also particularly interested in work related to eSports, for example new metrics for player performance and matchmaking algorithms, as they remain relatively unexplored and are a focal point for worldwide player interactions. Regardless of the specifics, we believe the papers presented at this workshop can provide a wealth of knowledge for researchers studying not only games, but online social systems in general.

We invited research on qualitative and quantitative analysis of games and gamer behavior, as well as systems to support such analysis from both academia and industry.

Topics of interest included:

- Understanding, detecting, and mitigating extreme and unethical behavior in online games.
- Big data systems for efficient storage and processing of gaming related data.
- Diffusion of optimal strategies from higher skill players to lower skill players.
- Improvements in matchmaking algorithms.
- Methods for annotating subjective events in eSports (e.g., successful fight initiations).
- Extrinsic rewards and intrinsic motivation in social games.
- The relationship between the roles players take in-game and personality.
- Methods for providing sensitive data for 3rd party analysis.
- Analysis of virtual goods economies, both things like MMO economies as well as out of band markets like the Steam Trading platform.
- Community/user generated content and relationships to game popularity, longevity, etc.
- Improvements to player tutorials.

3   Program Committee

The program committee for EGG 2014 was composed of a set of industry and academic experts on video games responsible for both ground breaking research as well as major commercial successes:

- Christian Bauckhage, B-IT institute of the University of Bonn
- Alessandro Canossa, Northeastern University
- Alexandru Iosup, Delft University of Technology

- Brian Keegan, Northeastern University
- Jina Lee, NC Soft
- Jiyoun Lim, ETRI
- Nick Lim, Sonamine
- Juyong Park, KAIST
- Cuihua (Cindy) Shen, University of California, Davis
- Kyong Jin Shim, Singapore Management University
- John Simon, 5rocks
- Michael Szell, MIT
- Ji Young Woo, Korea University

4   Submissions and Acceptance

EGG 2014 received 7 submissions, representing authors from 7 countries and 9 institutions. Of the 7 submissions, 3 were short papers and 4 were full length papers. Each paper received a minimum of 3 reviews. In the end, 6 submissions (2 short, 4 full length) were accepted. The accepted papers represented research on interaction methods for mobile games [3], the spread of altruistic behavior in massively multiplayer online games [13], context sensitive match making [8], linguisitc analysis of toxic players [6], the ways in which players receive help in games [9], and analysis of the social structure of high-skill players [10].

References

1. Blackburn, J., Kourtellis, N., Skvoretz, J., Ripeanu, M., Iamnitchi, A.: Cheating in Online Games: A Social Network Perspective. ACM Transactions on Internet Technology **3**(9), May 2014
2. Blackburn, J., Kwak, H.: STFU NOOB!: Predicting crowdsourced decisions on toxic behavior in online games. In Proceedings of the 23rd International Conference on World Wide Web, WWW 2014, pp. 877–888 (2014)
3. Bock, M., Fisker, M., Fischer Topp, K., Kraus, M.: Initial exploration of the use of specific tangible widgets for tablet games. In: Proceedings of the 1st Exploration on Games and Gamers Workshop, EGG 2014 (2014)
4. Kang, A.R., Jiyoung, W., Park, J., Kim, H.K.: Online game bot detection based on party-play log analysis. Computers & Mathematics with Applications **65**(9), 1384–1395 (2013)
5. Keegan, B., Ahmed, M.A., Williams, D., Srivastava, J., Contractor, N.: Sic transit gloria mundi virtuali?: promise and peril in the computational social science of clandestine organizing. In: WebSci (2011)
6. Kwak, H., Blackburn, J.: Linguistic analysis of toxic behavior in an online video game. In: Proceedings of the 1st Exploration on Games and Gamers Workshop, EGG 2014 (2014)
7. Lazer, D., Pentland, A., Adamic, L., Aral, S., Barabasi, A.L., Brewer, D., Christakis, N., Contractor, N., Fowler, J., Gutmann, M., Jebara, T., King, G., Macy, M., Roy, D., Van Alstyne, M.: Life in the network: the coming age of computational social science. Science **323**(5915), 721–723 (2009)

8. Mylak, M., Deja, D.: Developing game-structure sensitive matchmaking system for massive-multiplayer online games. In: Proceedings of the 1st Exploration on Games and Gamers Workshop, EGG 2014 (2014)

9. Okopny, P., Musabirov, I., Alexandrov, D.: Informal in-game help practices in massive multiplayer online games. In: Proceedings of the 1st Exploration on Games and Gamers Workshop, EGG 2014 (2014)

10. Park, H., Kim, K.J.: Social network analysis of high-level players in multiplayer online battle arena game. In: Proceedings of the 1st Exploration on Games and Gamers Workshop, EGG 2014 (2014)

11. Shores, K.B., He, Y., Swanenburg, K.L., Kraut, R., Riedl, J.: The identification of deviance and its impact on retention in a multiplayer game. In: Proceedings of the 17th ACM Conference on Computer Supported Cooperative Work & Social Computing, CSCW 2014, pp. 1356–1365. ACM (2014)

12. Szell, M., Thurner, S.: Measuring social dynamics in a massive multiplayer online game. Social Networks **32**(4), 313–329 (2010)

13. Woo, J., Kwak, B.I., Lim, J., Kim, H.K.: Generosity as social contagion in virtual community. In: Proceedings of the 1st Exploration on Games and Gamers Workshop, EGG 2014 (2014)

Initial Exploration of the Use of Specific Tangible Widgets for Tablet Games

Mads Bock, Martin Fisker, Kasper Fischer Topp, and Martin Kraus[✉]

Aalborg University, Aalborg, Denmark
{mbch10,mfiske09,kfsj10}@student.aau.dk,
martin@create.aau.dk

Abstract. In this paper we investigated the use of tangible widgets vs. the use of finger touch for tablet games, which to our knowledge has not been researched so far. A user test was conducted where participants would report which of the two interaction methods they preferred for playing two tablet games: a fast-paced and a slow-paced game. We conclude that some of the participants found tangible widgets to be an interesting and potentially entertaining interaction method, even though our implementation had technical shortcomings compared to finger touch. Further study is needed to investigate how to fix these shortcomings, and how to increase the game experience of tablet games using tangible widgets.

Keywords: Tangible widget · Tablet · Finger touch · Games · User interface · Capacitive screen · Multi-touch

1 Introduction

It is safe to say that tablets, and thereby touch screens, have become a household object. Due to the popularity of games on tablets, it is interesting to look into alternative possibilities of interacting with games on touch devices, in particular because the usual way of interacting with these touch devices, i.e. through the use of finger touch, has some limitations. For example, touch devices are not able to distinguish between different users, and most devices are not able to determine the orientation of fingers. Furthermore, tactile feedback of a flat screen is limited. In this study, we investigate the use of tangible widgets for playing games on tablets where a physical object, similar to a board game piece, is used to interact with the device instead of one's fingers. To our knowledge no prior research exists about the use of tangible widgets as an interaction method for games, and whether or not players prefer this method of interaction compared with finger touch. In order to investigate this topic, we conducted user tests on two tablet games, one fast-paced and one slow-paced, using both finger touch and tangible widgets in order to assess players' preference for one or the other. We found that the participants' preferences about widgets were polarized, with some participants being very interested and others being very critical. When the participants played the slow-paced game, issues with the detection and tracking algorithm turned

© Springer International Publishing Switzerland 2015
L.M. Aiello and D. McFarland (Eds.): SocInfo 2014 Workshops, LNCS 8852, pp. 183–190, 2015.
DOI: 10.1007/978-3-319-15168-7_23

out to be more problematic than when they played the fast-paced game. We also found that when designing games for widget interaction, it was important to adapt the game design to make full use of the widgets. Section 3 describes the design of the games and the widgets, which we used in the tests that are described in Section 4. Conclusions and future work are described in the last two sections.

2   Previous Work

Tangible widgets for touch screens have been researched since the mid-nineties. Studies have focused on the physical design of the widgets themselves [1,2,3,5,6] and different approaches to detecting widgets on a screen [4,7]. Some studies have created their own touch surface, while others focused on getting the widgets to work on off-the-shelf capacitive screens, both in the form of touch tables, and mobile devices [5]. However, few of the studies have included user tests [1,3], and none of those worked with games, even though a commercial product has already been released [8].

3   Methods and Materials

This section describes the implemented game designs and the design of the widgets used in this study.

Two games were developed to investigate whether widgets or certain aspects of them are better suited to either fast-paced or slow-paced games. In this context, pace is determined by the intensity of action experienced by the player, i.e., it is related to the concentration the player must apply in order to complete a task. Slow-paced gameplay generally needs contemplative and deeper thought while fast-paced gameplay consists of elements necessitating split-second decision-making and fast reactions.

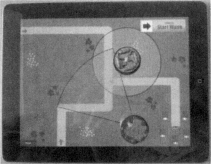

Fig. 1. Pictures of the two developed games while using widgets. To the left is the Breakout game and to the right is the Tower Defense game.

The fast-paced game is a version of the classic arcade game Breakout that has been remade many times, e.g., as popcorn and DX-Ball. The basic gameplay revolves around destroying layers of bricks by hitting them with a ball that moves across the screen and bounces off the screen edges and game objects. The player must keep the ball within the screen by preventing it from hitting the bottom using a bat that can be moved from side to side in the lower part of the screen; see Fig. 1 (left).

For this game the widget was made to represent the bat and used to move the bat around the screen. An additional version of this game was made where the bat could be rotated to take advantage of the ease of this movement afforded by a widget. In the finger touch version, the bat was moved from side to side by a finger and in a second version rotated according to the orientation of the line between two fingers.

The slow-paced game is of the Tower Defense genre, where the goal is to stop separate waves of enemies following a predetermined path, before they reach a village at the end of said path. In our game, the player must choose a given number of 3 different kinds of towers that differ in damage inflection and firing rate. The chosen towers must be placed around the enemies' path and aimed towards it. Then a wave consisting of a mix of 3 kinds of enemies with varying speed and health can be initiated. The towers cannot be moved once a wave has been started and if the village survives, the player chooses new towers to place and continues this way until all waves are beaten.

For the Tower Defense game, widgets representing each of the 3 towers are used to position and aim the towers by moving and rotating the widgets on screen. In the finger touch version, towers can be positioned by placing a finger on the virtual tower on the screen and dragging it to the desired location. Rotation is achieved by putting a finger on an arrow icon in front of the tower and dragging the finger to either side of it.

We created our own system of tangible widgets and detection- and tracking software. The widgets communicate three pieces of information to the device on which they are used: position, orientation and identity. Position refers to the widget's 2d position on the screen; orientation refers to the rotation of the widget around the screen normal; and identity refers to the unique identity of the specific widget, different from the other widgets in use.

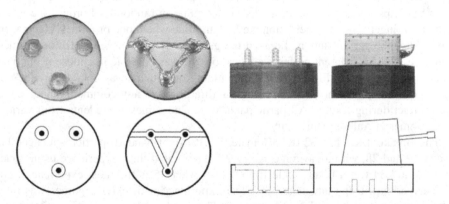

Fig. 2. Top row shows pictures of a widget. Bottom row shows corresponding sketches. From left to right: widget base bottom-view, widget base top-view, widget base side-view and widget top side-view.

Our test was conducted using an iPad 2, model MC769KN, and our software was implemented in C# using the Unity engine and editor.

Each widget was designed to have 3 touch points on the screen set in a triangular pattern (Fig. 2). This shape was altered to create different identities for the widgets. The 3 touch points were generated by using the heads of 3 nails set into the base of the widget. The nails were connected by placing aluminum foil around each nail point and into grooves cut into the top of the widget base leading to the widget's sides. Foil was wrapped around the widget base, which was connected to the foil in the grooves in order to connect the user's touch on the foil surface to the nail heads. A top piece with a decoration corresponding to the represented game piece placed on top of the base covers both the nail points and grooves.

An algorithm was developed to detect widgets on the screen. It was designed to read touch points from the Unity engine, identify the widgets, and output their position, orientation, and identity. This was achieved by going through each potential set of three touch points, and determining whether they describe a widget. The evaluation is done by comparing the relative lengths between the points with preset values for each widget calibrated to the game. If a widget is detected, the program updates its position and orientation. The algorithm runs continuously while the game runs, ensuring that the widgets' positions and orientations are constantly updated.

4   Tests and Results

Two tests have been conducted, one testing the Breakout game and one the Tower Defense game. In both tests, the participants were asked to fill out a questionnaire containing demographic questions when entering the room. They were also asked to rate their level of experience with using touch devices in general and tablets specifically as well as their level of experience of playing games on touch devices and tablets. After these questions, the participants got an introduction to one of the games. Each participant had two playthroughs of the game in randomized order: one where they used finger touch as interaction method and one where one or more widgets were used. After the participants had played the game, they were asked to fill out a questionnaire with 11 different preference questions. It was possible to choose if the preference was for either "Finger Touch", "Widget" or if there was "No difference". In addition to the preference questions, the facilitator noted any comments made about the product during testing. All participants were 2nd semester students from various programmes at Aalborg University.

The Breakout test had 32 (84.3% male, 81.2% right-handed) participants aged between 19 and 28, with an average age of 21. They rated their experience using touch devices at 4.34 (on a Likert scale from 1 to 5 where 5 is the most experience), and their experience using tablets at 3.31. The experience with playing games was rated 3.44 on touch devices, and 2.72 on tablets. They had to play the game for 3 minutes using finger touch and 3 minutes using a widget. A total of 24 negative and 16 positive comments were given about widgets in the Breakout test. The negative comments concerned occlusion issues, tracking issues, and that too low friction of the widget made it difficult to control it. The positive comments concerned low friction of the widget, easy control of the widget, that the widget was pleasant to use, and increased immersion. Half of the participants played the version with a rotatable bat and the other half played with a non-rotatable bat, but the results showed no significant difference between the two versions.

The Tower Defense test had 30 (83.3% male, 76.6% right-handed) participants aged between 18 and 35, with an average age of 22. They rated their experience using touch devices at 4.87, and their experience using tablets at 2.80. The experience with playing games was rated 3.53 on touch devices, and 2.20 on tablets. They played the game with both finger touch and widgets for either 5 minutes or until they won or lost the game. For being able to lose the game, they had to play the game for at least 3 minutes. A total of 14 negative and 12 positive comments were given about widgets in the Tower Defense test. The negative comments concerned tracking issues, too little conductive surface on the widgets, and occlusion. The positive comments concerned the widgets being pleasant and entertaining to use, increased immersion, and it being possible to do simultaneous actions.

Percentage of preference for widgets	Movement followed the best	Best method for precisely placing objects	Easiest to see screen	Most fun interaction method	To win, interaction method	Overall preferred interaction method
Breakout	**37.5%** (0.2153)	**54.8%** (0.7201)	34.4% (0.1102)	**56.3%** (0.5966)	**50.0%** (1.0000)	**56.3%** (0.5966)
Tower Defense	16.7% (**0.0003**)	26.7% (**0.0161**)	27.6% (**0.0241**)	**66.7%** (0.0987)	26.7% (**0.0161**)	**50.0%** (1.0000)

Fig. 3. Questionnaire results from both user tests. The percentages indicate how many participants preferred the use of widgets for the given question. Bold-faced percentages indicate tendencies in favor of widgets or a neutral result. The value in parentheses shows the calculated p-value for the given question. Bold-faced p-values indicate significant results in favor of finger touch.

Percentage preferences for widgets are listed in Fig. 3, where a two-tailed binomial test for the deviation from 50% has been used to calculate the p-values, which are listed in parentheses. The answers "No difference" have been evenly distributed as "Finger Touch" and "Widget" answers. In case of an odd number of "No difference" answers, one answer has been removed from the total sample size.

5   Discussion

There were no significant differences to be seen in the preference responses from the Breakout test. In the Tower Defense test, however, there were four significant response differences. When a question yields no difference in results, one might be tempted to conclude that participants in general had no preference one way or the other. That was not the case, however, as many of the questions actually showed a polarization of the replies, with very few neutral answers. In order to get a clearer and more nuanced result, it would have been preferable to use a Likert scale for the questionnaires, instead of the preference questions used in this study.

When asked the questions "Which interaction method followed your movement the best?" and "Which interaction method was the easiest to precisely place your game objects where you wanted them to be?", the participants strongly preferred the finger touch interaction method for the Tower Defense game. Both of these questions are related to certain tracking issues with the implementation of the widget interaction. Comments made by some participants in both tests further indicated that this problem was present. When they were asked "If you want to win the game, which interaction method would you then choose?", a significant difference in favor of finger touch also proved that this tracking issue was present. Optimizing the detection algorithm is likely to resolve these issues.

It was assumed prior to the test that tracking issues would be more of a problem in fast-paced games, but the results showed that the participants found it more of an issue in our slow-paced Tower Defense game. A reason for this might be that users see the inaccuracy more clearly when they have the time to position something very precisely.

Although there were no significant differences between responses in either test when the participants were asked "If you want to have the most fun, which interaction method would you then choose?", we noted that it was the only question where participants tended to prefer widgets over finger touch as the interaction method. This might indicate that the use of tangible widgets has the potential to create a more entertaining game experience. If the tracking issues in these tests were minimized, we might be able to get a significant response saying that using widgets is more entertaining.

When asked, "With which interaction method was it the easiest to see what happened on the screen?" in the Tower Defense test, participants preferred the use of finger touch. In both tests, participants commented that occlusion was an issue when using widgets. The size of the iPad, and the resolution of the electrode grid made it impossible to make widgets smaller than the ones used in the test, and still make them detectable by our detection algorithm. A higher resolution electrode grid or a larger touch screen would arguably make occlusion less of a problem.

When using the widgets, test participants experienced less friction than when they used finger touch. Most participants who commented on this found it to be one of the advantages of using the widget. A few participants on the other hand felt that it made them lose control of the widget. Different choices of materials for the contact points of a widget have to be considered in order to achieve a preferable level of friction.

It was observed that several participants failed to hold the widget in a way that electrically connected the user to the screen. Having only part of the widget surface being conductive puts a natural constraint on how the widget can be held. In order to make the interaction with the widget feel as natural as possible, this constraint needs to be addressed. Increasing the conductive surface of the widget, potentially covering the entire widget, would therefore make the interaction with the widget feel more natural.

The iPad used in this study had the capacity to detect 11 touch points simultaneously. Given that our design for widgets requires three touch points per widget, this does not allow for more than three widgets being used at the same time. Generally, all off-the-shelf multi-touch devices have a similar limit on the number of touch points.

In order to give developers more creative freedom to create widget-based games, it can be argued that commercial multi-touch devices would have to increase the number of touch points.

6   Conclusion

In this paper we implemented and tested two iPad games in order to investigate the use of tangible widgets vs. the use of finger touch to address the lack of research on the use of tangible widgets as an interaction method for games. Some participants found the concept of tangible widgets interesting, and in several cases more entertaining than using finger touch, whereas others did not like using the widgets at all. The participants showed a clear preference for widgets or finger touch, with only few participants having no preference. The two games gave different results in user preference, implying that the game design has an impact on the user's preference for either widgets or finger touch. Tracking issues were problematic if the user had to place a game object very precisely. This proved to be more of a problem in the slow-paced Tower Defense game than in the fast-paced Breakout game. We assume that optimizing the detection algorithm for the widgets, might lead to more reliable results.

7   Future Work

For future work, we propose three different directions. We would like to improve the overall detection of the widgets. This means optimizing the detection and tracking algorithm, as well as investigating if the design of the widgets can be improved to this end. We would also like to investigate other game designs than the ones already used, in order to map out which genres are most appropriate for the use of widgets. Finally, we would look into using other platforms than the iPad. Specifically, we would look into using different screen sizes and a higher number of touch points, in order to get a better user experience.

References

1. Blagojevic, R., Chen, X., Tan, R., Sheehan, R., Plimmer, B.: Using tangible drawing tools on a capacitive multi-touch display. In: Proceedings of the 26th Annual BCS Interaction Specialist Group Conference on People and Computers, pp. 315–320. British Computer Society, Swinton (2012)
2. Chan, L., Müller, S., Roudaut, A., Baudisch, P.: CapStones and ZebraWidgets: sensing stacks of building blocks, dials and sliders on capacitive touch screens. In: Konstan, J.A., Chi, E.H., Höök, K. (eds.) Proceedings of the SIGCHI Conference on Human Factors in Computing Systems, pp. 2189–2192. ACM, New York (2012)
3. Kratz, S., Westermann, T., Rohs, M., Essl, G.: CapWidgets: tangile widgets versus multi-touch controls on mobile devices. In: Mackay, W.E., Brewster, S. (eds.) CHI 2011 Extended Abstracts on Human Factors in Computing Systems, pp. 1351–1356. ACM, New York (2011)

4. Schaper, H.: Physical Widgets on Capacitive Touch Displays, Master's Thesis, pp. 1–118. RWTH Aachen University, Aachen, Germany (2013)
5. Voelker, S., Nakajima, K., Thoresen, C., Itoh, Y., Øvergård, K.I., Borchers, J.: PUCs: detecting transparent, passive untouched capacitive widgets on unmodified multi-touch displays. In: Quigley, A., Jacucci, G., Horn, M., Nacenta, M. (eds.) Proceedings of the 2013 ACM International Conference on Interactive Tabletops and Surfaces, pp. 101–104. ACM, New York (2013)
6. Wiethoff, A., Schneider, H., Rohs, M., Butz, A., Greenberg, S.: Sketch-a-TUI: low cost prototyping of tangible interactions using cardboard and conductive ink. In: Spencer, S.N. (ed.) Proceedings of the Sixth International Conference on Tangible, Embedded and Embodied Interaction, pp. 309–312. ACM, New York (2012)
7. Yu, N.-H., Chan, L.-W., Cheng, L.-P., Chen, M.Y., Hung, Y.-P.: Enabling tangible interaction on capacitive touch panels. In: Perlin, K., Czerwinski, M., Miller, R. (eds.) Adjunct Proceedings of the 23rd Annual ACM Symposium on User Interface Software and Technology, pp. 457–458. ACM, New York (2010)
8. AppMATes. http://www.appmatestoys.com (last accessed: September 6, 2014)

Generosity as Social Contagion in Virtual Community

Jiyoung Woo[1], Byung Il Kwak[1], Jiyoun Lim[2], and Huy Kang Kim[1(✉)]

[1] Graduate School of Information, Korea University, Seoul, South Korea
{jywoo,kwacka12,cenda}@korea.ac.kr
[2] Electronics and Telecommunications Research Institute, Daejeon, South Korea
kusses@etri.re.kr

Abstract. Online social network platform becomes a good arena to observe generous behaviors of humans. Among various online social platforms, online games mimic real world closely and embed various social interactions between players. In online games, players show generosity each other even to strangers by donating their cyber asset generously. We focus on analyzing the generous behaviors giving items or money to lower-level strangers. In this research, we focus on analyzing random acts of kindness that resembles generous behaviors in the real world, especially donation. Using a large-scale real data from a major online game company, we find that benefiting from a generous behavior increases a player's generosity. On the other hand, we also notice that social influence does not work effectively in case that these generous behaviors are not recognizable or visible to their friends.

Keywords: Generosity · Generous behavior · Social contagion · Online games

1 Introduction

The Ice Bucket Challenge, recently diffused throughout the world, is an activity of involving dumping a bucket of ice water. Its goal is to promote awareness of the disease amyotrophic lateral sclerosis (ALS) and encourage donations to research related ALS. ALS Ice Bucket Challenge went viral on social media by sharing a video of dumping ice bucket and calling out friends to invite the next try. The ice bucket challenge has raised $53.3 million in donations for the ALS Association at the end of August since July 29, compared with $2.1 million at this time last year, according to [1]. One of the reasons why people involve in the Ice Bucket Challenge is because of their friends. The participants are recognized and called by friends. At the same time, by joining this challenge, they can let their friends know their involvement to show their generosity. As like this, many studies show that friends play an important role in generous behaviors [2, 3]. In 2013 Christmas Eve, it happened that a customer paid for next customer's coffee [4]. More than 1,000 customers participated in pay-it-forward after they received suspended coffee from former customers. This case shows that people who received generosity are willing to show generosity to others.

Likewise the above cases, it is well known that generous behaviors are contagious [3, 5, 6]. People show generosity to others because of (a) learning, (b) social and

© Springer International Publishing Switzerland 2015
L.M. Aiello and D. McFarland (Eds.): SocInfo 2014 Workshops, LNCS 8852, pp. 191–199, 2015.
DOI: 10.1007/978-3-319-15168-7_24

personal standards, and (c) arousal and affect [7]. In perspective of learning, we can observe direct reciprocity and generalized reciprocity in generous behaviors. Generalized reciprocity refers which those who received generosity from strangers show generosity to others in future [8]. Direct reciprocity refers the cases which those who receive generosity give it back to givers. Regarding social standard, generous behaviors can be affected by social influence. The second case, the suspended coffee, shows that social contagion of generosity can be explained with generalized reciprocity. The first case, the Ice Bucket Challenge, shows that generosity is affected by social influence.

As digital technology develops, new types of generous behaviors are emerging in cyber space such as informational support and emotional support in a message board, boosting the donation campaign via a social networking web site, sharing and diffusion of open source software via web community site, and etc. Online social network platforms, especially online games are a good arena to observe generous behaviors of humans. Online games mimic variety of activities in the real world and embed various social interactions (e.g. chat, trade, party-play, duel and battle) between players. In online games, players show generosity to each other. They show generosity to even strangers. Beginners usually need items and cyber money to level up and enjoy game contents. Although they can exchange their own cyber assets into real money, higher-level players sometimes donate their items to lower-level players without expecting anything in return.

We will focus on analyzing the generous behavior giving items or money to lower-level players in Massively Multiplayer Online Role-Playing Games (MMORPGs). It resembles generous behaviors in the real world, such as donation. While previous research dealt with the donation campaign in cyber space, large-scale observational study on random acts of generosity is lack. Our research is not limited to donation campaign; we focus on the whole aspect of random acts of kindness. Further, we investigate how generalized reciprocity and social influence affect people's generosity.

2   Related Works

Tsvetokv and Macy [6] found out some events such as "an extra-large sized order of generosity" [9] and "customers pay for next car's order at Mass" [10]. They claimed that these examples give us an explanation: generous acts are contagious. In human behavior study, the networks of indirect reciprocity are crucial for understanding human behavior dynamics regarding to networks in economics [11, 12], especially cooperation in social networks [13, 14].

The concept of networks of indirect reciprocity has been studied in economic psychology field. Greiner and Levati [15] conducted an experimental investment game and analyzed data using generalized linear mixed-effects regression and Wilcoxon signed-rank test. In this research area, there were two different aspects of reciprocity study. One is outcome-based models focusing the distribution and diffusion of cooperative of selfish behavior. Fehr and Schmidt [16] and Bolton and Ockenfels [17] applied model of inequity aversion to investigate reciprocity in various networks.

On the other hand, Levine [18] proposed the model of altruism. The other is the intention-based model focusing on the 3rd party effect, the effect of other person's behavior. McCabe and Smith [19] and Dufwenberg and Kirchsteiger [20] dealt with this model for analyzing indirect cooperative behaviors.

Recent studies using web data for experiments of indirect reciprocity. Suri and Watts [3] studied indirect cooperative behavior and contagion of generosity based on networked public goods experiments. They tested their hypothesis through regression with data collected from Amazon Mechanical Turk (AMT) and found that significant contagion occurs in web-based and networked public goods. Tsvetokv and Macy [6] motivated by the generosity contagion examples observed in real world and tested whether receiving generosity and observing other's generous behaviors have positive effect on one's generous behaviors with regression analysis. Most of these previous studies have used Amazon Mechanical Turk (AMT) for examining their models. AMT is the online crowdsourcing platform and appropriate for these studies. However, it has to be exquisitely designed and controlled by examiners to replicate real world situation, however it has limit to show sufficient complex dynamics of human behaviors.

In using game data for studying the contagion of human behaviors in networks, Lofgren and Fefferman [21] inclined that the analysis in the gaming system could advance the capabilities of simulation modeling in epidemiology. They referred to the accident of one of the popular MMORPGs, World of Warcraft that highly contagious disease accidently occurred as an unintentional game error in 2005 [22]. They observed game user's behaviors which resemble real-world human behaviors. Consequently, they concluded that dynamics of real human behaviors in MMORPGs are clearer than the simulation-based research.

3   Results

We investigate whether receiving generosity increases the chance of showing generosity to strangers or not. Further, we also investigate whether friends' act of showing generosity to strangers increases the chance of showing generosity or not.

We set our testbed up for a leading MMORPG company in Korea, NCsoft. NCsoft provides a world-wide game service with well-known online games such as Lineage, Lineage II, Guildwars, and AION. We used the data set from AION, which was released in South Korea on November 25, 2008, and has been subsequently released in China, Japan, Taiwan, Australia, Europe, North America, and Russia. For our experiments, complete in-game action log of all players of a particular server was retrieved. We analyzed the trade log and social relationship log including party-play and friendship (having friends in the friend list) from December 21, 2010 to March 21, 2011.

For the first, we performed the following preprocessing to exclude noisy data. Activities that involve the sale of virtual in-game resources for real money through exchanges outside of the game are referred to as "real money trading" [23]. Users who give items to others and receive real money for that, which cannot be detected in the game world, should be excluded in this study. We measured the ratio of free transactions over total transactions per individual, namely free money ratio. Free transactions refer the case which the player gives items/money to others for free. We assume that users with free money ratio over 40% involve in real money trading in our previous work [24]. Recently, game sweatshop workers mostly do this real money trading. Game sweatshop also known as gold-farming workshop is a factory-sized professional illegal organization in order to gain profit by real money trading. In addition, to boost up the efficiency of gaining cyber money, game sweatshop workers use game BOT programs. Game BOT program is a well-crafted AI program designed for conducting tedious and labor-intensive jobs on behalf of human players. Thus, we get the whole bot-detection logs and banned user information from NCSoft in order to exclude all malicious users who may involve in real money trading. To launder money trails, malicious users give free money or items between them in the middle of establishing transaction of real money trading; it apparently looks like generous donations. We excluded the users who are detected for frequent use of the game bot and whose free money ratio exceeds 40% [24].

To purify generosity in the game, we investigated the level difference from givers to recipients in free transactions. When high-level users give free money or items to low-level users, this transaction may be a generous behavior. However, in the opposite case, the free transaction from low-level users to high-level users may involve other types of reward. In addition, players with a similar level tend to perform party-plays together, and they have many chances to trade items during or after party-plays. Thus, we limited our analysis to cases which higher-level players give item/money to lower-level players with 10-level difference at least. In Aion, the maximum level is 50 and the minimum level which users can enjoy major game contents is 10, when they reach 10-level, they can battle with another race and collaborate with other players in the same race.

To analyze generosity towards strangers, we limited the focus on the cases which users receive or give item/money from users who are not in friendship relationship nor frequently involved in the same party-play. Involving in a same party-play more than a day indicates that two players have relationship. During the period studied, there were 166,322 transactions excluding game bot users and game sweatshops. The number of transactions that satisfy the level difference is 18,808. This number reduces to 3,487 when limited to strangers. 3,019 players involved in 3,487 transactions confirmed as conducting generous behaviors.

First, we tested the generalized reciprocity theory. Generalized reciprocity indicates that individuals may base cooperative behavior on prior experience irrespective of the identity of their partners [25]. Their research differentiates generalized reciprocity from direct reciprocity that individuals base their behavior on the outcome of previous interactions with the present partner. In addition, generalized reciprocity is different from indirect reciprocity in perspective that latter refers the case that individuals show generosity to others expecting to receive generosity from others for that [26].

Our analysis focuses generalized reciprocity by limiting the analysis focus on giving behavior from higher-level to lower-level. Such manipulation excludes direct reciprocity since higher-level players do not donate expecting receiving rewards.

In addition, players hardly know about others' past behaviors. Further, we excluded generous behaviors between acquaintances to remove opportunities for rewards. The result for testing generalized reciprocity is shown in Table 1. We strictly kept the level difference between givers and recipients, which is 10, in counting the number of players who show generosity after they receive generosity.

Table 1. #, players who show generosity according to whether they receive it before or not

	#, players who give generosity to strangers after they receive it	#, players who do not give genorisity to strangers after they receive it
#, players who receive generosity from strangers	314	1,617
#, players who do not receive generosity	1,088	31,682

The fraction of showing generosity is 3% when they did not receive generosity from others in advance. Around 16% of users, ———— , give it back to strangers when they receive generosity from strangers. This increases up to 37.5% when they receive generosity over 8 times. We compared the fraction of showing generosity to others according to how many times they receive generosity. We observed that almost monotonic increase in the fraction as shown in Fig. 1.

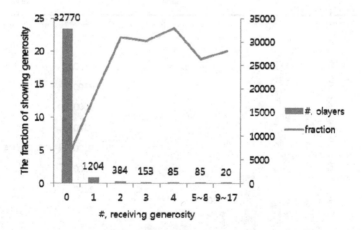

Fig. 1. The fraction of showing generosity according to the number of receiving generosity

The results in Table 1 are consistent with previous research that generosity generates more generosity. We also found that number of receiving generosity increases individuals' likelihood of showing generosity. Another factor explaining the mechanism of generosity contagion is social influence. Social influence is characterized with third party influence and peer influence. Third party influences indicates the cases which individuals show generosity to others after observing others' generosity [6]. Peer influence explains social influence with which individuals want to behave to meet others' expectation. In our data set, we cannot distinguish players' observation on others' generosity. However, under the assumption that information sharing by frequent interaction between friends, social influence can be measured through how many friends show generosity to others. To analyze the effect of social influence on the fraction of showing generosity, we investigated the fraction values according to the degree of social influence. Social influence is estimated as the number of the player' friends who show generosity to strangers. The results are displayed in Table 2 and Fig. 2. When friends shows generosity, the fraction of showing generosity is estimated at 9.1%, ————. The fraction when friends do not show generosity drops to 7.1%. As the number of friends who show generosity to others increases, the fraction of showing generosity also increases until the number of friends who show generosity reaches 4. However, after that, the value rather drops.

Table 2. #, players who show generosity according to whether their friends show generosity

	#, players who show generosity to strangers	#, players who do not show generosity to strangers
#, players whose friends show generosity to strangers	155	1,540
#, players whose friends do not show generosity	260	3,492

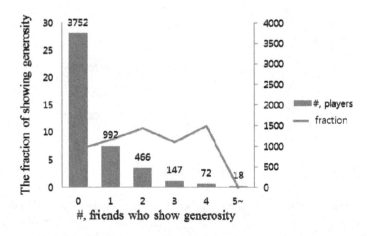

Fig. 2. The fraction of showing generosity according to the number of generous friends

As the number of friends who show generosity increases, the fraction of showing generosity according to the number of generous friends also increases up to 4, but the increase rate is not high. Moreover, after the number of friends who show generosity exceeds 4, the fraction drops to 0. We compared the effect of generalized reciprocity and social influence through the odd ratio. For generalized reciprocity, the odd ratio is calculated at 5.6 $\left(\frac{314/1088}{1617/31682}\right)$ from Table 1. The odd ratio of social influence is 1.4 $\left(\frac{155/260}{1540/3491}\right)$ from Table 2.

To sum up, people become more generous when they receive generosity. In addition, more generosity generates more generosity. However, social influence in the case that their generous behaviors are not surely exposed to their friends does not effectively increase people's generosity. Even the effect of social influence turned out to be negative. This possibly happens because people may feel that their friends fulfill their groups' normative obligation for showing generosity to low level players.

4   Conclusions and Future Studies

In this work, we conducted a large-scale data analysis for investigating social contagion of generous behaviors in online social network platforms, specifically from an MMORPG. Generous behaviors mainly take form of giving game items/money without reward back. In this work, we focused on the generous behavior of donating items or game money to strangers. We used a data set from AION, which was released world-wide and has nearly 240,000 concurrent users. We found that people become more generous when they receive generosity. However, social influence in the case that their generous behaviors are not guaranteed to be noticed by their friends does not effectively increase people's generosity as much as generalized reciprocity. For future research, we will investigate how the level of players and the degree of social interaction affect people' generosity. This will help us to understand who show generosity and who get generosity back to others. Then, we will trace generous behavior to identify cascades of generosity and their distribution. This will give us knowledge on how long generosity continues through giving it back to others.

Acknowledgement. This research was supported by Basic Science Research Program through the National Research Foundation of Korea (NRF) funded by the Ministry of Science, ICT & Future Planning (2014R1A1A1006228) and Ministry of Culture, Sports and Tourism (MCST) and Korea Creative Content Agency (KOCCA) in the Culture Technology (CT) and Research Development Program 2014. This work was also partially supported by the National Research Foundation of Korea Grant funded by the Korean Government (NRF-2013R1A1A3011816) and the ICT R&D program of MSIP/IITP [10044577, Development of Knowledge Evolutionary WiseQA Platform Technology for Human Knowledge Augmented Services].

References

1. http://knowledge.wharton.upenn.edu/article/ice-bucket-challenge-viral/
2. Barry, C.M., Wentzel, K.R.: Friend influence on prosocial behavior: The role of motivational factors and friendship characteristics. Developmental Psychology **42**, 153 (2006)
3. Suri, S., Watts, D.J.: Cooperation and contagion in web-based, networked public goods experiments. PLoS One **6**, e16836 (2011)
4. Starbucks Customers Break 1,000 in Pay-It-Forward Record 2013. Source: ABC News. http://abcnews.go.com/blogs/headlines/2013/12/starbucks-customersbreak-1000-in-pay-it-forward-record/
5. Jordan, J.J., Rand, D.G., Arbesman, S., Fowler, J.H., Christakis, N.A.: Contagion of cooperation in static and fluid social networks. PloS One **8**, e66199 (2013)
6. Tsvetkova, M., Macy, M.W.: The Social Contagion of Generosity. PloS One **9**, e87275 (2014)
7. Penner, L.A., Dovidio, J.F., Piliavin, J.A., Schroeder, D.A.: Prosocial behavior: Multilevel perspectives. Annu. Rev. Psychol. **56**, 365–392 (2005)
8. Bauman, Z.: Postmodern ethics. Blackwell Oxford (1993)
9. Mallough, R.: An extra-large sized order of generosity. http://www.macleans.ca/news/canada/an-extra-large-sized-order-of-generosity/
10. Memmott, M.: 55 customers pay for next car's order at Mass. doughnut shop. http://www.npr.org/blogs/thetwo-way/2013/07/15/202365926/55-customers-pay-for-next-cars-order-at-mass-doughnut-shop
11. Fudenberg, D., Rand, D.G., Dreber, A.: Slow to anger and fast to forgive: Cooperation in an uncertain world. The American Economic Review **102**, 720–749 (2012)
12. Christakis, N.A., Fowler, J.H.: Social contagion theory: Examining dynamic social networks and human behavior. Statistics in Medicine **32**, 556–577 (2013)
13. Jackson, M.O.: Networks and economic behavior. Annu. Rev. Econ. **1**, 489–511 (2009)
14. Rand, D.G., Arbesman, S., Christakis, N.A.: Dynamic social networks promote cooperation in experiments with humans. Proceedings of the National Academy of Sciences **108**, 19193–19198 (2011)
15. Greiner, B.: Vittoria Levati, M.: Indirect reciprocity in cyclical networks: An experimental study. Journal of Economic Psychology **26**, 711–731 (2005)
16. Fehr, E., Schmidt, K.M.: A theory of fairness, competition, and cooperation. Quarterly Journal of Economics **114**, 817–868 (1999)
17. Bolton, G.E., Ockenfels, A.: ERC: A theory of equity, reciprocity, and competition. American Economic Review **90**, 166–193 (2000)
18. Levine, D.K.: Modeling altruism and spitefulness in experiments. Review of Economic Dynamics **1**, 593–622 (1998)
19. McCabe, K.A., Smith, V.L., LePore, M.: Intentionality detection and "mindreading": Why does game form matter? Proceedings of the National Academy of Sciences **97**, 4404–4409 (2000)
20. Dufwenberg, M., Gneezy, U., Güth, W., van Damme, E.E.: An experimental test of direct and indirect reciprocity in case of complete and incomplete information. Discussion Papers, Interdisciplinary Research Project 373: Quantification and Simulation of Economic Processes (2000)
21. Lofgren, E.T., Fefferman, N.H.: The untapped potential of virtual game worlds to shed light on real world epidemics. The Lancet Infectious Diseases **7**, 625–629 (2007)
22. Reimer, J.: Virtual plague spreading like wildfire in World of Warcraft. Ars Technica 21 (2005)

23. Keegan, B., Ahmed, M.A., Williams, D., Srivastava, J., Contractor, N.: Dark gold: statistical properties of clandestine networks in massively multiplayer online games. In: 2010 IEEE Second International Conference on Social Computing (SocialCom), pp. 201–208. IEEE (2010)
24. Kwon, H., Mohaisen, A., Woo, J., Kim, Y., Kim, H.K.: Crime scene reconstruction: Online gold farming network analysis. Working paper
25. Rutte, C., Taborsky, M.: Generalized reciprocity in rats. PLoS Biology 5, e196 (2007)
26. Nowak, M.A., Sigmund, K.: Evolution of indirect reciprocity. Nature 437, 1291–1298 (2005)

Developing Game-Structure Sensitive Matchmaking System for Massive-Multiplayer Online Games

Mateusz Myślak[1](✉) and Dominik Deja[2]

[1] Gdańsk University of Technology, Gdańsk, Poland
matmysla@student.pg.gda.pl
[2] Polish-Japanese Institute of Information Technology, Warsaw, Poland
dominik.deja@pjwstk.edu.pl

Abstract. Providing a fair matchmaking system is an essential issue, while developing every online video game. In the article, we show that the currently existing matchmaking system in League of Legends, one of the most popular online video games currently existing, is built on a base of conditions which do not hold true in the presence of empirical data. This, in short, decreases the effectiveness of the ranking system, and negatively affects users experience. Therefore, we propose a new ranking system, which genuinely answers the needs, which arise from League of Legends gameplay. As League of Legends gameplay model is nowadays highly popular amid online video games, the proposed system can be easily generalized and adopted by other online video games that are currently popular among gamers.

Keywords: Game design · Online games · e-Sport · Matchmaking · Ranking systems

1 Introduction

The Rise of Massive-Multiplayer Online Games (MMOG) changed how online video games are perceived today by general public. Due to the games such as Starcraft, Warcraft, and Counter-Strike, an activity of game playing, which was commonly viewed as immature, or juvenile, became a fully professionalized e-sport. League of Legends (LOL) represents one of the younger branches which derives from the MMOG family - Massive Online Battle Arena (MOBA). Games from this genre are based on relatively short matches, where players compete in teams in order to archive various goals (typically to kill another team members, or to destroy another's team base). Recently, a peak of 5 million concurrent LOL players has been noted[1].

---

[1] http://www.riotgames.com/articles/20130312/700/league-legends-players-summit-new-peak (If not stated otherwise, all Internet sources were retrieved 08.09.2014).

© Springer International Publishing Switzerland 2015
L.M. Aiello and D. McFarland (Eds.): SocInfo 2014 Workshops, LNCS 8852, pp. 200–208, 2015.
DOI: 10.1007/978-3-319-15168-7_25

Key feature of almost all MOBA is matchmaking. It is an essential part of a game, because it makes a game enjoyable. Basically, matchmaking ensures that players always face opponents who are no better and no worse than them. A faulty matchmaking system deters good and bad players alike. Seasoned players will get bored, while laymen frustrated.

In the article, we propose a new matchmaking system for LOL, as we found out that the currently implemented system is providing suboptimal results. It is due to the fact, that LOL does not make use of the internal structure of a gameplay. The primary goal of our article is to show, how underlying structure of a gameplay can be used and leveraged in order to obtain the best possible matchmaking system. While we provide results for LOL, the solution can be generalized and implemented in wide range of MOBA.

All the data acquisition, data preprocessing, data processing and final computations for this article were done using C#, Python, and R.

2   Related Works

In 1959 Arpad Elo developed his chess rating system [4], which soon gained its popularity and became one of the most commonly used system in chess, as well as other disciplines. Arpad's work was based on the earlier system, developed by Harkness [7]. Both systems are based, and variants of Bradley-Terry model [2]. Glickman generalized Elo's sytem by putting modeling belief about a player's skill into Bayesian framework [5].

Recent advancement is TrueSkill system, which is inspired by Glickman's system, and which is wholesomely based in Bayesian approach [8]. TrueSkill is made specifically as an answer to the needs of multiplayer games, and its effectiveness has been tested on Xbox Halo 2 video game. Guo et al. [6] improved the system by allowing it to work on scores of matches. Also, their version allows to rate different aspects of player's play separately, such as offence and defense competences. Dangauthier [3] showed that the TrueSkill can effectively replace the Elo system in chess.

The variety of multiplayer games gave birth to different rating systems. Most of them are based on the Elo system. Probably, the most well known games such as World of Warcraft II[2], or Dota 2[3]. Some games, due to their specific characteristics have their own systems, such as Ticket to Ride[4], Smite[5], or World of Tanks[6].

In connection to its growing popularity, LOL and e-sport in general, became research topics. Hinnant [9] analyses phenomenon of e-sports from an economic point of view. Toxic behavior of players was analyzed by Blackburn and Kwak [1], whereas Warner and Raiter [10] explore ethical questions which arise in MMOG context.

---

[2] http://eu.battle.net/wow/en/
[3] http://blog.dota2.com/
[4] http://www.daysofwonder.com/en/
[5] http://www.hirezstudios.com/smite
[6] http://worldoftanks.eu/

3   About League of Legends

League of Legends is a multiplayer online battle arena video game. It was developed by Riot Games and released at the end of 2009[7]. In general, the game is free-to-play, but players might pay in order to receive additional features (which, however, do not change player's chances of winning). Currently, LOL is one of the most popular online games worldwide with approximately 27 million players, playing it every day[8]. The game is highly competitive and official tournaments are conducted on regular basis. Such events gather huge interest, with 32 million viewers watching annual finals in 2013 via the Internet[9].

League of Legends offers a number of game modes. However, the most important is Summoner's Rift, which creation was heavily inspired by mod for the video game Warcraft III: The Frozen Throne, called Defense of the Ancients. In this article we will focus only on this mode, as all tournaments and ranked games use only this one mentioned above. In this 5 versus 5 game mode (blue versus purple team), player controls behaviour of his/hers champion and cooperates with teammates in order to destroy enemy's base. A game ends, when one of the sides destroys an enemy's core building, called "Nexus". As it is located in the middle of a base, a team has to raze a number of defensive facilities located on the way to enemy's base. There are three lanes which connects two bases, and a jungle in between. The map is rather symmetrical, and chances of winning depends slightly on starting side in favor of blue team (53.3%, $\alpha < 0.001$). Usually, it takes about 30 minutes to play one match.

Summoner's Rift can be played in normal or ranked mode. Difference between those lies in ranking system, which is hidden for those who play normal games, and revealed for those who play ranked games. After first 10 ranked games, each players is assigned to a tier and division. In total, there are six tiers: bronze, silver, gold, platinum, diamond, and challenger. Each of those is divided into five divisions (apart from challenger, which is a tier for top 200 players). An assignment to a tier and division is based on Riot's ranking system, which is not publicly known.

The gameplay enforces cooperation between players, and winning highly depends on ability to play in team, especially in the later phases of a match. At the beginning, most of the time is spent on small, one-on-one fights and gathering gold and experience to increase power of one's champion. As the time passes, duels become more rare, and team fights start to occur. This are decisive points of a game, as after each death of player's champion, he/she has to wait a certain amount of time for revival. The later it happens, the longer one has to wait.

Effectiveness of a team depends on three factors. Skill of individuals who build up a team, champion selection, and used "meta" - an overall role distribution between teammates. They are correlated, as better players tend to pick

---

[7] http://www.riotgames.com/about

[8] http://www.riotgames.com/our-games

[9] http://www.economist.com/news/business/21614175-why-amazon-buying-video
-game-streaming-site-streaming-down-amazon

champions that complement with each other and use more efficient metas. Champions fall into one of categories such as: assassin, fighter (also called bruiser, or off-tank), tank, mage, marksman, or support. A strong team almost always consists of a marksman with support, tank and two champions from the rest of the list. Such differentiation is necessary, as every type plays important role. For example, tank protects more "squishy" champions by intercepting enemy's fire, while marksman tries to inflict as much damage as possible.

Still, the most important is meta. Our research shows that this is currently the bottle-neck of the matchmaking system. Professional teams tend to stick to one, standard meta: solo top, solo mid, jungler and duo bot with ad carry and support. It means that in early phase of a game, one player, usually a fighter, bruiser or tank, goes for a top lane, another one, usually assassin or mage, goes for mid lane, two (marksman and support) goes for the bot lane, and the last one (bruiser, assassin or tank) for the jungle. This strategy allows players to maintain high overall efficiency and build strength which will allow them to win in the later game.

Yet, players with less experience tend to use it less frequently. Table 1 shows that the teams that consist of players from the lowest tiers deviate from the standard mets over three and a half times more frequently than teams made of the best players.

Table 1. Standard meta usage amid the best and the worst players

	Bronze Teams	Champion Teams
Standard Meta	71.97%	91.16%
Non-Standard Meta	28.03%	8.84%

This is highly undesirable, because in teams with non-standard meta risk of having an AFK[10] is substantially higher than in those which use the standard one (23% : 6%). Additionally, a meta usage influences final results. Winning depends on used meta and professional players know what they do. Table 2 shows the results.

Table 2. Meta usage correlates with chances of a victory

	Victory	Defeat
Standard Meta	51.02%	48.98%
Non-Standard Meta	41.50%	58.50%

The main reason for this problem is the matchmaking system currently implemented in LOL. In the next chapter, its mechanics are analysed, deficiencies revealed, and, as a result of our work, a new model is proposed.

---

[10] Away From Keyboard - term used when someone stops playing in the middle of a game.

4   Matchmaking Based on Roles

The problem with the currently existing matchmaking system starts, in fact, even before a match commences. A screen from the queue process, fig. 1, captures the moment when a row between players begins.

Fig. 1. Screen from the game, made during one of matches played by authors. One of players, unsatisfied that his role is taken, starts to behave aggressively.

Before a match starts, players are put in a matchmaking queue, where every player chooses a champion he/she wishes to play in an upcoming match. Players have the right to choose their champions in order of diminishing ranking. This is a moment, when worse players, who chooses their champions as the last ones, may start arguments. It occurs, when better players take roles which worse players would like to take themselves. It may lead to rows, aggressive behavior, game leaving, and non-standard metas, which significantly decrease teams' chances of winning a match.

This happens especially often amid low tier players, as their abilities are limited, and they are not able to play on different positions with the same effectiveness. Although the ranking system used by LOL is not officially exposed, and it is highly unlikeable that it takes into account role-specific skill of a player. In fact, Riot has tested a system, where roles are chosen *before* matchmaking happens. However, even though the system exists, it is highly possible that it is not preferred by players, as Riot has not implemented it for ranked games.

Therefore, we propose to rebuilt the matchmaking process, in a way it could be implicitly role-specific. The system will always try to match five players into one team, in a way that every player's favorite position will be non-overlapping with other players preferences. This will require to treat player's skill as a vector of skill estimates for every position, rather than a scalar. So the skill of $player_i$, who played $\mathbf{games}_i : \{\mathbf{games}_i \subset \mathbf{Games} \text{ and } player_i \in \mathbf{games}_i\}$ will look like

$$\mathbf{Skill}_i(\mathbf{games}_i) = \begin{cases} Skill(\mathbf{games}_{i1}) \\ ... \\ Skill(\mathbf{games}_{ij}) \\ ... \\ Skill(\mathbf{games}_{im}) \end{cases} \tag{1}$$

where $1 \leq j \leq m$, $m = \#roles$, and **games**$_{ij}$ denote all the games of $player_i$, where he played on $role_j$.

To assign a player to a game, the matchmaking system would use information about players preferred position via estimated skill vector. This would end nerve-racking rows between players fighting for a role, and would result in better enjoyment drawn from a game. After all, no one likes to play a game, which is doomed to fail from the very beginning.

Still, one may ask, whether this system would work efficiently, as some positions are more preferable than others. This is not the case with LOL, as it is shown in fig. 2. Clustering reveals that there are separate groups of players who have their favorite position, and those groups do not overlap. Moreover, the better the player is, the more he/she plays on one position.

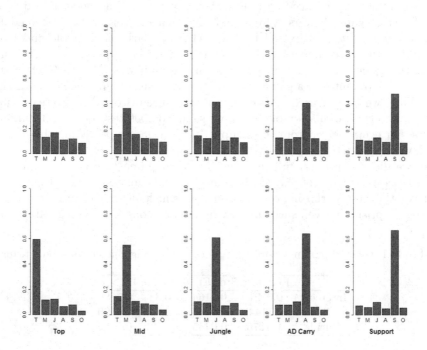

Fig. 2. Results from clustering (using k-means with k = 5) roles' choices for players from bronze tier (first row) and challenger tier (second row). Bar letters stands for: {Top, Mid, Jungle, Ad Carry, Support, Other}.

5   Results

To verify effectiveness of our solution, we decided to use data obtainable via official LOL api[11]. Although we could not test our system by deciding who

---

[11] https://developer.riotgames.com/

will play with whom, we could check, whether we are able to efficiently predict who will win a match on a base of our assumptions. LOL's matchmaking system matches teams in a way, that every team has got nearly 50% chances of winning. If, while using skill estimated on a base of role's performance, we can predict a match's outcome with a result significantly better than 50% (which is similar to a coin toss), then it means that our mechanism works better.

From July to August 2014 we gathered over 200 thousands of randomly selected ranked games played in the ongoing season 3, on Western European platform. By picking games from a such narrow time period we can assume, that the standard meta has not changed over time. Every game was played by 10 players, therefore, in total, we collected 2 million observations of individual gameplay. For every player from this set, we obtained his/hers league data, such as tier and division, which are public LOL's skill estimates. The total amount of chosen games was reduced by removing the ones where a non-standard meta was played or game leavers were found. The players roles were classified by consolidating two tags delivered by Riot API, the each players role and lane. Afterwards, the outcome was verified by analyzing player position on the map during the game. If the players position on the map was constantly changing during first 15 minutes of a game, we were marking such games as non-standard meta. Thus, we have cleared our sample to make sure it wouldl generate credible results. From this population of games, we sampled 2000 test games with unique players. For every player from the sample, his past games preceding the sample match were gathered - from 10 up to 30.

As we did not possess full information about game history, we could not obtain precise estimates of players elo. Thus, we made an assumption that player archieves the best performance on positions, which he/she chooses most frequently. Surprisingly, even such simplifying assumptions has given good results.

Table 3. Estimated parameters of logit model for wining chances of a blue team

	Estimate	Std. Error	z value	Pr($>|z|$)
(Intercept)	0.0721	0.2164	0.33	0.7389
Blue	0.1144	0.0438	2.61	0.0090
Purple	-0.1076	0.0445	-2.42	0.0156

For each game from the test set, we counted how many players from blue and purple team play on theirs favorite positions. Each player's favorite position was estimated on his/hers past games. Then, for prepared data, a logit model was estimated, in which dependent variable was binary (Win/Lose) score of a blue team.

Table 3 shows parameters. With $\alpha = 0.05$, variables are significant. The intercept does not pass this threshold, yet it cannot be excluded from the model. Each variable shows number of players in a team playing on their favorite position. The interpretation of parameters is that with each player playing his/hers "right" position, teams chances of winning increases, while with each player in

Table 4. Probabilities, according to the logistic model, of winning for blue team for different numbers of team members on their favorite positions

		0	1	2	3	4	5
	5	65.57%	62.94%	60.24%	57.47%	54.65%	51.8%
	4	63.1%	60.4%	57.63%	54.82%	51.97%	49.11%
Blue Team	3	60.56%	57.8%	54.99%	52.14%	49.28%	46.43%
	2	57.96%	55.15%	52.31%	49.45%	46.6%	43.77%
	1	55.32%	52.48%	49.62%	46.77%	43.93%	41.14%
	0	52.65%	49.79%	46.94%	44.1%	41.3%	38.56%

Purple Team

an enemy's team playing his/hers "right" position chances of blue team winning decreases. It is especially visible from the tab. 4. In a situation, where team perfectly matched plays versus team in total disorder (left-top corner) the probability of winning exceeds 65%. In reversed situation (right-bottom corner), probability of winning falls down to less than 40%. This shows, that having a team, in which everyone is on the "right" position, have a big impact on the overall score of a match.

6   Conclusions

One of the biggest advantages of the implicit matchmaking system based on game-structure from a developers point of view, is that it can improve users experience without any need to make sacrifices. In fact, players do not even have to be informed that they are matched on a base of their preferences and skill.

Though we tested our system on LOL, a game-structure oriented matchmaking system can be easily generalized and adopted to other MOBAs, such as Dota 2, or Smite. While every game is different, if there exists one, best "meta", the system can be easily implemented. For games, which already implements any kind of a skill rating system, then it can be easily expanded to register role information of every player.

In order to avoid "locking" players to roles which they play the best, the freedom to choose which role they want to play would be maintained via traditional champion selection stage. While the system will be trying to match players accordingly to their skills, the players will still have an open possibility to choose a role they would like to play.

References

1. Blackburn, J., Kwak, H.: Stfu noob!: predicting crowdsourced decisions on toxic behavior in online games. In: Proceedings of the 23rd International Conference on World Wide Web, pp. 877–888. International World Wide Web Conferences Steering Committee (2014)
2. Bradley, R.A., Terry, M.E.: Rank analysis of incomplete block designs: I. The method of paired comparisons. Biometrika, 324–345 (1952)

3. Dangauthier, P., Herbrich, R., Minka, T., Graepel, T.: Trueskill through time: revisiting the history of chess. In: Advances in Neural Information Processing Systems 20, pp. 931–938. MIT Press (2008). http://research.microsoft.com/apps/pubs/default.aspx?id=74417

4. Elo, A.E.: The rating of chessplayers, past and present. Arco Pub., New York (1978)

5. Glickman, M.E.: Parameter estimation in large dynamic paired comparison experiments. Journal of the Royal Statistical Society: Series C (Applied Statistics) **48**(3), 377–394 (1999)

6. Guo, S., Sanner, S., Graepel, T., Buntine, W.: Score-based bayesian skill learning. In: Flach, P.A., De Bie, T., Cristianini, N. (eds.) ECML PKDD 2012, Part I. LNCS, vol. 7523, pp. 106–121. Springer, Heidelberg (2012). http://research.microsoft.com/apps/pubs/default.aspx?id=193839

7. Harkness, K.: Official Chess Handbook. McKay Company (1967)

8. Herbrich, R., Minka, T., Graepel, T.: Trueskill(tm): a bayesian skill rating system. In: Advances in Neural Information Processing Systems 20, pp. 569–576. MIT Press, January 2007. http://research.microsoft.com/apps/pubs/default.aspx?id=67956

9. Hinnant, N.C.: Practicing work, perfecting play: League of legends and the sentimental education of e-sports (2013)

10. Warner, D.E., Raiter, M.: Social context in massively-multiplayer online games (mmogs): Ethical questions in shared space. International Review of Information Ethics **4**(7) (2005)

Linguistic Analysis of Toxic Behavior
in an Online Video Game

Haewoon Kwak[1]([⊠]) and Jeremy Blackburn[2]

[1] Qatar Computing Research Institute, Doha, Qatar
hkwak@qf.org.qa
[2] Telefonica Research, Barcelona, Spain
jeremyb@tid.es

Abstract. In this paper we explore the *linguistic* components of toxic behavior by using crowdsourced data from over 590 thousand cases of accused toxic players in a popular match-based competition game, League of Legends. We perform a series of linguistic analyses to gain a deeper understanding of the role communication plays in the expression of toxic behavior. We characterize linguistic behavior of toxic players and compare it with that of typical players in an online competition game. We also find empirical support describing how a player *transitions* from typical to toxic behavior. Our findings can be helpful to automatically detect and warn players who may become toxic and thus insulate potential victims from toxic playing in advance.

Keywords: Toxic behavior · Verbal violence · Tribunal · League of Legends · Cyberbullying · Online games

1 Introduction

Multiplayer games provide players with the thrill of *true* competition. Players prove themselves superior to other humans that exhibit *dynamic* behavior far beyond that of any computer controlled opponent. Additionally, some multiplayer games provide another wrinkle: teamwork. Now, not only is it a test of skill between two individuals, but cooperation, strategy, and communication between teammates can ensure victory. Unfortunately, the presence of teammates and their influence on victory and defeat can result in *toxic* behavior.

Toxic behavior, also known as cyberbullying [1], griefing [4], or online disinhibition [7], is bad behavior that violates social norms, inflicts misery, continues to cause harm after it occurs, and affects an entire community. The anonymity afforded by, and ubiquity of, computer-mediated-communication (CMC) naturally leads to hostility and aggressiveness [3,8]. A major obstacle in understanding toxic behavior is its subjective perception. Unlike unethical behavior like cheating, toxic behavior is nebulously defined; toxic players themselves sometimes fail to recognize their behavior as toxic [6]. Nevertheless, because of the very real impact toxic behavior has on our daily lives, even outside of games, a deeper understanding is necessary.

© Springer International Publishing Switzerland 2015
L.M. Aiello and D. McFarland (Eds.): SocInfo 2014 Workshops, LNCS 8852, pp. 209–217, 2015.
DOI: 10.1007/978-3-319-15168-7_26

To further our understanding, in this paper we explore the *linguistic* components of toxic behavior. Using crowdsourced data from over 590 thousand "judicial trials" of accused toxic players representing over 2.1 million matches of a popular match-based competition game, League of Legends[1], we perform a series of linguistic analyses to gain a deeper understanding of the role communication plays in the expression of toxic behavior. In our previous work [2], we found that offensive language is the most reported reason across all the three regions. Also, in North America, verbal abuse is the second most reported reason. In other words, linguistic components are a prime method of expressing toxicity.

From our analyses we draw several findings. First, the *volume* of communication is not uniform throughout the length of the match, instead showing a bi-modal shape with peaks at the beginning and end of a match. By comparing the distribution of frequency of communications between normal players and toxic players, we find subtle differences. Typical players chat relatively more at the beginning of a match, which is mainly for ice breaking, morale boosting, and sharing early strategic information. In contrast, toxic players chat less at the beginning but constantly more than typical players after some time point, i.e. phase transition. Next, we find discriminative uni- and bi-grams used by typical and toxic players, as signatures of them, examine the differences, and show that certain bi-grams can be classified based on *when* they appear in a match. Temporal patterns of the linguistic signature of toxic players illustrate what kind of toxic playing happens as the match progresses. Deeper analysis of temporal analysis of words used by toxic and typical players reveals a more interesting picture. We focus on how a player transitions to toxic by comparing the temporal usage of popular uni-grams between typical players and toxic players.

Our contribution is two-fold. First, we characterize linguistic behavior of toxic players and compare it with that of typical players in online competition games. Second, we find empirical support to describe how a player turns to be toxic. Our findings would be helpful to automatically detect and warn players who may turn to be toxic and thus save potential victims of toxic playing in advance.

2   Dataset

The League of Legends (LoL) is the most popular Multiplayer Online Battle Arena out today, and suffers from a high degree of toxic behavior. The LoL Tribunal is a crowdsourced system for determining the guilt of players accused of tocix behavior.

We collected 590,311 Tribunal cases from the North America region representing a total of 2,107,522 individual matches. Each Tribunal case represents a single player and includes up to 5 matches in which he was accused of toxic behavior. In LoL players can communicate via chat, which is ostensibly used to

---

[1] http://leagueoflegends.com

share strategic plans and other important information during the game. However, chat is also a prime vector for exhibiting toxic behavior. Thus, although a variety of information is presented to Tribunal reviewers [2], in this paper we focus exclusively on the in-game *chat logs*.

We extract 24,039,184 messages from toxic players and 33,252,018 messages from typical players. Because the teammates of toxic players are directly impacted by toxic playing and readily express aggressive reactions to a toxic player, we define *typical players* as the set of players on the opposite team when none of them report the toxic player.

Before continuing, we report some basic statistics about the size of vocabulary and the length of messages. We found 1,042,940 unique tokens in toxic player messages and 1,176,356 unique tokens in typical player messages. While typical players send 38% more messages than toxic players, the messages are composed of only 13% more unique tokens. Interestingly, we find that toxic players send longer messages than typical players; the average number of words per message is 3.139 and 2.732 for toxic and typical players, respectively.

3   Chat Volume over a Match

We begin our analysis by exploring chat volume over time. A LoL match can be broken up into logical stages. First is the *early game* (also known as the "laning phase"), where characters are low level and weak. In the early game, players expend great effort towards "farming" computer controlled minions to gain experience and gold, with aggressive plays against the other team usually coming as the result of an over extension or other mistake. As players earn gold and experience, they level up and become stronger, and the match transitions to the *mid game*. During the mid game, players become more aggressive and tend to group up with teammates to make plays on their opponents. Finally, once players are reaching their maximum power levels, the match transitions into the *end game*, where teams will group together and make hard pushes towards taking objectives and winning the match.

While these phases are not dictated by the programming of LoL, and thus there is no hard cut off point for when the transitions between phases occur, we suspect that each phase has an associated pattern of communication. Thus, in Figure 1 we plot the density of chat messages written by toxic and typical players as a function of the normalized time during a match. The plot confirms our suspicions: communication is not uniform throughout the match. Instead, we see three distinct levels of communication, likely corresponding to the three phases of a match, with relative peaks at the beginning and end of the match.

This finding can be explained with a deeper understanding of how a LoL match progresses. As mentioned above, in the early game players are relatively weak and must focus on farming for resources. Early game farming occurs via players choosing one of three lanes to spend their time in. The lanes are quite far from each other on the map (10+ seconds or so to travel between them) and thus players on the same team tend to be relatively isolated from each other.

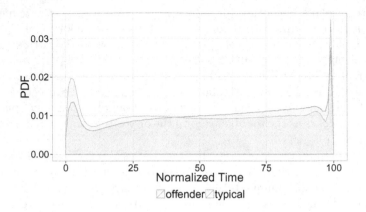

Fig. 1. Change of chat volume during a match

To take advantage of this isolation, and to get an early lead, players might roam from the lane they chose to play in to another lane. In turn, this provides their teammate in the other lane with a numbers advantage over opposing player in the lane. Colloquially, this roaming to provide a temporary numbers advantage is known as a "gank." To deal with ganks in the early game, players tend to communicate via chat when the opposing player in their lane has gone missing.

As the match transitions to mid game, teammates start grouping up. Since they are no longer so isolated the fear of ganks dissipates, and the need to communicate missing players diminishes. Additionally, since teammates are grouped together, they are seeing the same portion of the map, and there is not really that much additional information they can convey to each other.

Finally, as late game comes around, teams must focus and work together to complete objectives and win the match. In practice, this might involve coming to agreement on a final "push" for an objective, or agreeing on which lane the team should travel down. Also, there are some customs in e-sports, saying 'gg (good game)' at the end of the game. The sharp spikes contain those messages as well. While this might explain some of the spike seen at the end of Figure 1 another, simpler explanation is that players are simply communicating their (dis)pleasure in winning or losing the match.

A more interesting finding is the subtle difference in the distributions of typical and toxic players. At the early stage we see more active communication by normal players. We suppose that it includes all the messages for ice breaking or cheering (e.g. gl (good luck) or hf (have fun)). However, at some point after the short period, toxic players begin to chat more than typical players and keep such pattern until by the last stage. At the last stage of the match, typical players again chat more socially, for example, sending smile emoticons, which are :D or :), and also saying gg, as we mentioned. The transition point, where the distribution of toxic players cross over that of typical players, is a basis of our further analysis in Section 5.

Rank	Typical player		Toxic player	
	1-gram	2-gram	1-gram	2-gram
1	oops	group push	retards	fucking retard
2	o.o	wanted kill	nigger	report noob
3	midmia	wolves leash	garbage	fking noob
4	mis	gotta kill	uninstall	fucking useless
5	comin	ill ward	piece	fuck team
6	=/	ill start	pathetic	report fucking
7	:c	push hard	fuckign	stupid noob
8	:o	group mid	fukin	pussy ass
9	._.	frozen heart	nooob	play bots
10	afk?	thought guys	bots	play fucking

Fig. 2. Top 10 discriminative uni- and bi-grams

4   Discriminative Words of Toxic and Typical Players

The linguistic approach to the chat log characterizes toxic players with context. We conduct n-gram analysis because it is intuitive and straightforward. We filter the stopwords and then count the frequency of uni- and bi-grams from the chat log involving toxic reports of either verbal abuse or offensive language.

In order to find discriminative n-grams of toxic players we need a reference for comparison. We conduct the same n-gram analysis from enemy's chat log when verbal abuse or offensive language is *not* reported from the enemies. We consider it as a normal conversation among players and call those enemies typical players. We create the top 1,000 uni- and bi-grams for toxic and typical players, respectively. We find 867 uni- and 748 bi-grams in common. Then we obtain 133 non-overlapped uni- and 252 bi-grams for toxic and typical players; they appear only in either toxic or typical players. We define them as discriminative uni- and bi-gram for toxic and typical players, respectively.

Figure 2 shows top 10 discriminative uni- and bi-grams of toxic and typical players. Top 10 discriminative uni- and bi-grams of toxic players are filled with bad words. That is, Riot Games does not offer even the basic level of bad word filtering, and such bad words can be used as the signatures of toxic players who used verbal abuse or offensive language. We find that several discriminative bi-grams of typical players are about strategies, while most of toxic players' bi-grams are bad words. We note that some variations of 'fucking' are discriminative uni-grams but 'fucking' itself is not. It means that 'fucking' is often used not only by toxic players but also by typical players as well. This shows the difficulties of filtering bad words by a simple dictionary-based approach.

As the next step of the linguistic approach, we are interested in *when verbal abuse occurs* from a temporal perspective during a match. We divide 252 discriminative bi-grams of toxic players into three classes, early-, mid-, and late-bi-grams, based on when their highest frequencies occur.

Figure 3 presents an example of three temporal classes of bi-grams. Interestingly, 209 (82.94%) out of 252 bi-grams are late-bi-gram. The early-bi-gram

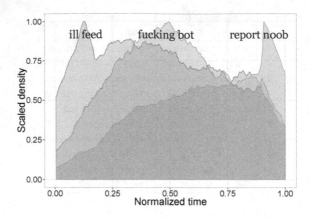

Fig. 3. Example of early-, mid-, and late-bi-gram

"ill feed" is a domain specific example of toxic behavior. In LoL, one of the ways players earn gold and experience during a match is by killing players on the opposite team. Intentional feeding is when a player deliberately allows the other team to kill them, thus "feeding" the enemies with gold and experience, in turn allowing them to become quite powerful.

The mid-bi-gram "fucking bot" is the toxic player expressing his displeasure for the performance of the bottom lane. The bottom lane is usually manned by characters that have a primarily late-game presence, and thus being behind during the mid-game has a significant impact on the remainder of the match.

Most verbal abuse of toxic players occurs in the late stage of the game. For example, "report noob" is the toxic player requesting that the rest of his team report a player (the "noob") that he singled out for his ire. We believe the most likely explanation for this is that verbal abuse is most likely a response to losing a game, which is often not apparent until the late-game. For example, consider a scenario where one player on the team has a bad game, perhaps making poor decisions resulting in the enemy team becoming quite strong. In the early-, and even mid-game phases, a toxic player might still be able to hold his own, however, when the enemy team groups up and makes coordinated pushes in the late-game, their relative strength will often result in quick and decisive victories in team-fights. If toxic playing can be detected in real-time, we could protect potential victims from verbal violence, for example via alerts or simply not delivering such messages.

Temporal dynamics of bi-grams might help to create a mental model of toxic players. For instance, 10 bi-grams containing 'bot' are divided into 1 early-bi-gram, 5 mid-bi-grams, and 4 late-bi-grams. Through manual inspection, we confirm that the early-bi-gram ('go bot') is strategic and non-aggressive, the mid-bi-grams are cursing, and the late-bi-grams are blaming the result of the match on the bot player(s). This provides us with a rough idea of how toxic players might behave and think over time: initially they have a similar mindset

One-gram	Time diff.	One-gram	Time diff.
:)	100	come	68
sorry	100	ult	57
:D	100	blue	56
ggwp	100	ty	50
op	100	care	47
well	99	re	44
end	98	brb	35
wait	97	k	34
lets	96	ward	33
back	96	gj	31
b	95	omw	31

Fig. 4. Time difference of last used time of uni-gram

as typical players, but, as the game plays out contrary to their desires, they grow increasingly aggressive, eventually lashing out with purely abusive language. We leave more sophisticated modeling of toxic players' thought process as future work.

5 Phase Transition of Toxic Players

In the previous section we recognize which words are exclusively used by toxic and normal players. However, some words are used by both toxic players and normal players. For these, the emerging patterns in a temporal sense could be quite different. If we assume that toxic players exhibit toxic behavior in reaction to certain events happening during the match, then the linguistic behavior of such toxic players *should be the same as typical players before those events happen.*

To validate the above hypothesis, we conduct the following experiment which is focused on finding some words that are not used after some time point by toxic players, while they are continuously used by normal players. We extract the top 30 uni-gram at every normalized time unit (ranging from 0 to 100) for toxic players and normal players, respectively. Since top 30 uni-grams are quite stable during the match, we obtain unique 80 uni-gram for toxic players and 91 uni-grams for normal players. We first observe that toxic players have slightly smaller vocabularies than that by normal players. For each of these uni-grams, we compute the normalized time of last use by toxic players and normal players, respectively. Finally, we compute the difference of the last used time between toxic and normal players for the common uni-grams.

Figure 4 lists the uni-grams with a time difference greater than 30. I.e., words in the list are used later into the match by normal players. Some interesting patterns are present in the results.

First, emoticons, particularly smile emoticons, are almost never used by toxic players. Second, apologies (e.g., 'sorry') are also exclusively used by normal players. Third, some words for strategic team maneuvers (e.g., 'come', 'ult', 'blue', 'ward') are used by toxic players, but this ceases at some point during the match. Fourth, some words primarily used for communicating movements with partners in the same lane (e.g. 'back', 'b', 'brb' (be right back), 'omw' (on my way), 'k' (okay)) are also used by toxic players, but again, after some point toxic players stop this form of communication. Fifth, toxic players stop praising (e.g., 'gj' (good job)) their teammates after some point in time.

All these findings reveal how toxicity is born during a match. It seems to be a kind of phase transition. They behave the same as normal players during the early stage of the match, but at some point they change their behavior. After some point, they utter neither apologies nor praise to express their feelings, and also stop strategic communication with team members.

By combining this finding with discriminative words of toxic players, we see the possibility for detecting a certain point that a player transitions to be toxic without using detailed in-game action logs, but just chat logs. Thus, linguistic analysis of toxic players shows not just how different they are and *when* they become different as well.

6   Conclusion and Future Work

In this work we have examined crowdsourced data from 590 thousand cases of accused toxic players in a popular match-based competition game, League of Legends. We have performed a series of linguistic analyses to gain a deeper understanding of the role communication plays in the expression of toxic behavior. We have several interesting findings: a bi-modal distribution of chats during a match, a difference between temporal chat patterns between toxic and typical players, a list of discriminative uni- and bi-grams used by typical and toxic players as signatures of them, temporal patterns of the linguistic signature of toxic players, and a possible footprint of transitions from typical behavior to toxic behavior. Our findings would be helpful to automatically detect and warn players who may turn to be toxic and thus save potential victims of toxic playing in advance.

Finally, we suggest several directions for future work. First, is focusing on interaction between typical and toxic players. In this work the unit of our analysis is a message, but we do not delve into the *flow* of messages. Interaction analysis could reveal more clear narratives of how a player transitions to toxic behavior. Next, is building a pre-warning system to detect toxic playing earlier. The main challenge here is to build a dictionary of words that are signs of toxic playing. As we have seen a list of discriminative uni- and bi-grams of toxic and typical players, some bad words are also used by typical players as well. This behavior is prevalent in "trash talk" culture, and an important factor in immersing players in a competitive game [5]. Thus, any pre-warning system must be effective in detecting toxic playing while being flexible enough to allow for trash talk to avoid breaking the immersive gaming experience. We believe that the signature of toxic and typical players we found is a first step for building the dictionary for a pre-warning system.

References

1. Barlińska, J., Szuster, A., Winiewski, M.: Cyberbullying among adolescent bystanders: role of the communication medium, form of violence, and empathy. Journal of Community & Applied Social Psychology **23**(1), 37–51 (2013)
2. Blackburn, J., Kwak, H.: STFU NOOB!: Predicting crowdsourced decisions on toxic behavior in online games. In: Proceedings of the 23rd International Conference on World Wide Web, WWW 2014, pp. 877–888 (2014)
3. Chen, V.H.-H., Duh, H.B.-L., Ng, C.W. : Players who play to make others cry: The influence of anonymity and immersion. In: Proceedings of the International Conference on Advances in Computer Entertainment Technology, ACE 2009, pp. 341–344 (2009)
4. Chesney, T., Coyne, I., Logan, B., Madden, N.: Griefing in virtual worlds: causes, casualties and coping strategies. Information Systems Journal **19**(6), 525–548 (2009)
5. Conmy, O.B.: Trash Talk in a Competitive Setting: Impact on Self-efficacy, Affect, and Performance. In: ProQuest (2008)
6. Lin, H., Sun, C.-T.: The "white-eyed" player culture: Grief play and construction of deviance in MMORPGs. In: Proceedings of DiGRA 2005 Conference (2005)
7. Suler, J.: The online disinhibition effect. Cyberpsychology & Behavior **7**(3), 321–326 (2004)
8. Thompson, P.: Whats fueling the flames in cyberspace? a social influence model. Communication and Cyberspace: Social Interaction in an Electronic Environment, 293–311 (1996)

Informal In-Game Help Practices in Massive Multiplayer Online Games

Paul Okopny, Ilya Musabirov$^{(\boxtimes)}$, and Daniel Alexandrov

National Research University Higher School of Economics,
16 Ulitsa Soyuza Pechatnikov, St. Petersburg 190121, Russia
{imusabirov,dalexandrov}@hse.ru

Abstract. In this paper we explore helping behavior of support agents and regular players in browser-based MMORTS/RPG Castlot. Using chat logs from 12 servers, we analyzed differences between support agents and regular players. We have found that the major in-game verbal help is being provided by players and not by support agents. We have also found that support agents' helping behavior drops dramatically as a server ages, while regular players preserve helping practice, that is mostly transferred from public to guild chat channels.

Keywords: Online games · Help practices · MMOG · Online communities

1 Introduction

Integration of newcomers in Massive Multiplayer Online Games is an important part of overall player experience. The first period of gameplay is crucial to the adaptation process as a newcomer faces unknown rules, concepts, and features of game mechanics. Though it is obvious that taking into account potential players' unawareness of all rules and features in game is extremely important, [2] shows that some games have usability issues when it comes to players inexperienced with the genre. Help availability can have significant impact on players retention [1].

Game-playing support can be a valuable addition to gameplay mechanisms of players' adaptation; although it could be hard to draw the line where it stops working as an adaptation mechanism and starts disrupting a gameplay. Inability to provide such support and integrate newcomers into an in-game social environment can lead to player's churn, which can spread via communication and friendship networks [3,4].

This paper is concerned with studying formal and informal in-game help practices. In the case of Multiplayer Online Strategy Castlot we quantify and compare activity of formal support agents and informal helpers, using in-game chat logs as a source of data.

© Springer International Publishing Switzerland 2015
L.M. Aiello and D. McFarland (Eds.): SocInfo 2014 Workshops, LNCS 8852, pp. 218–222, 2015.
DOI: 10.1007/978-3-319-15168-7_27

2   Methods and Data

The game we are studying is a browser-based strategy with role-playing game elements. The game process can be divided into two components: city development and combats. City development includes constructing and upgrading different buildings. Combat activity includes player-versus-player combats and player-versus-environment 'dungeon raids.'

Castlot game servers have explicit lifecycles. When a new server is deployed, it becomes the default destination for all registering players. After approximately two months, a new server is launched and replaces previous as a default option, thus redirecting the inflow. Since then, servers are isolated, unless merge of servers is initiated due to low number of players in late stages of server lifecycle.

Castlot has common adaptation mechanics including tutorial on basic interface and game elements, a system of simple introductory quests, and protection from other players' attacks until the player reaches a certain level.

Game playing support is performed by hired experienced players. Besides performing moderators' functions (e.g. ban players for chat rules violation), they are required to answer players' questions in the in-game chat. Chat is divided into several channels, including public channel and the channel of a player's guild. 'Helpers', as they are called in the game, are recruited from experienced players and paid with virtual currency. They are not allowed to perform their duty on the same server where they play. One game server can have up to 20 in-game support agents.

Our research was driven by initial research questions and then the data available. Our initial intention was to investigate main obstacles that new players encounter when entering the game by analyzing the answers given by in-game support agents.

For this purpose, we analyzed anonymized in-game chat logs taken from 12 servers at the 15th of December, 2013 (Table 1).

Table 1. Server activity statistics

Activity measure	Mean	Median	IQR
Server age, weeks	23.85	24.75	11.6
Active users	4629	4504	1286
Messages, mln.	1.17	1.16	0.72

The length of a chat messages is limited to 200 characters each, they tend to have a simple structure, and to be saturated with abbreviations and in-game slang. Traditional topic modelling techniques do not produce good results on such data. We used classification tree model [5] as our tool to extract and explore simple word patterns. For that purpose, a tree classifier was built with normalized word frequencies as predictors and a binary variable indicating whether a player is a support agent or not as the outcome variable.

Extracted rules were divided into three groups. Words in the first group were related to moderator duties of in-game support agents (e.g. 'ban', 'flood', 'warning', 'insult', 'permanent ban'). The second group involved citations and links to official help guides. The third group consisted of action words that were directly associated with helping activity.

Considering that we were interested in making sense of topics of communication connected to game-playing advice, we retrained the model excluding messages related to moderation activity.

3   Results

Discovered discriminative terms for helping messages were mostly action verbs that give direct instructions as answers to newcomers' questions.

We found that besides in-game support agents (working formally for in-game pay) there is a fraction of regular players who communicate similarly with support agents.

In particular, one player can give advice to another player on developing their city (which buildings to build and upgrade first), army (what troops and heroes to hire and what skills should be developed), and on how to solve quests (what exact actions to perform in order). There are also pieces of advice about the game interface.

Examples (translated from Russian):

- "If you want a battle hero upgrade his 'strength' and 'stamina', if you want a healer upgrade 'intellect', then you will give him healing cands and that's it."
- "Upgrade hall of heroes, barracs, then cottages, resources, and academy."

Those players were tagged as 'informal helpers'. The existence of these 'informal helpers' was confirmed by the company managers, who monitor in-game activities.

We investigated further 'informal helpers' activity in contrast to support agents during the beginning and mature stages of servers' lifecycles. We analyzed this activity on a server level across all 12 servers (Table 2).

We can clearly see that during both periods under consideration, the number of helping messages on servers sent by regular players exceeds the number of support agents' helping messages ($t(23) = 6.82$, $p < .001$). We should also emphasize that the share of helping messages from support agents plummeted compared to (just) twofold decrease of regular players' helping messages share. We suggest that as a server matures, support agents almost stop carrying out their duties, while informal helping activity decreases but stands.

When it comes to the structure of informal helpers' activity, we can see (Fig. 1) that at the beginning of server's lifecycle, the informal helping activity is performed mostly in the public channel. As a server matures, the share of helping messages in the public channel decreases and help is usually provided via in-guild channel. We propose two reasons for that. First, new players learn the rules and

Table 2. Support agents and informal helpers activity

User category, measure	First month	Last month
Support agents		
number	4.5 (SD=2.4)	2.3 (SD=1.2)
messages, per week	429.4 (SD=201.6)	117.0 (SD=144.3)
share of helping messages	3.8%	0.4%
Informal helpers		
messages, per week	871.0 (SD=473.8)	241.4 (SD=271.3)
share of helping messages	1.0%	0.5%

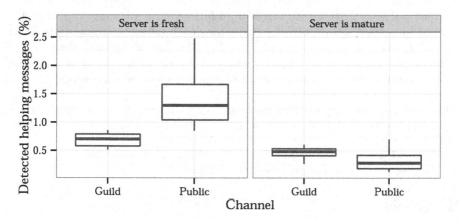

Fig. 1. Helping messages share at different server lifecycle periods

game mechanics and need less help as they become more experienced. Second, focus of communication moves to helping, mentoring, and self-organizing among peers inside a guild.

4   Conclusion and Future Work

In this paper we described a simple way to study helping practices in online games. We explored language features that can help in detecting acts of such practices. We compared formal and informal helping practices and concluded that while formal practices decrease, informal ones stay consistent during the servers lifetime.

Detecting and counting helping acts and helping players can be useful when determining whether an overall social climate in the in-game community is newbie-friendly or not. We suppose that this work will be crucial when studying network effects on players integration, adaptation, and churn.

Direction of our current and future work is twofold. First, we are going to continue to improve technical aspects of helping behavior detection using thread detection techniques in multiparticipant chats [7] and extensions of topic modeling algorithms for short messages. We should bear in mind not only helping-like language patterns, but also preceding requests for help and subsequent gratitudes for help. Second, we are going to look at the adaptation process from social stratification point of view, considering it as a part of Rich Club-like [8] process of in-game elite formation with a communicative exclusion of slowly adapting newcomers. This setting will allow us to test the efficiency of different adaptation mechanisms, including formal and informal game-playing support, form a Social Network Analysis point of view.

One of the applied future steps is to explore how gamification techniques can be used to improve newcomers' adaptation. Provided that we have an efficient technique of detecting transactions of helping behaviour, we propose an experimental setting where the institute of formal game-playing support will be replaced by a small game currency reward for each detected transaction. While susceptible to manipulation by exploiting Type I errors of the algorithms, overall efficiency of such a system, if taking into account social factors of churn, could be comparable with the current way of organizing game-playing support.

Acknowledgments. We would like to express our gratitude to Ekaterina Mekhnetsova, Grigoriy Lysov, Denis Bulygin, and Ksenia Tenisheva for their ideas and help with this research.

We would like to thank Maxim Barinov and Dmitry Stolyarov of Playvision for their cooperation and making this research possible.

References

1. Andersen, E., O'Rourke, E., Liu, Y.-E., Snider, R., Lowdermilk, J., Truong, D., Cooper, S., Popovic, Z.: The impact of tutorials on games of varying complexity. In: Proceedings of the SIGCHI Conference on Human Factors in Computing Systems, CHI 2012, pp. 59–68. ACM, New York (2012), doi:10.1145/2207676.2207687
2. Cornett, S.: The usability of massively multiplayer online roleplaying games: Designing for new users. In: Proceedings of the SIGCHI Conference on Human Factors in Computing Systems, CHI 2004, pp. 703–710. ACM, New York (2004), doi:10.1145/985692.985781
3. Patil, A., Liu, J., Price, B., Sharara, H., Brdiczka, O.: Modeling Destructive Group Dynamics in Online Gaming Communities (2012)
4. Kawale, J., Pal, A., Srivastava, J.: Churn Prediction in MMORPGs: A Social Influence Based Approach. In: International Conference on Computational Science and Engineering, CSE 2009, pp. 423–428 (2009)
5. Breiman, L., Friedman, J., Stone, C.J., Olshen, R.A.: Classification and Regression Trees. Chapman and Hall/CRC, New York (1984)
6. Williams, D., Ducheneaut, N., Xiong, L., Zhang, Y., Yee, N., Nickell, E.: From Tree House to Barracks The Social Life of Guilds in World of Warcraft. Games Cult. **1**, 338–361 (2006)
7. Uthus, D.C., Aha, D.W.: Multiparticipant chat analysis: A survey. Artif. Intell. **199**, 106–121 (2013)
8. Vaquero, L.M., Cebrian, M.: The rich club phenomenon in the classroom. Sci. Rep. **3**, 1174 (2013)

Social Network Analysis of High-Level Players in Multiplayer Online Battle Arena Game

Hyunsoo Park and Kyung-Joong Kim(⊠)

Department of Computer Engineering, Sejong University, Seoul, South Korea
hspark8312@gmail.com, kimkj@sejong.ac.kr

Abstract. Recently, multiplayer online battle arena (MOBA) games have become one of the most popular video game genres. They are also known as Defense of the Ancients (DotA)-like games. As an online-based matching game, it is interesting to analyze players' social structure. In League of Legends (LOL), the most popular MOBA game, players form a team and fight against an enemy together. In the game, they build communities like other conventional social network services (SNSs). In this paper, we analyze the social network of LOL, constructed from team/player data extracted with an official application programming interface (API). In particular, the ranks of players are considered in the analysis. The experimental results show the important features in the social structure of LOL that would be useful for applications in player modeling and match making.

Keywords: Social network · Online game · Multiplayer Online Battle Arena

1   Introduction

Recently, multiplayer online battle arena (MOBA) games such as League of Legends (LOL) have become one of the most popular video game genres. They are online matching games with simplified real-time strategy (RTS) game environments. In the games, several players are grouped into two teams and compete with each other as teams. It looks like an RTS game but each player has control of only one powerful character (a champion). Other parts of the game are handled by artificial intelligence (AI), and human players focus on their character. Interestingly, the games have a social network of players similar to conventional social network services (SNSs) such as Twitter and Facebook. In the SNS, each user connects to others with friend relationships. In this work, we investigated the social network of LOL to find useful knowledge. LOL has become very popular and provides an application programming interface (API) to access team/player data.

There have been a number of previous studies on social networks and community analyses of online games. Lim and Harrell proposed a novel approach for player preference modeling based on social network data [1]. They used social network data in *Steam* to predict player customization in their profile of *Team fortress 2*. Bialas *et al.* surveyed the relationship between culture and game playing style in

© Springer International Publishing Switzerland 2015
L.M. Aiello and D. McFarland (Eds.): SocInfo 2014 Workshops, LNCS 8852, pp. 223–226, 2015.
DOI: 10.1007/978-3-319-15168-7_28

Battlefield 3 [2]. They used game statistics from *Battlefield 3* to measure the competitiveness, cooperation, and tactics of each player and compared them based on the nationality of the players.

In this paper, we analyzed the LOL social network. To our knowledge, it is the first report applying social network analysis to the MOBA game genre. We implemented data crawlers using the official API to collect user data. In LOL, there are leagues based on ranks and player performance. These are important features in match making. Thus, we analyze the players' leagues in the same team. This can help in understanding the way in which users create teams.

2   Data Collection

The data for LOL includes information about the summoner, ranks, leagues, teams, games, and statistics of games. LOL provides easy access to in-game data and we built a data crawler based on the API. Like web crawlers, it starts from some seed players. It sends queries with the players' ids to collect players' detailed information and corresponding teams. In fact, each player can create several teams and it is similar to friendship in conventional social networks. In the network analysis, two players in the same team are friends. The crawler continuously extracts the friends of the player and sends queries with the friend's id.

We used the top 100 ranked players overall as the seed players, because it is easy to get high-ranked players' names from the game community site. However, collecting low-ranked (common) players' ids is more difficult. Thus, we concentrated our efforts on the collection of high-ranked player data. Because they are loyal to the game, we expect that they may show important features of the social structure of this game.

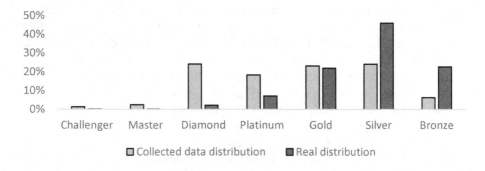

Fig. 1. Distribution of player leagues

We collected data for about 23,000 players for 2 weeks (August 2014) on a Korean server. Fig. 1 shows the distribution of players based on their ranks. In LOL, there are seven layers of players and they are called leagues. The Challenger is the highest league and Bronze is the lowest. Also, there are unranked players, but we did not consider them in this study. The figure shows that the crawlers collected data mainly from the high ranked players (Challengers, Master, Diamond, and Platinum). Because the crawler starts from the top (best) players, it takes a considerable time to get enough low-ranked players. Also, the official API has several constraints that limit the speed of data crawling.

3   Social Network Analysis

Fig. 2 shows the social network structure of players in higher. At the center of the network, there are approximately 6,000 nodes (players) and 12,000 edges (friend relationships). The average number of friends is 2.139±3.644 for Challengers, 2.839±4.097 for Masters, 3.103±4.092 for Diamonds, and 2.891±3.778 for Platinums. In most leagues, each player has, on average, two or three friends. There are trends that the number of friends of higher-ranked players (Challengers and Masters) is slightly lower than medium-ranked players (Diamonds and Platinums).

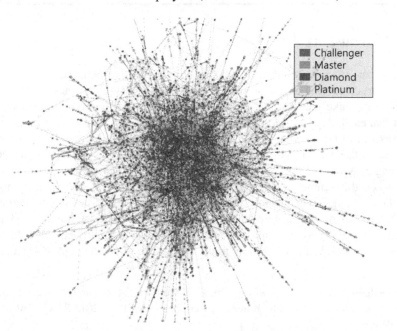

Fig. 2. Social network visualization

Typically, we would expect each player to make teams with others from the same or similar leagues because this would seem to be the most natural strategy to form a team. However, sometimes players can create a team with players from different leagues. We might anticipate that this could occur in special situations - for example, the players are friends in the real world although they are not at the same level. Table 1 shows how many players make a team with those from different leagues. Each league in the vertical row is the team owner's league and the horizontal lists the team participants (friends of the team owner). This table shows results similar to the number of friends analysis. Diamond and Platinum players set up many teams and players and Challengers and Masters make fewer teams. It also seems that Diamond and Platinum players make teams with players from the same league, but sometimes Challenger and Master players make teams with lower league (Diamond) players. Probably, this occurs because the numbers of Challenger and Master players are limited.

Table 1. Distribution of friends in different leagues

	Challenger	Master	Diamond	Platinum
Challenger	19.2 %	3.4 %	9.5 %	1.5 %
Master	1.4 %	25.2 %	14.2 %	2.2 %
Diamond	0.6 %	1.5 %	41.3 %	4.2 %
Platinum	0.2 %	0.3 %	5.7 %	36.3 %

4   Conclusions

In this paper, we performed basic analyses of the League of Legends (LOL) social network structure. LOL is the one of the most popular MOBA games. We focused on how players make teams. Each player can make several teams. Usually, we might expect that each player would make a team with others at a similar performance level. To investigate LOL players' social structure, we collected data using our crawler. It used the LOL official API and collected data on players in the higher leagues (Challenger, Master, Diamond and Platinum) on a Korean server for 2 weeks. We investigated the number and types of friends for each league. The results show that each player creates teams with players in the same league and the average numbers of friends are two or three. Also, there are differences between high-ranked players (Challenger and Master) and lower-ranked players (Diamond and Platinum). Typically, high-ranked players made fewer teams than the lower-ranked players.

Acknowledgements. This work was supported by the National Research Foundation of Korea (NRF) grant, funded by the Korean government (MSIP) (2013 R1A2A2A01016589, 2010-0018950).

References

1. Lim, C.-U., Harrell, D.F.: Modeling player preferences in avatar customization using social network data. In: IEEE Conference on Computational Intelligence in Games (2013)
2. Bialas, M., Tekofsky, S., Spronck, P.: Cultural influences on play style. In: IEEE Conference on Computational Intelligence in Games (2014)

2nd International Workshop on Computational History (HistoInformatics)

The 2nd HistoInformatics Workshop - Introduction

Adam Jatowt[1], Gaël Dias[2], Marten Düring[3], and Antal van den Bosch[4]

[1] Kyoto University, Yoshida-Honmachi, Sakyo-ku, Kyoto 606-8501, Japan
adam@dl.kuis.kyoto-u.ac.jp
[2] Normandie University, Campus Côte de Nacre, 14032 Caen Cedex, France
gael.dias@unicaen.fr
[3] Centre Virtuel de la Connaissance sur l'Europe, Château de Sanem, 4992
Sanem, G.-D. Luxembourg
marten.duering@cvce.eu
[4] Radboud University, PO Box 9103, 6500 HD Nijmegen, The Netherlands
a.vandenbosch@let.ru.nl

Abstract. The 2nd HistoInformatics Workshop[1] (the 2nd International Workshop on Computational History) was held in conjunction with the 6th International Conference on Social Informatics (Socinfo2014) in Barcelona, Spain on the 10th November 2014. The objective of the workshop is to provide for two research communities, Computer Science and History Sciences, a place to meet and exchange ideas and to facilitate discussion and collaboration. This report briefly summarizes the workshop.

1   Introduction

The HistoInformatics2014 workshop was held on November 10, 2014 in conjunction with the SocInfo2014 conference, as the second installment of the workshop series devoted to the interaction between Computer Science and Historical Science fields. This interdisciplinary initiative is a response to the growing popularity of Digital Humanities, particularly in historical research, and an increased tendency to apply algorithms and computer techniques for fostering and facilitating new research methods and tools in the Humanities. History as a representation of the past has many functions. It helps to create meaning, coherence, and orientation both individually and collectively, and it aims to settle the foundations of our nations, identities and our memories. As such, it is one of the fundamental subjects taught from elementary schools onwards. Traditionally, historical research is based on manual investigation of preserved records and artifacts to provide a reliable account of the past and verify different hypotheses. Alongside this hermeneutic approach historians have always translated primary sources into data and used statistics to analyze them. More recently, the field of Digital History has received attention with its aim to dematerialize patrimonial resources in order to explore them in the near future through the usage of automatic methods. This near future is already becoming the reality.

---

[1] http://www.dl.kuis.kyoto-u.ac.jp/histoinformatics2014/

L.M. Aiello and D. McFarland (Eds.): SocInfo 2014 Workshops, LNCS 8852, pp. 229–233, 2015.
DOI: 10.1007/978-3-319-15168-7_29

Nowadays, due to the increasing activities in digitizing and opening historical sources, the field of History can greatly benefit from the advances of Computer and Information sciences, through automated processing, organizing, and making sense of data and information. New computational methods can be applied to help verify and validate historical assumptions based on text analytics, image interpretation, or through comparing multiple perspectives. Hence, Digital History has now entered a new era that we call HistoInformatics, analogous to Bioinformatics and ChemoInformatics, which have respectively proposed new research trends in Biology and Chemistry. Many subareas of Computer Science are relevant and have potential to advance historical studies. These include Information Retrieval, Information Extraction, Text Analytics, Natural Language Processing, Artificial Intelligence (Machine Learning, Knowledge Representation), Image Processing, and others.

This year 12 presentations were delivered including the keynote talk given by Juan A. Barceló (University Autónoma de Barcelona, Spain) titled: *Simulating the Past to understand the Present*. This report introduces the workshop and overviews its papers.

2   Workshop Topics

The main topics of the workshop are that of supporting historical research and analysis through the application of Computer Science theories or technologies, analyzing and making use of historical texts, and simulating past courses of actions, analyzing collective memories, visualizing historical data, and providing efficient access to the large wealth of historical knowledge. The workshop papers are expected to have some technical traits. Either they are describing a particular computational approach, method or algorithm, or, at least, are pointing to those as being applicable to historical studies. The detailed workshop topics are (but are not limited to):

·   Natural language processing and text analytics applied to historical documents
·   Analyses of longitudinal document collections
·   Search methods in document archives, historical collections, associative search
·   Causal relationship discovery based on historical resources
·   Entity relationship extraction, detecting and resolving historical references in text
·   Computational linguistics for old texts
·   Digitizing and archiving
·   Modeling evolution of entities and relationships over time
·   Automatic multimedia document dating
·   Applications of Artificial Intelligence techniques to History
·   Simulating the past course of actions, social relations, motivations, figurations
·   Analysis of language change over time
·   Handling uncertain and fragmentary text and image data
·   Finding analogical entities, entity linking in historical collections
·   Named entity recognition and disambiguation
·   Automatic biography generation

- Mining Wikipedia for historical data
- OCR and transcription old texts
- Effective interfaces for searching, browsing, visualizing historical data collections
- Modelling collective memory in texts
- Automatically gathering, comparing multi-perspective views on historical events
- Studying and modeling forgetting and remembering processes
- Vulgarization of History through new media
- Probing the limits of HistoInformatics, epistemologies in HistoInformatics

3   Accepted Papers

This year we have received 21 submissions. Based on the feedback from the PC we have accepted seven full and four short papers. We briefly discuss them below.

With *"Learning to Identify Historical Figures for Timeline Creation from Wikipedia Articles"* *Sandro Bauer, Stephen Clark* and *Thore Graepel* present an original approach to the automated creation of timelines from historical Wikipedia articles. They start by processing roughly 600 manually created timelines and related history articles and use them as a baseline. Their approach lets them identify the most important persons and links them to time frames.

In *"Mapping the Early Modern News Flow: an Enquiry by Robust Text Reuse Detection"*, *Giovanni Colavizza, Mario Infelise*, and *Frédéric Kaplan* study text borrowings in early modern printed gazettes, focusing their evaluation on Turin and Genova gazettes from 1648. The method, which is demonstrated to be robust to noise from OCR, unveils that the two gazettes often drew upon the same news sources. A closer analysis reveals aspects of the underlying non-linear editorial system.

Andrea Bravo Balado, Victor de Boer and *Guus Schreiber* talk about a study in which they link domain-specific databases on Dutch maritime events, mostly from the 19th century, with the large digital newspaper archive offered by the Netherlands National Library. In *"Linking Historical Ship Records to a Newspaper Archive"* they illustrate how filters can be developed that offer high-precision matching of database entries and newspaper articles that talk about the same ship. The resulting database is offered as Linked Open Data.

Cathal Gurrin, Havard Johansen, Thomas Sodring and *Dag Johansen* authored position paper titled: *"Digital Chronofiles of Life Experience"* in which they discuss the data that lifelogging can generate and argue that such data will be useful for historians and archivists of the future. They overview the way in which life logging tools operate today and look at the future developments that should increase the quantity and quality of captured data. They also discuss how the work of future historians may change when they will have complete recorded life of individuals for their use.

Pim van Bree and *Geert Kessels* describe their experiences with collecting records of oral history in relation to anti-communist violence in Indonesia in: *"Mapping Memory Landscapes in nodegoat"*. They explore a collaborative and participatory research process as a use case of nodegoat system. nodegoat[2] is a web-based data management, analysis and visualisation environment that allows scholars building datasets based on own data model and offers relational modes of analysis with spatial and chronological forms of contextualisation.

In *"Mining Ministers (1572-1815). Using Semi-structured Data for Historical Research"*, *Serge Ter Braake*, *Antske Fokkens* and *Fred van Lieburg* study the automated charting of the works and lives of Dutch reformed ministers in the pre-kingdom Netherlands. The study exemplifies the enrichment of an old historical database, using its semi-structure to infer more structure and opportunities for linking with other datasets.

Mariona Coll Ardanuy, *Maarten van den Bos* and *Caroline Sporleder* present their paper titled *"Laboratories of Community: how Digital Humanities can further new European Integration History"*. They combine Named Entity Recognition with social network analysis to study the co-occurrences of political actors in Dutch newspapers between 1945 and 1955. The authors describe a sophisticated yet simple method to extract persons as nodes and to automatically enrich node attributes by collecting additional co-occurring keywords. They find that the early phase of EU integration was in fact a political process, "with its own vocabulary, central actors and use of concepts".

In *"The EHRI Project - Virtual Collections Revisited"* *Mike Bryant*, *Linda Reijn-houdt*, *Reto Speck*, *Thibault Clerice* and *Tobias Blanke* give insight into the project's architecture. Sources related to the Holocaust are currently spread all over the world, document collections have been broken up and searching specific documents is very difficult. The EHRI project creates an infrastructure to connect metadata of these sources by linking archival metadata in virtual collections. In their paper, Bryant et al. provide a definition of the elusive term "virtual collection", describe the challenges of their project and demonstrate how they reunite sources across different repositories.

Yanne Broux and *Mark Depauw* present paper *"Developing Onomastic Gazetteers and Prosopographies for the Ancient World through Named Entity Recognition and Graph Visualization: Some Examples from Trismegistos People"*. They illustrate, on the basis of Trismegistos[3], a metadata database and interdisciplinary platform for sources predominantly from ancient Egypt, how the data collection through Named Entity Recognition and visualization through Social Network Analysis can speed up the creation of onomastic lists and the development of prosopographies.

Günter Mühlberger, *Sebastian Colutto* and *Philip Kahle* address the challenging topic of handwriting recognition in their contribution *"Handwritten Text Recognition (HTR) of Historical Documents as a Shared Task for Archivists, Computer Scientists and Humanities Scholars. The Model of a Transcription & Recognition Platform (TRP)"*. The paper reports on advances made in the FP7 EU project "tranScriptorium" on a platform that integrates human transcription and automated recognition of handwritten texts, similar in spirit to the earlier "Monk" system[4] developed by Lambert Schomaker and colleagues at the University of Groningen.

---

[2] http://nodegoat.net/
[3] http://www.trismegistos.org
[4] http://www.ai.rug.nl/~lambert/Monk-collections-english.html

In his paper titled *"Can Network Analysis Reveal Importance? Degree Centrality and Leaders in the EU Integration Process"* Marten Düring addresses the limited technical skillset of humanists and asks to which extent even very basic tools can be effective helpers in the course of historical research. He asks whether network analysis can be a robust tool to help to identify key actors in the process of European integration and compares to co-occurrence networks to each other. One is based on historical photographs, the other on Wikipedia pages. Düring concludes that Degree centrality indeed outperforms other centrality measures for this task.

4   Programme Committee

We made sure each submission was reviewed by reviewers from both Computer and History Science. The following researchers served on the Programme Committee:

- *Robert Allen* (Yonsei University, South Korea)
- *Ching-man Au Yeung* (Huawei Noah's Ark Lab, Hong Kong)
- *Frederick Clavert* (Paris Sorbonne University, France)
- *Antoine Doucet* (Normandie University, France)
- *Roger Evans* (University of Brighton, United Kingdom)
- *Christian Gudehus* (University of Flensburg, Germany)
- *Iris Hendrickx* (Radboud University, The Netherlands)
- *Pedro Rangel Henriques* (Minho University, Portugal)
- *Pim Huijnen* (Utrecht University, The Netherlands)
- *Nattiya Kanhabua* (LS3 Research Center, Germany)
- *Tom Kenter* (University of Amsterdam, The Netherlands)
- *Mike Kestemont* (University of Antwerp, Belgium)
- *Adam Kosto* (Columbia University, USA)
- *Günter Mühlberger* (University of Innsbruck, Austria)
- *Andrea Nanetti* (Nanyang Technological University, Singapore)
- *Daan Odijk* (University of Amsterdam, The Netherlands)
- *Marc Spaniol* (Max Planck Institute for Informatics, Germany)
- *Shigeo Sugimoto* (University of Tsukuba, Japan)
- *Nina Tahmasebi* (University of Gothenburg, Sweden)
- *Lars Wieneke* (Centre Virtuel de la Connaissance sur l'Europe, Luxemburg)

Acknowledgments. We thank the SocInfo2014 conference organizers for helping to organize this workshop. We also express our gratitude to all the Program Committee members for their dedicated work and to the participants for their contribution to the workshop's success.

Learning to Identify Historical Figures for Timeline Creation from Wikipedia Articles

Sandro Bauer[1](✉), Stephen Clark[1], and Thore Graepel[2]

[1] University of Cambridge, Cambridge, UK
{sandro.bauer,stephen.clark}@cl.cam.ac.uk
[2] Microsoft Research Cambridge, Cambridge, UK
thore.graepel@microsoft.com

Abstract. This paper addresses a central sub-task of timeline creation from historical Wikipedia articles: learning from text which of the person names in a textual article should appear in a timeline on the same topic. We first process hundreds of timelines written by human experts and related Wikipedia articles to construct a corpus that can be used to evaluate systems that create history timelines from text documents. We then use a set of features to train a classifier that predicts the most important person names, resulting in a clear improvement over a competitive baseline.

1 Introduction

Creating a timeline that contains the most important events in a country's history from a history article can be seen as an instance of text summarisation; while the most prominent events in the country's history will figure in the timeline, less important details are likely to be ommitted. Timelines of this kind would be useful tools in education, for instance, in particular with the emergence of web applications that let users learn about the history of the world in new, interactive ways. Our goal is to use historical information available in Wikipedia to construct these timelines automatically.

This paper examines an important sub-problem of this task. We try to learn which historical figures from a textual article (on a country, a field of science, or similar) should be included in the corresponding history timeline. Our work differs from previous approaches in that we use a corpus of 279 gold-standard timelines and related Wikipedia articles. The material used for this purpose includes timelines created by human experts (on concepts such as *History of New York*), as well as textual Wikipedia articles about the same concepts. This data is then used to train a classifier that predicts, for a set of textual articles, which person names should appear in the corresponding timeline. We use a diverse set of features and obtain a clear improvement over a competitive frequency-based baseline. This study will provide a basis for more complex systems that identify events relevant to the history of a concept.

© Springer International Publishing Switzerland 2015
L.M. Aiello and D. McFarland (Eds.): SocInfo 2014 Workshops, LNCS 8852, pp. 234–243, 2015.
DOI: 10.1007/978-3-319-15168-7_30

2   Timeline Corpus Construction

We have processed about 600 timelines written by human experts and an equal number of sets of related textual history articles. This corpus can be used beyond the task described in this paper; it will make it possible to evaluate future automatic timeline construction systems that construct entire timelines from a set of history articles.

The history articles are Wikipedia pages whose titles start with "History of", for example "History of Iran" or "History of biology". When there was no such article available, we instead used the concept's main article. When the title of a timeline mentions two concepts, for instance "Timeline of biology and organic chemistry", but there is no single textual article on the same two topics, we use more than one textual article (in this case, "History of biology" and "Organic chemistry"). A timeline is a set of sentences, each of which is associated with a date, e.g. "2008" or "05/03/2009". The timelines come from Wikipedia and other history websites: *HistoryWorld*[1], www.timelines.ws, *WorldAtlas*[2], *HistoryMole*[3], the BBC and datesandevents.org. Where there are multiple timelines available for a concept, we take the union of all timeline entries, since it is assumed that all entries present in *any* of the timelines on a topic are relevant to that topic.

For addressing the sub-problem of learning important person names, we first extract all **PERSON** named entities from the timelines and the corresponding textual articles in order to construct a gold-standard data set of names. There are two problems that complicate the creation of this gold standard: First, the same people are often referred to in different ways in a timeline and a textual article. For example, the names in the timeline might not contain umlauts ("Schroder"), but those in the Wikipedia article do ("Schröder"). Similarly, a person might be mentioned in the same article using more than one name (e.g. "Friedrich I." and "Fritz"). Second, it is not obvious when a history article "corresponds" well enough to a timeline to be used as training data. The following subsections describe how we address these problems.

2.1   Creating a Gold Standard of Person Names

We start by extracting all **PERSON** NEs using the Stanford NE classifier [5]. Mentions that have only one entity candidate in the YAGO knowledge base [11] are filtered out if that candidate is not a person; this corrects for obvious cases where a named entity has been misclassified as a person.

In what follows, **TIML** designates a timeline and **TXTA** the corresponding textual article(s). For each **TIML** and **TXTA**, we infer a collection of *name sets*. A name set is a set of strings that represent the same entity, such as {*Friedrich I, Frederick I., Barbarossa*}. To construct this set, we start with the multi-word names (such as *Pete Sampras*). Each of these names is expanded into a name set

---

[1] www.historyworld.net

[2] www.worldatlas.com

[3] www.historymole.com

by adding versions with all umlauts removed, all diacritics removed, all titles of nobility removed, and so forth. If the name string has only one candidate entity in YAGO that is a person, we add all the *alternative names* contained in YAGO for that entity too. Finally, we check whether any of the names in the current name set are contained in one of the name sets already constructed. If this is the case, the two sets are merged.

Once we have a set of such name sets for each TIML and TXTA, we need to infer which name set in TIML corresponds to which one in TXTA (if any). We use a method which ensures that whenever a name set from the timeline and one from the textual article have a name in common, the two sets are linked to each other. For each name set tl from TIML, we check whether any name set txt_1 from TXTA contains one of the names in tl. If so, we create an overlap pair. If a second name set txt_2 in TXTA contains one of the names in tl, we merge the two name sets txt_1 and txt_2. The same applies in the opposite direction.

Note that we cannot simply use entity linking systems since some of the persons do not have a YAGO entry, and hence different versions of the same name can only be grouped together using the rules above. In addition, our scenario does not even require names to be disambiguated to canonical entities in a knowledge base. We merely want to avoid that two names referring to the same person are not matched only because, for example, some diacritics are missing. We found our heuristic to work well on the development set.

Next, we check whether any name with more than two tokens can be matched to a two-word name in a different name set; this way two names such as *David William Cameron* and *David Cameron* end up in the same name set. Finally, we add all single-word person names (such as "Cameron") to the name sets using a heuristic. For each short name in TIML and TXTA respectively, we obtain all name sets in both TIML and TXTA in which at least one of the multi-word names ends with the same last name. If there is more than one such name set, we pick the one with the highest total number of occurrences of its member names.

2.2   Finding High-Quality Pairs of Timelines and Textual Articles

Another problem is that we cannot assume that a timeline on a particular subject is an accurate reflection of the textual article in our corpus, since it is not known which textual resources the timeline authors used when putting together the timeline. Some Wikipedia timelines do contain hints in the form of links to related textual articles (e.g., the Wikipedia timeline on French history contains the following sentence: "To read about the background to these events, see *History of France.*"), but even in these cases it is not clear that the timelines represent all of the underlying textual content. A timeline author who creates a timeline from a textual article might decide that a part of the article is not relevant at all to the target concept, or a timeline might cover a different time window than the corresponding textual article. For example, there are timelines that only contain events after 1900, or textual articles that cover very recent events, while the corresponding timeline was last updated two years ago. It is also possible that either the timeline or the textual article is biased towards a particular subject area; for example, a timeline on a country might be biased towards armed conflicts. To alleviate this problem, a set of filters is used to ensure that there is sufficient overlap between a timeline and a textual article. We require a minimum number of 5 persons from the textual page that also appear on the timeline. In addition, we require the proportion of persons from the textual article that are also in the timeline to be between 0.1 and 0.9; cases where very few or almost all of the people in the textual article are mentioned in the timeline should be avoided. In the former case, we expect that the timeline sentences are not a good representation of the textual article's content. In the latter case, the timeline might not focus on important events only.

Finally, two more constraints are used to filter out low-quality pairs. Firstly, we require an absolute mininum number of 5 persons on both the timeline and the textual page. This filters out cases where one of the documents is too short. Secondly, a timeline is not allowed to contain more than 5 times the number of persons in the corresponding textual article. This removes cases where the timeline is too fine-grained and hence not a succinct description of the most important events on a topic, but rather a detailed event log (such as what happened in the last minutes before the first airplane hit the World Trade Center). Applying all these constraints resulted in a set of 279 pairs of timelines and textual articles.

3   System Description

The task of the system is to decide for each of the persons in the textual article(s) whether it should be mentioned in the timeline. To give an example, consider the following sentence taken from a Wikipedia article: "(...) the Hohenstaufen empire under *Frederick I Barbarossa* reached its peak in (...) the marriage of his son *Henry* (...) to (...) *Constance* (...)." *Frederick I Barbarossa* is present in the timeline, while *Henry* and *Constance* are not. To make these decisions, all mentions of all names in a name set such as {*Frederick I Barbarossa, Friedrich I*} are considered by the system.

In a first setting, a separate feature vector is created for each mention of one of the names in a name set. Alternatively, we use one combined feature vector for all mentions with the same name, where the feature values of overlapping features are either averaged or summed. At test time, a name set is accepted if at least 50% of all vectors receive a score above a threshold value tuned on the development set. As scores for the individual vectors we use the pseudo-probabilities output by LibLINEAR[4] (which uses a linear kernel).

4   Feature Set

We experiment with features that take into account the local and global context of the mentions, as well as external knowledge available about the persons. This

---

[4] www.csie.ntu.edu.tw/~cjlin/liblinear/

Table 1. Structural features

frequencyOfEachNEPerTextualPage: the frequency of each name on the textual page(s)   **frequencyOfEachNEPerTextualPage_dividedByAllNEs**: the frequency of each name on the textual page(s) divided by the total number of NEs
wordIdInSentence: the position of the NE in the containing sentence (word index of the first word of the NE)   **numberOfNEsInSentence**: the number of NEs in the containing sentence
indexOfCurrentStanfordNE: the index of the NE in question in the list of all NEs in the current sentence   **indexOfCurrentSentence**: the index of the sentence that contains the NE in question in the list of all sentences of the current paragraph   **indexOfCurrentParagraph**: the index of the paragraph that contains the NE in question in the list of all paragraphs of the current subsection
numberOfDifferentWritings: the number of different writings of the current name (i.e. the size of the corresponding name set)
occursInHeader: whether or not the current NE is in the Wikipedia document's header

includes structural features intended to capture effects such as: historical figures central to a concept will appear more often in an article; or important names are unlikely to appear in a sentence with a high number of other names. We also investigate the influence of document-level structure; for instance, some names might be so important for the article's topic that they are mentioned in the document's header; or the most important figures tend to appear early on in a paragraph.

Next, we build n-gram features (uni- and bigrams in a window of 3 words around the mention), as well as syntactic features that capture effects such as whether important historical figures are more or less likely to occur in a subject position or in a list of names. The length of co-reference chains that a name is part of (given by the Stanford NER toolkit) is also used, since important people might be mentioned multiple times in the form of pronouns.

Finally, we use semantic features to exploit the fact that many of the person names in the Wikipedia articles are linked to the person's own article. For each such article, there is a corresponding entity in YAGO that has types associated with it. Types in YAGO can be divided into WordNet types (at the top of the hierarchy) and Wikicategory types. We construct one feature per WordNet type of the target entity; we do not use Wikicategory types since these are too fine-grained.

Further semantic features include co-occurrences of the person name (e.g. *Charles de Gaulle*) and the concept name (such as *France*) in the same sentence; for this, we consider all sentences in the same article as well as in the person's Wikipedia article (that of *Charles de Gaulle* in this case). There is also a feature that indicates whether the concept name occurs in one of the section headers of the person's article.

Table 2. Linguistic features

unigrams: all unigrams (lemmatised) in a window size of +/- 3 around the mention, e.g. *abdicate* **unigrams_dist**: all unigrams (lemmatised) in a window size of +/- 3 around the mention, annotated with the distance in words from the NE, .g. *abdicate_+1* **bigrams**: all bigrams (lemmatised) in a window size of +/- 3 around the mention, e.g. *abdicate_after* **bigrams_dist**: all bigrams (lemmatised) in a window size of +/- 3 around the mention, annotated with the distance in words from the NE, e.g. *abdicate_after_+1* **postags**: all POS tags in a window size of +/- 3 around the mention, e.g. *VBD* **postags_dist**: all POS tags in a window size of +/- 3 around the mention, annotated with the exact distance, e.g. *VBD_-1*
dep_degree1_in: the types of all incoming dependency edges of any word that is part of the NE (e.g. *dobj*) **dep_degree1_out**: the types of all outgoing dependency edges of any word that is part of the NE (e.g. *xcomp*) **dep_degree2_in**: the types of all incoming dependency chains of length 2 starting from any word that is part of the NE (e.g. *dobj_det*) **dep_degree2_out**: the types of all outgoing dependency chains of length 2 starting from any word that is part of the NE (e.g. *xcomp_det*) **dep_is_local_or_global_subject**: indicator features that indicate whether any of the words in the NE are the subject of any clause of the current sentence or of the main clause **dep_is_local_or_global_object**: indicator features that indicate whether any of the words in the NE are the object of any clause of the current sentence or of the main clause **dep_numOfsisterDeps**: the number of "sister dependencies" of the same type (i.e. dependencies of the same type starting from a "parent token" of the current token in the dependency graph). This measures how long the list of names is that a name occurs in), and categorical features that fire if there are at least one, two or three sister dependencies.
part_of_corefchain: a binary feature that fires if the current name is part of a coreference chain **part_of_corefchain_longestChain**: the length of the longest co-reference chain the current name mention is part of **part_of_corefchain_atleast5sentences**: a feature that fires if the longest co-reference chain is longer than 5 sentences **part_of_corefchain_atleast_x_InBetweenSentence**: features that fire if there are at least x sentences between the sentences of the co-reference chain involving a person name **part_of_corefchain_lengthOfBiggestGapAtLeast_x**: features that fire if there are at least x sentences between any two sentences of the co-reference chain involving a person name **part_of_corefchain_distanceFromFirstToLastSentenceAtLeast_x**: the distance (in number of sentences) between the first and last sentences of any co-reference chain the current mention is part of

Table 3. Semantic features

conceptName_thisSentence: a feature that indicates whether the name of the concept (we remove "History of" from the article title, so hat concept names are "Germany" or "Biology") co-occurs with the name of the person in the same sentence **conceptName_allSentences**: a feature that indicates whether the name of the concept co-occurs with the name of the name of the person in **any** sentence in the textual document
entity_linked_to: a feature that fires if the name is linked to the person's Wikipedia article
sentenceOnTargetArticle_containsConceptName: a feature that indicates whether the name of the concept co-occurs with the name of the name of the person in **any** sentence in the person's Wikipedia article (if the name is linked to this article)
section_or_subsectionOnTargetArticle_containsConceptName: a feature that indicates whether the name of the concept occurs in a section or subsection title in the person's Wikipedia article (if the name is linked to this article)

5 Experiments

The 279 timelines which pass the areforementioned criteria are divided into a development set of 20 timelines (with an average of 81.9 name sets per timeline), a test set of 30 timelines (with an average of 83.7 sets) and a training set comprising the remaining 229 timelines. In order to ensure that the various sets contain timelines that are comparable in terms of how well they represent the textual article, we first divide the timelines into ten buckets based on what percentage of the name sets from the timeline is also present in the textual article, and then pick timelines from each of the buckets at random until the test and development sets are full. The rest becomes the training set.

Two different sets of metrics are used to evaluate our approach. First, we calculate precision, recall and F-score values across all timelines (micro-averaged), based on the tuned threshold value of 0.6. Since there are some names in the gold standard timeline that do not appear in the textual article, we restrict our evaluation to those that are contained in the article.

Alternatively, the task can be interpreted as trying to assign higher scores to those names from a textual document that occur in a timeline on the same topic than to those that are not contained in the timeline. To obtain an indication of the quality of the ranking provided by the pseudo-probabilities, we calculate Average Precision (AP) scores for each timeline individually, and from this an aggregate MAP score across all timelines.

Evaluating our system is complicated by the errors made by the Stanford NER system. For instance, there are named entities that are misclassified as persons. Therefore, a second evaluation setting is used where erroneous PERSON instances are removed manually; we do not investigate which person names the tagger missed out on since we are primarily interested in the goodness of the ranking for the person names detected.

Table 4. Results

Set and system		P	R	F1	MAP
DV+fp	SVM	0.5430	0.6619	0.5966	0.6454
DV+fp	BL	0.4916	0.4905	0.4911	0.5813
DV-fp	SVM	0.5347	0.6616	0.5914	0.6658
DV-fp	BL	0.5052	0.4924	0.4987	0.6020
TE+fp	SVM	0.4551	0.6391	0.5316	0.6002
TE+fp	BL	0.3379	0.6116	0.4353	0.5245

An obvious choice for a baseline is the number of times a person occurs on the textual page. The ranking is provided by the total frequency of all names in the name set and is compared to the one output by the classifier. To resolve ties, we order all name sets with the same frequency count by the position where the first mention occurs in the article; in other words, the baseline ranking assumes that persons mentioned early on in a document are more important. For deciding whether a name set is accepted by the frequency baseline we similarly tune a threshold value on the development set (a proportion of the maximum number of times that the names of any single name set occur in the textual article; here set to 0.1).

6   Results

Results for the setting where one feature vector is constructed per mention are given in Table 4; "-fp" and "+fp" indicate whether erroneous PERSON instances are removed or retained; DV and TE refer to the development and test sets, respectively. Whether we use separate feature vectors for each NE or combined vectors does not influence the performance too much. Using the frequency baseline leads to competitive results; many important names occur more than once in an article, while others mostly occur only once. In all cases, the classifier achieves an improvement of more than 5% over the baseline. We also experimented with non-linear kernels, but this did not improve the results.

7   Related Work

We are not aware of any existing work that has addressed the problem of constructing historical timelines from free-form text using a large corpus of timelines and textual documents on the same topic in the way we are proposing.

Some existing work on timeline generation is based on temporal information extraction techniques. Events and timestamps are first extracted from unstructured text in the form of TimeML EVENT [9] and TIMEX instances; the task of extracting the timestamps is usually referred to as *time normalisation* [2]. Relations among these events, such as BEFORE, AFTER and CONTAINS are then learned using a variety of approaches. This has been the focus of the TempEval shared tasks (see [12] for the most recent one) which are all based on the TimeML language. Kolomiyets et al. [7] are the first to learn a global timeline for a document based on such information extraction techniques. They use dependency parsing algorithms to arrange all the events in a document along a timeline. All these approaches, however, do not discuss the selection of important events for a particular downstream application such as the creation of a history timeline.

A second strand of research deals with timeline generation from news streams based on a user query. Chieu and Lee [4] apply extractive summarisation techniques to a collection C of documents to generate a timeline containing the top n most relevant events on a user query. They ask annotators to do their own research to produce a timeline on a given query, such as Bush (they are free to use whatever resource they like). Yan et al. [13] use gold-standard timelines created by professional editors and define four desirable criteria for timelines (relevance to a query, coverage, relevance, coherence). As many other similar works, they have access to a large number of documents on a single topic and the creation date for each document. Nguyen et al. [8] use a corpus of newswire texts along with timelines authored by journalists to extract salient events from news streams; they too make use of temporal processing techniques based on the TimeML framework. Their system can exploit co-occurrences of terms in multiple documents to identify salient events. Our task is more difficult in that the algorithm has to identify important entities from the local context alone.

A number of approaches focus on placing search engine results to a given user query (e.g. *Barack Obama*) along a timeline. They assume that important events appear frequently. Some approaches have used temporal information extraction techniques to process temporal information available in retrieved text documents [1]. The most closely related work is that of Chasin et al. [3]; they address the problem of creating history timelines from Wikipedia articles by classifying TimeML events into more and less important ones. The authors obtain human relevance judgments for events contained in a small number of textual documents, which is costly; they also point out that reaching inter-annotator agreement is difficult. Our study, on the other hand, is based on a novel, automatically constructed corpus of gold-standard timelines created by humans.

Finally, a great amount of work has gone into visualising information that is readily available in the form of time-labelled events [6,10].

8   Conclusion

In this paper, we have addressed a sub-task central to the goal of creating informative history timelines from Wikipedia articles automatically: inferring the most important person entities that should be contained in the timeline. For this, we have created a corpus of timelines and textual history articles which can also be used to evaluate systems that construct complete timelines. For the person detection task, it has been demonstrated that using a variety of features results in a clear improvement over a competitive baseline. We are going to use this study as a building block in an algorithm that constructs full timelines.

Acknowledgments. SB is funded by a Microsoft Research PhD Scholarship.

References

1. Alonso, O., Gertz, M., Baeza-Yates, R.: Clustering and exploring search results using timeline constructions. In: Proceedings of the 18th ACM Conference on Information and Knowledge Management, CIKM 2009, Hong Kong, China, pp. 97–106 (2009)
2. Bethard, S.: A synchronous context free grammar for time normalization. In: Proceedings of the 2013 Conference on Empirical Methods in Natural Language Processing, (EMNLP 2013), pp. 821–826 (2013)
3. Chasin, R., Woodward, D., Witmer, J., Kalita, J.: Extracting and Displaying Temporal and Geospatial Entities from Articles on Historical Events. The Computer Journal, 403–426 (2013)
4. Chieu, H.L., Lee, Y.K.: Query based event extraction along a timeline. In: Proceedings of the 27th Annual International ACM SIGIR Conference on Research and Development in Information Retrieval, SIGIR 2004, Sheffield, United Kingdom, pp. 425–432 (2004)
5. Finkel, J.R., Grenager, T., Manning, C.: Incorporating non-local information into information extraction systems by Gibbs sampling. In: Proceedings of the 43rd Annual Meeting on Association for Computational Linguistics, ACL 2005, Ann Arbor, Michigan, USA, pp. 363–370 (2005)
6. Hienert, D., Luciano, F.: Extraction of Historical Events from Wikipedia. CoRR abs/1205.4138 (2012). http://dblp.uni-trier.de/db/journals/corr/corr1205.html#abs-1205-4138
7. Kolomiyets, O., Bethard, S., Moens, M.: Extracting narrative timelines as temporal dependency structures. In: Proceedings of the 50th Annual Meeting of the Association for Computational Linguistics, pp. 88–97 (2012)
8. Nguyen, K.H., Tannier, X., Moriceau, V.: Ranking multidocument event descriptions for building thematic timelines. In: Proceedings of COLING 2014, the 25th International Conference on Computational Linguistics: Technical Papers, Dublin, Ireland, pp. 1208–1217 (2014)
9. Saurí, R., Knippen, R., Verhagen, M., Pustejovsky, J.: Evita: a robust event recognizer for QA systems. In: Proceedings of the Conference on Human Language Technology and Empirical Methods in Natural Language Processing, HLT 2005, Vancouver, British Columbia, Canada, pp. 700–707 (2005)
10. Sipoš, R., Bhole, A., Fortuna, B., Grobelnik, M., Mladenić, D.: Demo: HistoryViz – visualizing events and relations extracted from wikipedia. In: Aroyo, L., et al. (eds.) ESWC 2009. LNCS, vol. 5554, pp. 903–907. Springer, Heidelberg (2009)
11. Suchanek, F.M., Kasneci, G., Weikum, G.: YAGO: a core of semantic knowledge unifying wordnet and wikipedia. In: Proceedings of the 16th International Conference on World Wide Web, WWW 2007, Banff, Canada, pp. 697–706 (2007)
12. UzZaman, N., Llorens, H., Derczynski, L., Allen, J., Verhagen, M., Pustejovsky, J.: SemEval-2013 task 1: TempEval-3: evaluating time expressions, events, and temporal relations. In: Second Joint Conference on Lexical and Computational Semantics (*SEM), Volume 2: Proceedings of the Seventh International Workshop on Semantic Evaluation (SemEval 2013), Atlanta, Georgia, USA, pp. 1–9 (2013)
13. Yan, R., Wan, X., Otterbacher, J., Kong, L., Li, X., Zhang, Y.: Evolutionary timeline summarization: a balanced optimization framework via iterative substitution. In: Proceedings of the 34th International ACM SIGIR Conference on Research and Development in Information Retrieval, SIGIR 2011, Beijing, China, pp. 745–754 (2011)

Mapping the Early Modern News Flow:
An Enquiry by Robust Text Reuse Detection

Giovanni Colavizza[1]($\boxtimes$), Mario Infelise[2], and Frédéric Kaplan[1]

[1] EPFL, CDH, DH Laboratory, Station 10, 1015 Lausanne, Switzerland
giovanni.colavizza@epfl.ch
[2] Humanities Department, Ca' Foscari University of Venice, Dorsoduro 3484/D,
Calle Contarini, 30123 Venice, Italy

Abstract. Early modern printed gazettes relied on a system of news exchange and text reuse largely based on handwritten sources. The reconstruction of this information exchange system is possible by detecting reused texts. We present a method to individuate text borrowings within noisy OCRed texts from printed gazettes based on string kernels and local text alignment. We apply our methods on a corpus of Italian gazettes for the year 1648. Beside unveiling substantial overlaps in news sources, we are able to assess the editorial policy of different gazettes and account for a multi-faceted system of text reuse.

Keywords: Early modern newssheets · Gazettes · News flows · Information exchange · Media history · Text reuse · OCR

1 Introduction

The first printed gazettes developed during the Seventeenth century in an already structured environment of information exchange, which largely leveraged on handwritten gazettes as primary sources of texts to be borrowed, rearranged and printed. Such information system encompassed all Europe from at least the Sixteenth century onwards, with a small set of hubs playing a pivotal role in information gathering and redistribution. Hubs changed in importance over time according to their geographic, economic and political relevance. This multimedia system of information exchange endured well into the Eighteenth century, going through a process of incremental standardization of its products: news.[1]

Our aim is to contribute towards the reconstruction of a dynamic fine-grained picture of the news exchange network. To this end the main method is to map text reuse across gazettes: since most issues organized news by place of origin and date, it is possible to detect which gazettes borrowed from the same source.[2] Unfortunately the difficulties of gathering and mastering the available evidence, not to mention language barriers, jeopardize the field in a set of loosely linked

---

The author would like to acknowledge the financial support of Ca' Foscari University of Venice for the digitisation of the sources required for this study.

[1] As overall introductions to the topic refer to [6] and [1].

L.M. Aiello and D. McFarland (Eds.): SocInfo 2014 Workshops, LNCS 8852, pp. 244–253, 2015.
DOI: 10.1007/978-3-319-15168-7_31

national efforts, hindering our grasp of the phenomenon as a whole.[10] Several efforts are currently undergoing to address the lack of available sources in digital form,[2] and the study of news flows in a transnational perspective.[3]

Despite these efforts, the application of digital research methods for the detection of text borrowings on early—pre-XVIII century—gazettes is still wanting, as it is more generally the study of information supply and exchange. There are several concrete obstacles: the presence of both handwritten and printed sources demands a unified method to extract text from images, which is not possible with current state of the art OCR techniques. Secondly, to restrict ourselves to the OCR of printed sources, the quality of the results is usually very bad. Thirdly, we lack a clear knowledge of text reuse practices: translation, paraphrase, reorganization, summary, etc. are all phenomena we must assume were part of the manifold processes of text reuse. Lastly, each European language at the time is bound to present sensible orthographic variability. For all these reasons we cannot apply the standard procedures for text borrowing detection based on n-gram overlap and the assumption of low to none orthographic variability.

We propose here a method to overcome these limitations which is as generic as possible (i.e. maximizes recall at the expenses of precision) and is robust to bad quality OCR and orthographic variation. We are interested in detecting similarities among news from the same chronological period, to reconstruct the immediate propagation of news more than their persistence. There are three main steps in our process: 1) finding text pairs likely to contain an overlap (global comparison); 2) performing a local alignment to find similar passages within these text pairs (local comparison); 3) evaluating the typology of text similarity and eventually identify a shared source between the two gazettes presenting a text borrowing. We focus our attention on printed gazettes and test our method on the Turin and Genoa gazettes for the year 1648. This is one of the earliest dates with almost complete records for the two gazettes, whilst the implications of contemporary events, namely the ending phases of the Thirty Years War, are out of our scope here. The Turin gazette has been digitised from the Turin National Library, the Genoa gazette from the Vatican Secret Archives.[4]

This paper is organized as follows: section 2 provides a brief overview of related work on text reuse detection for our domain. Section 3 details our method in terms of data collection and preparation, and explains our algorithms for borrowing detection. Section 4 evaluates our results and section 5 concludes.

2   Related Work

Initial work on text borrowing detection for historical newspapers brings us back to the Crouch tool. This software relied on stemming pre-processing and

---

[2] See for example the projects: *La Gazette de Renaudot*, also mostly available on *Gallica*, and the *Fuggerzeitungen*. Digitisation projects for more recent newspapers are instead a growing reality, for example Europeana Newspapers.

[3] Especially relevant the recent News Networks in Early Modern Europe project.

[4] RIS.43/1-3; *Segreteria di Stato, Avvisi*, bb. 21 and 101, respectively.

synonym maps extracted from WordNet, to then apply text alignment by n-gram and similar words matching.[9] The most recent research on newspapers using the Crouch tool further augmented these methods by considering basic stylometric features and finally perform a hierarchical-clustering classification of borrowings.[5] The good results obtained with these methods lack in generality: reliance on WordNet and stemming greatly restrains applicability to modern English and the use of n-grams assumes very good OCRed or manually transcribed texts.

Smith et al. working on Nineteenth-century American newspapers proposed a more generic approach designed to be robust to noisy OCRed transcripts and unknown boundaries for reused text passages. Their three-step method includes a global alignment process based on skip n-gram shingling, a local alignment process on positive global matches based on the Smith-Waterman algorithm and finally passage clustering on matching sub-sequences with strong overlap.[13] Albeit more robust, this method is not applicable to very noisy OCR, where the assumption of correct word separation is not possible. Secondly, Smith et al. look for substantial amounts of text reuse, whilst we make no assumption on the length of the reused passages.

Lastly, the automatic detection of text reuses in literary texts is a subject close to our domain. In [4] the authors propose a fingerprint approach resilient to gaps in reused passages, able to detect short and ill-defined borrowings such as paraphrasing. The nature of our sources, where facts are narrated and interpolated by opinions and subjective statements, is very close to literary texts for the purpose of designing text reuse detection algorithms. We adopt the intuition of resilience to gaps in overlaps, and the focus on ill-defined and short borrowings. Eventually, our proposed approach specifically addresses very noisy OCRed texts of any length, with language-independent methods.

A key topic in both the study of early newspapers and text borrowing detection is the unit of comparison and its connection with the text formatting on the page. The methods presented before have refrained from using a unit of formatting as unit of comparison (e.g. paragraphs), preferring instead to focus on groups of sentences with no connection to contents or reading technologies established by an editorial process. Text in early modern gazettes is often systematically organized into paragraphs grouped by provenance and date. This incidentally applies to both printed and handwritten gazettes. In tracing the development of the paragraph until its widespread adoption in different genres during the Eighteenth century, Will Slauter reminds us of the importance of printed gazettes as a laboratory for its development during the previous century. It is by following the paragraphs and their alterations, that we can "reconstruct the trajectory of news."[12] More recently Brendan Dooley argued that it would be more appropriate to track periods, or sentences of coherent meaning, as news "building blocks".[2] In the effort to evaluate the historiographical debate, our method entails comparison at paragraph level, with the further aim to assess editorial policies of different gazettes and leverage on the semantic link between form and meaning.

3   Method

The internal structure of printed gazettes is very regular. Each gazette is a unique sheet folded once (*in-folio*), resulting in 4 pages of text. Most often news are organized in paragraphs, by place of origin and date. It is this information identifying groups of news within each issue that allows scholars to reconstruct news flows. Our method implies the comparison of paragraphs to detect text borrowings or similarities, which allows us to know when two different issues had the same source of information, the extent of the overlap, and if there was a different editorial policy according to text formatting. We refrain from providing a clear definition of what we consider a text reuse and what not since we do not want to limit ourselves to strictly *verbatim* borrowings. An *a posteriori* classification of borrowings will be instead proposed below.

Our pipeline is as follows: from images we extract the text of news in digital form by OCR. This text is then manually annotated with the necessary metadata and normalized. Finally, each paragraph of each news is compared with all paragraphs of all other news from different gazettes within a time window of one month ahead and backwards of the issue date. Each positive result above a given threshold is submitted to the user for direct evaluation and classification.

3.1   Text Extraction, Annotation and Pre-processing

All OCR has been done with ABBYY Fine Reader 11, Corporate Edition.[5] We trained the software on a random sample of 10% of the pages for both gazettes, expanding the character training set and the verification vocabularies. Results varied greatly according to the print and conservation quality of the original documents, therefore we do not report error rates for the OCR process, and threat all texts as bad quality. We then manually annotated OCRed texts with xml metadata on issue place and date, source date and place of origin, and paragraph division. Lastly, in a normalization step we removed all stopwords, punctuation, words shorter than 2 characters, whitespace, and we brought everything to lowercase.

An example of text after OCR is:

```
Daumarelatsonc defaeficltdell^^ 1 p.siriedrà quantoforfogilitosin à qual
 ^ giorno,;à Che aggipngOno qiielle de Rome dalli 23 . che PArmata Fran-
cese partita da Portolcsigone alli r 4oseguitatada'5 . Vasselli di Portu-
gallochen'ehe n.altriFranCrsifossero rimastitnLiuornoànstàrCiesogiòn-
```

Which after pre-processing becomes (in yellow the most relevant informations retained, despite the loss of word segmentation):

```
daumarelatsoncdefaeficltdell1psiriedràquantoforfogilitosinqual
giornocheaggipngonoqiielleromedalli23parmatafran
cesepartitaportolcsigoneallir4oseguitatada5vasselliportu
gallochenehenaltrifrancrsifosserorimastitnliuornoànstàrciesogiòn
```

---

[5] finereader.abbyy.com

3.2   Comparison Algorithms

The problem of finding patterns in sequences of symbols is a well-developed topic in the field of bioinformatics, especially for the task of protein classification, since proteins are represented as sequences of amino acids. The field makes an heavy use of *string kernels* in conjunction with kernel machine learning models.[3]

We use the subsequence string kernel (SSK), originally proposed in [8], which is the non-truncated version of the computationally cheaper gap kernel proposed in [7], an alternative we tested with comparable outcomes. The SSK does not rely on any domain knowledge, but only on the subsequences of characters as they appear in documents. The feature space is generated by the set of all non-contiguous k-mers, weighted by an exponentially decaying factor over their full length of the text. This actually means that the algorithm is configured with two parameters, λ, the decaying factor, and n, the length of the subsequences to consider. The subsequences can be non contiguous, and their score in the feature vector will be proportional to their contiguity. The drawback of the computation cost, which is quadratic, can be overcome by adopting more efficient options such as the gap kernel. After some fine-tuning we set the SSK parameters to $\lambda = 0.5$ using 5-mers.

Local alignment is computed with the Smith-Waterman algorithm as in [13]. We set out parameters like this: matching characters have a weight of 2, mismatches of -1, opening a gap -2 and continuing a gap -0.5. The only parameter out of the commonly adopted values for this algorithm is the opening gap penalty, which we set to -2 instead of -5 to be less strict on proximity mismatches due to bad OCR.

For each pair of paragraphs to compare, we apply SSK as global metric, keep the 5 higher-scoring results, proceed to locally align by Smith-Waterman and keep the 2 higher-scoring results for direct evaluation. To maintain the manual evaluation feasible, we discarded all results with SSK below 0.2 or local alignment lower than 80.

4   Evaluation of Results

The accurate measurement of precision and recall is a recognized problem in text reuse detection studies. In fact researchers have been using pseudo measures on pooled samples as in [13], manual evaluation as in [11], skipped evaluating recall completely as in [5], or used previously manually annotated corpora as in [4]. Unfortunately our case is even more problematic: recall is intractable given the amounts of comparisons to be manually verified, whilst precision is difficult to assess given the generic definition of text reuse we adopted. We were in fact able to verify the presence of several typologies of text reuse within our small corpus: 1) *verbatim* copy of a whole paragraph or parts of it, 2) paraphrasing or translations from the same source, 3) the same event narrated from different sources or perspectives, and finally 4) the same or similar topic but different news. The variety of typologies and our desire to consider them all but the last one, compelled us to adopt a very tolerant approach for the selection of matching pairs to be manually evaluated.

We selected a sample of 6 months on our data[6] and manually evaluated all pairs left after the filtering step. Furthermore each match we assigned to categories 1, 2 or 3 has been double-checked directly on sources. The results tells us that a negligible amount of pairs are within category 1 or 3 (less than 1%), and a substantial amount are within categories 2 (circa 30%) and 4 (circa 43%). The rest are non-matching false positives. Given half pairs were supposed not to be matches (because we retained two candidates to evaluate per paragraph), and several news had no matches at all (especially significant in this respect are local or minor events), the level of overlap is considerable. Another clear result is the almost complete absence of *verbatim* borrowings, which is probably a limitation of our corpus since all scholars in the field account for the frequency of such phenomenon, albeit in the absence of systematic surveys for this period. Lastly, it was hard to detect clear cases of a multiplicity of sources for the same news: the editorial line of the gazettes was usually enforced by cuts and by comments inserted within the text, for example undermining the reliability of the source.

In the last part of this section we discuss in detail the quantitative analysis of the page formatting and its link to the editorial process, and we provide an overview of the news flow of which the Genoa and Turin gazettes were part.

4.1 Paragraphs, Formatting and Editorial Policies

We initially looked at the provenance of sources in each issue of the two gazettes, and at the order in which news were grouped by source and paginated. It is important to remind at this point that the gazette from Genoa was published weekly, whilst the one from Turin bi-weekly. This, as we explain, has an impact on the overall amount of text per issue, but not on its internal organization. In the Genoese gazette there are 7 places with regular presence in each issue (frequency above 80%): Barcelona, Genoa, Germany, London, Milan, Paris and Venice. Places which appear above 50% of the times are: Lisbon, Naples, Rome and Turin. The organization of information within the gazette is far from random as well. A typical issue contains news in this order: Genoa first, then Rome or Naples or Marseille and the Provence, then Milan, Lisbon, Barcelona, Paris, London, Germany and Venice. A similar strong regularity is to be found in the gazette from Turin, plus the orders substantially overlap in the two gazettes. Table 1 provides an overview for the month of February 1648, with places in order of publication.

The systematic organization of information in each gazette hints at the exchange system in action: it is very likely that the news were composed and imposed on the form as they arrived, to gain time. Therefore their order of publication reflects the regularity of the postal system, delivering news on an almost weekly basis at fixed dates.

---

[6] Roughly less than half of it. The selected months were January to June 1648, but all summer months have faults in the issue sequence. From now onwards we report results obtained on this subset of the corpus, unless otherwise specified.

Table 1. Places of origin of sources in each February issue of the Turin gazette

Issue date	Sequence						
1648-02-05 Turin	Barcelona	Paris	London	Germany	Rome	Milan
1648-02-08 Milan	Lyon	Candia	Rome			
1648-02-12 Turin	Barcelona	Paris	London	Germany	Munster	Turin
1648-02-15 Milan	Genoa	Naples	Rome			
1648-02-19 Turin	Barcelona	Paris	London	Turin		
1648-02-22 Milan	Genoa	Naples	Rome	Venice		
1648-02-26 Turin	Barcelona	Lyon/Paris	London	Germany	Turin	
1648-02-29 Milan	Genoa	Rome	Venice			

We then focused on the quantity of matter (character types). Table 2 provides the numbers for the two gazettes. Besides the bi-weekly Turin gazette being richer in contents during the same time span, we are able to identify a different use of paragraphs between the two gazettes. More specifically, in Genoa the average length of paragraphs reflects the editorial policy of grouping together all the news from one place, which are split in several paragraphs in Turin. We believe this fact reflects the practice of reorganizing the information into single paragraphs in Genoa, and instead the practice of mimicking the paragraph organization of news as it was in the handwritten sources for Turin. We underline this phenomenon because it has a direct impact on text borrowing detection: on the one hand the paragraph is undermined in its role of comparison unit, on the other it retains interest because it conveys some information of the editorial practices.

Table 2. Basic statistics on Genoa and Turin gazettes, before and after pre-processing

Statistic	Genoa before	Genoa after	Turin before	Turin after
total char count	281206	186301	579381	415311
total number of paragraphs	263	263	1221	1221
average chars per paragraph	1069	708	474	340

The averages text per month, per issue and per paragraph are remarkably regular throughout the period under consideration. More specifically, the average amount of text per paragraph (roughly 1000 for Genoa and 400 for Turin) is consistent over time, proving an adherence to an established editorial policy. For further evidence table 3 and 4 provide the details of matter distribution into paragraphs per classes of size: the first column dives the % of paragraphs of less than 500 characters, the second column the proportion of text they contain, etc.

The evidence suggests a strong regularity in the flow of information reaching the two gazettes' presses. Each issue reproduced information from roughly the same places in similar amount and order. It also hints at very different editorial processes in action: the grouping of sources by provenance in Genoa, possibly to maximize the use of space, direct reproduction of the source format in Turin. We can finally demonstrate the alignment of sources' contents by borrowing detection.

Table 3. Details of paragraph distributions for Genoa

	500	% of text	1000	% of text	2000	% of text	3000	% of text
January	35.1	10	21.6	17.3	37.8	59.1	5.4	13.1
February	39.3	13.2	25	21.1	33.9	61.4	1.8	4.2
March	31	10.6	34.5	28.8	29.3	46	5.2	14.6
April	51.1	21	20	17.9	24.4	44.7	2.2	6.4
May	33.3	13.5	31.5	28.7	31.5	48.2	3.7	9.6
June	30.8	11.8	38.5	29.8	23.1	35.9	7.7	22.6

Table 4. Details of paragraph distributions for Turin

	500	% of text	1000	% of text	2000	% of text	3000	% of text
January	74.4	43.4	21.8	42.2	3	9.9	0.7	4.4
February	78.8	48.6	16.5	33.8	4.7	17.6	0	0
March	80.9	50.9	13.5	25.9	4.8	18.9	0.7	4.3
April	80.9	53.9	14.7	29.6	4	14.1	0.4	2.5
May	77.6	49.6	19.2	37.7	2.7	9.9	0.4	2.7
June	81.6	57.3	14.4	28.5	4	14.1	0	0

4.2   Information Exchange Networks

Our results on text reuse detection strongly confirm the preliminary insights exposed before. We were able to find systematic news overlap from the main source origins. Both gazettes present the same news from the Iberian peninsula (Barcelona and Lisbon), France (Paris), England (London) and Italy (Turin, Venice, Milan) with a frequency above 80% for the period of evaluation. The news match in their original date, date of publication (allowing for the different issue date of the two gazettes) and their contents with only marginal lack of overlap. What is nevertheless surprising is the absence of regular overlaps from Germany and Rome, and the very low amount of *verbatim* reuse in the detected matches. We are able to conclude that Genoa and Turin were part of the same information exchange system to a considerable extent, yet the process of text reuse was not simply that of a copy, but of a more complex set of practices.

At a more closer look we were able to identify the following processes of text rearrangement in action:

— alteration of order: paragraphs could be switched in order, reduced with cuts or assembled together.
— Paraphrasing: even the strongest matches were clear examples of free copy from the same source. The same news was narrated with slightly different words.
— Translations: we found hints at possible translations from the same source, usually for news from Spain. See figures 3 and 4 for an example: figure 3 (Genoa) says "Baya de todoslos Santos", figure 4 (Turin) "Baya di tutti i Santi".

– Cross referencing and news narrations: the different publication timings allowed a gazette to present some information before or only after the other one. Sometimes a narration was constructed to link the new information with previous issues.

– Reformulation of contents: it is frequent to find changes in contents, for example towards simplification or removal of details. See again figure 3 and 4: Genoa mentions the names of the commanders fighting over Baya, and the precise amounts of troops involved on Dutch side. Turin is more generic (no proper names, only overall amount of troops). These simplifications probably hint at details deemed to be uninteresting or not relevant for the local public.

– Partial overlap of sources: sometimes we detected a misalignment in the news. One part of the information was matching, others were not: it is either possible that the two gazettes had a partially non overlapping set of sources, or that they cut different parts of the news for opposite reasons.

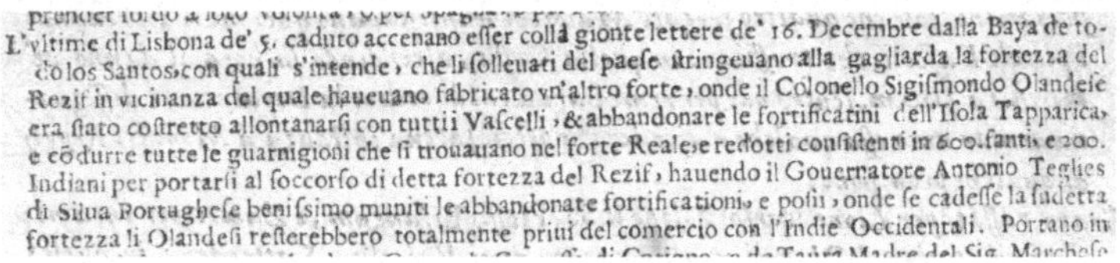

Fig. 1. Genoa issue of 28th March 1648. News from Lisbon

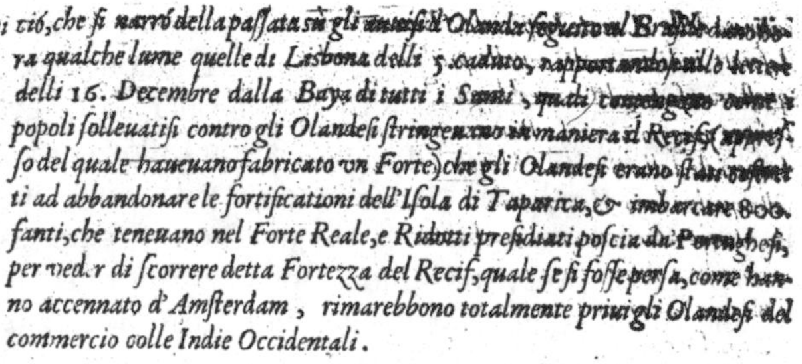

Fig. 2. Turin issue of 25th March 1648. News from Lisbon

We could eventually individuate three categories of matches, linked with different score ranges: 1- there can be an almost full match, which entails high scores both globally and locally; 2- a partial match, for example if a shorter text matches into a longer one, which delivers low global and high local alignment scores; 3- a topic match, which is distinguishable by high global and low local scores.

5 Conclusion

We described a method for the identification of text reuse in Seventeenth century printed gazettes, which is resilient to very noisy OCR and makes only minimal assumptions on the texts to compare. We applied our method on two Italian gazettes from 1648, with a very open definition of the borrowings to detect. Our overall results prove the existence of a substantially shared information supply system between the two gazettes. It is also evident that we discovered a more complex set of editorial practices than expected by the field literature, which will require further investigation. We consider this work as a first step into the development of digital methods to study the early modern information exchange system. Our next goal is to add handwritten sources to the equation.

References

1. Dooley, B. (ed.): The Dissemination of News and the Emergence of Contemporaneity in Early Modern Europe. Ashgate, Farnham (2010)
2. Dooley, B.: International news flows in the Seventeenth Century – problems and prospects. In: News and the Shape of Europe, 1500-1750 Conference, London (2013)
3. Fu, Y.: Kernel methods and applications in bioinformatics. In: Springer Handbook in Bioinformatics, Springer, Heidelberg (2014)
4. Garcia, J.-B., Glaudes, P., Del Lungo, A.: Automatic detection of reuses and citations in literary texts. LLC 29(3), 412–421 (2014)
5. Hardie, A., McEnery, T., Songlin, P.S.: Historical text mining and corpus-based approaches to the newsbooks of the commonwealth. In: [1]
6. Infelise, M.: Prima dei giornali: Alle origini della pubblica informazione. Laterza, Bari (2002)
7. Leslie, C., Kuang, R.: Fast string kernels using inexact matching for protein sequences. JMLR 5, 1435–1455 (2004)
8. Lodhi, H., Saunders, C., Shawe-Taylor, J., Cristianini, N., Watkins, C.: Text classification using string kernels. JMLR 2, 419–444 (2002)
9. Piao, S.L., McEnery, T.: A tool for text comparison. In: Proceedings of the Corpus Linguistics 2003 Conference, pp. 637–646 (2003)
10. Raymond, J.: Newspapers: a national or international phenomenon? Media History 18(3–4), 249–257 (2012)
11. Seo, J., Bruce Croft, W.: Local text reuse detection. In: SIGIR, Singapore (2008)
12. Slauter, W.: The paragraph as information technology: how news travelled in the eighteenth-century Atlantic world. Annales HSS 67(2), 253–278 (2012)
13. Smith, D.A., Cordell, R., Maddock Dillon, E.: Infectious texts: modeling text reuse in nineteenth-century newspapers. In: 2013 IEEE International Conference on Big Data, pp. 86–94 (2013)

Linking Historical Ship Records
to a Newspaper Archive

Andrea Bravo Balado[(✉)], Victor de Boer, and Guus Schreiber

Department of Computer Science, VU University Amsterdam,
Amsterdam, The Netherlands
a.c.bravobalado@student.vu.nl, {v.de.boer,guus.schreiber}@vu.nl

Abstract. Linking historical datasets and making them available on the
Web has increasingly become a subject of research in the field of digital
humanities. In this paper, we focus on discovering links between ships
from a dataset of Dutch maritime events and a historical archive of newspaper articles. We apply a heuristic-based method for finding and filtering links between ship instances; subsequently, we use machine learning
for article classification to be used for enhanced filtering in combination
with domain features. We evaluate the resulting links, using manually
annotated samples as gold standard. The resulting links are made available as Linked Open Data, thus enriching the original data.

Keywords: Text classification · Machine learning · Record linkage ·
Entity linkage · Historical research · Digital humanities · Digital history

1 Introduction

Digital Humanities is a rising area of research at the intersection of disciplines in
humanities with information technologies. This paper focuses on issues in *digital
history*. Recently, many historical archives have been digitized. A key challenge
in this area is increasing interoperability of heterogeneous datasets. Researchers
in interdisciplinary settings are now focusing their efforts on linking historical
datasets for enrichment and availability on the Web [1,12].

In this paper we develop and evaluate a method for finding identity links
between ships in two different datasets[1]. Our work is part of the Dutch Ships
and Sailors (DSS) project. In this project maritime digital datasets have been
made available as Linked Open Data [3]. The maritime history has been essential
in the development of economic, social and cultural aspects of Dutch society. It
has been well documented by shipping companies, governments, newspapers and
other institutions.

Given the importance of maritime activity in every day life in the XIX and
XX centuries, announcements on the departures and arrivals of ships or mentions of accidents or other events, can be found in historical newspapers, and

---

[1] This paper has an online appendix with technical details available at http://dx.doi.
org/10.6084/m9.figshare.1189228

© Springer International Publishing Switzerland 2015
L.M. Aiello and D. McFarland (Eds.): SocInfo 2014 Workshops, LNCS 8852, pp. 254–263, 2015.
DOI: 10.1007/978-3-319-15168-7_32

having these links available in the DSS data cloud would enrich the data, adding value for researchers. In this paper we describe how, using domain knowledge as well as machine learning text classification approaches, we are able to establish such links between different datasets for enrichment and help ease collaboration among historical researchers.

The method we use for linking involves a hybrid approach in which we use both domain-specific features to generate and filter candidate links, but also employ machine-learning techniques to improve the filtering process. We evaluate different combinations of these techniques, using manually annotated samples as gold standard and training set.

2   Related Work

Many approaches for linking datasets can be found in the literature. For instance, the idea of using domain knowledge for entity linkage is not new. In [9], the task of entity linkage is focused on linking named entities extracted from unstructured text to the entities on a knowledge base. Although our approach is essentially the opposite, where we use a structured dataset (instead of a knowledge base) to find entities in the unstructured text and the domain is different, this area of research is related to ours. Even though the domain is different, the most similar to our goals is the research done in [13], where the authors present a system to disambiguate entity mentions in texts and link them to a knowledge base, the main difference being our use of a database in place of a knowledge base. Furthermore, in [5], in addition to domain knowledge, the authors take an information retrieval approach for linking entities. Moreover, finding and linking relevant newspaper articles has been done in [2] using a vector space model with a similarity function. The main difference with our research, besides the domain, is that the authors intend to link similar and current archives, while ours are essentially different and historical. Linking relevant newspaper articles from the Dutch National Library archives has been done in [6] and [8], albeit on a different domain, linking parliamentary and political debates with media outlets. Similarly, although their approach is by means of a semantic model and topic modeling, as well as using named entities for ranking, our experimental setup and evaluation procedure is based on [7].

Machine learning text classification has also been used for entity disambiguation and linkage. In [16], the authors experiment with text classification methods for literary study. Yu goes into detail about the importance of preprocessing and choice of classifiers, in which we have based some of our work. Moreover, in [15] the authors present information extraction as a classification problem to be solved using machine learning algorithms, such as Support Vector Machines (SVM) and Naive Bayes (NB), among others in order to extract information related to natural disasters from newspaper articles in Spanish.

Our work is part of recent efforts into linking historical datasets in the Netherlands, namely the works on linking datasets from German occupied Dutch society in [4] and historical census data in [11].

3   Approach

3.1   Datasets

We use two datasets which both contain descriptions of ship instances. The first dataset is the "Northern muster rolls databases" (in Dutch: *Noordelijke Monsterollen Databases*). This dataset contains official lists of crew members, known as "muster rolls", for ship companies in the three northern provinces of the Netherlands (Groningen, Friesland and Drenthe). The data was curated from mustering archives by historian J. Leinenga and covers the period 1803–1937. It was made available as Linked Open Data in the DSS project [3]. In this collection names of ships are not unique and may appear several times. In a preprocessing step we group ships which share (i) the same ship name, (i) the same last name of the captain, (iii) the same type of ship, and (iv) the same period (through a proximity relation of the respective record years).

The second dataset is the historical newspaper archive of the Dutch National Library (in Dutch: *Koninklijke Bibliotheek*. This data contains text and images of newspaper articles from 1618 to 1995 in the Dutch language. The newspaper archive is not limited to the maritime domain. The text of the articles has been digitized through OCR (Optical Character Recognition). The Dutch National Library indicates that the quality of the OCR text is not 100% reliable[2], due to common problems, such as old spelling, complex page layouts, difficult fonts, discoloration of the paper and fading of the ink. The data is available through a public website and API[3].

3.2   Evaluation

We perform a manual evaluation of the candidate links generated. Given the size of the dataset, it is unfeasible to manually assess every instance. Therefore, we have randomly selected a subset of 50 instances to be included in the evaluation for every experiment. Stasiu *et al.* [14] suggest that a sample of 50 instances is enough to extrapolate the evaluation to the rest of the dataset, according to their experiments for a similar problem.

For every candidate link we present the evaluator with full record information as well as the text of the linked article. For the experiments, which do not involve text-classification algorithms, the evaluation criterion is based on a 5-point Likert scale, ranging from strong disagreement (1) to strong agreement (5) on whether the newspaper text should be linked to a given ship. The 5-point Likert scale was requested by the domain expert and is also used for the calculation of mean and standard deviation. For precision, recall and F1 score calculations the Likert scale is transformed into binary scale, where values 1, 2 and 3 are considered non-relevant items (label 0) and values 4 and 5 are considered relevant (label 1). This is done to facilitate calculations. For the text-classification experiments a

---

[2] http://kranten.delpher.nl/nl/pages/ocr
[3] http://www.delpher.nl/

binary scale was used, where 0 indicates that there is no mention of a ship or ships in the text; 1 otherwise.

The evaluation was performed by historian and domain expert J. Leinenga (rater C), as well as by two co-authors of this paper (raters B and A). We measured the inter-rater agreement for each pair of raters by means of the weighted Cohen's Kappa coefficient (κ). Between raters A and B (0.76) as well as raters A and C (0.62) there is substantial agreement, whereas the degree of agreement between B and C is moderate (0.58).

For the assessment of our experiments, we have chosen to calculate the standard precision and F_1 scores, as well as an approximate recall. Precision is the fraction of candidate links that are evaluated as correct while the F_1 score is a weighted harmonic mean of precision and recall [10]. In order to calculate a recall score, given the difficulty to assess the actual number of relevant results in the newspaper archives, we propose an approximation, based on the estimated number of correct links retrieved by an algorithm divided by the estimated number of correct instances in the dataset, for which we take the baseline experiment, i.e. our most inclusive algorithm. The approximate recall is calculated by:

$$ApproximateRecall_x = \frac{\text{retrieved\_items}_x \cdot \text{precision}_x}{\text{retrieved\_items}_\text{baseline} \cdot \text{precision}_\text{baseline}} \tag{1}$$

4   Linking Method

The linking method we deploy is a combination of processing steps. In the first step we generate a large candidate set of links; subsequent (alternative and/or consecutive) steps filter this large set with the aim to increase the link quality.

4.1   Baseline: Name of the Ship and Date Restriction

We created a baseline by generating a large set of candidate links. We expect this baseline to have high recall and low precisions, as ship names are hardly unique: ships have typically names of females, of geographical locations, or of concepts such as friendship, hope and faith. The baseline was constructed by querying the API of the second dataset using the name of all ship instances from the first dataset. The baseline contains for every ship instance the first 100 links to newspaper articles provided by the API.

4.2   Domain Feature Filtering

For these processing steps our approach is to identify domain knowledge features that are suitable for distinguishing different ship instances and thus work well for filtering candidate links:

Filter 1a: Captain's last name. In this filter we test a particular feature that domain experts have indicated can help on the disambiguation of candidate links from newspaper archives: the last name of the captain. This is mainly due to the fact that the captain of a ship, with few exceptions, is unlikely to change over time, unless the ship gets lost or destroyed. Note that this time, we are not performing queries on the full newspaper archive but only on the articles that contain at least a ship name and the publication year is within a range relevant for the ship instance at hand.

Filter 1b: Year restriction. This filter helps to make sure that the year of publication of the candidate links from the newspaper archive is within the original muster-roll year interval for each ship instance. The rationale behind it is that ship instances that have already been found in historical records within given years, are less likely to be mentioned in newspapers published outside the typical lifespan of a ship, which is, according to domain experts, about 30 years.

Filter 2: Combining captain's last name and year restriction. By combining the two filters 1a and 1b we expect to be able to boost precision, at the likely cost of recall.

4.3   Text Classification

The processing steps using text classification are focused on exploring the structure of newspaper articles in order to train a classifier that would be able to predict labels for unseen data. The main difference with previous experiments is that the text classification process is not intended for generating or filtering links directly; they only return a value for whether or not this article describes a historical ship. We used two different classifiers: Naive Bayes and Support Vector Machine (SVM) with Sequential Minimal Optimisation (SMO).

We used the WEKA's[4] off-the-shelf supervised learning algorithms to train and evaluate a classifier model and then used the classifier to predict labels for the rest of the dataset. As training set we used the 200 labeled samples (121 positive and 79 negative instances), obtained during the manual evaluation of the previous steps (baseline, filters 1a, 1b, and 2). From these samples, we selected only the text of the corresponding newspaper article and we converted the 5-point Likert scale label, as explained before.

The next step was to choose and set multiple filters for data transformation. We make use of a multi-filter in order to apply all chosen filters at once. We chose the *string-to-word-vector* filter to represent the newspaper texts as feature vectors. For this experiment, we implemented a bag-of-words model, where the frequency of occurrence of each term is used as a feature, ignoring their order in the document [10]. We remove short words (< 3 characters) using the *remove by name* filter. Furthermore, we perform feature selection using a ranking based on the information gain metric. As recommended by WEKA documentation, the classifier is defined and evaluated but not yet trained. The evaluation is performed using both Naive Bayes and SMO classifiers and consists of a 10-fold cross validation using training data. Once the Naive Bayes and SMO classifiers were evaluated, these could be used for learning. The test set contains 413,663

---

[4] http://www.cs.waikato.ac.nz/ml/weka/

instances. The algorithm returns a prediction; all new labels are imported into a new table for each classifier in the database to make it possible to associate labels to ship instances afterwards.

4.4   Combining Domain Feature Filtering and Classifier Labels

The final step of our method involves combining techniques from the previous experiments. More specifically, we combined Filter 2 with the labels assigned by the classifiers as an additional feature. For these experiments, our method is to restrict the number of candidate links, as done during domain filtering. Similar to Filter 2, the last name of the captain and the restriction of the year of publication of the article are the domain features chosen for filtering. Additionally, we selected the label provided by the classifiers as positive examples in order to refine filtering of the candidate links, in the hope of improving our previous results. We test two variants of this combination, one with the Naive Bayes Classifier and the other with the SMO classifier.

5   Results

Table 1 summarises the results. The baseline contains 413,863 candidate links, corresponding to 5,078 ship instances. This baseline was used in all consecutive steps.

The first filter (captain's name) results in precision going up from 0.23 to 0.90, at the cost of a decrease in (approximate) recall from 1.00 to 0.40. The second filter (year restriction) gives a much smaller gain in precision (0.23 to 0.28) at a higher cost in recall (from 1.00 to 0.19). When we combine the two filters precision goes up to 0.96, at the cost of a further drop of recall to 0.13.

Domain filtering combined with the two text classification methods resulted in a precision score of 0.94 and a similar approximate recall, of 0.09 and 0.10,

Table 1. Results for six (combinations of) processing steps: precision, approximate recall, F1 score, number of links retrieved, mean (λ) score, standard deviation (σ) of the score. * The two classifiers were evaluated using a binary scale instead of 5-point Likert scale and do not analyse candidate links but instead indicate whether an article is about ships.

Step	Prec.	Approx. recall	F1	#Links	(λ)	(σ)
Baseline	0.23	1.00	0.37	413,863	2.37	1.35
Filter 1a: Captain's last name	0.90	0.40	0.56	51,925	4.62	0.88
Filter 1b: Year restriction	0.28	0.19	0.23	79,113	2.58	1.58
Filter 2: 1a + 1b	0.96	0.13	0.23	16,037	4.80	0.49
Filter 2 + Naive Bayes	0.94	0.09	0.17	11,356	4.82	0.72
Filter 2 + SMO	0.94	0.10	0.18	12,215	4.84	0.51
Naive Bayes text classifier*	1.00	0.42	0.59	413,663	0.22	0.42
SMO text classifier*	1.00	0.45	0.63	413,663	0.30	0.46

respectively. These low recall scores affect the F1 scores, which are consequently low as well. This is mainly due to the restrictive nature of these algorithms, as evidenced by the number of retrieved links, being the lowest of all the experiments performed for this project.

The manual evaluation for the labels generated by the Naive Bayes and the SMO classifiers results in a precision of 1 and an approximate recall of 0.42 and 0.45, respectively. There were no false positives, thus the classifiers did not label relevant instances as irrelevant. Overall, the scores for the SMO classifier are somewhat better than the results of the Naive Bayes classifier.

6   Discussion

The baseline results show that it is indeed possible to retrieve a considerable amount of relevant links from a maritime historical dataset to historical newspaper articles. This despite the fact that OCR quality is imperfect and only a small part of the newspaper articles in the target dataset are about the maritime domain. Analysis of the baseline results also provided information for subsequent filtering steps.

When applying Filter 1a we found that the last name of the captain of a ship appears to be a good indicator for candidate link selection. This has also helped us gain more insight on the way ship instances are featured on the newspaper archives. By analysing the texts, we noticed that it is common to find the name of the ship along with the last name of the captain (either before or after), a port name and a date at the beginning of the sentence. For Filter 1b, on the one hand, we found that using the publication year and appearance in the muster-roll dataset do not yield successful results in terms of boosting precision. Even when the ship name appears in the text, only limiting the links to those of the years we have knowledge of is not enough for record linkage. However, we believe that this domain feature could be used either as a preprocessing step or in combination with more suitable domain features. Other features such as ship types were considered, but preliminary inspection showed that this feature does not appear in newspaper articles.

Precision can be further improved by combining domain features, as the results of Filter 2 show. We decided to concentrate on obtaining high precision scores because in general, historians prefer to have fewer but accurate links than the opposite. The results obtained by these experiments are satisfactory and have also given us an indication of the extent to which we can use domain knowledge for record linking.

The text-classification results by themselves (last two rows in Table 1) show that text classification in this domain is potentially a useful approach, regardless of the size of the training set. By analysing the feature vectors for both classifier models, we have found that the vectors consist mostly of port names (places) and female names, indicating that maritime activity terms are not mentioned on newspaper texts, at least not on common ship mentions. Also, our choices for data transformation and classifier configuration seem to be appropriate for the task at hand.

Our aim was to improve the link results by combining domain filtering and text classification. However, when we compare the scores of Filter 2 by itself to the scores of Filter 2 combined with either classifier we see that the latter have a negative impact on the results. Especially the loss in precision might be an artifact of the evaluation setup, especially given that the precision was already very high before this filter. Also, the restrictive nature of adding more features to the query causes loss of recall given that less links are retrieved. In retrospect, we think that a more sensible use of the classifier labels, e.g. as a filter before querying instead of it being part of the query, could have resulted in better scores. Still, more testing with bigger evaluation samples would be needed in order to decide whether combining both techniques is a suitable approach for this task.

We did not use the article titles in the training data for the classifiers. However, after updating the labels in the database, it was possible to see a distribution of article titles associated with each of the labels. Although there is some overlapping, it is noticeable that some newspaper sections seem more likely to be associated to ships than others, e.g. titles like "Advertentie" and "Familiebericht" (Eng: "Advertisement" and "Obituaries") seem to be indicative of texts unrelated to ships while titles like "ZEETIJDINGEN." and "Buitenl. Havens." (Eng: "Sea messages" and "Foreign harbours") are the opposite. These findings could be used as a feature for a different algorithm, e.g. for topic discovery. We believe it could also give an indication of the possible structures within the text articles given the distinctions between titles.

7 Conclusions

A total of 16,037 links resulting from Filter 2 have been used to enrich the main dataset as part of the DSS Linked Data cloud by De Boer et al. [3]. We chose the Filter 2 results because of the high precision, as this was high priority for the domain experts. These links provide new opportunities for analysis of the source material. Most found links are listings of arrivals or departures, including information about the destination. But other interesting examples of found links include links between ships and articles reporting on the sinking of that ship or the sale of the ship (including the price for which it was sold). These links are found to be interesting by maritime historical researchers. The data and example queries are available at http://dutchshipsandsailors.nl/data. Example queries include "return all newspaper articles between 1840 and 1850 for ships that sailed to Riga".

In summary, we have successfully enriched a dataset of historical Dutch ships by linking its instances to corresponding mentions on newspaper archives. We explored different strategies for record linking and used both domain knowledge features and machine learning algorithms to link a dataset of historical Dutch ships with relevant entries in the newspaper archive of the National library of the Netherlands. Overall, we believe that our methods provide a limited but valuable set of links for historians and history enthusiasts that would have otherwise needed many hours of manual search and/or classification by experts. This is important for the accessibility of historical datasets on the Web as well as the preservation of these through time.

Acknowledgments. We would like to thank Jurjen Leinenga and our contacts at the Royal Library for their contributions. This work was supported by CLARIN-NL (http://www.clarin.nl) and by the BiographyNet project (Nr. 660.011.308), funded by the Netherlands eScience Center (http://esciencecenter.nl/).

References

1. Boonstra, O., Breure, L., Doorn, P.: Past, present and future of historical information science. Historical Social Research / Historische Sozialforschung **29**, 2 (2004)
2. Bron, M., Huurnink, B., de Rijke, M.: Linking archives using document enrichment and term selection. In: Gradmann, S., Borri, F., Meghini, C., Schuldt, H. (eds.) TPDL 2011. LNCS, vol. 6966, pp. 360–371. Springer, Heidelberg (2011)
3. de Boer, V., van Rossum, M., Leinenga, J., Hoekstra, R.: Dutch ships and sailors linked data. In: Mika, P., Tudorache, T., Bernstein, A., Welty, C., Knoblock, C., Vrandečić, D., Groth, P., Noy, N., Janowicz, K., Goble, C. (eds.) ISWC 2014, Part I. LNCS, vol. 8796, pp. 229–244. Springer, Heidelberg (2014)
4. de Boer, V., van Doornik, J., Buitinck, L., Marx, M., Veken, T., Ribbens, K.: Linking the kingdom: enriched access to a historiographical text. In: Proceedings of the Seventh International Conference on Knowledge Capture, K-CAP 2013, pp. 17–24. ACM, New York (2013)
5. Gottipati, S., Jiang, J.: Linking entities to a knowledge base with query expansion. In: Proceedings of the Conference on Empirical Methods in Natural Language Processing, EMNLP 2011, pp. 804–813. Association for Computational Linguistics, Stroudsburg (2011)
6. Juric, D., Hollink, L., Houben, G.: Bringing parliamentary debates to the semantic web. In: Proceedings of the Workshop on Detection, Representation and Exploitation of Events in the Semantic Web (DeRIVE 2012) November 12, 2012 (to appear, 2012)
7. Juric, D., Hollink, L., Houben, G.-J.: Discovering links between political debates and media. In: Daniel, F., Dolog, P., Li, Q. (eds.) ICWE 2013. LNCS, vol. 7977, pp. 367–375. Springer, Heidelberg (2013)
8. Kleppe, M., Hollink, L., Kemman, M., Juric, D., Beunders, H., Blom, J., Oomen, J., Houben, G.: Polimedia: analysing media coverage of political debates by automatically generated links to radio and newspaper items. In: LinkedUp Veni Competition 2013, Proceedings of the LinkedUp Veni Competition on Linked and Open Data for Education, vol. 1124, pp. 1–6. CEUR Workshop Proceedings (2014)
9. Lv, Y., Moon, T., Kolari, P., Zheng, Z., Wang, X., Chang, Y.: Learning to model relatedness for news recommendation. In: Proceedings of the 20th International Conference on World Wide Web, WWW 2011, pp. 57–66. ACM, New York (2011)
10. Manning, C.D., Raghavan, P., Schtze, H.: Introduction to Information Retrieval. Cambridge University Press, Cambridge (2008)
11. Meroño-Peñuela, A., Ashkpour, A., Rietveld, L., Hoekstra, R.: Linked humanities data: the next frontier? a case-study in historical census data. In: Proc. of the 2nd Int. Workshop on Linked Science 2012, vol. 951 (2012)

12. Meroño-Peñuela, A., Ashkpour, A., van Erp, M., Mandemakers, K., Breure, L., Scharnhorst, A., Schlobach, S., van Harmelen, F.: Semantic technologies for historical research: A survey. Semantic Web Journal, 588–1795 (2014)
13. Rao, D., McNamee, P., Dredze, M.: Entity linking: finding extracted entities in a knowledge base. In: Poibeau, T., Saggion, H., Piskorski, J., Yangarber, R. (eds.) Multi-source, Multilingual Information Extraction and Summarization. Theory and Applications of Natural Language Processing, pp. 93–115. Springer, Heidelberg (2013)
14. Stasiu, R.K., Heuser, C.A., da Silva, R.: Estimating recall and precision for vague queries in databases. In: Pastor, Ó., Falcão e Cunha, J. (eds.) CAiSE 2005. LNCS, vol. 3520, pp. 187–200. Springer, Heidelberg (2005)
15. Téllez-Valero, A., Montes-y Gómez, M., Villaseñor Pineda, L.: A Machine Learning Approach to Information Extraction, pp. 539–547 (2005)
16. Yu, B.: An evaluation of text classification methods for literary study. LLC **23**(3), 327–343 (2008)

Digital Chronofiles of Life Experience

Cathal Gurrin[1,2]([⊠]), Håvard Johansen[2], Thomas Sødring[3], and Dag Johansen[2]

[1] Insight Centre for Data Analytics, Dublin City University, Dublin, Ireland
cathal@gmail.com
[2] UIT The Arctic University of Norway, Tromsø, Norway
[3] Oslo University College, Oslo, Norway

Abstract. Technology has brought us to the point where we are able to digitally sample life experience in rich multimedia detail, often referred to as lifelogging. In this paper we explore the potential of lifelogging for the digitisation and archiving of life experience into a longitudinal media archive for an individual. We motivate the historical archive potential for rich digital memories, enabling individuals' digital footprints to contribute to societal memories, and propose a data framework to gather and organise the lifetime of the subject.

1 Introduction

Earlier societies have left legacies informing us of their actions. Society has a need to record and document its events and has used whatever means possible. From Newgrange, Stonehenge and the Pyramids in Egypt, to the headstones on Easter Island, we are left with clues from a distant society. In many ways these societies created durable objects that tell a story that transcends time and sometimes these legacies leave us with a mystery to be solved in modern times. Historically the interaction and communication between individuals bore witness to events, and such material is today studied by historians and archivists. Whether stone carvings, exchange of letters, recorded phone calls, or the eyewitness details, this is what leaves the historical trace and forms the basis of the historical record.

As technology evolved, so too have the recording tools; hammer and stone, pen and paper, have been replaced by computers and digital recording devices. The ease at which we can create the historical trace is ever increasing and our ability to create an *evidence of me* has no bounds. Continual advancement in sensing technologies has lead us this point at which it becomes possible, should one wish, to continually record all of life activities into a personal media-rich archive, or as we refer to it in this paper, a *personal chronofile*. This process is called lifelogging and can quickly generate terabytes of information about the individual, in particular using wearable sensors and cameras, which are already flourishing on the consumer market [7].

Compare this to the most detailed life chronicle from the past, the Dymaxion Chronofile [18] where Richard Buckminster-Fuller documented his activities in detail day-by-day into a lifetime archive. Buckminster-Fuller referred to his archive as a "very accurate record of a human being", consisting of 140,000

© Springer International Publishing Switzerland 2015
L.M. Aiello and D. McFarland (Eds.): SocInfo 2014 Workshops, LNCS 8852, pp. 264–273, 2015.
DOI: 10.1007/978-3-319-15168-7_33

papers and 1,700 hours of audio and video. It is our conjecture that as lifelogging becomes a normative activity, archivists will have access to rich and unimaginably detailed records of many such individuals, not just those with the time or resources to manually curate a lifetime archive. These chronofiles would provide a first-hand, non-interpreted account of the past from people whose lifelogs provide a direct connection to historical activities and events.

In this paper we suggest that the chronofile generation process of lifelogging can revolutionise the concept of the historical archive. With minimal overhead, any individual will be able to maintain a chronofile. There are many challenges to be solved along the way, some of them documented in this paper, but the early adopters have shown that this is possible and as the benefits of lifelogging become apparent, it is likely to become the norm, rather than the exception. We propose a model of life-long personal chronofile management that takes the onus off manual curation, storage, and access to the digital objects by employing a set of transformation rules that filter or modify the digital objects.

2   Lifelogging and Life-Long Preservation

2.1   Personal Lifelogging

Lifelogging represents a phenomenon whereby individuals can digitally record their own daily lives in varying amounts of detail and for a variety of purposes. It offers great potential to mine or infer valuable knowledge about life activities. An example of a lifelog archive is shown in Figure 1, in which the activities of the lifelogger (a sequence of about 3,000 images) on the 29th May 2006 are organised automatically into a small set of logical events. Typically, early adopters to lifelogging considered it to be an activity for their own benefit. If lifelogging becomes more pervasive, one can imagine that many users would be willing to share aspects of their lifelog [17] with friends and family while alive or with archivists and researchers when passed away.

Lifelogging becomes possible as a result of three parallel advances in technology. Firstly, sensors are becoming cheap, reliable, robust, power-efficient and portable. There are many low-cost devices such as the OMG Autographer or the Narrative Clip that capture thousands of images per day. Digital audio recorders can record in detail 24/7 audio, a new generation of wearable video cameras can capture much of a day in high definition. Even our mobile phones include enough sensors to digitally lifelog our activities. It is now possible to gather a media-rich representation of our activities in detail that is previously unimaginable. Secondly, the cost of storing and transmitting large quantities of data from sensors and cameras has decreased. From [7] we know that we can currently store 6–8 years of wearable camera images on a $100 hard drive. Thirdly, we have new search and artificial-intelligence techniques to allow us to convert large volumes of raw sensor data into meaningful semantic information that can derive new and aggregated knowledge from this data. All these three technological advancements have brought us to this point: the advent of the era of the lifelogged individual.

Fig. 1. An example lifelog browser [12]

There are many potentially life enriching benefits that could encourage an individual to engage in lifelogging, such as the potential for better self-awareness leading to longer and more active lifespans, new personalised healthcare applications, enhanced methods of learning, increased productivity in the workplace, increased independence, or mobility for people suffering from various memory and cognitive impairments, and new forms of offline and online social interaction [7]. It is considered that as these benefits become apparent, that lifelogging will become a normative activity.

Many use-cases of lifelogging have been proposed, for example, to assist the lifelogger in tasks such as personal healthcare, memory reminiscence [3], and browsing a digital record of past activities [12]. There is now real potential that we are on the cusp of an era of, what Gordon Bell and Jim Gemmell refer to as *total capture* [2]. In fact, this has already begun with the market availability of lifelogging devices.

2.2   Lifelogs as Societal Records

We know from [14, p.139] that "all events have their witnesses, their memory: the trace" and that witness is born through communication of events. The tools we employ for communication today far outweigh the pen and paper of yesterday. Chronofiles promise a new dimension to witness, memory and trace. Consider if you will, a historian in 2114; he will have access to vast chronofile archives from the deceased first generation of lifeloggers. He will have access to orders of magnitude more information about the individual than we are currently gathering in 2014. The events, as before, will be witnessed and memorised, but the form they leave in the trace is so much richer in a world of lifelogging. Mis-interpretation of events and generating historical narrative based on only snapshots of historical communications will be a problem of the past.

One example is the story [15] of the sinking of the "Olong" and the subsequent misinterpretation of events and witness accounts. Human error and distant reporting of a chaotic scene taking place far from land where a sinking boat and a father gesturing the Navy to take his child becomes the story of desperate refugees willing to use all means possible to force the Navy to rescue them, including risking the lives of their children by throwing them overboard. This event has been documented and analysed in detail. Witness statements and logs are placed within a kind of system-centric approach to documenting, which means that the story is documented from societies point of view, placed in system so that we can learn more about society. The story is about a group of people trying to make it to Australia for a better life, but we are missing the story about the individual. The individual's search for a better life, the journey, the sinking and what subsequently happened to the individuals is lost. The true story lies distributed in peoples memory and portions of this story die as memories fade. The story of the individual takes second place to society's story. In the era of chronofiles the story about the individual does not have to be a footnote in a formal document.

2.3   Data Formats

While most historians will find lifelogging a treasure trove of information, it will also certainly pose problems in terms of long term preservation that may not be obvious yet. When it comes to electronic material it is already clear that archivists have a lot of trouble maintaining collections of electronic material. The reason for this is the short lived timespan that some file formats have and their evolutionary nature. Today we even have trouble correctly interpreting some word-processing documents from twenty years ago.

3   A Life Digitised

To understand the potential sources of knowledge and evidence contained in chronofiles, we can look to the early adopters and the data that they store. The manually generated chronofile of Richard Buckminster-Fuller, that we mentioned earlier, is a detailed first-hand record of a life lived. It is unlikely that there are many others willing to put in so much effort. Recent early adaptors, such as Bell [1] and Mann [13] show the potential of what can be captured for a basic first-generation chronofile and they motivate the necessity for chronofiles to be generated automatically by wearing a small set of non-intrusive sensing devices. These first generation chronofiles, which are called lifelogs, are simple data capture, storage, processing, and interaction frameworks that store the data in fixed formats and do not take into consideration the archival challenges of long-term storage and curation of the data. Figure 2 shows an example architecture of a first generation, widely deployable lifelog that is concerned with capturing rich data about the user experiences; organising and enriching it to make it usable for the individual; and finally supporting pervasive access via current access devices.

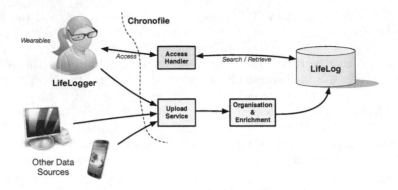

Fig. 2. The Structure of a Basic Lifelog Archive

3.1   Data Storage Requirements

The lifelogs being captured today already provide detailed knowledge about the minutiae of life in 2014, with many potential sources of information that can be included. The list of sources from [7] includes passive visual capture devices that take up to 4,000 images per day or short-durations of video, passive capture audio to record the sounds of life, personal biometrics to understand the physical state of the individual, mobile device context to understand the individuals place in the environment, the communications of the individual, the content they create and consume, their environmental context, media consumption, and any annotations to that content. To illustrate the variety of data sizes and quantities, a summary table of a selection of lifelog data is shown in Table 1. In this table we include the annual storage requirements as well as a lifetime (85 years) storage requirement.[1]

All this data is inherently unmanageable if left to the individual. The huge data volumes involved require the development of a suite of organisation and search tools that allow the individual to gain benefit from the lifelogging process. At present, these search tools, described in more detail in [7] allow for the conversion of a raw chronofiles into a manageable set of digital objects. To take a human memory analogy, these roughly align with the idea of an event in the life of a human (see the event list in Figure 1). The digital objects then act as the unit of observation and retrieval for the chronofile. In order to be located by a search mechanism, these events need to be enriched with appropriate metadata, indexed by search tools and made available via an appropriate interaction mechanism (e.g., Google Glass for the lifelogger or a desktop archive search tool for an archivist).

With the exception of digital video data, one can easily imagine storing a lifelog of an individual indefinitely. Because at current capture rates, it requires about 1 TB per year to capture wearable camera photos from an off-the-shelf

---

[1] Extrapolating across a lifetime, when there is an assumption that data bit rates remain static is merely for illustrative purposes only. Data sources, qualities, resolutions, and bit rates are constantly increasing.

Table 1. An illustration of the data quantities and data sizes for a selection of chronofile data in 2014, over a day, year and a lifetime (using 85 year lifespan and 16 hour days)

Content Type	Data/year	One year	Lifetime
4K Video	5,840 hours	342 TB	28.3 PB
HD Video	5,840 hours	32.8 TB	2.65 PB
Autographer Camera	1.1 million images	479.6 GB	40.8 TB
Audio (mono - 22 KHz)	5,840 hours audio	227.8 GB	19.4 TB
Accelerometer (1 Hz)	21 million readings at 1 Hz	0.05 GB	4.25 GB
Locations (0.2 Hz)	3.9 million GPS points	0.01 GB	1 TB
Reading Log	User dependent	1 GB+	80 GB

5 Mega Pixel wearable camera, along with various other continually sampling sensor data (e.g., accelerometer, GPS, and audio snippets). Consider the Autographer wearable camera. If one wore it for an 85 year lifespan, the storage requirements of six photos per minute would only require ten of today's hard drives. Today, it is therefore feasible to store this data permanently and provide direct non-interpreted knowledge about individuals.

Although the data produced by lifeloggers today is manageable with current technologies, information technology seemingly has a tendency to follow an exponential pathway of advancement. We have already seen this in Moore's Law for CPU transistor densities, Kryder's Law [4] for disk storage, and in Kurzweil's Law of Accelerating Returns [11] for general information technology advancement. Assuming lifelogging archive sizes follow similar growth curves, a capture rate of one Terabyte per year today has the potential to become 1 Zettabyte of data per year by 2045, or 1 Geopbyte by 2075.[2]

Some might argue that ever growing storage device capacities coupled with efficient compression algorithms will adequately support any future storage demands of personal lifeloggers. Others argue the contrary; that the modern society already produces way more data than available storage can handle. In particular, IDC [5] already predicted in 2007 that the 255 Exabytes of information created and replicated that year was for the first time to surpass the 246 Exabytes aggregate storage capacity available globally. Also, they predicted that the gap between disk demand and supply would just be larger. Some years later, their prediction may be correct.

3.2   Curation

Expecting an individual to curate their chronofile in a fine-grained manner to fit within available storage space, to migrate to new file formats, to address potential legal and privacy issues, is not realistic. Even today, the early adopters see chronofile archives as a form of data dump into which all possible data is

---

[2] This only assumes a simple lifelog configuration including the equivalent of an OMG Autographer and various other forms of sensed media. Were one to consider recording 4K video 24/7, then the storage requirements increase by an order of magnitude.

stored, either because it is too troublesome to manually curate the data, or because it is considered more prudent to keep all data on the chance that it could potentially be useful at some point in the future. Therein lies the problem that we foresee; the chronofile needs to be self-organising. We therefore propose a model for chronofiles, based on the Gardi model [6] we proposed for multimedia collections, which iterates over data sources temporally and applies higher-order information transformation rules directly on the stored digital objects. Gardi was positively evaluated for security video archives, home video, recordings and a very early stage visual lifelog.

In previous work, we have successfully applied such application specific data curation techniques for a concrete lifelog scenario in the sports domain. A light-weight lifelogging service was built and deployed for head coaches as part of elite soccer performance development. Soccer arenas and training grounds are populated with stationary [9] and portable cameras [8], and mobile devices provide support for hindsight annotations of sequences worth capturing. This also includes prototypes with Google Glasses used on the field by coaches. This way, coaches determine after a certain event has unfolded whether to permanently store this or not, and, if so, touches the cellular screen. Experience from a complete soccer series in Norway for a specific team over a year indicates that about 5% of video footage from complete games are persisted this way and made use of for analytics and feedback procedures. The other 95% of the video footage rendered useless with regard to events worth examining, can still be stored somewhere for archival purposes or permanently deleted. We conjecture similar techniques have broad applicability for personal chronofiles and long-term preservation.

3.3   Privacy

Since we do not envision that chronofiles will be curated by individual users, we suggest that policies regarding use and curation will be of concern. This implies that chronofiles also have the potential to be damaging if accessed inappropriately during the individual's life, or if accessed insensitively after death. Consider the case of the Norwegian explorer Fridtjof Nansen; he was an explorer, a scientist, a diplomat, a humanitarian and Nobel Peace Prize laureate. In 2011 a book was published detailing explicit exchanges between Nansen and his much younger partner. His once private collection had been put on display. This resulted in a change in the perception of Nansen, and is testament to the fact that the story the archive tells about a person can be damaging. A chronofile, assessed after an individual's death may contain deeply personal data.

Hence the need for automatic curation to ensure privacy and reputation would be very necessary. Privacy regulations and personal privacy constraints must be properly supported by the software hosting and maintaining these chronofiles. This must be provided for the computer-illiterate as a rule, not exception. Also, the chronofiles will be stored and maintained in a virtual network, not a centralised physical digital library, including enterprise silos, public services, specialised cloud providers, and even private utilities.

4   Chronofiles Transformation Model

Based on the ideas and discussions listed above, we propose an approach for lifelong and post-life management of personal chronofile data. Our model extends the basic lifelogging architecture described in Section 3 with the the concept of lifecycles of lifelog data using a set of transformation rules that operate over the chronofile data as needed, as illustrated in Figure 3. These transformation rules, in their present form, are classified as:

- *Robustness Transformations.* Maintain robustness of the data in the chronofile to hardware errors.
- *Migration Transformations.* Maintain data in currently accessible formats through periodic automated digital format migrations.
- *Enrichment Transformations.* Maintain modern and accurate metadata by means of new generations of semantic enrichment tools.
- *Storage Transformations.* Maintain an appropriate quantity of content by deleting content only if necessary, but keeping as much rich detail as possible, for example, by deleting repetition, but keeping novel content.[3]
- *Legal Transformations.* Protect the individual owner, and people captured in the archive, by adhering to data storage and privacy laws[4] as they apply to the individual.
- *Reputation Transformations.* Protect the reputation of the individual after control of the chronofile is relinquished, for example, after death.

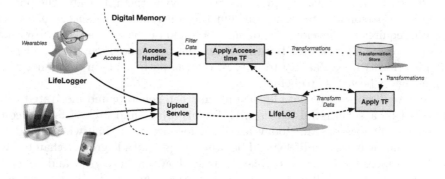

Fig. 3. An initial model of a Chronofile (TF = Transformation)

These data transformations can be independent tools that are automatically executed as required by the chronofile management software and permanently modify the data. There would also be access-time transformations, the aim of

---

[3] For more information on transformation rules for lifelogs, see the initial set in [6].

[4] Privacy and the Right to Privacy are concepts that vary across time and jurisdiction. In many cases, it may be more appropriate that the chronofile applies access-time, rather than permanent transformations on the data.

which is to limit what a user can see, while maintaining the integrity of the underlying data. For example privacy restrictions on lifelog data may require the chronofile to hide private or intimate content from some or all viewers, or display transformations which format chronofile data to take advantage of whatever access mechanism is being employed.

We have embarked on building a series of systems targeting long-term virtual storage infrastructure for early-stage personal chronofiles [6,10,16]. Our fundamental approach is to add self-contained and autonomic meta-code to the data collections or individual data items complementing traditional meta-data of today. In this way, expressive transformation or curation rules live alongside the data to be curated and can be maintained over a long timespans.

5   Conclusion

A traditional and important source of information when archivists and historians try to piece together the story of someones life is the subjects own diary. Combined with the contents of exchanges of information (letters) and other sources, the historian will carefully analyse and create an understanding of a person. In the traditional archive sense, there are few people that have their entire lives documented. The chronofile changes everything—forever. In many ways the chronofile reduces the influence of historians on the historical narrative. Historians will no longer have to fill gaps by matching various information pieces together, guessing and interpreting. This has the potential to give the individual a lot more control of how history will view them, but also the potential to have personal data examined. On the other hand the sheer volume of material requires the development of new tools and opens for many new exciting research areas for historians. Both inter and intra chronofile analysis will provide historians with an ability to understand the path-of-life in a manner that we have never been able to before.

We have discussed the data lifelogging that can generate and motivated why this could be a very useful data source for historians and archivists. We considered how lifelogs operate today and look forward to a time when the data quantity and richness of a lifelog will be orders of magnitude greater than today. We then proposed a model for chronofiles that allows them to grow and be managed by software, yet still maintain detailed representations of life activities and migrate automatically to latest formats, so that they are available for the lifelogger, and later the historians and archivists. Chronofiles gives the individual the ability to decide in advance what material should be available and to whom. Perhaps chronofiles will allow historians of the future to trace certain life-events of the individual and better understand their consequences for society as a whole. The analysis of multiple chronofiles within in social sciences setting may lead to a much better and deeper understanding of human behaviour. Chronofiles have the potential to positively impact on the life of the individual, the historian and society as a whole.

References

1. Bell, G., Gemmell, J.: A digital life. Scientific American **296**, 58–65 (2007)
2. Bell, G., Gemmell, J.: Total Recall: How the E-Memory Revolution Will Change Everything. Penguin Books (2009)
3. Berry, E., Kapur, N., Williams, L., Hodges, S., Watson, P., Smyth, G., Srinivasan, J., Smith, R., Wilson, B., Wood, K.: The use of a wearable camera, sensecam, as a pictorial diary to improve autobiographical memory in a patient with limbic encephalitis. Neuropsychological Rehabilitation **17**(4), 582–601 (2007)
4. Chip, W.: Kryder's law. Scientific American pp. 7–25 (2005)
5. Gantz, J.F., Reinsel, D., Chute, C., Schlichting, W., McArthur, J., Minton, S., Xheneti, I., Toncheva, A., Manfrediz, A.: The Expanding Digital Universe. White paper, IDC Corporate USA (2007)
6. Gurrin, C., Aarflot, T., Sav, S., Johansen, D.: Addressing the challenge of managing large-scale digital multimedia libraries. Journal of Digital Information Management **7**(5), 262–270 (2009)
7. Gurrin, C., Smeaton, A.F., Doherty, A.R.: Lifelogging: Personal big data. Foundations and Trends in Information Retrieval **8**(1), 1–125 (2014)
8. Johansen, D., Stenhaug, M., Hansen, R., Christensen, A., Hogmo, P.M.: Muithu: Smaller footprint, potentially larger imprint. In: 2012 Seventh International Conference on Digital Information Management (ICDIM), pp. 205–214 (August 2012)
9. Johansen, D., Halvorsen, P., Johansen, H., Riiser, H., Gurrin, C., Olstad, B., Griwodz, C., Kvalnes, Å., Hurley, J., Kupka, T.: Search-based composition, streaming and playback of video archive content. Multimedia Tools and Applications **61**(2), 419–445 (2012)
10. Johansen, H.D., Zhang, W., Hurley, J., Johansen, D.: Management of body-sensor data in sports analytic with operative consent. In: Proceedings of the 2014 IEEE Ninth International Conference on Intelligent Sensors, Sensor Networks and Information Processing (ISSNIP). IEEE (April 2014)
11. Kurzweil, R.: The law of accelerating returns. In: Teuscher, C. (ed.) Alan Turing: Life and Legacy of a Great Thinker, pp. 381–416. Springer, Berlin Heidelberg (2004)
12. Lee, H., Smeaton, A.F., O'Connor, N.E., Jones, G.J., Blighe, M., Byrne, D., Byrne, D., Doherty, A., Gurrin, C.: Constructing a SenseCam Visual Diary as a Media Process. Multimedia Systems Journal, Special Issue on Canonical Processes of Media Production **14**(6), 341–349 (2008)
13. Mann, S.: Continuous lifelong capture of personal experience with EyeTap. In: Proceedings of the the 1st ACM workshop on Continuous archival and retrieval of personal experiences, CARPE 2004, pp. 1–21. ACM, New York (2004)
14. Matsuda, M.K.: The memory of the modern. Oxford University Press (1996)
15. McKemmish, S., Piggott, M., REED, B., Upward, F. (eds.): Traces: Document, record, archive, archives by Sue McKemmish. Centre for Information Studies - Charles Sturt University (2005)
16. Nordal, A., Kvalnes, Å., Hurley, J., Johansen, D.: Balava: Federating private and public clouds. In: 2011 IEEE World Congress on Services (SERVICES), pp. 569–577 (July 2011)
17. O'Hara, K., Tuffield, M., Shadbolt, N.: Lifelogging: Privacy and empowerment with memories for life. Identity in the Information Society **1**(1), 155–172 (2009)
18. Quimby, S., Mandeville-Gamble, S., Pang, A., North, A., Chiu, P., O'Hanlon, B. (eds.): Dymaxion Chronofile. No. M1090 in Collections, Stanford University (2006)

Mapping Memory Landscapes in nodegoat

Pim van Bree[✉] and Geert Kessels

LAB1100, The Hague, The Netherlands
pim@lab1100.com

1 Introduction

nodegoat (http://nodegoat.net/) is a web-based data management, analysis and visualisation environment. nodegoat allows scholars to build datasets based on their own data model and offers relational modes of analysis with spatial and diachronic contextualisations. By combining these elements within one environment, scholars are able to instantly process, analyse and visualise complex datasets relationally, diachronically and spatially; trailblazing. nodegoat follows an object-oriented approach throughout its core functionalities. Borrowing from actor-network theory this means that people, events, artefacts, and sources are treated as equal: objects, and hierarchy depends solely on the composition of the network: relations. This object-oriented approach advocates the self-identification of individual objects and maps the correlation of objects within the collective.

In this paper we will explore a collaborative and participatory research process as a use case in nodegoat. This research is part of the project 'Memory Landscapes; Anti-Communist Violence in Semarang 1965' which aims to dynamically organise fuzzy data, gathered during multiple interview sessions and on-site research, in multimodal networks. This project has been initiated by Martijn Eickhoff (NIOD, Amsterdam; RU, Nijmegen) in cooperation with the UNIKA University Semarang. Students of UNIKA collected data on anti-communist/leftist violence by combining oral history and anthropological site research. The data includes relations between people as well as locations connected to the events of 1965-66 (e.g. places of mob violence, temporary detention, interrogation, torture, murder and mass burial). During a two week workshop in Semarang, all data gathered was entered into nodegoat, producing instant diachronic mappings and multi-modal networks.

2 Methodology

nodegoat combines data management functionalities with the ability to seamlessly analyse and visualise data. nodegoat functions as any other database application as it allows users to define, update and query multiple data models. nodegoat dynamically combines functionalities of a database application (e.g. Access/FileMaker) with visualisation possibilities (e.g. Gephi or Pajek) and extends these functionalities (e.g. with in-text referencing) in one web-based

© Springer International Publishing Switzerland 2015
L.M. Aiello and D. McFarland (Eds.): SocInfo 2014 Workshops, LNCS 8852, pp. 274–278, 2015.
DOI: 10.1007/978-3-319-15168-7_34

GUI. Working in a web-based environment allows for implementing collaborative projects and working simultaneously on the same dataset. Multiple users (who have been assigned varying clearance levels) can enter, update and inspect data. As soon as data is entered into the environment, various analytical tools and visualisations are available. In-depth filtering, diachronic geographical mappings, diachronic social graphs, content driven timelines, and shortest path calculation enable a user to explore the context of each piece of data. The explorative nature of nodegoat allows users to trailblaze through data; instead of working with static 'pushes' – or exports – of data, data is dynamically 'pulled' within its context each time a query is fired.

The methodological basis of nodegoat does not limit itself to one field only, but gives scholars of varying backgrounds new means, or more precise its object-oriented approach, to work with their data. nodegoat can not only be employed to navigate (aggregations of) collections and analyse social networks or proso-pographical spheres, but can also analyse correlations between literary themes in classical texts or co-occurrences of allegorical iconography in early modern paintings.

This open-ended approach makes nodegoat different from tools like the SNAC project (Social Networks and Archival Context), RoSE (Research Oriented Social Environment), SEASR (Software Environment for the Advancement of Scholarly Research), Prosop[1], or tools with a main focus on coding of qualitative data as seen in various computer-assisted qualitative data analysis software. With its object-oriented approach, nodegoat facilitates the aggregation of collections, coding of texts, and analysis of networks, but models these methods towards the creation and contextualisation of single objects that move through time and space.

The methodological basis of nodegoat is closely connected to actor-network theory (ANT).[4] nodegoat aims to provide scholars with an environment that allows them to bring the ideas associated with ANT into practice. The combination of tools and methodology offered by nodegoat distinguishes three levels brought together in an assemblage of objects: (1) the identification of all objects and their own possible definitions, relations and associations (cross-referencing); (2) the identification of all (contradictory) definitions, relations and associations related to each object (cross-referenced); (3) the identification of objects that are associated relationally, in space and in time.

The outcome of this process creates a dataset that not only includes objects that function as hubs or brokers, but also objects that are situated in the periphery of the network. Each object has their controversies and conflicting perspectives mapped, revealing their full complexity. The final result establishes the full contextuality in which the objects are to be approached.[2] Within this context, each object functions as a starting point for the exploration of the complete

---

[1] See:http://socialarchive.iath.virginia.edu/home_prototype.html,
http://liu.english.ucsb.edu/rose-research-oriented-social-environment/,
http://www.seasr.org/, http://www.prosop.org/

dataset. This allows for a continuous shift of perspectives, producing a multitude of different renderings based on the body of data.[5]

3   Use Case: Mapping Memory Landscapes

The project 'Memory Landscapes; Anti-Communist Violence in Semarang 1965' operates in the context of the events that took place from 1965 onwards during which outbursts of violence led to the killing of approximately half a million people in Indonesia. The project looks at these events from the local perspective of the city of Semarang. The acts of violence were carried out by anti-communist army units and civilian vigilantes.[3] The motivation of this violence was an alleged communist coup d'état in Jakarta on the first of October 1965. Although the manner in which the killings were carried out varied greatly per region, a recurring pattern was the arrival of anti-communist troops from outside.[3]

The stories of the victims of these events have never been integrated in state sanctioned narratives on the 1965 events.[1] During the first workshop within this project in January 2013, a group of 10 survivors were interviewed. After examination of these interviews, a relation in time and space between instances of violence was evident. The range of entities that were named in the interviews can be connected to each other by their shared identification, their co-occurrence, or their movement through space (e.g. people were being detained in a shared time frame, multiple persons could be linked to the same detention center, or multiple interviews mentioned the same mass grave).

The second workshop set out to integrate a networked approach by collecting and entering information gathered from interviews and site research directly into nodegoat. This meant that the students who conducted the interviews had to get a basic understanding of how relational data models function and how they could apply this knowledge to nodegoat. During the first days of the workshops we trained the students in working with nodegoat.

For this project we defined eight types in which objects were stored: 'workshop', 'interview', 'person', 'organisation', 'site', 'event', 'nuclear family' and 'group'. In the course of the workshop, a new type 'moment' was proposed by workshop participants and added to our data model. Each object is defined by a dynamic number of object descriptions and a dynamic number of sub-objects. Each bit of information is stored only once; namely in the object of which it describes an intrinsic aspect. All the information is subsequently connected by means of relations and associations.[2] Relations describe intrinsic aspects of the object (interviewee, organiser, etc) whereas associations reveal the circumstances of the object related to other objects (member of an organisation, presence during an event, etc).

As we solely rely on individual accounts based on personal memory we have to deal with a great variety of content, perspectives and reliability. We acknowledge this diversity and regard each bit of information gathered during the interview sessions as equally relevant.[6]

4   Gathering Data

The interviews were conducted at the homes of the survivors. Groups of students and academic staff recorded the interviews with a camera and took notes. As the project aims to expose a memory landscape, the interviewers did not need to focus on establishing 'facts' mentioned by the interviewee but to record an account based on the personal memory of the survivor.

The process of data collection resulted in a complex and heterogeneous dataset. We first set out to make one object for each interview within the type 'Interview'. This object is used as source reference for any input that would be made based on information from this interview. Secondly, we entered the basic biographical data of the interviewees. Thirdly, all the places of detainment of the interviewees were included in the objects of the interviewees as well as all the locations and relations of the institutions involved. As all the data was entered into one environment, the accumulated data immediately gives us a comprehensive overview of all the persons, institutes and locations that were mentioned in the separate interviews.

A challenge we faced during the data entry process regarded the definition of similar locations mentioned throughout the interviews. Sites that functioned as detainment centers were used for different purposes before 1965 (e.g. as a school), and again had various functions after 1966 (e.g. community building or shopping mall). This means that the names and descriptions used to identify one location vary greatly. As all the data was entered in a shared environment, decisions had to be made collectively whether we were dealing with one of a multitude of locations. The ability of nodegoat to immediately visualise a newly added location gave us instant feedback.

Next, a number of events that could be distilled from the interview (e.g. a meeting, demonstration or kidnapping) had to be identified. For this, the students had to make an object in the type 'Event', provide a description of the event, and provide the course of the event with the configuration of the attendees that were present (i.e. persons, groups). This proved to be a difficult task as the stories had to be broken down into separate events and can be modelled more freely.

After we had established a first overview of sites of violence in and around Semarang, the students visited a number of sites in order to conduct field research. During their field research, the students and research team interviewed people that lived or worked on the visited location. These interviews provided the project with new information relating to the landscape of violence.

At the end of the data entry process, students remarked that it was hard to store specific moments that could not be described as an event, but did contain valuable information about the interviewee during the interview itself. This extra information could relate to an emotional reaction, a non-verbal gesture or an expression of uncertainty connected to a statement in the interview. To accommodate this proposition, we created a new type in nodegoat called 'Moment' in which objects can be identified that describe considerations (with a relation to the interpreter) of the survivor and allows for the classification of these considerations by means of emotions. These moments can subsequently be used as a more specific source for instances originating from the interview.

5   Outcomes and Conclusion

The assemblage of personal memories within environment and the geographical visualisation of these memories produced a localised visual representation of the anti-communist violence in 1965-66. As the narratives of the victims are suppressed within the state sanctioned depictions of these event, this in itself proved to be a valuable outcome. Moreover, the geographical analysis of the locations mapped in Semarang revealed a number of patterns that allowed the research team to formulate new research questions. The most prominent pattern was found in the composition of sites where survivors were interrogated and temporarily detained in one area of Semarang and the location of a number of camps in another area. The research team focused specifically on questions regarding the confiscation of property and typologies of prisons.

The workshop demonstrated that nodegoat is able to support a participatory research process that aims to gather, connect and analyse personal stories. The flexible data design, collaborative working environment and the availability to visualise and analyse data throughout the process provided the project with the necessary equipment. The workshop has shown that an oral history research project does not necessarily need to end in a static end product (e.g. a collection of media files, an article or a book). The created actionable dataset is in itself open for scrutinisation or further contextualisation as a result of its non-hierarchical design. Our rhizomatic approach enables re-use and transcends debates on restrictions of content and constraints of research questions. By saving gathered data structurally in a shared environment, a new data resource is created that can be used by scholars who wish to continue this research or who want to use this dataset as context for a new research project.

References

1. Baskara, T., Wardaya, S.J.: Hearing Silenced Voices. A Foreword. In: Baskara, T., Wardaya, S.J. (eds.) Truth Will Out. Indonesian Accounts of the 1965 Mass Violence XXII-XLIII, Victoria (2013)
2. Bree, P. van, Kessels, G.: Trailblazing Metadata: a diachronic and spatial research platform for object-oriented analysis and visualisations. In: Cultural Research in the Context of Digital Humanities St Petersburg (2013)
3. Cribb, R.: The Indonesian Massacres. In: Totten, S., Parsons, W.S., Charny, I.W. (eds.) Century of Genocide. Eyewitness Accounts and Critical Views, pp. 236–263, New York (1997)
4. Latour, B.: Reassembling the Social. Oxford (2005)
5. Mol, A.: Actor-Network Theory: sensitive terms and enduring tensions. Kölner Zeitschrift für Soziologie und Sozialpsychologie **50**, 253–269 (2010)
6. Rothberg, M.: Introduction: Between Memory and Memory: From Lieux de mémoire to Noeuds de mémoire, Yale French Studies. Noeuds de mémoire: Multidirectional Memory in Postwar French and Francophone Culture **118**(119), 3–12 (2010)

Mining Ministers (1572–1815). Using Semi-structured Data for Historical Research

Serge ter Braake[1]([✉]), Antske Fokkens[2], and Fred van Lieburg[1]

[1] History, VU University Amsterdam, Amsterdam, Netherlands
{s.ter.braake,f.a.van.lieburg}@vu.nl
[2] Computational Linguistics, VU University Amsterdam, Amsterdam, Netherlands
antske.fokkens@vu.nl

Abstract. There is a long tradition of categorizing and storing historical data in databases. However, these databases cannot always be used readily for computational approaches. In this paper, we use a twentieth century dataset on Dutch ministers (1572–1815) for modern quantitative analyses. We describe our methodology, provide results on the mobility of ministers and make further suggestions for the questions that can be answered now that could not before.

1   Introduction

As long as computers exist historians have looked into the new opportunities they might provide for their research. The first database for historians, named after the Muse Clio, dates back to the late 70s of the 20th century [2, p. 20], but compatibility of these databases with more modern software can be difficult.Without a conversion of old datasets to a format that can endure the test of time there is a rich wealth of old data resources that may be lost or forgotten.

In this paper we analyze a dataset on 12,405 Dutch ministers [1], from the Reformation until the beginning of the nineteenth century, which was used in the nineties in Van Lieburg's (author of this paper) dissertation [3]. We describe the steps we made to make and keep these data compatible with up to date software.[1] We show how our approach facilitates computerized analyses that were impossible to do with data in old database formats, by the example of linking the data to GeoNames[2] to look at the mobility of the ministers through the centuries. In Section 2 we give a short account of the data we have at our disposal. In Section 3 we describe how we preserved the data for future historical analyses. In Section 4 we describe the results obtained from our exercises with these data. In Section 5 we conclude this paper, with suggestions for further research.

---

[1] The data and software used in this paper is available at https://github.com/antske/
Mining-Ministers
[2] http://www.geonames.org

L.M. Aiello and D. McFarland (Eds.): SocInfo 2014 Workshops, LNCS 8852, pp. 279–283, 2015.
DOI: 10.1007/978-3-319-15168-7_35

2   Dutch Ministers: The Available Data

In the last decades of the sixteenth century, the Reformed religion became dominant in the Northern Netherlands (now the Netherlands). The increasing dominance went hand in hand with the Dutch military successes during the revolt against Spain (1568-1648). Ministers began to form the core of public religious life in the Netherlands, responsible for the spiritual well being of their own Community, similar to the role played by catholic priests before that time. The database provided by Fred van Lieburg contains data on 12,405 ministers from 1575 to 1815 [1].

```
>Aalburg, van; Johannes | Geb. Zierikzee ca. 1717; pred. @Oudkarspel# 30
juni ~1743, overl. 14 maart ~1777.<
```

Fig. 1. Sample entry from Van Lieburg's corpus

The data include the names (and possible spelling variations) and when available dates and places of birth and death and start and end of their appointment as minister in a residence. Figure 1 provides a sample entry from the corpus. All entries were added manually and to a Word document. Entries may also contain short descriptions and sometimes contain minor inconsistencies in their patterns due to its manual creation. We therefore consider this data set semi-structured.

The main advantage of our data for historical research is that there was no discrimination in who to include: any known minister, and the estimate is that the database is nearly 100% complete [3], was added to the database. The chances of pollution in quantitative analyses due to a biased research population therefore are minimal.

3   Methodology

A dataset with over 12,000 people can be considered huge for historical research. All kinds of quantifications can be made investigating generalizations on a well defined group of people. Such (prosopographical) analyses were also made by Van Lieburg in the previous century. The dataset also offers new possibilities however, when we can link it to other datasets.

In order to address both classic and new research questions there are three tasks that need to be performed. First, the semi-structured data must be analyzed and turned into a consistently structured dataset. Second, location names must be disambiguated. Finally, basic calculations must be carried out on the extracted data. In this section, we describe the steps we take to carry out these tasks.

3.1   A Structured, Partially Disambiguated Database

As mentioned in the previous section, the data we used for this experiment is semi-structured. It was handed to us as a Word document where each minister was described in the form shown in Figure 1 in Section 2. The first step in this research was to retrieve as much information as possible from the corpus and store it in a form that is easy to handle for our interpretation software. The size of the corpus is small enough to be easily manageable, so we decided to store information as csv in a file, making it also easy to read for humans. During this step, we also normalized dates and performed the first step in disambiguating locations.

We use GeoNames to obtain information on the coordinates of specific locations. GeoNames provides rich information on a list of locations including alternative names in many languages, their coordinates and the country they are situated in. For each entry in the database, we extract strings that are likely to refer to a location and see if they occur as a place name in GeoNames. However, many place names are highly ambiguous. We therefore need to establish first which place name is meant. We use two principles in our disambiguation process: 1) proximity and 2) heuristics.

If a location name is associated with more than one name in GeoNames, our algorithm first checks whether Van Lieburg's corpus provides an additional specification (which can be indicated by a province or country in brackets or prepositions *bij* ("near") and *in* ("in")). If such a specification is given, we check whether they are (in) the same country as the ambiguous location. If more than one location qualifies, we calculate which location and specification are closest using their coordinates in GeoNames. In cases where there is uncertainty about the location and two are given, we use the location that is given first, disambiguating it by taking the GeoName entry that is nearest to the alternative. If there are no specifications about the exact location in the data, we apply heuristics based on the countries ambiguous locations are situated in.

Our algorithm prints out (partial) entries whenever it runs into unknown structures or when it identified strings that were not known locations in GeoNames. We used this output to correct errors that occur frequently or that may have a high input on our results.

3.2 Calculating Distances

We use the extracted and partially interpreted data to perform our calculations on the mobility of ministers. This involves an additional interpretation step, because many locations are still linked to more than one GeoNames entry after our initial disambiguation.

Places of birth and death are not always indicated in the original corpus. If they are unknown, but we do have information where the minister in question was baptized or buried, we use the location of their baptism or funeral instead. The place of death is typically not indicated in the corpus if the minister died in the place he last worked. We therefore use the location of the minister's final position if there is no other indication. In cases where the minister died on a trip, the conversion algorithm we applied to create our csv files already selected the destination of the journey. This means that in some cases, we use the intended mobility rather than the actual mobility of the minister.

We use the geographical coordinates from GeoNames to calculate distances. While calculating full mobility of ministers, we take their place of birth or baptism as starting point if known and else we take the first place they worked. We consider all places they worked and use their place of death or place of their funeral as their endpoint. Distances between place of birth and baptism or death and funeral are not taken into account in the rare case both are given. Our algorithm goes through all locations in chronological order of stay. If place names are ambiguous, we disambiguate them by taking the shortest possible distance between the two locations. Further calculations are carried out with the disambiguated location to make sure our calculations remain consistent. We add all distances the minister travelled according to our data and algorithms to determine his mobility.

4   Results

We verified our findings by comparing them to Van Lieburg's previous work with the original dataset. For instance, we checked whether the towns the ministers originated from correspond to the tables in [3]. The similarity of the results indicates that our results are reliable enough to indicate trends and overall tendencies. Further explorations with the data on classic historical questions can be found online.[3] These explorations could be done twenty years ago as well, although taking a longer time.

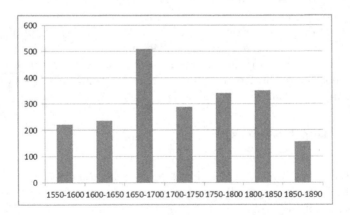

Fig. 2. Mobility in kilometres (distance moved between the known place of birth, work and death) per 50 years (based on dates of death of the ministers)

The benefit of the data we have at our disposal now is that it is not 'walled in' anymore and can communicate with other datasets. Now that we can extract structured names, normalized dates and location names, we can compare and

---

[3] http://www.biographynet.nl/a-prosopography-of-dutch-ministers-1575-1815/

relate Van Lieburg's data to other datasets we have at our disposal, such as GeoNames and the biographies from the Biography Portal of the Netherlands.[4] One of the questions which we can now address is on the geographical mobility of Dutch ministers (and Dutch elites in general). To this end we applied the algorithm described in Section 3 which adds up the distance between place of birth, places of work and place of death. Figure 2 shows a quite clear peak in the second half of the seventeenth century, which is hardly surprising (and again confirms the reliability of our system) since it was a golden age of exploration, trade, war and colonization for the Dutch Republic. Data on the mobility of people in other professions (politicians, wealthy merchants) could serve as an interesting base for comparison.

5 Conclusions and Further Work

In this paper we used modern methods to analyze Dutch ministers from the late sixteenth to the early nineteenth century with data from an old, exceptionally rich, 'traditional' semi-structured historical dataset. We converted the set breaking down the walls of the old database by making the data available for communication with other datasets. In future work, we will further facilitate communication with other datasets by converting the data to RDF.

This approach did not only ensure that the database of Van Lieburg can still be consulted in the future for classic historical questions. More importantly, it also enables new research questions, which would be out of the scope of digital historical methods in the previous century. In this paper we gave the example of research on geographical mobility by making a match with GeoNames. Other research questions with the help of other datasets will be possible, for example to match the ministers with biographical instances in DBpedia or other biographical resources to see what ministers became 'famous' or not and if this famous group is representative for the entire group. Another possibility is making links to descriptions of museum objects which are related to the ministers to enrich their biographies and see what cultural traces they have left over the centuries. With more structured and compatible datasets available in the future, the questions we can ask to our historical data will become more ambitious and might eventually change the academic field of history radically.

References

1. Van Lieburg, F.: Database Dutch Reformed Clergy 1555–2004 (Integration in Biography Portal of the Netherlands in preparation)
2. Haber, P.: Digital Past. Geschichtswissenschaft im digitalen Zeitalter, München (2011)
3. Van Lieburg, F.: Profeten en hun vaderland. De geografische herkomst van de gereformeerde predikanten in Nederland van 1572 tot 1816, Zoetermeer (1996)

---

[4] http://www.biografischportaal.nl/en

Laboratories of Community:
How Digital Humanities Can Further
New European Integration History

Mariona Coll Ardanuy[1]([✉]), Maarten van den Bos[2], and Caroline Sporleder[1]

[1] University of Trier, Universitätsring 15, 54296 Trier, Germany
{s2macoll,sporledc}@uni-trier.de
[2] University of Utrecht, Campusplein 1, 3584 ED Utrecht, The Netherlands
m.j.a.vandenbos@uu.nl

Abstract. It has been said that media is an important but mostly over-looked player in European integration history. Now, the mass digitisation of newspapers and the introduction of new digital techniques promise great potential to remedy this inattention. With the conjecture that people are drivers and carriers of change, we propose a people-centric approach to mine news articles in a way that can be most useful to further historical research. In this paper, we describe a methodology for building social networks from unstructured news stories, with the European integration scenario serving as a case study.

Keywords: Digital history · Text mining · European integration · International relations · Social network · Public discourse

1 Introduction

The historiography of European integration can be divided into three phases [21]. In the seventies, historians from a broad spectrum of backgrounds such as diplomatic history, economic history and the history of ideas began to analyse the origins of European cooperation. Subsequently, from the second half of the eighties, this fragmented field began not only to integrate but also to interact across disciplinary boundaries with international relations theory, judicial history and political philosophy. In the first half of the nineties, the international relations perspective gained dominance framing Europe as a political entity theoretically situated somewhere on a scale between a federation of states and a federal state. The third phase took off with a devastating critique of the dominance of the state as actor in the history and theory of international relations. Building upon the theoretical insights of early constructivists like Alexander Wendt, some scholars argued for not only a transnational history of the public opinion on the European project, but also for a shift of focus from interstate relations and government policy towards non-political actors, public discourses and popular images of Europe.

L.M. Aiello and D. McFarland (Eds.): SocInfo 2014 Workshops, LNCS 8852, pp. 284–293, 2015.
DOI: 10.1007/978-3-319-15168-7_36

The mass digitisation of books, newspapers and other historical materials and the introduction of new digital techniques promise new possibilities in furthering our knowledge of European integration. We propose a method to automatically extract networks of people mentioned in news stories, weighted according to their significance in the news and distributed according to their co-occurrence in the text. We suggest a simple strategy to incorporate shared contextual information for each pair of nodes in the network, based on word counts and tf-idf frequencies, implemented as edge attributes. The aim of the networks is to allow historians to have not only a bird's eye view of the scenario of a certain period of time (in our case, 1945–1955), but also to have an overview of which relevant topics were discussed when a certain historical actor was mentioned. By reducing the whole corpus of news into a network structure, we find some expected results and, more interestingly, some unexpected results. In this regard, we think of our method as a generator of hypotheses.

In this particular case study, we look at articles on the first steps of the integration process in the late forties and early fifties in the Netherlands. As one of the founding members of the European Union, the Netherlands proves an interesting case because of its diverse media landscape, in which different socio-political communities had their own ideological media outlet that coexisted with more neutral, general newspapers [2]. In a recent article, Hans-Jörg Trenz has named the media as an important but mostly overlooked player in integration history [22]. By using digitised newspapers from the large repository of the Dutch Royal Library to extract social networks and their main topics of conversation, we will develop a method to further the history of European integration in a digital fashion.

2   State of the Art

2.1   Historiographical Background

Theory and historiography of the European Union until the late nineties can be roughly divided into two fields of interest. In the first, the focus is on the current European institutions and treaties. In the second, the history of European integration is seen through the lens of international relations theory [26]. A landmark for this dominance was the publication of Alan Milward's *The European rescue of the Nation State*, in which he developed the argument that 'integration was not the supersession of the nation-state by another form of governance as the nation-state became incapable, but the creation of the European nation-states themselves for their own purpose, as an act of national will' [14]. From a more theoretical perspective, the leading scholar on European integration Andrew Moravcsik agreed as he concluded that the integration process did not supersede or circumvent the political will of national leaders, but reflected it [15].

Both their approaches however came under scrutiny in the late nineties. In his *Social Theory of International Politics*, Alexander Wendt developed a theory of the international system as a social construction. Following in his footsteps, a whole series of so-called constructivist studies focussed on the role of non-state actors, civil society and public opinion in international relations [28] [27].

Within the context of European integration historiography, constructivism got a firm boost from the 2005 rejection of the Treaty establishing a Constitution for Europe. Signed in October 2004 and quickly ratified by some member states, the ratifying process stranded only a summer later on the rejection of the treaty by French and Dutch voters. Especially the high turnout in both referenda sparked academic interest in the public image of and popular support for European integration [6] [16].

In recent years, a lot of work has been done broadening the research agenda by implementing transnational approaches, the history of interest groups, European bureaucracy and civil society organisations. In an attempt to set the future research agenda, the leading scholar Wolfram Kaiser has made a convincing plea for a network approach of the history of European integration. He introduced the concept 'epistemic communities' as a possibility to further what he labelled new European integration history. These communities essentially are networks of people who share expert knowledge and have a common understanding of a certain issue. Therefore, they function as 'channels through which new ideas circulate from societies to governments as well as from country to country' [27].

For historians, this network approach has distinct advantages over the other attempts to conceptualize the history of European Union. It is no rigid theory on the origins, functioning or development of European integration, but merely a heuristic concept that draws our attention to public debate, the emerging of new policy networks and the transfer of ideas and concepts across socio-political, academic and national borders. On the downside is the problem of operationalization. Networks of experts are only sometimes explicit (think tanks, for instance), work mostly behind the scenes and can be in competition with other networks; they are hard to find using traditional research strategies.

2.2   Computational Background

In the field of European Union studies, computational techniques to map out public discourse are, with counted exceptions [29], still in the earliest stage. A recent book on the role of national self-images in the perception of European integration in England, Germany and the Netherlands [5] uses a wide selection of more than a thousand editorials, but selection and analysis have been done merely by hand. Other studies that convincingly prove the investigatory value of newspapers also use traditional techniques to select and analyse the source material [12] [13]. The utility of using social networks in historical research has been demonstrated by several studies [18] [7] [20]. However, most of these studies create the networks either manually or drawn from structured data.

With the explosion of big data, there is a pressing need to improve techniques that address information extraction from unstructured data, which make for most of the real-world data with which historians have to deal. Text mining and other natural language processing techniques have been seeking since their beginnings a solution to the problem of unstructured data. In our method, we propose an entity-centric analysis of the data, an approach that has gained growing popularity in quantitative literary analysis [4] [17] [1] [3]. Some of these studies represent novels as social networks of characters that typify the skeleton representation of the plot. The self-containing nature of the literary works makes for the biggest difference between fiction and real world data. When a novel ends, its characters cease to exist. When working with news data, we are not in a microcosmos anymore, and thus networks are necessarily more spread out, and nodes more disseminated. In this paper we adjust the method from Coll Ardanuy and Sporleder (2014) [3] to suit historical news stories and adapt it to meet the needs of historians.

3   The Data

From the large repository of the Dutch Royal Library, we have selected three national newspapers that reflect the most relevant aspects of the Dutch political landscape. Although the concept of pillarization came under fierce scrutiny for the last two decades and the religious and socio-political stratification of Dutch society has been questioned, the press landscape remains to be seen as fragmented. Different socio-political communities had their own media outlets that — at least until the early sixties — were neglected by other groups. Here we use a distinct catholic newspaper (*De Tijd*) and a socialist one (*Het Vrije Volk*). Results from these newspapers will be compared and contrasted with articles from *De Telegraaf*, the largest Dutch daily that had no formal political and religious affiliation [23] [30].

We focus in this case study in the first post-war decade, the period between 1945 and 1955, in which the idea of a European Union started to take shape. In order to limit the data to the pieces of news relevant to European integration, we opted to consider only articles in which the words *'Europa'* (Europe), *'Europese'* (European) or *'Europeaan'* (European) appear. This is a wide search, but it is a first step in order to reduce the corpus to the topic in which we are interested. Only articles with a high OCR confidence were considered. After filtering the articles, our dataset consisted of 2327 articles from *De Tijd*, 2663 articles from *Het Vrije Volk*, and 1138 articles from *De Telegraaf*.

4   The Method

In this section, we describe the method that we use to build social networks from a collection of news articles. A network consists of two main components: nodes and edges. In a social network, the nodes are the actors and the edges represent the relations between them. We explain in subsection 4.1 our method for obtaining the nodes of the network. In subsection 4.2 we describe how we choose to define the edges between the nodes. The creation of the network is detailed in subsection 4.3.

4.1   Obtaining the Nodes

Human Name Recognition. A social network is a structure that captures the relations between a set of actors. Thus, the first step to the creation of a social network must necessarily be the extraction of human names from raw text. To that end, we use the `Stanford Named Entity Recognizer`.[1] We used training data for Dutch from the CoNLL-2002 shared task.[2] With the assumption that the more data, the better the entity recognition will be, we concatenated the training file together with the two test files in order to have more training data. The resulting training file consisted of 309683 tokens, 3032 of which were person names. Our training data is extracted from newspapers and, as we have already mentioned previously, we work on Dutch news text from the 1945–1955 decade. Considering that Dutch language has not changed significantly since, we expect the recognizer to work on our data as well as on modern-day data.

In order to enhance the performance of the named entity recognition module, we have applied some hand-made filtering steps, based on observation. We have realized that, on many occasions, newswire text introduces a person name by its description. In this way, it is normal to find occurrences in news text such as *'de 63-jarige Frank Donoghue'*[3], *'de kapitein Ben Shaw'*[4], or *'de 21-jarige pianist Theo'*.[5] Such linguistic cues are very reliable, since we can expect that most of the times a capitalized word following an age or a title/profession will be a person name. Two rules have been created to capture the age and the title/profession. The first one, very simple, captures every sequence of capitalized words (including initials and middle words such as *'van der'* or *'v.d.'*, typical of Dutch person names) following the expression XX-jarige, in which XX is a number (expressed numerically or alphabetically) and in which the dash is optional. To capture the title or profession, we have relied on a list of professions from the Wikipedia[6] as well as on a list of titles and professions automatically retrieved from our text, by capturing the uncapitalized word between an age expression and a capitalized word. We ended up with a list of 1650 titles or professions that are an indication that the next capitalized word will be a person name. These rules have been combined to also find entities introduced by both the age and the profession/title.

Newspapers tend to personalize institutions or organizations such as political entitites, which is the reason why, unlike in other domains such as literature, we could not rely on verbs of utterance to identify human names unequivocally. The only verbs of utterance that we have included in our filtering are mostly those that describe the manner in which something is said or which describe an action that cannot be (or is usually not) metaphorized, such as *think*, *laugh*, or *cry*, both in 3rd person present and past tense. We had to disregard verbs such as *admit*, *answer* or *maintain* since most of the times the subject of these verbs are institutions or organizations. Evaluated on a small sample of 10 articles, the linguistic patterns improve the f-score of the entity recognizer from 0.70 to 0.76.

---

[1] http://nlp.stanford.edu/software/CRF-NER.shtml

[2] http://www.cnts.ua.ac.be/conll2002/ner/

[3] Translation: 'the 63-year-old Frank Donoghue'.

[4] Translation: 'the captain Ben Shaw'.

[5] Translation: 'the 21-year-old pianist Theo'.

[6] http://nl.wikipedia.org/wiki/Lijst_van_beroepen

Co-reference Resolution. For each human name that we identify, we keep information such as the age, the profession or title in these cases in which there is such an information. For example, if a text talks about *de 20-jarige schipper Pim de Boer*, we keep as attributes of 'Pim de Boer' his title or profession ('shipper' in this case, but we could also have some less informative title such as 'Mr.') and the possible two years in which he was born (calculated by substracting his age from the year of publication of the article).

We resolve co-reference resolution per document by string matching. We assume that two identical surface forms from the same article will refer to the same person, unless it is indicated by means of the age, title or profession. When there is a contradiction of age between two surface forms, each surface form is supposed to be an entity on its own. When the contradiction is on the title, each surface form is supposed to be a different entity only when the titles indicate two different genders (such as *'heer de Muis'*[7] and *'vrouw de Muis'*[8]). In any other case, all identical surface forms are considered to correspond to one only entity. From each article, we extract a list of human entities, each of which having the following three attributes, which might be empty if the information is unknown:

1. The list of alternative names in which this entity may be referred, including initials instead of first and middle names, contractions for particles such as 'van', etc.
2. The year in which the person was born.
3. The list of titles or professions which precede the name in the text.

Co-reference resolution is performed in the whole dataset by string matching. We do not perform disambiguation of names. However, we give the possibility to the historian to check the list of titles and professions extracted for each entity so that we can manually correct whenever two different persons have been put together as one only entity. It is then up to the historian to decide if, for example, a farmer called Robert Schuman is the same person as the politician called Robert Schuman.

4.2   Establishing the Relations

Once we have found the nodes of the network, we need to define what kind of relation we want to draw between them. In our case we created an undirected graph based on the co-occurrence of nodes in each article. In other words, each pair of nodes is linked in our network if they co-occur in the same news article. Our network is weighted, so the more two entities interact throughout the collection, the stronger the relation between them will be. In an edge attribute we keep the list of articles in which both nodes of the edge co-occur. With this measure, we allow the historian to go back to the source files in which each two nodes co-occur. Each edge in the network has two more attributes apart from the

---

[7] Translation: 'Mr. de Muis'.
[8] Translation: 'Mrs. de Muis'.

weight and list of files: the list of the most common words (stopwords removed) of the articles in which both entities are mentioned and the list of the most relevant words using the tf-idf weighting for the concatenation of documents in which both nodes appear. An example of extracted attributes for a pair of nodes can be seen in Fig. 1.

Attributes of the node *Adenauer*
aka: Konrad Adenauer, Adenauers
born: unknown
title: heer, Bondskanselier, heren, kanselier, dr.

Attributes of the node *Schuman*
aka: Robert Schuman, Schumans, R. Schuman
born: unknown
title: heer, minister

Attributes of the edge *Adenauer-Schuman*
tfidf: sociaal-democraten, regeringsverklaring, Woensdagavond, Bondsdag, nota, Saarland, Commissie, goedgekeurd, Adenauer, plan-Schuman, Hoge, minister, Buitenlandse, verdrag, Zaken, gezet, gelijkheid, Kanselier
counts: minister, buitenlandse, europese, plan-schuman, zaken sociaal-democraten, acht, adenauer, bondsdag, commissie, duitse, europa, gemaakt, goedgekeurd, grote, hoge, kanselier, lang
co-occurring files: id0243.txt, id0566.txt, id0568.txt, etc.

Fig. 1. On the left, a simplified representation of a fragment from the network extracted from *De Tijd*, year 1951. On the right, attributes of the nodes *Adenauer* and *Schuman* and of the edge *Adenauer-Schuman*.

4.3   Building the Network

Since we are interested in the development of the network throughout history, we create dynamic networks, i. e., the succession of yearly static networks, for each collection. The python library `Networkx`[9] is used to construct the networks and the network analysis software `Gephi`[10] is used to visualize them. Both are open-source tools with an extensive functionality.

5   Analysis

The resulting social networks offer some expected results that prove to a certain degree the reliability of our approach, such as the important presence in the network of personae such as Robert Schuman, Dirk Stikker, Ernest Bevin, Konrad Adenauer, Winston Churchill, Georges Bidault, Willem Drees, Alcide de Gasperi, or Jean Monnet. It could also be expected that a socialist newspaper such as *Het Vrije Volk* would give more weight to local stories and relatively less weight to big names than other newspapers. Indeed, in our graphs, the weight

---

[9] http://networkx.github.io/
[10] http://gephi.org/

of the 10 most common nodes in *De Tijd* is 16% of the total weight, in *De Telegraaf* is 12%, and in *Het Vrije Volk* is 10%. While expected results are useful to understand that the method works and is able to predict correctly certain facts, it is when unexpected results come out that our approach is most interesting. Unexpected results are potential hypotheses that defy official history. It is then the task of the historian to verify, by looking at the pieces of news selected by our method, whether there is some truth in the information yielded by the network.

Looking at the results of our digital analysis, the importance of politics immediately stands out. Central actors in all networks continuously were politicians. This seems to be less surprising as it is. Milward [14] and Moravcsik [15] in their work on European integration named economic self-interest of the state the most important driver in the integration process. Combining our extracted networks with the word counts and tf-idf analysis, we come to the conclusion that early integration is better framed as essentially a political process. More than a cooperation of states, it was the creation of a new political sphere with its own vocabulary, central actors and use of concepts [27] [8].

The centrality of American politicians merits particular attention. In the literature, the importance of America as an actor in the early integration process is emphasised only for the late forties. After the presentation of the Schuman plan, the basis for the foundation of the Coal and Steel Union, in May 1950 the integration process more and more became truly a European matter [10]. But our networks clearly show that, at least in public discourse, America remained to be seen as an important actor. More specific research could be done here. Another issue raised is the concurrent ongoing emphasis on early integration being a technocratic process with a low political profile. As Mark Mazower concluded, the Second World War had left people with a deep antipathy towards ideological politics, which was reflected by mainstream politics steering away from polarized attitudes in favour of compromise. The European project after the presentation of the Schuman plan was one of the most important examples to support such a claim [11]. Recent studies however have reemphasized the role of ideology in early integration history and our research seems to prove them right, although the width and nature of the used material urges some caution here. Nonetheless, it is worth noticing that words like *'gemeenschapszin'* (sense of community) and *'solidariteit'* (solidarity) seemingly played a role in public discourse.

This corresponds with recent studies being done on political parties and civil society organisations that became laboratories of community in postwar Europe. After the Second World War, all over Europe new ideas on community arose out of the desire for stability, prosperity and welfare after years of devastating violence. Initiatives to reconcile and reunite European citizens reflected these debates. In that sense, European integration was merely a peace process [24]. Our material can be used to support such a claim, for instance by looking at the minor but significant differences in actors and vocabulary between the three newspapers. Seemingly, different moral communities formed different epistemic communities that supported or criticized the work of political leaders.

6   Conclusion

The central objective of this paper was to see how computational techniques could strengthen the empirical foundations of new European integration history. In the growing field of digital humanities, many voices have expressed a fear of a decline in the role of interpretative close reading [19] [25]. Although we do not completely share this fear, we do see the importance of combining different research strategies. In our paper, we have shown that using network extraction raises new questions on early European integration and suggests an outline for new and more refined research. The use of large digitised repositories and digital strategies to extract, select, analyse and read the material can be a potential way to overcome a problem immanent to European integration history: it is transnational, multilingual and ramified. Especially now that public discourse seems to have become the focal point in new historiography, digital search tools and data mining techniques can greatly further the scope of inquiry, as long as we remain critical towards some frames of big humanities. We have presented our approach as a showcase for digital humanities in the field of European integration history with the hope that it can become a stepping-stone for further research.

Acknowledgments. This project was funded as part of the HERA programme.

References

1. Bamman, D., O'Connor, B., Smith, N.A.: Learning latent personas of film characters. In: Proceedings of the 51st Annual Meeting of the Association for Computational Linguistics, pp. 352–361 (2013)
2. de Bruin, R.: Elastisch Europa. De integratie van Europa en de Nederlandse politiek, 1947–1968. Wereldbibliotheek, Amsterdam (2014)
3. Coll Ardanuy, M., Sporleder, C.: Structure-based clustering of novels. In: Third Workshop on Computational Linguistics for Literature at EACL 2014, pp. 31–39. Gothenburg, Sweden (2014)
4. Elson, D.K., Dames, N., McKeown, K.R.: Extracting social networks from literary fiction. In: Proceedings of the 48th Annual Meeting of the Association for Computational Linguistics, pp. 138–147 (2010)
5. de Roode, S.L.R.: Seeing Europe Through the Nation. TheRole of National Self-images in the Perception of European Integration inthe English, German, and Dutch Press in the 1950s and 1990s. Steiner, Stuttgart (2012)
6. Hooghe, L., Marks, G.: Europe's blues. Theoreticalsoul-searching after the rejection of the european constitution. Political Science & Politics **39**(2), 247–250 (2006)
7. Jackson, C.A.: Using Social Network Analysis to Reveal Unseen Relationships in Medieval Scotland. In: Digital Humanities Conference, Lausanne (2014)
8. Kaiser, W.: Transnational western europe since 1945. Integration as political society formation. In: Kaiser, W., Starie, P. (eds.) Transnational European Union. Towards a Common Political Space, pp. 17–35. Routledge, London (2005)
9. Kaiser, W.: Transnational networks in european governance. The informal politics of integration. In: Kaiser, W., Leucht, B., Rasmussen, M. (eds.) The History of the European Union. Origins of a Trans- and Supranational Polity 1950–1972, pp. 12–33. Routledge, New York/London (2009)

10. Lundestad, G.: "Empire" by Integration: The United States and European Integration, 1945–1997. Oxford University Press, Oxford (1998)
11. Mazower, M.: Dark Continent. Europe's Twentieth Century. Vintage Books, London (1998)
12. Medrano, J.D.: Framing Europe. Spain, and the United Kingdom. Princeton University Press, Princeton, Attitudes to European Integration in Germany (2003)
13. Meyer, J.H.: Tracing the European Public Sphere. A Comparative Analysis of British, French and German Quality Newspaper Coverage of European Summits (1969–1991). Steiner, Stuttgart (2010)
14. Milward, A.S.: The European Rescue of the Nation-state. Routledge, London (1992)
15. Moravcsik, A.: The Choice for Europe. Social Purpose and State Power from Messina to Maastricht. Cornell University Press, London/New York (1998)
16. Moravcsik, A.: What Can we Learn from the Collapse of the European Constitutional Project? Politische Vierteljahresschrift **47**(2), 219–241 (2006)
17. Oelke, D., Kokkinakis, D., Malm, M.: Advanced visual analytics methods for literature analysis. In: Language Technology for Cultural Heritage, Social Sciences, and Humanities (LaTeCH) at EACL 2012 Workshop. Avignon, France (2012)
18. Padgett, J.F., Ansell, C.K.: Robust action and the rise of the Medici, 1400–1434. American Journal of Sociology **98**(6), 1259–1319 (1993)
19. Piersma, H., Ribbens, K.: Digital Historical Research. Context, Concepts and the Need for Reflection. BMGN - Low Countries Historical. Review **128**(4), 78–102 (2013)
20. Rochat, Y., Fournier, M., Mazzei, A., Kaplan, F.: A network analysis approach of the venetian incanto system. In: Digital Humanities Conference, Lausanne (2014)
21. Seidel, K.: From pioneer work to refinement. publication trends. In: European Union History: Themes and Debates, pp. 26–44. Palgrave, Basingstoke (2010)
22. Trenz, H.J.: Media: The unknown player in european integration. In: Media. Democracy and European Culture, pp. 49–64. Intellect, Bristol (2008)
23. van Dam, P.: Staat van verzuiling. Over een Nederlandse mythe. Wereldbibliotheek, Amsterdam (2011)
24. van den Bos, M.: Mensen van goede wil. Pax Christi Nederland (forthcoming)
25. van Eijnatten, J., Pieters, T., Verheul, J.: Big Data for Global History: The Transformative Promise of Digital Humanities. BMGN - Low Countries Historical Review **128**(4), 55–77 (2013)
26. van Middelaar, L.: Telling Another Story of Europe. A Reply in Favour of Politics. BMGN - Low Countries Historical. Review **125**(4), 82–89 (2010)
27. van Middelaar, L.: The Passage to Europe: How a Continent Became a Union. Yale University Press, London (2013)
28. Wendt, A.: Social Theory of International Politics. Cambridge University Press, Cambridge (1999)
29. Wieneke, L., Düring, M., Sillaume, G., Lallemand, C., Croce, V., Lazzaro, M., Nucci, F.S., Pasini, C., Fraternali, P., Tagliasacchi, M., Melenhorst, M., Novak, J., Micheel, I., Harloff, E., Garcia Moron, J.: Building the social graph of the history of european integration. In: HistoInformatics Workshop at SocInfo 2013, Kyoto (2013)
30. Wolf, M.: Het geheim van De Telegraaf: geschiedenis van een krant. Boom, Amsterdam (2009)

The EHRI Project - Virtual Collections Revisited

Mike Bryant[1]($\boxtimes$), Linda Reijnhoudt[2], Reto Speck[1], Thibault Clerice[1],
and Tobias Blanke[1]

[1] Centre for e-Research, Department of Digital Humanities,
King's College London, London, UK
{michael.bryant,reto.speck,thibault.clerice,tobias.blanke}@kcl.ac.uk
[2] Data Archiving and Networked Services, The Hague, The Netherlands
linda.reijnhoudt@dans.knaw.nl

Abstract. This paper introduces details of EHRI's approach to
user-centric data integration across heterogeneous archival institutions
using virtual collections. Virtual collections provide the means to re-unite
archival material that has, through complex historical circumstances,
been deposited in many physical locations. They also allow the creation of
subject-specific groupings of material more closely comparable to archival
research guides, and provide users with the ability to organise their own
research in personalised ways.

1 Introduction

The overriding mission of the European Holocaust Research Infrastructure (EHRI)
project[1] is to integrate into an online portal information on Holocaust-related
archival documentation that is physically dispersed across repositories around the
world [1]. This is a particularly challenging mission as archival sources on the
Holocaust have, arguably more so than any other sources relating to contemporary history, undergone very extensive processes of destruction, fragmentation and
dispersal: the Nazis endeavoured to destroy evidence about the crime; survivors
migrated widely after the war and took important documentation with them; a
wide variety of post-war historical commissions and projects have sought to
reassemble surviving evidence, thereby frequently pulling material out of its original context, etc. All this has conspired to make historical research on the Holocaust a very complex undertaking. Indeed, relevant Holocaust source material can
be found in more than 1,800 institutions across the world, and it is frequently not
evident from available archival descriptions how the sources from one repository
may relate to the ones of another [2].

One of the key challenges we faced in EHRI was therefore to establish a platform for forming virtual collections that allows the re-establishment of latent, lost
or implied connections between archival material without further clouding the
provenance and physical arrangement of such material. This paper offers a concise outline of our approach. Section 2 provides an overview of the background

---

[1] http://www.ehri-project.eu

© Springer International Publishing Switzerland 2015
L.M. Aiello and D. McFarland (Eds.): SocInfo 2014 Workshops, LNCS 8852, pp. 294–303, 2015.
DOI: 10.1007/978-3-319-15168-7_37

behind this work, while section 3 describes the heterogeneous source data we encountered and includes an analysis of the main data integration challenges. Section 4 explains the specific rationale for EHRI's use of virtual collections to link together archival descriptions of physically dispersed material according to research themes, while section 5 describes our approach to the presentational issues we have faced. Section 6, finally, provides details about the technical implementation of virtual collections in the EHRI environment, including a sketch of some of the technical challenges we have encountered and a brief outlook of how we are planning to tackle these challenges in the future.

We believe that the platform we have established will enable researchers to virtually explore physically dispersed Holocaust collections, and to dynamically establish new connections, enabling the study of the Holocaust from a quantitatively increased and qualitatively more integrated empirical basis. At the same time, our approach to virtual collections will have general applicability to the challenge of how to develop interfaces to dispersed, fragmentary and complex historical collections that aim at offering researchers advanced search, browse and analysis capabilities across such collections.

2   Prior Work

Virtual collections have been subject to extensive debates. They are frequently seen as one of the main benefits digitisation of resources can deliver to libraries and archives, with the digitisation of resources and tools meaning their organisation can now be conducted in a distributed, decentralised manner. Through virtual collections, users of archives and libraries can engage in what Terry Cook [3] has termed "community-based archiving", developing their own view onto holdings not bound to the organisation by the collection professional. It is thus no surprise that virtual collections have attracted a lot of interest from professional users and especially researchers [4]. Blanke et al [5] discuss the case of classicists working through digital libraries who can build up their own virtual collection bringing together resources from multiple data stores. Classicists with a common interest in certain research topics can share these virtual collections with each other.

In addition to professional scholarly work, virtual collections also promise to support the integration of amateurs and armchair researchers, as they distribute access and means of data curation. In [6] a case study is presented where virtual collections help with involving amateurs in the digitisation work of museums. Other museum visitors seem to accept these kinds of virtual collections as useful. Neither Blanke et al [5] nor Terras [6], however, discuss the exact nature of what constitutes a virtual collection.

For archives, Bradley Westbrook [7] and William E. Landis [8] identify virtual collections as a tool for responding to the unmediated needs of users in ways that the descriptive aids developed by archivists themselves cannot. Traditional archival finding aids, concerned primarily with structure rather than substance, were developed with the assumption that the archivists themselves would be able to direct a user with a subject-based query to the appropriate material in their provenance-based fonds. "In these online systems", however, Landis writes, "mediation is not something we can impose on end users the way we have been able to at our reference desks." [8]

Historian Alessandro Salvador goes even further and welcomes the potential of virtual collections for overcoming complexity in fragmented archival landscapes by integrating archival records, repository information, bibliographies, and other descriptive data into online research guides [9, slide. 11] . This view aligns closely with Candela and Straccia's notion of virtual collections as "user defined un-materialized views over very heterogeneous information space" [10], and can narrowly be interpreted as a focussed application of the virtual research environment (VRE) in facilitating the "linking, integration and subsequent analysis of data" [11]. Because virtual collections offer these opportunities to access data across repositories in a "heterogenous information space", it is not surprising that their development is often seen as one of the main benefits of Linked Data approaches. For instance, [12] uses virtual collections to make cultural heritage metadata and vocabularies interoperable.

This paper adds to this existing work by offering details of a concrete implementation of virtual collections in a data integration context, aimed at mitigating real-world problems faced by researchers in their use of digital tools.

3   The Challenge of Heterogeneous Archival Data

Existing descriptions of Holocaust-related material are heterogeneous and reflect the diversity of institutions that hold such material; spanning the whole spectrum from national archives and large dedicated Holocaust memory and research institutions to small communities archives and private repositories [13]. Despite the fact that relevant conceptual and technical standards exist for the description of archival materials,[2] these standards are frequently not adhered to in practice. A survey we undertook of EHRI partner archives found that fewer than half of repositories follow international descriptive standards, and throughout our work, we have encountered a great variety of descriptive paradigms [2].

In terms of integrating existing descriptions and establishing connections between related material, institutional diversity in the following areas has proved particularly challenging:

Depth of hierarchies in the descriptions
In many cases a particular archival fonds might be described broadly at the collection level (all items together), with specific descriptions for each item. In other cases there can be many more levels of description, as the fonds is broken into subfonds and then perhaps into series, subseries, and files. Even with fonds of broadly comparable size, the number of levels used in the description varies widely between repositories depending on their specific organisational practices, and is not strongly guided by applicable standards.

---

[2] Principally those developed by the International Council on Archives (ICA).

Incompatible vocabularies

It is at present quite rare for archives that assign subject, place, and name (person, family, or corporate) classifiers to archival descriptions to do so from common vocabularies, such as the Library of Congress subject headings (LCSH)[3]. On the contrary, such "access points" (as the ICA refers to them) usually have a legacy basis within each institution.

Provenance vs. Pertinence

Organisation that *respect des fonds* by reflecting the provenance of the material, versus those that arrange collections on the pertinence principle, grouping together records according to subject content.

It very soon became apparent that a wholesale standardisation of the institutionally diverse descriptions prior to integration into the EHRI portal would be undesirable, and, indeed, infeasible. On the one hand, standardising to a common denominator would entail an unacceptable loss of information. On the other hand, institutionally idiosyncratic descriptions can, at times, reveal much about the complicated archival histories these collections have undergone, and as such constitute in themselves a valuable information resource.

Unlike other large-scale archival integration projects such as ApeX[4], we therefore decided to keep standardisation of structure to a minimum, and take a 'take it as it comes' approach to integrating data and building virtual collections. To enable this approach, we have dedicated much effort to establishing a platform that allows the expression of connections between related descriptions of archival items held in diverse repositories.

3.1   Case Study: Integration of Material by Hans G. Adler

Hans Gnther Adler was a Czech Jew born in Prague who, during the course of the war, was imprisoned in Theresienstadt, Auschwitz, and Buchenwald. Following liberation he worked at the Jewish Museum in Prague before emigrating to the United Kingdom in 1947. A prolific writer throughout his life, Adler's works and letters, both original manuscripts and copies, are distributed in many different institutions throughout Europe and beyond, including the EHRI partners Jewish Museum Prague, the Institute for War and Holocaust Studies (NIOD) in Amsterdam, the International Tracing Service (ITS) in Bad Arolsen, King's College London, and Yad Vashem in Jerusalem. Due to this wide distribution, it is difficult for contemporary researchers to gain a coherent overview of the output of this important figure in Holocaust scholarship.

Using virtual collections, we facilitate the creation of such integrated views on material of specific research interest; allowing descriptions of materials from

---

[3] http://id.loc.gov/authorities/subjects.html
[4] http://www.apex-project.eu

many archives to be aligned with each other. In addition to material from the same *fonds* but physically separated, there is also a case for including in such virtual collections that, from a purely archival sense, should be separately organised, such as letters sent by one individual to another. For example, the letters sent by Adler to Dora Philippson and kept at Beit Theresienstadt in Israel could belong within a virtual collection based on Adler's work.

4   Virtual Collections

Virtual collections serve therefore three main purposed within EHRI:

1. To assemble virtual fonds from multiple dispersed archives, reuniting material that belongs together under the provenance principal (figure 1).
2. To support "research guides" in EHRI's portal, overlaying the material itself with a higher-level thematic overview written from the perspective of the historian or the researcher (figure 2).
3. To allow users to create and organise personal lists of items, termed bookmark sets. Bookmark sets are, by default, private to individual users but can be made public and shared at the user's discretion.

Whereas archival finding aids often focus primarily on the structure of the material within a particular repository, research guides typically take a more subject-oriented approach, explicitly tailored to the user of the archives and often prepared by historians in the form of a book or pamphlet comprised of long-form narrative text.

There is, however, invariably some overlap between the descriptive finding aid and the archival research guide. This overlap can often be seen expressed in the areas that finding aids venture into narrative and research guides into structure, as they both must necessarily do. Virtual collections in EHRI embrace this overlap, allowing descriptive "glue" to complement structure in places where this would aid the understanding of the material itself.

Just as material within physical archives is organised hierarchically (from collection to item level), the EHRI research guides can provide their own nested sections that may be wholly or in-part comprised of references to physical documentary units. This arbitrary nesting allows items from separate physical collections to be combined in ways that maintain the coherence of their structure, regardless of the level at which the original archivists have chosen to place the descriptive detail. These intermediate virtual sub-levels are directly analogous to the sub-fonds, series, and sub-series commonly used by archivists, and the descriptive information that can be associated with individual components of EHRI virtual collections takes the same ISAD(G)-based format as standard archival descriptions. In this respect, virtual collections within EHRI more literally comprise virtual *finding aids*, composed of digital surrogates and not, as Westbrook [7] has proposed, of "discrete digital objects and digital objects borrowed from their established collection contexts."

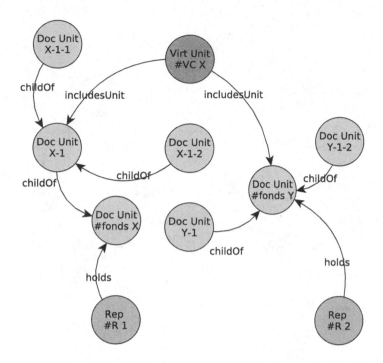

Fig. 1. Dispersed archives: repository R1 holds a fonds X, with a part missing, which is held by repository R2 there called fonds Y

Figures 1 and 2 illustrate two of the ways that virtual collections can be assembled, as, respectively, the gathering together of material from the same source into a dispersed virtual archive, and as a thematic collections organised by topics. Figure 1 shows the need to freely combine items at different levels of description (*VC X* incorporated both *fonds Y* in its entirety along with a child item from *fonds X*) in order to account for institutional differences in descriptive style. Figure 2, on the other hand, uses a structure solely based upon pertinence, with material from multiple different fonds included within subject-based intermediate levels.

5   Representational Challenges

As outlined in section 3, a key challenge for EHRI is to maintain clarity about the provenance and identity of information displayed in its online portal. Simultaneously, we wanted to avoid the "structural opacity" that Wendy Scheir [14] has identified as a major stumbling block for users of electronic finding aids. With material that can be either aggregated from many different archives, created directly by EHRI, or contributed by individual users, there exists potential for misattribution and confusion. Virtual collections, by presenting material in

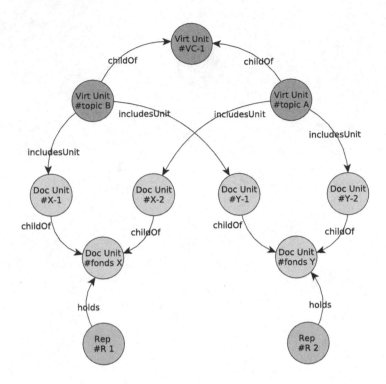

Fig. 2. Thematic collection: a new structure, based on topics, with units from different archives, and possibly different levels

new and different contexts to that represented by the archive in which they physically reside, heighten this danger.

There were two situations we identified that revealed the problems with identity and context in offering virtual collections alongside standard physically-derived digital finding aids, both involving navigation through item hierarchies via different contextual entry points.

In the standard mode of the EHRI portal the context of archival units (descriptions of material) is explicit in a hierarchy that typically reflects the way the material is physically stored, in a given collection or fonds, and by extension within a particular repository. Since a unit of material can only exist in one place at a time (copies notwithstanding) its archival context can be made fairly unambiguous.

Within the EHRI environment, however, a documentary unit can exist within *many different virtual collections* simultaneously, collections which may have been created for entirely different purposes and thus represent very different contexts. Respecting these different contexts implies respecting the manner in which a given item was arrived at by a particular user.

Similarly, we wanted to avoid a situation where a user, starting at the top level of a virtual collection, navigated through successive levels until they reached a non-virtual item and were thereupon removed from the context from which they began. In other words, when viewing a non-virtual documentary unit that was *discovered* through the context of a virtual collection, the discovery context should take precedent over that of the physical context.

The corollary of this situation is that, from an interface perspective (and indeed an interpretive one), the *identity* of a physical documentary unit viewed within the context of a virtual collection is different from its canonical identity. This distinction is, in practice, manifested in two ways:

– The URL for an item viewed in a virtual context always encapsulates its discovery path, allowing perma-linking to permit sharing of items with explicit context.
– User interface components such as "breadcrumbs" display the discovery path, rather than an item's physical context.

As an example, compare the physical path to an item (of which there can be only one) to one of potentially many virtual discovery paths:

Physical Path:
  – Czech Republic → Terezin Memorial → Photographic & Film Material → Dr. Weiglovi
Example Virtual Paths:
  – Terezin Collection → Research Guide → Dr. Weiglovi
  – Notable Czechs → Dr. Weiglovi

In implementing virtual collections in a web interface our key concern was to ensure that an item viewed in a virtual context was a web "resource" like any other, and did not depend on maintaining browser-side state to determine the path a user had taken to arrive at a given page, where many such paths potentially exist. For this reason, the path to a virtual context is encoded into the URL for the page and should always be consistent and shareable if the virtual collection is publicly visible.

6   Technical Implementation

While a detailed description of EHRI's technical implementation is beyond the scope of this paper, we include some details that may be of interest. Since a large portion of the data EHRI is integrating is in some form hierarchical (e.g. archival collections and subject vocabularies) a graph database was chosen as our primary data store [15] [5]. Archival descriptions are modelled as nodes, which are connected via edges to other descriptions, the repositories that hold them, and many other layers of the data model, such as researcher annotations and

---

[5] Specifically Neo4j (http://www.neo4j.org), which adheres to the pragmatic property-graph model, consisting of nodes, edges, and (typically scalar) property values which can be assigned to either.

archival thesaurus terms. The advantages of this approach, in purely practical terms, include simple and fast traversal of potentially unbounded node paths (e.g. from leaf item to root) and the ability to easily incorporate new and revised assumptions in the data model due to the lack of an explicit database schema.

Hierarchical virtual collections are one area where we feel the graph model particularly shows its strengths relative to traditional relational databases. In particular, it provides a very low-overhead environment in which to manage and reorganise tree structures without sacrificing performance when either navigating the hierarchy (for example, when traversing from an item-level unit to its top-level collection) or inserting new items (the typical trade-off in relational databases when employing optimisations such as the nested set model or adjacency lists.)

Our current implementation of hierarchical virtual collections *does* involve potentially expensive data retrieval queries. Due to the much more dynamic structure of VCs in comparison to the (largely static) underlying data, one particular implementation challenge is providing full-text search within the hierarchy of specific virtual collections. Our current approach depends on determining a set of the top-most virtual and non-virtual items within a given VC and applying a search constraint to the union of these items and their "descendants" (child, grandchildren, and so on.) This approach scales poorly, however, due to the unbounded number of items that can exist at each level of the VC hierarchy, and in future we may move to a system employing individual indexes specific to virtual collections.

7   Conclusion

We have outlined above the use of virtual collections in the EHRI project as a means to harmonise heterogeneous data from different archives, present coherent, thematically-based research guides, and to allow users to organise data in ways that best fit their research.

In section 2 we introduce the concept of virtual collections through some of the prior work and discussion addressing the topic in the context of archival integration and virtual research environments. Section 3 outlines the key characteristics of the data EHRI has encountered, including the fact that whilst hierarchical organisation is pervasive, data from individual archives varies greatly in both the depth of these hierarchies, the location of the descriptive detail within them, and the classification vocabularies used. Section 3.1 presents a case study of data integration in a fragmented archival environment

Section 4 describes the manner in which virtual collections can be used to lend coherence to thematic aggregations of data which span multiple physical archives, allowing differences in descriptive style to be harmonised via the use of synthetic groupings of material. Section 5 describes some of the representational challenges associated with this approach with regard to the provenance of items and the context in which they are discovered and viewed. We describe our attempts to mitigate these issues by including discovery context in our conception of a virtual collection "resource", providing an unambiguous handle to a given item within one of potentially many virtual contexts.

Finally, section 6 gives a brief overview of the technical architecture behind EHRI's platform and our plans for future work in this area.

References

1. Speck, R., Blanke, T., Kristel, C., Frankl, M., Rodriguez, K., Daelen, V.V.: The past and the future of holocaust research: From disparate sources to an integrated european holocaust research infrastructure. arXiv preprint arXiv:1405.2407 (2014)
2. Blanke, T., Kristel, C.: Integrating holocaust research. International Journal of Humanities and Arts Computing 7(1–2), 41–57 (2013)
3. Cook, T.: Evidence, memory, identity, and community: four shifting archival paradigms. Archival Science 13(2–3), 95–120 (2013)
4. Blanke, T., Hedges, M.: Scholarly primitives: Building institutional infrastructure for humanities e-science. Future Generation Computer Systems 29(2), 654–661 (2013)
5. Blanke, T., Candela, L., Hedges, M., Priddy, M., Simeoni, F.: Deploying general-purpose virtual research environments for humanities research. Philosophical Transactions of the Royal Society A: Mathematical, Physical and Engineering Sciences 368(1925), 3813–3828 (2010)
6. Terras, M.: Digital curiosities: resource creation via amateur digitization. Literary and Linguistic Computing, p. fqq019 (2010)
7. Westbrook, B.D.: Prospecting virtual collections. Journal of Archival Organization 1(1), 73–80 (2002)
8. Landis, W.E.: Nuts and bolts. Journal of Archival Organization 1(1), 81–92 (2002)
9. Salvador, A.: They're reading our minds: humanities research and digital thinking with cendari (2013) (accessed: August 20, 2014)
10. Candela, L., Straccia, U.: The Personalized, Collaborative Digital Library Environment CYCLADES and Its Collections Management. In: Callan, J., Crestani, F., Sanderson, M. (eds.) SIGIR 2003 Ws Distributed IR 2003. LNCS, vol. 2924, pp. 156–172. Springer, Heidelberg (2004)
11. Fraser, M.: Virtual research environments: Overview and activity. Ariadne (44) (2005)
12. Schreiber, G., Amin, A., Aroyo, L., van Assem, M., de Boer, V., Hardman, L., Hildebrand, M., Omelayenko, B., van Osenbruggen, J., Tordai, A., et al.: Semantic annotation and search of cultural-heritage collections: The multimedian e-culture demonstrator. Web Semantics: Science, Services and Agents on the World Wide Web 6(4), 243–249 (2008)
13. Speck, R., Links, P.: The missing voice. International Journal of Humanities and Arts Computing 7(1–2), 128–146 (2013)
14. Scheir, W.: First entry: Report on a qualitative exploratory study of novice user experience with online finding aids. Journal of Archival Organization 3(4), 49–85 (2006)
15. Blanke, T., Bryant, M., Hedges, M.: Back to our data—experiments with nosql technologies in the humanities. In 2013 IEEE International Conference on Big Data, pp. 17–20. IEEE (2013)

Developing Onomastic Gazetteers and Prosopographies for the Ancient World Through Named Entity Recognition and Graph Visualization: Some Examples from Trismegistos People

Yanne Broux[1(✉)] and Mark Depauw[2]

[1] Research Foundation - Flanders (FWO) / KU Leuven, KU Leuven, Belgium
yanne.broux@arts.kuleuven.be
[2] KU Leuven, Leuven, Belgium

Abstract. Developing prosopographies or onomastic lists in a non-digital environment used to be a painstaking and time-consuming exercise, involving manual labour by teams of researchers, often taking decades. For some scholarly disciplines from the ancient world this is still true, especially those studying non-alphabetical writing systems that lack a uniform transcription system, e.g. Demotic. But for many others, such as Greek and Latin, digital full text corpora in Unicode are now available, often even freely accessible. In this paper we illustrate, on the basis of Trismegistos, how data collection through Named Entity Recognition and visualization through Social Network Analysis have huge potential to speed up the creation of onomastic lists and the development of prosopographies.

Keywords: Named entity recognition · Graph visualization · Ancient prosopographies

1 Introduction

Developing prosopographies or onomastic lists in a non-digital environment used to be a painstaking and time-consuming exercise, involving manual labour by teams of researchers, often taking decades. For some scholarly disciplines from the ancient world this is still true, especially those studying non-alphabetical writing systems that lack a uniform transcription system, e.g. Demotic. But for many others, such as Greek and Latin, digital full text corpora in Unicode are now available, often even freely accessible. In this paper we illustrate, on the basis of Trismegistos (TM; www.trismegistos.org) [1], how data collection through Named Entity Recognition (NER) and visualization through Social Network Analysis (SNA) have huge potential to speed up the creation of onomastic lists and the development of prosopographies [2].

TM started out as a metadata database for sources from ancient Egypt, between 800 BC and AD 800, although at its roots lies a prosopography of Ptolemaic Egypt, the so-called Prosopographia Ptolemaica. Over the past years it has grown to a interdisciplinary platform, encompassing several interrelated databases of not only texts and the

© Springer International Publishing Switzerland 2015
L.M. Aiello and D. McFarland (Eds.): SocInfo 2014 Workshops, LNCS 8852, pp. 304–313, 2015.
DOI: 10.1007/978-3-319-15168-7_38

people mentioned in them, but also place names, ancient authors, ancient archives, collections, and publications. TM is now expanding its geographical scope to the ancient world in general (currently counting 359,107 texts), and TM unique numeric identifiers for source documents (clean URIs such as www.trismegistos.org/text/1234), are now used not only in the papyrological world (e.g. papyri.info) but also in epigraphy (e.g. the Europeana EAGLE consortium). The eventual goal of TM is to provide unique identifiers for all texts from the ancient world, both published and unpublished. This means that TM increasingly wants to be a platform pointing to places where information can be found about all texts from antiquity, thus facilitating cross-cultural and cross-linguistic research.

2   Named Entity Recognition for Onomastic Gazetteers

NER was originally developed by computational linguists in the 1990s, but quickly spread to other fields, such as biology and genetics [3] and is now gaining momentum in the Digital Humanities [4]. The problem with NER-systems, however, is that techniques designed for one genre or field do not necessarily work for others, due to specific text properties (some follow strict writing constraints, e.g. scientific or news articles, while others, such as email or tweets, are more informal), or due to language-related grammatical and syntactical formats. With their diacritic marks, their sometimes fragmentary state, the case system of ancient Greek and Latin, and the for the Western World aberrant onomastic systems with tria nomina or fathers' names instead of family names, our documentation provides a real challenge for the automated collection of names.

2.1   Creating a Multi-tiered Onomastic Gazetteer

In 2008 Bart Van Beek and Mark Depauw developed a database structure for the information on people occurring in the sources (TM People), and a NER procedure to extract references to the people in a Greek full text corpus [5]. The latter was made possible by the cooperation of the Papyrological Navigator, which just then released an Open Access Unicode version of the text of the roughly 50,000 papyri and ostraca from Egypt present in the Duke Database of Documentary Papyri. In early 2014 Mark Depauw developed a parallel system for Latin inscriptions

In each case the NER method was rule-based and relied on a gazetteer of personal names. Initially this consisted of a small set of some few thousand names from Ptolemaic Egypt. But of course many new names (fortunately easily recognizable through capitals) had to be added, and a strategy needed to be developed to cope with the multilingualism of the sources and the declensions of the inflected languages Greek and Latin. This resulted in the distinction of three layers of onomastic information, each with their own database: names, name variants, and declined name variants. The first database, NAM, currently has 34,094 entries, e.g. the Greek name Apollonios. Each of these names is connected to a set of transliterations and variants in all possible languages. As a rule, only very minor dialectal or orthographical variation is allowed in the 'native' language (e.g. Ἀπολλώνιος and Ἀπολλλώνιος); most of the variants are created by renderings of a name in other languages, e.g. ȝpwlnys, ȝpwrnys or ȝpll'ns in Egyptian. In all there are 148,637 variants in the NAMVAR database. Finally, for each of the variants the various declined forms were created, to cope with that special type of variation: examples are Ἀπολλώνιου (genitive) or Ἀπολλώνιωι (dative). This NAMVARCASE database is the largest with 628,351 entries, and it is this set which was used as a gazetteer for the rule-based NER. This resulted in 510,533 attestations of the name variants, as tagged in the full text.

2.2   Distilling Genealogical Information from Identifications

Building on the onomastic gazetteer, rules were then developed to cope with the combination of names, or more correctly declined name variants, in the identification of individuals. For the earlier texts in the Greek corpus, this was relatively uncomplicated, since in that onomastic system the standard way of identification is just a name followed by a father's name (in the genitival declined form). Already in the Ptolemaic period, however, there are complications with the use of double names, and in the Roman period not only are the names of more family members used (mother, paternal and maternal grandfather, ...), but also the Latin onomastic patterns are used more and more frequently. These imply the use of multiple names of different types (praenomen, nomen gentilicium, cognomen) for a single individual, as in Gaius Iulius Caesar.

To cope with this variation, for Greek a set of 164 rules was developed to interpret the clusters of onomastic identification. Criteria were the linguistic nature of the names (Latin names are not combined in the same ways as Greek or Egyptian ones), the case of the name (genitives being used to identify fathers), and the combination of the names with selected non-onomastic terms of identification, often referring to kinship (son, mother, ...). This allowed distillation of the genealogical information provided in the source. For the Latin inscriptions, a new start from scratch was made, because of the almost exclusive use of the Latin onomastic system and the very different composition of clusters, including also other types of elements such as the tribus (a geographical affiliation for Roman citizens).

2.3   Human Intervention for Quality Control and Intratextual Identification

At this stage a human check was performed on the NER. This included tasks which were not so easy to automate: interpreting declined name variants as attestations of a specific case where the mere form was ambiguous; deciding whether some ambiguous entries were toponyms or anthroponyms; and reviewing the results of the cluster interpretation rules and adding relevant information where necessary.

All this could be labelled 'quality control', but we also decided to rely exclusively on humans for the logical next step when developing a prosopography, i.e. the identification of namesakes as attestations of the same person. Since the systematic review was performed text per text, only intratextual identifications were implemented.

3   Data Visualization and Network Analysis to Assist the Creation of Prosopographies

In its current state, TM People can thus not be called a prosopography, since the identification of namesake individuals is a crucial aspect of this type of scholarly tool. Nevertheless TM People has already proven its worth through quantitative analysis, using descriptive statistics to chart the reflection of social and religious changes in name giving in Greco-Roman Egypt [6-9]. Now we are taking things a step further by using data visualization and network analysis, both to optimize the database and to gain new insights into the social structures of ancient Egypt.

3.1   The Problem of Homonymy

Homonymy was fairly common in the ancient world. In village communities similar names were common. In families, names were often passed down every other generation, a way to express kinship in many societies where family names did not exist, as e.g. in Egypt and the Greek world. Moreover, for many individuals, we have not much more than their name: no titles or other status markers, no occupation, no "address", often not even an exact date for the text in which they are mentioned. All this makes it difficult to distinguish between one person and another, or, reversely, one becomes (too) cautious when matching attestations. These prosopographical identifications involve complex reasoning and can thus not easily be automated, but on the other hand our data set is simply too large and complex to review each attestation individually. For this reason we decided to adopt network visualization to facilitate the identification of people appearing in multiple texts [10].

3.2   Network Visualization

With the help of network visualization, however, we are able to take into account an extra level: "communities", in this case in a rather abstract form, meaning people appearing together in different texts. Thanks to the interlock structure of the texts database (TEX) and the person attestation database (REF) in Trismegistos, a two-mode network of people-in-texts can easily be extracted and converted into a one-mode person-to-person network. This network can be checked swiftly for clusters of people reoccurring in several documents: these are most likely the same individuals. Visualizing our data in this manner presents us with a structured overview of the entire set, allowing us to achieve quicker results than when plodding through each individual record in the database.

A crucial element for the identification is of course the date of the document in which people are attested. Many ancient texts, however, do not mention a date, and in those that do, especially letters, the standard dating formula consists of the regnal year, followed by the month and the day. The name of the pharaoh (or king or emperor) is often omitted because it was obvious at the time of writing. In periods of unrest with contending rulers, perhaps even the year was left out because it allowed the scribe to remain impartial. In other cases, the part containing the date is damaged or lost. As a result, documents are often assigned to a broad span of time, e.g. 332-30 BC (= Ptolemaic period) on the basis of palaeography or content (a certain event, phrase, title, name, …). When exploring prosopographical identifications, for example, this can be particularly frustrating.

Again, data visualization can help us out here. When adding the dates of the texts in which the people appear as attributes to the same network generated above for the identification of individuals, broad date ranges can be narrowed down when these people are linked to others with a more accurate date. In a next stage, by combining the texts, the regnal years, and the people mentioned in the texts in one network, simple network concepts, such as the geodesic distance, can help to assign regnal years to a specific ruler when he is not mentioned in the text.

3.3   Letters from Elephantine

A group of Demotic letters from Elephantine, an island in the Nile on the border of Egypt and Nubia, serves as an excellent test case to illustrate the abovementioned methods. Trismegistos records some 146 letters from the fourth and third centuries BC, of which only 9 are (tentatively) dated to a specific year. The majority is simply attributed to 399-200 BC. Half of these texts mention a regnal year, but no ruler. We believe that a significant number should be assigned to the middle or the second half of the fourth century BC, around the time of Nectanebo II, the last pharaoh of the 30th dynasty (360-343 BC), and the Second Achaemenid period (343-332 BC).

These letters contain 450 attestations of individuals, but the identification of these people has only been carried out on a very limited scale, on the basis of the information given in the Prosopographia Ptolemaica [11]. By combining the two methods of personal identification and text dating, a pre-Ptolemaic date seems the most likely option for many of the texts, as we hope to show below.

Table 1. Excerpt of the nodelist of the one-mode Elephantine network

Id	Nodes	Nam_id	Date
8066	Eschnoumpmetis s. of E	175	303 BC
14501	Parates	752	216 BC
16284	Demetrios	2734	217 BC
16416	Es-onour-neb-shait	165	399-200 BC
16426	[ ]-sha-ti	1105	399-200 BC
16713	Esnebonychos	187	399-200 BC

Table 2. Excerpt of the edgelist of the Elephantine network

Source	Target
8066	16871
8066	17477
8066	57155
14501	57156
16284	16831
16284	16965

Fig. 1. Original Elephantine one-mode network

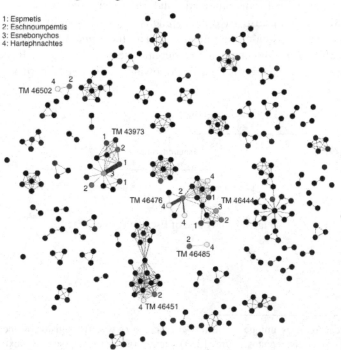

Fig. 2. Identifying individuals in the Elephantine network

People-in-Texts to People-to-People. We started out with a two-mode affiliation matrix, listing all the people and the texts in which they are attested. This was converted into a one-mode network connecting those people mentioned together in one or more texts. Table 1 is a sample of the nodelist: it includes the person's unique numeric identifier[1], the person's name and patronymic, the name ID, and the date of the text in which he appears (if a person is attested in more than one text, the most accurate date was chosen). The edgelist consists of a simple adjacency matrix linking the person IDs (Table 2).

In this network, we discerned four clusters where precisely dated nodes (green = 343 BC) were combined with broad ones (black) (Figure 1). The dates of these black nodes (= people), and consequently also the texts in which they appear, could therefore be narrowed down from 399-200 BC to 399-300 BC (green).

The next step was to check whether it was possible to identify any of the individuals, based on the reoccurrence of certain patterns of names (Figure 2). When highlighting the four most common names, several combinations appeared in six different texts: Eschnoumpmetis and Hartephnachtes are mentioned together in four (TM 46451, 46476, 46485 and 46502), the first of which is assigned to 343 BC; Espmetis (x2) and Esnebonychos in one (TM 43973); and Eschnoumpmetis, Hartephnachtes and Espmetis in another (TM 46444). Twice, both Eschnoumpmetis and Hartephnachtes are identified as sons of Esnebonychos (TM 46444 and 46476). In TM 43973, one of the men called Espmetis is a son of Esnebonychos as well: most likely the same Espmetis mentioned together with Eschnoumpmetis and Hartephnachtes before (TM 46444). Finally, in TM 43973 we also have an Espmetis son of Es-pa-nty-hut-neter and an Esnebonychos son of Es-pa-nty-hut-neter, perhaps the same Esnebonychos who is listed as the father of Eschnoumpmetis, Hartephnachtes and Espmetis? If these identifications are correct, we can reconstruct the following family tree (Figure 3):

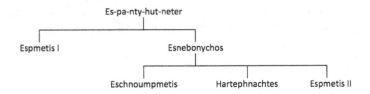

Fig. 3. Family tree of Eschnoumpmetis

---

[1] Since Trismegistos uses unique identifiers for people (www.trismegistos.org/person/1234), attestations (www.trismegistos.org/ref/1234), texts (www.trismegistos.org/text/1234) and names (www.trismegistos.org/name/1234), we use these instead of the actual names or publications to avoid confusion and spelling mistakes.

Fig. 4. New Elephantine one-mode network

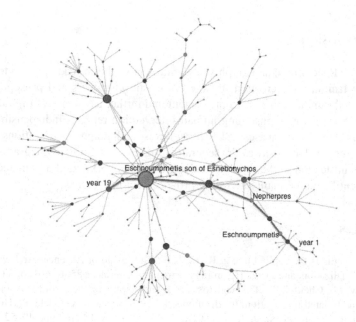

Fig. 5. Elephantine three-mode network

After carrying out these identifications, we reconstructed a new network, and this time a giant component connecting all the green nodes, and several new black ones, emerged (Figure 4). Again, the date of those black nodes could be narrowed down to the fourth century BC. Some extra identifications could also be performed. In this cluster, the name Osoroeris (son of Teos) appeared four times, as well as in one of the unconnected components: they were identified as one and the same person, as well as three attestations of Nepherpres, who is always mentioned in texts together with Eschnoumpmetis (son of Esnebonychos). Finally, three nodes labelled Eschnoumpmetis son of Psammetichos (of which one in the giant component) were also merged.

All-in-One Network. In a next stage, we gathered all the new prosopographical information, and constructed a three-mode network of people that appear in texts that in turn are linked to a regnal year (Figure 5). Our aim was to see if we could link year 19, which we believe to be the last year of Nectanebo II's reign, to year 1, the first of Artaxerxes III; they would correspond to 343 BC.

The shortest path between the two (red line), or geodesic distance, measures 8 in this case: year 19 – TM 46477 – Eschnoumpmetis son of Esnebonychos – TM 46451 – Nepherpres (or year 18) – TM 46615 – Eschnoumpmetis – TM 46443 – year 1. If we could identify the second Eschnoumpmetis with Eschnoumpmetis son of Esnebonychos, we would even get there in four hops, the absolute minimum to get from one year to another in this network. Unfortunately, there are at least two other people called Eschnoumpmetis (a son of Chnoum-machis and a son of Psammetichos), so this identification is far from certain. An alternative eight-hop route is year 19 – TM 46499 – P-oudja-metoues son of Psentaes – TM 46539 – year 18 – TM 46615 – Eschnoumpmetis – TM 46443 – year 1.

4   Conclusion

Named Entity Recognition and graph visualization have thus already proven to be tools that greatly facilitate the creation of new onomastic gazetteers and prosopographies. Yet there is substantial scope for improvement and further assistance of digital tools. In the current process, time-consuming human intervention remains indispensible at several stages. Also, the databases, NER-procedures, and graph visualizations and manipulations remain locked away in separate programmes. Further integration of e.g. database identification in the graph visualization or network-based automated suggestions for identification remain interesting prospects for the future.

References

1. Similar methods are applied in e.g. Klein, L.F.: The Image of Absence: Archival Silence, Data Visualization, and James Hemmings. American Literature 85(4), 661–688 (2013)
2. Depauw, M., Gheldof, T.: Trismegistos: An Interdisciplinary Platform for Ancient World Texts and Related Information. In: Bolikowski, Ł., Casarosa, V., Goodale, P., Houssos, N., Manghi, P., Schirrwagen, J. (eds.) TPDL 2013. CCIS, vol. 416, pp. 40–52. Springer, Heidelberg (2014)

3. Nadeau, D., Sekine, S.: A Survey of Named Entity Recognition and Classification. Linguisticae Investigationes **30**(1), 3–26 (2007)

4. van Hooland, S., De Wilde, M., Verborgh, R., Steiner, T., Van de Walle, R.: Exploring Entity Recognition and Disambiguation for Cultural Heritage Collections. Literary and Linguistics Computing. The Journal of Digital Scholarship in the Humanities, (2014) (forthcoming)

5. Depauw, M., Van Beek, B.: People in Greek Documentary Papyri. First Results of a Research Project. Journal of Juristic Papyrology **39**, 31–47 (2009)

6. Broux, Y.: Double Names and Elite Strategy in Roman Egypt (Studia Hellenistica 54). Peeters, Leuven (2015)

7. Coussement, S.: Because I am Greek: Polyonymy as an Expression of Ethnicity in Ptolemaic Egypt (Studia Hellenistica 55). Peeters, Leuven (forthcoming)

8. Depauw, M., Clarysse, W.: How Christian was Fourth-Century Egypt? Onomastic Perspectives on Conversion. Vigilae Christianae: A Review of Early Christian Life and Language **67**, 407–435 (2013)

9. Jennes, G.: Inspired by the Gods: Theophoric Names in the Late and Graeco-Roman Periods in Egypt. Unpublished PhD dissertation, Leuven (2012)

10. Our approach leans toward the methods applied by Rossi et al. to a large database of French notarial acts from the 13th-18th centuries: Rossi, F., Villa-Vialaneix, N., Hautefeullie, F.: Exploration of a Large Database of French Notarial Acts with Social Network Methods. Digital Medievalist **9** (2013)
http://www.digitalmedievalist.org/journal/9/villavialaneix/

11. Prosopographia Ptolemaica (Studia Hellenistica), 10 vols. Peeters, Leuven (1950-2002)

Can Network Analysis Reveal Importance?
Degree Centrality and Leaders in the EU
Integration Process

Marten Düring[✉]

CVCE, Luxembourg, Luxembourg
marten.duering@cvce.eu

Abstract. This paper describes ongoing work on the potential of simple centrality algorithms for the robust and low-cost exploration of non-curated text corpora. More specifically, this paper studies (1) a network of historical personalities created from co-occurrences in historical photographs and (2) a network created from co-occurrences of names in Wikipedia pages with the goal to accurately identify outstanding personalities in the history of European integration even within flawed datasets. In both cases Degree centrality emerges as a viable method to detect leading personalities.

Keywords: Historical network research · Wikipedia · Photos · Digital history

1   Introduction

Most scholars in the historical network research domain today work with carefully built datasets, some of which take years to complete. There is general scepticism towards automatically generated data [9]. Such data is however attractive given both the volume of texts which can be processed and the speed with which this can be done. Most scholars who specialise in text analytics work with tools far beyond the skill set of most humanists. The question therefore is: How to make the most of (in this case) Social Network Analysis without advanced and in many respects costly methods? To which extent can simple tools yield output which requires only basic technical skills, can be trusted and does not need to be subjected to manual verification? This is especially relevant for selection processes when facing large document collections and helps to reduce the number of potentially relevant nodes (e.g. persons, documents, etc.). The approach for this experiment is therefore consciously both naïve and simplistic. The goal is to find out whether easily obtainable yet by no means authoritative datasets (more on this below) can still be used to identify key actors. To which extent can photographs and Wikipedia pages be understood as proxies for real social relations and interactions? Any lessons learned in such a controlled environment will be beneficial for the analysis of similar approaches to unknown datasets.

Centrality measures developed in social network analysis are applied to two strongly biased network datasets and used to explore to which extent centrality measures are capable of identifying important actors in the history of European integration.

© Springer International Publishing Switzerland 2015
L.M. Aiello and D. McFarland (Eds.): SocInfo 2014 Workshops, LNCS 8852, pp. 314–318, 2015.
DOI: 10.1007/978-3-319-15168-7_39

There are many ways to define importance based on very different metrics and any definition will be based on more specific premises. Any understanding of importance attributed to individuals is the result of human-made, reversable selections which single out some while hiding others, some of which get rediscovered, some remain forgotten. But without doubt, some people left a greater mark on history than others. More specifically, importance in this context describes 1) having held high ranking offices in European institutions, 2) subjective judgment and best knowledge of the domain which leads me to attribute importance to Charles de Gaulle but not to Emilio Colombo, to Pierre Werner but not to Edward Heath (choices documented below). Any such list must be necessarily fuzzy; there can be no such thing as a universal, ranked list of important leaders and it would not be of much interest for historians anyways. Such choices are subject to debate, however a comparison between the persons with the highest and lowest scores does suggest plausibility to the overall findings of this paper. There are, I am sure, ways to find and compute abstract notions of importance. In this paper however I seek to understand to which extent centrality metrics applied to two imperfect datasets can still yield subjectively relevant results.

2   Literature Review

Historians in all subdisciplines have adapted methods and theories developed in Social Network Analysis in very different ways for several decades, in recent years interest as risen significantly [9]. The literature on social network extraction from photographs is still sparse and e.g. concerned with inferences of social ties based on celebrity photos [12] and race relations [1]. [2] find that (artificial) networks remain resilient to minor distortions. Wikipedia and the related DBpedia project have been used for a very large number of related research projects; only a subset of which can be listed here. Social Network Analysis has most often been used to study user interaction in Wikipedia [3]. [10] use Wikipedia for entity disambiguation, [11] use it to extract tripartite networks. More relevant to this topic is work on network extraction from texts in general. [6] note the importance of enriched and cleaned data and propose a meta-matrix approach for the detection of related concepts in texts, based on which they infer social ties. [4] apply sentiment analysis to extract positive and negative ties from biographies of 19th century Dutch socialists. [5] Infer social ties from geographic coincidences. Earlier work by the author analyzed covert historical networks of help for Jewish refugees during the Holocaust [8]. Nodes and edges were manually coded from text and the performance of centrality for a list of actors strongly involved in the respective networks was evaluated. In these networks, which were collected with great care, on average 67 percent of all strongly involved actors also appeared in a group of actors with the top 20 percent highest centrality scores. Degree centrality outperformed all other centrality measures.

3   Data Collection

Based on their collection of photographs, Centre virtuel de la connaissance sur l'Europe (CVCE) compiled a list of 468 personalities who are associated with the history of European integration. CVCE researches and tells the story of European integration based on corpora of primary sources, each of which explores a different aspect of this highly complex process. We assume that they have obtained at least one portrait photograph of all individuals they have considered to be of outstanding importance in this context. CVCE's focus on primary sources also means that every photograph with more than one person represents an historical event of some significance and by extension, at least some of the persons in the photograph must have played a significant role in the pictured event. Based on these considerations we can state that the list of 468 persons contains nearly all major actors in the process of European and that the list will also contain people of lesser importance who were photographed alongside others.

Wikipedia is the single most complete dataset for such information which is freely available and is an important source for information for many. For these reasons we can attribute it some significance as an indicator of a persons perceived status. A Python script was used to download the English Wikipedia page of each of the 468 persons. References to any of the other 467 persons in each personal page constitute an edge between the two. This applies to occurrences of Wikipedia-IDs (e.g. « Jean-Luc_Dehaene ») in the descriptive text and in the structured text (e.g. « Prime Ministers of Belgium »), additional occurrences increase an edge's weight. The data was cleaned using Google Refine and checked manually. This results in a graph containing 461 nodes and 5288 edges. Removal of isolates and self-loops reduced the graph to 369 nodes and 4628 edges with an overall low density of 0.068. This graph was used for the following computations of centrality scores.

The second graph was downloaded from histoGraph [13], a tool developed by the EC FP7-funded research project CUbRIK which brought together scholars in multimedia search and human-machine interaction. histoGraph combines automatic and crowd-based face recognition and identification. The tool currently contains a social network of 222 of the 468 individuals in CVCE's photograph collection. A weighted edge is created for each co-occurrence of two persons in a photograph. This yields 371 edges and an even lower overall undirected density of 0.024. Density describes the ratio of existing edges in a network to the number of possible edges.

4   Analysis

Commonly used centrality measures for both graphs were computed using Gephi's SNA Metrics Plugin. The following measures were selected: Degree, Betweenness, Closeness, Eigenvector, PageRank and Clustering Coefficient. For each measure the 25 highest scoring persons in both datasets were compared to get a first sense for their performance. Only Degree centrality scores came somewhat close to the expected results. Table 1 lists the highest scoring persons for degree centrality, which represents the number of ties a node has. An asterisk indicates importance attributed by me. It lists persons which fit the vague definition of importance such as Francois Mitterrand or Konrad Adenauer. In the Wikipedia network, among the 25 highest ranking persons 20 can be considered important and 14 in the histoGraph network. Others like Alois Mock seem to have a stronger profile in their respective home states. Still others such as US or Russian presidents can be considered important, albeit not primarily in the context of Europe. It would be misleading to filter the latter out based on these or other distinctions. Instead I chose to check all of the lower ranking persons in both networks for importance. Only three notable personalities in the Wikipedia network scored rather low in the histoGraph network (in brackets their degree): *Charles de Gaulle* (4), *Francois Mitterrand* (3), *Alcide de Gaspari* (4). In the Wikipedia network *Pierre Werner* (5) and *Jean Monnet* (5) have surprisingly low degrees. The complete dataset including all centrality scores is available online [7].

Table 1. Highest degree scores in both networks, cut-offs at 61 for the Wikipedia and 5 for the histoGraph network. Subjectively important persons are highlighted with an asterisk.

Rank	Wikipedia network		histoGraph network	
	Name	Degree	Name	Degree
1	Francois Mitterrand*	129	Konrad Adenauer*	27
2	Helmut Kohl*	114	Robert Schuman*	21
3	Walter Hallstein*	108	Margaret Thatcher*	17
4	Konrad Adenauer*	106	Walter Hallstein*	15
5	Felipe Gonzalez*	103	Paul-Henri Spaak*	14
6	Helmut Schmidt*	101	Pierre Werner*	13
7	Charles de Gaulle*	97	Helmut Kohl*	12
8	Alcide De Gasperi*	95	Joseph Bech	11
9	Margaret Thatcher*	93	Jean Monnet*	11
10	Winston Churchill*	92	Franz Vranitzky	10
11	Giulio Andreotti*	86	Amintore Fanfani	9
12	Aldo Moro	85	Jacques Santer*	9
13	George Marshall*	85	Willy Brandt*	8
14	Robert Schuman*	85	Helmut Schmidt*	8
15	Bettino Craxi	82	Hannelore Kohl	8
16	Willy Brandt*	80	Paul Finet	8
17	Anibal Cavaco Silva	77	Antoine Pinay	8
18	Guy Mollet	75	Klaus Hänsch	7
19	John F. Kennedy*	75	Valery Giscard d'Estaing*	6
20	Valery Giscard d'Estaing*	75	Franz Etzel	6
21	Jacques Delors*	74	Alois Mock	6
22	Jean-Claude Juncker*	73	Gaetano Martino	6
23	Jimmy Carter*	73	Georges Pompidou*	6
24	Ronald Reagan*	73	Paul Reynaud	6
25	Alain Poher	72	Leo Tindemans*	6
26	Dwight D. Eisenhower*	72	Winston Churchill*	6
27	Edward Heath	70	Hans-Dietrich Genscher	6
28	Jacques Chirac*	69	Gaston Thorn	6
29	Joseph Stalin*	69	Ronald Wilson Reagan*	6
30	Georges Pompidou*	68	Yasuhiro Nakasone	6
31	Paul-Henri Spaak*	67	Enzo Giacchero	5
32	Richard Nixon*	67	Thomas Klestil	5
33	Tony Blair	67	Giulio Andreotti*	5
34	Erich Honecker	66		
35	Harry S. Truman*	66		
36	Emilio Colombo	65		
37	George H. W. Bush*	65		
38	Harold Wilson*	65		
39	Leo Tindemans*	65		
40	Lester B. Pearson	65		
41	Urho Kekkonen	65		
42	Harold Macmillan*	63		
43	John Foster Dulles	63		
44	Vyacheslav Molotov	63		
45	Andrei Gromyko	62		
46	Ernest Bevin	61		
47	Fidel Castro*	61		
48	Jacques Santer*	61		
49	Romano Prodi*	61		

This suggests that we can safely expect to find a large majority of subjectively important persons among the highest ranking degree scores in both networks.

5   Future Work

At this stage I treated edges in both networks as undirected. Future work will consider the directionality of these co-occurrences since it does make a difference whether for example King Albert II is mentioned on Dehaene's page or Dehaene on King Albert's. The surprisingly poor performance of other centrality measures to detect importance must not mean that they are useless. At this stage it remains open whether high scores for less known persons indicate indeed some kind of influence or must be treated as artifacts.

References

1. Berry, B.: Friends for Better or for Worse: Interracial friendship in the United States as seen through wedding party photos. Demography **43**(3), 491–510 (2006)
2. Borgatti, S.P., et al.: On the robustness of centrality measures under conditions of imperfect data. Social Networks **28**(2), 124–136 (2006)
3. Brandes, U., et al.: Network analysis of collaboration structure in Wikipedia. In: Proceedings of the 18th International Conference on World Wide Web, pp. 731–740. ACM, New York (2009)
4. Van de Camp, M., van den Bosch, A.: The socialist network. Decision Support Systems **53**(4), 761–769 (2012)
5. Crandall, D.J., et al.: Inferring social ties from geographic coincidences. Proceedings of the National Academy of Sciences **107**(52), 22436–22441 (2010)
6. Diesner, J., Carley, K.: Exploration of communication networks from the enron email corpus. In: Proceedings of Workshop on Link Analysis, Counterterrorism and Security, SIAM International Conference on Data Mining 2005, pp. 3–14 (2005)
7. Düring, M.: Appendix for the HistoInformatics 2014 paper submission, https://dl.dropboxusercontent.com/u/132496/Permanent/Wikipedia-histoGraph-centrality-scores-histoInformatics2014.xlsx
8. Düring, M.: How reliable are centrality measures for data collected from fragmentary and heterogeneous historical sources? A case study. In: Proceedings of The Connected Past Conference. Oxford Publishing, Oxford (forthcoming)
9. Düring, M., Eumann, U.: Historische Netzwerkforschung. Ein neuer Ansatz in den Geschichtswissenschaften. Geschichte und Gesellschaft **39**, 369–390 (2013)
10. Gattani, A., et al.: Entity Extraction, Linking, Classification, and Tagging for Social Media: A Wikipedia-based Approach. Proc. VLDB Endow. **6**(11), 1126–1137 (2013)
11. Nazir, F., Takeda, H.: Extraction and analysis of tripartite relationships from Wikipedia. In: 2008 IEEE International Symposium on Technology and Society, ISTAS 2008, pp. 1–13 (2008)
12. Ravid, G., Currid-Halkett, E.: The social structure of celebrity: an empirical network analysis of an elite population. Celebrity Studies **4**(2), 182–201 (2013)
13. Wieneke, L., et al.: histoGraph – A Visualization Tool for Collaborative Analysis of Historical Social Networks from Multimedia Collections. In: Proceedings of 18th International Conference Information Visualisation (IV), 2014 Conference, Paris, France (2014)

Socio-Economic Dynamics, Networks and Agent-Based Models (SEDNAM)

SEDNAM - Socio-Economic Dynamics: Networks and Agent-Based Models - Introduction

Serge Galam[1], Marco Alberto Javarone[2](✉), and Tiziano Squartini[3]

[1] CEVIPOF - Centre for Political Research, Sciences Po, Paris, France
[2] Department of Mathematics and Computer Science, University of Cagliari,
Cagliari, Italy
marcojavarone@gmail.com
[3] CNR - Institute for Complex Systems, Sapienza University of Rome, Rome, Italy

Summary

Recent years have witnessed the increasing interest of physicists, mathematicians and computer scientists for socio-economic systems. In our view, the many reasons behind this can be summarized by observing that traditional approaches to disciplines as sociology and economics have dramatically shown their limitations.

The most prominent example is provided by the recent financial crisis which has clearly shown how necessary a paradigm-shift is. However, a merely philosophical change of perspective wouldn't have been of help at all. What has attracted, and strongly motivated, scientists to approach socio-economic systems is the unprecedented amount of data which has become available. The analysis of these big-data has immediately required the combined effort of experts even coming from traditionally distant disciplines (computer science, physics, applied mathematics, sociology, economics) and pointed out the need of a new, strongly data-driven approach. In this respect, the new interdisciplinary attitude has greatly benefited from the experimental character of physics, the analytical character of mathematics and the numerical character of computer science, which have not only provided data-rooted algorithms to model the systems of interest but also made the birth of the two new fields of *econophysics* and *sociophysics* possible. Such a paradigmatic shift contrasts substantially with the traditional approach of social and economic disciplines, resting upon the axiomatic notion of representative agent. According to the latter (which is a sort of emanation of the reductionist view) an economic system can be decomposed into many subsystems obeying the same behavioral principles of perfect rationality, complete knowledge, homogeneity, stability, etc. and acting in the same way, i.e. trying to optimize an utility function appropriately defined. In so doing, it is implicitly assumed that people can be faithfully represented by a sort of idealized agent whose solely analysis would allow to understand society and economy.

Reversing the perspective, econophysics and sociophysics aim at reconciling theories with observations: on the one hand, interactions do count or, in other words, "the whole is more than the sum of its parts"; on the other hand, the discovery of the ubiquity of power law distributions has clarified that the distribution average is rarely representative of real socio-economic systems. Thus, econophysics

© Springer International Publishing Switzerland 2015
L.M. Aiello and D. McFarland (Eds.): SocInfo 2014 Workshops, LNCS 8852, pp. 321–322, 2015.
DOI: 10.1007/978-3-319-15168-7_40

and sociophysics have adopted the view typical of statistical physics, considering ensembles of interacting units (instead of isolated agents) and properties emerging from microscopic dynamics within a probabilistic framework (instead of a simple, deterministic, function optimization). This has implied the adoption of techniques as agent-based modeling, often embedded onto multiple networks.

While agent-based models allow to describe the dynamics of systems composed by interacting agents characterized by individual behaviors (e.g. conformists VS non-conformists), embedding agents on networks allows to consider realistic scenarios to model interactions, of deep interest for the communities of sociologists, social psychologists and economists. Just to cite few examples, let us think of people interacting on different online and offline social networks, countries exchanging different kinds of commodities, financial shocks propagating through interwoven banks and institutions, etc. This approach reveals all its power when considering that strongly heterogeneous agents and strongly heterogeneous interactions can be accounted for simultaneously. Thus, while agents locally interact with each other via a non-trivial network of connections, both the agents' state (e.g. people's opinion in a social system or banks' liquidity in a financial system) and the agents' interactions (e.g. their number and intensity) are allowed to change in response to the neighbors' output, thus co-evolving in a continuous interplay and giving origin to a complex, dynamical process. As result, some statistical regularities emerge, not derivable from the microscopic behavior of the single agents. The formidable task represented by the interpretation of this complex outcome can be approached by using the tools of statistical mechanics: the statistical regularities emerging from the agents collective behavior can be interpreted in terms of phase transitions (the ordered phase representing consensus and agreement, characterized by a low social temperature, for example), diffusive processes (as the evolution of the price of stocks or options), turbulent phenomena (as the fluctuations in exchange-rates between foreign currencies), magnetization (as the difference between the density of agents having different opinions), etc. However, since the vast majority of the work behind agent-based modeling is feasible only via massive computer simulations, a deeper understanding of the possibilities of the latter is needed: smart storage techniques are required as much as fast and robust algorithms to clean huge amounts of data, visualize the systems and simulate their behavior.

From all the previous considerations, the interdisciplinary character of these new fields clearly emerges, whose aim is a deeper understanding of the intrinsic complexity of socio-economic systems, via the adoption of new models firmly established on empirical evidence. Under this light, the workshop SEDNAM represents the ideal occasion for researcher coming from different fields to discuss together and to strengthen the foundations of this relatively new field of science. All manuscripts have been reviewed by referees belonging to different fields, in order to ensure the novelty, the soundness and the interdisciplinarity of each accepted contribution.

Serge Galam
Marco Alberto Javarone
Tiziano Squartini

Reconstructing Topological Properties of Complex Networks Using the Fitness Model

Giulio Cimini[1]([✉]), Tiziano Squartini[1], Nicolò Musmeci[2],
Michelangelo Puliga[3], Andrea Gabrielli[1,3], Diego Garlaschelli[4],
Stefano Battiston[5], and Guido Caldarelli[3]

[1] Institute for Complex Systems (ISC-CNR) UoS "Sapienza",
University of Rome, Rome, Italy
giulio.cimini@gmail.com
[2] King's College, London, UK
[3] IMT Institute for Advanced Studies, Lucca, Italy
[4] Lorentz Institute for Theoretical Physics,
University of Leiden, Leiden, The Netherlands
[5] Department of Banking and Finance, University of Zurich, Zurich, Switzerland

Abstract. A major problem in the study of complex socioeconomic systems is represented by privacy issues—that can put severe limitations on the amount of accessible information, forcing to build models on the basis of incomplete knowledge. In this paper we investigate a novel method to reconstruct global topological properties of a complex network starting from limited information. This method uses the knowledge of an intrinsic property of the nodes (indicated as *fitness*), and the number of connections of only a limited subset of nodes, in order to generate an ensemble of *exponential random graphs* that are representative of the real systems and that can be used to estimate its topological properties. Here we focus in particular on reconstructing the most basic properties that are commonly used to describe a network: density of links, assortativity, clustering. We test the method on both benchmark synthetic networks and real economic and financial systems, finding a remarkable robustness with respect to the number of nodes used for calibration. The method thus represents a valuable tool for gaining insights on privacy-protected systems.

Keywords: Complex networks · Network reconstruction · Exponential random graphs · Fitness model

1 Introduction

The reconstruction of the statistical properties of a network when only limited information is available represents one of the outstanding and unsolved problems in the field of complex networks [1,2]. A first example is the case of financial networks, for which systemic risk estimation is based on the inter-dependencies among institutions [3,4]—yet, due to confidentiality issues, the information that regulators are able to collect on mutual exposures is very limited [5]. Other

© Springer International Publishing Switzerland 2015
L.M. Aiello and D. McFarland (Eds.): SocInfo 2014 Workshops, LNCS 8852, pp. 323–333, 2015.
DOI: 10.1007/978-3-319-15168-7_41

examples include social networks, for which information may be unavailable because of privacy problems or simply for the impossibility to sample the whole system.

Network reconstruction has been typically pursued through Maximum Entropy (ME) algorithms [6–8], which obtain link weights via a maximum homogeneity principle; however, the strong limitation of these algorithms resides in the assumption that the network is fully connected (for this reason they are known as "dense reconstruction methods"), while real networks show a largely heterogeneous connectivity distribution. More refined methods like "sparse reconstruction" algorithms [2] allow to obtain a network with arbitrary heterogeneity, but still cannot set an appropriate value for such heterogeneity. Recently, a novel *bootstrapping* (BS) method [9, 10] has been proposed in order to overcome these problems. The BS method uses the limited information on the system to generate an ensemble of networks according to the *exponential random graph* (ERG) model [11]—where, however, the Lagrange multipliers that define it are replaced by *fitnesses*, *i.e.*, known intrinsic node-specific properties related to the network topology [12]. The estimation of the network topological properties is then carried out within the ERG-induced ensemble. The method builds on previous results [13] which showed that, in the particular case of the World Trade Web (see below), the knowledge of a non-topological property (the Gross Domestic Product), if coupled to that of the total number of links, allows to infer the topological properties of the network with great accuracy. This procedure can be restated within a maximum-likelihood framework [14]. The BS method uses these preliminary observations to provide a reconstruction procedure valid in the case when the the degree sequence of the network (*i.e.*, the number of connections for each node) is known only partially.

While past works [2, 6–9] mainly dealt with using the limited information available on the network to estimate specific high-order properties such as systemic risk, in the present paper we employ the BS method to reconstruct the fundamental properties that are commonly used to describe a network: density of links, assortativity, clustering (see sec. 3). By focusing on these previously untested properties, we are able to enlarge the basket of quantities that are properly estimated by the BS approach. To validate our method we study how its accuracy depends upon the size of the subset of nodes for which the information is available; our case-study includes synthetic networks generated through a *fitness* model [12] as well as real instances of networked systems: 1) the World Trade Web (WTW), [15], *i.e.*, the network whose nodes are the countries and links represent trade volumes among them, and 2) the network of interbank loans of the e-mid (E-mid) interbank money market [16].

2   Method

We start by briefly describing the ERG model and the fitness model, on which the BS method builds.

The ERG model is one of the most common network generation framework [11, 17, 18], which consists in defining an ensemble Ω of networks which is maximally random, except for the ensemble average of a set of network properties

$\{\langle C_a \rangle_\Omega\}$—constrained to some specific values $\{C_a^*\}$. The probability distribution over Ω can then be defined via a set of control parameters $\{\theta_a\}$, namely the set of Lagrange multipliers associated with the constraints $\{C_a^*\}$. A particular yet widely used case of the ERG model is known as the Configuration Model (CM) [11], which is obtained by specifying the mean degree sequence $\{k_i^*\}_{i=1}^N$ of the network. In this case, each node i is identified by the Lagrange multiplier θ_i associated to its degree k_i. By defining $x_i \equiv e^{-\theta_i} \ \forall i$, the ensemble probability that any two nodes i and j are connected reads [11]:

$$p_{ij} = \frac{x_i x_j}{1 + x_i x_j} \tag{1}$$

so that x_i quantifies the ability of node i to create links with other nodes (induced by its degree k_i) [19].

On the other hand, the *fitness* model [12] assumes the network topology to be determined by an intrinsic non-topological property (known as *fitness*) associated with each node of the network, and has successfully been used in the past to model several empirical economical networks [13,16,20].

The BS method [9] combines these two network generation models, working as follows. We start from incomplete information about the topology of a given network G_0 (consisting of N nodes): we assume to know the degree sequence $\{k_i^*\}_{i \in I}$ of only a subset I of the nodes (with $|I| = n < N$) and an intrinsic, non-topological property $\{y_i\}_{i \in V}$ for all the nodes—that will be our fitness (see below). Using this information, we want to find the most probable estimate of the value $X(G_0)$ of a topological property X computed on the network G_0, compatible with the aforementioned constraints. The method builds on two important assumptions:

1. The network G_0 is interpreted as drawn from an ERG-induced ensemble Ω. We then expect the quantity $X(G_0)$ to mostly vary within the range $\langle X \rangle_\Omega \pm \sigma_X^\Omega$, where $\langle X \rangle_\Omega$ and σ_X^Ω are respectively average and standard deviation of property X estimated over the ensemble Ω.
2. The non-topological fitnesses $\{y_i\}$ are assumed to be proportional the degree-induced exponential Lagrange multipliers $\{x_i\}$ through a universal (unknown) parameter z:[1] $x_i \equiv \sqrt{z} y_i \ \forall i$. Therefore eq. (1) becomes:

$$p_{ij} = \frac{z y_i y_j}{1 + z y_i y_j}. \tag{2}$$

Thanks to these two assumptions we can turn the problem of evaluating $X(G_0)$ into the one of choosing the optimal ERG ensemble Ω compatible with the

---

[1] Fitnesses are often used within the ERG framework provided an assumed connection between them and the Lagrange multipliers. For instance, countries Gross Domestic Products (GDPs) work well as fitnesses when modeling the WTW, and eq. (1) accurately describes the WTW topology when $-\theta_i \propto \log(GDP_i)$ [13]. In any case, this second assumption (or any other relation $y_i = f(x_i)$) can be appropriately tested on the subset I of nodes for which the degree is known.

constraints on G_0, which is the most appropriate to extract the real network G_0 from—given that we know only partial information. Once Ω is determined (by the set $\{x_i\}$ and thus by the set $\{y_i\}$), we can use the average $\langle X \rangle_\Omega$ as a good estimation for $X(G_0)$ and σ_X^Ω as the typical statistical error. Now, since we know the rescaled fitness values $\{y_i\}$, the problem becomes equivalent to that of finding the most likely value of z that defines the ensemble Ω according to eq. (2).

An estimation for the value of z can be found using the incomplete degree sequence through the following relation [9]:

$$\sum_{i \in I} \langle k_i \rangle_\Omega \equiv \sum_{i \in I} \sum_{\substack{j=1 \\ j \neq i}}^{N} p_{ij} = \sum_{i \in I} k_i^* \tag{3}$$

in which the first equality comes from the definition of the ERG model, and the second one is the application of the maximum-likelihood argument [11]—the whole equation being restricted only to the nodes belonging to the subset I. Since $\langle k_i \rangle_\Omega = \sum_{j(\neq i)} p_{ij}$ contains the unknown z through eq. (2), and $\{y_i\}$ and $\sum_{i \in I} k_i^*$ are known, eq. (3) defines an algebraic equation in z, whose solution can be used to estimate the degree-induced Lagrange multipliers $x_i = \sqrt{z} y_i \ \forall i$ of the ERG ensemble $\Omega(z)$, and at the end to obtain an estimation of $X(G_0)$.

Summing up, the BS algorithm consists in the following steps. Given a network G_0, the knowledge of some non-topological property $\{y_i\}$ for all the nodes and the knowledge of the degrees of a subset I of nodes:

- compute the sum of the degrees of the nodes in I ($\sum_{i \in I} k_i^*$) and use it together with $x_i = \sqrt{z} y_i \ \forall i$ to solve eq. (3) and to obtain the corresponding value of z;
- using the estimated z and the knowledge of $\{y_i\}$, generate the ensemble $\Omega(z)$ by placing a link between each pair of nodes i and j with probability p_{ij} given by eq. (2);
- compute the estimate of $X(G_0)$ as $\langle X \rangle_\Omega \pm \sigma_X^\Omega$, either analytically or numerically.

3   Topological Properties

As stated in the introduction, in testing the BS method we will focus on the topological properties (each playing the role of X in the previous discussion) which are commonly regarded as the most significant for describing a network. To define these properties, we use the formalism of the adjacency matrix—where $a_{ij} = 1$ if nodes i and j are connected, and $a_{ij} = 0$ otherwise. We consider:

- link density (or connectance):

$$D := \frac{\sum_{i<j} a_{ij}}{N(N-1)/2} = \frac{2L}{N(N-1)} \tag{4}$$

which is the ratio between the actual number of links in the network and the maximal one compatible with the number of nodes N;

- mean average nearest-neighbors degree:

$$k_{nn} := \frac{\sum_i k_{nn,i}}{N} \quad \text{where} \quad k_{nn,i} := \frac{\sum_{j(\neq i)} a_{ij} k_j}{k_i} = \frac{\sum_{j(\neq i)} \sum_{k(\neq i,j)} a_{ij} a_{jk}}{\sum_{j(\neq i)} a_{ij}}$$

(5)

i.e., the arithmetic mean of the degrees of the neighbors of each node, averaged over all nodes;

- the mean clustering coefficient:

$$c := \frac{\sum_i c_i}{N} \quad \text{where} \quad c_i := \frac{\sum_{j(\neq i)} \sum_{k(\neq i,j)} a_{ij} a_{ik} a_{jk}}{\sum_{j(\neq i)} \sum_{k(\neq i,j)} a_{ij} a_{ik}}$$

(6)

i.e., the ratio between the number of observed links in each node neighborhood and the maximum possible number of such links, averaged over all nodes [21];

- average rich-club coefficient:

$$\phi = \sum_k P(k) \phi(k) \quad \text{where} \quad \phi(k) = \frac{\psi - D}{1 - D} \quad \text{and} \quad \psi(k) = \frac{2E_{>k}}{N_{>k}(N_{>k} - 1)}$$

(7)

with $P(k)$ representing the fraction of nodes having degree equal to k and $\phi(k)$ the ratio between the $E_{>k} = \sum_{i:k_i>k} \sum_{j:k_j>k} a_{ij}$ edges actually connecting the $N_{>k} = \sum_i \Theta\left[\sum_j a_{ij} - k\right]$ nodes with degree higher than k and the maximum possible number $N_{>k}(N_{>k} - 1)/2$ of such edges (or, in other words, the density of links of the subgraph consisting of only the nodes with degree higher than k) [22].

4   Dataset

In order to validate our BS method we use two instances of real economic systems. The first one is the World Trade Web [15], i.e., the network whose nodes represent the world-countries and links represent trade volumes between them:[2] thus, w_{ij} is the total amount of the export of country i to country j. The second one is the interbank loan network of the so-called E-mid interbank money market [16]. In this case, the nodes represent the banks and a link w_{ij} between banks i and j represents the amount of the loan from bank i to bank j.[3] These datasets are particularly suited for our study, as the node fitnesses $\{y_i\}$ can be naturally identified with country GDP for the WTW and with the banks total exposures (i.e., the total lending) for E-mid. Thus in both cases each node fitness coincides with its total strength: $y_i \equiv s_i = \sum_j w_{ij}$. The binary undirected version of these networks (that we want to reconstruct) is then built as $a_{ij} = \Theta[w_{ij} + w_{ji}]$.

---

[2] For WTW, we use trade volume data for the year 2000.

[3] For E-mid, we consider snapshots of loans aggregated on a monthly scale (as also done in other works [16]) because of the high volatility of the links at shorter time scales. In the following, we report the results about the snapshot for February 1999. We performed the same analysis also for other monthly snapshots and we found comparable results.

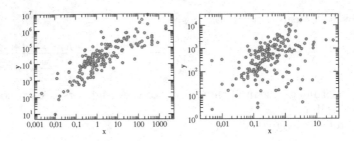

Fig. 1. Scatter plot of node fitness $\{y_i\}$ vs exponential Lagrange multiplier $\{x_i\}$ for WTW (left panel) and E-mid (right panel)

5 Test of the BS Method

Before proceeding to results, we remark that the BS method is subject to two different types of errors. The first one is due to the limited information available for calibrating the ERG model: since we know only the degrees of a subset I of nodes, we can just obtain an estimate of the best z of the ERG ensemble through eq. (3). The second error comes from the assumption that the node fitnesses $\{y_i\}$ are proportional to the degree-induced Lagrange multipliers $\{x_i\}$. Fig. 1 shows the relation between $\{y_i\}$ and $\{x_i\}$ for the two empirical networks. Indeed, there are deviations from linearity—which would correspond to a perfect realization of the fitness model. Note that a better correlation is observed for the WTW: thus, we can expect the BS method to work better in this case.

The quantitative estimation of the BS method effectiveness in reconstructing the topological properties of the two case-studies networks thus proceeds in two steps, as follows.

Test on synthetic networks. To assess the errors which are only due to the limited information available about the degree sequence, we first perform a benchmark test on *synthetic* networks generated through the fitness model. This means that we use the fitnesses $\{y_i\}$ (GDPs for the WTW and total loans for E-mid) to evaluate the "real" z of the ERG ensemble by solving eq. (3) with all nodes included in I (*i.e.*, assuming to know the whole degree sequence), and then draw a network G_0 from $\Omega(z)$ by numerically generating it through eq. (2). G_0 is now the network to reconstruct through the BS method (*i.e.*, with partial information), and the value of X is computed both on G_0 itself as $X(G_0)$, as well as on the whole ensemble $\Omega(z)$ as $\langle X \rangle_{\Omega(z)}$.[4] Inferring G_0 then consists of the following operative steps:

- choose a value of $n < N$ (the number of nodes for which the degree is known);
- build a set of $M = 100$ subsets $\{I_\alpha\}_{\alpha=1}^{M}$ of n nodes picked at random;

---

[4] In the latter case, we use $p_{ij} = \langle a_{ij} \rangle_{\Omega(z)}$ as the expected values of the adjacency matrix elements a_{ij} in the definitions (4,5,6,7).

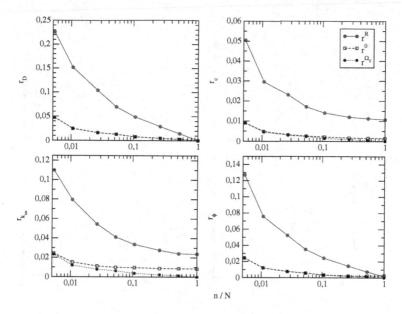

Fig. 2. rRMSE of various topological properties for different values of n, obtained by the BS method on the real WTW network and on its synthetic version obtained through the fitness model. Top left: density D; top right: clustering coefficient c; bottom left: average nearest-neighbor degree k_{nn}; bottom right: rich-club coefficient ϕ.

- for each subset I_α, use the degree sequence in I_α to evaluate z_α from eq. (3), and use it to build the ensemble $\Omega(z_\alpha)$;
- use the linking probabilities from eq. (2) to compute the value of property X over the ensemble $\Omega(z_\alpha)$ as $X_\alpha = \langle X \rangle_{\Omega(z_\alpha)}$;
- compute the relative root mean square error (rRMSE) of property X over the subsets $\{I_\alpha\}$:

$$r_X \equiv \sqrt{\frac{1}{M} \sum_{\alpha=1}^{M} \left[\frac{X_\alpha}{X_0} - 1 \right]^2} \qquad (8)$$

In the rRMSE expression, X_0 denotes a reference value of property X, which can be either $X(G_0)$ (the value of X measured on G_0), as well as $\langle X \rangle_{\Omega(z)}$ (the value of X on the whole ensemble $\Omega(z)$). The consequent two alternative rRMSEs (which we denote as r_X^0 and $r_X^{\Omega_0}$, respectively) provide different estimates of the BS method accuracy. In fact, r_X^0 tests the ability to reproduce a single outcome of the ensemble sampling, whereas, $r_X^{\Omega_0}$ refers to the theoretical values of X expected on the ensemble. Note that since the ensemble $\Omega(z)$ is generated through the fitness model, by construction $r_X^{\Omega_0} \to 0$ for $n \to N$; however, r_X^0 does not necessarily tend to zero, because the generated configuration G_0 is a single realization of $\Omega(z)$ and thus in general $X(G_0) \neq \langle X \rangle_{\Omega(z)}$.

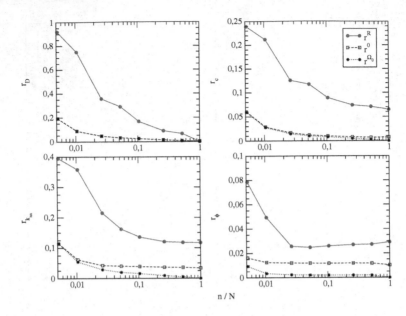

Fig. 3. rRMSE of various topological properties for different values of n, obtained by the BS method on the real E-mid network and on its synthetic version obtained through the fitness model. Top left: density D; top right: clustering coefficient c; bottom left: average nearest-neighbor degree k_{nn}; bottom right: rich-club coefficient ϕ.

Test on real networks. The testing procedure for real networks is equivalent to the one described above, with the only difference that G_0 and X_0 are now the empirical network and the value of X computed on such network respectively—the rRMSE in this case is denoted as r_X^R. We recall again that since the fitness model is only an approximation for real networks, in this case we expect larger errors from the BS reconstruction than those computed for the synthetic networks.

Results. In order to study the accuracy of the BS reconstruction, we study how the rRMSE for the various topological properties we consider varies as a function of the size n of the subset of nodes used to calibrate the ERG model (*i.e.*, for which information about the degrees is available). Results are shown in Fig. 2 for WTW and in Fig. 3 for E-mid. We observe that in all cases there is a rapid decrease of the relative error as the number of nodes n, used to reconstruct the topology, increases. This is an indication of the goodness of the estimation provided by the BS method. As expected, the rRMSE is higher for real networks than for synthetic networks, and the difference between the two respective curves gives a quantitative estimation of the error made in modeling real networks with the fitness model. The fact that such difference is higher for E-mid than for WTW is directly related to the better correlation between node fitnesses and node degrees observed in the latter case. Note also that the errors for E-mid are higher than the ones for WTW also for the corresponding synthetic networks. This feature is easily explained by the higher link density of WTW ($D \simeq 0.59$) with respect to that of E-mid ($D \simeq 0.20$): denser networks are easier to reconstruct because nodes have more links, and thus carry more information for the BS method to exploit (as fluctuations are tamed out).

6   Conclusions

In this paper we tested a novel network reconstruction (BS) method that allows to estimates the topological properties of a network by using only partial information about its connectivity, as well as a non-topological quantity (interpreted as fitness) associated to each node. This method is particularly useful to overcome the lack of topological information which often hinders the study of complex networks. We tested the method on empirical networks, as well as on synthetic networks generated through the fitness model, and studied how well it can estimate the fundamental topological properties which are widely employed to describe network patterns: connectivity, assortativity, clustering coefficient and rich-club coefficient. We found that these properties are reconstructed accurately, for instance with a tolerance usually varying from 2% to 15% (depending on the property examined) using only 5% of the nodes. We also found that the BS method brings to better estimates in denser networks (where more information is available); additionally, the method effectiveness strongly depends on the accuracy of the fitness model used to describe the empirical dataset. In the case of the WTW, the fitness model is fairly accurate in describing how links are formed across countries depending on their GDP [13] and the BS is thus efficient in reconstructing the network topological properties. In the case of E-mid, the fitness model is less accurate and so is the BS method, but the latter can still lead to useful outcomes.

While at first thought it can be surprising that a small fraction of nodes enables to estimate with high accuracy global emerging properties of the network, it is important to remark that the BS method assumes the knowledge of the fitness of all nodes and the validity of the fitness model in describing the data. Therefore, a limitation of this method could arise when considering higher-order topological properties as the community structure. Possibly, in these situations the method could require a larger initial information to obtain the same results. Investigation of these cases is left for future research. Finally note that, contrarily to past works [2,6–9], in this paper we focused on estimating previously untested network quantities, namely the most fundamental properties of a network. This allows us to enlarge the number of properties whose estimations are in remarkable agreement with observations. Indeed, any network reconstruction method must be tested against these basic quantities before being employed for more demanding tasks that are specific for a class of networks (such as systemic risk estimation in financial networks). Thus, the validation of the BS method we presented here also allows us to extend its applicability to any set of dependencies among components in a complex system.

Acknowledgments. This work was supported by the EU project GROWTHCOM (611272), the Italian PNR project CRISIS-Lab, the EU project MULTIPLEX (317532) and the Netherlands Organization for Scientific Research (NWO/OCW). DG acknowledges support from the Dutch Econophysics Foundation (Stichting Econophysics, Leiden, the Netherlands) with funds from beneficiaries of Duyfken Trading Knowledge BV (Amsterdam, the Netherlands).

References

1. Clauset, A., Moore, C., Newman, M.: Hierarchical structure and the prediction of missing links in networks. Nature **453**(7191), 98–101 (2008)
2. Mastromatteo, I., Zarinelli, E., Marsili, M.: Reconstruction of financial networks for robust estimation of systemic risk. J. Stat. Mech. Theory Exp. **2012**(03), P03011 (2012)
3. Battiston, S., Gatti, D., Gallegati, M., Greenwald, B., Stiglitz, J.: Liaisons dangereuses: increasing connectivity, risk sharing, and systemic risk. J. Econ. Dyn. Control **36**(8), 1121–1141 (2012)
4. Battiston, S., Puliga, M., Kaushik, R., Tasca, P., Caldarelli, G.: DebtRank: too central to fail? Financial networks, the fed and systemic risk. Sci. Rep. **2**, 541 (2012)
5. Wells, S.: Financial interlinkages in the United Kingdom's interbank market and the risk of contagion. Bank of England's Working paper 230 (2004)
6. van Lelyveld, I., Liedorp, F.: Interbank contagion in the dutch banking sector. Int. J. Cent. Bank. **2**, 99–134 (2006)
7. Degryse, H., Nguyen, G.: Interbank exposures: an empirical examination of contagion risk in the Belgian banking system. Int. J. Cent. Bank. **3**(2), 123–171 (2007)
8. Mistrulli, P.: Assessing financial contagion in the interbank market: maximum entropy versus observed interbank lending patterns. J. Bank. Finance **35**(5), 1114–1127 (2011)
9. Musmeci, N., Battiston, S., Caldarelli, G., Puliga, M., Gabrielli, A.: Bootstrapping Topological Properties and Systemic Risk of Complex Networks Using the Fitness Model. J. Stat. Phys. **151**(3–4), 720–734 (2013)
10. Caldarelli, G., Chessa, A., Gabrielli, A., Pammolli, F., Puliga, M.: Reconstructing a credit network. Nature Physics **9**, 125 (2013)
11. Park, J., Newman, M.: Statistical mechanics of networks. Phys. Rev. E **70**(6), 066117 (2004)
12. Caldarelli, G., Capocci, A., De Los Rios, P., Muñoz, M.: Scale-free networks from varying vertex intrinsic fitness. Phys. Rev. Lett. **89**(25), 258702 (2002)
13. Garlaschelli, D., Loffredo, M.: Fitness-dependent topological properties of the World Trade Web. Phys. Rev. Lett. 93(18), 188,701 (2004)
14. Garlaschelli, D., Loffredo, M.: Maximum likelihood: Extracting unbiased information from complex networks. Phys. Rev. E **78**, 015101 (2008)
15. Gleditsch, K.S.: Expanded Trade and GDP Data. J. Confl. Res. **46**(5), 712–724 (2002)
16. De Masi, G., Iori, G., Caldarelli, G.: A fitness model for the Italian Interbank Money Market. Phys. Rev. E **74**(6), 066112 (2006)
17. Dorogovtsev, S.: Lectures on complex networks. Phys. J. **9**(11), 51 (2010)
18. Garlaschelli, D., Loffredo, M.I.: Generalized Bose-Fermi Statistics and Structural Correlations in Weighted Networks. Phys. Rev. Lett. **102**, 038701 (2009)

19. Squartini, T., Garlaschelli, D.: Analytical maximum-likelihood method to detect patterns in real networks. New Journ. Phys. **13**, 083001 (2011)
20. Garlaschelli, D., Battiston, S., Castri, M., Servedio, V., Caldarelli, G.: The scale-free topology of market investments. Physica A **350**(2), 491–499 (2005)
21. Watts, D.J., Strogatz, S.: Collective dynamics of 'small-world' networks. Nature **393**(6684), 440–442 (1998)
22. Colizza, V., Flammini, A., Serrano, M.A., Vespignani, A.: Detecting rich-club ordering in complex networks. Nature Physics **2**, 110–115 (2006)

The Structure of Global Inter-firm Networks

Takayuki Mizuno [1,2,3,6](✉) , Takaaki Ohnishi[4,6], and Tsutomu Watanabe[5,6]

[1] National Institute of Informatics, Tokyo, Japan
mizuno@nii.ac.jp
[2] Department of Informatics, The Graduate University for Advanced Studies,
Tokyo, Japan
[3] PRESTO, Japan Science and Technology Agency, Tokyo, Japan
[4] Graduate School of Information Science and Technology, The University of Tokyo,
Tokyo, Japan
[5] Graduate School of Economics, University of Tokyo, Tokyo, Japan
[6] The Canon Institute for Global Studies, Tokyo, Japan

Abstract. We investigate the structure of global inter-firm relationships using a unique dataset containing information on customers, suppliers, licensors, licensees and strategic alliances for each of 412,814 major incorporated non-financial firms in the world. We focus on three different networks: customer-supplier network, licensee-licensor network, and strategic alliance network. In/out-degree distribution of these networks follows a Pareto distribution with an exponent of 1.5. The shortest path length on the networks for any pair of firms is around six links. The networks have a scale-free property. We also find that stock price returns tend to be more highly correlated the closer two listed firms are to each other in the networks. This suggests that a non-negligible portion of price fluctuations stems from the propagation of a particular firm's shocks through inter-firm relationships.

Keywords: Inter-firm network · Scale-free network · Global supply chain · Chain-reaction

1 Introduction

The structural weakness of supply chains in the world was exposed by the 2011 Thailand floods. On 8 October 2011, Rojana industrial estate which housed many manufacturing plants flooded by the 2.5 meter high water. The economies of countries besides Thailand were significantly impacted by the flood. For example, many of the factories that make hard disk drives were flooded. As a result, most hard disk drive prices nearly doubled worldwide. Thailand's flood contributed to a total estimated US$259 billion in economic losses for the first nine months of 2011. These losses represented 80% of the world's total economic losses, and the floods emphasized the importance of understanding the structure of inter-firm networks to avoid production disruptions.

The study of networks, which is an active area of scientific research inspired by the small-world network model published in 1998 [1], has attracted attention

© Springer International Publishing Switzerland 2015
L.M. Aiello and D. McFarland (Eds.): SocInfo 2014 Workshops, LNCS 8852, pp. 334–338, 2015.
DOI: 10.1007/978-3-319-15168-7_42

as a new paradigm that explains such real-world phenomena as computer and social networks. In previous works, network scientists also studied inter-firm networks, e.g. the relationship between firms and banks [2], customer-supplier networks [3][4][5][6][7], and shareholder and ownership networks [8]. In this paper, we introduce the key structures of three different networks of major international firms: customer-supplier network, licensee-licensor network, and strategic alliance network. We empirically evaluate to what extent stock price returns of listed firms are affected by the propagation of idiosyncratic shocks of listed firms through inter-firm relationships.

Our dataset was compiled by Standard & Poor's Financial Services LLC (S&P). The dataset covers 412,814 major incorporated non-financial businesses, including all the listed companies in the world. Information on global inter-firm relationships is recorded in this dataset. The dataset records the lists of core partners (i.e. customers, suppliers, licensors, licensees, and strategic alliances) for a firm, with their IDs. For example, numbers of core customers and suppliers for IBM are 446 firms and 216 firms, respectively for recent two years (2012 and 2013). There is the relationship between customers and suppliers. When firm j is a supplier to firm i, firm i is a customer of firm j. We also use an inverted list of customers and suppliers from the above list of core partners. We also make an inverted list of licensors and licensees, and one of strategic alliances by the same method.

2   Scale-Free Networks of Major Global Firms

We show the global network of customer-supplier relationships in Fig. 1. We will investigate the network structure. In Fig. 2 We show the cumulative distribution functions (CDFs) of links across firms for the customer linkages, supplier linkages, licensor linkages, licensee linkages, and strategic alliance linkages. The horizontal axis is the number of links, and the vertical axis represents the cumulative densities. Both the horizontal and vertical axes are in logarithm. The CDFs of the supplier links show a linear relationship between (the log of) the number of links and (the log of) the corresponding cumulative probability. The slope is about -1.5:

$$\text{Supplier}: P_>(N_s) \propto N_s^{-1.5}. \tag{1}$$

For the number of customer links, licensee links, licensor links and strategic alliance links, we again find a linear relationship between (the log of) the number of links and (the log of) the corresponding cumulative density. Moreover, these slopes of the linear relationship are close to the slope for the supplier links. These linkage slopes are about -1.5, and thus the CDFs for the number of links, which are denoted by N_c, N_{le}, N_{lo} and N_{sa}, can be characterized by

$$\text{Customer}: P_>(N_c) \propto N_c^{-1.5}, \tag{2}$$

$$\text{Licensee}: P_>(N_{le}) \propto N_{le}^{-1.5}, \tag{3}$$

$$\text{Licensor} : P_>(N_{lo}) \propto N_{lo}^{-1.5}, \tag{4}$$

$$\text{Strategic alliance} : P_>(N_{sa}) \propto N_{sa}^{-1.5}. \tag{5}$$

Equations (1)-(5) show that the number of links follows a Pareto distribution. Such a network is called a scale-free network. Moreover, those exponents are close to unity. Pareto distributions with exponent of 1, which are found in various phenomena including firm size distributions, are referred to as Zipf's law. This result suggests that firm size is related to the number of links.

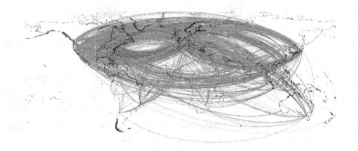

Fig. 1. Global network of customer-supplier relationships. The color expresses a community structure in the network. The nodes show top 1000 firms which have a lot of links.

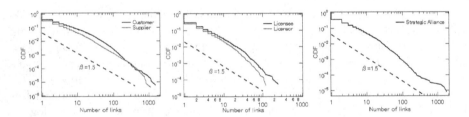

Fig. 2. Cumulative distributions for numbers of (left) customer and supplier links, (center) licensee and licensor links, (right) strategic alliance links. Dashed lines show Pareto distributions with an exponent of 1.5.

3   Closely Interconnected Firms and Stock Return

The number of firms that did business continuously on the customer-supplier network was 345,909, so there are about 119 billion pairs of firms. We calculated the shortest path lengths for each pair of firm i and firm j (i.e. the shortest cut among alternative paths connecting firm i to firm j) on the non-directed customer-supplier network. The number of firms in the maximum connected component of this network is 318,080, that is 92% of all firms. It is observed that 65.5% of all pairs are connected, but 34.5% cannot be connected regardless of how many path lengths there are. Figure 3 shows the distribution of the shortest path lengths for those connected pairs. The mode of distribution is five path lengths, and about 78.8% of the pairs are connected by six path lengths or fewer. We also investigate the mode for the directed customer-supplier network in order to consider the money and intermediate product flow. The mode is also short, only seven path lengths. We also show the mode is short for the non-directed licensee-licensor network and for the non-directed strategic alliance network in Fig. 3. Their modes are six path lengths.

Closely interconnected networks are called small-world networks. A representative example is an airline route map. Hub airports create close interconnections between areas. World inter-firm networks also have hub firms that collect many linkages, as is the case for airline route maps, because the number of links follows a Pareto distribution. The presence of such hub firms implies that even a local firm can be connected to a large number of firms in the world; once a local firm finds a path to one of the hub firms (probably by several path lengths), it is then connected to many firms in the world to which the hub firm is linked.

Close interconnectedness among firms implies that an idiosyncratic shock to a firm could diffuse widely to other downstream firms through business relationships on the networks. To investigate such diffusion on the networks, we compute the correlation in daily stock price returns between two firms, firms i and j, which is represented by ρ_{ij}. We use logarithm price returns in the all listed firms in NYSE from 01/04/2010 to 05/27/2014. We then examine how ρ_{ij} is related to the shortest path length between firms i and j. The results are shown in Fig. 4, which depicts the logarithm price return correlation between firm i and j is related to the shortest path length l_{ij} between them. Y-axis expresses the average of ρ_{ij} conditional on that the shortest path length is l. The correlation decreases with the shortest path length. This result indicate that there is a positive correlation between the stock price return s for firms i and j if they are close to each other in the networks.

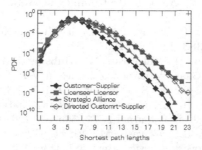

Fig. 3. Probability density function of shortest path lengths for all pairs of firms

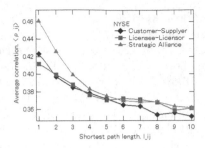

Fig. 4. Average of the stock price return correlations between pairs of listed firms conditional on the shortest path length between the pairs

4   Conclusion

We investigated the structure of global inter-firm relationships using a unique dataset that contains information of business relationships for each of 412,814 firms. We focused on the characteristics of the number of customer, supplier, licensor, licensee and strategic alliance links per firm. The distribution for the number of links has a heavier upper tail follows a Pareto distribution. Firms are closely interconnected with many other firms by hub firms in the Pareto distribution's tail. The mode of the shortest path lengths for all pairs of firms is about six links. We find that the stock price returns of a pair of listed firms tend to be more highly correlated when the two listed firms are closer to each other in the network, suggesting that a non-negligible portion of the price fluctuations stems from the propagation of microeconomic shocks - that is, shocks affecting only a particular firm - through inter-firm relationships.

References

1. Watts, D.J., Strogatz, S.H.: Collective dynamics of 'small-world' networks. Nature **393**, 440–442 (1998)
2. Souma, W., Fujiwara, Y., Aoyama, H.: Complex networks and economics. Physica A **324**, 396–401 (2003)
3. Saito, Y.U., Watanabe, T., Iwamura, M.: Do larger firms have more interfirm relationships? Physica A **383**, 158–163 (2007)
4. Ohnishi, T., Takayasu, H., Takayasu, M.: Hubs and Authorities on Japanese Inter-Firm Networks: Characterization of Nodes in Very Large Directed Networks. Progress of Theoretical Physics Supplement **179**, 157–166 (2009)
5. Fujiwara, Y., Aoyama, H.: Large-scale structure of a nation-wide production network. The European Physical Journal B **77**, 565–580 (2010)
6. Miura, W., Takayasu, H., Takayasu, M.: Effect of Coagulation of Nodes in an Evolving Complex Network. Physical Review Letters **108**, 168701 (2012)
7. Mizuno, T., Souma, W., Watanabe, T.: The Structure and Evolution of Buyer-Supplier Networks. PLoS ONE **9**(7), e100712 (2014)
8. Garlaschelli, D., Battiston, S., Castri, M., Servedio, V.D.P., Caldarelli, G.: The scale-free topology of market investments. Physica A **350**, 491–499 (2005)

Generalized Friendship Paradox: An Analytical Approach

Babak Fotouhi[1,2], Naghmeh Momeni[1](✉), and Michael G. Rabbat[1]

[1] Department of Electrical and Computer Engineering, McGill University,
Montreal, Canada
[2] Department of Sociology, McGill University, Montreal, Canada
{babak.fotouhi,naghmeh.momenitaramsari}@mail.mcgill.ca,
michael.rabbat@mcgill.ca

Abstract. The friendship paradox refers to the sociological observation that, while the people's assessment of their own popularity is typically self-aggrandizing, in reality they are less popular than their friends. The generalized friendship paradox is the average alter superiority observed empirically in social settings, scientific collaboration networks, as well as online social media. We posit a quality-based network growth model in which the chance for a node to receive new links depends both on its degree and a quality parameter. Nodes are assigned qualities the first time they join the network, and these do not change over time. We analyse the model theoretically, finding expressions for the joint degree-quality distribution and nearest-neighbor distribution. We then demonstrate that this model exhibits both the friendship paradox and the generalized friendship paradox at the network level, regardless of the distribution of qualities. We also show that, in the proposed model, the degree and quality of each node are positively correlated regardless of how node qualities are distributed.

1 Introduction

The friendship paradox is a phenomenon observed in various social networks. The term was coined by Feld [1]. It has been empirically observed that people's perception of their own popularity is self-aggrandizing; most people believe that they are more popular than their friends on average [2]. However, Feld observed that in reality, most people have fewer friends than their friends do. In [3], this phenomena is used for the early detection of flu outbreaks among college students. In [4], it is utilized to efficiently sample early-warning sensors during catastrophic events such as hurricanes.

In addition to degree, the same paradox has been observed about other individual attributes (called the *generalized friendship paradox* [5], or GFP). For example, in [6] it has been observed that on Twitter, for most people, their friends share, on average, more viral content and also tweet more. In [5], it has been observed that in scientific collaboration networks, one's co-authors have, on average, more citations, more publications and more co-authors.

© Springer International Publishing Switzerland 2015
L.M. Aiello and D. McFarland (Eds.): SocInfo 2014 Workshops, LNCS 8852, pp. 339–352, 2015.
DOI: 10.1007/978-3-319-15168-7_43

In this paper, we consider a network growth model which is a generalization of the preferential attachment scheme [7]. In our model, nodes are endowed with 'qualities' (ak.a. 'fitness' or 'attractiveness' in the literature [8–11]). Qualities are discrete positive numbers drawn from a given distribution $\rho(\theta)$ and assigned to a node upon its birth (remaining the same thenafter). We assume that the probability that node x with degree k_x and quality θ_x receives a link from subsequent nodes is proportional to $k_x + \theta_x$.[1] We obtain two statistical measures of this model: one is the degree-quality joint distribution, which is the fraction of nodes that have degree k and quality θ in the steady state. The second quantity is the nearest-neighbor distribution of quality and degree: it gives the fraction of nodes with degree ℓ and quality ϕ that are connected to a node with degree k and quality θ. Equipped with these distributions, we can quantify the paradox and study how it depends on the underlying quality distribution $\rho(\theta)$. To our knowledge, no similar theoretical result is available in the literature for any network growth model (either purely preferential [7], or fitness-based [9–11]).

We show that employing the above scheme as the attachment mechanism renders the occurrence of the GFP contingent upon the underlying distribution of node qualities. We then employ measures defined in the literature for assessing the GFP on the network level, and we investigate the dependence of these measures on the model parameters and the quality distribution. We demonstrate that, in the proposed model, the network exhibits a quality paradox at the network level for any quality distribution. We contend that this is indicative of a positive correlation between degree and quality; i.e., those with higher qualities are more likely to have higher degrees, and vice versa.

2   Model, Notation and Terminology

In the growth model considered in this paper, nodes are added successively to the network. The initial network has $N(0)$ nodes and $L(0)$ links. At each time step, one new node is added to the network. We assume that each node has an intrinsic quality, which is drawn from a given distribution $\rho(\theta)$. The quality is assigned to each new incoming node upon birth, and will remain the same thenafter. The mean of the distribution $\rho(\theta)$ is denoted by μ. A node of degree k and quality θ is also referred to as a (k, θ) node throughout.

Each new incoming node attaches to $\beta \leq N(0)$ existing nodes in the network. We consider the simplest additive model that incorporates both degree (popularity) and quality in the dynamics of connection formation: the probability that an existing node with degree k and quality θ receives a link from the new node is proportional to $k + \theta$. This means that, for example, a paper that is new and has very few citations can compensate for its small degree with having a high quality. Or in the social context, a newcomer who does not have many friends in the new social milieu but is gregarious and sociable can elevate the chances

---

[1] Note that for example in [8], the attachment probability is proportional to the product of degree and quality. This model however, has not be solved in closed form. Also, it assigns zero link reception probability to nodes with degree zero.

of making new friends. The new node is called the *child* of the existing nodes that it connects to, and they are called its *parents*. By a (ℓ, ϕ)-(k, θ) *child-parent pair*, we mean a node with degree ℓ and quality ϕ that is connected to a parent node of degree k and quality θ.

The probability that an existing node x receives a new link is $\frac{k_x + \theta_x}{A}$, where the normalization factor A is given by $\sum_x (k_x + \theta_x)$. The sum over all node degrees at time t, which equals twice the number of links at time t, is equal to $2[L(0) + \beta t]$. For long times, the sum over the quality values of all the nodes will converge to the mean of the quality distribution times the number of nodes, that is, we can replace $\sum_x \theta_x$ by $[N(0) + t]\mu$. So at time t, the probability that node x receives a link equals $\frac{k_x + \theta_x}{2L(0) + N(0) + (2\beta + \mu)t}$.

Throughout the present paper, the steady-state joint distribution of quality and degree is denoted by $P(k, \theta)$. The expected number of nodes with degree k and quality θ at time t is denoted by $N_t(k, \theta)$. We denote by $N_t(k, \theta, \ell, \phi)$ the expected number of (ℓ, ϕ)-(k, θ) child-parent pairs.

3   Degree-quality Joint Distribution

We seek the steady-state fraction of nodes who have degree k and quality θ. In Appendix A we derive the following expression for this quantity:

$$P(k, \theta) = \rho(\theta) \left(2 + \frac{\mu}{\beta}\right) \frac{\Gamma(k + \theta)}{\Gamma(\beta + \theta)} \frac{\Gamma\left(\beta + \theta + 2 + \frac{\mu}{\beta}\right)}{\Gamma\left(k + \theta + 3 + \frac{\mu}{\beta}\right)} u(k - \beta). \quad (1)$$

Note that in the special case of a single permitted value for the quality (that is, when $\rho(\theta) = \delta[\theta - \theta_0]$) this model reduces to the shifted-linear preferential attachment model analyzed, for example, in [13]. The solution in this special case simplifies to

$$P_{sh}(k) = \left(2 + \frac{\theta_0}{\beta}\right) \frac{\Gamma(k + \theta_0)}{\Gamma(\beta + \theta_0)} \frac{\Gamma(\beta + 2 + \theta_0 + \frac{\theta_0}{\beta})}{\Gamma(k + 3 + \theta_0 + \frac{\theta_0}{\beta})}. \quad (2)$$

This coincides with the degree distribution of shifted-linear kernels given in [12] and [13]. Furthermore, when $\rho(0) = 1$, all nodes will have zero quality and attachments will be purely degree-proportional, synonymous with the conventional preferential-attachment model proposed initially in [7]. For the special case of $\theta = \mu = 0$ we obtain

$$P_{BA}(k) = \frac{2\beta(\beta + 1)}{k(k + 1)(k + 2)}. \quad (3)$$

This is equal to the degree distribution of the conventional BA network (see, e.g., [12,14]).

Let us also examine the behavior of (1) in the limit of large k. In this regime, we can use the asymptotic approximation that for large values of x, the function $\Gamma(x) \approx x^{x-\frac{1}{2}} \exp(-x)$. Then we replace $\frac{\Gamma(k+\theta)}{\Gamma(k+\theta+3+\frac{\mu}{\beta})}$ with $k^{-3-\frac{\mu}{\beta}}$, independent of θ. Therefore, the steady-state joint degree-quality distribution $P(k,\theta)$ is proportional to $k^{-3-\frac{\mu}{\beta}}$. Marginalizing out θ to recover the degree distribution, we obtain the well-known power law, $P(k) = k^{-3-\frac{\mu}{\beta}}$.

4   Nearest-Neighbor Quality-Degree Distribution

To quantify how qualities and degrees of adjacent nodes correlate, we need to go beyond the quality-degree distribution obtained in the previous section. The closed-form expression for the nearest-neigbor correlations under the preferential attachment model is derived in [13]; that work only considers degrees and does not address qualities. We would like to quantify the conditional distribution $P(\ell, \phi | k, \theta)$, the fraction of neighbours of a given node with degree k and quality θ that have degree ℓ and quality ϕ. We refer to this as the *nearest-neighbor quality-degree distribution* (NNQDD).

In Appendix B we study the rate equation describing how the distribution $P(\ell, \phi | k, \theta)$ evolves as nodes are added to the network. This gives rise to a system of difference equations which we solve to obtain that, in the steady-state,

$$
P(\ell, \phi | k, \theta) = \frac{\rho(\phi)}{k} \frac{\Gamma\left(k + \theta + 3 + \frac{\mu}{\beta}\right)}{\Gamma\left(k + \theta + 3 + \frac{\mu}{\beta} + \ell + \phi\right)} \frac{(\ell - 1 + \phi)!}{(\beta - 1 + \phi)!} \Gamma\left(\beta + 2 + \phi + \frac{\mu}{\beta}\right) \times
$$
$$
\left[\sum_{j=\beta+1}^{k} \frac{\Gamma\left(j + \theta + 2 + \frac{\mu}{\beta} + \beta + \phi\right) \binom{k-j+\ell-\beta}{\ell-\beta}}{\Gamma\left(j + \theta + 2 + \frac{\mu}{\beta}\right) \Gamma\left(\beta + 2 + \phi + \frac{\mu}{\beta}\right)} + \sum_{j=\beta+1}^{\ell} \frac{\Gamma\left(j + \theta + 2 + \frac{\mu}{\beta} + \beta + \phi\right) \binom{\ell-j+k-\beta}{k-\beta}}{\Gamma\left(j + \phi + 2 + \frac{\mu}{\beta}\right) \Gamma\left(\beta + 2 + \theta + \frac{\mu}{\beta}\right)} \right].
$$
$$(4)$$

In order to obtain the nearest-neighbor quality distribution $P(\phi | \theta)$, one needs to perform the calculations $P(\phi | \theta) = \sum_{\ell} \sum_{k} P(k) P(\ell, \phi | k, \theta)$, which requires knowledge of $P(k)$. In turn we have $P(k) = \sum_{\theta} P(k, \theta)$, which according to (1), yields different sums for different quality distributions $\rho(\theta)$.

5   Quantifying the Friendship and Generalized Friendship Paradoxes

As discussed in Section 1, GFP refers to an average alter superiority in arbitrary aspects (e.g., number of citations, exposure to viral online content). In this paper, we use the 'quality' dimension that is incorporated in the model as the subject of the GFP. Our objective is to compare the degrees and qualities of nodes with their neighbors. We say that a node experiences the friendship paradox if the degree of that node is less than the average of the degrees of its neighbors.

Similarly, we say that a node experiences the quality paradox if the quality of the node is less than the average of the qualities of its neighbors.

The above-mentioned definitions characterize individual-level paradoxes. Our primary interest is to what fraction of nodes experience the friendship and quality paradoxes. To this end, we compare the average degree of the nodes with the average degree of the neighbors of all nodes (and similarly for quality). Comparing these two average values yields a macro measure for the system, indicating whether it exhibits paradoxes on average. We call these as the *network-level friendship paradox* and *network-level quality paradox*.

Our measure of the network-level quality paradox is defined as NQP $= \frac{\sum_i k_i \theta_i}{\sum_i k_i} - \frac{1}{N} \sum_i \theta_i$. The summations are performed over all nodes in the network. Note that the numerator of the first sum is actually the sum of the qualities of the neighbors of all nodes. Node i is repeated k_i times in this sum, once for each of its neighbors. Focusing on the limit as $t \to \infty$, we can use the law of large numbers and express the NQP as follows

$$\text{NQP} = \frac{\sum_{k,\theta} k\theta P(k,\theta)}{\sum_{k,\theta} kP(k,\theta)} - \mu. \tag{5}$$

The greater NQP becomes, the more strongly the paradox holds. Negative NQP is indicative of the absence of a quality paradox at the network level.

Undertaking similar steps to above, we can measure the network-level friendship paradox via

$$\text{NFP} = \frac{\langle k^2 \rangle}{\langle k \rangle} - \langle k \rangle = \frac{\langle k^2 \rangle - \langle k \rangle^2}{\langle k \rangle}. \tag{6}$$

Note that the numerator is the variance of the degree distribution, so it is positive. The denominator is the average degree and is also positive. So the NFP is always positive, which means that by this definition: *any network exhibits the friendship paradox at the network level.* So the task of the present paper with regard to the NFP is to investigate its magnitude, i.e., to measure how strongly the paradox holds. For example, in the conventional Barabasi-Albert scale-free model, where the degree variance diverges, the NFP also diverges, which is a result of the presence of macro hubs.

6   Results and Discussion

To study the NFP and the NQP in concrete settings, we confine ourselves to two quality distributions $\rho(\theta)$ for illustrative purposes. We consider a finite support for θ, so that $0 \le \theta \le \theta_{\max}$. For each distribution, we are going to consider four different values β, and four different values of $\theta_{\max}$.

The first distribution we consider is the Bernoulli case, where nodes can either have quality zero or quality $\theta_{\max}$. The probability of quality zero is p and the probability of quality $\theta_{\max}$ is $1 - p$, where $0 \le p \le 1$. The second distribution we consider is the discrete exponential distribution with decay factor q.

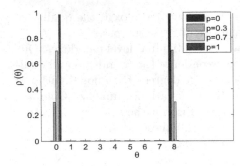
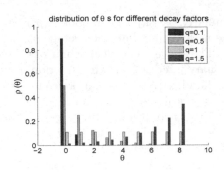

(a) Bernoulli distribution with $p = 0, 0.3, 0.7, 0.1$. The cases of $p = 0$ and $p = 1$ correspond to conventional Barabasi-Albert and shifted-linear preferential attachment networks, respectively.

(b) Exponential distribution for decay factor $q = 0.1, 0.5, 1, 1.5$. The special case of $q = 1$ corresponds to a uniform distribution supported in the interval $0 \leq \theta \leq \theta_{max}$.

Fig. 1. Examples of the quality distributions used in this paper with $\theta_{max} = 8$. Four instances of each type is depicted.

The probability that the quality is θ is proportional to q^{θ}. Note that in the case of $q = 1$, one recovers a uniform distribution as a special case. We consider both $q < 1$ and $q > 1$, yielding decreasing and increasing distributions in θ, respectively. These distributions are depicted in Figure 1.

The results for the Bernoulli quality distribution are depicted in Figure 2. As depicted in Figure 2a, for a fixed θ_{max}, the NQP decreases as β (the initial degree of nodes) increases. Also, it is observable that the sensitivity of the NQP to the variations of the quality distribution diminishes for larger values of β.

As illustrated in Figure 2b, the NFP increases as β (the initial degree of nodes) increases. Hence, according to (6) *the variance of the degree distribution grows faster than the mean degree, as β increases.* On the other hand, for a given β, increasing θ_{max} (which is tantamount to increasing μ), increases the NQP. This means that according to (5) *as θ_{max} increases, the mean of the qualities of the neighbors increases faster than the mean of the qualities of the nodes.*

Figure 2c pertains to this case. Observe that as θ_{max} increases, the NQP becomes more sensitive to the distribution of qualities. Finally, Figure 2d represents the NFP for a fixed β and different values of θ_{max}. From Figures 2a, 2b, 2c and 2d, a general observable pattern is that as p increases, the NFP increases (monotonically for almost all values of p), whereas the NQP is concave and unimodal (it increases at first, achieves maximum, and then decreases).

Now we focus on the exponential quality distribution with the decay factor denoted by q. As depicted in Figure 3a, for a given θ_{max}, the NQP decreases as β increases. Also, it is observed that as β increases, the sensitivity of the NQP to the quality distribution diminishes. These are both similar to the results of the Bernoulli distribution. As can be seen in Figure 3b, the NFP increases as β

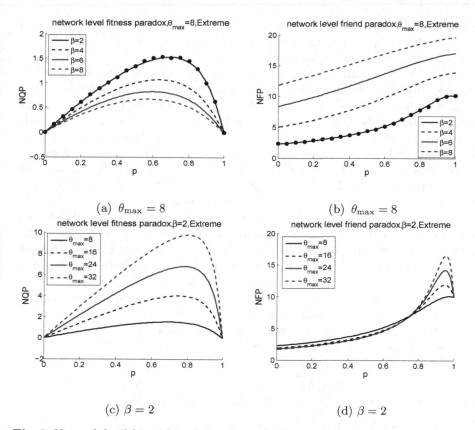

(a) $\theta_{\max} = 8$ (b) $\theta_{\max} = 8$

(c) $\beta = 2$ (d) $\beta = 2$

Fig. 2. Network level friendship and quality paradox for Bernoulli quality distribution. The markers in Figures (a) and (b) represent simulation results, and the solid curves are the theoretical expression. The depicted results are averaged over 100 Monte Carlo trials.

increases. So similar to the Bernoulli case, the variance of the degree distribution grows faster than the mean degree, as β increases.

From Figure 3c we observe that for a fixed β, increasing $\theta_{\max}$ increases the NQP. We observe that as $\theta_{\max}$ increases, NQP becomes more sensitive to the changes in the decay factor. Finally, Figure 3d represents the NFP for a fixed β and different values of $\theta_{\max}$. We observe that increasing $\theta_{\max}$ increases the NFP for positive decays. Also, for very small decay factors (which generate right-skewed distributions that are highly unequal), changing $\theta_{\max}$ has scant effect on the NFP. This is reasonable because when the decay factor is small, all large values of θ have small chances of occurrence. Consequently, changing $\theta_{\max}$ minimally changes the shape of the distribution for small decay factors.

A trend is discernible from Figures 3a, 3b, 3c and 3d: as q increases, the NFP decreases (monotonically for all values of q), whereas NQP is concave and increases up to a point around $q = 1$, and then decreases. Since $q = 1$ yields a uniform distribution, we can qualitatively conclude that the probability of the network-level quality paradox is higher when qualities are heterogeneous, as compared to when qualities are similar.

Finally, to verify our results, we run Monte Carlo simulations to synthesize networks that grow under the prescribed quality-based preferential attachment mechanism, and then calculate the desired quantities by averaging over nodes in the synthesized network. Due to computational limitations, we restrict this validation to the case where $\beta = 2$ and $\theta_{max} = 8$ for the Bernoulli quality distribution and the case where $\beta = 2$ and $\theta_{max} = 16$ for the exponential quality distribution. These results are shown in Figures 2a , 2b, 3a and 3b. The markers show the results of simulations, averaging over 100 Monte Carlo trials, and the solid curves correspond to our theoretical expressions.

We have tested the results on various other quality distributions and observed similar results; these additional simulations not reported here due to space limitations. In general, we observe that for a fixed θ_{max}, increasing β increases the NFP and decreases the NQP regardless of the quality distribution. Also, for a fixed β, increasing θ_{max} increases the NQP and decreases the NFP.

Note that in all cases the NQP is nonnegative. This has roots in the correlation between degree and quality of single nodes (intra-node correlation, rather than inter-node correlation). Let us denote the correlation between degree and quality for a node by $\rho_{k\theta}$, which is the Pearson correlation coefficient obtained from the joint distribution $P(k,\theta)$. From (5), we have:

$$\text{NQP} = \frac{\sum_{k,\theta} k\theta P(k,\theta)}{\sum_{k,\theta} kP(k,\theta)} - \mu = \frac{\sum_{k,\theta} k\theta P(k,\theta) - \mu \sum_{k,\theta} kP(k,\theta)}{\sum_{k,\theta} kP(k,\theta)}$$

$$= \frac{\sum_{k,\theta} k\theta P(k,\theta) - \mu \langle k \rangle}{\langle k \rangle} = \frac{\rho_{k\theta}\sigma_k\sigma_\theta}{\langle k \rangle}. \tag{7}$$

This implies that the sign of NQP is the same as the sign of $\rho_{k\theta}$ (since σ_k, σ_θ and $\langle k \rangle$ are nonnegative). The observation that NQP is always nonnegative indicates that $\rho_{k\theta}$ is also always nonnegative. We conclude that *the quality-dependent preferential attachment model generates networks in which degree and quality of a node are always positively correlated.* This is what we intuitively expect the model to exhibit; increasing quality increases degree. For example, in citation networks, papers with higher qualities receive more citations. Conversely, a paper with many citations is more likely to have a high quality. In the case of friendship networks, a person that is more sociable ends up with more friends than an anti-social person, and conversely, a popular person is more likely to be friendly than an isolated person.

We also observe that in all cases, μ (equivalently, θ_{max}) and β have opposite effects on both the NFP and the NQP. That is, the effect of increasing β is akin to that of decreasing μ, and vice versa. We observed similar trends for other quality distributions; these results are omitted here due to space limitations. What causes this disparity is the following: as can be seen in (1) and (22), μ only appears in the distributions in the form of $\frac{\mu}{\beta}$. Thus increasing μ and decreasing β have the same effect on this variable, and consequently, on the distribution.

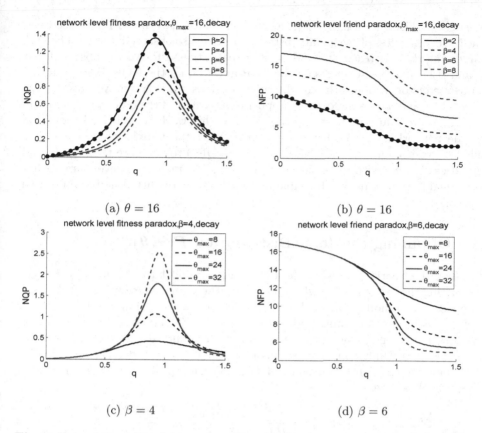

(a) $\theta = 16$

(b) $\theta = 16$

(c) $\beta = 4$

(d) $\beta = 6$

Fig. 3. Network level friendship and quality paradox for exponential quality distribution. The markers in Figures (a) and (b) represent simulation results and the solid curves are from the theoretical expressions. The depicted results are averaged over 100 Monte Carlo trials.

7   Summary and Future Work

The aim of the present paper was to put in crisp theoretical focus the seemingly prevalent phenomena of the friendship paradox and the generalized friendship paradox. We proposed a network growth model that incorporates quality. In this model, the probability that a node receives a link increases with both its degree and quality. We analysed the model theoretically in the steady-state (large size limit), and found two theoretical quantities that characterize the interrelation between quality and degree. The first quantity is $P(k, \theta)$, which is the joint degree-quality distribution, and equals the fraction of nodes who have degree k and quality θ. The second quantity characterizes nearest-neighbor correlations, and is the nearest-neighbor quality-degree distribution, denoted by $P(\ell, \phi | k, \theta)$.

We then defined two network-level measures for the quality and friendship paradoxes and computed them for two particular examples of quality distributions.

We observed that for a fixed $\theta_{\max}$, increasing β increases the NFP and decreases the NQP regardless of the quality distribution. We also observed that for a fixed β, increasing $\theta_{\max}$ increases the NQP and decreases the NFP. We also observed that μ and β have opposite effects on the NFP and also on the NQP. We also tested these results on various other quality distributions, and they proved robust; the effects of β and μ on paradoxes are opposite regardless of the quality distribution.

There are many interesting extensions of this work to pursue. In addition to the network-level paradox, we can also study the individual-level paradox, which would require the utilization of the NNQDD to compare the degrees and qualities of nodes with those of their neighbors. The individual-level paradox has empirical implications which enable us to assess the quality distribution of real networks.

A   Obtaining the Joint Distribution $P(k, \theta)$

We seek the fraction of nodes who have degree k and have quality θ. We begin by writing the rate equation which quantifies the temporal evolution of $N_t(k, \theta)$. Suppose that a node with quality θ and degree $k - 1$ at time $t - 1$, receives a link from the new incoming node. Consequently, its degree will become k and $N_t(k, \theta)$ increments. Conversely, if a node with quality θ and degree k at time $t - 1$, receives a link from the new incoming node, $N_t(k, \theta)$ decrements. Finally, each new incoming node increments $N_t(\beta, \theta)$ with probability $\rho(\theta)$. The rate equation thus reads

$$N_{t+1}(k, \theta) - N_t(k, \theta) = \frac{\beta(k - 1 + \theta)N_t(k - 1, \theta)}{2L(0) + N(0) + (2\beta + \mu)t}$$
$$- \frac{\beta(k + \theta)N_t(k, \theta)}{2L(0) + N(0) + (2\beta + \mu)t} + \rho(\theta)\delta_{k,\beta}. \tag{8}$$

Replacing $N_t(k, \theta)$ by $[N(0) + t]P_t(k, \theta)$, this can be expressed in terms of $P_t(k, \theta)$ as follows:

$$[N(0) + t][P_{t+1}(k, \theta) - P_t(k, \theta)] + P_{t+1}(k, \theta) =$$
$$\frac{\beta(k - 1 + \theta)[N(0) + t]P_t(k - 1, \theta)}{2L(0) + N(0) + (2\beta + \mu)t} - \frac{\beta(k + \theta)[N(0) + t]P_t(k, \theta)}{2L(0) + N(0) + (2\beta + \mu)t} + \rho(\theta)\delta_{k,\beta}. \tag{9}$$

In the limit as $t \to \infty$, the transients vanish. So, we drop the t in the arguments and rewrite (9) as:

$$P(k, \theta) = \frac{\beta(k - 1 + \theta)P(k - 1, \theta)}{2\beta + \mu} - \frac{\beta(k + \theta)P(k, \theta)}{2\beta + \mu} + \rho(\theta)\delta_{k,\beta}. \tag{10}$$

This can be rearranged and expressed equivalently as follows:

$$P(k, \theta) = \frac{(k - 1 + \theta)P(k - 1, \theta)}{2 + \frac{\mu}{\beta} + k + \theta} + \frac{2 + \frac{\mu}{\beta}}{2 + \frac{\mu}{\beta} + \beta + \theta}\rho(\theta)\delta_{k,\beta}. \tag{11}$$

Multiplying both sides by $2\beta + \mu$ and rearranging the terms, this can be recast as follows

$$P(k,\theta) = \frac{(k-1+\theta)P(k-1,\theta)}{2+\frac{\mu}{\beta}+k+\theta} + \frac{2+\frac{\mu}{\beta}}{2+\frac{\mu}{\beta}+\beta+\theta}\rho(\theta)\delta_{k,\beta}. \qquad (12)$$

Setting $k = \beta$, this yields $P(\beta,\theta) = \dfrac{2+\frac{\mu}{\beta}}{2+\frac{\mu}{\beta}+\beta+\theta}\,\rho(\theta)$. For all $k > \beta$, the second term on the right hand side vanishes, and this equation reduces to a straightforward recursion $P(k,\theta) = \dfrac{(k-1+\theta)}{2+\frac{\mu}{\beta}+k+\theta}P(k-1,\theta)$, whose solution is

$$P(k,\theta) = P(\beta,\theta)\prod_{j=\beta+1}^{k}\frac{(k-1+\theta)}{\left(2+\frac{\mu}{\beta}+k+\theta\right)} = P(\beta,\theta)\frac{(k-1+\theta)!}{(\beta-1+\theta)!}\frac{\Gamma\left(3+\frac{\mu}{\beta}+\beta+\theta\right)}{\Gamma\left(3+\frac{\mu}{\beta}+\beta+\theta\right)}$$

$$= \rho(\theta)\left(2+\frac{\mu}{\beta}\right)\frac{\Gamma(k+\theta)}{\Gamma(\beta+\theta)}\frac{\Gamma\left(\beta+2+\theta+\frac{\mu}{\beta}\right)}{\Gamma\left(k+3+\theta+\frac{\mu}{\beta}\right)}. \qquad (13)$$

B   Obtaining the Conditional Distribution $P(\ell,\phi|k,\theta)$

We begin by writing the rate equation to quantify the evolution of $N_t(k,\theta,\ell,\phi)$, which is the number of nodes with degree ℓ and quality ϕ who are connected to a parent node of degree k and quality θ. Upon introduction of a new node, regardless of its quality, the following is true: if it attaches to a node of degree ℓ and quality ϕ who is the child of a parent of degree k and quality θ, then the degree of the receiving node increments and consequently $N_t(k,\theta,\ell,\phi)$ decrements. Also, $N_t(k,\theta,\ell,\phi)$ decrements if the new node attaches to the parent node in such a pair of nodes. Another way that $N_t(k,\theta,\ell,\phi)$ can increment is if either there is a child-parent pair of $(k,\theta,\ell-1,\phi)$ or $(k-1,\theta,\ell,\phi)$. If the new node attaches to the child node in the former case or to the parent node in the latter case, then $N(k,\theta,\ell,\phi)$ increments. Finally, with probability $\rho(\phi)$, the new node will have quality ϕ, and if the new node attaches to an existing node of degree $k-1$ and quality θ, then $N_t(k,\theta,\ell,\phi)$ increments. The rate equation reads

$$N_{t+1}(k,\theta,\ell,\phi) - N_t(k,\theta,\ell,\phi) = \beta\left[\frac{(\ell-1+\phi)N_t(k,\theta,\ell-1,\phi) - (\ell+\phi)N_t(k,\theta,\ell,\phi)}{2L(0)+N(0)+(2\beta+\mu)t}\right]$$

$$+\beta\left[\frac{(k-1+\theta)N_t(k-1,\theta,\ell,\phi) - (k+\theta)N_t(k,\theta,\ell,\phi)}{2L(0)+N(0)+(2\beta+\mu)t}\right] + \rho(\phi)\delta_{\ell,\beta}\frac{\beta(k-1+\theta)N_t(k-1,\theta)}{2L(0)+N(0)+(2\beta+\mu)t}$$

$$(14)$$

Undertaking the same steps that let us transform (8) into (9), and denoting the fraction $\frac{N(k,\theta,\ell,\phi)}{N(0)+t}$ by $n_t(k,\theta,\ell,\phi)$, this can be re-written in terms of

$n_t(k, \theta, \ell, \phi)$ instead of $N_t(k, \theta, \ell, \phi)$. In the limit as $t \to \infty$, we can drop the t subscript and obtain:

$$n(k, \theta, \ell, \phi) = \frac{(\ell - 1 + \phi)n(k, \theta, \ell - 1, \phi)}{2 + \frac{\mu}{\beta} + k + \ell + \theta + \phi} + \frac{(k - 1 + \theta)n(k - 1, \theta, \ell, \phi)}{2 + \frac{\mu}{\beta} + k + \ell + \theta + \phi}$$

$$+ \rho(\phi)\delta_{\ell,\beta} \frac{(k - 1 + \theta)P(k - 1, \theta)}{2 + \frac{\mu}{\beta} + k + \ell + \theta + \phi}. \tag{15}$$

Let us define the new sequence $m(k, \theta, \ell, \phi) = \frac{\Gamma(3 + \frac{\mu}{\beta} + k + \ell + \theta + \phi)}{(k - 1 + \theta)!(\ell - 1 + \phi)!}n(k, \theta, \ell, \phi)$. Using this substitution and applying the properties of the Gamma function as well as the delta function, we can rewrite (15) equivalently as

$$m(k, \theta, \ell, \phi) = m(k, \theta, \ell - 1, \phi) + m(k - 1, \theta, \ell, \phi)$$

$$+ \frac{\Gamma\left(2 + \frac{\mu}{\beta} + k + \beta + \theta + \phi\right)}{(k - 1 + \theta)!(\beta - 1 + \phi)!}\rho(\phi)\delta_{\ell,\beta}(k - 1 + \theta)P(k - 1, \theta). \tag{16}$$

Using the expression in (1) to rewrite the last term on the right hand side of this equation, we can express it equivalently as follows

$$m(k, \theta, \ell, \phi) = m(k, \theta, \ell - 1, \phi) + m(k - 1, \theta, \ell, \phi)$$

$$+ \rho(\phi)\rho(\theta)\delta_{\ell,\beta}\left(2 + \frac{\mu}{\beta}\right) \frac{\Gamma\left(2 + \frac{\mu}{\beta} + k + \beta + \theta + \phi\right)}{(\beta - 1 + \theta)!(\beta - 1 + \phi)!} \frac{\Gamma\left(\beta + 2 + \theta + \frac{\mu}{\beta}\right)}{\Gamma\left(k + 2 + \theta + \frac{\mu}{\beta}\right)}. \tag{17}$$

Now define the generating function $\psi(z, \theta, y, \phi) = \sum_k m(k, \theta, \ell, \phi)z^{-k}y^{-\ell}$. Multiplying both sides of (16) by $z^{-k}y^{-\ell}$, summing over all values of k, ℓ and rearranging the terms, we arrive at

$$\psi(z, \theta, y, \phi) = \frac{\rho(\phi)\rho(\theta)\left(2 + \frac{\mu}{\beta}\right)\Gamma\left(\beta + 2 + \theta + \frac{\mu}{\beta}\right)}{(\beta - 1 + \theta)!(\beta - 1 + \phi)!}$$

$$\times \sum_{j=\beta+1}^{\infty} \frac{\Gamma\left(2 + \frac{\mu}{\beta} + j + \beta + \theta + \phi\right)}{\Gamma\left(j + 2 + \theta + \frac{\mu}{\beta}\right)} \frac{z^{-j}y^{-\beta}}{1 - z^{-1} - y^{-1}}. \tag{18}$$

(The lower bound of the sum is $\beta + 1$ because $P(k - 1, \theta)$ is zero for $k < \beta + 1$.) The inverse transform of the factor $\frac{z^{-j}y^{-\beta}}{1 - z^{-1} - y^{-1}}$ in the summand can be taken through the following steps:

$$\frac{z^{-j}y^{-\beta}}{1-z^{-1}-y^{-1}} \xrightarrow{z^{-1}} \frac{1}{(2\pi i)^2} \oint \oint \frac{z^{k-j-1}y^{\ell-\beta-1}}{1-z^{-1}-y^{-1}}dzdy$$

$$= \frac{1}{(2\pi i)^2} \oint \oint \frac{z^{k-j}y^{\ell-\beta}}{z-\frac{y}{y-1}} \frac{1}{y-1}dzdy$$

$$= \frac{1}{(2\pi i)} \oint \oint y^{\ell-\beta} \left(\frac{y}{y-1}\right)^{k-j} \frac{1}{y-1}dzdy$$

$$= \frac{1}{(k-j)!} \frac{d^{k-j}}{dy^{k-j}} y^{k+\ell-\beta-j}\Bigg|_{y=1} = \binom{k-j+\ell-\beta}{\ell-\beta} \quad (19)$$

So we can invert (18) term by term. We get

$$m(k,\theta,\ell,\phi) = \frac{\rho(\phi)\rho(\theta)\left(2+\frac{\mu}{\beta}\right)\Gamma\left(\beta+2+\theta+\frac{\mu}{\beta}\right)}{(\beta-1+\theta)!(\beta-1+\phi)!}$$

$$\times \sum_{j=\beta}^{\infty} \frac{\Gamma\left(2+\frac{\mu}{\beta}+k+\beta+\theta+\phi\right)}{\Gamma\left(k+2+\theta+\frac{\mu}{\beta}\right)} \binom{k-j+\ell-\beta}{\ell-\beta}. \quad (20)$$

From this, we readily obtain

$$n(k,\theta,\ell,\phi) = \rho(\phi)\rho(\theta) \frac{\Gamma\left(\beta+2+\theta+\frac{\mu}{\beta}\right)}{\Gamma\left(3+\frac{\mu}{\beta}+k+\ell+\theta+\phi\right)} \frac{(k-1+\theta)!(\ell-1+\phi)!}{(\beta-1+\theta)!(\beta-1+\phi)!}$$

$$\times \left(2+\frac{\mu}{\beta}\right) \sum_{j=\beta}^{k} \frac{\Gamma\left(2+\frac{\mu}{\beta}+j+\beta+\theta+\phi\right)}{\Gamma\left(j+2+\theta+\frac{\mu}{\beta}\right)} \binom{k-j+\ell-\beta}{\ell-\beta}. \quad (21)$$

The last step is to abridge this quantity and the desired NNQDD distribution, that is, $P(\ell,\phi|k,\theta)$. Remember that the NNQDD is the fraction of (ℓ,ϕ) nodes among the neighbors of a (k,θ) node. To obtain this fraction, we first need to obtain the total number of neighbors of (k,θ) nodes, then find the number of (ℓ,ϕ) nodes among these nodes, and divide the latter by the former. The total number of neighbors of (k,θ) nodes is simply $kNn(k,\theta)$. The number of (ℓ,ϕ) nodes among them equals $\big[n(k,\theta,\ell,\phi)+n(\ell,\phi,k,\theta)\big]N$, because the (ℓ,ϕ) node can both be the parent or the child of the a (k,θ) node to be connected to it. So we have $P(\ell,\phi|k,\theta) = \frac{n(k,\theta,\ell,\phi)+n(\ell,\phi,k,\theta)}{kP(k,\theta)}$. Inserting the results of (21) and (1) into this expression and simplifying the results, we obtain

$$P(\ell,\phi|k,\theta) = \frac{\rho(\phi)}{k} \frac{\Gamma\left(k+\theta+3+\frac{\mu}{\beta}\right)}{\Gamma\left(k+\theta+3+\frac{\mu}{\beta}+\ell+\phi\right)} \frac{(\ell-1+\phi)!}{(\beta-1+\phi)!} \Gamma\left(\beta+2+\phi+\frac{\mu}{\beta}\right) \times$$

$$\left[\sum_{j=\beta+1}^{k} \frac{\Gamma\left(j+\theta+2+\frac{\mu}{\beta}+\beta+\phi\right)\binom{k-j+\ell-\beta}{\ell-\beta}}{\Gamma\left(j+\theta+2+\frac{\mu}{\beta}\right)\Gamma\left(\beta+2+\phi+\frac{\mu}{\beta}\right)} + \sum_{j=\beta+1}^{\ell} \frac{\Gamma\left(j+\theta+2+\frac{\mu}{\beta}+\beta+\phi\right)\binom{\ell-j+k-\beta}{k-\beta}}{\Gamma\left(j+\phi+2+\frac{\mu}{\beta}\right)\Gamma\left(\beta+2+\theta+\frac{\mu}{\beta}\right)}\right].$$

$$(22)$$

References

1. Feld, S.L.: Why Your Friends Have More Friends than You Do. American Journal of Sociology **96**(6), 1464–77 (1991)
2. Ezar, W., Zuckerman, J.T.: What Makes You Think You're So Popular? Self-evaluation Maintenance and the Subjective Side of the "Friendship Paradox". Social Psychology Quarterly **64**(3), 207–223 (2001)
3. Gracia-Herranz, M., Moro, E., Cebrian, M., Christakis, N., Fowler, J.: Using Friends as Sensors to Detect Global-Scale Contagious Outbreaks. PLos ONE **9**, e92413 (2014)
4. Kryvasheyeu, Y., Chen, H., Moro, E., Van Hentenryck, P., Cebrian, M.: Performance of Social Network Sensors During Hurricane Sandy (2014). arXiv preprint arXiv:1402.2482
5. Eom, Y.H., Jo, H.H.: Generalized Friendship Paradox in Complex Networks: The Case of Scientific Collaboration, Nature Scientific Reports, 4 (2014)
6. Hodas, N.O., Kooti, F., Lerman, K.: Friendship paradox redux: your friends are more interesting than you. In: 7th International AAAI Conference on Weblogs and Social Media, pp. 225–233 (2013)
7. Barabási, A.L., Albert, R.: Emergence of Scaling in Random Networks. Science **286**, 509–512 (1999)
8. Bianconi, G., Barabási, A.L.: Competition and Multiscaling in Evolving Networks. Europhysics Lettres **54**(4), 436–442 (2001)
9. Caldarelli, G., Capocci, A., de Los Rios, P., Muñoz, M.A.: Scale-free Networks from Varying Vertex Intrinsic Fitness. Physical Review Letters **89**(25), 258702 (2002)
10. Servedio, V.T.P., Caldarelli, G., Butta, P.: Vertex Intrinsic Fitness: How to Produce Arbitrary Scale-free Networks. Physical Review E **70**(5), 056126 (2004)
11. Smolyarenko, I.E., Hoppe, K., Rodgers, G.J.: Network Growth Model with Intrinsic Vertex Fitness. Physical Review E **88**(1), 012805 (2013)
12. Dorogovtsev, S.N., Mendes, J.F.F., Samukhin, A.N.: Structure of Growing Networks with Preferential Linking. Physical Review Letters **85**(21), 4633–4436 (2000)
13. Fotouhi, B., Rabbat, M.G.: Degree Correlation in Scale-free Graphs. European Physical Journal B, **86**(12) (2013)
14. Krapivsky, P.L., Redner, S.: Organization of Growing Random Networks. Physical Review E **63**(6), 066123 (2001)

Collective Intelligence-Based Sequential Pattern Mining Approach for Marketing Data

Kazuaki Tsuboi[✉], Kosuke Shinoda, Hirohiko Suwa, and Satoshi Kurihara

The University of Electro-Communications,
1-5-1 Chofugaoka, Chofu, Tokyo 182-8585, Japan
tsuboi@uec.ac.jp

Abstract. It is important to understand consumer needs correctly and clarify target of goods and service in marketing. In recent years, as information processing technology develops, video image analysis also has become as important tool for customer behavior analysis. It is said that discovering consumers' purchase patterns of choosing purchased goods may be possible by using video data. Video is sequential temporal data, so time-series data mining technique is necessary. And generally consumer behavior is ambiguous. To respond to these situation, we are now developing a collective intelligence-based sequential pattern mining approach with high robustness and adaptability, and this time, we have succeeded in visualizing the relation of goods that they are continuously touched up by consumer.

Keywords: Sequential pattern mining · Ant colony optimization · Marketing

1 Introduction

Understanding consumer needs correctly and clarifying target of goods and service are quite important for marketing. Furthermore, it is quite useful to understand consumer insights such as consumers' action, a state of mind and so on.

In conventional marketing approaches, POS data has been mainly used for analysing. But, in recent years, as information processing technology develops, video data also has become as important consumer data for considering marketing. That is, by using the video data of the customer in a store, not only purchase results but also consumers' continuous actions are utilizable. And, it is said that mental background and/or intention of consumer can be extracted by analyzing a sequential action of touched goods.

Purpose of this study is to extract various typical purchase pattern of consumers from consumer action video data. To utilize the video data, segmentation of video stream and tagging each segment as goods which consumer touched are necessary.

As for data mining technique, time-series data mining technique is necessary, and in this paper, we will propose a new ACO-based sequential pattern mining

© Springer International Publishing Switzerland 2015
L.M. Aiello and D. McFarland (Eds.): SocInfo 2014 Workshops, LNCS 8852, pp. 353–361, 2015.
DOI: 10.1007/978-3-319-15168-7_44

approach having high robustness and adaptability, because consumer behavior is basically ambiguous. ACO (Ant Colony Optimization)[1] algorithm is one of collective intelligence-based approach and the optimization method which modeled the behavior of ant seeking for food in a nature. ACO algorithm is famous as a solution of a traveling salesman problem. ACO algorithm consists of leaving a pheromone to the course which the ant passed and tending to choose the course in which the concentration of a pheromone is high. By this property, as a result, whenever ants act, the ants which pass a shortest path increase in number and the concentration of the pheromone which remains in a shortest path becomes more great. On the other hand, the concentration of pheromone will become low if time passes, because the pheromone is volatile chemical material. Therefore, the path which ants rarely pass, that is path other than a shortest path, of the concentration of pheromone becomes lower. As a result, the concentration of the pheromone which remained shows the answer to a shortest path problem. So, the property of ACO algorithm is extremely robust against and adaptable to dynamic change.

The rest of this paper is organized as follows. The section 2 shows related works about pattern mining and ACO algorithm. The section 3 describes our proposing sequential pattern mining algorithm based on ACO. The section 4 shows the first experimental results. This time, we are using the real marketing data about toothbrush. And, in the section 5 we will conclude this paper, and in the section 6 we will describe the future works.

2   Related Works

The apriori algorithm [2] is so famous for discovering the pattern which occurs frequently, and combination of items which meets a certain standard can be extracted. Apriori All[3] algorithm discovers the pattern in consideration of a time series. GSP algorithm[4] which aiming at improvement of the mining speed by imposed time pressure constraints. SPADE algorithm[6] which also aiming at improvement of the mining speed by dividing a candidate of sequential pattern by the concept of "lattice". In [8], sequential pattern mining algorithm using rough set theory are proposed. But, in all of these conventional approaches, goal is pattern extraction, that is, the point of view of time series is out of scope. So, the change of frequent pattern by progress of time cannot be caught.

Tamaki et al. proposed ACO-based algorithm as data mining technique for sensor-network application[5]. They proposed the technique of presuming the contiguity relation of a sensor using ACO algorithm by focusing on a sensor reacting to people's action. By using ACO-based algorithm, it has succeeded in presuming the contiguity relation of a sensor without receiving the influence of noises which is the simultaneous reaction by two or more persons and is the reaction by malfunction of a sensor. So, in this study, we will also propose a sequential pattern extraction algorithm based on ACO.

3   Pattern Mining Algorithm Base on ACO

The goal of this study is to extract various typical purchase patterns which occur frequently from consumers' action in a retail store. Time series data of the goods touched by consumer one by one from the behavior which choose consumers' purchase goods is input data. We try to extract consumers' purchase pattern from this data by ACO-based approach.

3.1   Consumer Data

The data used in the proposed algorithm consists of various kinds of goods which each consumer picked up in sequence. In this paper, each goods are denoted by a number as an item set. Consumers represented $C = \{c_1, \cdots, c_n\}$. For example, the Fig.1 shows that consumer c_1 touches item s_1, s_2, s_3, s_4 in order, consumer c_2 touches item s_5, s_6, s_7 in order, consumer c_3 touches item s_8, s_9, s_{10}, s_{11} in order and consumer c_4 touches item s_{12}.

$$c_1 = \{ s_1, s_2, s_3, s_4 \}$$
$$c_2 = \{ s_5, s_6, s_7 \}$$
$$c_3 = \{ s_8, s_9, s_{10}, s_{11} \}$$
$$c_4 = \{ s_{12} \}$$
$$\vdots$$

Fig. 1. Data set of input

3.2   Sequential Pattern Mining Algorithm Base on ACO

Generally, ACO algorithm consists of two processing phases: accumulation phase of pheromone to the environment, and evaporation phase with the time progress. In the proposed approach, pheromone accumulation and evaporation are performed by each consumer. And frequent pattern is extracted by processing this pheromone calculation for all consumers.

Virtual Graph. At first, a virtual environment for virtual ants is prepared. The environment is represented as virtual graph G. $G = (S, D)$ is a directed graph. Each node in virtual graph represents each goods $s_i \in S$ in a real store. Each edge $d_{i,j} \in D$ represents path which touches goods s_j after touching s_i. Pheromone is accumulated on an edge, and cumulative dosage is represented as τ. When mining process starts, there is no information about consumers' purchase pattern, so the initial value of distribution of the pheromone τ is 0 .

Accumulation and Evaporation of Pheromone. Accumulation and evaporation of the pheromone to the virtual graph G are processed by each consumer c_n. First, the frequency distribution $d_{i,j}$ that consumers moved between goods is calculated. For example, the frequency distribution $d_{i,j}$ represents the number of times of touching the goods s_j after consumer touched the goods s_i. According to eq.(1), the pheromone is updated using the frequency distribution $d_{i,j}$.

$$\tau_{i,j}(c_n) = \tau_{i,j}(c_{n-1}) + d_{i,j}(c_n) \qquad (1)$$

Second, the pheromone is evaporated after accumulation phase of the pheromone. Evaporating the pheromone depend on the evaporative rate ρ. Equation (2) represents calculation of evaporation.

$$\tau_{i,j}(c_n) = \tau_{i,j}(c_n)\,(1 - \rho) \qquad (2)$$

By the feature of evaporation pheromone, old behavior is discarded little by little and new behavior is reflected in an analysis result at a constant ratio always. So, the evaporation rate ρ shows the speed of update.

3.3 Adaptation to Ambiguous Behavior

It is easy to imagine that consumer usually take many ambiguous behavior. We usually pick up goods without much attention in shopping. So, in order to correspond to ambiguous consumers' behavior, we will improve the pheromone accumulation phase.

Disregarding Same Goods Touched Continuously. Generally consumers may touch the same goods several times continuously. This situation is often seen at shopping cart. When the difference between goods is not in sight easily, it often happens. So, the goods that has been touched continuously should be disregarded as noise. To be more precise, pheromone is not added to the edge containing the disregarded goods. And, instead, pheromone is added to the edge between the goods touched before and behind the disregarded goods.

Easing Transitive Relations. With the basic algorithm based on ACO, the pheromone is added along the only order of a time series of a consumer behavior (Fig.2), and the more two goods have high relation and high popularity the more high pheromone is accumulated.

But, usually consumer's behavior is not always intentional, that is, we usually pick up goods ambiguously. For example, let's assume that a consumer c_a picked up three goods one by one in order like: goods s_a, goods s_b, then goods s_c, and assume that this pattern is included many times in the data. In this case, of course this pattern can be extracted by our proposed methodology. But, we must also consider a possibility of the following pattern: consumer c_a picked up two goods one by one in order like: goods s_a, then goods s_c. Because the consumer c_a's real interest may be in the goods s_a and s_c, and he may pick up the goods s_b ambiguously not a little.

So, when we assume that the behavior of consumer n is $c_n = \{s_1, s_2, s_3, s_4\}$, then we generate not only $\{d_{1,2}(c_n) = 1, d_{2,3}(c_n) = 1, d_{3,4}(c_n) = 1\}$ but also $\{d_{1,3}(c_n) = 1, d_{1,4}(c_n) = 1, d_{2,4}(c_n) = 1\}$ (Fig.3).

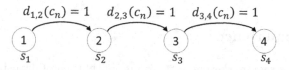

Fig. 2. The edge which adds a pheromone with the basic algorithm based on ACO (Each node number means the order in which consumer touched)

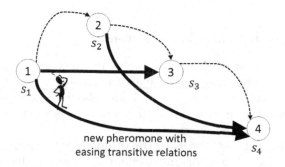

Fig. 3. The edge which adds a pheromone with easing transitive relations (Each node number means the order in which consumer touched)

Introduction of Node Pheromone. Let's assume following situation: there are three edges like $d_{1,2}, d_{2,3},$ and $d_{1,3}$. And if value of $d_{1,2}, d_{2,3}$ was smaller than the threshold of pheromone evaporation, then these two edge were deleted. But, it is important that the goods s_2 connect goods s_1 and goods s_3 as mediator (in social science research area, mediator of this context is called "weak tie"). So, if $d_{1,2}, d_{2,3}$ is smaller than the threshold of pheromone evaporation for node (θ_s), we generate $d_{1,3}$ in substitution for $d_{1,2}$ and $d_{2,3}$, then delete $d_{1,2}$ and $d_{2,3}$ (Fig.4).

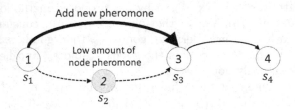

Fig. 4. The edge which adds the pheromone with introduction of Node Pheromone (Each node number means the order in which consumer touched)

4   Initial Experience

This time we used real marketing data about toothbrush of drugstore. The evaporation rate is set as 0.01 ($\rho = 0.01$). Consumers' behavior extracted from the video stream data of toothbrush sales floor of retail store is used as input data. Input data consists of 1552 consumers, 1758 kinds of goods and 7834 touched goods.

4.1   Mining Result Before Three Extensions

We visualized our mining result, that is virtual graph G, by using Cytoscape [9]. In G, nodes means goods and edges means the amount of the pheromone. θ is the threshold to decide whether node and edge should be deleted or not. Edge and Node are deleted, if the amount of the pheromone is less than a lower bound ($\tau_{i,j} < \theta$). In this experiment θ was set as 0.25.

G is clustered about nodes by using the community clustering algorithm that is an implementation of the Girvan-Newman fast greedy algorithm as implemented by the GLay Cytoscape plugin [10]. Each circle represents each community which is based on the kinds of goods.

As you can see the Fig.5, it turns out that consumers' purchase pattern is to touch the goods with which the kind is alike when consumers think what to buy.

4.2   Effect of the Easing Transitive Relations

By applying the extension of easing transitive relations, mining result was changed from the Fig.5 to the Fig.6. Here, θ was set as 0.4. The Fig. 6 shows that the number of nodes which constitute each cluster was increased, on the other hand the number of community clusters was decreased. In the Fig.5, each cluster shows the feature of toothbrush (soft or hard, etc.) , but in the Fig.6, each cluster shows each toothbrush manufacturer. For example the cluster of tooth powder in the Fig.5 was merged in the cluster of toothbrush. This phenomenon is considered to be the tooth powder bought along with the goods of others in many cases.

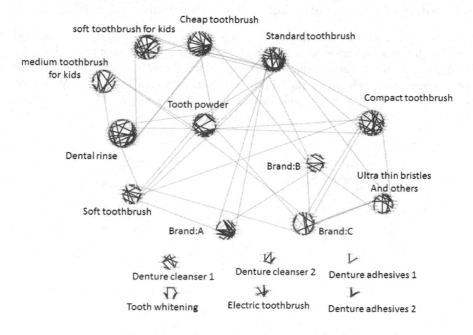

Fig. 5. Mining result without three extensions

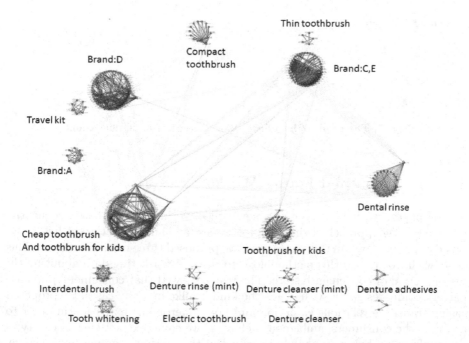

Fig. 6. Effect of the easing transitive relations

4.3   Effect of the Introduction of Node Pheromone

In this experiment, we set θ_{nodes} as 5, which means that if a goods s_a is touched less than 5 times, the node of the goods s_a is disregarded, and result was shown as the Fig.7. As you can see, a cluster which consists of tooth powder bought along with other goods deleted in the Fig.6, can be restored in the Fig.7. Moreover, some edges between related goods in same cluster are generated (see the Fig.7), due to the bypass function of this extension.

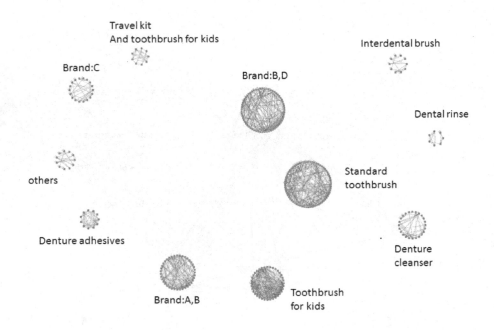

Fig. 7. The result of introduction of concept of node pheromone

5   Conclusion and Future Works

In this paper, we have proposed a new collective intelligence-based sequential pattern mining approach having high robustness and adaptability, which is ACO-based approach, and, in this paper, we have proposed three more extensions. This time, we have applied this methodology to the real marketing data about toothbrush section of convenience store. The result showed that consumers' purchase pattern compares goods with which the kind is alike in many cases. By proposed easing transitive relations extension and node pheromone extension in order to adapt to the consumers' ambiguous behavior, we could extract consumer's typical and frequent behavior unambiguously. But these result is only at initial stage, so experiment by more big data is necessary.

In this study, pheromone is only added on the edge between goods. But considering more meta level behavior is also important for marketing, for example, typical movement from drink section to food section. To make this, it is necessary to consider more complex algorithm which can form hierarchy structure. And, it is necessary to propose a new visualization method.

On the other hand, this type of mining technique has high readability. That is, for example, SVM is high performance methodology but it is difficult to understand why mining result is calculated. And, mining tools having high readability are quite important for marketer and/or medical adviser ,etc to explain the reason of mining process to their customers and/or patient. So, developing a high useful user interface of the proposed pattern mining methodology for end users is necessary.

References

1. Dorigo, M., Gambardella, L.M.: Ant colony system: a cooperative learning approach to the traveling salesman problem. IEEE Transactions on Evolutionary Computation **1**(1), 53–66 (1997)
2. Agrawal, R., Srikant, R.: Fast algorithms for mining association rules. In: Proc. 20th Int. Conf. Very Large Data Bases, VLDB, vol. 1215, pp. 487–499 (1994)
3. Agrawal, R., Srikant, R.: Mining sequential patterns. In: Proceedings of the Eleventh International Conference on Data Engineering, 1995, pp. 3–14. IEEE (1995)
4. Srikant, R., Agrawal, R.: Mining sequential patterns: generalizations and performance improvements. In: Apers, P.M.G., Bouzeghoub, M., Gardarin, G. (eds.) EDBT 1996. LNCS, vol. 1057, pp. 1–17. Springer, Heidelberg (1996)
5. Tamaki, H., Fukui, K. I., Numao, M., Kurihara, S.: Pheromone approach to the adaptive discovery of sensor-network topology. In: Proceedings of the 2008 IEEE/WIC/ACM International Conference on Web Intelligence and Intelligent Agent Technology, vol. 2, pp. 41–47. IEEE Computer Society (2008)
6. Zaki, M.J.: SPADE: An efficient algorithm for mining frequent sequences. Machine Learning **42**(1–2), 31–60 (2001)
7. Girvan, M., Newman, M.E.: Community structure in social and biological networks. Proceedings of the National Academy of Sciences **99**(12), 7821–7826 (2002)
8. Kaneiwa, K., Kudo, Y.: A sequential pattern mining algorithm using rough set theory. International Journal of Approximate Reasoning **52**(6), 881–893 (2011)
9. http://www.cytoscape.org/. Accessed 14 Sept 2014
10. The Resource for Biocomputing, Visualization, and Informatics (RBVI). RBVI Cytoscape Plugins. http://www.rbvi.ucsf.edu/cytoscape/clusterMaker2/. Accessed 10 Sept 2014

Workshop on Social Influence (SI)

Workshop on Social Influence – SI 2014 - Introduction

Radosław Michalski[1(✉)], Paulo Shakarian[2], Ingo Scholtes[3],
and Jarosław Jankowski[4]

[1] Wrocław University of Technology, Wrocław, Poland
radoslaw.michalski@pwr.edu.pl
[2] Arizona State University, Tempe, AZ, USA
shak@asu.edu
[3] ETH Zurich, Zurich, Switzerland
ischoltes@ethz.ch
[4] West Pomeranian University of Technology Szczecin, Szczecin, Poland
jjankowski@wi.zut.edu.pl

1   Introduction

The enormous popularity of the Internet and the evolution of social media create new areas for observing and modelling processes related to social sciences, such as social influence or diffusion of innovations. Now it is possible to evaluate different strategies of targeting people and observing the outcome of the process, since social graphs and social activity logs are definitely easier to obtain than two decades before. In this area several interesting topics can be distinguished, such as modelling the spread of influence, implementing and evaluating epidemiological models, tracking dynamics of diffusion processes or designing new algorithms towards these processes prediction or optimisation. This workshop aims to connect research related to both social and technical systems and one of key topics is social influence in socio-technical systems.

The website of the workshop is http://www.wosinf.org.

2   Scope of the Workshop

The digital era creates new possibilities for observing humans' behaviour, especially the one expressed on the Internet, but we also leave traces during everyday activity by making phone calls, using GPS devices or using any kind of transportation. People who meet together or communicate over the Internet or other channels constantly exchange information, rumours, spread opinions and attitudes. Sometimes it is just an information that is being passed from one to another, but it may also become the beginning of a huge change, either of an individual or even of the whole society – but in both cases it starts with becoming influenced or influencing others. Social influence is the process of a complex nature which involves our location in social network, the network structure and dynamics, time and psychological and sociological factors. At the level of an individual it is rather a psychological process but at the network scale it is strongly dependent on the network structure and its dynamics. Hence, studying

© Springer International Publishing Switzerland 2015
L.M. Aiello and D. McFarland (Eds.): SocInfo 2014 Workshops, LNCS 8852, pp. 365–367, 2015.
DOI: 10.1007/978-3-319-15168-7_45

social influence is a challenging interdisciplinary task, which, if succeeded, leads to better understanding of the surrounding world. The goal of this workshop devoted to the social influence process is to present the research on:

- how the social influence occurs in society at the level of an individual and at the network level (empirical research),
- how to simplify or find theoretical representation for this complex phenomenon (models),
- how to target the society to maximize the spread of influence or innovations diffusion (heuristics, analytical solutions),
- how to influence individuals (psychological and sociological factors, the impact of social media on the influence),
- how to achieve different goals related to social influence, like minimizing the cost of change or slowing down or speeding up this process.

As the era of static networks analysis is now moving towards dynamic networks analysis, it is a topic of great importance to observe the dynamics of the networks as well as the dynamic processes like the spread of influence in order to better understanding of the human behaviour. Here, the dynamics is being observed at two levels – the social network itself changes and this network becomes a transmission layer for another dynamic process – spread of influence. This is why there is still the open debate what plays more important role – the underlying layer or the social influence process itself. By organizing this workshop we would like to bring us closer to the answer on this question.

This workshop aims to gather researchers studying the phenomenon of social influence in networks and it is indented to be a cross-domain knowledge exchange. That is why we are willing to present the state of the art and current research in this area from different perspectives: sociology, computer science, psychology as well as mathematics and physics, making this event interdisciplinary. We believe that only by taking the advantage of all the above mentioned fields it is possible to move forward in understanding how this complex works and how the society may benefit from understanding it better.

3   Statistics on Accepted Papers

In total 18 papers were submitted to the workshop, whereas 17 were submitted as full research papers and one as a demo paper presenting spread of influence phenomenon in social networks. They followed double-blind peer review process, i.e. the names and affiliations of authors were not revealed to the reviewers. Because of this authors were asked to remove all the details that could unveil their identity. In total 17 papers were sent for reviews (authors of one paper did not prepare anonymized version of it, despite asking them to make so) and each paper was reviewed by at least two and at most four Program Committee members. Finally, five papers were accepted as research papers and one has been accepted as a demo paper – that gives the acceptance rate of 31,25% for research papers.

4   Program Committee

Chairs of the Workshop on Social Influence would like to express their gratitude to all the members of Program Committee for their commitment in the review process. It resulted in the high quality of reviews.

The PC members are the following:

Renaud Lambiotte, University of Namur, Belgium
José Fernando Mendes, University of Aveiro, Portugal
Frank Schweitzer, ETH Zurich, Switzerland
Reda Alhajj, University of Calgary, Canada
Huan Liu, Arizona State University, United States
Naoki Masuda, University of Bristol, United Kingdom
Kiran Lakkaraju, Sandia National Labs, United States
György Korniss, Rensselaer Polytechnic Institute, United States
Przemysław Kazienko, Wrocław University of Technology, Poland
Patrick Roos, University of Maryland, United States
B. Aditya Prakash, Virginia Tech, United States
Luis E C Rocha, Karolinska Institutet, Sweden
David García, ETH Zurich, Switzerland
Feng Xia, Dalian University of Technology, China
Ricardo Colomo-Palacios, Østfold University College, Norway
Dariusz Król, Bournemouth University, United Kingdom and Wrocław University of Technology, Poland
Peter-Paul van Maanen, Netherlands Organisation for Applied Scientific Research, The Netherlands
Katarzyna Musiał, King's College London, United Kingdom
Piotr Bródka, Wrocław University of Technology, Poland
Tomasz Kajdanowicz, Wrocław University of Technology, Poland
Matthias Hirth, University of Würzburg, Germany
Michał Kozielski, Silesian University of Technology, Poland
Juwel Rana, Luleå University of Technology, Sweden
Wojciech Filipowski, Silesian University of Technology, Poland
Luca Tummolini, Institute of Cognitive Sciences and Technologies, Italy

5   Organizing Committee

Paweł Knuth, Wrocław University of Technology, Poland

Acknowledgements. The workshop has been supported by the SINTELNET[1], the European Network for Social Intelligence as well as by the ENGINE project[2] that received funding from the European Union's Seventh Framework Programme for research, technological development and demonstration under grant agreement no. 316097.

---

[1] http://www.sintelnet.eu
[2] http://engine.pwr.edu.pl

Naming Game Dynamics on Pairs of Connected Networks with Competing Opinions

Albert Trias Mansilla[1(✉)], Mingming Chen[2],
Boleslaw K. Szymanski[2,3], and Josep Lluís de la Rosa Esteva[1]

[1] EASY Innovation Center, University of Girona, Girona, Spain
{albert.trias,joseplluis.delarosa}@udg.edu
[2] Network Science and Technology Center, RPI, Troy, NY, USA
{chenm8,szymab}@rpi.edu
[3] Computer Science and Management, Wroclaw University of Technology, Wroclaw, Poland

Abstract. We study the Naming Game (NG) dynamics when two disjoint networks with nodes in consensus on competing opinions are connected with new links. We consider two sets of networks; one contains several networks with real-life communities, the other networks generated with the Watts-Strogatz and Barabási-Albert models. For each set, we run NG on all the possible pairs of networks and observe whether a consensus is reached to determine network features that correlate highly with such outcome. The main conclusion is that the quality of network community structure informs network's ability to resist or exert influence from/on others. Moreover, the outcomes depend on whether Speaker-First of Listener-First NG is run and on whether a speaker or listener is biased towards high or low degree nodes. The results reveal strategies that may be used to enable and accelerate convergence to consensus in social networks.

Keywords: Social networks · Social influence · Naming Game · Simulations

1 Introduction

Research on opinion dynamics [1,2] has been concerned with the effect of social influence. Prior research has shown that the interpersonal relationships often drive large-scale changes to the opinions in the network and thus have a dominant effect on opinion adoption and spread [3]. Several models have been proposed to incorporate this effect such as the Voter Model [4], Threshold Model [5], Bass Model [6], and the Naming Game (NG) [7,8]. Unlike the other models, the Naming Game allows each node to possess more than one opinion at a time. This paper focuses on the Naming Game.

The model consists of a social network of $|V|$ agents where each of these agents has a list of opinions. In each step of the Naming Game, there are $O(|V|)$ pairwise communications between two randomly selected agents, one of which plays the role of speaker and the other the role of listener. The speaker transmits to the listener an opinion from its list. If the opinion sent is on the listener's list then both agents reduce their list to a single opinion sent by the speaker. Otherwise, the listener adds the opinion sent to its list. The order in which speaker and listener are selected has a

© Springer International Publishing Switzerland 2015
L.M. Aiello and D. McFarland (Eds.): SocInfo 2014 Workshops, LNCS 8852, pp. 368–379, 2015.
DOI: 10.1007/978-3-319-15168-7_46

strong impact on the model. Choosing the listener first increases the chance for select-ing a speaker with the degree higher than average. Consequently, in scale free net-works, hubs will be the most frequent speakers, giving rise to faster convergence to consensus [9].

Empirical social graphs exhibit strong community structure that inhibits achieving consensus. Methods and conditions for achieving it in social networks have been stu-died and included use of committed agents [8] or global external signals [10, 11].

In this paper, we study the outcomes of Naming Game in which two disconnected networks with nodes in consensus on competing opinions are joined by newly added links. We study which network has higher chance to converge the joined network to its opinion. Consequently, we focus on the so-called Binary Naming Game, in which only two opinions, A and B, and their union, AB, can appear on the list of opinions of any agent.

2   Network Properties and Community Quality

The most basic properties of a network are the number of nodes ($|V|$) and the number of edges ($|E|$). The assortative coefficient (r) measures the tendency of a node connecting to other nodes with similar degrees. A positive r indicates that most connections exist between nodes with similar degrees (assortative network), while a negative r implies a disassortative network which is often more vulnerable to random failures and targeted attacks [12]. The diameter (d) defines the longest shortest path in a network, so it is representative of the linear size of the network. Finally, the spectrum that contains the eigenvalues of the adjacency matrix is an important characteristic, especially the largest eigenvalue (λ), where a higher value of λ means a smaller diameter and more robustness of the network [12].

Among community quality metrics, modularity [13] is widely used to effectively measure the strength of the community structure found by community detection algo-rithms. This metric measures the difference between the fraction of all edges that are within the actual community and such a fraction of edges that would be inside the community in a randomized graph with the same number of nodes and the same de-gree sequence. For the given community partition of a network G= (V, E) with $|E|$ edges and $|V|$ nodes, modularity (Q) is given by

$$Q = \sum_{c \in C} \left[\frac{|E_c^{in}|}{|E|} - \left(\frac{2|E_c^{in}| + |E_c^{out}|}{2|E|} \right)^2 \right],$$

where C is the set of all the communities, $|E_c^{in}|$ is the number of edges between nodes within the specific community c, and $|E_c^{out}|$ is the number of edges from the nodes in community c to the nodes outside c.

To address well-known modularity shortcomings, Chen et al. [14] propose to modify modularity by subtracting from it the fraction of edges connecting nodes of different communities and by including community density in formula. The resulting metric, called modularity density (Q_{ds}), is defined as

$$Q_{ds} = \sum_{c \in C} \left[\frac{|E_c^{in}|}{|E|} d_c - \left(\frac{2|E_c^{in}| + |E_c^{out}|}{2|E|} d_c \right)^2 - \sum_{\substack{c' \in C \\ c' \neq c}} \frac{|E_{c,c'}|}{2|E|} d_{c,c'} \right],$$

$$d_c = \frac{2|E_c^{in}|}{|c|(|c|-1)}, \quad d_{c,c'} = \frac{|E_{c,c'}|}{|c||c'|}.$$

In the above, |c| is the size of community c, d_c is the internal density of community c, and $d_{c,c'}$ is the pair-wise density between communities c and c'.

We also use the following community quality metrics.

The number of Intra-edges $|E_c^{in}|$ is the total number of edges in the community c and it tends to be high for communities of high quality.

Intra-density, d_c in the definition of Q_{ds}, tends to be high for high quality communities.

Contraction $2|E_c^{in}|/|c|$ measures the average node intra-edge degree for edges internal to the community and it tends to be high for communities of high quality.

The number of Boundary-edges $|E_c^{out}|$ that connect nodes in community c to nodes outside c and it tends to be low for high quality communities.

Expansion $|E_c^{out}|/|c|$ measures the average inter-edge node degree for edges that connect to nodes outside the community c; it tends to be low for high quality communities.

Inter-density $|E_c^{out}|/(|c|(|V|-|c|))$ measures the inter-edge density and it tends to be low for communities with high quality.

Conductance $\frac{|E_c^{out}|}{2|E_c^{in}|+|E_c^{out}|}$ measures the fraction of edges that point outside community c; it tends to be low for communities of high quality.

Additionally, we also considered the number of communities (|C|) and the largest (highest value of) size of community (HSC) in the network.

3 Naming Game on Pairs of Networks

We study the Naming Game dynamics on pairs of networks to analyze what properties of a network define its resilience to external opinions and its ability to impose its opinion on other networks. Like in [15], we start with two disjoint networks, each with nodes in consensus on opinion different from consensus opinion in the other network. Then, we introduce links from one network to the other, modeling the response to incentives for forming new links between agents from different networks. After the NG stabilizes the opinion distribution, we record the outcome. Since our goal is to observe under what conditions the joint network reaches consensus, we discard from our results cases in which no consensus on a single opinion is reached.

We investigate the following research questions: What are the network properties that influence the outcome? How does the outcome depend on the type of Naming Game and the selection of a partner for opinion exchange? In term of influence, answers to these questions may help to identify sub-networks which are good influencers, or, opposite, which are easy to be influenced. These answers may also be useful in designing strategies for increasing the selected sub-networks resilience to influence or their ability to influence other sub-networks.

It is clear [15] that too small number of added links will not yield the consensus and very large number of links will benefit the network with the larger number of nodes. The interesting region is right in middle of these two extremes, when the outcome depends on structural properties of networks and their communities. For simplicity and brevity sake, in this paper, we only investigate the addition of a constant number of links (100), but the sizes of the two joined networks vary in our analyses, thus, also the percentage of added links does.

3.1   An Example of NG Dynamics on a Pair of Networks

Given are two networks with four nodes each. The network A has a ring topology (4Ring) while network B is fully connected (4All). All nodes in network A have opinion A, while in network B they all have opinion B. We connect both networks by a single link, and for simplicity of the analysis, change the opinions of nodes connected by this link to a mixed opinion {A, B}. The start of the scenario is shown in Fig. 1.

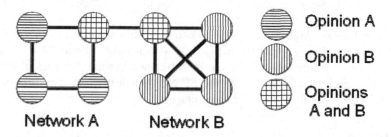

Fig. 1. The start of scenario

For the Speaker First Naming Game (SF-NG), a straightforward analysis (omitted here for the sake of the brevity) shows that both networks have a same probability, 1/8 of removing the outsiders' opinion from their nodes. However, the probability of propagating the outsiders' opinion inside each network is 3/64 for opinion A and 1/24 for opinion B. Thus, for networks with the comparable number of nodes, the one that has weaker community structure or fewer links has higher probability of propagating its consensus opinion to the other network and, at the same time, it has lower probability of getting the outsiders' opinion propagated to its own nodes.

Similar elementary analysis for the Listener First Naming Game (LF-NG) case shows that both networks have the same probability of propagating the outsiders' opinion inside each network. But network B is more likely than network A to resist permanent holding of the outsiders' opinion by its nodes. Here, the conclusion is reversed compared to the previous case and the network with more links or stronger community structure is favored to impose consensus to its opinion in LF-NG.

The simulation results corresponding to the discussed cases are shown in Tables 1 and 2.

Table 1. Percentage of games that network A wins over network B in the SF-NG followed by the difference in the number of links and by the difference in their intra-densities

A/B	3	4Ring	4All	5Ring	5All
3	0.5;0;0	0.40;-1;0.25	0.47;-3;0	0.33;-1;0.5	0.43;-7;0
4Ring	0.61;1;-0.25	0.5;0;0	0.56;-2;-0.25	0.43;-1;0.25	0.55;-6;-0.25
4All	0.52;1;-0.25	0.43;2;0.25	0.5;0;0	0.35;1;0.5	0.47;-4;0;
5Ring	0.67;2;-0.5	0.57;1;-0.25	0.65;-1;-0.5	0.5;0;0	0.61;-5;-0.5
5All	0.573;7;0	0.46;6;0.25	0.54;4;1	0.40;5;0.5	0.5;0;0

Table 2. Percentage of games that network A wins network B in the LF-NG, followed by the difference in the number of links and by the difference in intra-densities

A\B	3	4Ring	4All	5Ring	5All
3	0.5;0;0	0.42;-1;0.25	0.30;-3;0	0.37;-1;0.5	0.17;-7;0
4Ring	0.57;1;-0.25	0.5;0;0	0.36;-2;-0.25	0.44;-1;0.25	0.23;-6;-0.25
4All	0.706;3;0	0.63;2;0.25	0.5;0;0	0.56;1;0.5	0.33;-4;0
5Ring	0.64;2;-0.5	0.56;1;-0.25	0.42;-1;-0.5	0.5;0;0	0.27;-5;-0.5
5All	0.84;7;0	0.78;6;0.25	0.68;4;1	0.73;5;0.5	0.5;0;0

Tables 1 and 2 show high correlation between the difference of the number of links and the percentage of games that the network A wins network B with LF-NG. There is also a high inverse correlation between the difference in intra-densities of the networks and the percentage of wins with the SF-NG. When the intra-densities are the same, the network with more nodes has advantage.

4   Method

23 networks were generated using the Watts-Strogatz and Barabási-Albert models. Then, we used the fine-tuned Q_{ds} algorithm to detect the community structures of these networks [16]. Finally, we calculated the values of the community quality metrics on the discovered community structure of each generated network.

In terms of properties, the sizes of generated networks ranged from 100 to 1000 nodes and from 191 to 7,000 edges. The other parameters ranged as follows: the number of communities, $|C| \in [1, 104]$, the assortative coefficient $r \in [-0.1772, 0.2697]$, the network diameter $d \in [3, 38]$, the modularity density $Q_{ds} \in [0.039, 0.471]$, and the modularity $Q \in [0, 0.684]$. The quality metrics have the following ranges: intra-density, ID [0.16, 0.788], conductance CND $\in [0, 0.788]$, expansion EXP $\in [0, 5.991]$, border density BD $\in [0, 0.04]$, the number of boundary-edges BE $\in [0, 76.789]$, contraction CNT [1.418, 15.84], the number of intra-edges IE $\in [2.904, 1175.67]$. In addition we measured the number of converged games over 100 Naming Game runs, CG $\in [41,100]$, and the mean number of steps, s, that were needed to bring the game to consensus (s $\in [20, 3618]$).

Then, we selected all possible pairs of all networks for the games. Each pair was connected with $\Delta L=100$ new links between nodes of different networks. Both SF-NG and LF-NG were run 5000 times with different random generator seed for each configuration for up to M=5,000 steps. The executed algorithm is sketched in Table 3. We used three strategies for selecting the second agent for each conversation (speaker or listener) in each case. The strategies are selected by parameter x={0,1,-1} that defines probability of selecting the node i with the degree n_i is as follows:

$$p(i) = \frac{n_i^{x}}{\sum_{j=1}^{|V|} n_j^{x}}. \tag{1}$$

Thus, strategy with x=0 is the usual one, where all the neighbors have the same probability of being chosen. For strategy with x=1, the selection is biased towards high degree nodes while the opposite bias arises for strategy with for x = -1.

Table 3. Implemented NG Algorithm

```
Function NG
    End:=false; maximumSteps:=M; steps:=0;
    While !End
        For( i to |V| )
            Speaker,Listener:=SelectPairofNodes();
            localCommunication(Speaker,Listener);
        endFor
        steps:=steps+1;
        End:= convergedGame || steps==maximumSteps;
    EndWhile
EndFunction


Function localCommunication(Speaker,Listener)
    Word:=Speaker.selectWord();
    If(Listener.hasWord(Word))
        //Successful communication
        Speaker.newSynonimList(Word)
        Listener.newSynonimList(Word)
    Else
        //Unsuccessful communication
        Listener.addToSynonimListWord(Word)
    EndIf
EndFunction
```

We collected the following results.

$W_{i,j} \in [0,1], D_{i,j} \in [0,1], L_{i,j} \in [0,1], S_{i,j} \in [-1,1]$ indicate, respectively, the fraction of wins, draws, losses, and the fraction of wins less the fraction of losses over the converged games between networks c_i and c_j. However, only S was used in analysis.

Each input variable is the ratio of the differences of values of the corresponding property or community metric for networks c_i and c_j to its maximum absolute value.

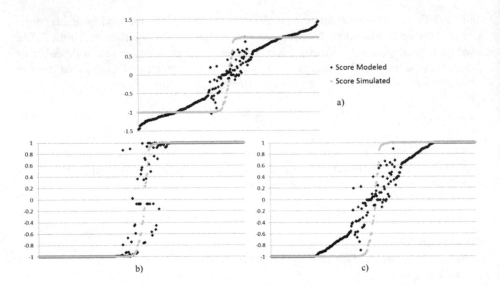

Fig. 2. Sample values of modeled score and simulated score values

We obtained linear models (lm's) using the software R [17] and the package leaps
[18].. Fig 2. shows the pairs of values obtained from simulations compared
with the ones obtained with the lm's. Fig. 2 a) shows the values of the variable
Score and a sample lm output. One can observe that the value of the modeled variable goes out of the range [-1, 1]. In such case, one option is to apply correction to
the outputs out of the boundaries, as it is shown in Fig. 2 c), to bring them into the
range. We will refer to the resulting model as the corrected lm. Another option is
to transform the variable Score to a saturated growth model, as represented in
Equation (2); and then obtain the lm of the transformed variable a. In that case, it
is important to avoid the numerical error of computing logarithm for argument 0,
thus, we rescaled outputs of the model into the range [-0.9999, 0.9999].

$$
\begin{aligned}
score &= 1 - e^a \\
1 - score &= e^a \\
a &= \begin{cases} \ln(1 + score), & score < 0 \\ -\ln(1 - score), & score \geq 0 \end{cases}
\end{aligned}
\tag{2}
$$

These models are used to predict the scores of each network pairing, and we compute the mean absolute error (MAE), the mean squared error (MSE), and the Pearson
correlation of the simulated scores with the modeled scores.

5   Results

The first observation is that there are many games that did not converge with the
$\Delta L_{AB} = 100$. Thus, in the future work, we will use ΔL_{AB} proportional to the community size to avoid that effect of a contact number of links.

The several strategies produce small variation on outcomes over all games. Yet, if we consider the global outputs, the best strategy for the LF-NG is x=-1 while the worst is x=1; opposite is true in the case of SF-NG. Even though the results show that numbers of wins in each of the two NG variants are the same, the wins come from pairings between different networks in each case. Moreover, the outcome may also be affected by the quality metrics of network communities, with modularity density Q_{ds}, being the predictor. More discussion of this case is included in Section 5.2.

5.1   Modeling Pairing Results

Table 4 shows the results obtained from the models described in Section 4. We can observe that the saturated models have a lower mean absolute error, MAE, than the corrected-lm. However, for the mean squared error, MSE, there are cases when it is higher for the saturated model than for the corrected-lm; this happens when the saturated model fits correctly more points, but when it errs, the errors are usually high compared to the corrected-lm errors, as can be observed in Fig. 2 b and Fig. 2 c.

Table 4. Evaluation metrics of the obtained models. Rows MAE, MSE and Correlation show the values for the corrected lm and the saturated model.

Game	MAE	MSE	Correlation	Lm
Speaker 0 0	0.231; 0.0924	0.1205;0.1057	0.9417;0.9395	Eq (3)
Speaker 1 0	0.3244;0.1526	0.2025; 0.1384	0.8887;0.9231	Eq(4)
Speaker -1 0	0.197; 0.099	0.105; 0.1064	0.946; 0.944;	Eq(5)
Speaker 1 -1	0.334;0.233	0.2275; 0.314	0.871; 0.832	Eq(6)
Speaker 1 1	0.2339;0.1225	0.1295;0.1365	0.923; 0.9303	Eq(7)
Speaker -1 -1	0.1329;0.05158	0.0571;0.0467	0.9696; 0.9729	Eq(8)
Listener 0 0	0.1596; 0.078	0.0799;0.099	0.935;0.9429	Eq(9)
Listener 1 0	0.2123; 0.0905	0.120; 0.0912	0.935; 0.9474	Eq(10)
Listener -1 0	0.2074; 0.1152	0.1145; 0.1156	0.9389; 0.9369	Eq(11)
Listener 1 -1	0.2425; 0.1622	0.1636;0.1939	0.9109; 0.8946	Eq(12)
Listener 1 1	0.205;0.0580;	0.1097;0.05212	0.941; 0.969	Eq(13)
Listener -1 -1	0.2291; 0.1252;	0.1054;0.1384	0.9465;0.9234	Eq(14)

In general, we can observe that in SF-NG, the networks with low community quality perform well; as indicated by their low or even negative modularity density Q_{ds}, large number of border-edges, BE, high conductance CND, expansion EXP, and the number of nodes, |V| (an exception is Equation (8)), but negatively correlated with contraction CNT. The score equations for SF-NG are listed below.

$$score = -7.25 \ 10^{-4} + 1.468|V| - 0.852Qds - 0.9093d - 0.892HSC + 0.2811\,BE \quad (3)$$
$$score = 0.1065 + 1.14|V| - 0.671s + 1.40CND - 0.279HSC - 0.857BD \quad (4)$$
$$score = -0.0609 + 1.42|E| - 0.457CNT + 0.1366r - 0.233HSC - 0.8123d \quad (5)$$
$$score = 0.1009 + 1.032|V| + 0.5058|E| - 0.371CNT - 0.389s + 0.103EXP \quad (6)$$
$$score = -0.001158 + 1.64|V| - 0.892|E| + 0.983|C| + 0.68966CG - 0.6978s \quad (7)$$
$$score = -5.64 \ 10^{-4} - 1.65|V| + 2.373|E| + 0.585|C| - 0.1748CNT - 0.242d \quad (8)$$

In case of LF-NG, we can observe that models correlate negatively with contraction CNT and the number of nodes |V| (with the exception of Equation (14).). At the same time, the models correlate positively with expansion EXP, conductance CND and the number of boarder edges, BE. This suggests that networks with low Q_{ds} perform well. The score equations for LF-NG are listed below.

$$score = 5.31 \ 10^{-5} - 1.818|V| + 2.216|E| + 0.7939|C| + 0.6381\lambda - 0.2589 \ CNT \qquad (9)$$
$$score = -0.00949 - 1.7685|V| + 1.674|E| + 0.878|C| + 0.95\lambda + 0.2188EXP \qquad (10)$$
$$score = -0.01625 + 1.4|E| - 0.4479CNT - 0.6352d + 0.0926r - 0.170HSC \qquad (11)$$
$$score = 0.005394 - 1.315|V| + 1.719|E| + 0.647|C| + 0.6157\lambda + 0.3485CND \qquad (12)$$
$$score = -3.62 \ 10^{-4} - 1.477|V| + 1.212|E| + 0.7831|C| + 1.265\lambda + 0.2234BE \qquad (13)$$
$$score = -5.15 \ 10^{-4} + 0.959|V| + 0.335|E| - 0.586s - 0.335HSC + 0.448EXP \qquad (14)$$

In Section 3.1, we observed that LF-NG with strategy x=0 is highly correlated with the number of edges |E|; while SF-NG with strategy x=0 is highly correlated with border-density BD. Our simulations show that for LF-NG with x=0, Score S is highly correlated with the number of edges |E| and inversely correlated with the number of nodes, |V|. In the case of SF-NG with x=0, Score S it is directly proportional to |V| and seems that networks with lower community quality have an advantage.

5.2   Selection of Communication Partners in NG

In Section 4, we proposed a set of three strategies for selecting the second agent in each conversation. It is interesting question which strategy provides the best performance in various situations. To answer this question, we used the real social networks with known community structures: football [19], dolphin [20], karate [21] and Santafe [22]. We simulated each network paired with its copy using strategies x=1 and x=-1, (for example [football x=1] vs. [football x=-1]) with the addition of 100 links. Table 5 shows for each network which strategy is the best when each network is paired with its copy. These preliminary results suggest that the best strategy selection can be affected by the community structure quality of the networks, estimated with Q_{ds}.

Table 5. Performance of strategies x=1 and x=-1 in the game of two copies of the same network. A value of 1 indicates winning by x=1 strategy, while -1 indicates advantage of x=-1 strategy.

	Q_{ds}	SF-NG	LF-NG
Football	0.4281	1	-1
Karate	0.1828	-1	1
Dolphin	0.1368	-1	1
Santafe	0.1043	-1	1

We tested the effect of increasing the number of links being added between communities until the NG converged and reached consensus on a single opinion. This avoided the annoying lack of convergence in many relatively poorly connected networks. The results are shown in Table 6; the conclusions implied by results in Table 6 are in agreement with the ones drawn on the basis of results shown in Table 5. Networks with low Q_{ds} obtained better results with x=-1strategy for SF-NG and with x=1

Table 6. Performance of strategy x=1 and x=-1 in the game of two copies of the same network. A value of 1 indicates advantage of x=1 strategy, while -1 indicates winning by x=-1 strategy; values of 0.5 or -0.5 indicate slight advantage of the corresponding strategy.

Q_{ds}	SF-NG	LF-NG
0.039	-1	1
0.039	-1	1
0.046	-1	1
0.084	-1	1
0.134	-1	1
0.163	-1	1
0.173	-1	1
0.21	-0.5	-1
0.246	0.5	-1
0.323	1	-1
0.339	1	-1
0.343	1	-1
0.356	1	-1
0.378	1	-1
0.407	1	-1
0.408	1	-1
0.418	1	-1
0.422	1	-1
0.424	1	-1
0.439	1	-1
0.449	1	-1
0.469	1	-1
0.471	1	-1

strategy for LF-NG. In contrast, networks with high Q_{ds} obtained better results with x=1 strategy for SF-NG and with x=-1 strategy for LF-NG. The results were obtained by treating $Q_{ds} \geq 0.343$ as high and $Q_{ds} \leq 0.173$ as low. Which strategy is the best for Q_{ds} values between (0.173, 0.343) is not clear, and the answer may also depend on the type of game (SF-NG or LF-NG). In our results, we can observe that with $Q_{ds} = 0.246$, SF-NG with x=1 strategy has an advantage while with $Q_{ds} = 0.21$, x=-1 strategy preforms better. Hence, the turning point is likely to be between these two values. We will further investigate the position of this turning point in future work.

The results also indicate that the behavior of each strategy depends on network structure as measured by parameters, such as Q_{ds}. This probably limits the precision of prediction that can be obtained with linear models. It should also be noted that the set of networks used contains more networks with high Q_{ds} than with the low one; it may indicate why the best strategies on average were x=-1 for LF-NG and x=1 for SF-NG.

6   Conclusions

It is important to notice that when we stage a NG, we modify the initial properties of the networks by adding new links that may introduce significant change to the community structures. The preliminary case study described here has shown that the type of NG and bias in selecting the speaker or listener influence to which opinion the two networks are likely to converge.

The main conclusion of this paper is that the quality of a network community structure is directly related to network's ability to resist or exert influence from/on others. We also observe that the modularity density Q_{ds} is highly predictive of which network is most likely to impose its opinion for consensus in the merged networks. LF-NG scores are highly correlated with the number of edges |E| and highly inversely correlated with the number of nodes |V|. In contrast, SF-NG scores are highly positively correlated with the number of nodes |V|. Furthermore, when the two networks have similar sizes (both in terms of the numbers of edges |E| and nodes |V|), the network with higher community structure quality performs poorly in SF-NG but well with LF-NG.

Acknowledgments. This work was supported in part by the Army Research Laboratory under Cooperative Agreement Number W911NF-09-2-0053, by the Army Research Office Grant W911NF-12-1-0546, by the Office of Naval Research Grant No. N00014-09-1-0607, by the Polish National Science Centre, the decision no. DEC-2013/09/B/ST6/02317, by the EU's 7FP under grant agreement no 316097, by the TIN2013-48040-R (QWAVES) *Nuevos métodos de automatización de la búsqueda social basados en waves de preguntas*, the IPT20120482430000 (MIDPOINT) *Nuevos enfoques de preservación digital con mejor gestión de costes que garantizan su sostenibilidad*, and VISUAL AD, RTC-2014-2566-7 and GEPID, RTC-2014-2576-7, as well as the *grup de recerca consolidat* CSI-ref. 2014 SGR 1469. The views and conclusions contained in this document are those of the authors and should not be interpreted as representing the official policies, either expressed or implied, of the Army Research Laboratory or the U.S. Government.

References

1. Schellings, T.C.: Micromotives and Macrobehavior. Norton (1978)
2. Castellano, C., Fortunato, S., Loreto, V.: Statistical physics of social dynamics. Rev. Mod. Phys. **81**, 591–646 (2009)
3. Carr, J.: Applications of Centre Manifold Theory. Springer, US (1982)
4. Clifford, P., Sudbury, A.: A model for spatial conflict. Biometrika. **60**, 581–588 (1973)
5. Granovetter, M.: Threshold Models of Collective Behavior. Am. J. Sociol. **83**, 1420–1443 (1978)
6. Bass, F.M.: A New Product Growth for Model Consumer Durables. Manage. Sci. **15**, 215–227 (1969)
7. Steels, L.: A self-organizing spatial vocabulary. Artif. Life. **2**, 319–332 (1995)
8. Lu, Q., Korniss, G., Szymanski, B.K.: The Naming Game in social networks: community formation and consensus engineering. J. Econ. Interact. Coord. **4**, 221–235 (2009)
9. Dall'Asta, L., Baronchelli, A., Barrat, A., Loreto, V.: Nonequilibrium dynamics of language games on complex networks. Phys. Rev. E **74**, 036105 (2006)
10. Mazzitello, K.I., Candia, J., Dossetti, V.: Effects of Mass Media and Cultural Drift in a Model for Social Influence. Int. J. Mod. Phys. C **18**, 10 (2006)
11. Candia, J., Mazzitello, K.I.: Mass media influence spreading in social networks with community structure (2008)
12. Mahadevan, P., Krioukov, D.: The Internet AS-level topology: three data sources and one definitive metric. In: ACM SIGCOMM (2006)

13. Newman, M., Girvan, M.: Finding and evaluating community structure in networks. Phys. Rev. E **69**, 026113 (2004)
14. Chen, M., Nguyen, T., Szymanski, B.: A new metric for quality of network community structure. ASE Hum. **2**, 226–240 (2013)
15. Schecki, K., Holyst, J.: Bistable-monostable transitoin in the Ising model on two connected complex networks. Physical Review E, 031110 (2009)
16. Chen, M., Kuzmin, K., Szymanski, B.: Community Detection via Maximization of Modularity and Its Variants. IEEE Trans. Comput. Soc. Syst. **1**, 46–65 (2014)
17. R Core Team: R: A Language and Environment for Statistical Computing (2013). http://www.r-project.org/
18. Lumley, T.: leaps: regression subset selection (2009). http://cran.r-project.org/package=leaps
19. Girvan, M., Newman, M.E.J.: Community structure in social and biological networks. Proc. Natl. Acad. Sci. U. S. A. **99**, 7821–7826 (2002)
20. Lusseau, D.: The emergent properties of a dolphin social network. Proc. R. Soc. London. Ser. B Biol. Sci. **270**, S186–S188 (2003)
21. Zachary, W.: An information flow model for conflict and fission in small groups. J. Anthropol. Res. **33**, 452–473 (1977)
22. Newman, M.E.: The structure of scientific collaboration networks. Proc. Natl. Acad. Sci. U. S. A. **98**, 404–409 (2001)

Threshold of Herd Effect for Online Events in China

Tieying Liu[1(✉)], Kai Chen[2], and Yang Zhong[1]

[1] School of International and Public Affairs, Shanghai Jiao Tong University, Shanghai, China
(tyliu,zhongyang)@sjtu.edu.cn
[2] Institute of Image Communication and Information Processing,
Shanghai Jiao Tong University, Shanghai, China
kchen@sjtu.edu.cn

Abstract. Herd effect, as a way people are influenced by others, is popular in Internet. Prior empirical work has shown that when the online purchase passes one particular threshold, it is more likely that people are influenced by the product purchase may become hot. For online events, is there the same phenomena? Based on the data collected from SinaWeibo, the largest microblog in China, we use the fluctuation scaling method to analyze the influence process online. We also found the particular threshold for online events. Once the follow-up number of some event surpasses a particular threshold of popularity, collective behavior is easily to be observed. Interestingly, we classified all events into three types, political events, social events and non-public events. The threshold for these different types of events varies. The lowest threshold for social events can be explained by some offline surveys too.

Keywords: Herd effect · Online events · Collective behavior · Social influence

1 Introduction

In our society, individual's decision is often influenced by others. For these decisions, some are rational, but others are not. When facing with the incomplete information, people are easily to follow others' behavior and make the same decision. This kind of phenomena that people do what others do, is commonly defined as herd effect.

Nowadays, with the popularity of internet, the herd behavior is more likely to be observed for online shopping behavior. It seems that more goods and products are exposed to consumers online, but compared with the traditional offline purchase, people have less chance to try and experience the products. When people face more uncertainty, herd behavior is more possible. They rely more on the others' comments about it. People's decision is more liked to be influenced by others. The persuasive use of internet change social influence among people[1].

Likely, people prefer to download software or purchase something just based on other users' comments or hit number instead of their own information and judgment. This kind of herding has been observed in many occasions. But we wonder whether there is a threshold that may help promote the herding phenomena? That means we wonder how many previous hits may push others to follow others' action.

© Springer International Publishing Switzerland 2015
L.M. Aiello and D. McFarland (Eds.): SocInfo 2014 Workshops, LNCS 8852, pp. 380–389, 2015.
DOI: 10.1007/978-3-319-15168-7_47

Onnela & Reed-Tsochas[2] tracked the popularity of a complete set of applications installed to study social influence processes. They captured and analyzed collective behavior with standard fluctuation scaling method and found that when applications' popularity crosses a particular threshold of around 50 times per day, social influence processes become highly correlated among the users, thus propelling some of the applications to extraordinary levels of popularity. Below this threshold, the collective effect of social influence appears to vanish almost entirely.

This inspires our curiosity about the popularity process of online events. The software downloading is one kind of online shopping behavior. People follow others' comment or choice to determine their own commercial action. Such herd effect has rational idea behind of that, because people can benefit from others experience. But in the social area, we wonder whether herd effect is also a major factor of social influence that propel online collective behavior, whether there is such a threshold for online spontaneous action, and if so, for different types of events, whether the threshold varies.

In this paper, we designed to test the social influence threshold for online events in China. In order to find the factor correlated to the social influence, we classified all online events into three categories: political public events, social public events and non-public events. Such classification may help understand people's interest on different types of events and their tendency to make collective behavior.

We found that people do intend to behave collectively when the participation for one online event surpasses a particular threshold. Such collective intention has a difference on varied events. We found that people easily collectively behave on social events most, and while on non-public events least.

We begin Section 2 by introducing our data collection and classification. Section 3 explains fluctuation scaling method we use. Section 4 gives experimental results. Section 5 concludes.

2   Data

2.1   Data Collection and Screening

Our research is based on hot events from Sina Weibo. As the largest microblog platform in China, Sina Weibo has 57 percent of Chinese microblog users. People catch, share and diffuse information across the site. We collected over 14 million of posts that were collected from Sina Weibo between September 14, 2012 and July 11, 2013.

We intend to study people's collective behavior and correlated influence. So we prefer to study the hot events that attract people's attention. Hot events surely refer to the incidents attracting much attention, as quantitatively expressed with great number of replies and follow-up threads. It is very possible that many users initiate their own microblogs with the same topic. So to define hot events, one way for us is to collect all the threads about these hot events, combine the threads of the same topic together, and analyze one event's attention received and predict other events based on data we collect. But collecting all data from the SinaWeibo may be regarded as the risky attack to the website server. On the other hand, such definition based on all the threads from only one website does not consider online hot events as a whole, and may exclude some events which are hot but not under much discussion on SinaWeibo. The hot events defined with this method cannot represent the Internet as a whole.

People use microblog to get information and talk about the hot events. Generally, the hot events online as a whole also draw attention in the microblog world. The authoritative websites hot events rankings offer us a good reference. These authoritative websites cover a larger landscape of data and have their own unique algorithms to ensure its credibility and reliability. We adopted real-time hot events ranking lists from famous search engines in China as our microblog hot events topic source, including Baidu Ranking (top.baidu.com), Souhu Ranking (top.sogou.com), Tenet Ranking (top.soso.com), and Sina Ranking (huati.weibo.com).

We caught the top-ten hot events every ten minutes from the rankings of these websites real-time updated list. We searched the titles of these hot events from Google news (news.google.com) and Baidu news (news.baidu.com) and obtained more text information and key words of this hot events using TF-IDF(Term Frequency–Inverse Document Frequency)[3]. With the text information and key words, we parsed and crawled the data from Sina Weibo to get all the posts on these topics.

In our ongoing study, we followed the online data for ten months and caught over 14 million of threads. But there are many spammers online. To remove such noises we select the active users by calculating the users and their friends' activities and relationship. We use the following formula to calculate each user's score.

$$s_i = \sum_n n|U_i^n| + N_i^{(1)} \tag{1}$$

Where,

$N_i^{(0)}$ the number of user i's posts and reposts.

$N_i^{(1)}$ the number of user i's friend posts and reposts.

$|U_i^n|$ the cardinality of the set U_i^n

$s_i = 0 \; if \; N_i^{(0)} < T_c \; (T_c = 3)$

We used 24 hours as a study window. The popularity of the first five hours was given and we used these data to predict and observe the following 19 hours popularity for the present event. We suppose if the prediction result was between 20% higher or lower than the real figure, we set the prediction result as accurate.

2.2   Data Classification

This study manually divided all events into three categories: political public affairs, social public affairs and non-public affairs, based on relative political and public theories about the definition of political and public affairs.

Public affairs can be defined from different perspectives. Based on the state theory, states originated from the transfer of public power, carry three basic functions, legislation, administration and jurisdiction. From this perspective, public affairs refer to events with regard to state sovereignty and legitimacy. It is also defined as the management of social affairs, which is concerned with common interests. In addition, it can also be regarded as personal experience of public activities [4].

Political public affairs are related to the political system, including legislation, maintenance of social order, public safety, sovereignty, diplomatic relationships, and derivative administrative issues such as bureaucratic administration, fiscal administration and government internal control. Political public affairs are not directly related to public interests. People's concern on political affairs shows their attitudes, values, and beliefs toward the society and government. People's agreement on this kind of public affairs represents the fundamental support for the political system and government governance, so the political participation ties to the evaluation of how well political institutions conform to a person's sense of what is right [5]. The conflicts arising from political disagreement are tough to solve since they are concerned with basic values and beliefs. That is why it is difficult to reach agreement on the political appeal of collective events in reality.

The other kind of public affairs are closely related to people's daily life and interest. Public affairs involve members of the whole society and affect people's interests most. They are broadly defined as social public affairs, including education, science and technology, medical and health system, and transportation etc. [6]. Social public affairs influence people's interests, so people's concern on social public affairs is interest driven and unrelated to personal values and beliefs. Due to the close relationship with the public interest, people may pay great attention, and behave radically or emotionally to express their appeal or satisfaction. However, such conflicts are not caused by fundamental values or beliefs, but due to their temporary benefit requirement or emotional contagion. Once their interest is satisfied or their outrage calms down, their behaviors will stop. People's support for some social events may change very quickly once their interests are harmed. Generally, social events pose little harm on the political system or the regime.

Beside political public events and social public events, all other events are defined as non-public events here. These events consists of entertaining incidents that attract people's attention, which basically have no influence on the public, such as pop stars' private affairs or fancy and funny events. People's concern on these affairs is purely out of their curiosity, unrelated to their own interests or personal values.

Table 1 displays the descriptive findings of the collective hot events data obtained from Sina Weibo. Among all hot events, 54.1% are non-public events, 33.5% are social public events, and 12.4% are political public events. Over half of the total hot events are non-public events. The number of political hot events is the least among them all, with a total number of 513. The total number of public events, including both political events and social public events, is 1897, which accounts for 46% of the total.

Table 1. Descriptive data of three types of online hot events

	Political events	Social events	Non-public events	All events
Number of events	513	1384	2238	4135
Average follow-up	2046	2171	1656	1877*
Percent of total events	12.4%	33.5%	54.1%	100%

*The average follow-up of all events here is the weighted average of the three types of events.

3   Research Methodology

We use fluctuation scaling method to study to what extent an individual's behavior is influenced by others. Fluctuation scaling has been applied to study the complex systems whose interacting elements participate in dynamic process. The activity of various elements is often different and the fluctuation in the activity of an element grows monotonically with the average activity. This relationship is often of the form "fluctuations ≈ const. × average_", where the exponent α is predominantly in the range [1/2, 1]. This power law has been observed in a very wide range of disciplines, ranging from population dynamics through the Internet to the stock market and it is often treated under the names Taylor's law or fluctuation scaling [7]. Here we use fluctuation scaling method to study the possible social influence of online behavior.

In our study, we define $f_i(t)$ as the number of follow-ups for event i between times t-1 and t. Fluctuation scaling methodology relates the temporal average and SD of $f_i(t)$ through the relationship $\sigma_i \propto \mu_i^{\alpha}$. This motivates us to identify whether there is region where the relationship between $\log \mu_i$ and $\log \alpha_i$ for different values of i is linear. The exponent α , as the fluctuation scaling index expressed on the line, is the slope. Although α lies in the rather narrow range [1/2,1], its value is crucial as an indicator of statistical coupling in the system. If the follow-up behavior of an event is independent of the behaviors of others, one would expect α =1/2, whereas if the follow-up behavior is fully correlated with others, one would expect α =1.

μ_i and σ_i are obtained from the following equation:

$$\langle f_i \rangle \equiv \mu_i = \frac{1}{T_i} \sum_{t=1}^{T} f_i(t)$$

$$\sigma_i = (\frac{1}{T_i - 1} \sum_{t=1}^{T} [f_i(t) - \langle f_i \rangle]^2)^{1/2}$$

Where T_i is the specific time series length for event i.

Throughout the paper we use life length to mean the time it takes for event to receive 90% of all their retweets in our dataset.

4   Results and Discussion

We use fluctuation scaling method to test different types of events to see whether people's behavior online is influenced by others.

Table 2. Experimental results of fluctuation scaling for different types events

Events type	log(μx) of transition	Average daily follow-up of the threshold	α1	α2
All events	-1.0	29	0.56205	0.83714
Political events	-1.1	23	0.50625	0.82301
Social events	-1.2	18	0.59116	0.84246
Non-public events	-0.7	57	0.56662	0.82916

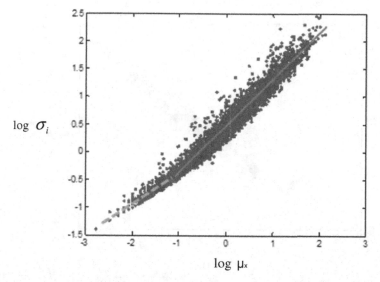

Fig. 1. Results for all online hot events. Two qualitatively different regimes emerge, and are separated by a cross-over point located at log μx = -1 The first individual regime is characterized by the exponent α I ≈ 0.56, and the second, collective regime by α C ≈ 0.83.

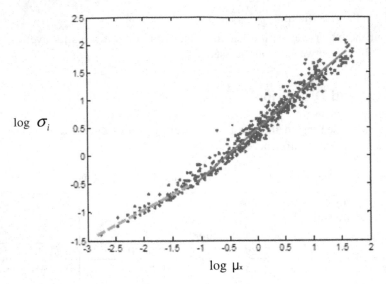

Fig. 2. Results for the online political events are plotted here. Two qualitatively different regimes emerge, and are separated by a cross-over point located at log μ_x = -1.1. The first individual **regime** is characterized by the exponent $\alpha_I \approx 0.50$, and the second, collective regime by $\alpha C \approx 0.82$.

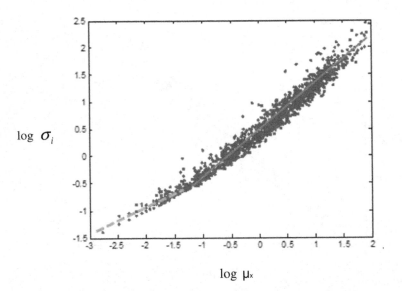

Fig. 3. Results for the online social events are plotted here. Two qualitatively different regimes emerge, and are separated by a cross-over point located at log μ_x = -1.2. The first individual regime is characterized by the exponent $\alpha I \approx 0.59$, and the second, collective regime by $\alpha C \approx 0.84$.

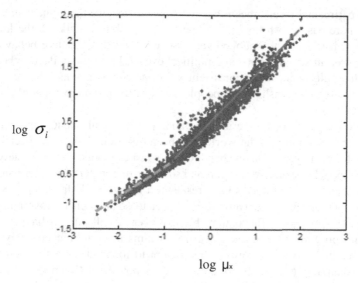

$\log \sigma_i$

$\log \mu_x$

Fig. 4. Results for the online non-public events are plotted here. Two qualitatively different regimes emerge, and are separated by a cross-over point located at log μ_x= -0.7. The first individual regime is characterized by the exponent α I ≈ 0.57, and the second, collective regime by α C ≈ 0.83.

In Fig.1 of all events, when μ_x= -1, we obviously observe that the events in the figure are separated into two parts. For the first part α ≈ 0.56 which is close to 1/2, it means people's follow-up behavior is not influenced by the system. They make their decision individually not collectively. For the second part α ≈ 0.83 which is close to 1, it means people follow-up the events based on the systematic information given. We record the data every 5 minutes. The transition between the two regimes takes place at approximately log(μ_x) = -1, which translates into an average daily activity of $24 \times 12 \times 10^{-1}$ ≈ 29 new follow-up a day. So, 29 follow-ups for one event is the threshold. If the number of follow-up is less than 18 per day, the follow-up behavior is nearly uncorrelated and social influence is negligible. If the number of follow-up is more than 18 per day, the follow-up behavior is influenced by others. Such influence will induce collective behavior easily.

This result shows that people's online behavior is really influenced by others once the number of follow-up surpass some level. We wonder whether some influence varies for different types of events and test for the classified events separately.

Different types of events results are shown in Fig. 2, 3, 4. We find that for different types of events, the thresholds vary. Social Events have the lowest threshold of transition from individual behavior to collective behavior. Once the number of some social event surpasses 18 per day, people's behavior starts to correlate with others. While the threshold for political events is a little bit higher, that is 23 per day. The highest threshold is for non-public events is 57.

The above experimental results mean that social events receive the highest attention and people are more easily to follow these events. Non-public events are the largest part of all, but it is harder for non-public events to be followed. Collective behavior is easily to be observed in social events, and political events. From the collective behavior's angle, such results seem to be consistent with our common sense. Since social events have the closest relationship with people's daily life and interest, people easily collectively behave.

Chinese collective behavior online also explains partly social phenomenon. China, as the second largest economy in the world, has been questioned about its social and political stability for many years. On one hand, China's fast economic growth ensures the government to get people's extensive support and social prosperity. On the other hand, its mounting political and social problems have resulted in many fragile factors [8]. Social influence may gather people collectively with respect to some events. Government is worried about the possible social fluctuations brought over by collective behaviors. The online censorship program of Chinese government aims at curtailing collective actions. Such censorship is oriented toward the attempt to forestall collective activities [9]. However, the anxiety about collective events does not affect China's regime stability and social prosperity. The 2013 Pew Survey of Global Attitudes showed that 85% of Chinese were "very satisfied" with their country's direction, compared with 31% of Americans.

Yu [10] elaborates Chinese society's resilience from the perspective of the nature of social influence and conflict in China. He explains that nowadays, collective events are becoming increasingly frequent year by year, but eighty percent of the collective events are attributed to the conflict of social interest [11]. These events are featured with the safe-guard of participants' rights. In other words, such events are brought about by conflicts of people's interest against the government, rather than conflicts of fundamental values or beliefs. Participants only want to pursue their own rights and interests within the current legal system, involving no intention to challenge current legal and social rules. Collective behaviors are passive in nature. People can be easily influenced when their interests are harmed and their needs cannot be satisfied. They do not take actions purely for political purposes. Social influence is more effective when people's personal interests are affected. In one word, the current collective events are about issues of social interests rather than politics. That is why Chinese society can maintain stable though facing mounting social problems.

A recent survey conducted in five of China's biggest cities reveals that Chinese are concerned with public affairs, but they have more concern on affairs that are closely related to livelihood issues such as house price, inflation, medical care, education, income and social welfare. In contrast to the high concern on social affairs, people show low interest on political reform, human right and freedom [12].

The above offline survey results actually support our experimental results. That is people are most easily collectively behave on social events, followed by political events. Although non-public events share the largest part of online information, but people are not easily collectively to pay much attention on this type of events.

5   Conclusions

We collected over four thousand online events and classified them into three types to analyze people's online behavior and influence. We found that people's online behavior has obvious herd effect once the number of follow-up for some event surpass a particular threshold 29 follow-ups per day. At the same time, we found the collective behavior varies for different type of events. For the social events that have closely relate to people's interest and benefit, people are easily to be influenced by others. 18 follow-ups will attract people's attention and induce collective behavior online. While for the political events, the threshold of herd effect is 23 follow-ups per day, which shows that people has less attention on political events than social events. Non-public events are the largest part of online information, which accounts 54 percent of total, but the threshold for non-public events is 57 per day. People do not easily collectively behave on non-public events.

Acknowledgement. This work was supported in part by 973 Program (2010CB731401, 2010CB731406), NSFC (61025005, 61129001), and the 111 Program (B07022)".

References

1. Duan, W., Gu, B., Whinston, A.B.: Analysis of herding on the internet-an empirical investigation of online software download. In: AMCIS (2005)
2. Onnela, J.-P., Reed-Tsochas, F.: Spontaneous emergence of social influence in online systems. Proceedings of the National Academy of Sciences 107(43), 18375–18380 (2010)
3. Salton, G., McGill, M.J., Introduction to modern information retrieval (1983)
4. Wang, Y.K.: Research on Fundamental Issues of Public Administration. China Administration Management 11, 11 (2001). (in Chinese)
5. Muller, E.N., Jukam, T.O.: On the meaning of political support. The American Political Science Review, 1561–1595 (1977)
6. Wang, L.F.: Social Intension of Public Administration. Political Research 3(78.84) (2001) (in Chinese)
7. Eisler, Z., Bartos, I., Kertesz, J.: Fluctuation scaling in complex systems: Taylor's law and beyond 1. Advances in Physics 57(1), 89–142 (2008)
8. Shirk, S.L.: China: The fragile superpower. Oxford University Press (2007)
9. King, G., et al.: How Censorship in China Allows Government Criticism but Silences Collective Expression. American Political Science Review 42, 1–38
10. Yu, J.R.: Interest, Authority and Order: Collective Events Analysis of Villagers against Local Governments. China Countryside Observation 4, 70–76 (2000). (in Chinese)
11. Yu, J.R.: Dilemma of Controlling Social Revenge Events in China. Contemporary World and Socialism 1, 4–9 (2008). (in Chinese)
12. Zhong, Y., Chen, Y.: Regime Support in Urban China. Asian Survey 53(2), 369–392 (2013)

Identifying Bridges for Information Spread Control in Social Networks

Michał Wojtasiewicz$^{(\boxtimes)}$ and Krzysztof Ciesielski

Institute of Computer Science, Polish Academy of Sciences, Warsaw, Poland
m.wojtasiewicz@phd.ipipan.waw.pl, k.ciesielski@ipipan.waw.pl

Abstract. In this paper scalable method for cluster analysis based on random walks is presented. The main aim of the algorithm introduced in this paper is to detect dense subgraphs. Provided method has additional feature. It identifies groups of vertices which are responsible for information spreading among found clusters. The algorithm is sensitive to vertices assignment uncertainty. It distinguishes groups of nodes which form sparse clusters. These groups are mostly located in places crucial for information spreading so one can control signal propagation between separated dense subgraphs by using algorithm provided in this work.

Keywords: Information spread · Clusters · Scalable · Signal transfer · Random walks

1 Introduction

One of the most general occurences in the world is formation of structures of elements connected with different relations. These are called networks. Knowledge about subsets that contain information about the network has high potential of use in data mining. The most desired subsets to find in networks are called clusters. Dense subsets can be interpreted in many ways. This creates a necessity for algorithms that can cope with diversity of possible meanings. Commonness of networks in everyday life (e.g. the Internet, data sets of citings) implies using advanced methods to analyze them. The most common and natural coding method for networks are graphs. Graph structure and the way of information spread in networks are the most interesting fields of research in social network community detection. In this paper scalable method of cluster analysis based on random walks is presented. The method divides a graph into subsets, where some of them can be used for information spread control. The main aim of the algorithm presented in this paper is to detect dense subgraphs. The method provides clustering sensitive to vertices assignment uncertainty. As a result of a introduced Locally Aggregated Random Walks (LARW) algorithm one receives division which distinguishes groups of nodes responsible for signal transfer between clusters.

© Springer International Publishing Switzerland 2015
L.M. Aiello and D. McFarland (Eds.): SocInfo 2014 Workshops, LNCS 8852, pp. 390–401, 2015.
DOI: 10.1007/978-3-319-15168-7_48

2   Related Works

So far many algorithms for detecting communities in networks has been developed. From most popular and most frequent used techniques one has to distinguish four categories. Because of the diversity of cluster analysis problems, each of the areas is used in different situations. Choice of a method of identifying clusters should be made so that the available knowledge about the data could be used the most effectively. These are methods from categories: *bisection methods, hierarchical methods, combinatorical methods* and *spectral methods* [3]. In practical questions one mostly deals with large graphs, which frequently consist of houndreds of thousands nodes and millions of edges. In such situations there is a limited number of methods which provide a solution in a short time. This is because of complexity problems and difficulty of finding dense sets in large networks. Initial analysis, e.g. estimation of expected number of dense sets, is hard to perform as well. These are the reasons why hierarchical methods are most preffered to use in such situations. The most efficient algorithms operate on smaller sets and then agregate results with a determined stop condition. [7][6]. In this paper authors introduced a hierarchical, scalable algorithm of cluster analysis. This algorithm returns a very special division. Among standard clusters one can distinguish subgraphs which are sparse and cannot be assigned to any dense clusters. These special subgraphs enable control of signal propagation in between clusters. This subject is connected to feature of MCL algorithm and it was fully discussed in section 3.3.

Many of articles speaking about modeling or controlling the information spread in networks focus on greedy selection of vertices that have the highest influence in graph [5]. The main problem with this approach is that user starts with one most influential vertex and then greedy algorithm searches for most influential node in given neighbourhood. It can be easily seen that this kind of thinking produces very local result. Additionaly it is very probable that first most influential vertex is deep in cluster. Finding few most influential nodes in social networks in that way do not solve problem of signal propagation between clusters. An occurence similar to the feature connected to the MCL algorithm (section 3.3) was noticed in paper [2]. The author of [2] paper noticed that vertices of high degree gather more information in their neighborhood, while vertices of lower degree quickly transfer information inside the graph. It was noticed, that in dense subsets information are transfered relatively fast. It happens because such subsets have many internal edges and fewer on the outside. That creates the problem of communication between the clusters, which should be solved by initiating signal transfer on the boundaries of clusters. This is what LARW does. Interesting approach for identifing influential veritices was presented in [1]. Authors analyzed dynamic social networks and they developed algorithm which assigns *dynamic influential value*. This coefficient is based on probability of spreading influence through time. It is calculated in a greedy way so there is again problem with local optimum. Because it takes into account information from future states of network it is useless in static case analysis. In work [4] authors introduced approach in which there can be more than one type of influence. Every node can have a *opinion* which is continous function of time. Despite that interesting approach authors assume that influence of node is given by its degree. This is not so simple. It is easy to imagine that vertex can have small degree but signal started in this vertex will propagate very fast. This will happen in situation when that node is connected to several dense clusters.

In every work mentioned above vertices were considered singly. Introduced in this paper algorithm provides division in graph where some groups of vertices can be used to signal diffusion control.

3   LARW Algorithm

3.1   Motivation

Popular way of dealing with a complex problem is to divide it into smaller parts. The point of this process is to minimize the complexity without losing key data. One has to find optimal trade-off between global and local approach. Algorithm presented in this paper is an answer to a problem of scalability of MCL method [10]. That algorithm relies on simulating random walks on network. This procedure comes down to multiplication of stochastic matrices. There is a computational problem related. Because of multiplying very large matrices one has to have huge amount of operation memory and computational power. At the beginning of the process stochastic matrix is sparse but it becomes dense after several steps. As the matrix gets more and more dense the operation memory starts to become insufficient. It regards even small graphs. Solution suggested by the authors is based on execution computations on specific subsets of graph. Dense subsets are seperated by using the MCL algorithm locally and then aggregating results. This is a hierarchical method which gives in result multilevel clustering. That division has an important advantage. Among selected clusters there are subgraphs which are not dense in a sense of internal edges. Authors have named these sparse subgraphs *bridges* and defined as follows:

Bridges are subgraphs which have less internal edges than external ones. Additionaly they have at least two neighbouring clusters and at least two of those clusters are dense.

This definifion implies that bridge can be connected to more than just two clusters and several bridges can be connected to each other. Simulations in section 4 show that the role of these bridges is transfering signal/information between clusters.

3.2   Scheme

In this section authors introduced a scheme of proposed algorithm. The scheme consists of three main steps which were discussed briefly below and can be seen on figure 1.

1. Find spanning tree $T(G)$ of a given graph G. Now find vertex v which fulfills condition:

$$V(T(G))_{min} = \operatorname*{argmin}_{u \in V(T(G))} (deg(u)) \tag{1}$$

$$v = \operatorname*{argmax}_{w \in G}(deg(w) : w \in V(T(G))_{min}) \tag{2}$$

where $V(T(G))$ is set of all vertices in graph G and $deg(v)$ is a degree of vertex v. Next, cut out neighbourhood of rank r of found vertex v. Save the rest of a graph as G'. Repeat this step for all next G' until reaching situation when all nodes are assigned to some neighbourhood. This first division will be called *initial clustering*.

2. Apply MCL method for every cluster in initial clustering. Save received results.

3. Aggregate every cluster from second step to one *supernode*. Create a new graph from supernodes and assign transition probabilities between them as a sum of probabilities between vertices from given clusters.

Whole procedure have to be repeated until graph becomes a separated set of supernodes.

First step of the scheme above contains an important rule for choosing vertices. This rule should cause a situation where vertices chosen firstly are located near borders of clusters. Neighbourhood of that vertex probably consists of vertices from different actual clusters. MCL algorithm should find out that certain initial cluster has to be divided according to borders of actual dense subsets.

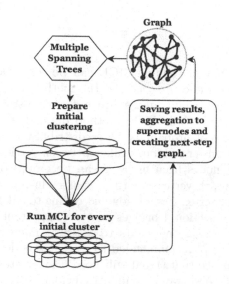

Fig. 1. Flowchart of LARW algorithm

Aggregating results of clustering by grouping vertices to a supernode is a typical technique of hierarchical algorithms.

The main idea of algorithm is to recognize where in the graph are located borders and then dividing initial clusters along them. Local approach satisfies requirement of scalability of algorithm for large datasets. Hierarchical way ensures that vertices near to a border which are from different clusters will be still separated.

Scalability of algorithm is really good. LARW performs tens or hundreds times faster than MCL [10] for large sets and that advantage becomes higher with larger graphs.

3.3   MCL Feature

During work on the scalable modification of Markov Clustering Algorithm very interesting feature was revealed. Figure 2 shows behaviour of the algorithm in certain situation of three vertices.

Feature of MCL Based on Random Walks

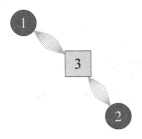

Fig. 2. MCL feature

In the figure 2 result of running MCL can be seen. Despite that there is no distinction between these three nodes, the method has found two clusters. It happened because probability mass run out very fast from vertex number *3* to other vertices. This is why MCL method decided to mark vertex *3* as a different one in a sense of probability mass distribution. Role of a node with number *3* is just to transfer random walker between vertices *1* and *2*. It is not hard to imagine that nodes from figure 2 can be groups of vertices. If one of groups hidden underneath vertex *3* form a sparse cluster and its neighbouring clusters are dense then vertex *3* is a bridge according to a definition from section 3.1. As can be seen in section 4 bridges play an important role in information spread through networks. If one wants to reach as many units as possible in shortest time then it is not recommended to start in a node which is deep in the cluster. In a situation like that signal will need a lot of steps until it travels to a different cluster. The best way is to identify bridges (if they exist) and initate signal in one or some of them. When it is wanted to target nodes only from one cluster identifying bridges will be helpful. Removing bridges adjacent to a considered cluster will make leaving that cluster more difficult. One can control signal propagation on a graph by opening and closing flow through bridges.

4 Simulations and Results

In this section results of several simulations were provided. Authors considered two directions of checking role of bridges in graphs. First direction is to compare pace of signal spreading in two situations: initialized in bridges and initialized in a cluster. Second is to analyze how important role bridges play in transferring information between neighbouring clusters. Both directions were presented in sections 4.2 and 4.3 respectively. It was difficult to make a comparison with presented LARW algorithm. This is because most of hierarchical clustering algorithms do not find any subsets which fulfill definition of bridge. Authors found one algorithm - Walktrap [6] which can find at least one bridge. Comparison of clusterings was placed in section 4.

LARW algorithm gives in a result multilevel clustering therefore for analysis of signal propagation division with highest modularity [8] was taken.

4.1 Datasets

In this section a basic statistics of chosen graphs was provided. In table 1 one can see parameters for degrees of nodes in given graphs. All of these datasets can be found on [9]. As can be seen in table 1 LARW algorithm found couple bridges. In section 4 one can see that despite of the fact there is little number of bridges they play crucial role in signal transferring.

Table 1. Statistics of analyzed graphs

Graphs	#V(G)	#E(G)	Minimum	Median	Maximum	Bridges found by LARW
Coauthorship	16264	47594	1	4	107	40
Zachary	34	75	1	3	16	1
Dolphins	62	159	1	5	12	5
Lesmis	77	254	1	6	36	1
Football	115	615	7	11	12	1
Polblog	1490	16726	0	7	351	0

4.2 Signal Initialization

First way of analyzing bridges influence is to simulate how fast signal discovers a graph when it was started in a bridge against one initialized in a cluster. To do that the Markov Chain was involved again. For every bridge authors did the same procedure:

1. Identify bridge and remove subgraph induced by vertices from considered bridge and adjacent clusters. Call it G_{sub}. Set of neighbouring clusters can contain other bridges as well.
2. Simulate signal propagation by multiplying stochastic matrices 1,2,...,d times where d is diameter of G_{sub}. For every cluster G_{sub} in every step calculate how many vertices were visited outside given cluster in certain number of steps.

Potential of Signal Diffusion

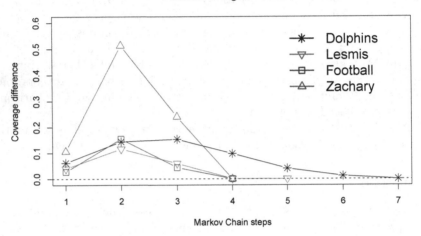

Fig. 3. Signal Initialization by LARW

Step 2. can be done by calculating fraction of positive transition probabilities from given cluster to the rest of a graph. Now it is enough to compare fractions derived from considered bridge and other clusters. For that purpose authors calculated average fraction for all clusters except bridge. Then for every G_{sub} difference between bridge fraction and average fraction from other clusters was derived. In result one recives a list of differences between visited fraction of nodes in certain number of steps. Of course number of steps as well as diameter can be different in different G_{sub}. At the end authors calculated average difference between considered fractions. Average was taken over all G_{sub}'s for every number of steps separately. In result one receives mean coverage of signal spread in graph in two situations: starting in a bridge cluster and starting in any other. Figure 3 shows results for different datasets.

Figure 4 shows comparison between information spreads induced by bridges detected by LARW and bridges detected by Walktrap algorithm.

Figure 3 proves that by initializing signal in a bridge, one will achieve higher coverage of a network than initializing it in any other cluster. All coverage differences are positive which means that signal recovers graph faster when it was started in one of found bridges. In figure 4 one can see that bridges found by Walktrap are very different from those found by LARW. As can be seen in a

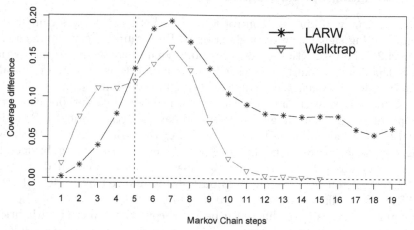

Fig. 4. Signal Initialization in Coautorship network

figure 4 Walktrap bridges are in fact parts of clusters. This is why signal is spreading very fast in first five steps and then it stucks while signal from LARW bridges recovers more and more nodes. This situation implies that Walktrap bridges are less influential after several steps of random walker.

In figure 5 one can see result of simulations when LARW did not find any bridges but Walktrap found four. These bridges are mistakes. Signal spreads faster initialized in cluster than in one of these bridges.

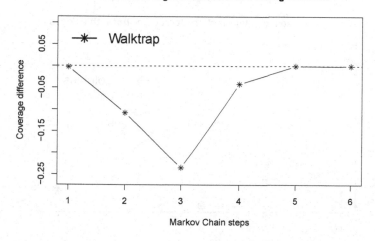

Fig. 5. Signal Initialization in Polblog network by Walktrap

4.3   Information Spread Control

Analysis of how well one can control travelling between clusters can be done by manipulating signal flow through bridges. Procedure is very similiar to one used in 4.2. The distinction is that authors computed difference in fractions of visited nodes in a clustering with bridges and without them. Potential of information flow between dense clusters through bridges in G_{sub} was calculated in 4.2. The same way of thinking was performed here but authors considered subgraph of G_{sub}. That subgraph does not have analyzed bridges. So this is a situation in which information cannot travel through a bridge. At the end average difference between fractions of visited nodes with using bridges and without them was calculated. Figure 6 shows results for several datasets. In figure 7 comparison between information spreads induced by bridges detected by LARW and Walktrap algorithm was shown.

In figure 6 one can see difference between coverage achieved with bridges and coverage without them. Positive values provide that removing bridges is a method that impede signal dispersion. When comparing figures 3 and 6 one can see that without bridges even number of steps needed to uncover the whole graph is larger. Clearly bridges are located between clusters and they transfer large amount of information.

In figure 7 comparison of quality between bridges found by Walktrap and bridges found by LARW has been shown. One can see that coverage given by LARW algorithm in step number five exceeds the one achieved by bridges from Walktrap clustering. The difference between signal spreads with and without bridges is even negative. This means that spreading information is easier without bridges found by Walktrap. This is because some of them are connected stronger to one of neighbouring clusters and should be part of them. After removing

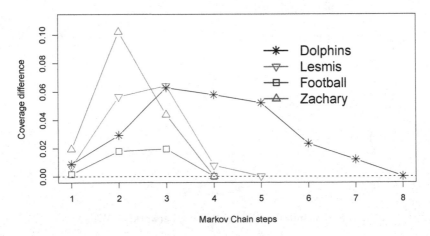

Fig. 6. Bridges Influence by LARW

Influence of Information Spread Control with Bridges in Coauthorship Network

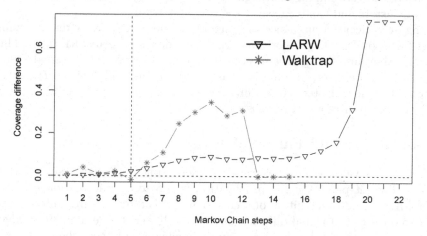

Fig. 7. Bridges Influence in Coautorship network

Influence of Information Spread Control with Bridges in Polblog network

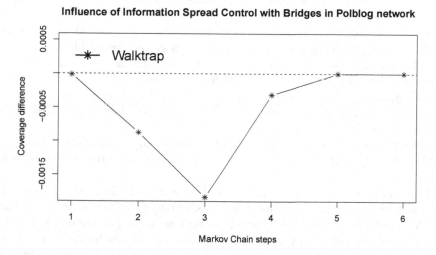

Fig. 8. Bridges Influence in Polblog network by Walktrap

bridges nodes there is simply less vertices to visit when information propagate through network.

Interesting thing is that the diameter of G_{sub}'s in case of LARW clustering becomes longer after removing bridges. It can be seen in figure 7. It means that some of found bridges are located in the most important for signal dispersion places in a graph. Influence of found bridges is so big that even after a number of steps equal to diameter of analyzed G_{sub} the difference in coverages is very high. The monotonic behaviour of coverage difference with respect to the Markov Chain steps is a consequence of splitting G_{sub} into two separated subgraphs. Clearly situation in which after a large number of steps difference did not converge to zero implies that signal started in G_{sub} without bridges stucks in one of clusters and cannot recover the rest of a graph.

In figure 8 negative influence of a signal spread is visible. After removing bridges found by Walktrap algorithm signal spreads faster than with them. This is because they are strongly connected to one of clusters. When signal starts to spread from a cluster, information has to get to this bridge which is weakly connected to other clusters. Identyfing these bridges gives nothing because in fact they are a part of a certain cluster.

5   Conclusion and Future Work

In this section several conclusions were provided. Firstly, one can easily see that the most difficult part of signal propagation is spreading information between clusters. According to definition of a cluster which is a dense subgraph one can expect to observe fast signal diffusion inside the cluster. Large number of edges forming cluster ensures that most of vertices in cluster will be reached in several steps. This is why random walker will rather stay in cluster than travel between clusters. Presented LARW algorithm provides clustering which has important probabilistic feature. It can separate groups of vertices which form a sparse cluster but should not be included in any of dense ones. Authors found out those groups are bridges defined in section 3.1 and they are responsible for transferring information between clusters. Simulations presented in section 4 shows that bridges are very important as a neighbours of dense clusters. Without them pace of signal dispersion in a graph becomes slower. Futhermore one can control spreading of information by removing certain bridges or lowering probability of passing information through them.

Clustering provided by LARW enables control of information diffusion in social networks by identyfing subgraphs crucial for transferring signal between clusters.

Algorithm presented in this work shows how much is still to be done in control of signal propagation by community detection. One of topics is a situation when LARW cannot find any bridge. Where is an optimal place for signal initialization then? One of possible solutions is to find groups of vertices from every clusters that are on borders of them. Then one has to remove number of vertices without quality loss of signal dispersion. This topic will be a part of future research. Second interesting subject is to identify bridges connected to other bridges. It is better to manipulate signal with small number of influential subgraphs. This have to be done carefully because one can easily lower resolution of influence and ability to control signal diffusion. Another important direction of research is a situation when LARW finds lots of bridges. Reduction of influence removing part of them can be huge so one has to examine importance of every of those subgraphs and choose best ones for given problem.

Acknowledgments. The paper is co-founded by the European Union from resources of the European Social Fund. Project PO KL ,,Information technologies: Research and their interdisciplinary applications", Agreement UDA-POKL.04.01.01-00-051/10-00.

References

1. Aggarwal, C., Lin, S., Yu, P.S.: On influential node discovery in dynamic social networks. In: SDM, pp. 636–647 (2014)
2. Doerr, B., Fouz, M., Friedrich, T.: Why rumors spread fast in social networks. Communications of the ACM **55**(6), 70–75 (2012)
3. Fortunato, S.: Community detection in graphs. Complex Networks and Systems Lagrange Laboratory ISI Foundation (2010)
4. Ju, C., Cao, J., Zhang, W., Ji, M.: Influential node control strategy for opinion evolution on social networks. Abstract and Applied Analysis, Article ID 689495 (2013)
5. Kempe, D., Kleinberg, J., Tardos, É.: Influential nodes in a diffusion model for social networks. In: Caires, L., Italiano, G.F., Monteiro, L., Palamidessi, C., Yung, M. (eds.) ICALP 2005. LNCS, vol. 3580, pp. 1127–1138. Springer, Heidelberg (2005)
6. Pons, P., Latapy, M.: Computing communities in large networks using random walks (2005)
7. Blondel, V.D., Guillaume, J.-L., Lambiotte, R., Lefebvre, E.: Fast unfolding of communities in large networks. J. Stat. Mech. P10008 (2008)
8. Newman, M.E.J.: Modularity and community structure in networks. PNAS **103**(23), 8577–8582 (2006)
9. Newman, M.: http://www-personal.umich.edu/mejn/netdata/
10. van Dongen, S.M.: Graph clustering by flow simulation. PhD thesis, Universiteit Utrecht (2000)

Think Before RT: An Experimental Study of Abusing Twitter Trends

Despoina Antonakaki[1]([✉]), Iasonas Polakis[2], Elias Athanasopoulos[1],
Sotiris Ioannidis[1], and Paraskevi Fragopoulou[1]

[1] FORTH-ICS, Heraklion, Greece
{despoina,elathan,sotiris,fragopou}@ics.forth.gr
[2] Columbia University, New York, USA
polakis@cs.columbia.edu

Abstract. Twitter is one of the most influential Online Social Networks (OSNs), adopted not only by hundreds of millions of users but also by public figures, organizations, news media, and official authorities. One of the factors contributing to this success is the inherent property of the platform for spreading news – encapsulated in short messages that are tweeted from one user to another – across the globe. Today, it is sufficient to just inspect the trending topics in Twitter for figuring out what is happening around the world. Unfortunately, the capabilities of the platform can be also abused and exploited for distributing illicit content or boosting false information, and the consequences of such actions can be *really* severe: one false tweet was enough for making the stock-market crash for a short period of time in 2013.

In this paper, we analyze a large collection of tweets and explore the dynamics of popular trends and other Twitter features in regards to deliberate misuse. We identify a specific class of trend-exploiting campaigns that exhibits a stealthy behavior and hides spam URLs within Google search-result links. We build a spam classifier for both users and tweets, and demonstrate its simplicity and efficiency. Finally, we visualize these spam campaigns and reveal their inner structure.

Keywords: Spam · Twitter · Microblogging · Social influence · Spammer · Spam campaign · Trending topic · Machine learning · Classification · Regression trees · Gain more followers campaign · Online social networks · Privacy

1 Introduction

Twitter is one of the most prominent OSNs, characterized as the SMS service of the Internet. This is mainly due to its simple and intuitive design: users are only allowed to post short messages of up to 140 characters. This behavior, also called microblogging, has attracted more than 645 million registered users as of 2014 [20], has over 115 million active users per month with an average of 58 million tweets sent each day and a search engine that performs 2.1 billion

© Springer International Publishing Switzerland 2015
L.M. Aiello and D. McFarland (Eds.): SocInfo 2014 Workshops, LNCS 8852, pp. 402–413, 2015.
DOI: 10.1007/978-3-319-15168-7_49

queries per day. All this amount of information has established Twitter as a very important service for disseminating the news in our society. Therefore, it is vital that all information originating from Twitter can be practically checked for false (or spam) messages. Consider that about a year ago, a single tweet was enough for making the stock-market crash for a short time [19].

But, how can an attacker leverage Twitter? Twitter provides the ability to enrich the semantics of a simple tweet with special characters that prefix specific words. One of the most known prefixes is the hash symbol (#) that denotes a specific word in the tweet as a hashtag. Hashtags are keywords in a tweet that assign context to the entire tweet by associating it with a topic. Even though hashtags started as an intuitive way to categorize and provide context to a message, it became a social phenomenon and their use was adopted by other media (even non electronic) as a simple method to signify, idealize and conceptualize a single word (or phrase) in a short message. Twitter collects popular hashtags and popular search queries and compiles a list referred to as the popular trends, trending topics or, simply, *trends*. Popular trends are becoming part of the social collective memory regarding a specific topic or event. Trends are also dynamic since they change daily and are strongly correlated to a specific location (although some can reach worldwide interest). Unfortunately, trends are a very effective method for tricking users into visiting malicious or spam websites, a technique called *trend-jacking* [12]. According to this, the attackers collect information regarding the most popular (*trending*) topics and include them in tweets pointing to spam sites.

In this paper, we perform a comprehensive study of this phenomenon. Initially we download a large collection of tweets that contain popular trends. Then we extract the contained URLs and we measure the number of contained trends as well as other features. We use 86 different Real-time Blackhole Lists (RBLs) to obtain the spam status of the collected URLs. We refer to this class of spam as *RBL*.

We also identify a specific type of spam campaigns that evade detection by masquerading URLs as Google search results. Spam campaigns are orchestrated, with large amounts of tweets coming mostly from hijacked accounts [8] that are promoting a specific service or product. These campaigns attempt to attract victims by offering to increase the number of accounts that follow the user. We refer to this class of spam as *GMF* (Get More Followers). Tweets of this campaign, trick users into giving permission to a malicious website, e.g., by trusting a site that advertises some type of meta-analysis of the user's account. Usually these fraudulent services offer to report usage statistics, analysis on user's followers, which followers retweet most of the user's tweets or who viewed the user's profile. Interestingly, most of the services that these sites offer can actually be performed without giving any special permission to the third-party. Even more surprising is the fact that there are legitimate sites that perform most of this analysis, for example: [1]. This points to the fact that there is a serious lack of public awareness regarding the actions that third-party services can perform when explicit authorization is permitted, as opposed to what actions can be performed by simply accessing a user's public data. Moreover, either as a paid service or a free one, these "get-more-followers" campaigns [17] consist a serious threat since it is a multi-million dollar scheme [15]. Our analysis shows that spammers propagating these campaigns follow a stealthier approach (compared to other spammers) as it hides URLs redirecting to spam sites within Google search results links. From all the Twitter features we study, the amount of different popular trends, included by a user in tweets, exhibits the highest divergence between spammers and legitimate users.

Based on our findings, we build a classifier that uses these features to differentiate between spammers and legit users. Our classifier on GMF class spam, is able to achieve a True Positive Rate (TPR) of 75%, which is comparable to existing studies, while maintaining a False Positive Rate (FPR) of 0.26% that is significantly lower than existing studies. We also extend the classifier to focus on individual tweets rather than users with similar results (81% TPR and 0.58% FPR). Finally we visualize the GMF campaigns and reveal that, while all spam domains originate from only 2 IPs, they are posted by thousands of users.

2 Background

A natural consequence of Twitter's rapid growth was to become a very popular medium for deploying spam campaigns [11]. Furthermore, Twitter's architecture facilitates the rapid propagation of phishing and spam attacks [9]. As a first line of defense, Twitter has employed a URL shortener service that preemptively checks for reported malware and phishing sites before shortening a URL [2]. With this defense spam in Twitter has reportedly dropped to 1% [3]. Additional studies have suggested methods for feature extraction from tweets and application of machine learning methods for spam identification. The main requirements when developing these techniques are high TPR, low FPR, simplicity and low computational requirements [9,13,14].

The analysis pipeline followed in most existing studies starts by extracting various features from tweets. These features can be either content based [4,5, 10,12,21] or graph based [4,5,10,21]. Some studies analyze specific spam strategies [16]. Then they proceed to flag (or label) the tweets or user in order to form a ground truth. Techniques to do that are: manual inspection [5,6,21], consult online blacklists [4,12], honeypots [10] or delegate this task to Twitter itself via the embedded URL shortening service [4,7]. Then they proceed to train a Machine Learning algorithm to classify either users [4–6,10,21] or individual tweets [5,21] between spam and legit categories. They employ various algorithms such as Naive Bayesian [21], Decision Trees [7,12], Random Forrests [10], Support Vector Machines [5], Aggregate methods [4] and web search [6]. Some studies also perform Unsupervised learning (clustering) [4,7].

It is in general difficult to perform comparisons between existing studies, since they measure different features and they follow diverse analysis pipelines. In general best studies are considered the one that achieve True Positive Ratio (TPR) higher than 80% and False Positive Ratio (FPR) lower than 1%. In

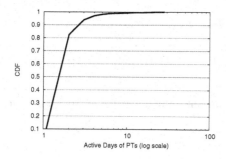

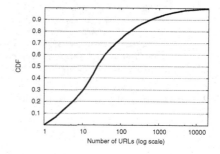

(a) Prevalence of PTs for March of 2014   (b) Number of different URLs associated with a specific trending topic

Fig. 1

our implementation, we demonstrate how we can achieve similar classification results, with simpler and computationally lighter techniques while relying on separate features that can lead to a previously undetected set of spam campaigns.

3   Methodology

Twitter has released a public API for interacting with the service. Through this API we collect daily Popular Trends (PTs) and tweets that contain these trends. Subsequently, since all URLs are automatically shortened by Twitter, we apply a URL expansion process that allows us to collect the final URL that is contained within each tweet. On average we downloaded 240 PTs per day and 1.5 million tweets. Our data collection phase lasted for three months, specifically January—March of 2014, during which we collected 150 million tweets.

In Figure 1a we plot a Cumulative Distribution Function (CDF) of the duration of Popular Trends during March of 2014. This plot contains the ratio of Popular Trends that were active for less or equal days than the values in x axis. We can see that 80% of the trends are active for 2 days or less. However, certain trends remain active and very popular for more than 20 days.

Another interesting observation is the different number of URLs posted per trend. In Figure 1b we plot a CDF of the number of different URLs associated with a particular popular topic. We observe that approximately 90% of trends are associated with less than 1,000 URLs.

3.1   Feature Extraction

The next step was to extract various user metrics, that will be used as *features* for our classifier. For each user we collected: The total number of tweets, the number of Total and Unique Popular Trends, Hashtags, User Mentions and URLs, the number of followers and the number of followings.

```
http://www.google.com.tr/url?
sa=t&rct=j&q=&esrc=s&frm=1&source=web&cd=1&cad=rja&sqi=2&v
ed=0CC4QFjAA&url=http%3A%2F%2Fwww.twitterfollowers.mobi
%2F&ei=r_aHUpyLM43FswbmolGACw&usg=AFQjCNFmozWrfrRT-
vcGzpNi4O5HOMxkZg&sig2=evyaeNnWIS4lbzl1pq5sUw&bvm=bv.
56643336,d.Yms&refer=YcUzgMRkPi
```

Fig. 2. An example of a get-more-followers spam link camouflaged as a Google search result

Grouping Potential Spam Campaigns. After calculating these metrics, we build a graph containing the users and group them according to the URLs they sent, i.e., creating subgraphs for each URL that contain all the users that included it in a tweet. Since we are interested in URLs that are posted in bulk, we extract all link nodes that have a degree smaller than 10. Subsequently we collect the domain name of each URL. This results in the collection of 24.000 different domain names during our 3 month collection period. Next, we attempt to obtain the ground truth by identifying which URLs belong to spam domains. We follow two methods for obtaining that information. First, we utilize various blacklists and, second, we employ a heuristic to identify spam that belong to the GMF class.

3.2 Real-Time Blackhole Lists (RBL)

Initially, we query various Real-Time Blackhole Lists (RBLs) to identify spam campaigns contained within our dataset. The advantages of RBLs is that they offer a fast and low-bandwidth method for spam detections. The main disadvantage, however, is that they exhibit delays for updating and including new spam domains [9]. For our experiments we used 86 RBLs.

3.3 Get-more-followers (GMF) Campaigns

During the manual inspection of the collected URLs, we observed a large percentage that appeared to be Google search results. Finding Google search results URLs within Twitter can be simply attributed to the following scenario: users that copy URLs from a Google search results' page and paste them into a tweet. Even though these URLs appear in the browser to be from domains other than Google, when copied they actually are Google URLs. When clicked, Google redirects the user to the desired link but, first, records the fact that this specific user clicked this link. After a more detailed inspection, we found that spammers exploit this and use it as a mechanism for *link obfuscation*. We present an example of such a case in Figure 2. Thus, spammers are able to masquerade spam URLs as Google results and conveniently bypass any blacklists or filtering mechanisms. We collected all Google results URLs from our dataset and identified 44 domains belonging to the get-more-followers (GMF) domains. We subsequently searched in RBL blacklists for domains that contained the word "follow" and we enriched this list with another 62 domains. These 106 domains mapped to 33 different IP addresses.

4   Data Analysis

In this section we present the results from our analysis of collected data, following the methodology presented in Section 3.

Using the list of 86 blacklists and our GMF heuristic, 1,911 domains from our dataset were flagged as spam, accounting for 7.9% of all the checked domains. These 1,911 domains traced back to 1,429 different IP addresses. After manual inspection we removed 91 domains that were obvious false positives. Surprisingly, we found that out of the 4,593,229 different URLs that we collected during March of 2014, 250,957 pointed to a single spam domain. This is 5.4% of all URLs, which is significantly higher that the 1% that Twitter reports [3]. This demonstrates that a notable amount of spam is able to bypass Twitter's spam detection mechanism.

Having acquired a significant labelled dataset of spam URLs, we proceed with identifying all spam users by examining which users posted spam URLs. From a total of 8.2 million users, we locate 590,000 that have posted at least one spam link which accounts for 7.2% of the users. As we mentioned in Section 2, these users are most likely victims whose accounts have been compromised rather than being spammers themselves.

The next step is to examine the features we have collected and see how different they are for spammers (including compromised accounts) and legitimate users. Our results show that all metrics exhibit a larger mean value for spam users compared to legitimate ones. Among them, Total Trends and Total Hashtags exhibit the highest mean increase, (2-fold). We also observe that the Different Trends and Different Hashtags exhibit similar average increases (both from 1.0 to 1.6) This is expected given the similarity of these two features (PTs and Hashtags). Moreover the difference of the average values for Twitter features between spammers and legitimate users is wider in the case of the GMF domain dataset. Surprisingly, we don't observe any significant difference for the number of User Mentions compared to the RBL+GMF dataset. This leads us to the conclusion that this feature is not exploited by spammers.

Having identified the features that present the largest divergence between legitimate users and spammers, we continue with plotting the distribution of users for each of those features. Figure 3a presents the distribution of PTs for legitimate users and spammers. The left subplot contains the unique PTs per day and the right one, the total PTs per day. We plot two different sets of spammers; one for both the RBL and GMF datasets and one for the GMF alone. We follow the same approach in Figure 3b that contains the distribution of Hashtags. The two figures demonstrate the extent to which spammers exploit the PTs and Hashtags for promoting their campaigns and reaching as many users as possible. A key observation is that the unique Trends and unique Hashtags exhibit higher differentiation than the total Trends and total Hashtags. Thus, spammers incorporate a large number of different trending topics so as to show up in various

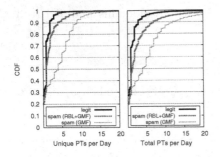

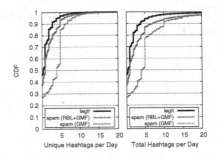

(a) CDF of Popular Trends of users weighted by the number of Active Days

(b) CDF of Hashtags of users weighted by the number of Active Days

Fig. 3

user queries and achieve a larger coverage and more diverse set of users, while maintaining a constrained approach to the total number of hashtags tweeted in a day. That is an indication of spammers following a stealthy approach and not flooding the system, to avoid being flagged by Twitter's spam detection mechanism. This confirms our initial intuition that posting many different trending topics is more suspicious than just posting many tweets containing trending topics. Moreover, we notice that GMF spam is far more active in exploiting PTs and Hashtags compared to RBL. We also performed a statistical analysis (two-sample Kolmogorov-Smirnov test) to test if these features (unique Trends and unique Hastags) belong to the same distribution regardless if it is measured in spam or legit users. The p-value ($<$1e-10) reveal that they belong to different distributions.

5   The Classifier

In this section we describe the classification schema that we used as a mechanism to discriminate between spam and legit users. Each user has a class information that is defined as the average number of spam tweets per active days. This metric indicates not only if a user is a spammer or not, but also the level of spam activity that he/she exhibits. The next part was to split the dataset into two random subsets. The first was used to train the machine learning algorithm and the second was used as a test dataset in order to assess the predictive ability of the model. We used a random 90% of the initial dataset as train and the remaining 10% as test.

After the construction of the train and test datasets we train a Decision Tree Regression (DTR) classifier. This method takes advantage of the rich information that is conveyed in the class feature (average number of spam tweets per active days). After training the DTR model, we assess the TPR and FPR metrics of the classification on the test dataset. We repeat this procedure 100 times. Each

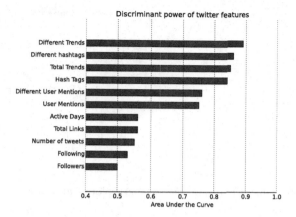

Fig. 4. The Area Under the Curve (AUC) metric for each feature

time we construct a novel train and test dataset as presented above, we train a DTR and assess the TPR and FPR metrics. Finally we report the average TPR and FPR metrics. This approach is called repeated random sub-sampling validation. We used the python package scikit-learn to train and assess the DTR classifier.

We applied this classification schema on tweets collected throughout March 2014. This collection contained 622,428 users from which 5,152 have posted at list one GMF spam tweet. These users have posted in total 6,658,2825 tweets. The average TPR was 75.2% (95% CI [74.8, 75.5]) and the average FPR was 0.25% (95% CI [0.246, 0.255]). Finally we performed an analysis of the discriminatory ability of each feature. We did this by measuring the performance of the classification scheme when we apply only one of each feature and we blind the rest. Then we measured the Area Under the Curve (AUC) of the Receiver Operating Characteristic (ROC) plot of the trained model. An AUC equal to 1.0 indicates a perfect classifier, whereas 0.5 indicates that the model does not perform better than a random classifier. This analysis show that both total and different trends and hashtags perform good as features for spam detection (Figure 4).

5.1   Tweets Classification

In this section we present the ability of the features to discriminate individual tweets that belong to the GMF campaigns. In this experiment every tweet that does not belong to the GMF campaign was assigned a negative class. We used again the tweet collection from March 2014 which contains 63,612 tweets belonging to the GMF campaigns (out of 6.6 million). The features that were extracted for each tweet were: Total Links, Hash Tags, User Mentions, Retweet Status, and Total Trends. We applied the same learning and validation schema as in the user classification experiment. The only difference is that we applied a Decision Tree Classifier (DTC) instead of a DTR. DTC is more applicable to this

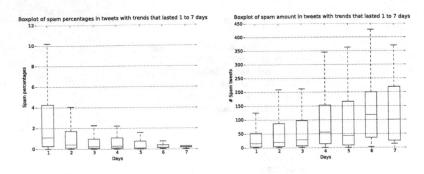

(a) Boxplot of spam percentages   (b) Boxplot of absolute spam amount

Fig. 5

task since we are facing a binary classification problem. The average TP rate of the classifier was 81% (95% CI [78.2, 82.7]) and the average FP rate was 0.58% (95% CI [0.56, 0.6]). In comparison, [7] succeeded 55% TPR and 0.4% FPR on twitter data and 80.8% TPR and 0.32% on Facebook data. Of course identifying spam that belong in the GMF campaign is a relatively easy task since it is based largely on hijacking of trending topics.

In decision trees the most discriminant rule is located on the root node. In our case this rule was: if Total_Trends <3.5 then legit else spam. This single rule has 79.6% TPR and 0.77% FPR. Practically this means that just by checking the number of Trends in a single tweet, an algorithm can identify 4 out of 5 tweets that belong in the GMF campaign. The rest 1 out of 5 are False Negatives. As a future work, we intend to inspect closer the nature of these tweets hoping that we will get insights that might increase the accuracy of the classifier.

5.2   Time Scale Analysis of Popular Trends

We also analyzed the time period that is usually takes before a Hashtag is exploited after it becomes a PT. During March of 2014 we collected 5,780 different PTs. From these 3,193 (55%) had been used in at least one spam tweet. The 74.5% of these trends where involved in spam tweets for only a single day and 15% for two days. This show that the vast majority of PTs are exploited the very first days that they are created. Since acquiring a list of PTs from Twitter is an easy task, spammers seem to do this daily in order to add them on spam tweets. In figure 5a we present the boxplots of spam percentages in tweets containing PTs that lasted from 1 to 7 days. Trends that lasted more than 7 days were very few (<1%) and were excluded from our analysis. It is impressive that 1% of tweets that contain trends that are active only for a single day is spam. We also observe a downward trend, meaning that PTs that are active for more days contain a lower percentage of spam. Nevertheless if we repeat the same plot with the absolute number of spam (rather than percentages), we observe an upward

Fig. 6. Plot of a spam campaign involving 17 GMF domains and 1.604 users

trend (figure 5b). This means that PTs that are active for more days contain a higher amount of spam. As we have seen PTs that are active for more days are more generic, thus they are exploited in a higher level. Nevertheless targeting PTs with shorter duration is more effective since it is exploiting novel trends and potential unsuspicious users.

6   Spam Campaigns

As we have previously discussed, in most cases spam delivery happens on a massive scale with well orchestrated behavior [18]. To further illustrate this, we plot a recreation of a spam campaign that was captured on a single day (January 10th 2014) in Figure 6. This campaign comprised of 17 different spam domains belonging to the GMF class, which involved 1,604 different users. 16 out of these 17 domains belong to a single IP address. This IP also hosted 2 more domains that were contained in the blacklists, but that did not take part in this campaign. The average edge degree for a node that represents a spam domain is 125, i.e., every spam domain in the graph could be found in average, in the tweets of 125 different users. In contrast, the average edge degree for the graph depicting users and the URLs they tweeted for that day, is 2.3 for legitimate URLs. Various graph properties can be exported either from spam campaign graphs, or user-URL graphs, that can potentially assist in identifying spam users and campaigns. We plan to explore this as part of our future work.

The most successful domain is tweeted by 337 users, while the least by 40. These numbers demonstrate the stealthy approach of this type of campaigns that do not flood Twitter with multiple messages advertising the campaign, which would result on being detected by Twitter's spam detection mechanism. The average number of tweets per user ranges from 1.07 to 1.58, meaning that in the worst case only half the users will promote the spam domain a second time.

7 Conclusions

As the impact of Online Social Networks (OSNs) becomes more prominent in modern societies, it is crucial to study the emergent patterns of both benign and malign user behaviors. In particular, spam distribution can be disruptive for the finances and the privacy of individual users. For this reasons delving into the methods and techniques employed for spam distribution is essential for protecting users and uncovering potential system vulnerabilities.

In this paper we conduct a study regarding the characteristics of spam propagating through Twitter and, specifically, how spammers use certain features of the service to increase the effectiveness of their campaigns. Our exploration of our 3-month dataset revealed a set of spam campaigns that exhibited a stealthier approach than other campaigns and also masqueraded URLs pointing to spam websites as a Google search result. Using a set of 86 blacklists, and a heuristic for identifying these new campaigns, we create labelled datasets that we use for training a classifier. We then quantify the behavior of legitimate users and spammers using metrics for Twitter-specific keywords and content, and find a large divergence in categories such as the number of trending topics included in tweets.

We create a classifier for a spam detection mechanism that uses these metrics, and test it on a dataset containing all the tweets collected during a period of one month. Our detection mechanism is able to correctly identify 75% of the stealthy spammers, while maintaining a very low false positive ratio of 0.25%. Overall, our system offers a light detection mechanism for a stealthy and persistent class of Twitter campaigns, while maintaining a very low false positive rate that is a very significant requirement for deployment in a real environment. It also relies on features that require low to zero computational resources since they are widely available from Twitter's API.

Acknowledgments. We would like to thank the anonymous reviewers for their valuable comments. This work was supported by the FP7 Marie-Curie ITN iSocial funded by the EC under grant agreement no 316808. This work was also supported by the: NSF Grant CNS-13-18415, FP7-PEOPLE-2010-IOF project XHUNTER, No. 273765, Prevention of and Fight against Crime Programme of the European Commission Directorate-General Home Affairs (project GCC), European Union's Prevention of and Fight against Crime Programme Illegal Use of Internet e ISEC 2010 Action Grants, grant ref. HOME/2010/ISEC/AG/INT-002.

References

1. http://followerwonk.com/
2. https://blog.twitter.com/2012/shutting-down-spammers
3. https://blog.twitter.com/2010/state-twitter-spam
4. Amleshwaram, A.A., Reddy, A.L.N., Yadav, S., Gu, G., Yang, C.: Cats: characterizing automation of twitter spammers. In: COMSNETS, pp. 1–10. IEEE (2013)

5. Benevenuto, F., Magno, G., Rodrigues, T., Almeida, V.: Detecting spammers on twitter. In: Annual Collaboration, Electronic messaging, Anti-Abuse and Spam Conference (CEAS) (2010)
6. Flores, M., Kuzmanovic, A.: Searching for spam: detecting fraudulent accounts via web search. In: Roughan, M., Chang, R. (eds.) PAM 2013. LNCS, vol. 7799, pp. 208–217. Springer, Heidelberg (2013)
7. Gao, H., Chen, Y., Lee, K., Palsetia, D., Choudhary, A.: Towards online spam filtering in social networks. In: Symposium on Network and Distributed System Security (NDSS) (2012)
8. Gao, H., Hu, J., Wilson, C., Li, Z., Chen, Y., Zhao, B.Y.: Detecting and characterizing social spam campaigns. In: Proceedings of the 10th Annual Conference on Internet Measurement. ACM (2010)
9. Grier, C., Thomas, K., Paxson, V., Zhang, M.: @spam: The underground on 140 characters or less. In: Proceedings of the 17th ACM Conference on Computer and Communications Security, CCS 2010, pp. 27–37. ACM, New York (2010)
10. Lee, K., Eoff, B.D., Caverlee, J.: Seven months with the devils: a long-term study of content polluters on twitter. In: ICWSM (2011)
11. Markatos, E., Balzarotti, D., Almgren, M., Athanasopoulos, E., Bos, H., Cavallaro, L., Ioannidis, S., Lindorfer, M., Maggi, F., Minchev, Z., et al.: The red book
12. Martinez-Romo, J., Araujo, L.: Detecting malicious tweets in trending topics using a statistical analysis of language. Expert Syst. Appl. **40**(8), 2992–3000 (2013)
13. O'Donovan, J., Kang, B., Meyer, G., Höllerer, T., Adalii, S.: Credibility in context: an analysis of feature distributions in twitter. In: SocialCom/PASSAT, pp. 293–301 (2012)
14. Ozdikis, O., Senkul, P., Oguztuzun, H.: Semantic expansion of hashtags for enhanced event detection in twitter. In: Proceedings of the 1st International Workshop on Online Social Systems (2012)
15. Perlroth, N.: Fake twitter followers become multimillion-dollar business. The New York Times (2013)
16. Sridharan, V., Shankar, V., Gupta, M.: Twitter games: how successful spammers pick targets. In: Proceedings of the 28th Annual Computer Security Applications Conference, ACSAC 2012, pp. 389–398. ACM, New York (2012)
17. Stringhini, G., Wang, G., Egele, M., Kruegel, C., Vigna, G., Zheng, H., Zhao, B.Y.: Follow the green: growth and dynamics in twitter follower markets. In: Proceedings of the 2013 Conference on Internet Measurement Conference, pp. 163–176. ACM (2013)
18. Thomas, K., Grier, C., Song, D., Paxson, V.: Suspended accounts in retrospect: an analysis of twitter spam. In: Proceedings of the 2011 ACM SIGCOMM Conference on Internet Measurement Conference, IMC 2011, pp. 243–258. ACM, New York (2011)
19. Time.com. How does one fake tweet cause a stock market crash? http://business. time.com/2013/04/24/how-does-one-fake-tweet-cause-a-stock-market-crash/
20. Twitter, Huffington Post, e. Twitter Statistics (2014). http://www.statisticbrain. com/twitter-statistics/
21. Wang, A.H.: Don't follow me - spam detection in twitter. In: SECRYPT, pp. 142–151 (2010)

3rd International Workshop on Social Media in Crowdsourcing and Human Computation (SoHuman)

SoHuman 2014 – 3rd International Workshop on Social Media in Crowdsourcing and Human Computation - Introduction

Theme: Socially-aware Crowdsourcing – The Value of the Human Touch

Jasminko Novak[1,2(✉)], Alessandro Bozzon[3], Piero Fraternali[4], Petros Daras[5], Otto Chrons[6], Bonnie Nardi[7], and Alejandro Jaimes[8]

[1] European Institute for Participatory Media, Berlin, Germany
j.novak@eipcm.org
[2] University of Applied Sciences Stralsund, Stralsund, Germany
jasminko.novak@fh-stralsund.de
[3] Delft University of Technology, Delft, The Netherlands
a.bozzon@tudelft.nl
[4] Politecnico Di Milano, Como, Italy
piero.fraternali@polimi.it
[5] ITI CERTH, Thessaloniki, Greece
daras@iti.gr
[6] Microtask, Tampere, Finland
otto.chrons@microtask.com
[7] UC Irvine, Irvine, CA, USA
nardi@ics.uci.edu
[8] Yahoo Research, Barcelona, Spain
ajaimes@yahoo-inc.com

Abstract. This workshop aims at bringing together researchers and practitioners from different disciplines to explore the challenges and opportunities of novel approaches to collective intelligence, crowdsourcing and human computation that address social aspects as a core element of their design principles, implementations or scientific investigation.

Keywords: Crowdsourcing · Human computation · Collective intelligence · Social media · Collaborative systems · AI · Multimedia information retrieval · HCI · Socio-technical systems

1 Introduction

As research in the quickly grown field of crowdsourcing matures, there is an increasing awareness of the need to more explicitly address social aspects of crowdsourcing and human computation in order to identify and overcome limitations – of conceptual, technical, social or ethical nature – of overly mechanistic models often underlying current approaches. However, there is still relatively little work that explicitly addresses the importance, implications and opportunities that arise when incorporating

L.M. Aiello and D. McFarland (Eds.): SocInfo 2014 Workshops, LNCS 8852, pp. 417–420, 2015.
DOI: 10.1007/978-3-319-15168-7_50

the perspective of crowd workers as social collectives into the design of crowdsourcing and human computation systems and applications.

Based on the successful experience of the two previous SoHuman workshops in 2012 and 2013, this workshop aims at facilitating such questions to be considered in an interdisciplinary setting, from different perspectives at the intersection of the social sciences and computer science. The goal is to identify how experiences gained in the rich body of work on the design of socially-aware systems and applications and from the study of social dynamics in technologically-mediated, large-scale social systems can inform the conceptualization and the development of novel, socially-aware approaches to crowdsourcing and human computation.

1.1   Previous Workshops

We conduct this workshop due to a high interest in our SoHuman workshop series, voiced especially by participants of our two previous workshops. The first SoHuman workshop took place in 2012, at IEEE Social Computing 2012 in Amsterdam, and the second, SoHuman 2013, at ACM WebScience 2013 co-located with the ECRC 2013 and ACM CHI 2013 in Paris. Both workshops were organized as half-day workshops. They have attracted lively interest with 29 registrations both in the first and second year. The diverse backgrounds of attendees and their active participation and discussion made them both successful events. For SoHuman 2013, we received a total of 17 paper submissions out of which 5 were selected for presentation (29% acceptance rate).

2   Aims and Scope

This year's theme of the workshop highlights the intersections between the perspectives of computer science and the social sciences, such as: How can the experience gained from the design of crowdsourcing applications inform the development of new approaches to collective intelligence and social computing on the web? Can we conceptualize specific classes of human computation as instances of different forms of social collaboration? And vice versa: what lessons from the broader domain of the study of large-scale social systems can inform the design of new kinds of systems for crowdsourcing and human computation?

Both crowdsourcing and human computation consider humans as distributed task-solvers, with the latter embedding human users as a part of intelligent computational systems. They both leverage human reasoning to solve complex tasks that are easy for individuals but difficult for purely computational approaches (human computation) or for traditional organizational work arrangements (crowdsourcing). Effective realizations of these paradigms typically require participation of a large number of distributed users over the Internet, a careful design of task structures, participation incentives and mechanisms for coordinating and aggregating results of individual participants into collective solutions.

Though rarely explicitly addressed as such, social media and related technologies often provide the enabling methods and technologies for the realization of such models. Examples include crowdsourcing marketplaces (e.g. Amazon mTurk), crowdsourcing service providers (e.g. Microtask) or games with a purpose. While centralized platforms are also at the core of "traditional" approaches to collective intelligence (e.g. Wikipedia), attention is increasingly turning to the possibilities of harnessing existing social platforms (e.g.Facebook, Twitter) that already gather huge numbers of users into webs of social relationships.

For instance, such relationships allow the development of new kinds of task routing mechanisms (e.g. identifying the best or most trusted participants for a specific task), while social incentives can reflect community-like phenomena (e.g. the reputation economy). This is already leading to experiments such as expert-based crowdsourcing or solutions for task-injection across distributed social platforms. It is also partially reflected in growing research on inferring social influence, attention or trust from online social exchanges with the aim of providing mechanisms for more effective information exchanges or collective problem solving.

Socially-aware human computation and crowdsourcing systems call for new mechanisms of work division and execution, where the traditional individual "tayloristic" model evolves into a collaborative labor environment featuring different kinds of communication and collaboration between the users, going beyond private exchanges between the task-owner and the task-solver.

This begs the question of how such more open, participatory models of collective action can inform the development of new kinds of crowdsourcing and human computation systems and approaches:

- Can we conceptualize specific classes of human computation as instances of different forms of social collaboration?
- How can we design crowdsourcing and human computation systems where the involvement of a large number of diverse human users as providers, aggregators or "processors" of information leads to outcomes that benefit the entire collective rather than only individual contributors or commissioners of task assignments?
- How can the theory of collective action inform the design of such collaborative approaches to socially-aware crowdsourcing and human computation?
- What are the different sources of value of the "human touch" that can be brought to bear through such new approaches?

In order to effectively address such questions the workshop has invited contributions from researchers from computer science and social sciences working at the intersections of studying and/or designing the described classes of socio-technical systems, with a focus on socially-aware crowdsourcing and human computation. We are especially interested in novel approaches to understanding social dynamics and designing applications for a range of domains such as collective action and social deliberation, multimedia search and exploration, cultural heritage, social data analysis or citizen science. By highlighting the importance of domain-specific challenges and specific use cases we can also enrich a technology-driven perspective with a user-centered view and system-level social dynamics.

By explicitly discussing the social aspects of collective systems and relating them to experiences from the practice of crowdsourcing and social computing (i.e. in terms of specific problems, models and use cases) the exchange between commonly disparate research communities from social sciences and different fields of computer science but which are working on related problems can be facilitated. Such orientation to the social aspects of crowdsourcing and human computation and its linking to broader classes of social systems involving the shared production of collective goods and large-scale online social exchanges has been a specific focus of this workshop.

The workshop is of interest to: 1) researchers and practitioners concerned with the development and evaluation of methods, technologies and applications for crowd-sourcing and human computation, and 2) researchers and practitioners in social sciences, computational social science, web science and related fields working on the analysis, theory building and evaluation of large-scale social exchanges.

3   Accepted Papers

We received 9 submissions out of which 5 were accepted as full research papers and 2 as application demonstrators. All submissions were reviewed by at least 2 reviewers in a double-blind review process.

For the list of accepted papers and the workshop program see http://eipcm.org/sohuman2014.

4   Program Committee

- Lora Aroyo, VU University Amsterdam
- Klemens Böhm, Karlsruhe Institute of Technology
- Alessandro Bozzon, Delft University of Technology
- Marco Brambilla, Politecnico di Milano
- Simon Caton, Karlsruhe Institute of Technology
- Gianluca Demartini, University of Fribourg
- Fausto Giunchiglia, University of Trento
- Martha Larson, Delft University of Technology
- Pietro Michelucci, Strategic Analysis, Inc.
- Ville Miettinen, Microtask
- Jasminko Novak, European Institute for Participatory Media / Univ. of Applied Sciences Stralsund
- Naeem Ramzan, University of West of Scotland
- Wolfgang Prinz, Fraunhofer FIT / RWTH Aachen
- Marcello Sarini, University of Milano-Bicocca
- Aaron Shaw, Northwestern University and Harvard University
- Mohammad Soleymani, University of Geneva
- Maja Vukovic, IBM T.J. Watson Research
- Pietro Michelucci, ThinkSplash LLC

Acknowledgements. This workshop is partially supported by the EU FP7 project CUbRIK (grant agreement n° 287704), by the European Institute for Participatory Media in Berlin and by the IACS - Institute for Applied Computer Science at the University of Applied Sciences Stralsund.

CrowdMonitor: Monitoring Physical and Digital Activities of Citizens During Emergencies

Thomas Ludwig[✉], Tim Siebigteroth, and Volkmar Pipek

Institute for Information Systems, University of Siegen, Siegen, Germany
{thomas.ludwig,volkmar.pipek}@uni-siegen.de,
tim.siebigteroth@student.uni-siegen.de

Abstract. In recent times, emergencies such as the 2013 flood in mid Europe have clearly shown that besides the professional emergency services and authorities, citizens get a more and more active role in crisis response work. They organize themselves and coordinate private relief activities. Those activities can be found in (physical) groups of affected local citizens, but also within (digital) social media groups. To detect and use this civil potential by professional emergency services, approaches are needed that support the instructing of citizens and coordinating of their actions to avoid needless duplications or conflicts. In this paper we present a concept, based on a mobile crowd sensing approach, which was designed as well as implemented as the system prototype CrowdMonitor and facilitates the monitoring of physical and digital activities of and the assignment of specific tasks to citizens.

Keywords: Crowdsourcing · Emergency management · Mobile crowd sensing · Social media

1 Introduction

Events such as the big flood in mid Europe 2013 or the typhoon Haiyan in Philippines 2013 clearly show that ordinary citizens already take a more and more active role in responding to emergencies. Citizens already organize themselves independently within relief communities often via social media for coordinating private response activities[1]. Currently, symbiotic approaches already exist for combining the civil activities with those of the professional emergency services. Citizens can help for one thing physically, e.g. by filling sandbags[2], for another thing they can help online, e.g. by providing crisis-related information[3]. Although the emergency services have already recognized the relevance of civil physical and digital activities – besides legal issues – the problem still remains, how on-site as well as online activities can be managed in very time-critical and uncertain situations and thus be integrated usefully into the current professional work practice.

In the recent years, open innovation concepts – emerging from Web 2.0 – have been geared to citizen engagement. *Crowdsourcing* is a *"type of participative online activity in which an individual, an institution, a non-profit organization, or company proposes to a group of individuals via a flexible open call, the voluntary undertaking of a task"*[4]. Within crisis management, crowdsourcing can be applied within different

© Springer International Publishing Switzerland 2015
L.M. Aiello and D. McFarland (Eds.): SocInfo 2014 Workshops, LNCS 8852, pp. 421–428, 2015.
DOI: 10.1007/978-3-319-15168-7_51

areas. One of them is the field of situation assessment, where a crowd can be used for the provision of on-site information[5,6] and the online community acts as a group of reporters[7]. Community members already create, provide, share, evaluate and discuss photos, videos, posts, news, etc. in social media groups. But how professional emergency services can use and make sense out of this mass of citizen-generated content with regard to their physical on-site activities in order to better respond to the emergency remains a big issue.

A subset of crowdsourcing is the concept of participatory sensing[8,9], in which the public is requested to gather, analyze and share data and information with the integrated sensor capabilities of mobile devices[10,11]. Such sensors can be the camera, GPS or microphone for providing and transmitting e.g. locations or noises[8]. For crisis management, social media services such as Facebook or Twitter are of great interest[5], because on the one hand such services contain relevant information about an emergency[12] and on the other hand affected citizens already can be found within them. This is demonstrated by the fact that citizens communicate via social media and share information directly from the incident's location[6]. The concept of *mobile crowd sensing*[13] tries to combine the participatory sensing concept with a "collective" sensing view by supplementing environmental or sensor data collected via mobile devices on-site with citizen-generated content within social media[14],. This creates a great amount of information, which supplements sensor data with opinions and experiences of citizens[15].

Within this paper, we analyze the related work and specific approaches to crowdsourcing and mobile crowd sensing in emergencies. In a qualitative empirical study of emergency services, we explored the impact of citizen-generated content of social media as well as on- and off-site citizen involvement. Based on our pre-studies we derived an approach, which allows the combination of both on-site civil as well as digital activities. We used the empirical findings to implement the web-based application "CrowdMonitor" which is based on the mobile crowd sensing concept and is intended to support the situation assessment and collaboration between emergency services and citizens.

2   Crowdsourcing Systems for Emergencies

There are a lot of existing approaches that try to make use of crowdsourcing during emergencies. Such systems focus on supporting the actions of emergency services and those of citizens, especially in very time-critical situations. In the following section we will present different types of crowdsourcing systems.

CrisisTracker is a platform for exploring Twitter within a specific type of disaster. It pre-filters tweets by a keyword and location with the aim of creating a 'social awareness'. In addition, tweets can be visualized on a map or a timeline. Although CrisisTracker can provide important information, it does not use other social media sources or include civil interactions or sensing capabilities[16]. Ushahidi is a platform, which tries to support professional organizations with options for requesting citizens or digital assistants to gather, structure or share information[17]. This information mainly contains reports about the intensity of a disaster like medical needs[17]. In addition, those reports originate from different sources, like social media[18], E-Mail[3] or SMS[19].

Within Ushahidi, reports are visualized on a map to improve the situation assessment[19] and they are frequently updated[17]. Ushahidi was used during different emergencies such as the tsunami in Japan 2011 for the allocation of food[3]. Although it embeds information from citizens as well as different sources, information from social media is not used. With Mobile4D, emergency services request affected citizens to submit reports about their local situation by using a dedicated mobile application. Emergency services use this application to directly communicate with the public and verify submitted information. In addition Mobile4D supports the warning of citizens, depending on submitted reports. Mobile4D was used within smaller incidents in 2013 Luang Prabang in Laos, where reports about floods and the avian flu were collected. Affected people can be contacted directly[20]. By providing citizen-interaction and participatory sensing approaches, the potential of digital volunteers still remains unused.

Compared to the systems previously described, CROSS uses social media to initiate the using of a mobile application of citizens by a public call. With the help of this application, citizens can collect information from the incident's place and transmit it with location data. The location allows the emergency services to coordinate and monitor participating citizens[5]. Although using social media for a first interaction, CROSS does not embed it as an additional source of information. With CrowdHelp, citizens can submit information about their medical conditions, which is then visualized and clustered by its urgency on a map. The clustering allows emergency services to allocate units on-site more effectively[18]. But an integration of social media information within CrowdHelp is not apparent.

The system DIADEM represents another way of gathering and validating civil information. Here a pre-selected expert group of citizens are requested by emergency services to use a mobile application for identifying strange smells with the help of surveys during chemical disasters[21]. The collected responses are shared between experts and visualized on a map, so that emergency services can derive possible locations of an affected chemical factory[22]. Although providing interaction and participatory sensing functionality, the use of social media is not part of DIADEM.

Microtasking-applications like MicroMappers (http://micromappers.com/) enable performing small tasks by citizens with just a few mouse clicks. Emergency services request digital volunteers to fulfil tasks by a crowdsourcing-platform[23]. Such applications were used e.g. during the 2013 typhoon in the Philippines to categorize photos[7]. On the one hand those approaches use the potential of digital volunteers, but on the other hand they do not integrate physical activities on site.

The approaches presented above are mainly used to request citizens for information gathering or its evaluation. Especially the potential of local physical activities often remains unused. Moreover the systems neither use the potential of social media, where crowds of citizens submit crisis-relevant information, nor a combination of those with the activities on-site. Within the approaches social media is occasionally used for initiating participation or rarely as additional information sources. Addressing this gap, an approach that allows both digital and physical involvement of citizens during emergencies is still an open research question. In the next step, we examine the potential of citizen-generated information for situation assessment and integrating local involvement into the current work practices of emergency services.

3   Empirical Study

Our objective is to examine the potential of citizen-generated content from social media in situation assessment as well as of a physical involvement into current work practices of emergency services. The research question of this paper is how physical as well as digital activities of citizens can be combined and made manageable to emergency services during emergencies. We first must understand the current potentials of an integration of citizens in professional emergency response work. We therefore conducted and analyzed 42 interviews (Table 1) from 2010-2014 with different organizations involved in emergencies (members of police, fire department and regulatory authority) in Germany as well as in the European Union with a view to establishing, inter alia, the potential of citizen-initiated activities as well as citizen-generated content from social media in emergency management. The interviews (I1-24; IM-15; IS1-4) were audio recorded and later transcribed or documented (C1-11) for subsequent data analysis.

Table 1. Interviews (2010-2014)

Name	Title and Focus	Year	Quantity	Place
I1-24	Work Practices and IT Support	2010 - 2011	22	GER
IM1-5	Mobile Collaboration Practices	2012	5	GER
C1-11	Social Media in Emergencies	2014	11	EU
IS1-4	Citizen Involvement in Crisis	2014	4	GER
Sum:			42	

3.1   Integration of Citizens into Emergency Practices

During the everyday work practices, citizens are not involved by emergency services, *"because someone [a citizen] cannot work for fire services without any qualification"* (IS03). But during large-scale or long-term emergencies the collaboration of citizens is appreciated, because activities like *"filling sandbags does not require any special training"* (IS03). In order to integrate the public, it is *"extremely important that we instruct the citizens"* (IS04), because only professional emergency services have an appropriated knowledge about the overall situation: *"What is the use of having 150 people and 50 bags or maybe nothing to do at all? I must also get an overview on the entire area of operations and the situation itself"* (IS01). Emergency services must therefore *"allow them [citizens] to act under our command, to try to convince them through conversations and to make them adapt our operational strategy"* (IS01), because otherwise citizens can hamper the official actions (IS03) or can take damage in hazardous areas, e.g. if a breach in a dam occurs (IS04). So, coordination and instructions in accordance with the organizational structure and the overall emergency management strategy is essential (IS01). In addition to those physical activities, special local knowledge and abilities (e.g. foresters, chimney sweepers) or language skills might be needed in a situation (IS01): *"There are many special things for which you need basic knowledge or foreknowledge. But there are also things for which you can make use of the knowledge and skills of citizens because it is their daily bread"* (I11).

Beside physical activities, citizens can provide and collect important information directly from the disaster's location or validate existing information to achieve situational awareness, especially in inaccessible areas and large-scale disasters such as flooding. But acquiring information from citizens only makes sense until the professional emergency services arrive (IS04). However, such citizen-generated content can differ from the actual situation on-site (IS04), because citizens *"are not very capable of assessment"* (IS03) and therefore often consciously or unconsciously mislead task forces. A validation and review on crisis-relevant information is therefore required. This can be achieved either by a number of on-site-reports or by virtual activities, like monitoring social media (IS02), e.g. giving an overview on what is going on and where people meet (IS01) or supporting the communication via social media.

3.2   Integration of Off-Site Citizen Activities

As already mentioned – apart from the physical activities on the ground – emergency services already have recognized the potential of social media and citizen-generated content. Especially the communication with citizens during emergencies was highlighted, which normally does not take place during everyday incidents due to time constraints (IS03) or a lack of additional value. With the help of social media data, emergency services can *"control activities and volunteers better"* (IS02). Moreover such information contains relevant information of an emergency, like *"location information, [...] which can achieve a better overview of the situation"* (IS02). But this has to be filtered (L10) to avoid incorrect and overwhelming information (L10). Problems that can occur during the communication with the public via social media were described as *"problems of understanding"* (IS04), such as different meanings or different use of specific terminologies that citizens do not understand. Furthermore information provided on-site could on the one hand *"attract nosy bystanders"* (IS03), but on the other hand *"prevent that many people will go into hazardous areas"* (IS04).

4   Implementation of the Monitoring System: CrowdMonitor

As our empirical study has shown, emergency services already recognized that they need support in handling citizen-generated content of social media and instructing on the ground physical civil activities. However, the current approaches[5,7,16–23] do not facilitate a combined assessment and management of social media and citizen-initiated activities. To proof the findings from the empirical study we argue that a support could be achieved by monitoring social media and physical civil activities. We therefore developed the system *CrowdMonitor*.

CrowdMonitor consists of two parts: (1) a web platform, described within this paper and (2) a mobile crisis application. The first is an administrative tool (Figure 1) for actors of professional emergency services with the aim of supporting situation assessment practices. The central part of CrowdMonitor is an Open Street Map, which displays all information on different layers (1). As the literature already has shown a layer-based map is an important part for situation assessment activities during

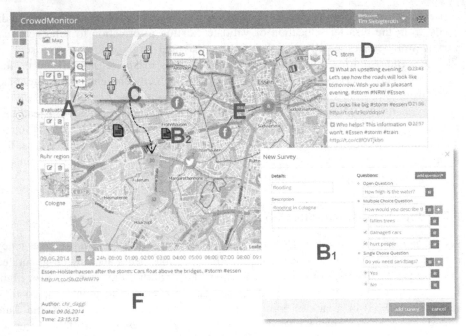

Fig. 1. CrowdMonitor

emergencies[24]. Besides showing different layers like hydrants or the weather, emergency services can request citizens to fulfil special kinds of tasks (A) such as information gathering or physical activities. The emergency services must therefore define a title, a description and the specific questions (B_1). If a citizen enters a pre-specified location area, he gets a push notification on the mobile application to participate and help in an emergency situation by answering the survey or following official instructions. All responses are displayed on the map by time of transmission and its location (B_2). In addition, CrowdMonitor collects sensor data from participants. Thus, emergency services can see e.g. movements on the platform's map (C). By assessing the locations of citizens on-site, emergency services gets a better situation overview and have the option for directly communicate with the individuals.

Beyond this, the map offers possibilities to search social media (e.g. Twitter, Facebook, Google+) by a keyword and time (D). The results of this search are automatically filtered by an algorithm that focuses on the location and content[25] and will be displayed on the map (E). Depending on the zoom-level, all information is clustered to provide a better situation overview. Furthermore it is possible to directly answer social media messages. All information, either social media messages or on-site reports are presented in detail within the 'detail area' (F).

Compared to the previously described approaches, CrowdMonitor embeds citizen-generated content from different sources, including various social media services as well as the important civil on-site reports. In addition, it provides different functionality of participatory and mobile crowd sensing functionality to request and instruct citizens along crisis-related activities.

5   Conclusion and Outlook

The work of professional emergency services has been confronted with (at least) two separate issues: The first and newly emergent issue is the appropriated handling of citizen-generated content from social media and the second a management of physical citizen-initiated on-site activities (newly coordinated through social media). Our paper contributes a mobile crowd sensing approach that focuses on both types of citizen involvement during emergencies by combining the citizens' digital as well as physical activities could support the work of professionals.

Based on our empirical work, which outlines the current intersection between citizens and professional emergency services during emergencies, we developed the web application CrowdMonitor. It facilitates the concept of mobile crowd sensing as part of crowdsourcing and provides functionality for gathering on-site movements and requesting data forum the ground as well as digital social media information and therefore covers both real and virtual activities. With the help of our approach, emergency services can request information from local citizens or collect it from social media, especially in non-reachable areas, and therefore can get a first overview of a situation.

As a next step, we are looking forward to evaluate our system with several actors from the emergency services to derive first implications for its practical usage and improvements.

Acknowledgements. The EmerGent project has received funding from the European Union's Seventh Framework Programme for research, technological development and demonstration under grant agreement no. 608352.

References

1. Reuter, C., Heger, O., Pipek, V.: Combining real and virtual volunteers through social media. In: Proc. ISCRAM 2013, pp. 780–790 (2013)
2. Kaufhold, M.-A., Reuter, C.: Vernetzte selbsthilfe in sozialen medien am beispiel des hochwassers 2013. In: Pipek, V., Reuter, C. (eds.) Hrsg. i-com - Zeitschrift für Interaktive und Kooperative Medien, vol 13, 13(1) Aufl. (2014)
3. Gao, H., Barbier, G.: Harnessing the Crowdsourcing Power of Social Media for Disaster Relief. Intell. Syst. IEEE. **26**(3), 10–14 (2011)
4. Estelles-Arolas, E., Gonzalez-Ladron-de-Guevara, F.: Towards an integrated crowdsourcing definition. Journal of Information Science **38**(2), 189–200 (2012)
5. Chu, E.T., Chen, Y., Lin, J., Liu, J.W.S.: Crowdsourcing support system for disaster surveillance and response. In: Proc. WPMC 2012, Taipei, pp. 21–25 (2012)
6. Chatfield, A.T., Brajawidagda, U.: Crowdsourcing hazardous weather reports from citizens via twittersphere under the short warning lead times of EF5 intensity tornado conditions. In: Proc. HICSS 2014, pp. 2231–2241 (2014)
7. Poblet, M., García-Cuesta, E., Casanovas, P.: IT enabled crowds: leveraging the geomobile revolution for disaster management. In: Poblet, M., Noriega, P., Plaza, E. (eds.) Hrsg. Proc. Sintelnet WG5 Workshop on Crowd Intelligence: Foundations, Methods and Practices, Barcelona, pp. 16–23 (2014)

8. Kanhere, S.S.: Participatory sensing: crowdsourcing data from mobile smartphones in urban spaces. In: Proc. MDM 2011, pp. 3–6. IEEE (2011)
9. Jiang, M., McGill, W.: Human-centered sensing for crisis response and management analysis campaigns. In: Proc. ISCRAM 2010, pp. 1–11 (2010)
10. Burke, J., Estrin, D., Hansen, M., et al.: Participatory Sensing, pp. 1–5 (2006)
11. Ludwig, T., Scholl, S.: Participatory sensing im rahmen empirischer forschung. In: Mensch and Computer 2014: Interaktiv unterwegs – Freiräume Gestalten. Oldenbourg-Verlag, München (2014)
12. Schulz, A., Paulheim, H., Probst, F.: Crisis Information Management in the Web 3.0 Age, pp. 2–6 (April 2012)
13. Zaslavsky, A., Jayaraman, P.P., Krishnaswamy, S.: ShareLikesCrowd: mobile analytics for participatory sensing and crowd-sourcing applications. In: Proc. ICDEW 2013, pp. 128–135 (2013)
14. Guo, B., Yu, Z., Zhou, X., Zhang, D.: From participatory sensing to mobile crowd sensing. In: Proc. of the Workshop on Social and Community Intelligence, Budapest (2014)
15. Sherchan, W., Jayaraman, P.P., Krishnaswamy, S., Zaslavsky, A., Loke, S., Sinha, A.: Using on-the-move mining for mobile crowdsensing. In: Proc. MDM 2012, pp. 115–124. IEEE (2012)
16. Rogstadius, J., Vukovic, M., Teixeira, C.A., Kostakos, V., Karapanos, E., Laredo, J.A.: CrisisTracker: Crowdsourced social media curation for disaster awareness. IBM Journal of Research and Development 57(5), 4:1–4:13
17. Heinzelmann, J., Waters, C.: Crowdsourcing Crisis Information in Disaster-Affected Haiti, Washington DC (2010)
18. Besaleva, L.I., Weaver, A.C.: CrowdHelp: A crowdsourcing application for improving disaster management. In: Global Humanitarian Technology Conference (GHTC), 2013 IEEE, pp. 185–190. IEEE, San Jose (2013)
19. Chohan, A.F., Hester, V., Munro, R.: Pakreport: Crowdsourcing for Multipurpose and Multicategory Climate related Disaster Reporting. (Cdi), pp. 1–9 (2010)
20. Frommberger, L., Schmid, F.: Mobile4D: crowdsourced disaster alerting and reporting. In: Proc. ICTD 2013, vol. 2, pp. 29–32 (2013)
21. Winterboer, A., Martens, M.A., Pavlin, G., Groen, F.C.A., Evers, V.: DIADEM: a system for collaborative environmental monitoring. In: Proc. CSCW 2011, pp. 589–590. ACM, New York (2011)
22. Asadi, S., Badica, C., Comes, T., et al.: ICT solutions supporting collaborative information acquisition, situation assessment and decision making in contemporary environmental management problems: the DIADEM approach. In: Pillmann, W., Schade, S., Smits, P. (eds.) Hrsg. Proc. EnviroInfo 2011, pp. 920–931. Shaker Verlag, Aachen (2011)
23. Meier, P.: MicroMappers: Microtasking for Disaster Response (2013). http://irevolution. net/2013/09/18/micromappers/ (accessed May 19, 2014)
24. Birregah, B., Top, T., Perez, C., et al.: Multi-layer crisis mapping: a social media-based approach. In: 2012 IEEE 21st International Workshop on Enabling Technologies: Infrastructure for Collaborative Enterprises (WETICE), pp. 379–384 (2012)
25. Reuter, C., Ritzkatis, M., Ludwig, T.: Entwicklung eines SOA-basierten und anpassbaren Bewertungsdienstes für Inhalte aus sozialen Medien. In: Informatik 2014 - Big Data - Komplexität meistern. Stuttgart: GI-Edition-Lecture Notes in Informatics (LNI), pp. 977–988 (2014)

Crowd Work CV: Recognition for Micro Work

Cristina Sarasua$^{(\boxtimes)}$ and Matthias Thimm

Institute for Web Science and Technologies, University of Koblenz-Landau,
Koblenz-landau, Germany
{csarasua,thimm}@uni-koblenz.de

Abstract. With an increasing micro-labor supply and a larger available
workforce, new microtask platforms have emerged providing an extensive
list of marketplaces where microtasks are offered by requesters and completed by crowd workers. The current microtask crowdsourcing infrastructure does not offer the possibility to be recognised for already accomplished and offered work in different microtask platforms. This lack of
information leads to uninformed decisions in selection processes, which
have been acknowledged as a promising way to improve the quality of
crowd work. To overcome this limitation, we propose Crowd Work CV, an
RDF-based data model that, similarly to traditional Curriculum Vitae,
captures crowd workers' interests, qualifications and work history, as well
as requesters' information. Crowd Work CV enables the representation
of crowdsourcing agents' identities and promotes their work experience
across the different microtask marketplaces.

Keywords: Microtask crowdsourcing · CV · Ontology · Crowd worker ·
Requester · Marketplace

1 Introduction

One of the challenges in human computation systems is to involve the humans
who, as intelligent and independent beings with a particular knowledge, are
crucial to solve problems that machines can hardly solve alone. Crowdsourcing
alleviates this challenge, as it provides a mechanism to distribute a task among a
potentially large group of people who subscribe to an open call on the Web [10].
A promising strategy to improve the quality of crowd work, which is particularly relevant for knowledge-intensive crowdsourced tasks, is to find the most
suitable worker(s) for a microtask (or vice versa), as Kittur and colleagues highlighted [8]. With the current increasing order of magnitude (in available micro
work and workforce), and the evidence of the crowd being diverse in terms of
background [11], personality [6], and motivation [5], analysing different aspects
of the agents involved in crowdsourcing in order to improve microtask assignment accordingly becomes meaningful. However, the realisation of such process is
hindered by the current microtask crowdsourcing infrastructure, which is highly
focused on independent marketplaces. Even if many of them have adopted some
common patterns (e. g. consider majority voting as aggregation method), each

© Springer International Publishing Switzerland 2015
L.M. Aiello and D. McFarland (Eds.): SocInfo 2014 Workshops, LNCS 8852, pp. 429–437, 2015.
DOI: 10.1007/978-3-319-15168-7_52

of them acts as a data silo. When crowd workers are registered and work in several marketplaces, the work they perform is registered in the marketplace they worked at and only visible there. If a requester is interested in knowing further information on the achievements and proven skills of a worker (e. g. through obtained qualifications) in other marketplaces, this information is not accessible programmatically, even though the data exists and it is visible to the worker. The same applies to requester information. This lack of data interoperability between marketplaces has a negative impact in the process of finding the best combination of workers and microtasks and may result in uninformed decisions. In Section 2 we describe a motivational scenario in more detail.

To overcome this limitation and as a solution to what we proposed in our previous work [12], we introduce Crowd Work CV, an RDF-based data model to represent someone's crowd work life, equivalently to what traditional Curriculum Vitae reflect. Crowd Work CV enables the aggregation of valuable information about crowd workers and requesters, which may be exchangeable if the data owner—the agent represented in the Crowd Work CV—decides to do it. The approach is conceived to boost transparency among crowdsourcing agents, which has a positive effect in crowdsourcing environments, too [4]. The contributions of this work are:

- The definition of a conceptual model to represent Crowd Work Curriculum Vitae information (see Section 3)
- The implementation of the data model into an OWL vocabulary (see Section 3)

The description of the Crowd Work CV data management system is out of the scope of this paper.

2   Motivational Scenario

Let us imagine Alice, who has registered in several marketplaces[1]. She is being assessed as a candidate crowd worker for a group of microtasks published at ClixSense about sentiment analysis of Spanish Web sites. The requester who published the microtasks trusts experienced crowd workers more than unexperienced crowd workers. 1) Alice registered at *ClixSense* but did not work there yet. 2) Alice worked on text translation at *Neobux*, where she obtained a Spanish qualification that a requester defined. 3) At *GetPaid* Alice successfully completed several microtasks which are equivalent to those for which she is going to be assessed, because CrowdFlower distributed the group of microtasks over several marketplaces (ClixSense and GetPaid). 4) At *MTurk* Alice worked with very good performance on other microtasks, which required her to analyse the sentiment of Tweets—similar purpose, with different type of data.

At ClixSense, Alice will be poorly evaluated because her ClixSense work history is empty. Other candidate crowd workers who have worked on Web site

---

[1] ClixSense http://www.clixsense.com, GetPaid http://www.getpaid.com, Neobux http://www.neobux.com, MTurk http://www.mturk.com.

sentiment analysis microtasks with a much lower performance than what Alice did at GetPaid will be better considered. Alice has a language qualification and she has proven to be capable of solving the type of job being analysed, and even other related microtasks dealing with a similar problem. Still, due to a lack of shared information, the requester will not consider her work experience. This has drawbacks for both parties: the requester is not taking advantage of a potentially good worker for the task at hand, and the crowd worker is missing an opportunity to work on something she might be interested in because of its similarity to previously completed crowd work.

3 Modelling the Crowd Work CV

With Crowd Work CV, we aim at adopting the procedure of reporting work experience from the traditional workplace, where there are plenty of guidelines about the information that should be included in CVs. We identify 5 requirements for a CV in microtask crowdsourcing: First, **domain independence**, i. e. a clear separation between the domain knowledge (e. g. media, fashion, biology) and the management of crowd work history needs to be ensured in order to enable the reusability of crowd work activity reports. Second, **marketplace independence**; the model needs to guarantee a certain level of generality, representing well-established processes instead of particular isolated characteristics provided by one particular marketplace. Third, **semantic and syntactic interoperability**; an agreement on vocabulary should be ensured. The semantics should be explicitly defined and shared separately from the data using a common (in our case) Web-based syntax. Fourth, **extensibility**, because the appearance of new features in marketplaces, or the definition of new workflows in crowd work should not interfere in the already specified model and existing crowd work CV descriptions. Fifth, **compatibility with traditional CV information** defined in standard systems like Europass and LinkedIn[2].

3.1 The Crowd Work CV Ontology

The Crowd Work CV ontology describes crowdsourcing agents (i. e. crowd workers and requesters), their **interests**, obtained **qualifications** and **work history**. The ontology is available online, and written in OWL[3]. We followed the ontology engineering methodology proposed by Noy and McGuiness[9] and considered reusing related ontologies. We decided to reuse some classes and properties of FOAF[4] for the description of agents and SIOC[5] for the description of user

---

[2] Europass http://europass.cedefop.europa.eu/en/documents/curriculum-vitae and LinkedIn https://www.linkedin.com/.

[3] Implementation of the Crowd Work CV data model: https://github.com/criscod/CrowdWorkCV/tree/master/ontology.

[4] FOAF vocabulary http://xmlns.com/foaf/spec/.

[5] SIOC Core Ontology Specification http://www.w3.org/Submission/sioc-spec/.

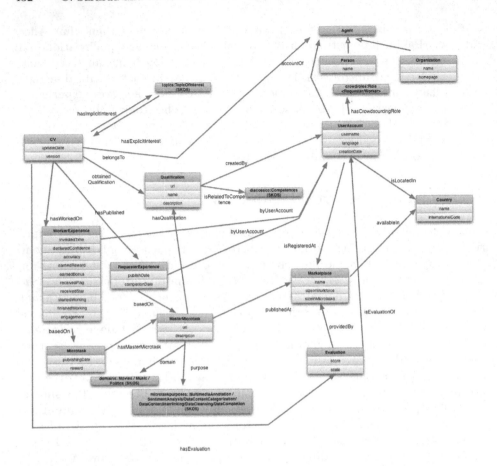

Fig. 1. Overview of the Crowd Work CV ontology. With Crowd CV it is possible to describe agents, their user accounts, CVs, qualifications, work experiences, microtasks and their master microtasks, marketplaces.

accounts, because their definition fits directly our needs and information annotated with such vocabularies on the Web becomes reusable. While the Crowd Work CV elements share some commonalities with the ResumeRDF[6] ontology, for modularity reasons, we decided to define our own ontology elements (which are more oriented to crowdsourcing) and align the CV concept to this ontology. We list the most relevant elements in the Crowd Work CV ontology and describe their purpose. Figure 1 shows the graphical representation of the ontology.

CV is the core class of the ontology. It aggregates all the information that is used to report the crowd work life of an Agent, which (from FOAF) can be either a Person or an Organisation (subclasses). A CV may refer

---

[6] ResumeRDF http://www.w3.org/wiki/ResumeRDFOntology.

to the interests of its owner, which might have been explicitly stated by the owner (hasExplicitInterest), or might have been inferred by the interaction in the marketplace (hasImplicitInterest). When we think of crowd workers, a CV may be related to obtained qualifications, which are related to competencies. We propose the use of the SKOS vocabulary for competences included in the Europass[7], but any taxonomy about crowdsourcing-oriented skills can be connected in the same way. For each piece of work accomplished, the CV connects the relation hasWorkerExperience to a new WorkerExperience, which consists of information about the way the crowd worker solved the microtasks (e. g. the time the worker invested, whether the requester gave flags or stars in such work, and the engagement of the worker in the complete group of microtasks). When we think of requesters, a CV is related to the RequesterExperience, which refers to the work they offer. The CV may have an Evaluation associated, which reflects usually a global evaluation connected to a particular UserAccount (e. g. the global reputation of a worker in a marketplace). We align our CV class to the CV class in the ResumeRDF vocabulary (with owl:equivalentClass).

UserAccount represents the account that an Agent may have in a marketplace. It is a SIOC class, to which we associate a role defined in SKOS (Requester or Worker). Besides the geographical information related to a UserAccount, what is relevant for the CV is the relation between the UserAccount and the Marketplace where the account belongs to. A crowd worker may have several accounts (one per marketplace), which are described with a username, the language(s) spoken by the owner and its creationDate.

Qualification refers to the achievement that determines whether an agent (usually a crowd worker) has the required knowledge on a particular topic. Qualifications—which are obtained through qualification tests—can be specified as requirements of microtasks (hasQualification), to restrict the set of crowd workers who may accomplish the microtasks. Requesters can write their own tests or reuse the questions provided by marketplaces. In the Crowd Work CV, qualifications may be defined with a textual description, a URL with a deployed example and a name. This class may be extended in the future if categories of qualifications are defined (e. g. language qualifications could be a subclass).

MasterMicrotask is a set of Microtasks grouped by the same structure, description and configurations. Usually microtasks are generated applying a template (for the UI and other crowdsourcing settings). Templates are combined with data and the Marketplaces convert these into specific microtasks. We have collected a set of common microtask purposes (e. g. from the task templates published by CrowdFlower) and defined a SKOS vocabulary with these. The taxonomy can be further extended. In the same way, we have included in a SKOS vocabulary some examples of possible domains.

---

[7] ESCO https://ec.europa.eu/esco/download/-/Download/skos.

New domains and purposes that marketplaces or requesters may define can also be included.

Microtask represents the particular instances of `MasterMicrotasks`. The specific unit of work that crowd workers need to solve. `WorkerExperience` is related to `Microtask`, since the information associated to the WorkerExperience (e. g. accuracy, invested time) is based on (`basedOn`) the results obtained in the microtasks. A `Microtask` is related to the `MasterMicrotask` which from it originated (after combining a template with data).

Marketplace represents the crowdsourcing platform containing a Website where microtasks are offered and accomplished. Such platforms provide support for both requesters (for creating the microtasks, defining basic restrictions on who to accept in their microtasks, monitoring the evolution of the work, and obtaining the crowdsourced results) and crowd workers (for browsing available microtasks, acquiring qualifications, submit their work, monitoring their activity in the marketplace and sending their feedback). `Marketplaces` may be described by a `name` and their `sizeInMicrotasks` and `sizeInWorkforce` to have some statistical information about them.

Evaluation reflects the assessment of an `Agent` in a `Marketplace`. It is generally described by a `score` within a `scale`, but it could easily be extended, for example with new intermediate properties that following the criteria suggested by Turkopticon express that a `Requester` is evaluated by its communicativity, generosity, fairness and promptness[8]

Figure 2 shows an excerpt of the serialisation of the motivational scenario. The complete data can be found at the GitHub repository[9].

```
ex:rex a cwcv:RequesterExperience;       ex:mm2 a cwcv:MasterMicrotask;
    cwcv:byUserAccount ex:acc1;              cwcv:hasQualification ex:q1;
                                             cwcv:publishedAt ex:Neobux;
ex:cv1 cwcv:hasRequesterExperience
ex:rex;                                  ex:cv2 cwcv:hasWorkerExperience ex:mex1;
                                         ex:mex1 a cwcv:WorkerExperience;
ex:mm1 cwcv:publishedAt ex:ClickSense;       ex:mex cwcv:basedOn ex:m1;
    cwcv:publishedAt ex:GetPaid;             cwcv:byUserAccount ex:acc2;
    cwcv:purpose                             cwcv:accuracy "0.9";
microtaskpurposes:SentimentAnalysis     ex:m1 a cwcv:Microtask;
                                             cwcv:hasMasterMicrotask ex:mm1;
ex:cv2 cwcv:obtainedQualification
        ex:q1;

ex:q1 a cwcv:Qualification;
    cwcv:name "Spanish A1";
    cwcv:isRelatedToCompetence
      disco:Capability1;
```

Fig. 2. Crowd Work CV data to describe the work accomplished in marketplaces. For each work done or published an experience is created.

---

[8] Turkopticon's evaluation criteria http://turkopticon.ucsd.edu/help.

[9] Example of generated Crowd Work CV:
https://github.com/criscod/CrowdWorkCV/tree/master/ontology.

3.2   Ontology Verification

In order to ensure that we are following best practices in ontology engineering, we validated our ontology with the OOPS! pitfall scanner[10], which considers a list of 40 common pitfalls in ontology specifications. Except for the imported concepts and properties from other ontologies, we ensured that we do not have important nor critical piftalls.

We also verified the fulfillment of the aforementioned Crowd Work CV requirements: the main elements of the Crowd Work CV ontology refer to **domain-independent** objects in crowdsourcing systems (e. g. microtasks, user accounts and marketplaces). The SKOS vocabularies connected to the core of the Crowd Work CV ontology, which express the purpose of microtasks or the domain, are responsible for bringing the specific knowledge domain into the CV data. Along the same lines, the ontology elements are general enough to be used in **different marketplaces**. For instance, the overall evaluation of a worker in a marketplace or the qualifications do not refer to particular evaluation schemes that MTurk or Clickworker have—which might be different from other market-places. The **semantic and syntactic interoperability** of the Crowd Work CV data is achieved with the use of the OWL ontology language. Furthermore, the Crowd Work CV ontology can be **extended** by defining subclasses (e. g. sub-classes of qualifications), subproperties, or adding new relations between existing and new ontology concepts. The SKOS vocabularies can also be easily extended in order to have for example, a broader catalogue of microtask purposes. The Crowd Work CV ontology is compliant with existing **standard traditional CV information**, describing the particular instances of work experience, the edu-cational achievements (in our case qualifications) and related skills and compe-tences. More details on the comparison can be found in the GitHub repository[11].

4   Related Work

Several authors have proposed new methods for matching crowd workers and tasks in crowdsourcing environments. Khazankin and colleagues [7] defined a framework for selecting suitable crowd workers to solve a task based on skill requirements attached to tasks, the availability workers report they have, and the skills workers have. Goel and colleagues [2] introduced a method for assigning tasks to workers, which analyses both skills and costs. Difallah and colleagues [1] implemented in a Facebook App a recommendation strategy that pushes suit-able tasks to users based on information extracted from their Facebook profiles and previously accomplished HITs, following various assignment strategies (i. e. category-based, text-based, and graph-based). These approaches do not offer a shareable and reusable description of worker expertise that could be used across-platforms. Ul Hassan and colleagues [3] proposed the SLUA ontology for

---

[10] OOPS! http://oeg-lia3.dia.fi.upm.es/oops/index-content.jsp.
[11] Comparison   https://github.com/criscod/CrowdWorkCV/blob/master/ontology/ EuropassLinkedIncomparison.txt.

matching users and actions in crowdsourcing scenarios. While the authors raised the problem of lacking interoperability between platforms aligned to our initial proposition [12], their approach has a different focus: they describe tasks, users, rewards and capabilities primarily for routing. In contrast, our goal is to gather more information and be able to share it as a means to recognition for work. We in addition consider microtasks, marketplaces, qualifications and requesters' information. Moreover, our data leads to a workflow for building CV summaries out of large sets of RDF triples. ResumeRDF[12] is an RDFS vocabulary to express information of Curriculum Vitae, including personal details, attended courses, skills and work experience. Celino[13] proposed the Human Computation ontology, which enables the annotation of crowdsourced data and is mapped to the Provenance Ontology. These data models share some common concepts with ours but do not cover all the crowdsourcing-specific domain required in a Crowd Work CV.

5   Conclusions and Future Work

Because microtask crowdsourcing builds a social system, with humans who invest time and money with a purpose, we need to define methods that satisfy the needs and expectations of all involved agents. We have presented Crowd Work CV, an approach for modelling and sharing knowledge about crowd work experience across different marketplaces, which could facilitate a fruitful requester-crowd worker interaction in microtask marketplaces and weave relations of trust. Our approach would considerably enrich the way reputation and credentials are managed in the current crowd workplace. The Crowd Work CV would also encourage job specialisation policies in microtask crowdsourcing.

Future work will focus on the development of the infrastructure of the Crowd Work CV data management system. An interesting area we would like to investigate is the automatic generation of Crowd Work CV summaries out of large sets of Crowd Work CV RDF triples.

The research leading to these results has received funding from the Seventh Framework Programme of the European Union, technological development and demonstration under grant agreement no. 611242 Sense4Us

References

1. Difallah, D.E., Demartini, G., Cudré-Mauroux, P.: Pick-a-crowd: tell me what you like, and I'll tell you what to do. In: Proceedings of the 22nd International Conference on World Wide Web (WWW 2013) (2013)
2. Gagan Goel, A.K., Singla, A.: Matching workers expertise with tasks: incentives in heterogeneous crowdsourcing markets. In: NIPS 2013 Workshop on Crowdsourcing: Theory, Algorithms and Applications (2013)

---

[12] ResumeRDF http://rdfs.org/resume-rdf/.
[13] Human Computation Ontology http://swa.cefriel.it/ontologies/hc.html.

3. ul Hassan, U., O'Riain, S., Curry, E.: Slua: Towards semantic linking of users with actions in crowdsourcing. In: CrowdSem (2013)
4. Huang, S., Fu, W.: Don't hide in the crowd! increasing social transparency between peer workers improves crowdsourcing outcomes. In: Proceedings of the ACM SIGCHI Conference on Human Factors in Computing Systems (2013)
5. Kaufmann, N., Schulze, T.: Worker motivation in crowdsourcing and human computation. In: Proceedings of the AAAI Workshop on Human Computation (HCOMP) (2011)
6. Kazai, G., Kamps, J., Milic-Frayling, N.: Worker types and personality traits in crowdsourcing relevance labels. In: Proceedings of the 20th ACM International Conference on Information and Knowledge Management (2011)
7. Khazankin, R., Psaier, H., Schall, D., Dustdar, S.: QoS-based task scheduling in crowdsourcing environments. In: Proceedings of the 9th International Conference on Service-Oriented Computing (2011)
8. Kittur, A., Nickerson, J.V., Bernstein, M.S., Gerber, E.M., Aaron, S., Zimmerman, J., Lease, M., Horton, J.J.: The future of crowd work. In: 16th ACM Conference on Computer Supported Cooperative Work (CSCW 2013) (2013)
9. Noy, N.F., McGuinness, D.L., et al.: Ontology development 101: a guide to creating your first ontology. Tech. Rep. 2 (2001)
10. Quinn, A.J., Bederson, B.B.: Human computation: a survey and taxonomy of a growing field. In: Proceedings of the SIGCHI Conference on Human Factors in Computing Systems (2011)
11. Ross, J., Irani, L., Silberman, M.S., Zaldivar, A., Tomlinson, B.: Who are the crowdworkers?: shifting demographics in mechanical turk. In: CHI 2010 Extended Abstracts on Human Factors in Computing Systems (2010)
12. Sarasua, C., Thimm, M.: Microtask available, send us your cv! In: International Workshop on Crowd Work and Human Computation (CrowdWork 2013) (2013)

Means and Roles of Crowdsourcing Vis-À-Vis CrowdFunding for the Creation of Stakeholders Collective Benefits

Angelo Miglietta and Emanuele Parisi[✉]

Department of Economics, IULM University, Milan, Italy
{angelomigliettaprof,emanuelemarioparisi}@gmail.com

Abstract. This work aims at assessing characteristics and roles of Crowdsourced activities vis-à-vis online CrowdFunding platforms, assessing potential collective benefits for stakeholders that arise from social media individual activities and investment decisions of users-investors. CrowdFunding platforms in fact leverage crowds and undefined pools of potential investors to screen, select and spread each CrowdFunding initiative in a detailed and thorough way – hence allowing users to perform several tasks that are traditionally carried out throughout IT models and static criteria.

We identify 5 key roles played by Crowdsourcing Systems (CS) and we develop a potential model aimed at screening positive outcomes that benefit the collectivity (stakeholders). The model evaluates Crowdsourced activities as indicators for the creation of sustainable value for the enterprise and therefore for the collectivity of stakeholders. In order to test the model, we are currently deploying an Equity CrowdFunding platform embedding strong Crowdsourced tasks.

In conclusion, we classify opportunities, limits and potential for a successful deployment of Crowdsourced tasks in CrowdFunding.

Keywords: CrowdFunding · Human Computation · Crowdsourcing Systems · Collaborative Computing

1   Introduction

The fast development of Crowdsourcing Systems (CS) in both public and private industry has provided adequate amount of research, endorsing that CrowdSourced activities may improve collaboration within communities - through the organization of users to perform tech-integrated tasks - eventually providing collective benefits (Doan, Ramakrishnan, Halevy 2011).

The literature in this field traditionally refers to the deployment of Crowdsourcing Systems in the operating phase in private companies and/or governmental organizations (Biewald 2012, Iperiotis, Paritosh 2011) hence mostly referring to established firms. There is little evidence focused on the impact of CrowdSourced activities in the startup

© Springer International Publishing Switzerland 2015
L.M. Aiello and D. McFarland (Eds.): SocInfo 2014 Workshops, LNCS 8852, pp. 438–447, 2015.
DOI: 10.1007/978-3-319-15168-7_53

phase, picturing roles and extents of *crowds leveraging* for the startup quality assessment, made of financial due diligence, campaigns selection and business development.

Since Startups do not generally offer financial records - and are highly reliant on external investments in order to fully develop their potential – the first *market perception* of early investors is the main driver of subsequent investor's decision.

The Startup *quality assessment* is increasingly being performed online by prospective investors – involving a great deal of user involvement, and there are several Crowd sourced activities and tools that startups can use in order to test the consistency of their business model before a single investment is made.

In recent years especially, an innovative tech-based fundraising model has gathered investors and startups to a new *quality assessment* paradigm – allowing crowds to invest discretional amounts of money in startups through online platforms. It is called CrowdFunding; a phenomenon that arose in the early years of the noughties that is recently experiencing an intense growth (Andreini, Pedeliento 2014).

CrowdFunding allows Crowds to invest in potentially profitable projects, while also being closely involved in the decision making process - both as investors and as potential consumers (Belleflamme, Lambertz, Schwienbacher 2012).

The literature mostly considers Equity CrowdFunding as a novel way for entrepreneurial ventures to secure funds without having to seek out venture capital or other forms of investments (Mollick 2013) - and its success features a number of CrowdSourced activities that are enabled by the technology underneath CrowdFunding platforms and the users involvement. This subject is partially covered in the literature in little though thorough research (Hui, Greenberg, Gerber, 2014).

CrowdFunding projects online features several *users performed activities*, each involving a high degree of personal involvement. Users interact and cooperate for performing specific complex tasks and activities - that traditionally require well instructed entity and models - in a qualitative better and less biased way.

Each user is eventually responsible for the success of the campaign. Among others, these activities can be identified in 5 key roles such as: 1) Information asymmetry; 2) Widespread discovery; 3) Widespread promotion; 4) Steering of investments and Due Diligence; 5) Reshaping of Project. These will be analyzed in detail in section 3.

In this paper, in particular in the domain of Equity CrowdFunding, we assess the human touch played CrowdSourced activities for the creation of *long time collective value* for stakeholders - illustrating how social media individual activities and investment decisions played by users-investors address the screening, selection, diffusion and success of each initiative in a detailed and thorough way.

2   Crowfunding as Collective Practice

The latest assessments on the CrowdFunding domain report that aggregated volume of transactions is doubling every two months, in parallel with the global disruptive shift in capital formation. As of the first quarter of 2014, overall global Pledges reached of 351,174,819.50 dollars and the growth trend is rising. *All or Nothing* campaigns tend to collect more pledges, and people are more likely to invest in *equity*

CrowdFunding platforms rather than *Donation* or *Merchandising* systems, due to eventual returns on equity investment[1].

Reasons behind the success of CrowdFunding have been largely analyzed in the literature (Agrawal, Catalini, Goldfarb, 2011; Lambert, Schwienbacher 2010) stressing the importance of aspects such as: 1) the ability to generate preliminary scenarios of the project success - thus screening unprofitable projects from succeeding; 2) the potential to gather nominally minor investments - although from larger sources; 3) the potential to generate stronger social and entrepreneurial interactions within stakeholders; 4) the ability to address investment portfolio diversification and pooling of risks within larger groups; 5) its role as systemic response to the credit crunch and shortage of funds experienced globally in the financial System.

The Creators are generally the startup owners in charge of sponsoring and broadcasting their projects on online dedicated platforms aimed at the solicitation of investments. Investors are individuals such as retail customers, financial institutions and Organizations. The online dedicated Platform is in charge of promoting the collection of funds, targeting the campaigns to adequate investors and monitoring the overall process. The platform is a web provider of the intermediation service between creators soliciting for investments and investors willing to sponsor the project. All users may leave feedback and remarks on the project – allowing creators to adjust and revise possible aspects of the business model according to potential investor's needs and expectations. User's investment decision is based upon open-ended different drivers: the business plan, the team structure and functions, the growth prospective, the scalability, the motivation of the leaders and of course the assessment and feedback of other users.

This process can be synthesized as a flux involving 1 input (the startup project presentation on the platform), following 3 levels of judgment from individual user#1 hence: 1) project analytics 2) personal perception 3) other users feedback; and 1 output as final effect of investments collected - that provides a leveraging effect on subsequent investments (post-user#1) that is strongly affected by *user#1* output. Every level may lead to different *threads of action*, finally stirring the overall investment decision of *post-user#1*, and determining the campaign success. Possibilities are unlimited and levels may be unconstrained.

The literature has focused on the aspects of level 1 and 2 (personal perception and projects feedbacks), in particular ascertaining what features of the campaign shall be emphasized and how – establishing empirical models eager to forecast the likelihood of the campaigns success (Joenssen, Michaelis, Müllerleile 2014). However, such models traditionally require well instructed entity and models and rely on activities that may not be computed[2] - although can be CrowdSourced.

---

[1] Assessment of Sept. 5th 2014 can be retrieved at:
http://www.crowdfundinsider.com/2014/05/38941-crowd-data-center-releases-q1-crowdfunding-data/

[2] We make reference to *computed evaluation criteria* and *IT models* traditionally used by companies, investors and funds to perform selection of projects or ideas.

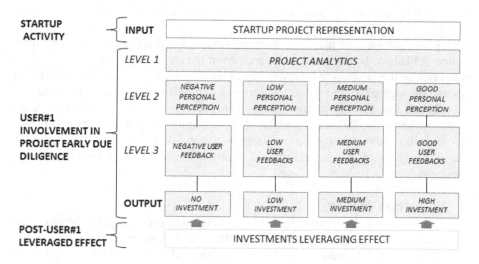

Fig. 1. Investors judgment Flux

By leveraging the crowds to perform the due diligence on projects based upon the individual appreciation of each user and the subsequent activities carried online regarding other users activities (in picture 1 represented in level 2, 3 and 4) leads to safer and more detailed startup quality assessments.

Users distribute comments, submit feedback and perform several activities on social media outlets on the project, which generates a viral spread of the initiative. This spread follows different threads according to user decisions at each level, every time creating new threads. Eventually, this activity leads to a virtuous cycle of *"approval – positive sharing – setting investment thresholds – raising of new investors"* that may set the business success also in the long term creating collective added value for the shareholders. On the other hand, a negative thread of activities (a vicious cycle of *disapproval – negative sharing – not investing – discouraging new investors*) may lead the campaign to fail and the business to be negatively affected also by reputational risk.

The relation between CrowdFunding and CrowdSourced systems establishes a specific social media behavior ensuing safer, more detailed and more effective startup quality assessment on startups that can be identified in the following 5 key roles.

3   Roles of Computational Technology in Crowdfunding

1) Information asymmetry

Information Asymmetry refers to the situation where the entrepreneur is in a position to learn the true quality of the product before the consumers/investors, establishing asymmetric information. In general terms, two situations can be considered: a) *Hidden information*: when the realization of quality escapes the entrepreneur's control (also referred as adverse selection problem) b) *Hidden Action*: when the entrepreneur sets the level of quality prior to the launch (also referred to as *moral hazard*) (Belleflamme 2013).

Due to the levels of judgment aforementioned, CrowdFunding campaign information is likely to be disclosed in advance from the creator in order to avoid reputational risk of the business. Moreover, due to the CrowdSourced due diligence activities and the technology employed by users, relevant information can be detected individually and shared with the community. This prevents both *hidden information* and *hidden actions* from the creator and avoids potential losses on investments. However, this may play a dire role for the campaign as a negative due diligence performed by one user may establish a negative thread within his network and a long-term reputational risk.

2) Widespread discovery

Startups frequently face difficulties in reaching potential investors through basic means due to the technical constraints of traditional investment rounds with single or organized investors (Brydon et al, 2012). Investors often have to be encountered in person, and projects presented to single investors – with a high opportunity cost for the startup. Online and broad sponsoring of investment rounds may ease such constraints, but can hardly reach specific target investors.

Online CrowdFunding enables projects to reach virtually anyone, due to the viral capability of the World Wide Web – while also providing time limits for the collection of funds. Due to the activities performed by users with regards to CrowdFunding campaigns (sharing, posting, promoting), chances of projects reaching investors notably increase. Likewise, there is a surge in the possibility that investors interested in a particular business area can discover a specific campaign for that topic.

3) Widespread promotion

Startups normally experience budget limits in their early stages, especially for business advertising (Davila, Foster 2007). Moreover, not all advertising strategies reach the expected target – creating further constraints for additional advertising promotions.

Online CrowdFunding is a bottom-up activity that bases its strength in its users and crowdsourcing of activities. They are not only investors and they are stakeholders of the business thus sharing - for their own profit - the business success expectations. Positive Activities performed by users on social media account to a low cost advertising campaign – where investors introduce the sponsored business to potential investors and consumers. The latter are finally encouraged to act likewise on the base of user#1 feedbacks and investment threshold. Lastly, providing feedbacks on social media strengthens the commitment and trust of investors, which stimulates additional commitments by other investors (Sargeant, Ford, West 2006).

4) Steering of investments and due diligence

It is commonly considered that CrowdFunding is a risky investment due to its illiquidity, its lack of economic records and the lack of adequate monitoring presidia for the post-funding phase (Agrawal, Catalini, Goldwarb 2013).

However crowdfunded campaigns rely on due diligence carried out by single investors (as mentioned in section 3.1) or by organized communities of investors; or again by professional investors that act as *Early investors*. According to the reliability of the latter and the profits made in their previous investments - when available online - the benchmark set for their specific investment positions also determines future investor's choices.

Financial literature on the matter has emphasized the role played by *Early investors* in establishing trend-following benchmarks, involving other venture capitalist and attracting further investments.

With particular regard to CrowdFunding, Business Angels and Professional investors play one of the most crucial role in the early stage of investment round. By acting as *Early investors*, they perform projects preliminary screening and due diligence; they set benchmarks and pace for subsequent investments and they yield for themselves tactical benefits including easier syndication. The investment trend can also be tracked online by users and this rapidly stirs investors to follow the trend established by *Early investors* [3].

5) Reshaping of Project

CrowdFunding platforms generally establish a specific a minimum threshold of investments to collect before the campaign can be considered as completed. This approach consists of a peculiar *"market test"* that provides valuable information and forecasts on the businesses success.

At first the platform shows the project and its *Goal* threshold. Next, users can post comments, ask questions to the creator, indicate weaknesses of the project and point out favorable/unfavorable aspects. Subsequently, they can decide whether and how to fund the projects, setting also the financial commitment they intend to subscribe.

The projects that reach the goal will be launched and funders will be given equity shares. Projects that do not reach the threshold will not be realized, and sums paid will be fully refunded to the lender without entailing any loss. In either case, the Creator will benefit from this test by gaining advice from investors (potential consumers) and may eventually decide to adjust or reshape some aspects of the business model. Finally, this process allows a very efficient selection of "profitable" projects starting from the design stage of the activity, due to the impact that the project has on investors-consumers.

4   Model

This section considers two models that additionally describes CrowdSourced activities role in CrowdFunding, picturing a complete vision of technology-assisted CrowdFunding while highlighting the 5 key roles of crowdsourcing discussed in section 3.

---

[3] As of today, most CrowdFunding platforms require projects to be sponsored by a professional investor. The Italian Regulatory framework in this extent, requires a mandatory 5% professional investor's subscription on any equity campaign.

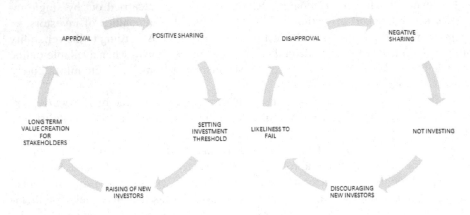

Fig. 2. Positive CrowdSourced activities   **Fig. 3.** Dire CrowdSourced activities

The analysis of the 5 roles of CrowdSourced activities for CrowdFunding campaigns indicate in picture 2 a "virtuous cycle" based upon *approval – positive sharing – setting investment threshold – raising of new investors – long term value creation for stakeholders.* Figure 3 is a negative reflection based upon *disapproval – negative sharing – not investing – discouraging new investors – likeliness to fail.*

Personal approval from funders and especially *Early users* may lead to stronger syndication of users around the project, allowing the flow to function and eventually resulting in the creation of collective value for the stakeholders. The model of picture 2 can be integrated with any of the 5 key roles detected in section 3, establishing different degrees of success of the initiative and higher likelihood of creation of value for the collectivity.

On the contrary, disapproval from users and especially *Early users* leads to an opposite result: *disapproval – negative sharing – not investing – discouraging new investors – likeliness to fail.* This model can also be integrated with any of the 5 key roles detected in section 3.

Technology and CrowdSourced activities play a significant role in both models. First, it enables the widespread and sharing of a great deal of relevant information easily and in aggregated ways. The information is processed according to *threads of communication* and personal approval / disapproval. A satisfied user that has a positive market perceptions of the campaign will set a high investment scale on the campaign, and will share positive information about his investment on social media outlets – establishing a positive thread with a cascade effect on other potential investors of his network.

The opposite will happen with an unsatisfied user, that may not repost or share information on the campaign (hence blocking a thread that becomes neutral) or in a worse scenario, he may repost negative information on the project thus establishing a negative thread in his network that will be hard to invalidate from following users, unless his peers decide to perform the due diligence themselves.

The creation of added value results in the network of satisfied users that sponsor the initiative. These individuals are real stakeholders of the company, and they are hence motivated to help and sustain the business within their community for the profit of their equity investment.

5   Aggregation Experiment

In order to test the consistency of this model, we have developed an online Equity CrowdFunding platform that verifies the soundness of all 5 crowdsourcing systems key roles described in section 3 as compared with the output of *long time collective value*. We consider a generated collective value in case of occurrence of a net *stock increased value* (with regard to initial pledged equity value).

The Equity CrowdFunding Platform created entails a system where users can favor their projects and share their investments on virtually any social media outlet. We will be able to track investor profits, create a hierarchy of the most successful investors and offer the possibility for other users to follow these.

Since the platform requires any startup to nominate a Professional Investor prior to the launch of the campaign, we will consider the acknowledgment of a project from such investors as an auxiliary degree of *project screening and* an initial positive thread - that will further decrease the chances of a business failure.

Likewise, we have programmed a software that allows users through an internal mailing system to provide feedbacks on any project or investment trends. The platform allows the startup to provide polls on the project to the investors - both in the funding phase and in the rollout phase.

The platform is purposely designed to track all activities performed by users according to *threads*. We are hence able to track online activities of users, and categorize them under different threads. To do so, we generate hash tags according to individual user's choices such as *#positive #mediuminvestment #negative #neutral* etc.. We also generate hashtags for investment threshold set by the investor (*#numerical*). The threads structural path, both qualitative and quantitative, will allow us to perform an assessment on whether there is a *chain impact* on investments from users - based upon individual online activities - and the estimated degree of such impact on the overall campaign.

The aim is to test the consistency of the assumption that CrowdSourced activities are relevant to the campaign success, and results will be useful in outperforming possible flaws of each project by timely detecting negative threads. The latter can be mitigated, for example, by reshaping the project as mentioned in section 3.

Also, we aim to assess the *long time collective value* of startups in their roll out phase for the collectivity - based upon the degree of positivity of the threads in scope and the due diligence on profits after each semester. We require each startup to nominate an accountant to track impartially such data. As startups usually do not share dividends in their first years, we will compute only data from startups that have not encountered dilution or dividends distribution, and we will give a time span for the evaluation of 18 months for the first assessment.

The platform is currently ongoing and we have started collecting preliminary data on campaigns. The launch of the platform is planned for the 1st of October 2014 – and first assessments on results will be available starting from the end of 4Q of 2014 with the preliminary evaluation of threads impact and Crowdsourcing on CrowdFunding projects.

6 Concluding Thoughts

Nowadays, there are scarce available set of data worldwide from which to construct a model to assess the specificity of Equity CrowdFunding. At this early stage, prior to carrying out a detailed quantitative analysis, it is necessary to formulate hypotheses and correlations of the different variables that relate to the phenomenology of Equity CrowdFunding and the impact of Crowdsourcing activities. This is a logical-intuitive path, however essential in substantiating empirically the assumptions of the paper.

The data will be analyzed taking also into consideration the international experience of Equity CrowdFunding, and state of the art in the literature of the role of investment in start-ups and business incubators. Further analysis will start from data gathered from the aggregation experiment in order to verify the consistency of the model, and results of may indicate further model development and higher degree of details.

Endogenous and exogenous limits to the model shall be recalled. The success of a startup – even if successfully crowd-funded – depends on many factors (social, economic, juridical, financial) that may not be adequately recorded in the aggregation experiments. The *long time collective value* created by an enterprise for its stakeholder can be assessed by different means, such as the number of new jobs created or the decrease in market price arising from competition, and may not be fully reflected in the net value nor the stock price used in our experiments also due to the current volatility of markets.

Moreover, there are aspects of the threads mechanism that may not be aggregated in the assessment. Updates and amendments in the regulatory setting of equity CrowdFunding - aimed at protecting investors from subscribing risky investments - are currently intensifying in many countries. In some instances, the administrative tasks that must be performed before funding a project may discourage investors and affect the output of the campaign, but not the success of the startup itself.

Equity CrowdFunding is a phenomenon that will enlarge notably in the next years.

This research may provide development of current state of the art analysis and raise questions that may lead to the definition of best practice and models to be replicated worldwide.

References

1. Agrawal, A.K., Catalini, C., Goldfarb, A.: The geography of CrowdFunding. Working paper, National Bureau of Economic Research, Cambridge, MA, USA (2011)
2. Andreini, D., Pedeliento, G.: CrowdFunding: a financing alternative for new ventures: the kickstarter experience. Journal of Investor Relations 1, 26–29 (2013)

3. Anhai, D., Raghu, R., Alon, Y.H.: Crowdsourcing systems on the World-Wide Web. Communications of the ACM (CACM) **54**(4), 86–96 (2011)
4. Belleflemme, P., Lambert, T., Schwienbacher, A.: CrowdFunding: Tapping the Right Crowd (April 25), CORE Discussion Paper, n. 2011/32, pp. 1–20 (2012)
5. Biewald, L.: Current Trends in Web Engineering, Workshops, Doctoral Symposium, and Tutorials, Held at ICWE 2011, Paphos, Cyprus, 20–21 June 2011
6. Brydon, J., Ferguson T., Hoang, J., Israel, A., Tulusan, K.,: Private equity CrowdFunding, SUS6175: Capital Markets, SP12, San Francisco, pp. 6–21 (2012)
7. Freund, J.: How to Overcome the Barriers Between Economy and Sociology With Open Innovation, Open Evaluation and CrowdFunding? International Journal of Industrial Engineering and Management, Martin - Luther University **1**(3), 107–109 (2012)
8. Hui, J.S., Greenberg, M.D., Gerber, E.M.: Understanding the role of community in CrowdFunding work. In: Proceedings of the 17th ACM Conference on Computer Supported Cooperative Work & Social Computing, CSCW 2014, pp. 62–74 (2014)
9. Joenssen, D.W., Michaelis, A., Müllerleile, T.: A Link to New Product Preannouncement: Success Factors in CrowdFunding (2014)
10. Mollick, E.: The dynamics of CrowdFunding: Determinants of success and failure, University of Pennsylvania, Working paper series , Wharton School, pp. 12–24 (2012)
11. Mollick E.: Swept Away by the Crowd? CrowdFunding, Venture Capital, and the Selection of Entrepreneurs University of Pennsylvania, Working paper series, Wharton School, pp. 7–31 (2012)
12. Panagiotis, G., Ipeirotis, M., Paritosh, P.K.: Managing Crowdsourced human computation: a tutorial. In: WWW 2011 Proceedings of the 20th International Conference Companion on World Wide Web, pp. 287–288 (2011)
13. Sargeant, A., Ford, J.B. and West, D.C.: Perceptual determinants of nonprofit giving behavior. Journal of Business Research, 155–165 (2006)
14. Wash, R., Solomon, J.: CrowdFunding and the Return Rule: Reducing Risk but Increasing Spread, Michigan State University Working papers. Communication Arts and Sciences **X**(X), 18–20 (2011)

On Utilizing Player Models to Predict Behavior in Crowdsourcing Tasks

Carlos Pereira Santos[1,2(✉)], Vassilis-Javed Khan[2], and Panos Markopoulos[1]

[1] Eindhoven University of Technology, Eindhoven, The Netherlands
{c.a.pereira.santos,p.markopoulos}@tue.nl
[2] NHTV Breda University of Applied Sciences, Breda, The Netherlands
{santos.c,khan.j}@nhtv.nl

Abstract. Player Modeling is a research field that studies player characteristics by analyzing in-game behavior. We aim to develop independent models, which are transferable and useful beyond a game's context. We shall demonstrate the feasibility of this approach by applying player models to crowdsourcing to predict workers' task completion effectiveness. Specifically, we model a user's Need for Cognition based on in-game behavior, and based on that try to assign appropriate tasks to workers.

1 Introduction

Every single player interaction within a video-game has the potential of generating data. Each player's in-game behavior can be tracked, for example, the sequence of pressed buttons, the usage of specific words, the response time for a certain part of the game, or the frequency of game-specific actions such as walking, picking up items or purchasing items.

By using data analysis techniques like simply counting the occurrences of specific events [1], or more complex clustering techniques [2] it is possible to obtain general information about the player, like: personality traits, age groups and skill sets. Player modeling is a recent research field directly applied to games, which recent research studies show to attain not only player skills but also predict specific players' traits.

Those models are currently used to improve video-game experiences, during new development cycles like associating specific play styles with player age [3], or using avatars to profile personality traits [4], or even to reduce a game's difficulty and improve player experience [5].

In a recent chapter [6] defined four different purposes for using player models: *i)* game balancing, i.e., adapt the game experience based on the player skill, *ii)* personalized content, i.e., procedural generation of more content, *iii)* game authoring, i.e., playtest to determine whether it provides the desired player experience and *iv)* monetization, i.e., increase revenue, popular in free-to-play games.

However, we think that there is a greater potential for player models. The work we have been developing is focused on creating Context Independent Player Models (CIPMs) by building player models which can be applied for other than game

© Springer International Publishing Switzerland 2015
L.M. Aiello and D. McFarland (Eds.): SocInfo 2014 Workshops, LNCS 8852, pp. 448–451, 2015.
DOI: 10.1007/978-3-319-15168-7_54

systems. More specifically we aim to investigate whether and to what extent player models can be utilized to identify more suitable workers in crowdsourcing systems and increase value of the human touch.

2 Prior Art

Crowdsourcing tasks are making an important contribution to society by providing jobs, while still allowing enterprises to maintain quality and cut costs. Apart from the obvious motivation of financial benefits there are more reasons for people to engage on crowdsourcing such as: altruism, enjoyment, reputation and socialization [7].

There are already some examples that illustrate the potential of our approach. The Malaria Training Game [8] is a first example combining gaming aspects and crowd intelligence. It utilizes learning capabilities of human crowds to conduct reliable microscopic analysis of biomedical samples. A second example is Quizz [9]. It is a crowdsourcing game, which assesses a user's knowledge within a specific field and enrich the system's knowledge base. In both systems, the game results (answers) are used to improve or validate knowledge. The difference in our approach is that these and other similar systems can be improved if the in-game player behavior is analyzed, providing a richer knowledge about the player, not only using the game results but also the way game is played. Hence the need to create CIPMs, which would be valid not only within the game context, but also, as a cross-domain profiling tool.

Most of crowdsourcing task platforms do not consider individual workers abilities, personality, and context when assigning tasks. Recent studies have showed that user profiling tools could improve quality and workers satisfaction [10]. Integration of CIPM to profile crowdsourcing workers would bring advantages such as: i) keep workers more motivated, ii) it would be more difficult for workers to cheat in self-reported profiling tools, iii) it would be an unobtrusive way of creating a player model and iv) can complement existing services or be integrated within the task.

3 Case Study: Need for Cognition as CIPM

Most of player modeling studies are performed based on data-mining techniques which try to statistically correlate (large) set of collected variables about player in-game behavior. In the research line we propose a different approach: to design game mechanics, which are able to determine specific player models.

For this reason we focused our research on a specific personality trait – Need for Cognition (NC). NC is a personality trait associated with the extent a certain person is inclined to perform cognitive activities. NC researches the link between personality and behavior, and can be reliable measured through a self-report questionnaire [11].

NC is a simple and stable personality model, and it has been applied across contexts to make predictions of user behavior[12]. High NC defines a personality which is more inclined to mental problem solving, assessment of situations with higher degree of elaboration; persons with lower NC are prone to less elaboration and follow more heuristic/empirical strategies. The dualism of this personality trait creates an area to explore inference using CIPM.

NC is also important for specific crowdsourcing tasks. Studies on profiling labor compared crowdsourcing workers to other recruiting methods and concluded that workers are representative of the general population and substantially less expensive to recruit also observer NC as a personality trait [14].

In practice, this may allow assigning specific tasks which require more reasoning to high cognition workers, even classify workers into crowdsourcing categories (e.g. low NC workers to crowd labor, or high NC workers to crowd creativity); this categorization is based on industry website Crowdsourcing.org, and depicted in infographic about crowdsourcing companies and services [15].

To our knowledge NC is being used to serve as profiling tool within both contexts (games and crowdsourcing), but, never being inferred through game behavior or being used to predict and influence crowd tasks; this makes NC a good and credible personality trait for us to study as CIPM.

Based on the aforementioned analysis of existing studies, the key research questions we are interested in addressing are:

- Can Need for Cognition predict people's behavior in crowdsourcing applications?
- Can certain game mechanics be designed to reliably infer Need for Cognition?

3.1   Method and Current Study

We are currently in an exploratory phase, where we are evaluating the possibility of inferring NC based on users' gameplay. We have already developed a game which integrates a mechanic to specifically to measure NC (Fig. 1). This mechanic is based on the work of Boatman [13] which states that individuals with a high NC are process-oriented as opposed to outcome-oriented. More specifically, in our game we ask players to control the movement of a set of units. We embedded a hint system (using game AI) which provides one possible (non-optimal) movement to support the decision making process. In theory, higher NC players are driven by the cognition and the process, not the outcome, hence, we should observe that high NC players will use and follow less hints, unlike lower NC which are goal oriented and opt to take mental

Fig. 1. The mobile game we developed to integrate mechanics to infer a player's NC

shortcuts, consequently, follow hints more frequently. The in-game data will be compared to NC measured using the 18-item self-report questionnaire [11]. The game is available online and we are gathering data.

For the experiments we are conducting all user collected information is fully anonymous, and used exclusively for research purposes, we agree that the integration such techniques should be subjected to a clear privacy policies with user consent.

References

1. Drachen, A., Canossa, A.: Towards gameplay analysis via gameplay metrics. In: Proceedings of the 13th International MindTrek Conference: Everyday Life in the Ubiquitous Era on - MindTrek 2009, pp. 202–209. ACM Press (2009)
2. Mahlmann, T., Drachen, A., Togelius, J., Canossa, A., Yannakakis, G.N.: Predicting player behavior in Tomb Raider: underworld. In: Proceedings of the 2010 IEEE Conference on Computational Intelligence and Games, CIG 2010, pp. 178–185 (2010)
3. Tekofsky, S., Spronck, P., Plaat, A., van den Herik, J., Broersen, J.: Play style: showing your age. In: 2013 IEEE Conference on Computational Intelligence in Games (CIG), pp. 1–8. IEEE (2013)
4. Yee, N., Ducheneaut, N.: Introverted elves & conscientious gnomes: the expression of personality in world of warcraft. In: Proc. SIGCHI Conf. Hum. Factors Comput. Syst., pp. 753–762 (2011)
5. Zook, A.E., Riedl, M.O.: A temporal data-driven player model for dynamic difficulty adjustment. In: Proceedings of the 8th AAAI Conference on Artificial Intelligence and Interactive Digital Entertainment, AIIDE 2012, pp. 93–98 (2012)
6. Yannakakis, G.N., Spronck, P., Loiacono, D., André, E.: Player Modeling (2013). http://drops.dagstuhl.de/opus/volltexte/2013/4335/
7. Quinn, A.J., Bederson, B.B.: Human computation: a survey and taxonomy of a growing field. In: Proceedings of the SIGCHI Conference on Human Factors in Computing Systems, pp. 1403–1412. ACM (2011)
8. Luengo-Oroz, M.A., Arranz, A., Frean, J.: Crowdsourcing malaria parasite quantification: an online game for analyzing images of infected thick blood smears. J. Med. Internet Res. **14**, e167 (2012)
9. Ipeirotis, P.G., Gabrilovich, E.: Quizz: targeted crowdsourcing with a billion (potential) users. In: Proc. 23rd Int. Conf. World Wide Web, pp. 143–154 (2014)
10. Sarasua, C., Thimm, M.: Microtask Available, Send us your CV! In: 2013 International Conference on Cloud and Green Computing, pp. 521–524. IEEE (2013)
11. Cacioppo, J.T., Petty, R.E., Kao, C.F.: The efficient assessment of need for cognition. J. Pers. Assess. **48**, 306–307 (1984)
12. Kaptein, M., Markopoulos, P., de Ruyter, B., Aarts, E.: Can you be persuaded? individual differences in susceptibility to persuasion. In: Gross, T., Gulliksen, J., Kotzé, P., Oestreicher, L., Palanque, P., Prates, R.O., Winckler, M. (eds.) INTERACT 2009, Part I. LNCS, vol. 5726, pp. 115–118. Springer, Heidelberg (2009)
13. Boatman, P.R., Day, E.A., Kowollik, V., Espejo, J., McEntire, L.E.: Modeling the links between need for cognition and the acquisition of a complex skill (2007)
14. Berinsky, A., Huber, G., Lenz, G.: Evaluating Online Labor Markets for Experimental Research: Amazon.com's Mechanical Turk. Polit. Anal. **20**, 351–368 (2012)
15. Blattberg, E.: Crowdsourcing Industry Landscape (2011)

Comparing Human and Algorithm Performance on Estimating Word-Based Semantic Similarity

Nils Batram[1(✉)], Markus Krause[1], and Paul-Olivier Dehaye[2]

[1] Leibniz University, Hannover, Germany
nils.batram@gmx.de, markus@hci.uni-hannover.de
[2] University of Zurich, Zurich, Switzerland
pdehaye@math.ethz.ch

Abstract. Understanding natural language is an inherently complex task for computer algorithms. Crowdsourcing natural language tasks such as semantic similarity is therefore a promising approach. In this paper, we investigate the performance of crowdworkers and compare them to offline contributors as well as to state of the art algorithms. We will illustrate that algorithms do outperform single human contributors but still cannot compete with results gathered from groups of contributors. Furthermore, we will demonstrate that this effect is persistent across different contributor populations. Finally, we give guidelines for easing the challenge of collecting word based semantic similarity data from human contributors.

1 Introduction

Semantic similarity plays an important role for many natural language processing tasks, especially word sense disambiguation and information retrieval [1, 2]. Humans are better than algorithms at rating semantic similarity between two words. The employment of human knowledge however is inflexible, time-consuming and expensive. Involving paid online workers on a crowdsourcing platform (crowdworkers) can reduce costs, but the response quality is harder to predict. The incentive structure for crowdworkers is mostly financial and purposefully under-performing crowdworkers are still a major challenge for crowdsourcing [3]. Different algorithmic approaches do exist [4–6] but are not yet able to reproduce human level results [7]. We aim to answer the question whether crowdworkers provide results at a quality level that justifies the extra costs compared to state of the art algorithms. In this article, we compare three identical data sets generated by offline contributors with native command of the English language, crowdworkers, and state of the art algorithms. We will illustrate that although predictions based on individual human rater scores underperform compared to algorithms, predictions based on averaged human rater scores do outperform algorithms in estimating population averages.

© Springer International Publishing Switzerland 2015
L.M. Aiello and D. McFarland (Eds.): SocInfo 2014 Workshops, LNCS 8852, pp. 452–460, 2015.
DOI: 10.1007/978-3-319-15168-7_55

2   Related Work

Using crowdworkers is effective in many areas like paraphrase recognition [8], transcribing large amounts of text [9] or detecting accessibility problems on sidewalks in Google Streetview [10], but the response quality of crowdworkers judging semantic similarity is still unknown. Temporal Semantic Analysis (TSA) is a state of the art algorithm for predicting semantic similarity with good results on standardized data sets [7]. TSA uses statistical information about words, including usage over time. Radinsky et al. [7] already use results from crowdworkers and offline contributors on semantic similarity to estimate their algorithms quality. However, they do not compare crowdworkers with offline contributors directly, leaving the following questions open:

RQ1: Do averaged crowdworker results perform better than algorithms?
RQ2: Do averaged crowdworker results perform on the same level as offline contributors?

Both questions yield a sub question. As current research only observes average scores of human raters, we are interested in the performance on an individual level:

RQ1a: Do individual crowdworkers perform better than algorithms?
RQ2a: Do individual crowdworkers perform as well as offline contributors?

As explained above a rigorous quality management is sometimes necessary to achieve reasonable results from crowdworkers [11]. In most scenarios, experimenter only use simple quality control mechanisms such as ground truth questions [12] also called gold questions or control questions. We also want to investigate the relevance of this aspect:

RQ3: What level of quality control is necessary for optimal response quality?

Since human ratings are the baseline, we formulate the following hypotheses for the posed research questions:

H1: Crowdworkers do outperform algorithms when quality control is applied.
H2: The response quality of crowdworkers is comparable to offline contributors.

3   Study Design

Our study uses a between-group design with three conditions. The first two conditions are crowdworkers without ground truth questions (*uncontrolled*) and crowdworkers with ground truth questions (*controlled*). We performed all crowdsourcing-based experiments on the *CrowdFlower* online self-service platform. We accepted workers from Australia, UK and the US for all conditions. As other studies on word-based semantic similarity we use the WordSimilarity-353 test collection [13]. The set consists of 353 word pairs of the English language and contains 13 to 16 human judgments for each word pair with a continuous scale from 0 (totally unrelated) to 10 (very related). Finkelstein et al. [13] collected this set from offline contributors with near native command of the English language. We refer to this set as the *WS-353* condition. We compare the results of our human conditions to two state of the art algorithms from different authors namely *TSA* [7] and *ESA* (Explicit Semantic Analysis) [14].

For the *controlled* condition we used twelve word pairs from the *WS-353* data set as ground truth questions. We used their averaged similarity score as baseline and accepted all responses not more than two score points away from this mean as valid.

All crowdworkers in the *controlled* condition had to take an introduction test of four random ground truth questions. We only accepted workers with an accuracy of 70% or higher. While working on the actual task crowdworkers got a ground truth question every sixth task in the *controlled* condition. We discarded responses from workers when their accuracy dropped below 70%. For each word pair we collected 13-14 judgments in the *controlled* condition, for 4413 judgments.

Additionally we collected 73-113 judgments for ground truth questions, resulting in further 1096 judgments. 42 different crowdworkers added to the results, with an average of 107 judgments (without ground truth questions). For our analysis, we dropped all workers with less than 50 responses, leaving 23 workers and 3894 judgments for evaluation. We also repeated the *controlled* condition two times with different settings for the introduction test. As the results were identical, we only refer to the first instance of the *controlled* condition.

For the *uncontrolled* condition, we collected 13 judgments for each word pair from 16 different workers, resulting in 4589 judgments with an average of approximately 287 judgments per worker. We did not use ground truth questions nor introduction tests in this task.

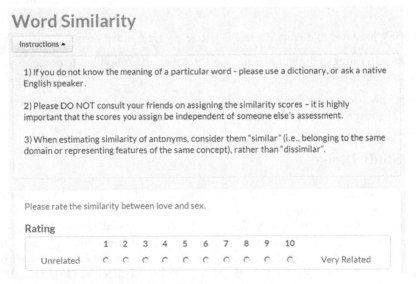

Fig. 1. Screenshot of the Word Similarity task on CrowdFlower

4   Procedure

We conduct both experiments for the *uncontrolled* and *controlled* conditions using CrowdFlower. We gave instructions identical to the *WS-353* survey. We left out some instructions specific to the *WS-353* implementation, e.g. crowdworkers did not have to state their name at the beginning of the survey since their ID is automatically stored. Every crowdworker had to rate the similarity between pairs of words on a Likert scale from 1 (unrelated) to 10 (very related). For technical reasons, the scale goes from 1 to 10 contrary to the *WS-353* data set with a scale from 0 to 10. We normalized all ratings to lie in the range [0.0, 1.0] for the evaluation process. Figure 1 shows a screen shot of the experiments interface as seen by our crowdworkers.

5   Measures

To estimate the performance of crowdworkers and offline contributors we use Spearman's Rank-Order Correlation (Spearman's ρ). To estimate the overall quality of a condition we calculate ρ for the condition and the average similarity scores from *WS-353*. For each condition we average the scores of each word pair over all contributors (averaged results). We calculate these average scores for each condition and the results of *WS-353*.

Correlation can only reveal relative differences. Therefore we also estimate mean squared error (*MSE*) and again use the average of the *WS-353* data set as an estimator for the population mean. To estimate *MSE* we normalize all scores to lie in the interval [0.0, 1.0]. So that:

$$X = \frac{X - X_{min}}{X_{max} - X_{min}}$$

We calculate the mean of these normalized scores for each word pair in each condition. We calculate *MSE* using the mean normalized scores of the WS-353 data set as an estimate for the true values. Although, semantic similarity is subjective we can estimate the *MSE* for a condition to be a predictor for the population average. If the results from a condition are close to the population average, we can assume a higher utility.

To measure the response quality of individual contributors within a condition we calculate Spearman's ρ to the average scores of WS-353 for every contributor. We then calculate mean and standard deviation (σ) of these resulting ρ scores (individual results). This allows us to compare individuals from each condition with each other. We also calculate individual *MSE* scores in the same way.

For the *TSA* algorithm we use the ρ values as reported by Radinsky et al. [7]. Beside correlation, another important quality indicator is inter-rater agreement (*IRA*). Although semantic similarity in general is a subjective task, the *WS-353* list of word pairs contains few controversial pairs. Therefore, *IRA* is a useful indicator for response quality. To estimate *IRA* we calculate Krippendorf's alpha coefficient α [15] for contributors in each condition.

6   Results

First, we investigate our first and third questions (**RQ1**, **RQ3**): Can crowdworkers outperform current state-of-the-art algorithms without quality control mechanisms. The *controlled* condition has the highest correlation of $\rho = 0.88$, followed by the *TSA* algorithm with $\rho = 0.79$ and *ESA* with $\rho = 0.75$. In the *uncontrolled* condition, crowdworkers achieved $\rho = 0.62$ without quality control. All correlations are significant on an α-level of 0.001. This supports hypothesis **H1** that without quality control state of the art algorithms do outperform crowdworkers in our task. The mean squared error of the crowdsourced conditions supports this hypothesis as well. After normalizing similarity scores the *MSE* for the *controlled* condition is 0.08 compared to 0.31 in the *uncontrolled* condition. The *MSE* scores of both algorithms are also higher with 0.29 for *TSA* and 0.31 for *ESA*.

Our second question **RQ2** compared crowdworkers and offline contributors. The *uncontrolled* condition had an individual average correlation of $\rho = 0.26$ ($\sigma = 0.24$). In the *controlled* condition crowdworkers had individual average correlations of $\rho = 0.69$ ($\sigma = 0.07$). Contributors in the *WS-353* condition have an average correlation of $\rho = 0.75$ ($\sigma = 0.07$). To calculate the individual average agreement for the *WS-353* condition we compare each contributor to the average score of the *WS-353* without this contributor. Figure 2 shows a boxplot of the individual results. Again all correlations are significant on an α-level of 0.001.

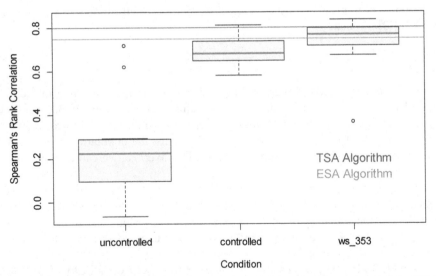

Fig. 2. Individual correlations between human based conditions and the average of the *WS-353* data set. Horizontal lines give results for *TSA* and *ESA* algorithms as reported in [7].

As the results of the *WS-353* condition are very close to the *controlled* condition, it is not clear if the differences originate from random effects, possible errors introduced through the normalization, or other effects. Therefore, we compare the *IRA* of both conditions. A higher *IRA* indicates better agreement within contributors and is an indicator for the quality of responses. Although semantic similarity is an inherently subjective task, the data set *WS-353* contains very few controversial word pairs. Consequently, results with a higher *IRA* are likely to be of higher quality than results with a low *IRA*. Table 1 reports Krippendorf's alpha scores for all human based conditions. The agreement between contributors in the *controlled* condition $\alpha = 0.444$ is lower than in the *WS-353* condition with $\alpha = 0.506$. Therefore, we cannot support our hypothesis *H2* that crowdworker perform on the same level as offline contributors with our experiment.

Table 1. Inter Rater Agreement within each condition estimated with Krippendorf's alpha

Uncontrolled	$\alpha = 0.004$
Controlled	$\alpha = 0.444$
WS-353	$\alpha = 0.506$

These findings are consistent with measured individual *MSE* scores. The average individual *MSE* score for the controlled condition is 0.19 ($\sigma = 0.05$) which is higher than the average *MSE* score for the *WS-353* condition 0.03 ($\sigma = 0.007$).

These results indicate that on an individual level the *TSA* algorithm can outperform offline human contributors' and crowdworkers alike. Yet the *MSE* score of both algorithms (TSA=0.29 ($\sigma = 0.14$), ESA=0.31 ($\sigma = 0.18$)) is higher than the average individual *MSE* in the uncontrolled and *WS-353* condition. Therefore, we cannot yet definitely answer our questions **RQ1a** and **RQ2a** that contributors are less accurate on an individual level in predicting population averages.

The results show that for our experiment aggregated human responses still outperform algorithms in predicting population averages. In order to estimate the number of contributors necessary to achieve good results we drew 7 sets of 1000 unique combinations of contributors from our 23 contributors in the *controlled* condition. Each of the 7 sets was selected so that each word pair aggregated n responses from different contributors, with n in the range of two to eight. We averaged the scores for each pair and calculated Spearman ρ for each sets average to the average of *WS-353*. Figure 3 shows the number of responses per word pair necessary to achieve certain Spearman ρ scores with crowdworkers from the *controlled* condition in our experiment.

As stated earlier we repeated the *controlled* condition with different settings for the introductory test. In the first repetition, we removed the test completely. In the second repetition, we used eight instead of four ground truth questions of which seven had to be correct. All repetitions and the *controlled* condition show nearly identical results for *IRA*, correlation, and *MSE*. The differences of Spearman's ρ are not significant at an α-level of 0.1 with power >95%. These results not only demonstrate that minimal precautions were already sufficient to enhance response quality in our experiment but also illustrate that the results are repeatable. We repeated the *controlled* condition three weeks after the initial trial.

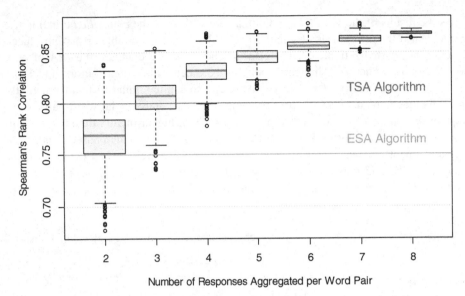

Fig. 3. Boxplot of correlation with different numbers of responses aggregated for each word pair. For each box, we used 1000 permutations of crowdworkers from our controlled set of 19 workers so that an average of *n* workers contributed to the result of a word pair. We compare each set to the average of the WS-353 data set. Horizontal lines indicate *TSA* and *ESA* scores as reported in [7].

7   Discussion and Future Work

Semantic similarity plays an important role in natural language processing, especially word sense disambiguation and information retrieval. In our experiment, we compare responses of crowdworkers, offline contributors, and two algorithms *TSA* (Temporal Semantic Analysis) and *ESA* (Explicit Semantic Analysis) on the same 353 word pairs.

In our experiment, we found that human contributors are better than algorithms at estimating population averages for word based semantic similarity when their responses are aggregated. The correlation of the best crowdsourced condition is $\rho = 0.88$ and therefore higher than the best score from any algorithm (TSA) with $\rho = 0.79$. In our experiment, aggregating responses from at least five contributors per word pair were necessary to achieve higher ρ-scores than the *TSA* algorithm.

On an individual level, the TSA algorithm achieves better Spearman's ρ correlation scores than individual contributors than any other condition. Yet individual contributors in our *controlled* condition still achieve better *MSE* (mean squared error) scores of 0.19 ($\sigma = 0.05$) than the *TSA* algorithm with a score of 0.29.

We found that for our experiment the design of the introductory test had no impact on response quality. The reason for this might be that spammers avoid tasks as soon as minimal precautions against spamming are taken.

The measured ρ-scores of the *controlled* condition are close to the offline contributors from the *WS-353* data set. However, measured *MSE* scores differ significantly. Future work should investigate whether more sophisticated quality control mechanisms and feedback methods [16, 17] can enhance response quality of crowdworkers. Furthermore, the *WS-353* data set was introduced in 2002 and contains words with a high temporal component. For instance, *Maradona* or *Arafat* might have had more relevance in 2002 than 2014. Future work should evaluate the influence of temporal differences by repeating the *WS-353* experiment at the same time as the crowdsourced conditions.

Acknowledgments. We would like to thank Kira Radinsky for responding so fast to our inquiry, although she had not visited her university for 3 years. This paper would have been much less concise without her help.

References

1. Feng, J., Zhou, Y., Martin, T.: Sentence similarity based on relevance. In: Proceedings of IPMU 2008, pp. 832–839 (2008)
2. Navigli, R.: Word Sense Disambiguation: A Survey. ACM Computing Surveys **41**(2), Article 10 (2009)
3. Krause, M., Porzel, R.: It is about time : time aware quality management for interactive systems with humans in the loop. In: CHI 2013 EA. ACM Press, Paris, France (2013)
4. Strube, M., Ponzetto, S.P.: WikiRelate! computing semantic relatedness using wikipedia. In: AAAI, pp. 1419–1424 (2006)
5. Yang, D., Powers, D.M.W.: Measuring semantic similarity in the taxonomy of WordNet. In: Conferences in Research and Practice in Information Technology, vol. 38, pp. 315–322 (2005)
6. Resnik, P.: Using information content to evaluate semantic similarity in a taxonomy. In: Proceedings of IJCAI 1995 (1995)
7. Radinsky, K., Agichtein, E., Gabrilovich, E., Markovitch, S.: A word at a time: computing word relatedness using temporal semantic analysis. In: Proceedings of WWW 2011, pp. 337–346 (2011)
8. Tschirsich, M., Hintz, G.: Leveraging crowdsourcing for paraphrase recognition. In: Proceedings of the 7th Linguistic Annotation Workshop & Interoperability with Discourse, pp. 205–213 (2013)
9. Williams, J.D., Melamed, I.D., Alonso, T., Hollister, B., Wilpon, J.: Crowd-sourcing for difficult transcription of speech. In: 2011 IEEE ASRU Workshop, pp. 535–540 (2011)
10. Hara, K., Le, V., Froehlich, J.: Combining crowdsourcing and google street view to identify street-level accessibility problems. In: Proceedings of CHI 2013, pp. 631–640 (2013)
11. Radinsky, K., Agichtein, E., Gabrilovich, E., Markovitch, S.: A word at a time: computing word relatedness using temporal semantic analysis. In: Proceedings of WWW 2011, pp. 337–346 (2011)
12. Wang, J., Ipeirotis, P., Provost, F.: Quality-Based Pricing for Crowdsourced Workers. NYU Working Paper No. 2451/31833 (2013)
13. Oleson, D., Sorokin, A., Laughlin, G., Hester, V., Le, J., Biewald, L.: Programmatic Gold: Targeted and Scalable Quality Assurance in Crowdsourcing. Human Computation: Papers from the 2011 AAAI Workshop, pp. 43–48 (2011)

14. Finkelstein, L., Gabrilovich, E., Matias, Y., Rivlin, E., Solan, Z., Wolfman, G., Ruppin, E.: Placing Search in Context : The Concept Revisited. ACM Transactions on Information Systems **20**(1), 116–131 (2002)
15. Gabrilovich, E., Markovitch, S.: Computing Semantic Relatedness Using Wikipedia-based Explicit Semantic Analysis. IJCAI **7**, 1606–1611 (2007)
16. Krippendorff, K.: Estimating the Reliability, Systematic Error and Random Error of Interval Data. Educational and Psychological Measurement **30**(1), 61–70 (1970)
17. Sheng, V.S., Provost, F., Ipeirotis, P.G.: Get another label? improving data quality and data mining using multiple, noisy labelers. In: Proceedings of the 14th ACM SIGKDD International Conference on Knowledge Discovery and Data Mining, p. 614 (2008)
18. Krause, M.: GameLab: A tool suit to support designers of systems with Homo Ludens in the loop. In: HComp 2013: Works in Progress and Demonstration Abstracts, pp. 38–39. AAAI Press, Palm Springs (2013)

Mobile Picture Guess: A Crowdsourced Serious Game for Simulating Human Perception

Michael Riegler[1]([✉]), Ragnhild Eg[1], Mathias Lux[2], and Markus Schicho[3]

[1] Simula Research Laboratory, Oslo, Norway
{michael,rage}@simula.no
[2] University of Klagenfurt, Klagenfurt, Austria
mathias.lux@itec.uni-klu.ac.at
[3] Econob, Klagenfurt, Austria
markus.schicho@econob.com

Abstract. In this paper we present a novel idea that combines a mobile game with a Crowdsourcing campaign. The game is designed for studies into the visual saliency of image segments, where the game objective is for players to guess what is depicted in an image that is gradually uncovering. Game scores depend on the number of correct answers and the speed at which these are provided. With these game mechanics, we can determine the image segments that are most essential to players when asked to guess the image content, thereby assessing the most salient image regions. Through the combination of this game scenario and a Crowdsourcing campaign, we also present a way to tackle the rising demands for higher salaries in this line of work. By providing workers with an entertaining task, we aim to increase player motivation and hopefully make them want to play longer than required. In this paper we also present a sample study that evaluates the visual saliency of 200 animal images from Flickr. We conclude with preliminary results from the study and with our insights on how this approach can be applied to improve the current understanding of human visual perception.

Keywords: Crowdsourcing · Human perception · Human computation · Game with a purpose

1 Introduction

Nowadays computer science can solve numerous problems without the help of humans, for instance in areas like computer vision and information retrieval. A wide range of algorithms and methods already exist and these are very efficient in emulating human behaviour. Yet there is still a huge gap between what computers can do and what humans can do. As a result, human computation has evolved as a research area, and recent years have seen its importance increase within related research communities. Human computation can be used to learn from human behaviour and cognition or can be applied to situations where computers cannot replace human performance, for instance in perceptual or preference tasks (such as Crowdsourcing). Research in this area has yielded promising

L.M. Aiello and D. McFarland (Eds.): SocInfo 2014 Workshops, LNCS 8852, pp. 461–468, 2015.
DOI: 10.1007/978-3-319-15168-7_56

results, but it also shows that we still have a lot to learn about humans' capabilities. In order to improve our understanding about human perception, we present a methodology that uses a Game With a Purpose (GWAP), as a variety of human computation, in conjunction with Crowdsourcing. The gathered information can also be applied to solve problems in other areas, for instance in content based image retrieval.

In this scenario, the game design facilitates the study of how players observe the content of an image and which elements are most salient in content recognition. Moreover, we explore how a well-designed Human Intelligence Task (HIT) may peak the interest of players and increase the amount of data generated by these workers. With these goals in mind, we developed a GWAP with an engaging task that occupies the attention of players and that collects data without disturbing their focus. The main contributions from this endeavour include, (i) a novel game with a purpose, designed to collect subconscious information from the user, (ii) the means to improve our understanding of human perception, (iii) a preliminary study of the image elements that are most vital in content recognition, and (iv) a dataset collected for further analyses and for future public availability. The paper is outlined in separate sections. We first present relevant results from related works, we then describe the design and the purpose of the game, before we provide details about the experiment and the HIT. Finally, we provide our preliminary findings and conclusions and share our plans for future work.

2   Related Work

The idea behind GWAP, or serious games, is to design them so that they provide fun to the players while simultaneously serving a greater purpose. This purpose could be to generate useful data, to communicate information, to teach concepts, or to animate to movement. Most serious games are based on the work of von Ahn [5], who developed *ESP Game* and *Peekaboom* to demonstrate the concept, along with other widely used games [6]. The ESP Game asks players to label random images, whereas Peekaboom involves adding locations to the previously labelled objects. This location information can later be used in algorithms for object detection or for classification tasks. In his paper, von Ahn outlines the purpose and the usefulness of these games and describes how serious games can be applied to a wide range of areas, such as computer vision and content filtering, as well as security and information retrieval.

A great challenge in the design of a GWAP is the balance between obtaining useful and sufficient amounts of data and creating a task that engages and encourages players. This challenge emphasises the importance of both the gameplay and the underlying game mechanics. Most serious games are designed to support multi-player mode, and Siu et al. [4] have demonstrated the benefits of collaborative and competitive game interactions over individual tasks. Single player serious games less common, mainly because they pose additional challenges relating to player motivation and input controls. In [2], the authors elaborate on these challenges, stating that the needs of researchers and developers are not easily combined with the entertainment desired by players. To overcome this challenge, we wanted to consider feedback from researchers and players alike and thus decided on an iterative development of our GWAP. Although crowdsourcing has become a well-known term in many research circles, the gamification seen through the development of serious games is a recent trend. The gamification of crowdsourcing emerged in response to the number of workers that seemed mostly motivated by any possible means to maximise profits, at the expense of work integrity and response accuracy. In casual terms, we can divide crowdsourcing workers into two groups, the financially driven and the entertainment driven ones. The need to isolate the second group from the first gave birth to the idea of transforming the questions at hand to game scenarios. Consequently, researchers gain the benefits of higher engagement and faithfulness to the task, common among gamers, along with the means to quickly extract results with higher accuracy and better cost-efficiency.

So far, many Crowdsourcing applications have been developed, but the use of serious games is not yet widespread. From the field of scientific research come some highly interesting applications that serve to exemplify the importance and efficiency of games of purpose in attacking problems that computers fail to resolve. For instance, using an online puzzle video game called Foldit [1], scientists from the University of Washington called on the help of gamers when they failed to solve the structure of the AIDS protein using advanced crystallography technology. It only took a few days for a team called *Contenders* to puzzle together a protein that fit almost perfectly with the answer the scientists were looking for. In a subsequent interview [1], the designer and developer of Foldit mentioned that the team's unfamiliarity with biochemistry worked as an advantage in this study. Hence, serious games take research problems that have been confined to scientific environments and present them to a larger and more diverse group of people. Being naïve to the background of a presented problem may enable these people to approach the question from a previously unseen angle.

The advantage of combining game mechanics with a crowdsourcing task has also been explored in a machine learning experiment. Eickhoff and colleagues [3] carried out a large-scale crowdsourced game task, in which workers played an annotation game to assess document relevance. In short, they observe that the game design motivates workers to play on even after they receive the required payment token. However, they note that players become frustrated when there is no real conclusion to the game, and they address the issue that some game tasks may inspire more towards a win than an accurate performance.

The design of our GWAP stands out with its single player experience and its research aim. We seek to investigate perceptual mechanisms in individual visual tasks, thereby collecting data that will contribute to increase our understanding of how humans process images. Furthermore, we have ensured a clear start and end-point in the game, and designed the task so that the survival rate is contingent on a player's accurate performance.

---

[1] http://www.gamesforchange.org/play/foldit/

3 The Game

With the aim to develop a GWAP that facilitates studies into human visual perception using single player game modes, we decided on the category of puzzle games. Our game was developed in an iterative manner, with new user tests following each iteration. Accordingly, we relied on the analyses from each completed test to point out game aspects in need of alteration, or new functionalities that should be added. Through this process, we improved permutations between our research goals and the players' requests. In the end, we have achieved a game that is both fun to play and collects the desired information in a fluent fashion. The entire system is comprised of two parts, the game and the back-end server solution. While the game collects data from the players, the server in the background stores this information and keeps it readily available for future use.

3.1 Gameplay

The main objective of our game is the study of perceptual mechanisms involved in image recognition, making the single player mode a requisite. To begin, players download the game to their own touch-screen Android phone, we include a detailed description of this process in section 3.2. At the start of the game, the player is allocated a period of time and the countdown commences with the game. The game is divided into rounds, and in each round the player is asked to guess the content of the image that is gradually revealed. The image is presented alongside four response options, illustrated in Figure 1, and the player uses the touch-screen of the phone to select their response. Considering that owners of this type of phone are generally familiar with using human touch in their technological interactions, we deemed this type of tactile input a familiar scenario that should only increase game involvement. The round concludes with a correct response, or when the image is entirely unveiled, whichever comes first. The full game is made up of as many rounds as the player can complete in the given amount of time.

The image material was selected over several steps. First, we identified a list of 124 visually different animals and annotated them with their respective names, from albatross to zebra. After that, we used these terms to query the images on Flickr, selecting those that are free to use or that are published under a Creative Commons attribution license. To ensure visually appealing content, we ranked the images by Flickr's interestingness score and kept the highest-ranked 25 images for each animal. This resulted in more than 3000 images, from which we selected 200 to use in the game. The criteria for this final selection were based on the visibility of the relevant animal and the absence of excessive editing, such as borders and overlays. For images under the Creative Commons license, we overlaid a license text in the lower left corner. Finally, we dedicated three random, but manually validated, wrong answers to each of the 200 images, in addition to the correct animal name.

For the visual aspect of the game, the order of the terms is randomised prior to every single presentation. At the start of each round, the image is completely masked by a black screen, but this then gradually disappears as blocks in a mosaic. With time, more and more of the image becomes visible as more and more of the blocks disappear. This implies that the guessing task becomes easier with time, and accordingly the point reward decreases steadily down to zero as the image unveils. This motivates the player to provide a response as quickly as possible. With a correct answer, the full image is displayed and the player receives points and extra seconds. With an incorrect answer, the player loses time; the more incorrect answers, the more seconds lost. Figure 1 shows a partly unveiled image of a duck for a game round where the player has already provided two incorrect answers, highlighted in red, and finally the correct answer, highlighted in green. The final game score is presented to the player upon the conclusion of the game, when time has run out.

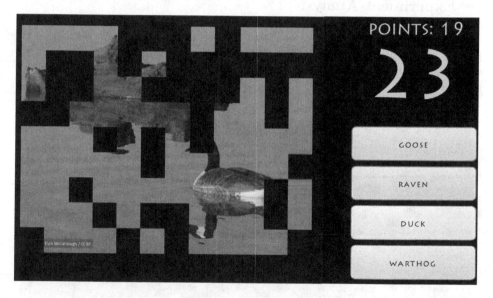

Fig. 1. The screenshot shows a game round with two selected wrong response terms (in red), the correct term (in green), as well as an unselected option (in blue)

3.2   Human Intelligence Task

We designed the game for Android devices and made it publicly available for download and play. To ensure that the workers performed the HIT correctly and played the game for an extended time, we added a special mechanic that did this check. Using a token system based on the timestamp, the worker ID, and the awarded points, we only provided payments to workers who reported a minimum of two tokens. Initially, a token would be earned when reaching 2.000 points in a game, but we noted that some players never accomplished this mark, and thus adjusted it down to 1.500 points. This lower bound for game scores served as a quality control, making it impossible to complete the HIT without adhering to the game rules and simply making random guesses. Moreover, even with the down-adjustment, we still collected around 50 played rounds per worker. This indicates that the gamification of crowdsourcing tasks can lead to higher motivation for the workers, and consequently yield more research data. During one week of running the HIT, we collected data from 111 workers that played more than 10.000 rounds combined. Based on recommendations by Microworkers, we payed each worker 0.80 Euros per HIT. In total, we spent 100 Euros on the entire experiment; this includes the Microworkers platform fee. Player feedback suggests that the game was well-accepted and enjoyable. However, one drawback relates to the time spent assessing the submitted HITs. For some of the older Android devices, glitches would appear in the game, but we plan to resolve this issue in the next version of the game.

4   Experiment Analysis

In total, we collected 13.264 responses, across 200 images, from 302 distinct players. With our 111 paid crowdsourcing workers completing approximately 40 rounds each, we had additional games played by workers after they finished the paid HITs.

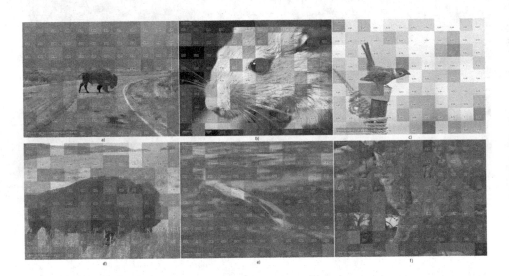

Fig. 2. Examples of the visually aggregated results from the experiment

With this preliminary analysis, we highlight the possible outcomes that our game can provide. Figure 2 depicts six game images, where the top three yield clear regions of higher visual salience and the bottom three fail to reveal any consistent visual patterns. The red overlays illustrate the aggregated distribution of revealed tiles; presented as inverse heat maps, the colour density corresponds to lower salience of a tile (the highest saliency is thus presented without any red overlay). The numbers in the lower left corners show how many times a tile was in view before a correct response was provided. The higher the number, the less important we deem the tile to the recognition of the image content. In the provided examples, pictures a), b) and c) show that the tiles uncovering the bison, the gerbil, and the bird, respectively, are important to their recognition. However, pictures d), e) and f) show more random distribution patterns, indicating that the image compositions may not work well for this particular task.

From our initial evaluation, we highlight two main findings. First, the size of the central object, or animal, is important to its recognition. Not surprisingly, the bigger depictions need more uncovered tiles than the smaller ones. An animal seen from afar takes up a smaller proportion of the image and consequently fewer tiles have to disappear before it can be identified. Secondly, the physical size of the animal also appears to be of import. The characteristic of an animal is connected to its body parts, and these may be more distinct for a small animal. For example, in Figure 2, picture f) illustrates the importance of the ear of the lynx, whereas picture d) show a trend where the body shape of the bison is required for recognition.

Originally, we expected a basic $F(x) = y$ response curve, with the percentage of tiles exposed directly related to the rate of correct responses provided. However, the graph in Figure 3 shows that the relationship instead corresponds to a psychometric curve. This is consistent with psychophysical studies on visual perception and can be explained by the amount of information needed to make sense of an image. Initially, the human visual system needs to aggregate and combine information, but after this initial stage, the additional information becomes redundant or irrelevant.

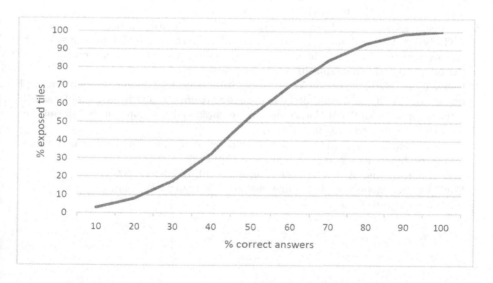

Fig. 3. Diagram of the overall coherence between exposed tiles and correct answers

5   Conclusion

With our mobile picture game, we have presented a novel way to run studies on human visual perception. The sophisticated design of our game with a purpose provides the means to run large-scale experiments while drawing from the benefits of crowdsourcing. To demonstrate the benefits of our approach, we have conducted an image recognition experiment and presented results that highlight salient regions for animal images. We surmise that our GWAP can be applied as an alternative to time-consuming eye-tracking studies. In future work, we will release a publicly available dataset based on our collected data. Furthermore, we plan investigations into the correlation between the results from this game-based method and a traditional eye-tracking study. Doing so, we hope to present our game design as an economic and time-saving alternative to existing eye-tracking approaches.

Acknowledgments. This work is partly funded by the FRINATEK project "EONS" (#231687) and the iAD Centre for Research-based Innovation (#174867) by the Norwegian Research Council and the Lakeside Labs GmbH, Klagenfurt, Austria and funding from the European Regional Development Fund and the Carinthian Economic Promotion Fund (KWF) under grant KWF-20214/25557/37319..

References

1. Boyle, A.: Gamers solve molecular puzzle that baffled scientists. http://www. nbcnews.com/science/science-news/gamers-solve-molecular-puzzle-baffled-scientists-f6C10402813 (last visited 10 July 2014)
2. Cooper, S., Treuille, A., Barbero, J., Leaver-Fay, A., Tuite, K., Khatib, F., Snyder, A.C., Beenen, M., Salesin, D., Baker, D., et al.: The challenge of designing scientific discovery games. In: Proceedings of the Fifth international Conference on the Foundations of Digital Games, pp. 40–47. ACM (2010)
3. Eickhoff, C., Harris, C.G., de Vries, A.P., Srinivasan, P.: Quality through flow and immersion: gamifying crowdsourced relevance assessments. In: Proceedings of the 35th International ACM SIGIR Conference on Research and Development in Information Retrieval, pp. 871–880. ACM (2012)
4. Siu, K., Zook, A., Riedl, M.O.: Collaboration versus competition: Design and evaluation of mechanics for games with a purpose (2014)
5. Von Ahn, L.: Games with a purpose. Computer 39(6), 92–94 (2006)
6. Von Ahn, L., Dabbish, L.: Designing games with a purpose. Communications of the ACM 51(8), 58–67 (2008)

histoGraph as a Demonstrator for Domain Specific Challenges to Crowd-Sourcing

Lars Wieneke[1(✉)], Marten Düring[1], Vincenzo Croce[2], and Jasminko Novak[3]

[1] CVCE, Sanem, Luxembourg
{lars.wieneke,marten.duering}@cvce.eu
[2] Engineering Ingegneria Informatica spa, Roma, Italy
crocev@eng.it
[3] EIPCM, Berlin, Germany
j.novak@eipcm.org

Abstract. histoGraph provides an integrated pipeline for the extraction of co-occurrence information in historical photos to build an exploreable social graph of relationships that can lead to new insights for historical research. The application leverages on the CUbRIK platform for human/machine computation and applies a hybrid approach to face-detection and -recognition that combines the strengths of algorithmic analysis with expert and generic crowd sourcing. Following a general overview of our approach, we explore the surplus value of human touch for the identification of identities in historical image collections through a uniform crowd-sourcing approach. We find that only a combination of generic and expert crowds yields promising results. Even though the application was designed and developed for a specific target audience, we aim not only at demonstrating the current functionality but also identify and discuss several core principles that can be transferred to other domains.

Keywords: Face identification · Crowdsourcing · Photographs · Digital humanities · European integration

1 Introduction

In this paper we explore the surplus value of human touch for the identification of identities in historical image collections through a hybrid crowd-sourcing approach. We will demonstrate that to solve this task efficiently in accordance with the quality demands of our target users we need to involve both a generic crowd and an expert crowd for specific tasks.

The application of computational methods to research questions from the humanities (often referred to as digital humanities) has been applied in different projects such as for example in the analysis of historical institutions [9], in mapping networks between historical actors [9,10,11] or in genealogical networks [13]. The analysis of multi-media sources has been reviewed and applied in different digital humanities projects (see [14] for an overview and Crowdsourcing approaches have been applied

L.M. Aiello and D. McFarland (Eds.): SocInfo 2014 Workshops, LNCS 8852, pp. 469–476, 2015.
DOI: 10.1007/978-3-319-15168-7_57

to the wider field as well [15,16]. Historical image archives on the other hand provide an immense wealth of implicitly encoded knowledge that has not been fully exploited up to now (see [1] for further details). Even though some archives provide information for images detailing for example who is depicted in a picture and when, where and in which context the image was taken, this information is often limited to high-level information (« Brussels » as free text rather than an entity that describes « Commission meeting room, 13th floor, Berlaymont Building Brussels Belgium ») or to specific political actors that were considered relevant at the time of indexation rather than all persons depicted in the image. Furthermore the information is not aggregated to achieve a distant view on all images in a dataset leaving aside the ability to fully explore relations derived from the co-occurrence of persons in time and space. Providing such a perspective on larger image archives could stimulate new research questions for historical research and provide new insights in the interactions of historical actors.

While the automatic recognition of persons in images has made significant process in recent years and now seems to challenge even human-level performance [2] a historical dataset of images that includes non-biometric images showing actors that were active across several decades thereby changing their appearance sometimes dramatically provides a significant challenge for any automatic recognition process. Human indexation on the other hand is highly time consuming and shows limited success when it comes to persons that are less known or currently unknown.

To tackle this problem histoGraph applies a hybrid strategy that combines both human and machine computation in the indexation of images as well as an integrated online application that enables exploration, annotation and discussion in one interface. histoGraph has been developed in the context of the FP7 funded CUbRIK project using a highly user-centred design process to take into account the specific requirements of researchers in European Integration studies, a field of the humanities that researches the process of European integration in an interdisciplinary fashion covering contributions from social sciences, law and history.

In the following section we want to provide an overview on the technical implementation of histoGraph while highlighting the specific benefits of the CUbRIK platform and our hybrid approach to crowdsourcing. After this overview we will discus the application itself as well as rationales for our design decision and give a critical reflection on the acceptance of generic and expert crowdsourcing in historical research. Afterwards we will discuss how elements of histoGraph can be generalized and transferred to other domains.

2   Development Process and Technical Implementation

The specific details for the technical implementation of histoGraph have been discussed elsewhere in greater detail [1,3]. The application was developed using an iterative process in which user-centered requirements analysis is performed in a way that aligns the existing needs of historians (user pull) with the identification of opportunities created by novel technologies (technology push). Our approach followed user-centered design principles, involved experts in computer science, HCI research and as interface design as well the development of user stories and focus groups. See [1] for a detailed description of this process.

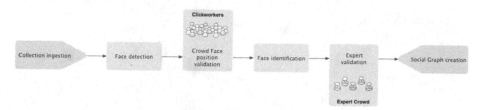

Fig. 1. Indexation pipeline of histoGraph

The histoGraph indexation pipeline (see Fig. 1.) starts with the ingestion of image collections in a face detection process where an algorithm tries to identify the faces of persons in the images. In the next step a group of clickworkers [5,6] validates or refuses the results of the automatic recognition process, thereby eliminating false positives. Once the position of faces has been validated a face identification algorithm is triggered that yields a list of potential identities for each face. This list is disseminated to a crowd of experts, which then review the proposals and cooperatively establishes the identity of the face. Finally co-occurrence information are calculated that feed into the creation of the social graph. At the end of this process, an identified person is assigned to its appropriate entity in Entitypedia, a repository for linked data on historical events and people [7].

In combination with the visualisation of the social graph on the histoGraph website using a spring-embedder layout and the different analytical and cooperative tools available there (see Fig.2, [3] and compare [1]), the current implementation allows for different types of use cases that go beyond the acquisition of identities alone. By incorporating a mechanism of research inquiries, users can leverage on their individual networks and address colleagues to verify identities but also to identify complex information such as date and location of the recording, but also context information such as related events or for example the name of the photographer.

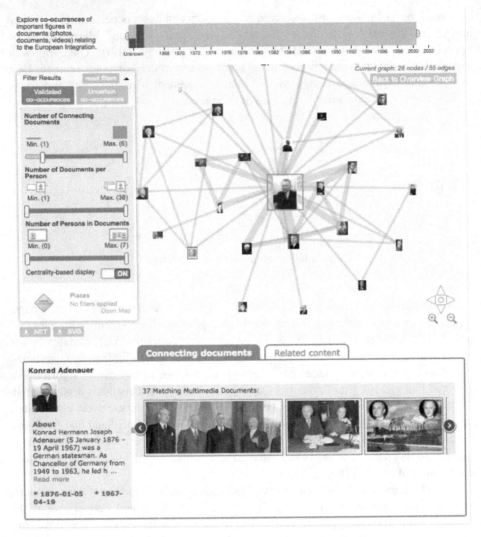

Fig. 2. Social graph exploration tool in histoGraph

3   Crowdsourcing for Historical Research

As discussed before, a highly user-centred design process was implemented to drive the development of histoGraph. This process included on-site observation of work practices as well as different user-workshops, questionnaires and interviews. Besides other findings two core practices of historical research were identified that showed a particular relevance for the design of the crowd-sourcing process: the specific role of sources and the concept of truth in historical research.

Fig. 3. Alternative identities and provision of sources for decisions in histoGraph

Like all research, historical research places significant emphasis on the provision of sources but exceeds other domains in its critical review of these sources emphasizing specific aspects like provenance, bias etc. In turn this critical distance towards sources led to specific challenges for the crowdsourcing of information. While researchers accepted in our workshops the verification of face positions by a generic and therefore unknown crowd they showed serious concerns about the validation of identities by unknown persons (see [1] for a more detailed discussion on this matter). We suppose today that the reasons for these concerns are caused in part from the fact that the verification has severe implications on the creation of the graph but also because the task of identification itself was closer to their existing research practices and should therefore reflect the standards of their work practices to become acceptable. To confront this issue it was decided to integrate a data model that captures the provenance of different information and to implement source information for the identity of persons as well as any other elements such as time or place of recording. As a practical consequence of this requirement, users of the application are invited to not simply accept a given statement but rather confirm it by finding another source that supports their claim. The crowd consists of CVCE's own EU studies department and their peers.

The second important factor for the design of crowd-tasks was identified in the notion of truth in humanities research. In contrast to computer science, where truth is either well defined (TRUE/FALSE) or can be quantified, historical research operates with multiple, sometimes contradicting truths. In the same way as the popular proverb "one mans terrorist, the other mans freedom fighter" illustrates, truth is not absolute but can depend on the point of view. Historians try to capture these different perspectives in order to draw their conclusions. The interface of the expert crowd application therefore includes a "discursive" interface inspired by the discussion structure in the Q&A platform "stack overflow". This approach allows the depiction of different interpretations and leaves room for discussions through the provision of arguments or sources to determine the interpretation that will be finally used in the social graph. The interface and its current implementation are shown in Figure 3.

Besides established research practices and their impact on the acceptance of crowdsourcing solutions our workshops and interviews also indicated that historical researchers already use their personal networks in the identification of persons or the dating of images. To incorporate such informal networks the concept of research queries was developed. Following this idea users can request information concerning specific sources or events and send out requests for help through their established networks, e.g. by using Twitter followers or by mail. This exposure to peers within an expert community allows users to tap highly specialized knowledge resources. The research inquiries allow the community to discuss and comment on competing answers and to vote them up or down (see [1,3] for further details). This ensures that contributions which are obviously out of place can be filtered out rather quickly. For the humanities, this is focused process of community-based answer finding is a new experience.

4   Outlook

histoGraph was developed for a specific target group of digital humanities researchers. However, during the validation phase the application has demonstrated the potential for a transfer to other contexts where similar issues exist. In fact the demonstrator evidenced the capability to scale up and tackle up to 30k images and filter them according to space and time constraints for a categorization. Besides the generic task of identifying persons and locations in time, which is applicable to different domains, specific functionalities such as the identification of connections between different persons, the identification of clusters (groups) and the identification of specific events, such as the forming of coalitions through the appearance and disappearance of connections in time show an interesting potential. For an overview of different kinds of research activities in histoGraph see [1].

The reference context for the original histoGraph demonstrator is the processing of static collections of photos from historical archives but its characteristics make it suitable for other context presenting similar conditions. In particular two contexts were analyzed so far:

- Broadcasters archives containing videos of specific period of times, such us the RAI archive *teche RAI*; this is the archive of video material produced by RAI during its whole history, including also material prior to 1950's.
- Security surveillance systems that use pattern analysis on shots and videos stream for threat identification

The adaptation of histoGraph to these contexts implies the development of further additional steps in the pipelines including video and video stream analysis. For the RAI Broadcaster scenario we identified that video shot detection, key frame extraction and frame reconciliation need to be performed as preliminary steps. This approach will allow us to produce a collection of images that is representative of the video collection and can be injected into the histoGraph pipeline thereby leveraging on the existing framework. In the context of this scenario, the broad view on a large set of content delivered by histoGraph provides a specific benefit while the time based view on relationships could help to identify specific preferences and biases of media coverage.

For the security surveillance system scenario, the pipeline needs to be adapted in order to manage the registration of already identified "key persons" and to support research inquiries based on the relationships between "key person" and faces detected and identified in existing photos, for example, from video surveillance cameras in airport or other sensitive sites. In this scenario the specific features of histoGraph to identify persons are highly valuable in particular in networked scenarios where security experts can identify suspects cooperatively. Furthermore the identification of fractions and exchanges between them over time can become valuable.

These examples demonstrate that the pipeline approach offers the flexibility to disassemble the media processing workflow, to reuse and reconfigure it according to specific domain needs while putting into practice a significant human computation component.

5   Conclusion

This paper discussed a demonstrator for a hybrid human/machine computation approach to the identification of identities in historical images thereby highlighting the value of the human touch in this specific domain. The application leverages on a combination of automatic and crowd verified face detection, automatic face recognition and crowd as well as experts verification. We find that only a combination of generic and expert crowds yields promising results. This approach was conceived to tackle uncertainty in automatic processing derived by low quality of sources or by uncontrolled environments at photos shooting time, i.e. the photos depicturing half-face or overlapped subjects. Uncertainty is restrained in order to avoid error propagation and overall low accuracy.

References

1. Wieneke, L., et al.: histoGraph – A visualization tool for collaborative analysis of histori-cal social networks from multimedia collections. In: 2014 Conference Proceedings of 18th International Conference Information Visualisation (IV), Paris, France (2014)
2. Taigman, Y., et al.: DeepFace: closing the gap to human-level performance in face verifi-cation. In: 2014 IEEE Conference on Computer Vision and Pattern Recognition (CVPR), pp. 1701–1708 (2014)
3. Wieneke, L., et al.: Building the social graph of the history of european integration. In: Nadamoto, Akiyo, Jatowt, A., Wierzbicki, A., Leidner, J.L. (eds.) SocInfo 2013. LNCS, vol. 8359, pp. 86–99. Springer, Heidelberg (2014)
4. Kee Square. http://www.keesquare.com/
5. Amazon Mechanical Turk. http://www.mturk.com/
6. Microtask. http://www.microtask.com/
7. Entitypedia. http://entitypedia.org/
8. D3.js – Data-Driven-Documents. http://d3js.org/
9. League of Nations. http://www.lonsea.de/
10. Athenikos, S.J., Lin, X.: WikiPhiloSofia: extraction and visualization of facts, relations, and networks concerning philosophers using Wikipedia. In: Conf. Abstracts of Digital Humanities 2009, pp. 56-62 (2009)
11. ePistolarium. http://ckcc.huygens.knaw.nl/
12. Republic of Letters. http://republicofletters.stanford.edu/
13. Kennard, D.J., et al.: Linking the past: discovering historical social networks from docu-ments and linking to a genealogical database. In: Proc. of the 2011 Workshop on Historical Document Imaging and Processing, pp. 43-50. ACM (2011)
14. Warwick, C., et al.: Digital humanities in practice. Facet Publishing (2012)
15. Operation War diary. http://www.operationwardiary.org
16. Ancient Lives. http://www.ancientlives.org

Author Index

Printed in the United States
By Bookmasters